READING LYRICS

ALSO BY OR EDITED BY ROBERT GOTTLIEB

The Everyman Collected Stories of Rudyard Kipling

The Journals of John Cheever

Reading Jazz: A Gathering of Autobiography,
Reportage, and Criticism from 1919 to Now

A Certain Style: The Art of the Plastic Handbag, 1949–1959

———

ALSO BY OR EDITED BY ROBERT KIMBALL

The Complete Lyrics of Cole Porter

The Complete Lyrics of Ira Gershwin

The Complete Lyrics of Lorenz Hart
(with Dorothy Hart)

The Complete Lyrics of Irving Berlin
(with Linda Emmet)

Cole (with Brendan Gill)

The Gershwins (with Alfred Simon)

Reminiscing with Sissle and Blake
(with William Bolcom)

READING LYRICS

Edited and with an Introduction by

Robert Gottlieb and Robert Kimball

PANTHEON BOOKS   NEW YORK

Permissions acknowledgments begin on page 665.

Library of Congress Cataloging-in-Publication Data

Reading lyrics / edited and with an introduction by
Robert Gottlieb and Robert Kimball.
p.   cm.
Includes index.
ISBN 0-375-40081-8
1. Songs, English–Texts.   2. Popular music–Texts.
3. Musicals–Excerpts–Librettos.
I. Gottlieb, Robert, 1931-   II. Kimball, Robert, 1939-
ML54.6 .R39   2000   782.42164'0268–dc21   99-088811

Random House Web Address: www.randomhouse.com

Printed in the United States of America

4   6   8   9   7   5   3

Contents

Contents

Introduction

───────◆◆◆───────

I T   H A S   B E E N a daunting challenge to choose a thousand or so of the "best" American and English lyrics of their time. As with all anthologies, the actual process of accumulating and assessing material has changed the original idea of the anthology itself. For instance, this book was originally going to span the years 1910 to 1970. In the abstract, it seemed that "Alexander's Ragtime Band," from 1911, would be an appropriate introduction to the mainstream of twentieth-century popular song–that it marked a real break from everything that preceded it. But eventually it became clear to us that it was George M. Cohan, so active in the first decade of the century, who made the effective break from the operetta conventions of, say, Victor Herbert, and the over-whelmingly sentimental nature of earlier American song. And so our beginning date got pushed back to 1900–at which point we were charmed by other clever and natural-seeming lyrics from this early decade.

Again, the date 1970, somewhat arbitrarily chosen, excluded a number of Broadway musicals–*Follies, Chicago,* etc.,–that were still in the tradition of the golden age, producing songs that have lasted. By 1975, though, it really was over, except for some isolated instances. In a few cases–Stephen Sondheim is the obvious example–this has meant excluding the interesting later work of contemporary writers, but only in a few cases. And the last two and one-half decades–the era of Andrew Lloyd Webber's sung-through pastiches–haven't produced many talented lyric writers; only recently are new voices emerging that may well come to have lasting value. In Hollywood, the musical was more or less gone by the late seventies, and pop music has increasingly become more about arrangement and performance than about words and music.

A more painful decision was to limit the field to the song as we know it from shows, movies, and pre-rock pop. Partly this was a matter of logistics: No single volume could stretch to include folk, country, blues, and rock. And though a collection of lyrics that excludes, say, Bob Dylan or Hank Williams is obviously one that is far from complete, their stories are not the stories we can tell here (or are equipped to tell).

Perhaps more important, as we listened to, or read the sheet music for, thou-sands of songs, our focus began to shift somewhat from individual lyrics to individual writers. That is, one of our chief goals became the desire to reveal the lyricists themselves, who they have been and what they accomplished–not just the obvious titans but those who had honorable and successful careers on Broadway or in Hollywood or in vaudeville or in cabaret or in pop, and are now more or less forgotten even if we haven't forgotten a few of their songs. In a modest way, the organization of the book–presenting the lyricists chronologically, with a short bio for each–is meant to reflect the history of songwriting in America and England during the twentieth century. One can follow the progress from the first masters of the colloquial–Cohan, Berlin, Wodehouse– to the more worldly sophistications of Porter and Hart and Coward, to the robust American vein of Hammerstein and Mercer, to the semi-art song of Alec Wilder. Or, looked at another way, the progress from providing personal material for vaudeville stars to writing for Broadway and then–with the coming of sound to movies–for Hollywood, and finally back to providing material for specific stars, as Sammy Cahn did for Frank Sinatra.

There are historical moments that trigger new ideas–the Depression, with both its serious laments ("Brother, Can You Spare a Dime?") and its brave upbeat defiances of poverty ("I Can't Give You Anything but Love"); World War II, with its romantic ballads ("Saturday Night Is the Loneliest Night of the Week") and the cheerful swing of songs like "Milkman, Keep Those Bottles Quiet!"–a good writer like Don Raye has to be considered in that latter context, which may be why he is not remembered enough today.

There were surprises along the way. Of course, the great masters remain unchallenged: No dark horse emerged as superior to Irving Berlin or Ira Gershwin. Nor had we overestimated Dorothy Fields, say, or Frank Loesser, or Andy Razaf, or Leo Robin, or Comden and Green. But it was both surprising and gratifying to realize just how good Johnny Burke was, and Ted Koehler, and Harold Rome; and how well giants of the twenties and thirties, such as Gus Kahn and DeSylva, Brown, and Henderson, hold up today. And it was exciting to rediscover–or just discover–a Bobby Troup, a Peggy Lee, a Tom Adair.

To emphasize our interest in the careers of lyricists, we decided to focus on those who had written at least three songs we really liked. On the other hand, so as not to exclude a number of one-hit wonders, we added a coda of individual songs: Don't expect consistency from anthologists in love with their subject!

As everyone understands, reading song lyrics is very different from reading poems. A lyric is one-half of a work, and its success or failure depends not only on its own merits as verse but on its relationship to its music. Possibly some of the lyrics we have included will not seem worthy to readers who don't know the music that is essential to them—indeed, the brilliance of certain lyrics lies in their perfect, natural marriage to their tunes rather than in their verbal ingenuity; Gus Kahn's "It Had to Be You" is an example. And there's almost no way to read certain lyrics without evoking their music: That's both the difficulty and the joy of reading lyrics. Again, some lyrics, not of the highest quality, are so deeply embedded in our minds that to have excluded them would have been perverse. But on the whole, whereas all hits certainly don't turn out to be first-rate (or even second-rate), the songs that have really lasted generally seem to deserve their place in our memories and affections.

Depending on his or her taste, every reader is going to find certain lyrics questionable: too overblown, too sardonic, too simple, too fussy, too politically incorrect. Tastes change, and it has been a complicated effort to adjust ourselves to the different periods we cover and approach them in the appropriate spirit. Since we were both born in the thirties, our memories cover most of the century, going back to the songs our parents cared for and forward from our childhoods. The only genre that seems really alien is the race song of the first decades of the century—the "wop" song, the "coon" song, the Irish and Jewish "comic" song. Luckily, none of these that we encountered had any merit, so there were no hard choices to make. Later songs that might make one slightly uncomfortable today—Peggy Lee's "Mañana," say—are so clearly good-natured, so little mean-spirited, that their merits seemed to outweigh one's mild embarrassment about them. On the other hand, one is struck by (and impressed by) the outspoken and angry stance of the lyrics by African-American writers of songs such as "That's Why They Call Me 'Shine' " and "Black and Blue"—songs from the twenties that laid it on the line, yet achieved commercial success. And by the loyalty to their political principals of such writers as Yip Harburg and Harold Rome.

When we were kids, the only songs forty or more years old that were still current were those of Stephen Foster and Gilbert and Sullivan (and the influence of Gilbert can be felt through the first half of the twentieth century). Today, the vast majority of the thousand songs in this book, which stretch back through an entire century, are still viable: that is, they are still singable—and are still sung, on records and in cabaret. The best American and English popular songs of the twentieth century have turned out to have tremendous staying power; they can now be seen as an intense flowering of a specialized yet widely appealing art form. It's no surprise that "serious" singers—of opera and lieder—increasingly include them in their repertoires (with varying degrees of success): these songs have achieved the longevity of classics. It is this quality of singableness that was our final test for every song considered for inclusion. The oldest songs may seem old-fashioned, but they don't (to us) seem dated; they're alive.

Our hope is that this book will serve readers in several ways–as a work of reference, as a chronicle of tastes and talents, as pure pleasure. We regret the absence of somebody else's favorites, and hope for a happy response to our own.

Robert Gottlieb and Robert Kimball
New York, August 2000

READING LYRICS

Anne Caldwell (1867–1936)

B<small>Y HALF</small> a dozen years the oldest contributor to this book, Boston-born Anne Caldwell was active in Broadway musicals for more than twenty years, beginning in 1907. An immensely successful librettist, she wrote the book for more than twenty-five successful shows, as well as the lyrics for many more. She worked on Montgomery and Stone's *Chin-Chin;* with Jerome Kern on such shows as *The City Chap* and *Stepping Stones;* and with Vincent Youmans on *Oh, Please!* before going to Hollywood in 1931. Several of her songs became popular, of which the best known today is probably "I Know That You Know." She had begun improvising words while playing the piano as a little girl, and she wrote until her death, working on such Hollywood musicals as *Flying Down to Rio, Babes in Toyland,* and *Dixieana.*

I KNOW THAT YOU KNOW

VERSE

Life's a game,
But who can play it
All alone?
Ev'ry chap
Should hold a heart
That's all his own.
Love may come at first sight,
They told me;
When I saw you,
I knew
I had found my only love,
When I met you.
So, darling . . .

REFRAIN

I know
That you know
That I'll go
Where you go.
I choose you;

Won't lose you.
I wish you knew
How much I long
To hold you
In my arms.

This time
Is my time,
'Twill soon be
Good-bye time;
Then in the starlight
Hold me tight.
With one more little kiss,
Say "Nighty-night!"

—*Vincent Youmans*

LEFT ALL ALONE AGAIN BLUES

I have the blues,
Ev'ry time my hubby leaves me
I have the blues,

Because it peeves me
To be left here, flat here,
Just like a bump on a log,
I said on a log!
No woman knows
If she has a travelin' husband
Just where he goes,
Unless she follows on
And nails him, trails him,
Just like a faithful old dog.

That old song
"Where Has My Highland
Laddie Gone?",
It says a mouthful.
We never do know
Just where they do go.
How they keep us guessing
Isn't it distressing!
I have the blues
When my hubby leaves,
Although I wouldn't accuse.
Each time he says "Good-bye"
I get those same old
Left-all-alone-again blues.

I have the blues,
Ever since he married me
I sure have the blues,
Because I used to have a
Good time, all time.
Every time I might roam,
I said when I'd roam!
When first we met
We could render a duet,
But now hubby sings
"I Won't Go Home 'Til Morning,"
Never one short stanza
Of "Home Sweet Home."

I like cats,
I'm fond of rabbits,
I like dogs,

And even goldfish.
It's lucky maybe
That there's a baby
Grand piano coming,
Then I'll start a-humming:
I have the blues,
Only hubby dear can cure
My terrible blues.
Each time he says "Good-bye"
I get those doggone
Left-all-alone-again blues.

—*Jerome Kern*

RAGGEDY ANN

VERSE I
When I was just a tiny tot, with
    tousled head,
I had two pals with whom I dearly loved
    to play.
The girl lived in a dollhouse, close beside
    my bed;
Beneath her window ev'ry night the boy
    would say,

REFRAIN
"My Raggedy Ann,
Come out when you can.
Your Raggedy Andy has a plan,
I've got a flivver sedan!
We'll rattle off to find a ragtime
    cabaret
Where we can rag our raggy rags till
    break of day.
Oo,
Raggedy Ann,
Do
Say that you can,
Come and dance with your raggedy man,
My Raggedy Ann!"

VERSE 2
I love a lady who has black shoe-
   button eyes,
I love a lady with a rag bag in her head.
In a parade of dumbbells she would take
   the prize;

But when it came to ragtime she can knock
'em dead.

REPEAT REFRAIN

—Jerome Kern

Otto Harbach (1873–1963)

T HE DEAN OF U.S. librettists" is what *Variety* called him in its obituary, and certainly Otto Harbach was a dominant figure on Broadway for almost half a century. Born in Salt Lake City, he worked as a professor of English, a reporter, and an advertising copywriter before launching his career in the theater at the age of thirty-five. Much of his most famous work was in the heyday of American operetta—he worked, often in collaboration with Oscar Hammerstein II, with composers Rudolf Friml (ten shows, including *The Firefly* and *Rose-Marie*), Sigmund Romberg *(The Desert Song),* Vincent Youmans *(Wildflower* and *No, No, Nanette),* and Jerome Kern, most memorably for *The Cat and the Fiddle* and *Roberta.* Many of his songs from these shows now seem dated—operetta lyrics are inevitably sentimental and are often drowned out by the soaring schmaltz of the music. But there are lighter songs, like his first hit, "Cuddle Up a Little Closer." And "Smoke Gets in Your Eyes" and "Yesterdays," at least, remain known and loved, partly through the luck of being sung so affectingly in the Astaire/Rogers/Irene Dunne film of *Roberta.*

LET'S BEGIN

VERSE

Before I met you no one attracted me,
No love thoughts worried or distracted me.
My disposition kept exempting me
Until you started in pre-empting me,
And all this while you've really been
　　tempting me.
Maybe you can tell me what we ought
　　to do.

REFRAIN

Now that you've got me goin',
Whatcha gonna do?
Is it up to me?
Is it up to you?
What kinda game is this
We've begun?

Was it done
Just for fun?
We have necked
Till I'm wrecked.
Won't you tell me
What you expect!
Is this to be a case of
Kiss and never tell?
Folly and farewell?
Heav'n or maybe Hell?
Which is it goin' to be,
Love or gin?
Wife or sin?
Let's begin . . .
And make a mess of
Both of our bright young lives.

—Jerome Kern

THE LOVE NEST

VERSE 1

Many builders there have been
Since the world began.
Palace, cottage, mansion, inn,
They have built for man.
Some were small, and some were tall,
Long or wide or low.
But the best one of them all
Jack built long ago.
'Twas built in bygone days,
Yet millions sing its praise.

REFRAIN

Just a love nest,
Cozy and warm,
Like a dove rest
Down on a farm.
A veranda with some sort of
    clinging vine,
Then a kitchen where some rambler
    roses twine.
Then a small room,
Tea set of blue.
Best of all room,
Dream room for two.
Better than a palace with a
    gilded dome
Is a love nest
You can call home.

VERSE 2

Building houses still goes on
Now as well as then.
Ancient Jack and Jill are gone,
Yet return again.
Ever comes the question old,
Shall we build for pride,
Or shall brick and mortar hold
Warmth and love inside?

The answer you may know.
Jack solved it long ago.

REPEAT REFRAIN

—*Louis A. Hirsch*

POOR PIERROT

Poor Pierrot
Loved his fair Pierrette,
Golden the glow
Of the happy hour when they met.
To their sweet retreat
Birds on the wing
Hastened to bring
Garlands of spring.
At her dainty feet
Wove on their loom
Carpets of bloom,
Breathing perfume.
What heav'n they knew
Only lovers may know.
For fair Pierrette
Loved her happy Pierrot.

Poor Pierrot
Loved his fair Pierrette.
How should he know
That a girl may vow and forget?
To her gay retreat
Comes one who brings
Rare golden rings,
Jewels and things.
At her dainty feet
Where flowers bled,
There now instead
Gay silks are spread.
What hell
Rages in one heart
None may know,

For fickle Pierrette
Has forgotten
Poor Pierrot.

—*Jerome Kern*

SHE DIDN'T SAY "YES"

She didn't say "yes,"
She didn't say "no,"
She didn't say "stay,"
She didn't say "go,"
She only knew that he had spied her
    there,
And then she knew he sat beside her
    there.
At first there was heard
Not one little word,
Then coyly she took
One sly little look,
And something awoke and smiled inside,
Her heart began beating wild inside.
So what did she do?
I leave it to you,
She did just what you'd do too.

She didn't say "yes,"
She didn't say "no,"
They very soon stood
Beside his chateau,
They lingered like two poor waifs
    outside,
For well she knew 'twas only safe outside.
In there it was warm,
Out there it was cold,
The sleet and the storm
Said "Better be bold!"
She murmured: "I'm not afraid of ice,
I only wish that I was made of ice."
So what did she do?
I leave it to you,
She did just want you'd do too.

She didn't say "yes,"
She didn't say "no,"
She wanted to stay,
But knew she should go,
She wasn't so sure that he'd be good,
She wasn't even sure that she'd
    be good.
She wanted to rest
All cuddled and pressed,
A palpable part
Of somebody's heart.
She loved to be "en rapport" with him,
But not behind a bolted door with him.
And what did she do?
I leave it to you,
She did just what you'd do too.

She didn't say "yes,"
She didn't say "no,"
For heaven was near,
She wanted it so.
Above her, sweet love was beckoning,
And yet she knew there'd be a
    reckoning.
She wanted to climb,
But dreaded to fall,
So bided her time
And clung to the wall.
She wanted to act ad libitum,
But feared to lose her equilibrium.
So what did she do?
I leave it to you,
She did just what you'd do too.

—*Jerome Kern*

SMOKE GETS IN YOUR EYES

They asked me how I knew
My true love was true.
I of course replied,
Something here inside

Cannot be denied.
They said someday you'll find,
All who love are blind.
When your heart's on fire,
You must realize
Smoke gets in your eyes.
So I chaffed
Them and I gaily laughed
To think they could doubt my love.
Yet today
My love has flown away,
I am without my love.
Now laughing friends deride
Tears I cannot hide,
So I smile and say,
"When a lovely flame dies,
Smoke gets in your eyes."

—Jerome Kern

YESTERDAYS

Yesterdays,
Yesterdays,
Days I knew as happy sweet
    sequester'd days.
Olden days,
Golden days,
Days of mad romance and love.
Then gay youth was mine,
Truth was mine,
Joyous, free and flaming life forsooth
    was mine.
Sad am I,
Glad am I,
For today I'm dreaming of
Yesterdays.

—Jerome Kern

George M. Cohan (1878–1942)

FOR FIFTEEN YEARS—from 1904 to 1919—George M. Cohan was the most successful figure in the American theater. He was born into vaudeville, and by the age of nine was a member of the family act, quickly joined by his sister and eventually by his first wife. He was publishing songs by the time he was sixteen, and in 1904 had his first great stage hit, *Little Johnny Jones*—a breath of fresh air in a musical theater dominated by European and British operettas. Cohan was composer and lyricist of his songs, star of most of his shows, and an immensely successful producer, with his partner, Sam Harris. (In 1911, they had six hit shows on Broadway and controlled seven theaters.) By the twenties, his spunky, Irish-American patriotic swagger had lost its magic for audiences, but he was a great success in Eugene O'Neill's *Ah, Wilderness* in 1933, and again in the Rodgers and Hart *I'd Rather Be Right* in 1937. Cohan lived to see himself immortalized in the 1942 movie *Yankee Doodle Dandy,* for which James Cagney won an Oscar. His life and songs also provided the basis for a 1968 Broadway musical, *George M!*

DOWN BY THE ERIE CANAL

If you want to make good in a
    Broadway show,
You must have a song that is sure to go.
The sort of refrain that gives you a pain
And drives you insane
When you hear it again.
The orchestras murder it near and far,
It's usually sung by the female star,
The publisher gives her a motor car,
And the chorus goes something like this:

Down by the Erie,
There waits my pal.
Tho' the days are long and dreary,
He declares he'll ne'er grow weary.
Poor John O'Leary,
I'm afraid you've lost your gal,

For she's left you flat, my dearie,
By the Erie Canal.

FORTY-FIVE MINUTES FROM BROADWAY

VERSE I

The West, so they say, is the home of
    the jay,
And Missouri's the state that can
    grind them.
This may all be, but just take it from me,
You don't have to go out west to find them.
If you want to see the real jay delegation,
The place where the real rubens dwell,
Just hop on a train at the Grand Central
    Station,
Get off when they shout "New Rochelle."

Only forty-five minutes from Broadway,
Think of the changes it brings;
For the short time it takes, what a
    diff'rence it makes
In the ways of the people and things.
Oh! What a fine bunch of rubens,
Oh! what a jay atmosphere;
They have whiskers like hay, and imagine
    Broadway
Only forty-five minutes from here.

VERSE 2
When the bunco men hear that their game
    is so near,
They'll be swarming here thicker than
    bees are.
In Barnum's best days, why he never
    saw jays
That were easier to get to than these are.
You tell them old jokes and they laugh till
    they sicken,
There's giggles and grins here to let.
I told them that one about "Why does a
    chicken,"
The rubens are all laughing yet.

REFRAIN 2
Only forty-five minutes from Broadway,
Not a café in the town;
Oh! The place is a bird, no one here ever
    heard
Of Delmonico, Rector or Browne.
With a ten-dollar bill you're a spendthrift;
If you open a bottle of beer
You're a sport, so they say, and imagine
    Broadway
Only forty-five minutes from here.

GIVE MY REGARDS TO BROADWAY

VERSE I
Did you ever see two Yankees part upon a
    foreign shore,
When the good ship's just about to start
    for old New York once more?
With tear-dimmed eye, they say good-bye,
    they're friends, without a doubt;
When the man on the pier shouts, "Let
    them clear," as the ship strikes out.

REFRAIN
Give my regards to Broadway,
Remember me to Herald Square.
Tell all the gang at Forty-second Street
That I will soon be there.
Whisper of how I'm yearning
To mingle with the old-time throng;
Give my regards to old Broadway
And say that I'll be there, e'er long.

VERSE 2
Say hello to dear old Coney Isle, if there
    you chance to be.
When you're at the Waldorf, have a smile
    and charge it up to me.
Mention my name ev'ry place you go, as
    'round the town you roam;
Wish you'd call on my gal, now remember,
    old pal, when you get back home.

REPEAT REFRAIN

I WANT TO HEAR A YANKEE DOODLE TUNE

VERSE I
I've always hated
That overrated

Pretentious music, complicated,
And compositions
That have conditions,
And intermissions that please musicians.
It's hard to hear it, or just be near it,
Upon my word I always fear it,
For I'm the original cranky, Yankee
    popular melody fool.

Give me a tune that's worth a listening,
Give me a tune that's worth a whistling.
I want a Sousa strain
Instead of a Wagner pain;
Give the trombones a chance to blow in it,
Give me a dash of rag and go in it.
What I'm stating
Is advocating
The popular melody school.

REFRAIN
I want to hear a Yankee Doodle tune,
Played by a military band.
I want to hear a Yankee Doodle tune,
The only music I can understand.
Oh! Sousa, won't you write another
    march,
Yours is just the melody divine.
You may have your William Tell,
And Faust and Lohengrin as well,
But I'll take a Yankee Doodle tune
    for mine.

VERSE 2
Give me the fellow
Who writes the mellow
Contagious strain that's rather yellow.
It may be hashy,
And may be trashy,
But still it's dashy and gets the cashy.
It's really clever
And lasts forever,
You hear it once, forget it never,

For now we are coming to hanky, panky,
    popular melody days.

That it's the music, there's no doubt of it.
Cut all the cheap cadenzas out of it.
Music to please the gang
With plenty of biff and bang;
Music that all the children hum a bit,
All the composer's glories come of it.
It's so ringing,
That's what is bringing
The popular melody craze.

REPEAT REFRAIN

IF I'M GOING TO DIE I'M GOING TO HAVE SOME FUN

VERSE I
Jim Jackson caught a cold,
And he laughed when he was told
That he'd better go to bed
And cover up his head.
A hot gin fizz was the thing, they said—
Jim laughed at this advice;
He had a date to shoot some dice.
He walk'd right out in the wind and snow,
The night was cold as ice.
Two weeks later a very sickly coon,
A doctor with a spoon
Says, "Jim, take your medicine."
Jim said, "Doc, am I bad, now, don't
    you lie."
The doctor said, "I'll tell the truth, I think
    you're goin' to die."
When Jim sat right straight up in bed,
He raised his head, to the doctor said:

REFRAIN
"I'm goin' to get right up and put on my
    clothes.

I'm goin' to go right out and take in all the
shows.
I'm goin' to drive around in an open
carriage.
If I meet my gal, there's goin' to be a
marriage.
I'll borrow from ev'rybody on my staff,
I'm goin' to eat and drink and drive and
laugh.
The doctor says my days are done,
So if I'm goin' to die, I'm goin' to have
some fun.
I'm goin' to have some fun."

VERSE 2
Jim jump'd right out of bed
And did just what he said.
He said, "Doctor, you're a scab,"
For his clothes he made a grab.
He ran outdoors and he called a cab.
He drove right down the line, and he
drank a lot of wine,
And strange to say, the next day
Jim was feeling very fine.
Two weeks later the doctor, he took sick,
And all the doctors quick
Came to hold a consultation;
They said, "Doc, you'd better make
your will."
The doctor said, "Please tell me, is Jim
Jackson living still?"
When someone said, "He's feeling fine,"
The Doc said, "Well, boys, that's
for mine."

REPEAT REFRAIN

IF WASHINGTON SHOULD COME TO LIFE

VERSE I
If Washington should come to life and see
how matters stand,
A smile from George's lips would
surely fall.
Instead of all the wasted fields and plains
and barren land,
He'd find the greatest country of them all.
He'd find he's not neglected, that his
mem'ry rends the air;
His monuments erected he would see most
ev'rywhere.
He'd find a mighty nation of men who do
and dare;
He'd find he's still the daddy of them all.

REFRAIN I
I wonder what he'd think of Mister
Morgan
And how he'd like political machines.
I wonder if he'd read what Thomas
Lawson
Is writing for the monthly magazines.
I wonder how he'd take to Teddy
Roosevelt,
I'd like to hear exactly what he'd say.
I wonder if he'd try to never tell a lie,
If Washington should come to life today.

VERSE 2
He'd marvel at the changes as he'd take a
look around,
At motor cars he'd surely stop and stare.
I wonder what he'd think of all these
railroads underground,
And elevated trains up in the air.
The Biograph would faze him when he'd
see the pictures walk;

The phonograph would daze him when the
   thing began to talk;
The rush and shove amaze him if he ever
   saw New York
With its wondrous big skyscrapers all
   around.

REFRAIN 2

He'd soon discover we're no second-raters,
I know he'd sing the "Yankee Doodle Boy."
I wonder if he'd visit our theaters,
I wonder if he'd laugh at Eddie Foy.
I wonder if he'd try to dope the horses,
I wonder what he'd think about Broadway.
He'd buy the *New York Journal* first,
And then he'd call on Willie Hearst,
If Washington should come to life today.

I'M MIGHTY GLAD I'M LIVING AND THAT'S ALL

VERSE I

"This life's a play," said Shakespeare;
   they're the truest words he spoke.
Mister Shakespeare is a man I wish
   I'd met.
For I've seen enough of life to understand
   that it's a joke,
It's a joke and no one's guessed the
   answer yet.
Why, it's all imagination. If you'll only
   stop to think,
To this positive conclusion you'll arrive:
We live and then we die,
And when we die, why it's good-bye.
So we ought to all be glad that we're alive.

REFRAIN I

I've seen a lot of sunshine, I've seen a lot
   of rain,
I've known a lot of happiness, I've known
   a lot of pain,

I've had a dozen fortunes, a dozen times
   been broke,
No matter how the winds may blow, I take
   it as a joke.
I've had a lot of worry, of fun I've had
   no ends,
I've made a lot of enemies, I've made a lot
   of friends.
No matter what may happen, whatever
   may befall,
I only know I'm mighty glad I'm living,
   and that's all.

VERSE 2

The man who takes life serious is an awful
   laugh with me,
Why, you'll dodge him if you see him on
   the street.
But the man who sees the funny side of
   ev'rything he'll see
Is the man that ev'rybody wants to meet.
Why, it's all just what you make it.
You can manufacture joy,
Or can find a lot of fault, that's if
   you try.
But a disposition bright and a corking
   appetite
Are two little things that bankrolls
   never buy.

REFRAIN 2

I never long for riches, I never long
   for fame,
I care not if posterity ignores or shouts
   my name.
I never envy Roosevelt, nor wish that I
   were he,
Just what I am and who I am, I'm satisfied
   to be.
The Pennsylvania Railroad, it isn't mine,
   and so
I care not if the stocks go up or down, or
   how they go.

I'm happy and I'm healthy, no doctors
  need to call,
And so I know I'm mighty glad I'm living,
  and that's all.

LIFE'S A FUNNY PROPOSITION AFTER ALL

VERSE I

Did you ever sit and ponder, sit and
  wonder, sit and think,
Why we're here and what this life is all
  about?
It's a problem that has driven many brainy
  men to drink,
It's the weirdest thing they've tried to
  figure out.
About a thousand diff'rent theories all the
  scientists can show,
But never yet have proved a reason why
With all we've thought and all we're
  taught, why all we seem to know
Is we're born and live a while and then
  we die.

REFRAIN I

Life's a very funny proposition after all,
Imagination, jealousy, hypocrisy and all.
Three meals a day, a whole lot to say;
When you haven't got the coin you're
  always in the way.
Ev'rybody's fighting as we wend our way
  along,
Ev'ry fellow claims the other fellow's in
  the wrong;
Hurried and worried until we're buried
  and there's no curtain call.
Life's a very funny proposition after all.

VERSE 2

When all things are coming easy, and
  when luck is with a man,

Why then life to him is sunshine
  ev'rywhere;
Then the fates blow rather breezy and they
  quite upset a plan,
Then he'll cry that life's a burden hard to
  bear.
Though today may be a day of smiles,
  tomorrow's still in doubt,
And what brings me joy, may bring you
  care and woe;
We're born to die, but don't know why, or
  what it's all about,
And the more we try to learn the less
  we know.

REFRAIN 2

Life's a very funny proposition, you
  can bet,
And no one's ever solved the problem
  properly as yet.
Young for a day, then old and gray;
Like the rose that buds and blooms and
  fades and falls away,
Losing health to gain our wealth as
  through this dream we tour.
Ev'rything's a guess and nothing's
  absolutely sure;
Battles exciting and fates we're fighting
  until the curtain falls.
Life's a very funny proposition after all.

MARY'S A GRAND OLD NAME

VERSE I

My mother's name was Mary,
She was so good and true;
Because her name was Mary,
She called me Mary too.
She wasn't gay or airy,
But plain as she could be;
I hate to meet a fairy
Who calls herself Marie.

REFRAIN

For it is Mary, Mary,
Plain as any name can be.
But with propriety, society
Will say Marie.
But it was Mary, Mary,
Long before the fashions came,
And there is something there
That sounds so square,
It's a grand old name.

VERSE 2

Now, when her name is Mary,
There is no falseness there;
When to Marie she'll vary,
She'll surely bleach her hair.
Though Mary's ordinary,
Marie is fair to see;
Don't ever fear sweet Mary,
Beware of sweet Marie.

REPEAT REFRAIN

NOTHING NEW BENEATH THE SUN

VERSE 1

Did you ever stop to figure that this very
    life we lead
Was led by our ancestors, don't you know?
We imagine that we're living in an age of
    mighty speed,
But to tell the truth we're absolutely slow.
For fashions, fads, and fancies always are
    and always were;
Tho' they rave about progression,
There's been nothing new occur.
Ev'rything is just the same as when they
    wrote the calendar,
And that's over nineteen hundred
    years ago.

REFRAIN 1

The same old hard luck stories from the
    hard luck boys;
Good luck boys have the good luck noise.
There is nothing surer,
The poor are growing poorer,
The rich are making money by the ton.
For it's the same old world, it's full of
    smiles and tears,
And ev'rything that's going on's been
    going on for years.
If the track is clear or muddy,
Size up ev'rybody
And you'll find there's nothing new
    beneath the sun.

VERSE 2

Just to prove we're not progressive, the
    theater of today
Is the place where people mimic and
    pretend;
There's a hero and a shero and a villain in
    the play,
And the hero whips the villain in the end.
Why don't someone write a drama where
    the villain wins the day,
Why don't someone have a show without a
    hero in the play?
Just because they've always had him it will
    always be that way,
The theater hasn't one progressive friend.

REFRAIN 2

You hear the same old songs about the
    same old coons,
Few new words but the same old tunes.
Dashing on before us,
We see the merry chorus,
And ev'rything they do you know's
    been done;
You hear the same old jokes that make the
    same old hit,

The scen'ry's just the same but it's been
    painted up a bit;
You can ask most any showman,
Inquire of Charley Frohman
And he'll say there's nothing new beneath
    the sun.

VERSE 3

For instance, take the City of New York
    and look around,
It's just where it originally laid.
There's Wall Street under cover, there's
    the subway underground,
And there's no one seen the money
    Morgan's made.
Why, the Brooklyn Bridge was thought of
    as a wonderful affair,
But we used to get to Brooklyn long before
    the bridge was there.
And before McClellan's time we had a City
    Hall and Mayor,
Things are as they were and will be, I'm
    afraid.

REFRAIN 3

Why there's the same old Bow'ry of the
    old-time day,
Same old town and the same Broadway;
Cut a few new capers,
One or two skyscrapers,
You'll see them all in twenty minutes run;
Then there's the same old Sullivan, the
    same old Tim,
In case you break a window, why it's best to
    be with him.
Why, it's just the same old city
As when Croker grabbed the kitty,
So there's really nothing new beneath
    the sun.

OVER THERE

VERSE 1

Johnnie get your gun, get your gun, get
    your gun.
Take it on the run, on the run, on the run.
Hear them calling you and me,
Ev'ry son of liberty.
Hurry right away, no delay, go today,
Make your daddy glad to have had such
    a lad.
Tell your sweetheart not to pine,
To be proud her boy's in line.

REFRAIN

Over there, over there,
Send the word, send the word over there,
That the Yanks are coming, the Yanks are
    coming,
The drums rum-tumming e'vrywhere.
So prepare, say a pray'r,
Send the word, send the word to beware.
We'll be over, we're coming over,
And we won't come back till it's over over
    there.

VERSE 2

Johnnie get your gun, get your gun, get
    your gun.
Johnnie show the Hun you're a son of
    a gun.
Hoist the flag and let her fly,
Like true heroes do or die.
Pack your little kit, show your grit, do
    your bit.
Soldiers to the ranks from the towns and
    the tanks,
Make your mother proud of you,
And to liberty be true.

REPEAT REFRAIN

So Long, Mary

VERSE 1

"It's awf'ly nice of all you girls to see me
    to the train."
"So long, Mary."
"I didn't think you'd care if you should
    ne'er see me again."
"You're wrong, Mary."
This reminds me of my family
On the day I left Schenectady,
To the depot then they came with me.
I seem to hear them say:

REFRAIN

"So long, Mary;
Mary, we will miss you so.
So long, Mary,
How we hate to see you go.
And we'll all be longing for you, Mary,
While you roam.
So long, Mary,
Don't forget to come back home."

VERSE 2

"It's awf'ly kind of all you boys to see me
    off today."
"So long, Mary."
"I didn't think you'd care if I should either
    go or stay."
"You're wrong, Mary."
Yes, I'm going to other lands to dwell,
Awf'ly nice of you to wish me well;
Hardly thought a soul in New Rochelle
Would even come to say:

REPEAT REFRAIN

Twentieth-Century Love

VERSE

What a modern age, modern age,
    modern age,
The whole world's racing;
Speed is all the rage, all the rage, all
    the rage,
As we go chasing.
Thomas Edison,
He's the one,
Who's begun
Accelerating.
Now with Mister Bell,
Sam'll Morse as well,
Why keep waiting?

REFRAIN 1

No time to pitch woo now,
The century's new now,
I'm singing my love songs in that new
    ragtime.
The minute I meet ya'
I send for the preacher
And order those wedding bells to chime.
I'm
A Yankee with know-how,
Don't want to go slow now,
Can't wait for that moon above
Or even a dove.
So, kiss me and run, kid,
It's nineteen-o-one, kid,
And I'm in twentieth-century love!

REFRAIN 2

No time to pitch woo now,
It's nineteen-o-two now,
"I love you" by telegraph is fast and clear.
Whenever we're parted,
We're not broken-hearted
As long as a telephone is near,
Dear.

It's love at first sight now,
By Edison's light now,
No waiting for stars above
Or even a dove.
So, hurry to me, kid,
It's nineteen-o-three, kid,
And be my twentieth-century love!

When a Fellow's on the Level with a Girl That's on the Square

VERSE I

There are lots of fellows think that they're
    in love,
There are lots of girls who think the
    very same.
When a gal likes a fellow just because he's
    got a bankroll
And he likes her because she is a
    pretty dame,
That ain't the proper kind of love,
That's a bunco game for fair.
It's ten to one that she ain't on the level,
And it's still a better price than that
That he ain't on the square.
There ain't no love-bee making any honey,
With him it's the looks and with her it's
    the money.

REFRAIN

When a fellow's on the level with a girl
    that's on the square,
There is no other kind of happiness that
    can compare,
But dodge the merry wedding bells if
    there's a single doubt,
It's the worry of the thing that makes it
    hard to string it out.
You can tell the way she chatters if it's
    coin she's thinking of;

With thirty cents you're rich enough if it's
    a case of love.
She needn't be a queen, he needn't be a
    millionaire,
When a fellow's on the level with a girl
    that's on the square.

VERSE 2

Ev'ry fellow ought to figure ev'rything
Long before he ever buys a wedding ring,
And a girl ought to size a fellow up and get
    his number
And make pretty sure he hasn't got her on
    a string.
Take lots of time before you fall, and be
    careful what you do;
It's ten to one that he is only kidding,
And I'll lay you still a better price
That she is skidding too.
We all have dreams, it seems, of
    matrimony,
We wake from the dream when we pay
    alimony.

REPEAT REFRAIN

The Yankee Doodle Boy

VERSE I

I'm the kid that's all the candy,
I'm a Yankee Doodle dandy,
I'm glad I am,
So's Uncle Sam.
I'm a real live Yankee Doodle,
Made my name and fame and boodle
Just like Mister Doodle did, by riding on
    a pony.
I love to listen to the Dixie strain,
I long to see the girl I left behind me;
And that ain't a josh,
She's a Yankee, by gosh,

Oh, say can you see
Anything about a Yankee that's phony?

REFRAIN
I'm a Yankee Doodle dandy,
A Yankee Doodle, do or die;
A real live nephew of my Uncle Sam's,
Born on the Fourth of July.
I've got a Yankee Doodle sweetheart,
She's my Yankee Doodle joy.
Yankee Doodle came to London, just to
    ride the ponies,
I am a Yankee Doodle boy.

VERSE 2
Father's name was Hezikiah,
Mother's name was Ann Maria,
Yanks through and through,
Red, White and Blue.
Father was so Yankee-hearted,
When the Spanish war was started
He slipped on his uniform and hopped up
    on a pony.
My mother's mother was a Yankee true,
My father's father was a Yankee too,
And that's going some,
For the Yankees, by gum,
Oh, say can you see
Anything about my pedigree that's
    phony?

REPEAT REFRAIN

You're a Grand Old Flag

VERSE I
There's a feeling comes a-stealing and it
    sets my brain a-reeling
When I'm list'ning to the music of a
    military band.
Any tune like "Yankee Doodle" simply
    sets me off my noodle,

It's that patriotic something that no one
    can understand.
"Way down South in the land of cotton,"
    melody untiring,
Ain't that inspiring!
Hurrah! Hurrah! We'll join the jubilee,
And that's going some
For the Yankees, by gum!
Red, White and Blue,
I am for you,
Honest, you're a grand old flag.

REFRAIN
You're a grand old flag,
You're a high-flying flag,
And forever in peace may you wave.
You're the emblem of
The land I love,
The home of the free and the brave.
Ev'ry heart beats true
Under Red, White and Blue,
Where there's never a boast or brag.
But should auld acquaintance be forgot,
Keep your eye on the grand old flag.

VERSE 2
I'm a cranky hanky panky, I'm a dead
    square honest Yankee,
And I'm mighty proud of that old flag that
    flies for Uncle Sam.
Though I don't believe in raving ev'ry
    time I see it waving,
There's a chill runs up my back that makes
    me glad I'm what I am.
Here's a land with a million soldiers, that's
    if we should need 'em,
We'll fight for freedom!
Hurrah! Hurrah! For ev'ry Yankee tar
And old G.A.R., ev'ry stripe, ev'ry star.
Red, White and Blue,
Hats off to you,
Honest, you're a grand old flag.

REPEAT REFRAIN

Henry Creamer (1879–1930)

ONE OF the most successful of America's black lyricists, Henry Creamer was born in Richmond, Virginia, the son of a minister, and was raised in New York City. He worked in a popular vaudeville act with his frequent co-writer J. Turner Layton, with whom he wrote material for Bert Williams (in the 1911 *Ziegfeld Follies*), Al Jolson, and Sophie Tucker. In 1922 they wrote the songs for, and starred in, *Strut Miss Lizzie* on Broadway.

AFTER YOU'VE GONE

VERSE 1
Now won't you listen, honey, while I say
How could you tell me that you're
    going away?
Don't say that we must part,
Don't break your baby's heart.
You know I've loved you for these many
    years,
Loved you night and day.
Oh, honey baby, can't you see my tears?
Listen while I say:

REFRAIN
"After you've gone
And left me crying,
After you've gone
There's no denying,
You'll feel blue,
You'll feel sad,
You'll miss the bestest pal you've ever had.
There'll come a time,
Now don't forget it,
There'll come a time
When you'll regret it.
Oh! Babe,
Think what you're doing,

You know my love for you will drive me
    to ruin,
After you've gone
After you've gone away."

VERSE 2
Don't you remember how you used to say
You'd always love me in the same old way?
And now it's very strange
That you should ever change.
Perhaps some other sweetie's won your
    heart,
Tempted you away.
But let me warn you, tho' we're miles
    apart,
You'll regret some day.

REPEAT REFRAIN

—*J. Turner Layton*

IF I COULD BE WITH YOU

VERSE
I'm so blue I don't know what to do,
All day through I'm pining just for you.
I did wrong when I let you go away

For now I grieve about you night
  and day.
I'm unhappy and dissatisfied,
But I'd be happy if I had you by my side.

REFRAIN

If I could be with you
I'd love you strong,
If I could be with you
I'd love you long.
I want you to know
I wouldn't go
Until I told you, honey, why I love
  you so.
If I could be with you
One hour tonight,
If I was free to do
The things I might,
I'm telling you true,
I'd be anything but blue,
If I could be with you.

VERSE 2

All dressed up but still nowhere to go,
How I wish that I could see a show.
Here I wait with no one to call me dear,
The one I love is many miles from here.
Central gave me one two three four J,
Oh won't you listen little sweetie while
  I say:

REPEAT REFRAIN

—*James P. Johnson*

'WAY DOWN YONDER IN
NEW ORLEANS

VERSE I

Guess!
Where do you think I'm goin' when the
  winds start blowin' strong?

Guess!
Where do you think I'm goin' when the
  nights start growin' long?
I ain't goin' East,
I ain't goin' West,
I ain't goin' over the cuckoo's nest.
I'm bound for the town that I love
  best,
Where life is one sweet song.

REFRAIN I

'Way down yonder in New Orleans,
In the land of dreamy scenes,
There's a garden of Eden,
That's what I mean,
Creole babies with flashing eyes
Softly whisper with tender sighs,
"Stop!
Oh! won't you give your lady fair
A little smile?
Stop!
You bet your life you'll linger there
A little while."
There is Heaven right here on earth
With those beautiful queens
'Way down yonder in New Orleans.

VERSE 2

Guess!
What do you think I'm thinkin' when you
  think I'm thinkin' wrong?
Guess!
What do you think I'm thinkin' when I'm
  thinkin' all night long?
I ain't thinkin' this,
I ain't thinkin' that,
I cannot be thinkin' about your hat.
My heart does not start to pit-a-pat
Unless I hear this song:

REPEAT REFRAIN

—*J. Turner Layton*

P. G. Wodehouse (1881–1975)

WHEN, in 1916, P(elham) G(renville) Wodehouse first wrote a few songs with Jerome Kern for a show called *Miss Springtime,* he had already been writing lyrics for more than a decade, beginning at Oxford. Less than four months after they began collaborating, they had a full show on, and a year later came their greatest success, *Oh, Boy!,* which was also the most successful of the famous Princess Theater shows; at last Broadway musicals were integrating their songs into the plot–a revolution! *Oh, Boy!* (1917) produced "Till the Clouds Roll By"; *Leave It to Jane* (also 1917) featured "Cleopatterer." Nineteen-eighteen saw *Oh, Lady! Lady!,* from which the original version of "Bill" was cut and so saved for *Show Boat,* nine years later. Kern and Wodehouse worked together only sporadically after that–a couple of successful shows in London and the 1924 *Sitting Pretty* ("Tulip Time in Sing Sing"). Kern went on to collaborate with Otto Harbach and Oscar Hammerstein II, and Wodehouse went on with the torrent of comic novels and stories that brought him worldwide fame and, eventually, a knighthood. Jeeves and Bertie Wooster are far more famous today than the musicals, but no one could really be influenced by Wodehouse's fiction–it was inimitable; whereas the shows that Kern, Wodehouse, and librettist Guy Bolton put together, and the relaxed vernacular of Wodehouse's lyrics, influenced generations of American musicals. *Bring On the Girls,* the memoir by Wodehouse and Bolton of their early theater days, is essential (and hilarious) reading for anyone interested in theatrical history.

BILL

(ORIGINAL VERSION)

VERSE I

I used to dream that I would discover
The perfect lover someday.
I knew I'd recognize him
If ever he came 'round my way.
I always used to fancy then
He'd be one of the godlike kind
 of men,
With a giant brain and a noble head
Like the heroes bold in the books
 I read.

REFRAIN I

But along came Bill
Who's quite the opposite
Of all the men
In storybooks.
In grace and looks
I know that Apollo
Would beat him all hollow,
And I can't explain,
It's surely not his brain
That makes me thrill.
I love him
Because he's wonderful,
Because he's just old Bill.

VERSE 2

He can't play golf or tennis or polo
Or sing a solo or row.
He isn't half as handsome
As dozens of men I know.
He isn't tall and straight and slim,
And he dresses far worse than Ted or Jim,
And I can't explain why he should be
Just the one, one man in the world for me.

REFRAIN 2

He's just my Bill,
He has no gifts at all:
A motor car
He cannot steer,
And it seems clear
Whenever he dances,
His partner takes chances.
Oh, I can't explain,
It's surely not his brain
That makes me thrill.
I love him
Because he's—I don't know—
Because he's just my Bill.

—Jerome Kern

BILL

(*with Oscar Hammerstein II, as rewritten
for* Show Boat)

REFRAIN I

But along came Bill,
Who's not my type at all,
You'd meet him on the street and never
        notice him.
His form and face,
His manly grace,
Are not the kind that you would find in a
        statue.
Oh, I can't explain,
It's surely not his brain

That makes me thrill.
I love him, because he's wonderful,
Because he's just my Bill.

REFRAIN 2

He's just my Bill,
An ordinary guy,
He hasn't got a thing that I can brag about.
And yet to be
Upon his knee,
So comfy and roomy seems natural to me.
Oh, I can't explain,
It's surely not his brain
That makes me thrill.
I love him,
Because he's—I don't know—
Because he's just my Bill.

—Jerome Kern

BUNGALOW IN QUOGUE

VERSE I

Oh, let us fly without delay
Into the country far away,
Where, free from all this care and strife,
We'll go and live the simple life.
How clear the voice of Nature calls;
I'll go and get some overalls,
And get a last year's almanac
To read at night when things are slack.

REFRAIN I

Let's build a little bungalow in Quogue,
In Yaphank, or in Hicksville or Patchogue,
Where we can sniff the scented breeze,
And pluck tomatoes from the trees,
Where there is room to exercise the dog.
How pleasant it will be through life
        to jog
With Bill the bull and Hildebrand
        the hog.

Each morn we'll waken from our doze,
When Reginold, the rooster, crows,
Down in our little bungalow in Quogue.

VERSE 2

Each day, if you will show me how,
I'll go and milk Clarice the cow,
Or for asparagus we'll dig,
Or slaughter Percival the pig.
And if we find a snail or slug
Or weevil or potato bug,
We'll track them down and wring their
    necks,
Regardless of their age or sex.

REFRAIN 2

Let's build a little bungalow in Quogue,
In Yaphank, or in Hicksville or Patchogue,
Where Hilda, our resourceful hen,
Will lay us omelettes now and then,
As easily as falling off a log.
The cheerful chirp of Frederick the frog
Will greet our ears from some
    adjacent bog
When we are sitting up at nights,
Comparing our mosquito bites,
Down in our little bungalow in Quogue.

REFRAIN 3

Let's build a little bungalow in Quogue,
In Yaphank, or in Hicksville or Patchogue.
If life should tend to be a bore,
We'll call on Farmer Brown next door
And get an earful of his dialogue.
When winter comes and brings the snow
    and fog
We'll fortify our systems with hot grog,
And listen, when the nights are still,
To Wilberforce the whippoorwill,
Down in our little bungalow in Quogue.

—Jerome Kern

CLEOPATTERER

VERSE 1

In days of old beside the Nile
A famous queen there dwelt.
Her clothes were few, but full of style,
Her figure slim and svelte.
On ev'ry man that wandered by
She pulled the Theda Bara eye,
And ev'ryone observed with awe
That her work was swift, but never raw.

REFRAIN 1

I'd be like Cleopatterer
If I could have my way.
Each man she met she went and kissed,
And she'd dozens on her waiting list.
I wish that I had lived there
Beside the pyramid,
For a girl today don't get the scope
That Cleopatterer did!

VERSE 2

And when she tired, as girls will do,
Of Bill or Jack or Jim,
The time had come, his friends all knew,
To say "Good-bye" to him.
She couldn't stand, by any means,
Reproachful, stormy farewell scenes.
To such coarse stuff she would not stoop,
So she just put poison in his soup!

REFRAIN 2

When out with Cleopatterer
Men always made their wills.
They knew there was no time to waste
When the gumbo had that funny taste.
They'd take her hand and squeeze it,
They'd murmur, "Oh, you kid!"
But they never liked to start to feed
Till Cleopatterer did.

VERSE 3

She danced new dances now and then,
The sort that make you blush.
Each time she did them, scores of men
Got injured in the rush.
They'd stand there gaping in a line
And watch her agitate her spine;
It simply used to knock them flat
When she went like this and went
    like that.

REFRAIN 3

At dancing, Cleopatterer
Was always on the spot.
She gave those poor Egyptian ginks
Something else to watch besides the
    Sphinx.
Marc Antony admitted
That what first made him skid
Was the wibbely wobbely wiggley dance
That Cleopatterer did!

—Jerome Kern

IT'S A HARD, HARD WORLD FOR A MAN

VERSE I

No woman yet has understood
We try our hardest to be good;
But something always seems to
    interfere.
No gratitude
Our attitude
Was ever known to win;
But still we persevere.
We do our best, as we have said,
The straight and narrow path to tread,
Ignoring temptations Fate may send.
But of snare the world has plenty, meant
To trap the man of sentiment;
And one is sure to get us in the end.

REFRAIN I

Oh, it's a hard, hard, hard, hard world for
    a man,
For he tries to be wise
And remain aloof and chilly.
But along comes something feminine and
    frilly.
So what's the use?
He will run loose,
Though he does the best he can.
It's a hard, hard, hard, hard world for
    a man!

VERSE 2

The hist'ry books are full of tales
Of fellows who were perfect whales
At virtue when they started their career.
Sir Lancelot
To glance a lot
At girls was never known,
Till he met Guinevere.
Marc Antony, the records show,
Was like a chunk of driven snow,
But Cleopatra sent the poor man wrong.
And King Henry was a paragon
Till Catherine of Aragon
And six or seven others came along.

REFRAIN 2

Oh, it's a hard, hard, hard, hard world for
    a man.
He'd be good, if he could,
But he can't, and there's a reason:
For the skirts are getting shorter ev'ry
    season.
So what's the use?
He will run loose,
Though he does the best he can.
It's a hard, hard, hard, hard world for
    a man!

—Jerome Kern

THE LAND WHERE THE GOOD SONGS GO

VERSE 1

On the other side of the moon,
Ever so far,
Beyond the last little star,
There's a land, I know,
Where the good songs go,
Where it's always afternoon.
And snug in a haven of peace and rest,
Like the dear old songs that we love
    the best,

REFRAIN

It's a land of flowers
And April showers,
With sunshine in between.
With roses blowing and rivers flowing
'Mid rushes growing green.
Where no one hurries
And no one worries
And life runs calm and slow.
And I wish someday I could find my way
To the land where the good songs go.

VERSE 2

Dear old songs forgotten too soon,
They had their day,
And then we threw them away,
And without a sigh we would pass them by
For some other, newer tune.
So off to a happier home they flew,
Where they're always loved and they're
    always new.

REPEAT REFRAIN

—*Jerome Kern*

NAPOLEON

VERSE 1

Napoleon was a little guy,
They used to call him Shorty.
He only stood about so high,
His chest was under forty.
But when they started joshing him,
His pride, it didn't injure.
He'd simply say,
"Ah, fade 'way!"
He knew he had the ginger.

REFRAIN 1

Napoleon, Napoleon,
They thought him quite a joke.
"Hey! Take a slant at the little pill!"
Was the line of chatter that they used to
    spill.
But they couldn't hold Napoleon
When he started in to scrap.
He was five feet high,
But he was one tough guy,
And I take after Nap.

VERSE 2

Napoleon was a homely gink,
He hadn't time to doll up,
But though he looked like thirty cents,
He packed an awful wallop.
And all the kings in Europe,
When they came to know his habits,
Pulled up their socks
And ran for blocks,
He got them scared like rabbits.

REFRAIN 2

Napoleon, Napoleon
Went out and got a "rep,"
He had a lot of 'em climbing trees,
Though he weighed a hundred in his
    B.V.D.'s.

It was easy for Napoleon,
And he wiped them off the map.
He was not so tall,
But he could lick them all,
And I take after Nap.

VERSE 3
Napoleon was the ladies' pet,
He liked to have them handy.
He used to blow in half his pay
On violets and candy.
He knew the game from soup to nuts
And worked it on a system!
He'd meet a queen at five-fifteen,
By six o'clock she'd kissed him.

REFRAIN 3
Napoleon, Napoleon,
The ladies thought him great,
They fell for him good and hard, they did,
When he came and handed them the "Oh,
     you Kid."
They were wild about Napoleon,
For his work was full of snap.
He was sawn off short,
But he was one good sport,
And I take after Nap.

—*Jerome Kern*

THAT WAS BEFORE I MET YOU

VERSE 1
HE: Prepare yourself to hear the worst!
     I'm sorry, but you're not the first
     My heart to claim,
     I own with shame.
     I'm thankful that I have confessed:
     My conscience now will be at rest.
     You may forgive me and love me just
          the same.
     To force myself to say so

I've had an awful tussle,
     Yet still the fact I can't conceal:
     I once loved Lillian Russell.

REFRAIN 1
But that was before I met you, dearie,
     dear,
That was before I met you.
Her image I've banished,
All passion has vanished,
I think you're a million
Times sweeter than Lillian.
Don't scold me,
You told me
To tell you the truth;
Just count it as one of the follies of youth:
I thought her a queen
When I was fourteen,
But that was before I met you.

VERSE 2
SHE: My pet, I know just how you feel,
     For I have something to reveal:
     For, dear, I too
     Once loved like you.
     I shall be happier, no doubt,
     When I have let my secret out.
     In days gone by, dear, I idolized
          John Drew.
     I used to hope that someday
     We might become acquainted.
     And when I got his autograph
     I thought I should have fainted.

REFRAIN 2
But that was before I met you, dearie, dear,
That was before I met you.
His wonderful profile
Made all girls, you know, feel
That nothing could cheer them
If he wasn't near them.
Romances
My fancies

Would weave about John!
But love seemed to wane as the long years
    went on.
I thought him divine;
But then I was nine,
And that was before I met you.

—Jerome Kern

Till the Clouds Roll By

(with Jerome Kern and Guy Bolton)

VERSE I

SHE: I'm so sad to
    Think that I have had to
    Drive you from your home so coolly.
HE: I'd be gaining
    Nothing by remaining,
    What would Mrs. Grundy say?
    Her conventions, kindly
        recollect them!
    We must please respect them
    Duly.
SHE: My intrusion needs explaining.
    I felt my courage waning.
HE: Please, I beg, don't mention it!
    I should not mind a bit,
    But it has started raining.

REFRAIN

TOGETHER: Oh, the rain
    Comes a-pitter-patter,
    And I'd like to be safe in bed.
    Skies are weeping
    While the world is sleeping,
    Trouble heaping
    On our head.
    It is vain to remain and chatter,
    And to wait for a clearer sky;
    Helter-skelter
    I must fly for shelter
    Till the clouds roll by.

VERSE 2

SHE: What bad luck, it's
    Coming down in buckets,
    Have you an umbrella handy?
HE: I've a warm coat,
    Waterproof, a storm coat,
    I shall be all right, I know.
    Later on, too, I will ward the
        grippe off
    With a little nip of
    Brandy.
SHE: Or a glass of toddy draining,
    You'd find that more sustaining.
HE: Don't be worried, I entreat,
    I've rubbers for my feet,
    So I don't mind it raining.

REPEAT REFRAIN

—Jerome Kern

Tulip Time in Sing Sing

VERSE

Up the river there's a college
Which authorities acknowledge
Is a cozy sort of place to go and dwell.
And with joy each student chortles
As he passes through its portals
And the faculty conduct him to his cell.
How I wish that there I'd waited,
Wish I'd never graduated,
For the memory of those days still stirs
    me so.
And the birdies every Spring sing,
Aren't you coming back to Sing Sing
Where you used to be so happy
    long ago?

REFRAIN I

When it's tulip time in Sing Sing,
Oh it's there that I would be.

There are gentle hearts in Sing Sing,
Watching and yearning for me.
Oh I wish I was back with a rock or two to
     crack
With my pals of the class of "ninety-
     nine."
How I miss the peace and quiet
And the simple wholesome diet
Of that dear old-fashioned prison of
     mine!

VERSE 2

Oh I'd give a lot to go there,
Life was never dull or slow there,
Every night there was a concert or a hop.
Or I'd sit discussing Coué
With my old pal bat-eared Louie,
Quite the nicest man that ever slugged
     a cop.
We were just a band of brothers,
Each as good as all the others
As the humblest sort of sneak thief you
     might rank,
But when you'd been there a week, well,
We were treated as an equal
By the high and mighty swells who'd
     robbed a bank.

REFRAIN 2

When it's tulip time in Sing Sing,
Oh it's there that I would be.
There are gentle hearts in Sing Sing,
Watching and yearning for me.
Oh, there's no place like home,
And I'm tired of having to roam
Through the world with its women and
     its wine.
So just bob my hair and shove me
Where I know the warders love me,
In that dear old-fashioned prison
     of mine!

—*Jerome Kern*

YOU CAN'T MAKE LOVE BY WIRELESS

(with George Grossmith)

VERSE 1

Charles Augustus Chaytor,
Wireless operator,
Loved the fair
Golden-hair'd
Bessie Magee.
She lived in Dargheeling
Avenue, West Ealing;
He was always out at sea.
Such was his devotion
That when on the ocean,
Ev'ry day
He'd relay
Greetings to Bess.
But I'm told that sometimes
There, alas, would come times
When he'd moan this S.O.S:

REFRAIN 1

"You can't make love by wireless;
It's like bread without the jam.
There is nothing girls desire less
Than a cold Marconigram.
For it's something you can't speak to
From a someone you can't see.
It's like a village church that's
     spireless,
Or a little home that's fireless,
Or a motorcar that's tireless,
And it isn't any good to me!"

VERSE 2

Mark the horrid sequel,
It is hard to equal;
Fate with grim
Tragic whim
Upset his dream.
For that maiden fickle

Wed a man from Crickle-
Wood who kept a laundry (steam).

Charles, poor man, thus jilted,
Naturally wilted.
Soured he grew,
Gloomy too,
Quite lost his smile.
Nevermore his jokes'll
Entertain the fo'csle.
He keeps mutt'ring all the while:

REFRAIN 2
"You can't make love by wireless,
It's like eggs without the ham.
There is nothing girls desire less
Than a cold Marconigram.
For it's something you can't speak to
From a someone you can't see.
It's like a village church that's
    spireless,
Or a Selfridge's that's buyerless,
Or a Pekinese that's sireless,
And it isn't any good to me!"

—*Jerome Kern*

You Never Knew About Me

VERSE 1
HE: We were children once long ago,
    dear, you and I.
    At the start our lives lay apart as lives
    will lie.
    Up I grew and I never knew
    That the world contained a darling
    like you,
    Nor did you dream you would see
    little me, too, by and by.

REFRAIN 1
I never knew about you, dear,
And you never knew about me.
Life might have been Heaven,
If I, then age seven,
Had but met you when you were three.
We'd have made mud pies like affinities.
We'd have known what rapture may be.
I'd have let you feed my rabbit
Till the thing became a habit, dear!
But I never knew about you,
(Ah! What we might have been.)
And you never knew about me.

VERSE 2
SHE: How I wish I'd known, dear, that one
    day you'd arrive,
    Just to feel I had an ideal for which to
    strive.
    Had I'd known I'd meet you, my own,
    I would not have lived for pleasure
    alone;
    I was frivolous and gay, sad to say,
    when I was five.

REFRAIN 2
I never knew about you, dear,
And you never knew about me.
I never missed chances
Of juvenile dances,
For my life was one mad spree.
I was often kissed 'neath the mistletoe
By small boys excited with tea.
If I'd known that you existed,
I'd have scratched them and resisted, dear!
But I never knew about you,
(Oh! the pain of it.)
And you never knew about me.

—*Jerome Kern*

Cecil Mack (1884–1944)

Cecil Mack (Richard C. McPherson)–born in Norfolk, Virginia, and educated at Lincoln University and the University of Pennsylvania–was one of the top black songwriters of the century. He wrote dozens of successful numbers for such popular entertainers as Nora Bayes and Bert Williams; collaborated with James P. Johnson on the show *Runnin' Wild,* which gave the Charleston to the world; and founded the first black publishing firm in America, the Gotham-Attucks Music Publishing Co. His "That's Why They Call Me 'Shine' "–one of the most telling comments on prejudice in popular song–became a hit four times, for white singers as well as black, over a period of twenty-four years: first with the California Ramblers in 1924; then in 1932 in the top ten with Bing Crosby; in the same year with Louis Armstrong; and back in the top ten in 1948 with Frankie Laine. Mack's wife, too, was a pioneer–she was the first registered dentist of her race in New York State.

CHARLESTON

VERSE

Carolina, Carolina,
At last they've got you on the map.
With a new tune,
A funny blue tune,
With a peculiar snap!
You may not be able to buck or wing,
Fox-trot, two-step, or even sing,
If you ain't got religion in your feet
You can do this prance and do it
    neat.

REFRAIN

Charleston!
Charleston!
Made in Carolina.
Some dance,
Some prance,
I'll say.

There's nothing finer than the
    Charleston,
Charleston.
Lord, how you can shuffle.
Ev'ry step you do
Leads to something new,
Man, I'm telling you
It's a lapazoo.
Buck dance
Wing dance
Will be a back number,
But the Charleston,
The new Charleston,
That dance is surely a comer.
Sometime
You'll dance it one time,
The dance called the Charleston,
Made in South Caroline.

–Cecil Mack and James P. Johnson

HE'S A COUSIN OF MINE

VERSE I

There's a scandal in the neighborhood
And it's all 'bout Julie Brown.
It seems her long lost cousin, Jeremiah,
Had lately arrived in town.
When Julie's feller came to call
That Sunday at her home,
He found the pair a-sitting there
Jes' a-spoonin' in the gloam.
The sight made him so riled
He started home at once,
But Julie said, "I'm s'prised at you,
Don't go act like a dunce."

REFRAIN

"Why, he's a cousin of mine, just a cousin
    of mine.
You're li'ble for to see him here any
    old time.
Jes like a bee, you're all the time a-buzzin',
'Taint no harm for to hug and kiss your
    cousin.
I haven't seen Jerry in the last ten years,
You know that's a mighty long time.
He's Mother's sister's angel child–
He's a cousin of mine."

VERSE 2

When she had explained her relationship,
He replied, "It may be so,
But he don't look like a thirty-second
    cousin
That I met a week ago."
She smiled at home quite innocently
And blushed up to her hair,
Then said, "If you don't want him
    'round,
I will tell him so, my dear."
She joined her cousin's side

And as they strolled away,
He heard him ask, "Who is that freak?"
And heard his Julie say:

REPEAT REFRAIN

—Christopher Smith and Silvio Hein

THAT'S WHY THEY CALL ME "SHINE"

VERSE I

When I was born they christened me plain
    Samuel Johnson Brown.
I hadn't grown so very big 'fore some folks
    in the town
Had changed it 'round to Sambo, I was
    Rastus to a few,
Then Choc'late Drop was added by some
    others that I knew,
And then to cap the climax I was strolling
    down the line
When someone shouted, "Fellers, hey,
    come on and pipe the Shine."
But I don't care a bit,
Here's how I figure it.

REFRAIN

'Cause my hair is curly,
'Cause my teeth are pearly,
Just because I always wear a smile,
Like to dress up in the latest style,
'Cause I'm glad I'm living,
Take troubles smiling, never whine;
Just because my color's shady,
Slightly diff'rent maybe,
That's why they call me "Shine."

VERSE 2

A rose, they say, by any other name would
    smell as sweet,

So if that's right, why should a nickname
    take me off my feet?
Why, ev'rything that's precious from a
    gold piece to a dime
And diamonds, pearls, and rubies ain't no
    good unless they shine.
So when these clever people call me
    "shine" or "coon" or "smoke,"

I simply smile, then smile some more, and
    vote them all a joke.
I'm thinking just the same,
What is there in a name?

REPEAT REFRAIN

—Ford Dabney

Bert Kalmar (1884–1947)
and Harry Ruby (1895–1974)

R UBY AND KALMAR not only wrote together for three decades but were the subject of a big M-G-M musical named after their most famous song, "Three Little Words." (Ruby was played by Red Skelton, Kalmar by Fred Astaire.) Bert Kalmar–he ran away from home at the age of ten–came up through tent shows and vaudeville as both a comedian and a magician, and Harry Ruby began as a movie-house pianist and song-plugger, but by the teens they were both in New York, writing songs and skits for musical revues. By the twenties they were writing successful Broadway shows, among them *Helen of Troy, New York,* and *Good Boy,* in which Helen Kane first sang "I Wanna Be Loved By You," the "Boop-boop-a-doop" song. Ruby worked with the Marx Brothers on the stage version of *Animal Crackers,* and when he and Kalmar went to Hollywood, they helped on the movie and on *Horse Feathers* and *Duck Soup* as well. In 1923 there were five top-ten versions of another of their biggest hits, "Who's Sorry Now?," and yet another when Connie Francis recorded it thirty-five years later.

GIVE ME THE SIMPLE LIFE

(Harry Ruby alone)

VERSE

Folks are blessed who make the best of
    ev'ry day,
Living by their own philosophy.
Everyone beneath the sun must find a way,
And I have found the only way for me.

REFRAIN 1

I don't believe in
Frettin' and grievin';
Why mess around with strife?
I never was cut out
To step and strut out.
Give me the simple life!
Some find it pleasant
Dining on pheasant,

Those things roll off my knife.
Just serve me tomatoes
And mashed potatoes;
Give me the simple life.
A cottage small is all I'm after,
Not one that's spacious and wide.
A house that rings with joy and
    laughter
And the ones you love inside.
Some like the high road,
I like the low road,
Free from the care and strife.
Sounds corny and seedy,
But yes, indeedy,
Give me the simple life!

REFRAIN 2

Living I find is
Best when your mind is

Keen as a carving knife.
I'm crazy about sleep,
Can't do without sleep.
Give me the simple life!
I love to whittle
And play a little
Tune on a ten-cent fife.
I don't aim to worry,
Hustle or hurry;
Give me the simple life.
I greet the dawn when I awaken,
The sky is clear up above.
I like my scrambled eggs and bacon
Served by someone that I love.
Life could be thrilling
With one who's willing
To be a farmer's wife.
Kids calling me Pappy
Would make me happy;
Give me the simple life!

—Rube Bloom

Nevertheless
(I'm in Love with You)

VERSE I

I knew the time had to come
When I'd be held under your thumb.
I'm like a pawn in your hand,
Moved and compelled, at your
      command.
Whether it's for bad or for good,
I would never change if I could.

REFRAIN

Maybe I'm right and maybe I'm wrong,
And maybe I'm weak and maybe I'm
      strong,
But, nevertheless, I'm in love
      with you.
Maybe I'll win and maybe I'll lose,

And maybe I'm in for cryin' the blues,
But, nevertheless, I'm in love with you.
Somehow, I know at a glance
The terrible chances I'm taking:
Fine at the start,
Then left with a heart that is breaking.
Maybe I'll live a life of regret,
And maybe I'll give much more than
      I'll get,
But, nevertheless, I'm in love
      with you.

VERSE 2

In spite of all I could do,
I went ahead falling for you.
So if I laugh or I cry,
I made my bed, that's where I'll lie.
For what happens there's no excuse,
I put my own head in the noose.

REPEAT REFRAIN

Three Little Words

VERSE I

Three words in my dictionary
I never could see,
But to my vocabulary
I've added those three.
I'm waiting for someone
To say them to me.

REFRAIN

Three little words,
Oh, what I'd give for
That wonderful phrase.
To hear those three little words,
That's all I'd live for
The rest of my days.
And what I feel in my heart
They tell me sincerely,
No other words

Can tell it half so clearly.
Three little words,
Eight little letters
Which simply mean,
"I love you!"

VERSE 2
I used to pay no attention
Whenever I'd hear
Some lonesome Romeo mention,
"I love you, my dear."
Now I want to hear it
Each time you draw near.

REPEAT REFRAIN

WHAT A PERFECT COMBINATION
(with Irving Caesar)

VERSE
I just fell
Hook, line and sinker
For the sweetest gal in town.
I'm all bound up
With a brand-new love affair.
I can't tell
Which way I'm going,
'Cause the world is upside down.
I know that I'm gone,
The panic is on.

REFRAIN I
She has lips that taste like wine,
I like hers and she likes mine,
What a perfect combination,
No wonder we're in love.
She has charms and perfect taste,
I have arms that fit her waist.
What a perfect combination,
No wonder we're in love.
She taught me one thing,
Love is only what you make it.

And I know one thing,
She can dish it out and I can take it.
We both want a family,
I want twins and so does she,
What a perfect combination,
No wonder we're in love.

REFRAIN 2
I like bread and she likes jam,
I like eggs and she likes ham,
What a perfect combination,
No wonder we're in love.
Can she cook and can she sew?
She can sew and so and so.
What a perfect combination,
No wonder we're in love.
Once she liked crooning,
Used to go for Rudy Vallee.
We started spooning,
Now her radio is in the alley.
When we neck we neck all night,
I'm a wreck and she's a sight.
What a perfect combination,
No wonder we're in love.

—Harry Akst

WHO'S SORRY NOW?

VERSE I
You smiled when we parted,
It hurt me somehow,
I thought there was nothing
    worthwhile.
The tables are turning
And you're crying now,
While I am just learning
To smile.

REFRAIN
Who's sorry now?
Who's sorry now?

Whose heart is aching
For breaking each vow?
Who's sad and blue?
Who's crying too?
Just like I cried over you.
Right to the end,
Just like a friend,
I tried to warn you somehow.
You had your way,
Now you must pay;
I'm glad that you're
    sorry now.

VERSE 2
Although I forgive you,
I cannot forget
How you shattered all my ideals.
You smiled when I told you
That you would regret,
And now you know just how
It feels.

REPEAT REFRAIN

—Ted Snyder

Joseph McCarthy (1885–1943)

BEFORE BECOMING one of his era's most successful lyricists, Joseph McCarthy, from Massachusetts, worked as a singing waiter, a song-plugger, and a music publisher. He supplied lyrics for a number of hit shows composed by Harry Tierney–1919's *Irene,* with Edith Day singing "Alice Blue Gown" for a then-record 675 performances; *Kid Boots* with Eddie Cantor; and *Rio Rita*–as well as four editions of the Ziegfeld Follies. His career slowed down in the thirties, but he wrote the American lyrics for "Underneath the Arches," a great English music hall favorite, and in 1940 he contributed to Billy Rose's Aquacade at the New York World's Fair. His son, Joseph McCarthy, Jr., followed in his father's footsteps as a successful songwriter.

ALICE BLUE GOWN

VERSE 1

I once had a gown, it was almost new,
Oh, the daintiest thing, it was sweet
    Alice blue;
With little forget-me-nots placed here and
    there,
When I had it on, I walked on the air,
And it wore, and it wore, and it wore,
Till it went and it wasn't no more.

REFRAIN

In my sweet little Alice blue gown,
When I first wandered down into town,
I was both proud and shy
As I felt ev'ry eye,
But in ev'ry shop window
I'd primp, passing by.
Then in manner of fashion I'd frown,
And the world seemed to smile all
    around.
Till it wilted I wore it,
I'll always adore it;
My sweet little Alice blue gown.

VERSE 2

The little silkworms that made silk for
    that gown
Just made that much silk and then crawled
    in the ground,
For there never was anything like it
    before,
And I don't dare to hope there will be
    anymore.
But it's gone, 'cause it just had to be,
Still it wears in my memory.

REPEAT REFRAIN

—Harry Tierney

I'M ALWAYS CHASING RAINBOWS

VERSE

At the end of the rainbow there's
    happiness,
And to find it how often I've tried,
But my life is a race, just a wild goose
    chase,

And my dreams have all been denied.
Why have I always been a failure,
What can the reason be?
I wonder if the world's to blame,
I wonder if it could be me?

REFRAIN

I'm always chasing rainbows,
Watching clouds drifting by.
My schemes are just like all my dreams,
Ending in the sky.
Some fellows look and find the sunshine,
I always look and find the rain.
Some fellows make a winning sometime,
I never even make a gain;
Believe me,
I'm always chasing rainbows,
Waiting to find a little bluebird in vain.

—Harry Carroll

You Made Me Love You
(I Didn't Want to Do It)

VERSE I

I've been worried all day long,
Don't know if I'm right or wrong,
I can't help just what I say,
Your love makes me speak this way.
Why, oh! why should I feel blue?
Once I used to laugh at you,
But now I'm cryin',
No use denyin',
There's no one else but you will do.

REFRAIN

You made me love you,
I didn't wanna do it,
I didn't wanna do it.
You made me want you,
And all the time you knew it,
I guess you always knew it.
You made me happy sometimes,
You made me glad,
But there were times, dear,
You made me feel so bad.
You made me sigh, for
I didn't wanna tell you,
I didn't wanna tell you.
I want some love that's true,
Yes I do, 'deed I do, you know I do.
Gimme, gimme what I cry for,
You know you got the brand of kisses that
    I'd die for,
You know you made me love you.

VERSE 2

I had pictured in my mind
Some day I would surely find
Someone handsome, someone true,
But I never thought of you.
Now my dream of love is o'er,
I want you and nothing more,
Come on enfold me,
Come on and hold me,
Just like you never did before.

REPEAT REFRAIN

—James V. Monaco

Sam M. Lewis (1885–1959) and Joe Young (1889–1939)

AMONG THE hundreds of lyrics written by the tremendously successful partnership of Samuel M. Lewis and Joe Young, many of the most famous are associated with Al Jolson: "My Mammy," "Rock-a-Bye Your Baby with a Dixie Melody," "I'm Sitting on Top of the World." Their "Dinah" was a hit for Jolson, Ethel Waters, Eddie Cantor, and eventually Dinah Shore, who made it her theme song. Lewis, a New Yorker, began his career at sixteen, singing and supplying skits and gags as well as lyrics for burlesque shows and variety performers. (He also tried the violin, Wall Street, and working in a theatrical ticket agency.) Without Young, he wrote "For All We Know" and "Just Friends." Young (born Judewitz, also in New York) wrote successfully on his own as well –"Was That the Human Thing to Do?" and "I'm Gonna Sit Right Down and Write Myself a Letter." He had begun in vaudeville and then worked as a song-plugger before going on to his great career as a lyricist and his important role in the early years of ASCAP.

DINAH

VERSE 1

Carolina gave me Dinah;
I'm the proudest one beneath the
    Dixie sun.
News is spreadin'
'Bout a weddin',
I hear church bells ringin'.
Here's the song my heart keeps
    singin':

REFRAIN

"Dinah,
Is there anyone finer
In the state of Carolina?
If there is and you know 'er,
Show 'er to me.

Dinah,
With her Dixie eyes blazin',
How I love to sit and gaze in
To the eyes of Dinah Lee.
Ev'ry night
Why do I
Shake with fright,
Because my Dinah might
Change her mind about me.
Dinah,
If she wandered to China,
I would hop an ocean liner,
Just to be with Dinah Lee!"

VERSE 2

Some designer modeled Dinah,
He must be the One who made the
    golden sun.

Heaven bless her,
She said "Yes, Sir,"
All day long I'm prayin',
Even in my dreams I'm sayin':

REPEAT REFRAIN

—Harry Akst

FIVE FOOT TWO, EYES OF BLUE
(HAS ANYBODY SEEN MY GIRL?)

VERSE I

I just saw a maniac,
Maniac, maniac,
Wild and tearing his hair.
Jumping like a jumpin' jack,
Jumpin' jack, jumpin' jack.
Child, you should have been there;
Laughed so loud I thought that I would
    cave in
When I heard that silly, daffy-dilly
    ravin':

REFRAIN

"Five foot two, eyes of blue,
But oh! what those five feet could do,
Has anybody seen my girl?
Turned-up nose, turned-down hose,
Flapper? Yes sir!, one of those.
Has anybody seen my girl?
Now if you run into
A five foot two
Covered with fur,
Diamond rings
And all those things,
Betcha' life it isn't her.
But could she love, could she woo?
Could she, could she, could she coo?
Has anybody seen my girl?"

VERSE 2

Love made him a lunatic,
Lunatic, lunatic.
Gee! he hollered and cried
Like a monkey on a stick,
On a stick, on a stick;
He was fit to be tied.
When we asked him for his wife's
    description,
He just answered all of us with this
    conniption:

REPEAT REFRAIN

—Ray Henderson

FOR ALL WE KNOW
(Sam M. Lewis alone)

For all we know
We may never meet again.
Before you go
Make this moment sweet again.
We won't say good night
Until the last minute,
I'll hold out my hand
And my heart will be in it.
For all we know
This may only be a dream.
We come and go
Like a ripple on a stream.
So love me tonight,
Tomorrow was made for some,
Tomorrow may never come,
For all we know.

—J. Fred Coots

How 'Ya Gonna Keep 'Em Down on the Farm?

(After They've Seen Paree)

VERSE 1

"Reuben, Reuben, I've been thinking,"
Said his wifey dear;
"Now that all is peaceful and calm,
The boys will soon be back on the farm."
Mister Reuben started winking,
And slowly rubbed his chin.
He pulled his chair up close to Mother,
And he asked her with a grin:

REFRAIN 1

"How 'ya gonna keep 'em down on
    the farm,
After they've seen Paree?
How 'ya gonna keep 'em away from
    Broadway;
Jazzin' aroun',
And paintin' the town?
How 'ya gonna keep 'em away
    from harm?
That's a mystery.
They'll never want to see a rake or plow,
And who the deuce can parley-vous
    a cow?
How 'ya gonna keep 'em down on the
    farm,
After they've seen Paree?"

VERSE 2

"Reuben, Reuben, you're mistaken,"
Said his wifey dear;
"Once a farmer, always a jay,
And farmers always stick to the hay."
"Mother Reuben, I'm not fakin',
Tho' you may think it strange.
But wine and women play the mischief
With a boy who's loose with change."

REFRAIN 2

How 'ya gonna keep 'em down on
    the farm,
After they've seen Paree?
How 'ya gonna keep 'em away from
    Broadway;
Jazzin' aroun',
And paintin' the town?
How 'ya gonna keep 'em away
    from harm?
That's a mystery.
Imagine Reuben when he meets his pa,
He'll kiss his cheek and holler "oo-la-la!"
How 'ya gonna keep 'em down on
    the farm,
After they've seen Paree?

—Walter Donaldson

I Wonder Why She Kept on Saying "Si-Si-Si-Si-Senor"

VERSE 1

In old Barcelona I met sweet Romana,
A cute little dancer was she.
Her dress was all spangled and when she
    fandangled,
Oh! boy what that gal did to me.
She threw her bolero way up in the air-o,
I think that they fed her on twist;
She had so much vigor, and oh! what a
    figure,
There wasn't a thing that I missed.

REFRAIN

I wonder why she kept on saying,
"Si-si-si-si-Senor."
I thought she'd stop in an hour or two,
I kept on shoutin', "More power to you."
With my little heart she kept playing,
And I wanted to si-si some more.

She wasn't too fat and she wasn't too lean,
But this little Queen shook a mean
    tambourine.
I wonder why she kept on saying,
"Si-si-si-si-Senor."

VERSE 2
With each little wiggle she'd look up and
    giggle
And make my poor heart beat like this.
And heaven preserve us, she had me so
    nervous
I couldn't ask her for a kiss.
We might have got chummy, but I was a
    dummy,
I couldn't speak Spanish a bit.
I tried to console 'er without Espagnola,
But it didn't make any hit.

REFRAIN 2
I wonder why she kept on saying,
"Si-si-si-si-Senor."
I thought that she'd stop in an hour
    or two,
So I started shoutin', "More power
    to you."
With my little heart she kept playing,
And I wanted to si-si some more.
I'll never forget just how we two first met,
And oh! how I raved about her castanet.
I wonder why she kept on saying,
"Si-si-si-si, si-si Senor."

—*Ted Snyder*

I'm Gonna Sit Right Down and Write Myself a Letter

(Joe Young alone)

VERSE
The mailman passes by,
And I just wonder why

He never stops to ring my front
    doorbell.
There's not a single line from that dear old
    love of mine,
No, not a word since I last heard
    "Farewell."

REFRAIN
I'm gonna sit right down and write myself
    a letter
And make believe it came from you.
I'm gonna write words, oh, so sweet,
They're gonna knock me off my feet.
A lot of kisses on the bottom,
I'll be glad I got 'em.
I'm gonna smile and say, "I hope you're
    feeling better,"
And close "with love" the way you do.
I'm gonna sit right down and write myself
    a letter,
And make believe it came from you.

—*Fred E. Ahlert*

I'm Sitting on Top of the World

VERSE I
Don't want any millions,
I'm getting my share.
I've only got one suit,
That's all I can wear.
A bundle of money
Won't make you feel gay.
A sweet little honey
Is making me say:

REFRAIN
"I'm sitting on top of the world,
Just rolling along,
Just rolling along.
I'm quitting the blues of the world,

Just singing a song,
Just singing a song.
Glory Hallelujah,
I just phoned the Parson,
'Hey, Par, get ready to call.'
Just like Humpty Dumpty,
I'm going to fall.
I'm sitting on top of the world,
Just rolling along,
Just rolling along."

VERSE 2

Some people have diamonds
And beautiful pearls,
While others have children,
Just kiddies with curls.
Keep all of your fortunes,
Keep all of your fame,
I just found a sweetie
Who's changing her name.

REPEAT REFRAIN

—Ray Henderson

JUST FRIENDS

(Sam M. Lewis alone)

VERSE I

We two were sweethearts,
But we said good-bye,
One with a handshake
And one with a sigh.
We two were sweethearts
By a sacred vow,
What are we now?
What are we now?

REFRAIN

Just friends,
Lovers no more.
Just friends,

But not like before.
To think of what we've been
And not to kiss again
Seems like pretending
It isn't the ending.
Two friends
Drifting apart,
Two friends,
But one broken heart.
We loved, we laughed, we cried,
And suddenly love died.
The story ends,
And we're just friends.

VERSE 2

Where are the sunbeams
That were in your eyes?
Sometimes I wonder
If they too were lies.
We who were lovers
Are now only friends,
That's how it ends,
That's how it ends.

REPEAT REFRAIN

—John Klenner

LIFE IS A SONG, LET'S SING IT TOGETHER

(Joe Young alone)

VERSE

Don't be afraid of the future,
All of our plans will come true.
How can they fail with love on
    our side?
They'll never fail, we won't be
    denied.
All the world's a symphony
For you,
For me.

Life is a song, let's sing it together.
Let's take our hearts and dip them in
    rhyme.
Let's learn the words, let's learn the music
    together,
Hoping the song lasts for a long, long time.
Life is a song that goes on forever,
Love's old refrain can never go wrong.
Let's strike the note
Mendelssohn wrote
Concerning spring weather,
Let's sing it together,
And make life a song.

—Fred E. Ahlert

Rock-a-Bye Your Baby with a Dixie Melody

VERSE I

Mammy mine,
Your little rollin' stone that rolled away,
Strolled away.
Mammy mine,
Your rollin' stone is rollin' home today,
There to stay.
Just to see your smilin' face,
Smile a welcome sign.
When I'm in your fond embrace,
Listen, Mammy mine:

REFRAIN

Rock-a-bye your baby
With a Dixie melody.
When you croon,
Croon a tune
From the heart of Dixie.
Just hang my cradle, Mammy mine,
Right on that Mason-Dixon line,
And swing it from Virginia
To Tennessee with all the love that's in yer.

"Weep no more, my lady,"
Sing that song again for me;
And "Old Black Joe,"
Just as though
You had me on your knee.
A million baby kisses I'll deliver
The minute that you sing the "Swanee
    River."
Rock-a-bye your rockabye baby
With a Dixie melody.

VERSE 2

Any time
I hear a Mammy sing her babe to sleep;
Slumber deep.
That's the time
The shadows 'round my heart begin to
    creep,
And I weep.
Wonder why I went away,
What a fool I've been,
Take me back to yesterday,
In your arms again.

REPEAT REFRAIN

—Jean Schwartz

Street of Dreams

(Sam M. Lewis alone)

VERSE I

Midnight,
You heavy laden, it's midnight.
Come on and trade in your old dreams
    for new,
Your new dreams for old.
I know where they're bought,
I know where they're sold.
Midnight,
You've got to get there at midnight,
And you'll be met there by others like you,

Brothers as blue,
Smiling on the street of dreams.

REFRAIN
Love laughs at a king,
Kings don't mean a thing
On the street of dreams.
Dreams broken in two
Can be made like new
On the street of dreams.
Gold, silver and gold,
All you can hold
Is in the moonbeams;
Poor, no one is poor
Long as love is sure
On the street of dreams.

VERSE 2
Midnight,
Look at the steeple, it's midnight.
Unhappy people, it's ringing with joy,
It's ringing with cheer,
'Cause yesterday's gone,
Tomorrow is near.
Midnight,
The heart is lighter at midnight,
Things will be brighter the moment
     you find
More of your kind,
Smiling on the street of dreams.

REPEAT REFRAIN

—*Victor Young*

Was That the Human Thing to Do?

(Joe Young alone)

VERSE
To err is human, I heard you say,
Forgiveness is divine.

But all the sweet things you may say
Can't mend this heart of mine.

REFRAIN
Never thought that anyone in their
     right mind
Could ever treat another human so
     unkind.
Didn't you sneak away and leave a note
     behind?
Was that the human thing to do?
Always thought that yours was such a
     heart of gold.
But after I was sold on all the tales
     you told,
Didn't you let your kisses turn from hot
     to cold?
Was that the human thing to do?

1. Now I'm not trying to patch
        things up,
     What's been done must be.
     Lord! I wouldn't ever treat a pup
     The way you treated me.
     How could anyone be so darn unfair?
     You let me hang around until I learned
        to care.
     Didn't you even laugh and leave me
        crying there?
     Was that the human thing to do?

2. Now I just want to be understood,
     I'm no false alarm.
     If I couldn't do a human good,
     I wouldn't do 'em harm.
     How you let me fall and how you let
        me be!
     And when I begged you for a little
        sympathy,
     Didn't you even try to hi de hi de me?
     Was that the human thing to do?

—*Sammy Fain*

You're Gonna Lose Your Gal

(Joe Young alone)

VERSE

Flowers need the sunshine
And the morning dew.
I need lovin' sometimes,
So I'm warning you:

REFRAIN

You're gonna lose your gal,
You don't know who's your gal,
Acting like a two-time lover,
Keeping kisses under cover,
You'll wake up and soon discover
You're gonna lose your gal.
You're gonna sail away
You're bound to get that way.
How can you be so conceited,
Take a heart and then mistreat it,
You can't have your heart and eat it,
You're gonna lose your gal.
And when she's gone
She won't come back,
They don't come back,
Won't come back,
Once they're gone.
You're gonna be surprised,
You never realized
Someone else can treat her nicer,
Someone else can shoes and rice her,
Someone else will paradise her,
You're gonna lose your gal.
And when she starts to break your date,
Make you stand or sit and wait,
Now listen to me, pal,
You're gonna lose your gal.

—James V. Monaco

Edgar Leslie (1885–1976)

T HE PROLIFIC Edgar Leslie was born in Stamford, Connecticut, and studied at Cooper Union in New York, quickly establishing himself as a purveyor of special material for a variety of vaudeville stars. Apart from his major standard successes, he has a number of popular specialty numbers to answer for: his first hit, in 1907, was "The Police Won't Let Mariuch-a Dance Unless She Move da Feet," followed by "I'm a Yiddish Cowboy," "When Ragtime Rosie Ragged the Rosary" (it was accused of sacrilege by the New York *Clipper*), and "All the Quakers are Shoulder Shakers Down in Quaker Town." No one can say he wasn't ecumenical! One of his early successes was "Sadie Salome, Go Home!," one of the rare well-known numbers for which Irving Berlin had a co-writer, and a song that helped make Fanny Brice a star. Like Berlin, Leslie produced patriotic songs for both world wars: "America, I Love You" for the first, "American Patrol" for the second. His collaboration with composer Joe Burke was so successful that in January 1936, their "A Little Bit Independent," "On Treasure Island," and "Moon Over Miami" were numbers one, two, and four on *Your Hit Parade!* As well as writing a string of hits over several decades, Edgar Leslie worked hard as a founding member of ASCAP.

AMONG MY SOUVENIRS

There's nothing left for me
Of days that used to be,
I live in memory
Among my souvenirs.
Some letters
Tied with blue,
A photograph or two,
I see a rose from you
Among my souvenirs.
A few more tokens rest
Within my treasure chest,
And though they do
    their best
To give me consolation,
I count them all apart,

And as the teardrops start
I find a broken heart
Among my souvenirs.

—Horatio Nicholls

FOR ME AND MY GAL

(with E. Ray Goetz)

VERSE I
What a beautiful day
For a wedding in May!
See the people all stare
At the lovable pair.
She's a vision of joy,
He's the luckiest boy.

49

In his wedding array
Hear him smilingly say:

REFRAIN

"The bells are ringing
For me and my gal.
The birds are singing
For me and my gal.
Ev'rybody's been knowing
To a wedding they're going
And for weeks they've been sewing,
Ev'ry Susie and Sal.
They're congregating
For me and my gal.
The parson's waiting
For me and my gal.
And sometime
I'm goin' to build a little home for two,
For three or four or more,
In Loveland
For me and my gal."

VERSE 2

See the relatives there
Looking over the pair!
They can tell at a glance
It's a loving romance.
It's a wonderful sight
As the fam'lies unite.
Gee! It makes the boy proud
As he says to the crowd:

REPEAT REFRAIN

—*George W. Meyer*

KANSAS CITY KITTY

VERSE 1

Chicago Charlie was a good time Romeo,
He'd love a gal, then whisper "Good-bye,
    cheerio."

Just like Napoleon, love got Charlie, too.
Here's how Chicago Charlie said he met
    his Waterloo.

REFRAIN 1

"I left Frisco Kate swingin' on the
    Golden Gate,
When Kansas City Kitty smiled at me!
I left Ma and Pa out in Omaha-ha-ha,
When Kansas City Kitty smiled at me!
She comes from Missouri and she
    showed me,
Like a Texas steer she buffaloed me.
Every Jim and Jack
Got the well-known Hackensack,
When Kansas City Kitty smiled at me!"

VERSE 2

Chicago Charlie's singing "No more
    wedding bells,"
He's got a sore throat singing "No more
    baby yells."
They wake the neighbors when they start
    to cry,
And Charlie has to pacify them with this
    lullaby:

REFRAIN 2

"I just played the chill for the famous
    Diamond Lil,
When Kansas City Kitty smiled at me!
Folks in New Rochelle said, "He ain't
    done right by Nell,"
Since Kansas City Kitty smiled at me!
I gave Georgia Brown my watchcase
    Sunday.
I gave Louisville Lou the "works" on
    Monday.
I passed up those queens
Like you'd pass up Boston beans,
When Kansas City Kitty smiled at me!"

—*Walter Donaldson*

A Little Bit Independent

A little bit independent
In your walk,
A little bit independent
In your talk,
There's nothing like you in Paris
Or New York,
You're awfully easy on the eye.
A little bit independent
When we dance,
A little bit independent
Towards romance,
A bit of sophistication
In your glance,
And yet you're easy on the eye.
Whenever I'm alone
You weave a magic spell,
And though it be a danger zone
I only know that you're swell.
A little bit independent
With your smile,
A little bit independent
In your style.
But how can I love you all the while?
You're so easy on the eye.

—Joe Burke

T'ain't No Sin to Dance Around in Your Bones

VERSE

Dancing may do this and that
And help you take off lots of fat,
But I'm no friend of dancing when
    it's hot!
So if you are a dancing fool
Who loves to dance but can't keep cool,
Bear in mind the idea that I've got.

REFRAIN 1

When it gets too hot for comfort
And you can't get ice cream cones,
T'ain't no sin to take off your skin
And dance around in your bones.
When the lazy syncopation
Of the music softly moans,
T'ain't no sin to take off your skin
And dance around in your bones.
Polar bears aren't green in
    Greenland,
They got the right idea,
They think it's great to refrigerate
While we all cremate down here.
Just be like those bamboo babies
In the South Sea tropic zones;
T'ain't no sin to take off your skin
And dance around in your bones.

REFRAIN 2

When you're calling up your
    sweetie
In those hothouse telephones,
Why it ain't no sin to take off
    your skin
And dance around in your bones.
When you're on a crowded dance
    floor
Near those red-hot saxaphones,
T'ain't no sin to take off your skin
And dance around in your bones.
Just take a look at the girls while
    they're dancing,
Notice the way they're dressed.
Wear silken clothes without any hose
And nobody knows the rest.
If a gal wears X-ray dresses
And shows everything she owns,
T'ain't no sin to take off your skin
And dance around in your bones.

—Walter Donaldson

Shelton Brooks (1886–1975)

THE HIGHLY SUCCESSFUL black composer/lyricist Shelton Brooks was born in Canada and raised in Detroit, the son of musical parents. He began by playing piano in cafés, then moved on to vaudeville. In 1910 he wrote "Some of These Days," and Sophie Tucker and fame quickly followed. (Alec Wilder was to call it a "landmark in popular music, perhaps *the* landmark song of early Tin Pan Alley.") He became a headliner on the Keith and Orpheum circuit and then, in 1917, wrote his second great hit, "The Darktown Strutters' Ball," one of the first two songs recorded by the Original Dixieland Jazz Band; eventually, the sheet music sold over three million copies. Brooks was in Europe in 1923, with Lew Leslie's *Blackbirds* and at a command performance for King George V and Queen Mary, and he appeared for two years in Ken Murray's *Blackouts*.

THE DARKTOWN STRUTTERS' BALL

VERSE I

I've got some good news, honey,
An invitation to the Darktown Ball.
It's a very swell affair,
All the "High browns" will be there.
I'll wear my high silk hat and a frock
 tailcoat,
You wear your Paris gown, and your new
 silk shawl.
There ain't no doubt about it, babe,
We'll be the best dressed in the hall.

REFRAIN

I'll be down to get you in a taxi, honey,
You better be ready about half past
 eight.
Now dearie, don't be late,
I want to be there when the band starts
 playing.
Remember when we get there, honey,

The two-steps, I'm goin' to have 'em all,
Goin' to dance out both my shoes,
When they play the "Jelly Roll Blues,"
Tomorrow night at the Darktown
 Strutters' Ball.

VERSE 2

We'll meet our high-toned neighbors,
An exhibition of the "Baby Dolls,"
And each one will do their best,
Just to outclass all the rest,
And there'll be dancers from ev'ry
 foreign land,
The classic, buck and wing, and the
 wooden clog:
We'll win that fifty-dollar prize,
When we step out and "Walk the Dog."

REPEAT REFRAIN

(That's the Way) Dixieland Started Jazz

VERSE

Syncopation, it has roused the nation to a
    red, red hot degree,
They're all getting so flustrated
'Bout how jazz first originated.
Down below the Mason-Dixon Line they
    organized the first jazz band;
They all got together in a honky-tonk, and
    here's how jazz began:

REFRAIN

The leader man, he played the
    saxophone,
The harmony came from the slide
    trombone,
The cornet player used a mute,
Oh boy! how he could toot!
The clarinet, it did nothing but moan,
From the banjo there came a wicked
    strum,
Tempo strict, with a stick, by the drum.

1. They took classics of the past
    And began to play them fast.
    That's the way Dixieland started jazz.

2. Each played like a fiendish elf,
    It was each man for himself.
    That's the way Dixieland started jazz.

Some of These Days

VERSE I

Two sweethearts courted happily for quite
    a while
Midst simple life of country folk.
When the lad told girlie he must go away,

Her little heart with grief 'most broke.
She said, "You know it's true I love you
    best of all,
So honey don't you go away."
Just as he went to go,
It grieved the girlie so,
These words he heard her say:

REFRAIN

"Some of these days
You'll miss me, honey.
Some of these days,
You'll feel so lonely.
You'll miss my hugging,
You'll miss my kissing,
You'll miss me, honey,
When you go away.
I feel so lonely
Just for you only,
For you know, honey,
You've had your way.
And when you leave me,
I know 'twill grieve me.
You'll miss your little baby,
Yes, some of these days."

VERSE 2

The little girlie, feeling blue, said, "I'll
    go too
And show him two can play this game."
When her honey heard this
    melancholy news,
He quickly came back home again.
But when he reached the house he found
    his girl was gone,
So down he rushes to the train.
While it was pulling out,
He heard his girlie shout,
This loving sweet refrain:

REPEAT REFRAIN

WALKIN' THE DOG

VERSE I

Now listen, honey, 'bout a new dance craze
Been 'riginated for about ten days.
It's there,
It's "a bear,"
And it's a new step,
A funny two-step.
In every cabaret and dancing hall
You see them doing it, yes, one and all.
If you'll just give me a chance,
I'll introduce this dance.

REFRAIN

Get 'way back
And snap your fingers.
Get over, Sallee, one and all.
Grab your gal
And don't you linger,
Do that slow drag round the hall.

Do that step,
"The Texas Tommy" drop,
Like you're sitting on a log.
Rise slow,
That will show
The dance called "Walkin' the Dog."

VERSE 2

You all were crazy 'bout the Bunny Hug,
'Most everybody was a Tango Bug,
But now
And somehow
The funny Dog Walk
Is all-the-town talk.
In every private home
This dance is known.
I called a friend a mine up on the
      phone,
Hearing on his graph-o-phone
The doggone raggy tone.

REPEAT REFRAIN

Gus Kahn (1886–1941)

I F THE ROSTER of absolute giants among lyricists is solid–Berlin, Gershwin, Hammerstein, Hart, Porter–the list of just-unders is more porous. Among them, but most likely to be forgotten today, is Gus Kahn, who from the mid-teens until his death turned out dozens–scores–of first-rate songs, most of them unpretentious, unself-conscious, and unforgettable. Kahn was born in Koblenz, Germany, and arrived in Chicago when he was five (and, unusually, he stayed at home until he went to Hollywood; no New York). Like so many writers, he cut his teeth producing specialty songs for vaudeville performers, then Broadway revues and musicals. By 1922, when he entered into his most fruitful partnership, with Walter Donaldson, he was an established craftsman and hit-maker. His range is suggested by the two most famous songs from Ziegfeld's 1928 show *Whoopee*–"Makin' Whoopee!," for Eddie Cantor, and "Love Me or Leave Me," for Ruth Etting. Half a year later, he was collaborating with the Gershwins on the score for Ruby Keeler's *Show Girl* (most famously, "Liza"), but soon he was off to Hollywood, where he wrote for more than fifty films. Like Irving Berlin, Kahn was a superb and meticulous craftsman who made a lyric seem easy, even inevitable, rather than calling attention to its ingenuity or wit. But no one was fooled; it was clear to his colleagues just how good he was. (Johnny Mercer, for instance, singled out "It Had to Be You" as the greatest popular song ever written.) The public got it, too: Through his career he averaged five hits a year, and he was still going strong when he died in 1941 at the age of fifty-five. In 1951 he became the subject of a film about his life, *I'll See You in My Dreams,* in which he was played by Danny Thomas and the long-suffering Mrs. Kahn by Doris Day.

AIN'T WE GOT FUN
(with Raymond B. Egan)

VERSE I

Bill collectors gather
'Round and rather
Haunt the cottage next door–
Men the grocer and butcher sent,
Men who call for the rent.
But within, a happy chappy
And his bride of only a year
Seem to be so cheerful.
Here's an earful
Of the chatter you hear:

REFRAIN I

"Ev'ry morning,
Ev'ry evening,
Ain't we got fun?
Not much money,

Oh, but honey,
Ain't we got fun?
The rent's unpaid, dear,
We haven't a bus,
But smiles were made, dear,
For people like us.
In the winter,
In the summer,
Don't we have fun?
Times are bum and
Getting bummer,
Still we have fun.
There's nothing surer,
The rich get rich and the poor get
    children,
In the meantime,
In between time,
Ain't we got fun?"

VERSE 2

Just to make their trouble
Nearly double
Something happened last night.
To their chimney a gray bird came,
Mister Stork is his name,
And I'll bet two pins a pair of twins
Just happened in with the bird.
Still, they're very
Gay and merry
Just at dawning I heard:

REFRAIN 2

"Ev'ry morning,
Ev'ry evening,
Don't we have fun?
Twins and cares, dear,
Come in pairs, dear,
Don't we have fun?
We've only started
As mommer and pop,
Are we downhearted?
I'll say that we're not!

Landlord's mad and
Getting madder,
Ain't we got fun?
Times are bad and
Getting badder,
Still we have fun.
There's nothing surer,
The rich get rich and the poor get laid off,
In the meantime,
In between time,
Ain't we got fun?"

VERSE 3

When the man who sold 'em
Carpets told 'em
He would take them away,
They said "Wonderful, here's our
    chance,
Take them up and we'll dance."
And when burglars came and
    robbed them,
Taking all their silver they say,
Hubby yelled, "We're famous
For they'll name us
In the papers today."

REFRAIN 3

"Night or daytime,
It's all playtime,
Ain't we got fun?
Hot or cold days,
Any old days,
Ain't we got fun?
If wifie wishes
To go to a play,
Don't wash the dishes,
Just throw them away.
Streetcar seats are
Awful narrow,
Ain't we got fun?
They won't smash up
Our Pierce Arrow,

We ain't got none.
They've cut my wages,
But my income tax will be so much
    smaller,
When I'm paid off
I'll be laid off,
Ain't we got fun."

     —Richard A. Whiting

ALL GOD'S CHILLUN GOT RHYTHM

VERSE
Chillun', listen here to me,
This is my philosophy
To see me through the day,
To scare my cares away.

REFRAIN
All God's chillun got rhythm,
All God's chillun got swing.
Maybe haven't got money,
Maybe haven't got shoes,
All God's chillun got rhythm
For to push away their blues,
Yeah!
All God's chillun got trouble,
Trouble don't mean a thing.
When they start to go
Ho ho ho de ho,
Trouble's bound to go 'way, say!
All God's chillun got swing.

    —Bronislaw Kaper and Walter Jurmann

CAROLINA IN THE MORNING

VERSE I
Wishing is good time wasted,
Still it's a habit they say;

Wishing for sweets I've tasted,
That's all I do all day.
Maybe there's nothing in wishing,
But speaking of wishing I'll say:

REFRAIN
"Nothing could be finer
Than to be in Carolina
In the morning.
No one could be sweeter
Than my sweetie when I meet her
In the morning.
Where morning glories
Twine around the door,
Whispering pretty stories
I long to hear once more.
Strolling with my girlie
Where the dew is pearly early
In the morning,
Butterflies all flutter up
And kiss each little buttercup
At dawning.
If I had Aladdin's lamp for only a day,
I'd make a wish and here's what I'd say:
'Nothing could be finer
Than to be in Carolina
In the morning.' "

VERSE 2
Dreaming was meant for nighttime,
I live in dreams all the day;
I know it's not the right time,
But still I dream away.
What could be sweeter than dreaming,
Just dreaming and drifting away.

REPEAT REFRAIN

    —Walter Donaldson

GUILTY

VERSE

Though you've decided that our love is
  wrong
And think that we should part,
It seems as though I have loved you so
  long,
You'll always be in my heart.

REFRAIN

Is it a sin,
Is it a crime
Loving you, dear, like I do?
If it's a crime, then I'm guilty,
Guilty of loving you.
Maybe I'm wrong,
Dreaming of you,
Dreaming the lonely night through.
If it's a crime, then I'm guilty,
Guilty of dreaming of you.
What can I do,
What can I say,
After I've taken the blame?
You say you're through,
You'll go your way,
But I'll always feel just the same.
Maybe I'm right,
Maybe I'm wrong,
Loving you, dear, like I do.
If it's a crime, then I'm guilty,
Guilty of loving you.

—Harry Akst and Richard A. Whiting

I'LL SEE YOU IN MY DREAMS

VERSE 1

Tho' the days are long,
Twilight sings a song
Of the happiness that used to be.

Soon my eyes will close,
Soon I'll find repose,
And in dreams you're always near to me.

REFRAIN

I'll see you in my dreams,
Hold you in my dreams,
Someone took you out of my arms,
Still I feel the thrill of your charms.
Lips that once were mine,
Tender eyes that shine,
They will light my way tonight,
I'll see you in my dreams.

VERSE 2

In the dreary gray
Of another day,
You'll be far away and I'll be blue.
Still I hope and pray,
Through each weary day,
For it brings the night and dreams
  of you.

REPEAT REFRAIN

—Isham Jones

I'M THROUGH WITH LOVE

VERSE

I have given you my true love,
But you love
A new love.
What am I supposed to do now,
With you now,
You're through now?
You'll be on your merry way,
And there's only this to say:

REFRAIN

"I'm through with love,
I'll never fall again,

Said 'Adieu' to love,
'Don't ever call again,'
For I must have you or no one,
And so I'm through with love.
I've locked my heart,
I'll keep my feelings there.
I have stocked my heart
With icy frigidaire.
And I mean to care for no one,
Because I'm through with love.
Why did you lead me to think you
    could care,
You didn't need me, for you had your
    share
Of slaves around you to hound you and
    swear,
With deep emotion, devotion to you.
Good-bye to Spring,
And all it meant to me,
It can never bring
The thing that used to be,
For I must have you or no one,
And so I'm through with love.

    —Joseph A. Livingston and
     Matt Malneek

IT HAD TO BE YOU

VERSE I

Why do I do just as you say,
Why must I just give you your way?
Why do I sigh,
Why don't I try to forget?
It must have been that something
Lovers call fate
Kept on saying I had to wait.
I saw them all,
Just couldn't fall
'Til we met.

REFRAIN

It had to be you,
It had to be you,
I wandered around
And finally found
The somebody who
Could make me be true,
Could make me blue,
And even be glad
Just to be sad,
Thinking of you.
Some others I've seen
Might never be mean,
Might never be cross
Or try to be boss,
But they wouldn't do.
For nobody else
Gave me a thrill,
With all your faults
I love you still,
It had to be you,
Wonderful you,
It had to be you.

VERSE 2

Seems like dreams like I always had,
Could be, should be, making me glad.
Why am I blue?
It's up to you to explain.
I'm thinking maybe, baby, I'll go away.
Some day, some way you'll come
    and say:
"It's you I need,"
And you'll be pleading in vain.

REPEAT REFRAIN

    —Isham Jones

Love Me or Leave Me

VERSE

This suspense is killing me,
I can't stand uncertainty.
Tell me now,
I've got to know,
Whether you want me to stay or go.

REFRAIN

Love me or leave me
And let me be lonely,
You won't believe me,
And I love you only.
I'd rather be lonely
Than happy with somebody else.
You might find the nighttime
The right time for kissing,
But nighttime is my time
For just reminiscing.
Regretting
Instead of forgetting with somebody else.
There'll be no one unless that someone
    is you.
I intend to be independently blue.
I want your love
But I don't want to borrow,
To have it today
And to give back tomorrow,
For my love is your love
There's no love for nobody else!

—*Walter Donaldson*

Makin' Whoopee

VERSE

Ev'rytime I hear that march from
    Lohengrin
I am always on the outside looking in.

Maybe that is why I see the funny side
When I see a fallen brother take a bride.
Weddings make a lot of people sad,
But if you're not the groom they're not
    so bad.

REFRAIN 1

Another bride, another June,
Another sunny honeymoon,
Another season, another reason
For makin' whoopee!
A lot of shoes, a lot of rice,
The groom is nervous, he answers twice,
It's really killing that he's so willing
To make whoopee!
Picture a little love nest
Down where the roses cling,
Picture the same sweet love nest,
Think what a year can bring.
He's washing dishes and baby clothes,
He's so ambitious he even sews.
But don't forget, folks,
That's what you get, folks,
For makin' whoopee!
Another whoopee!

REFRAIN 2

Another year, or maybe less,
What's this I hear? Well, can't you
    guess?
She feels neglected, and he's suspected
Of makin' whoopee!
She sits alone 'most ev'ry night,
He doesn't 'phone her, he doesn't write,
He says he's "busy," but she says,
    "Is he?"
He's makin' whoopee!
He doesn't make much money,
Only five thousand per,
Some judge who thinks he's funny
Says, "You'll pay six to her."
He says, "Now, Judge, suppose I fail?"

The judge says, "Budge right into jail.
You'd better keep her,
I think it's cheaper,
Than makin' whoopee!"
Another whoopee!

—Walter Donaldson

MY BABY JUST CARES FOR ME

VERSE

I'm so happy since the day
I fell in love in a great big way
And the big surprise is someone loves
    me, too.
Guess it's hard for you to see
Just what anyone can see in me,
But it simply goes to prove what love
    can do.

REFRAIN 1

My baby don't care for shows,
My baby don't care for clothes,
My baby just cares for me!
My baby don't care for furs and laces.
My baby don't care for high-toned places.
My baby don't care for rings,
Or other expensive things,
She's sensible as can be.
My baby don't care who knows it,
My baby just cares for me!

REFRAIN 2

My baby's no Gilbert fan,
Ron Colman is not her man,
My baby just cares for me!
My baby don't care for Lawrence Tibbetts
    [Tibbett]
She'd rather have me around to kibbitz.
Bud Rogers is not her style,
And even Chevalier's smile

Is something that she can't see.
I wonder what's wrong with baby?
My baby just cares for me!

—Walter Donaldson

NO, NO, NORA

VERSE 1

In the apartment above me,
There is the lovingest pair.
I don't know what she has to be
    jealous of,
He has a face that just a mother could love.
And still I know she's always worried
Some girl will steal her prize away.
She's always asking: "Is there
    somebody else?"
I guess it's just to hear him say:

REFRAIN 1

"No, no, Nora, nobody but you, dear,
You know, Nora, yours truly is true,
    dear.
When you accuse me of flirting,
I wouldn't, I couldn't, I love you so.
I have chances, too many to mention,
Never give 'em a bit of attention.
And would I trade you for Venus?
No, no, Nora, no, no."

VERSE 2

She has a lot of detectives
Who check him up ev'ry day.
She's read about those men who lead
    double lives,
She's making sure she won't be "one of
    those wives."
She thinks he looks like Douglas
    Fairbanks,
Altho' he has Ben Turpin's eyes.

A hundred times a day she calls on the
    phone,
And ev'ry time she does he sighs:

REFRAIN 2

"No, no, Nora, nobody but you, dear,
You know, Nora, that I stick like
    glue, dear.
And when you're speaking of Sheiking,
I wouldn't, I couldn't, I love you so.
I see eyes that are full of affection,
But I look in another direction.
And do I care for the Follies?
No, no, Nora, no, no."

—*Ernie Erdman and Ted Fiorito*

OKAY, TOOTS

VERSE 1

I know a couple of newlyweds,
They've been newlyweds for years.
Just a pair of spooners,
Sunny honeymooners,
This happy couple lives next to me
And it's music to my ears
After ev'ry kiss
To hear him saying this:

REFRAIN

"Okay, Toots,
If you like me like I like you,
We know nobody new will do,
It's okay, Toots.
Okay, Toots,
If you say "Yes," then I'll say "Yes,"
If you say "No," then it's no go,
It's okay, Toots.
You know I'm in favor of
Whatever you do.
I tasted the flavor of
One kiss and I knew

It was okay, Toots,
If you wash dishes,
I dry dishes.
I dry dishes, I'm ambitious,
Okay, Toots."

VERSE 2

I like a hubby who likes his wife,
And who likes to tell her so.
If you really feel love,
Why should you conceal love?
So if you ever try married life,
You will never find it slow
If you spend each day
Just talking in this way:

REPEAT REFRAIN

—*Walter Donaldson*

THE ONE I LOVE
(BELONGS TO SOMEBODY ELSE)

VERSE 1

I'm unhappy,
So unhappy,
For I can see
The one I love don't care for me.
I'd be happy,
Oh, so happy,
But it was fate
That it was too late
When I happened to find her.

REFRAIN

The one I love belongs to
    somebody else,
She means her tender songs for
    somebody else.
And even when I have my arms around her,
I know her thoughts are strong for
    somebody else.

The hands I hold belong to
    somebody else,
I'll bet they're not so cold to
    somebody else.
It's tough to be alone on the shelf,
It's worse to fall in love by yourself.
The one I love belongs to
    somebody else.

VERSE 2
I keep trying,
I keep trying
To stay away.
It can't be done one single day.
I keep saying,
I keep saying,
"Good-bye I'm through,"
But each time I see her I start in
    all over.

REPEAT REFRAIN

—*Isham Jones*

PRETTY BABY

VERSE 1
You ask me why I'm always teasing you,
You hate to have me call you
    pretty baby.
I really thought that I was pleasing you,
For you're just a baby to me.
Your cunning little dimples and your baby
    stare,
Your baby talk and baby walk and
    curly hair;
Your baby smile makes life worthwhile,
You're just as sweet as you can be.

REFRAIN
Ev'rybody loves a baby,
That's why I'm in love with you,

Pretty baby, pretty baby.
And I'd like to be your sister,
Brother, dad and mother too,
Pretty baby, pretty baby.
Won't you come and let me rock you in my
    cradle of love,
And we'll cuddle all the time.
Oh! I want a lovin' baby
And it might as well be you,
Pretty baby of mine.

VERSE 2
Your mother says you were the
    cutest kid;
No wonder, dearie, that I'm wild
    about you,
And all the cunning things you said
    and did.
Why, I love to fondly recall,
And just like Peter Pan, it seems you'll
    always be
The same sweet, cunning, little baby dear
    to me.
And that is why I'm sure that I
Will always love you best of all.

REPEAT REFRAIN

—*Tony Jackson and Egbert Van Alstyne*

TOMORROW IS ANOTHER DAY

REFRAIN
The day is through,
The sun descending
Has brought to you
No happy ending,
But you can face the setting sun
    and say,
"Tomorrow is another day."
You've had your share
Of tears and trouble,

But ev'ry care
Will be a bubble,
If you can face the setting sun and say,
"Tomorrow is another day."
Some days a little rain must fall,
The skies can't all be blue.
Sometimes a little tear must fall
To make a smile break through.
Today is gone,
It's all behind you,
A brighter dawn
Will surely find you
If you can face the setting sun and say,
"Tomorrow is another day."

—Bronislaw Kaper and Walter Jurmann

TOOT, TOOT, TOOTSIE!
(GOOD-BYE)

VERSE I

Yesterday I heard a lover sigh,
"Good-bye, oh me, oh my."
Seven times he got aboard his train
And seven times he hurried back
To kiss his love again, and tell her:

REFRAIN

"Toot, toot, Tootsie, good-bye!
Toot, toot, Tootsie, don't cry.
The choo-choo train that takes me
Away from you, no words can tell
How sad it makes me.
Kiss me, Tootsie, and then
Do it over again.
Watch for the mail,
I'll never fail,
If you don't get a letter
Then you'll know I'm in jail.
Toot, toot, Tootsie, don't cry,
Toot, toot, Tootsie, good-bye!"

VERSE 2

When somebody says good-bye to me,
I'm sad as I can be.
Not so with this loving Romeo,
He seemed to take a lot of pleasure
Saying bye-bye to his treasure:

REPEAT REFRAIN

—Ernie Erdman and Ted Fiorito

WHEN MY SHIP COMES IN

VERSE I

There is a ship that sails the sea
For little folks like you and me.
It carries all our dreams,
Our little hopes and schemes.
I've got a ship that sailed away,
It's coming home some day.

REFRAIN I

I'll have a golden castle grand and tall
With eighteen butlers standing in the hall
And Walter Disney paintings on the wall,
When my ship comes in.
I'll leave the choice of autos up to you,
And if you think a big Rolls-Royce will do,
I think I'll play it safe and order two,
When my ship comes in.
I'll buy Barnum and Bailey
And move 'em right next door,
They'll give two performances daily
For the kids who never saw a show before.
In golden chairs we'll sip our tea for two,
I'll have Paul Whiteman here to play
    for you,
I'll have Bing Crosby singing "Boo
    Boo Boo,"
When my ship comes in.

VERSE 2

We're bound to have our ups and downs,
There will be days when fortune frowns,
But if you wait a while,
The world will wear a smile.
Until the good things come along,
I'll sing myself this song:

REFRAIN 2

I'll buy out ev'ry ice cream factory
So all the kids can come and get it free,
And I'll throw all the spinach in the sea,
When my ship comes in.
I'll buy up all the public schools in sight
And all day long I'll have them closed up
    tight,
But they'll be used as picture shows at
    night,
When my ship comes in.
I'll have suits made to measure,
In fact I'll buy a store,
And can you imagine the pleasure
Wearing shoes that no one ever wore
    before?
I'll phone to each department store
    and say,
"Call up your Santa Claus and raise
    his pay,
And tell him we'll have Christmas
    ev'ry day,"
When my ship comes in.

—Walter Donaldson

YES, SIR! THAT'S MY BABY

VERSE I

Who's that coming down the street?
Who's that looking so petite?
Who's that coming down to meet me here?
Who's that, you know who I mean,

Sweetest "who" you've ever seen,
I could tell her miles away from here.

REFRAIN I

Yes, Sir, that's my baby,
No, Sir, don't mean "maybe,"
Yes, Sir, that's my baby now.
Yes, Ma'am, we've decided,
No, Ma'am, we won't hide it,
Yes, Ma'am, you're invited now.
By the way,
By the way,
When we reach the preacher I'll say,
Yes, Sir, that's my baby,
No, Sir, don't mean "maybe,"
Yes, Sir, that's my baby now.

VERSE 2

Who's the "who" I rave about?
Who do I feel blue without,
In the Winter, Summer, Spring and Fall?
What was I just gonna say,
I forget, but anyway,
Here's the most important thing of all.

REFRAIN 2

Yes, Sir, that's my baby,
No, Sir, don't mean "maybe,"
Yes, Sir, that's my baby now.
Well, well, "lookit" that baby,
Do tell, don't say "maybe,"
Nell's bells, won't she cause some row.
Pretty soon,
Pretty soon,
We will hear that Lohengrin tune.
Who for should she be, Sir,
No one else but me, Sir,
Yes, Sir, that's my baby now.

—Walter Donaldson

You Stepped Out of a Dream

VERSE
I've had a million dreams
That never came true
Until the lucky day
I discovered you.

REFRAIN
You stepped out of a dream,
You are too wonderful
To be what you seem!

Could there be eyes like yours,
Could there be lips like yours,
Could there be smiles like yours,
Honest and truly?
You stepped out of a cloud.
I want to take you away,
Away from the crowd
And have you all to myself,
Alone and apart,
Out of a dream,
Safe in my heart.

—Nacio Herb Brown

Clifford Grey (1887–1941)

C LIFFORD GREY, BORN IN Birmingham, England, and educated at Cambridge University, began writing lyrics in 1913 after half a dozen years as an actor in the West End, and quickly he became one of the most successful and prolific songwriters and librettists for the London and New York stages–he had three shows on Broadway in 1925 alone. In England he collaborated with, among others, Ivor Novello, Noel Gay, and Vivian Ellis (the huge hit *Mr. Cinders*). In America he worked with the young George Gershwin *(The Rainbow)*, Jerome Kern *(Sally)*, Vincent Youmans *(Hit the Deck* and *Smiles),* and operettists Sigmund Romberg and Rudolf Friml.

HALLELUJAH!

(with Leo Robin)

VERSE

I'm recallin'
Times when I was small, in
Light and free jubilee days.
Old folks prayin',
Ev'rybody swayin',
Loudly, I chanted my praise.
How I sang about the Judgment morn,
And of Gabriel tootin' his horn.
In that sunny
Land of milk and honey,
I had no complaints,
While I thought of Saints.
So I say to all who feel forlorn:

REFRAIN

"Sing 'Hallelujah! Hallelujah!'
And you'll shoo the blues away;
When cares pursue ya, 'Hallelujah!'
Gets you through the darkest day.
Satan
Lies awaitin'
And creatin'

Skies of gray,
But 'Hallelujah! Hallelujah!'
Helps to shoo the clouds away."

—Vincent Youmans

IF YOU WERE THE ONLY GIRL IN THE WORLD

VERSE

Sometimes when I feel bad
And things look blue,
I wish a pal I had,
Say one like you!
Someone within my heart
To build a throne,
Someone who'd never part,
To call my own.

REFRAIN

If you were the only girl in the world,
And I were the only boy,
Nothing else would matter in the world
     today,
We could go on loving in the same old way.

A Garden of Eden just made for two,
With nothing to mar our joy.
I would say such wonderful things to you,
There would be such wonderful things
    to do,
If you were the only girl in the world,
And I were the only boy.

—Nat D. Ayer

SPREAD A LITTLE HAPPINESS

VERSE 1
I've got a creed
For ev'ry need
So easy that it must succeed;
I'll set it down for you to read,
So please take heed.
Keep out the gloom!
Let in the sun!
That's my advice to ev'ryone.
It's only once we pass this way,
So day by day,

REFRAIN
Even when the darkest clouds are in
    the sky,
You mustn't sigh,
And you mustn't cry.
Just spread a little happiness
As you go by.
Please try!

What's the use of worrying and
    feeling blue?
When days are long
Keep on smiling through;
And spread a little happiness
Till dreams come true.
Surely you'll be wise to make the best of
    ev'ry blues day;
Don't you realize you'll find next Monday
    or next Tuesday
Your Golden Shoes day?
Even when the darkest clouds are in
    the sky,
You mustn't sigh,
And you mustn't cry;
Just spread a little happiness
As you go by!

VERSE 2
The rule is old,
So I've been told,
But still it's worth its weight in gold.
It pays you back a thousandfold,
So be enrolled
Upon the lists
Of optimists,
And disregard the pessimists.
This life is short, so try to smile
Each little while.

REPEAT REFRAIN

—Vivian Ellis

Haven Gillespie (1888–1975)

THE CAREER OF Haven Gillespie (born in Covington, Kentucky) ranged over thirty years, from the mid-twenties to the mid-fifties. His songs were greatly varied– from the tremendous novelty hit "Santa Claus Is Comin' to Town" to the ballad "You Go to My Head" to the neo-folkie Frankie Laine hit "That Lucky Old Sun." He claimed that his comfortable later years were entirely due to his annual royalties from "Santa Claus . . . ," which *Variety* cites as perhaps the most recorded song in American music history. (If he could have copyrighted the phrase "naughty and nice," he would have been even richer.)

BREEZIN' ALONG WITH THE BREEZE

VERSE I

I have been a rover
Since I was a child,
No one to love or care for me.
Knocked around all over,
Kinda grew up wild.
My home's wherever I may be.

REFRAIN

I'm just breezin' along with the breeze,
Trailin' the rails,
Roamin' the seas.
Like the birdies that sing in the trees,
Pleasin' to live,
Livin' to please.
The sky is the only roof I have over
    my head,
And when I'm weary, Mother Nature
    makes me a bed.
I'm just goin' along as I please,
Breezin' along with the breeze.

VERSE 2

Ain't no someone yearnin',
Wond'rin' where I be;

I'm gone but no one's missin' me.
Ain't no light a-burnin'
Ev'ry night for me;
I'm like a bird that's flyin' free.

REPEAT REFRAIN

*—Seymour Simons and Richard A.
Whiting*

SANTA CLAUS IS COMIN' TO TOWN

VERSE I

I just came back from a lovely trip
Along the Milky Way.
I stopped off at the North Pole
To spend a holiday.
I called on dear old Santa Claus
To see what I could see.
He took me to his workshop
And told his plans to me.
So,

REFRAIN I

You better watch out,
You better not cry,

Better not pout,
I'm telling you why:
Santa Claus is comin' to town.
He's making a list
And checking it twice,
Gonna find out
Who's naughty and nice,
Santa Claus is comin' to town.
He sees you when you're sleepin',
He knows when you're awake,
He knows if you've been bad or good,
So be good for goodness sake.
Oh! You better watch out,
You better not cry,
Better not pout,
I'm telling you why:
Santa Claus is comin' to town.

VERSE 2

Now Santa is a busy man,
He has no time to play.
He's got millions of stockings
To fill on Christmas day.
You'd better write your letter now
And mail it right away,
Because he's getting ready
His reindeers and his sleigh.
So,

REFRAIN 2

With little tin horns and little toy drums,
Rooty-toot-toots and rummy-tum-tums,
Santa Claus is comin' to town.
And curlyhead dolls that toddle and coo,
Elephants, boats, and kiddie cars too,
Santa Claus is comin' to town.
The kids in Girl- and Boyland
Will have a jubilee,
They're gonna build a Toyland town
All around the Christmas tree.
So! You better watch out,
You better not cry,
Better not pout,

I'm telling you why:
Santa Claus is comin' to town.

—J. Fred Coots

THAT LUCKY OLD SUN

Up in the mornin', out on the job,
Work like the devil for my pay.
But that lucky old sun got nothin' to do
But roll around Heaven all day.
Fuss with my woman, toil for my kids,
Sweat till I'm wrinkled and gray,
While that lucky old sun got nothin' to do
But roll around Heaven all day.
Dear Lord above, can't you know I'm
     pinin',
Tears all in my eyes.
Send down that cloud with a silver linin',
Lift me to Paradise.
Show me that river, take me across,
Wash all my troubles away.
Like that lucky old sun,
Give me nothin' to do
But roll around Heaven all day.

—Beasley Smith

YOU GO TO MY HEAD

You go to my head
And you linger like a haunting refrain,
And I find you spinning 'round in my brain
Like the bubbles in a glass of champagne.
You go to my head
Like a sip of sparkling Burgundy brew,
And I find the very mention of you
Like the kicker in a julep or two.
The thrill of the thought
That you might give a thought
To my plea

Casts a spell over me.
Still, I say to myself,
"Get ahold of yourself,
Can't you see
That it never can be."
You go to my head
With a smile that makes my
     temp'rature rise,
Like a summer with a thousand Julys

You intoxicate my soul with your eyes.
Though I'm certain that this heart
     of mine
Hasn't a ghost of a chance
In this crazy romance,
You go to my head.
You go to my head.

—J. Fred Coots

Irving Berlin (1888–1989)

H E *is* American music," said Jerome Kern of this extraordinary man who, unlike most of his major colleagues, came from a poor immigrant family and had little formal education, yet he went on to the most all-encompassing and triumphant career in American popular music. Irving Berlin (born Israel Baline) began as a singing waiter on New York's Lower East Side, graduated to song-plugger, and in 1907, when he was nineteen, had his first song published–"Marie from Sunny Italy." "Alexander's Ragtime Band" made him a worldwide figure in 1911, and his career never faltered. As composer and lyricist (although he famously could not read music) he produced three of America's anthems–"God Bless America," "White Christmas," and "Easter Parade"–as well as "Oh, How I Hate to Get Up in the Morning" for World War I and "This Is the Army, Mr. Jones" for World War II. His Broadway shows included *Face the Music, As Thousands Cheer, Louisiana Purchase, Annie Get Your Gun,* and *Call Me Madam.* Among the many films he provided songs for were three for Astaire and Rogers–*Top Hat, Follow the Fleet,* and *Carefree*–as well as *On the Avenue, Alexander's Ragtime Band, Holiday Inn, White Christmas, Easter Parade, Blue Skies,* and *There's No Business Like Show Business.* And, of course, he had countless pop hits unconnected to shows or movies. A hallmark of his style is how easy he makes it all look, yet no one ever worked harder; perhaps that helps to explain a success that lasted for half a century. His unique career spans the eras of ragtime and rock and roll, and includes everything in between.

ALEXANDER'S RAGTIME BAND

VERSE I

Oh, ma honey,
Oh, ma honey,
Better hurry
And let's meander,
Ain't you goin',
Ain't you goin'
To the leader man,
Ragged meter man?
Oh, ma honey,
Oh, ma honey,

Let me take you
To Alexander's
Grandstand,
Brass band,
Ain't you comin' along?

REFRAIN

Come on and hear,
Come on and hear
Alexander's Ragtime Band.
Come on and hear,
Come on and hear,
It's the best band in the land.

They can play a bugle call
Like you never heard before,
So natural
That you want to go to war.
That's just
The bestest band
What am,
Honey lamb.
Come on along,
Come on along,
Let me take you
By the hand
Up to the man,
Up to the man
Who's the leader
Of the band,
And if you care to hear
The Swanee River
Played in ragtime,
Come on and hear,
Come on and hear
Alexander's Ragtime Band.

VERSE 2
Oh, ma honey,
Oh, ma honey,
There's a fiddle
With notes that screeches,
Like a chicken,
Like a chicken,
And the clarinet
Is a colored pet.
Come and listen,
Come and listen
To a classical band
What's peaches,
Come now,
Somehow,
Better hurry along.

REPEAT REFRAIN

ALWAYS

VERSE
Ev'rything went wrong,
And the whole day long
I'd feel so blue.
For the longest while
I'd forget to smile;
Then I met you.
Now that my blue days have passed,
Now that I've found you at last,

REFRAIN
I'll be loving you,
Always.
With a love that's true,
Always.
When the things you've planned
Need a helping hand,
I will understand,
Always, always.
Days may not be fair,
Always.
That's when I'll be there,
Always.
Not for just an hour,
Not for just a day,
Not for just a year,
But always.

BLUE SKIES

VERSE I
I was blue,
Just as blue as I could be,
Ev'ry day
Was a cloudy day for me.
Then good luck
Came a-knocking at my door,
Skies were gray,
But they're not gray anymore.

REFRAIN

Blue skies
Smiling at me,
Nothing but blue skies
Do I see.
Bluebirds
Singing a song,
Nothing but bluebirds
All day long.
Never saw the sun
Shining so bright,
Never saw things
Going so right,
Noticing the days
Hurrying by,
When you're in love, my,
How they fly.
Blue days,
All of them gone,
Nothing but blue skies
From now on.

VERSE 2

I should care
If the wind blows east or west,
I should fret
If the worst looks like the best,
I should mind
If they say it can't be true,
I should smile,
That's exactly what I do.

REPEAT REFRAIN

Change Partners

Must you dance ev'ry dance
With the same fortunate man?
You have danced with him since the music
    began,
Won't you change partners and dance
    with me?

Must you dance quite so close
With your lips touching his face?
Can't you see I'm longing to be in his
    place?
Won't you change partners and dance
    with me?
Ask him to sit this one out, and while
    you're alone
I'll tell the waiter to tell him he's wanted
    on the telephone.
You've been locked in his arms
Ever since heaven knows when,
Won't you change partners, and then
You may never want to change partners
    again.

Cheek to Cheek

Heaven,
I'm in heaven,
And my heart beats so that I can hardly
    speak;
And I seem to find the happiness I seek
When we're out together dancing
Cheek to cheek.
Heaven,
I'm in heaven,
And the cares that hung around me
    through the week
Seem to vanish like a gambler's lucky
    streak
When we're out together dancing
Cheek to cheek.
Oh! I love to climb a mountain
And to reach the highest peak,
But it doesn't thrill me half as much
As dancing cheek to cheek.
Oh! I love to go out fishing
In a river or a creek,
But I don't enjoy it half as much
As dancing cheek to cheek.
Dance with me,

I want my arm about you.
The charm about you
Will carry me through to heaven.
I'm in heaven,
And my heart beats so that I can hardly
    speak,
And I seem to find the happiness I seek
When we're out together dancing
Cheek to cheek.

A COUPLE OF SWELLS

VERSE 1
We're a couple of swells,
We stop at the best hotels,
But we prefer the country
Far away from the city smells.
We're a couple of sports,
The pride of the tennis courts,
In June, July, and August
We look cute when we're dressed in
    shorts.
The Vanderbilts have asked us up for tea,
We don't know how to get there,
    no siree.

REFRAIN 1
We would drive up the avenue,
But we haven't got the price.
We would skate up the avenue,
But there isn't any ice.
We would ride on a bicycle,
But we haven't got a bike.
So we'll walk up the avenue,
And to walk up the avenue's what we like.

VERSE 2
Wall Street bankers are we,
With plenty of currency.
We'd open up the safe but
We forgot where we put the key.
We're the favorite lads

Of girls in the picture ads.
We'd like to tell you who
We kissed last night, but we can't be cads.
The Vanderbilts are waiting at the club,
But how are we to get there, that's the rub.

REFRAIN 2
We would sail up the avenue,
But we haven't got a yacht.
We would drive up the avenue,
But the horse we had was shot.
We would ride on a trolley car,
But we haven't got the fare.
So we'll walk up the avenue,
Yes, we'll walk up the avenue,
Yes, we'll walk up the avenue
'Til we're there.

EASTER PARADE

VERSE
Never saw you look
Quite so pretty before,
Never saw you dressed
Quite so lovely, what's more
I could hardly wait
To keep our date
This lovely Easter morning,
And my heart beat fast
As I came through the door,
For

REFRAIN
In your Easter bonnet
With all the frills upon it
You'll be the grandest lady
In the Easter Parade.
I'll be all in clover,
And when they look you over
I'll be the proudest fellow
In the Easter Parade.
On the Avenue, Fifth Avenue,

The photographers will snap us,
And you'll find that you're
In the rotogravure.
Oh, I could write a sonnet
About your Easter bonnet
And of the girl I'm taking to
The Easter Parade.

FOOLS FALL IN LOVE

VERSE

Why do I allow my heart
To make decisions for me?
Why do I keep list'ning to my heart?
Why do I get so involved
When I would rather be free?
Maybe it's because I'm not so smart.

REFRAIN

Fools fall in love,
Only lunatics fall in love,
And I'm a fool.
Fools seek romance,
Only idiots take a chance,
And I'm a fool.
I should be able to put all my feelings aside,
I should be able to take one free ride in my
    stride,
But fools cannot play,
They get serious right away,
And break the rule.
My heart's on fire
When I know I ought to keep cool,
Fools fall in love
And I'm such a fool.

HEAT WAVE

VERSE

A heat wave
Blew right into town last week,

She came from
The island of Martinique,
The can-can
She dances will make you fry,
The can-can
Is really the reason why

REFRAIN

We're having a heat wave,
A tropical heat wave.
The temp'rature's rising–
It isn't surprising–
She certainly can . . .
Can-can.
She started the heat wave
By letting her seat wave,
And in such a way that
The customers say that
She certainly can . . .
Can-can.
Gee!
Her anatomy
Made the mercury
Jump to ninety-three.
Yes sir!
We're having a heat wave,
A tropical heat wave.
The way that she moves that
Thermometer proves that
She certainly can . . .
Can-can.

PATTER

It's so hot,
The weatherman will
Tell you a record's been made.
It's so hot,
A coat of tan will
Cover your face in the shade.
It's so hot
The coldest maiden
Feels just as warm as a bride.
It's so hot

A chicken laid an
Egg on the street
And it fried!

REPEAT REFRAIN

How Deep Is the Ocean?
(How High Is the Sky?)

VERSE

How can I tell you what is in my heart,
How can I measure each and ev'ry part,
How can I tell you how much I love you,
How can I measure just how much I do?

REFRAIN

How much do I love you?
I'll tell you no lie,
How deep is the ocean,
How high is the sky?
How many times a day,
Do I think of you?
How many roses
Are sprinkled with dew?
How far would I travel
To be where you are?
How far is the journey
From here to a star?
And if I ever lost you,
How much would I cry?
How deep is the ocean,
How high is the sky?

I Got Lost in His Arms

VERSE

Don't ask me just how it happened,
I wish I knew.
I can't believe that it's happened,
And still it's true.

REFRAIN

I got lost in his arms
And I had to stay.
It was dark in his arms
And I lost my way.
From the dark came a voice
And it seemed to say,
"There you go. There you go."
How I felt as I fell
I just can't recall,
But his arms held me fast
And it broke the fall.
And I said to my heart
As it foolishly kept jumping all around,
"I got lost,
But look what I found."

I Got the Sun in the Morning

VERSE

Taking stock of what I have and what I
    haven't,
What do I find?
The things I've got will keep me
    satisfied.
Checking up on what I have and what I
    haven't,
What do I find?
A healthy balance on the credit side.

REFRAIN

Got no diamond, got no pearl,
Still I think I'm a lucky girl,
I got the sun in the morning
And the moon at night.
Got no mansion, got no yacht,
Still I'm happy with what I've got,
I got the sun in the morning
And the moon at night.
Sunshine
Gives me a lovely day,
Moonlight

Gives me the Milky Way.
Got no checkbooks, got no banks,
Still I'd like to express my thanks,
I got the sun in the morning
And the moon at night,
And with the sun in the morning
And the moon in the evening
I'm all right.

REFRAIN 2

Got no butler, got no maid,
Still I think I've been overpaid,
I've got the sun in the morning,
And the moon at night.
Got no silver, got no gold,
What I've got can't be bought
    or sold,
I've got the sun in the morning
And the moon at night.
Sunshine
Gives me a lovely day,
Moonlight
Gives me the Milky Way.
Got no heirlooms for my kin,
Made no will but when I cash in
I'll leave the sun in the morning
And the moon at night,
And with the sun in the morning
And the moon in the evening,
I'm all right.

REFRAIN 3

Got no honey, got no jam,
Lost my feller and here I am
With just the sun in the morning
And the moon at night.
Got no future, got no plan,
Things look different without a man.
What good is sun in the morning
And the moon at night?
Sunshine vanished beyond recall,
Moonlight just isn't there at all.

No ambition, things look black,
Won't be different till he comes back
And brings the sun in the morning
And the moon at night.
And with the sun in the morning
And the moon in the evening,
I'm all right.

ISN'T THIS A LOVELY DAY
(TO BE CAUGHT IN THE RAIN?)

VERSE

The weather is fright'ning;
The thunder and light'ning
Seem to be having their way.
But as far as I'm concerned,
It's a lovely day.
The turn in the weather
Will keep us together,
So I can honestly say
That as far as I'm concerned,
It's a lovely day.
And ev'rything's O.K.

REFRAIN

Isn't this a lovely day
To be caught in the rain?
You were going on your way,
Now you've got to remain.
Just as you were going,
Leaving me all at sea,
The clouds broke,
They broke and oh!
What a break for me.
I can see the sun up high,
Though we're caught in the storm.
I can see where you and I
Could be cozy and warm.
Let the rain pitter patter,
But it really doesn't matter
If the skies are gray;

Long as I can be with you,
It's a lovely day.

It's a Lovely Day Today

It's a lovely day today,
So whatever you've got to do
You've got a lovely day to do it in,
    that's true.
And I hope whatever you've got to do
Is something that can be done by two,
For I'd really like to stay.
It's a lovely day today,
And whatever you've got to do
I'd be so happy to be doing it with you.
But if you've got something that must
    be done,
And it can only be done by one,
There is nothing more to say
Except it's a lovely day for saying
It's a lovely day.

I've Got My Love to Keep Me Warm

The snow is snowing,
The wind is blowing,
But I can weather the storm.
What do I care how much it may storm?
I've got my love to keep me warm.
I can't remember
A worse December,
Just watch those icicles form.
What do I care if icicles form?
I've got my love to keep me warm.
Off with my overcoat,
Off with my glove,
I need no overcoat,
I'm burning with love.
My heart's on fire,

The flame grows higher,
So I will weather the storm.
What do I care how much it may storm?
I've got my love to keep me warm.

Let Me Sing and I'm Happy

VERSE
What care I who makes the laws of a
    nation?
Let those who will take care of its rights
    and wrongs.
What care I who cares
For the world's affairs,
As long as I can sing its popular
    songs?

REFRAIN
Let me sing a funny song
With crazy words that roll along,
And if my song can start you laughing,
I'm happy, happy.
Let me sing a sad refrain
Of broken hearts that loved in vain,
And if my song can start you crying,
I'm happy.
Let me croon a lowdown blues
To lift you out of your seat;
If my song can reach your shoes
And start you tapping your feet,
I'm happy.
Let me sing of Dixie's charms,
Of cotton fields and Mammy's arms,
And if my song can make you homesick,
I'm happy.

Let's Face the Music and Dance

There may be trouble ahead,
But while there's moonlight and music

And love and romance,
Let's face the music and dance.
Before the fiddlers have fled,
Before they ask us to pay the bill,
And while we still have the chance,
Let's face the music and dance.
Soon we'll be without the moon,
Humming a diff'rent tune,
And then
There may be teardrops to shed.
So while there's moonlight and music
And love and romance,
Let's face the music and dance.

LET'S HAVE ANOTHER CUP OF COFFEE

VERSE

Why worry when skies are gray?
Why should we complain?
Let's laugh at the cloudy day,
Let's sing in the rain.
Songwriters say the storm quickly
    passes,
That's their philosophy,
They see the world through rose-colored
    glasses,
Why shouldn't we?

REFRAIN

Just around the corner
There's a rainbow in the sky,
So let's have another cup o' coffee
And let's have another piece o' pie!
Trouble's just a bubble,
And the clouds will soon roll by,
So let's have another cup o' coffee
And let's have another piece o' pie!
Let a smile be your umbrella,
For it's just an April show'r.
Even John D. Rockefeller

Is looking for the silver lining.
Mister Herbert Hoover
Says that now's the time to buy,
So let's have another cup o' coffee
And let's have another piece o' pie!

THE LITTLE THINGS IN LIFE

VERSE

Great big houses with great big rooms
Were not fashioned for brides and
    grooms;
A little place is where we should be.
Great big troubles and great big cares
Come from houses with marble stairs;
A little place for you and me.

REFRAIN

Just a little room or two
Can more than do
A little man and wife.
That's if they're contented with
The little things in life.
Living on a larger scale
Would soon entail
A lot of care and strife.
We could be so happy with
The little things in life.
A little rain,
A little sun,
A little work,
A little fun,
A little time for loving
When the day is done.
And a little thing that cries
For lullabies
Could make a man and wife
Tell the world how much they love
The little things in life.

Manhattan Madness

Manhattan, Manhattan,
Manhattan, Manhattan,
Manhattan madness,
You've got me at last.
I'm like a fly upon a steeple
Watching seven million people
Do a rhythm
That draws me with 'em.
Manhattan, Manhattan,
Manhattan, Manhattan,
Manhattan madness,
You're going too fast.
I'm like a baby on a rocker
Watching Father Knickerbocker
Being busy,
I'm getting dizzy.
When shadows creep,
In my bed I tumble,
But never sleep,
For I hear the rumble
In the street,
The tramping of feet
That haunt me the whole night long.
And through the day
I'm watching the drama
That people play
In your panorama,
And I hear
In tones very clear
The sound of your restless song.
Subways below and trains above racing,
Packed with humanity,
Taxis and trucks and trolley cars
    chasing,
Busy as they can be.
Steaming machines and riveters grating,
Motors instead of men.
Buildings go up with wrecking crews
    waiting

To tear them down again.
Newsies that shout sensational
    headlines,
Children that scream and yell,
Whistles and bells and siren horns
    blowing,
Pistols that crack and roar,
Traffic that stops and goes without
    knowing
What's all the shootings for?

Manhattan, Manhattan,
Manhattan madness,
You've got me at last.
I'm like a fly upon a steeple,
Watching seven million people
Do a rhythm
That draws me with 'em,
And it's mad.

Oh! How I Hate to Get Up in the Morning

VERSE I
The other day I chanced to meet
A soldier friend of mine,
He'd been in camp for sev'ral weeks
And he was looking fine;
His muscles had developed
And his cheeks were rosy red.
I asked him how he liked the life
And this is what he said:

REFRAIN I
"Oh! How I hate to get up in the morning,
Oh! How I'd love to remain in bed.
For the hardest blow of all
Is to hear the bugler call:
'You've got to get up,
You've got to get up,
You've got to get up this morning!'

Some day I'm going to murder the
   bugler,
Some day they're going to find him dead.
I'll amputate his reveille,
And step upon it heavily,
And spend the rest of my life in bed."

VERSE 2

A bugler in the army
Is the luckiest of men,
He wakes the boys at five and then
Goes back to bed again;
He doesn't have to blow again
Until the afternoon.
If ev'rything goes well with me
I'll be a bugler soon.

REFRAIN 2
(SECOND ENDING OF LAST THREE
LINES OF FIRST REFRAIN:)

And then I'll get that other pup,
The one that wakes the bugler up,
And spend the rest of my life in bed.

ALTERNATIVE VERSE

I've been a soldier just a while
And I would like to state
The life is simply wonderful,
The army food is great.
I sleep with ninety-seven others
In a wooden hut.
I love them all, they all love me,
It's very lovely but:

REPEAT REFRAIN I

PACK UP YOUR SINS AND GO TO THE DEVIL

VERSE

Oh,
I got a message from below,

'Twas from a man I used to know
About a year or so ago,
Before he departed.
He is just as happy as can be,
I'll tell you what he said to me,
He said, "If ever you get heavy-hearted,

REFRAIN

Pack up your sins and go
To the devil. In Hades
You'll meet the finest of gentlemen
And the finest of ladies.
They'd rather be down below than up above.
Hades is full of thousands of
Joneses and Browns,
O'Hoolihans, Cohens, and Bradys.
You'll hear a heavenly tune
That went to the devil
Because the jazz bands
They started pickin' it,
Then put a trick in it,
A jazzy kick in it.
They've got a couple of old reformers in
   heaven
Making them go to bed at eleven.
Pack up your sins and go to the devil,
And you'll never have to go to bed at all.

PATTER

If you care to dwell where the weather
   is hot,
H-E-double-L is a wonderful spot.
If you need a rest and you're all out of
   sorts,
Hades is the best of the winter resorts.
Paradise doesn't compare;
All the nice people are there.
They come from ev'rywhere
Just to revel with Mister Devil.
Nothing on his mind but a couple of horns,
Satan is waitin' with his jazz band
And
His

Band
Came from Alabam'
With a melody hot.
No one gives a damn
If it's music or not.
Satan's melody
Makes you want to dance forever,
And you never have to go to bed at all."

THEN THE PATTER AND THE
REFRAIN ARE SUNG IN
COUNTERPOINT

A PRETTY GIRL IS LIKE A MELODY

VERSE I
I have an ear for music,
And I have an eye for a maid.
I link a pretty girlie
With each pretty tune that's played.
They go together, like sunny weather
Goes with the month of May.
I've studied girls and music,
So I'm qualified to say:

REFRAIN
"A pretty girl is like a melody
That haunts you night and day.
Just like the strain of a haunting
    refrain,
She'll start upon a marathon
And run around your brain.
You can't escape, she's in your
    memory.
By morning, night, and noon
She will leave you and then
Come back again.
A pretty girl is just like a pretty tune."

VERSE 2
Most every year we're haunted
By some little popular tune,

Then someone writes another,
The old one's forgotten soon.
A pretty maiden with beauty laden
Is like that kind of song:
Just when you think you love her,
Another one comes along.

REPEAT REFRAIN

PUTTIN' ON THE RITZ
(ORIGINAL VERSION)

VERSE
Have you seen the well-to-do
Up on Lenox Avenue?
On that famous thoroughfare
With their noses in the air,
High hats and colored collars,
White spats and fifteen dollars,
Spending ev'ry dime
For a wonderful time.

REFRAIN
If you're blue and you
Don't know where to go to,
Why don't you go where Harlem sits,
Puttin' on the Ritz?
Spangled gowns upon a bevy
Of high browns from down the levee,
All misfits,
Puttin' on the Ritz.
That's where each and ev'ry Lulu Belle
    goes
Ev'ry Thursday ev'ning with her swell
    beaus,
Rubbing elbows.
Come with me and we'll attend
Their jubilee and see them spend
Their last two bits,
Puttin' on the Ritz.

(REVISED VERSION)

VERSE

Have you seen the well-to-do
Up and down Park Avenue?
On that famous thoroughfare
With their noses in the air,
High hats and Arrow collars,
White spats and lots of dollars,
Spending ev'ry dime
For a wonderful time.

REFRAIN

If you're blue and you
Don't know where to go to,
Why don't you go where fashion sits,
Puttin' on the Ritz?
Diff'rent types who wear a day coat,
Pants with stripes and cutaway coat,
Perfect fits,
Puttin' on the Ritz.
Dressed up like a million dollar
    trouper,
Trying hard to look like Gary Cooper,
Super duper.
Come, let's mix where Rockefellers
Walk with sticks or umbrellas
In their mitts,
Puttin' on the Ritz.

REMEMBER

VERSE I

One little kiss,
A moment of bliss,
Then hours of deep regret.
One little smile,
And after a while,
A longing to forget.
One little heartache
Left as a token,

One little plaything,
Carelessly broken.

REFRAIN

Remember the night,
The night you said
"I love you,"
Remember?
Remember you vowed
By all the stars
Above you,
Remember?
Remember we found a lonely spot,
And after I learned to care a lot
You promised that you'd forget me not,
But you forgot
To remember.

VERSE 2

Into my dreams
You wandered, it seems,
And then there came a day;
You loved me, too,
My dreams had come true,
And all the world was May.
But soon the Maytime
Turned to December,
You had forgotten,
Do you remember?

REPEAT REFRAIN

SAY IT ISN'T SO

VERSE

You can't stop people from talking,
And they're talking, my dear.
And the things they're saying
Fill my heart with fear.
Now I could never believe them
When they say you're untrue,

I know that they're mistaken,
Still I want to hear it from you.

REFRAIN
Say it isn't so,
Say it isn't so,
Ev'ryone is saying you don't love me,
Say it isn't so.
Ev'rywhere I go,
Ev'ryone I know
Whispers that you're growing tired
    of me,
Say it isn't so.
People say that you
Found somebody new,
And it won't be long before you leave me.
Say it isn't true,
Say that ev'rything is still okay,
That's all I want to know,
And what they're saying,
Say it isn't so.

The Song Is Ended
(But the Melody Lingers On)

VERSE
My thoughts go back to a heavenly
    dance,
A moment of bliss we spent.
Our hearts were filled with a song of
    romance
As into the night we went
And sang to our hearts' content.

REFRAIN
The song is ended,
But the melody lingers on,
You and the song are gone,
But the melody lingers on.
The night was splendid,
And the melody seemed to say,

"Summer will pass away,
Take your happiness while you may."
There 'neath the light of the moon
We sang a love song that ended
    too soon.
The moon descended
And I found with the break of dawn
You and the song had gone,
But the melody lingers on.

Supper Time

Supper time,
I should set the table,
'Cause it's supper time.
Somehow I'm not able,
'Cause that man o' mine
Ain't comin' home no more.
Supper time,
Kids will soon be yellin'
For their supper time.
How'll I keep from tellin' that
That man o' mine
Ain't comin' home no more?
How'll I keep explainin'
When they ask me where he's gone,
How'll I keep from cryin'
When I bring their supper on?
How can I remind them
To pray at their humble board,
How can I be thankful
When they start to thank the Lord?
Lord!
Supper time,
I should set the table,
'Cause it's supper time,
Somehow I'm not able,
'Cause that man o' mine
Ain't comin' home no more,
Ain't comin' home no more.

There's No Business Like Show Business

VERSE 1
The butcher, the baker, the grocer, the
    clerk
Are secretly unhappy men because
The butcher, the baker, the grocer, the
    clerk
Get paid for what they do but no
    applause.
They'd gladly bid their dreary jobs
    good-bye
For anything theatrical, and why?

REFRAIN 1
There's no bus'ness like show bus'ness,
Like no bus'ness I know.
Ev'rything about it is appealing,
Ev'rything the traffic will allow.
Nowhere could you get that happy
    feeling
When you are stealing that extra bow.
There's no people like show people,
They smile when they are low.
Yesterday they told you you would not
    go far,
That night you open and there you are,
Next day on your dressing room they've
    hung a star.
Let's go on with the show.

VERSE 2
The costumes, the scen'ry, the makeup,
    the props,
The audience that lifts you when
    you're down,
The headaches, the heartaches, the
    backaches, the flops,
The sheriff who escorts you out of town.
The opening when your heart beats like
    a drum,

The closing when the customers
    won't come.

REFRAIN 2
There's no bus'ness like show bus'ness,
Like no bus'ness I know.
You get word before the show has
    started
That your fav'rite uncle died at dawn.
Top of that your Pa and Ma have parted,
You're brokenhearted, but you go on.
There's no people like show people,
They don't run out of dough.
Angels come from ev'rywhere with lots
    of jack,
And when you lose it, there's no attack.
Where could you get money that you don't
    give back?
Let's go on with the show.

VERSE 3
The cowboys, the tumblers, the wrestlers,
    the clowns,
The roustabouts who move the show
    at dawn,
The music, the spotlight, the people, the
    towns,
Your baggage with the labels pasted on.
The sawdust and the horses and the smell,
The towel you've taken from the last hotel.

REFRAIN 3
There's no bus'ness like show bus'ness
If you tell me it's so.
Trav'ling through the country will be
    thrilling,
Standing out in front on opening nights,
Smiling as you watch the theater filling,
And there's your billing out there in
    lights.
There's no people like show people,
They smile when they are low.
Even with a turkey that you know will fold,

You may be stranded out in the cold,
Still you wouldn't change it for a sack
    of gold.
Let's go on with the show.

They Say It's Wonderful

VERSE I
SHE: Rumors fly and you can't tell where
    they start,
    'Specially when it concerns a
    person's heart.
    I've heard tales that could set my
    heart aglow,
    Wish I knew if the things I hear
    are so.

REFRAIN I
SHE: They say that falling in love is
    wonderful,
    It's wonderful, so they say.
    And with a moon up above,
    It's wonderful,
    It's wonderful,
    So they tell me.
    I can't recall who said it,
    I know I never read it,
    I only know they tell me that love is
    grand,
    And
    The thing that's known as romance is
    wonderful,
    Wonderful,
    In ev'ry way, so they say.

VERSE 2
HE: Rumors fly and they often leave a
    doubt,
    But you've come to the right place to
    find out.
    Ev'rything that you've heard is
    really so,

    I've been there once or twice and I
    should know.

REFRAIN 2
HE: You'll find that falling in love is
    wonderful,
    It's wonderful.
SHE: So you say.
HE: And with a moon up above,
    It's wonderful,
    It's wonderful.
SHE: So you tell me.
HE: To leave your house some
    morning,
    And without any warning
    You're stopping people shouting that
    love is grand
    And
    To hold a man in your arms is
    wonderful,
    Wonderful
    In ev'ry way.
SHE: So you say.

This Is the Army, Mr. Jones

VERSE
A bunch of frightened rookies
Were list'ning filled with awe,
They listened while a sergeant
Was laying down the law.
They stood there at attention,
Their faces turning red.
The sergeant looked them over,
And this is what he said:

REFRAIN
"This is the army, Mister Jones,
No private rooms or telephones,
You had your breakfast in bed before,
But you won't have it there anymore.
This is the army, Mister Green,

We like the barracks nice and clean,
You had a housemaid to clean your floor,
But she won't help you out anymore.
Do what the buglers command,
They're in the army and not in a band.
This is the army, Mr. Brown,
You and your baby went to town,
She had you worried, but this is war,
And she won't worry you anymore."

Top Hat, White Tie, and Tails

VERSE

I just got an invitation through the
    mails.
"Your presence requested this evening,
    it's formal"–
A top hat, a white tie, and tails.
Nothing now could take the wind out of
    my sails
Because I'm invited to step out this
    evening
With top hat and white tie and tails.

REFRAIN

I'm puttin' on my top hat,
Tyin' up my white tie,
Brushin' off my tails.
I'm dudein' up my shirt front,
Puttin' in the shirt studs,
Polishin' my nails.
I'm steppin' out, my dear,
To breathe an atmosphere
That simply reeks with class;
And I trust
That you'll excuse my dust
When I step on the gas,
For I'll be there,
Puttin' down my top hat,
Mussin' up my white tie,
Dancin' in my tails.

What'll I Do?

VERSE 1

Gone is the romance that was so divine,
'Tis broken and cannot be mended.
You must go your way and I must
    go mine,
But now that our love dreams have
    ended,

REFRAIN

What'll I do
When you
Are far away
And I am blue,
What'll I do?
What'll I do
When I
Am wond'ring who
Is kissing you,
What'll I do?
What'll I do
With just
A photograph
To tell my troubles to?
When I'm alone
With only
Dreams of you
That won't come true,
What'll I do?

VERSE 2

Do you remember a night filled with
    bliss?
The moonlight was softly descending.
Your lips and my lips were tied with
    a kiss,
A kiss with an unhappy ending.

REPEAT REFRAIN

WHEN THE MIDNIGHT CHOO-
CHOO LEAVES FOR ALABAM'

VERSE 1

I've had a mighty busy day,
I've had to pack my things away,
Now I'm goin' to give the landlord back
    his key–
The very key
That opened up my dreary flat,
Where many weary nights I sat
Thinking of the folks down home who
    think of me.
You can bet you'll find me singing
    happily. . . .

REFRAIN

When the midnight choo-choo leaves for
    Alabam',
I'll be right there,
I've got my fare.
When I see that rusty-haired
    conductor man,
I'll grab him by the collar
And I'll holler,
"Alabam'! Alabam'!"
That's where you stop your train
That brings me back again,
Down home where I'll remain
Where my honey-lamb am.
I will be right there with bells
When that old conductor yells,
"All aboard! All aboard!
All aboard for Alabam'."

VERSE 2

The minute that I reach the place
I'm goin' to over-feed my face,
'Cause I haven't had a good meal since
    the day
I went away.
I'm goin' to kiss my Pa and Ma

A dozen times for ev'ry star
Shining over Alabama's new-mown hay;
I'll be glad enough to throw myself away.

REPEAT REFRAIN

WHITE CHRISTMAS

VERSE

The sun is shining, the grass is green,
The orange and palm trees sway.
There's never been such a day
In Beverly Hills, L.A.
But it's December, the twenty-fourth,
And I'm longing to be up north.

REFRAIN

I'm dreaming of a white Christmas
Just like the ones I used to know,
Where the tree-tops glisten
And children listen
To hear sleigh bells in the snow.
I'm dreaming of a white Christmas
With ev'ry Christmas card I write.
"May your days be merry and bright,
And may all your Christmases be white."

YOU CAN'T GET A MAN WITH
A GUN

VERSE

Oh, my mother was frightened by a
    shotgun they say,
That's why I'm such a wonderful shot.
I'd be out in the cactus and I'd practice
    all day,
And now tell me what have I got.

REFRAIN 1

I'm quick on the trigger,
With targets not much bigger

Than a pinpoint,
I'm number one.
But my score with a feller
Is lower than a cellar,
Oh, you can't get a man with a gun.
When I'm with a pistol,
I sparkle like crystal.
Yes, I shine like the morning sun.
But I lose all my luster
When with a bronco buster,
Oh, you can't get a man with a gun.
With a gu-un, with a gu-un,
No, you can't get a man with a gun.
If I went to battle
With someone's herd of cattle,
You'd have steak when the job was done.
But if I shot the herder,
They'd holler bloody murder,
And you can't get a hug
From a mug with a slug,
Oh, you can't get a man with a gun.

REFRAIN 2

I'm cool, brave and daring,
To see a lion glaring
When I'm out with my Remington.
But a look from a mister
Will raise a fever blister,
Oh, you can't get a man with a gun.
The gals with umbrellers
Are always out with fellers
In the rain or the blazing sun.
But a man never trifles
With gals who carry rifles,
Oh, you can't get a man with a gun.
With a gu-un, with a gu-un,
No, you can't get a man with a gun.
A man's love is mighty,
He'll even buy a nighty
For a gal who he thinks is fun.
But they won't buy pajamas
For pistol-packin' mamas,
And you can't shoot a male

In the tail like a quail,
Oh, you can't get a man with a gun.

REFRAIN 3

If I shot a rabbit
Some furrier would grab it
For a coat that would warm someone;
But you can't shoot a lover
And use him for a cover,
Oh, you can't get a man with a gun.
If I shot an eagle
Although it wasn't legal,
He'd be stuffed when the job was done.
But you can't stuff a feller
And watch him turning yeller,
Oh, you can't get a man with a gun.
With a gu-un, with a gu-un,
No, you can't get a man with a gun.
A Tom, Dick, or Harry
Will build a house for Carrie
When the preacher has made them one.
But he can't build you houses
With buckshot in his trousers,
For a man may be hot
But he's not—when he's shot!
Oh, you can't get a man with a gun.

You'd Be Surprised

VERSE 1

Johnny was bashful and shy.
Nobody understood why
Mary loved him,
All the other girls passed him by.
Ev'ryone wanted to know
How she could pick such a beau.
With a twinkle in her eye
She made this reply:

REFRAIN 1

"He's not so good in a crowd,
But when you get him alone,

You'd be surprised.
He isn't much at a dance,
But then when he takes you home,
You'd be surprised.
He doesn't look like much of a lover,
But don't judge a book by its cover.
He's got the face of an Angel, but
There's a Devil in his eye.
He's such a delicate thing,
But when he starts in to squeeze,
You'd be surprised.
He doesn't look very strong,
But when you sit on his knee,
You'd be surprised.
At a party or at a ball
I've got to admit he's nothing at all,
But in a Morris chair,
You'd be surprised."

VERSE 2
Mary continued to praise
Johnny's remarkable ways
To the ladies,
And you know advertising pays.
Now Johnny's never alone,
He has the busiest phone,
Almost ev'ry other day
A new girl will say:

REFRAIN 2
"He's not so good in the house,
But on a bench in the park,
You'd be surprised.
He isn't much in the light,
But when he gets in the dark,
You'd be surprised.
I know he looks as slow as the Erie,
But you don't know the half of it, dearie.
He looks as cold as an Eskimo,
But there's fire in his eyes.
He doesn't say very much,
But when he starts in to speak,
You'd be surprised.

He's not so good at the start,
But at the end of a week
You'd be surprised.
On a streetcar or in a train
You'd think he was born without any brain,
But in a taxicab,
You'd be surprised."

YOU'RE JUST IN LOVE

I hear singing and there's no one there.
I smell blossoms and the trees are bare.
All day long I seem to walk on air.
I wonder why,
I wonder why.
I keep tossing in my sleep at night,
And what's more I've lost my appetite.
Stars that used to twinkle in the skies
Are twinkling in my eyes,
I wonder why.

LYRIC FOR COUNTER MELODY
You don't need analyzing,
It is not so surprising
That you feel very strange but nice.
Your heart goes pitter patter,
I know just what's the matter,
Because I've been there once or twice.
Put your head on my shoulder,
You need someone who's older,
A rubdown with a velvet glove.
There is nothing you can take
To relieve that pleasant ache,
You're not sick, you're just in love.

YOU'RE LAUGHING AT ME

VERSE
I love you, which is easy to see,
But I have to keep guessing
How you feel about me.

You listen to the words that I speak,
But I feel that you listen
With your tongue in your cheek.

REFRAIN
You're laughing at me,
I can't be sentimental,
For you're laughing at me, I know.
I want to be romantic,

But I haven't a chance.
You've got a sense of humor,
And humor is death to romance.
You're laughing at me.
Why do you think it's funny
When I say that I love you so?
You've got me worried and I'm all at sea,
For while I'm crying for you,
You're laughing at me.

Maxwell Anderson (1888–1959)

BEFORE BEGINNING his prestigious career as a playwright, Maxwell Anderson–having played football for North Dakota University–worked for *The New Republic* and several New York newspapers. His first great hit was *What Price Glory?* (with Laurence Stallings); then came the verse dramas *Winterset* and *High Tor;* and the historical dramas *Elizabeth the Queen, Mary of Scotland, Valley Forge;* and, for Ingrid Bergman, *Joan of Lorraine.* He supplied the librettos and lyrics for two important Kurt Weill musicals, *Knickerbocker Holiday,* in which Walter Houston first sang his "September Song," and *Lost in the Stars,* based on Alan Paton's novel of South Africa, *Cry, the Beloved Country.*

IT NEVER WAS YOU

VERSE 1

I've been hunting through woods,
I've been fishing over water
For one certain girl
Who's a certain father's daughter.
I've been following trails,
I've been staring after ships
For a certain pair of eyes
And a certain pair of lips.
Yes, I looked ev'rywhere,
You can look without wings,
And I found a great variety
Of interesting things.

REFRAIN

But it never was you,
It never was anywhere you.
An occasional sunset reminded me,
Or a flower hanging high on a tulip tree,
Or one red star hung low in the west,
Or a heartbreak call from the
    meadowlark's nest
Made me think for a moment:

"Maybe it's true,
I've found her in the star,
In the call,
In the blue!"
But it never was you,
It never was anywhere you,
Anywhere, anywhere you, anywhere you.

VERSE 2

I've been running through rains
And the wind that follows after
For one certain face
And an unforgotten laughter.
I've been following signs,
I've been searching through the lands
For a certain pair of arms
And a certain pair of hands.
Yes, I tried a kiss here
And I tried a kiss there,
For when you're out in company
The boys and girls will pair.

REPEAT REFRAIN

—Kurt Weill

Lost in the Stars

Before Lord God made the sea and
    the land,
He held all the stars in the palm of
    His hand,
And they ran through his fingers like
    grains of sand,
And one little star fell alone.
Then the Lord God hunted through the
    wide night air
For the little dark star on the wind down
    there
And he stated and promised he'd take
    special care
So it wouldn't get lost again.
Now a man don't mind if the stars
    grow dim
And the clouds blow over and
    darken him,
So long as the Lord God's watching
    over them,
Keeping track how it all goes on.
But I've been walking through the night
    and the day
Till my eyes get weary and my head
    turns gray,
And sometimes it seems maybe God's
    gone away,
Forgetting the promise that we heard
    him say,
And we're lost out here in the stars–
Little stars, big stars, blowing through the
    night.
And we're lost out here in the stars,
Little stars, big stars, blowing through the
    night,
And we're lost out here in the stars.

—Kurt Weill

September Song

VERSE 1

When I was a young man courting the girls,
I played me a waiting game:
If a maid refused me with tossing curls,
I'd let the old earth take a couple of whirls
While I plied her with tears in lieu of pearls
And as time came around she came my way,
As time came around she came.

REFRAIN

Oh, it's a long, long while
From May to December,
But the days grow short
When you reach September.
When the autumn weather turns the
    leaves to flame,
One hasn't got time for the waiting game.
Oh, the days dwindle down to a
    precious few,
September,
November!
And these few precious days
I'll spend with you,
These precious days
I'll spend with you.

VERSE 2

When you meet with the young men early
    in spring,
They court you in song and rhyme,
They woo you with words and a clover ring,
But if you examine the goods they bring,
They have little to offer but the songs
    they sing
And a plentiful waste of time of day,
A plentiful waste of time.

REPEAT REFRAIN

—Kurt Weill

Noble Sissle (1889–1975)

NOBLE SISSLE—born in Indianapolis and educated at Butler College—is best known for his collaboration with Eubie Blake on two Broadway successes, *Shuffle Along,* with its great hit "I'm Just Wild About Harry" (decades later, Harry Truman's campaign song), and *The Chocolate Dandies,* but his career had started years earlier with the Jubilee Singers and various bands. He was the lead vocalist for the famous James Reese Europe Society Orchestra, which broke the color barrier in New York nightclubs; and in World War I, after fighting in an all-black regiment, he performed "Over There" with Europe's military orchestra, the Hellfighters. Back in America, he recorded and made film shorts, led his own orchestra, was one of the early members of ASCAP, and founded the Negro Actors Guild. Just after World War II he toured Europe with a USO troupe and then gave up his orchestra to focus on his music publishing firm and his nightclub. (He was also the first black DJ.) In 1950 Noble Sissle succeeded Bill "Bojangles" Robinson as the "unofficial mayor of Harlem."

BALTIMORE BUZZ

VERSE

There have been a thousand raggy, draggy
    dances
That are danced in ev'ry hall,
And there have been a thousand raggy,
    draggy prances
That are pranced at ev'ry ball.
But the bestest one that "wuzz"
Is called the Baltimore Buzz,
So

REFRAIN

First you take your babe and gently
    hold her,
Then you lay your head upon her shoulder,
Next you walk just like your legs were
    breaking,
Do a fango like a tango,
Then you start the shimmy to shaking.

Then you do a raggy, draggy motion
Just like any ship upon the ocean,
Slide
And then you hesitate,
Glide
Oh, honey, ain't it great!
You just go simply in a trance
With that Baltimore Buzzing dance.

—Eubie Blake

I'M CRAVING FOR THAT KIND OF LOVE

VERSE

I'm wishing and fishing
And wanting to hook
A man kind, like you find
In a book.
I mean a modern Romeo,

I do not want a phoneo,
He may be the baby
Of some vamp, oh, babe!
At vampin' and lampin'
I'm the champ.
And if I once get him,
Why, I'll just set him
Beneath my parlor lamp, and
    let him. . . .

REFRAIN

Kiss me, kiss me,
Kiss me with his tempting lips,
Sweet as honey drips.
Press me, press me,
Press me to his loving breast
While I gently rest.
Breathe love tender sighs,
Gaze into his eyes,
Eyes that will just hypnotize.
Then I know he'll
Whisper, whisper,
Whisper to me soft and low,
Something nice, you know.
Honey, honey,
Honey, when there's no one near
My baby dear will
Huddle me,
Cuddle me,
Sing to me,
Cling to me,
Spoon to me,
Croon to me,
Sigh to me,
Cry to me,
I'm craving for that kind of love.

—Eubie Blake

I'M JUST WILD ABOUT HARRY

VERSE 1

There's just one fellow
For me in this world,
Harry's his name,
That's what I claim.
Why, for ev'ry fellow
There must be a girl,
I've found my mate
By kindness of fate.

REFRAIN

I'm just wild about Harry,
And Harry's wild about me.
The heav'nly blisses
Of his kisses
Fill me with ecstasy.
He's sweet just like choc'late candy,
And just like honey from the bee.
Oh, I'm just wild about Harry,
And he's just wild about,
Cannot do without,
He's just wild about me.

VERSE 2

There are some fellows
That like all the girls,
I mean the vamps,
With cruel lamps,
But my Harry says I'm
The girl of all girls,
I'm his ideal,
How happy I feel.

REPEAT REFRAIN

—Eubie Blake

Grant Clarke (1891–1931)

GRANT CLARKE WAS born in Akron, Ohio, and was a stock-company actor and music publisher before starting to write. He had his first success at eighteen, and when he was just twenty-one, in 1912, his "Ragtime Cowboy Joe" became a number-one hit. He produced material for Fanny Brice ("Second Hand Rose"), Bert Williams, Eva Tanguay, and Nora Bayes, and was a steady hit-maker in the teens and twenties before becoming one of the first songwriters to take up a career in Hollywood, writing theme songs for movies. (One of them was "Mother o'Mine, I Still Love You" for Al Jolson–who else?–in *The Jazz Singer;* Clarke had written an earlier hit for Jolson, "Everything Is Peaches Down in Georgia.") He was only forty when he died, having worked on thirteen movies in his final two years.

AM I BLUE?

VERSE I

I'm just a woman,
A lonely woman,
Waitin' on the weary shore.
I'm just a woman
That's only human,
One you should be sorry for.
Got up this mornin' along about dawn,
Without a warnin' I found he
    was gone.
Why should he do it?
How could he do it?
He never done it before.

REFRAIN

Am I blue?
Am I blue?
Ain't these tears
In these eyes
Tellin' you?
Am I blue?
You'd be too

If each plan
With your man
Done fell through.
Was a time
I was his only one,
But now I'm
The sad and lonely one.
Lawdy,
Was I gay?
'Til today,
Now he's gone
And we're through.
Am I blue?

VERSE 2

It's aggravatin'
To stand here waitin',
Waitin' for a triflin' man.
It set me hatin'
To stand here waitin',
Suicide's my only plan.
I think it's awful, his treatment of me,
It's most unlawful how mean he
    can be.

I can't forget him,
I'm bound to get him,
I'll run him down if I can.

REPEAT REFRAIN

—Harry Akst

Everything Is Peaches Down in Georgia

VERSE I
Down in Georgia there are peaches
Waiting for you, yes, and each is
Sweet
As any peach
That you could reach for on a tree.
Southern beauties, they are famous,
Georgia's where they grow.
My folks, they invite me.
Don't you want to go?

REFRAIN
Ev'rything is peaches down in
Georgia,
What a peach of a clime
For a peach of a time.
Believe me, Paradise is waiting down
  there
For you.
I've got a peach of a Pa,
Peach of a Ma,
Oh, what a peach of a couple they are!
There's a preacher preaches down in
  Georgia
Always ready to say:
"Will you love and obey?"
I bet you'll pick yourself a peach of
  a wife,
Settle down to a peach of a life,
Ev'ry thing is peaches down in
Georgia.

VERSE 2
All of Georgia's full of peaches.
They're all gorgeous, each one reaches
Right
Into your heart
And makes you part of Georgia too.
Clingstone peaches cling to you,
Peaches haunt your dream.
Think of getting, always getting,
Peaches in your cream.

REPEAT REFRAIN

—Milton Ager and George W. Meyer

Ragtime Cowboy Joe

VERSE I
Out in Arizona where the bad men are
And the only friend to guide you is an
  evening star,
The roughest, toughest man, by far,
Is Ragtime Cowboy Joe.
Got his name from singin' to the cows and
  sheep;
Ev'ry night, they say, he sings the herd to
  sleep
In a basso, rich and deep,
Crooning soft and low.

REFRAIN
He always sings
Raggy music to the cattle as he swings
Back and forward in the saddle on a horse
That is syncopated, gaited;
And there's such a funny meter
To the roar of his repeater!
How they run,
When they hear that fellow's gun,
Because the Western folks all know
He's a high falutin',
Scootin', shootin'

Son of a gun from Arizona,
Ragtime Cowboy Joe!

VERSE 2

Dressed up ev'ry Sunday in his Sunday
   clothes,
He then beats it for the village where he
   always goes;
And ev'ry girl in town is Joe's,
'Cause he's a ragtime bear.
When he starts a-spielin' on the dance hall
   floor,
No one but a lunatic would start a war;
Wise men know his forty-four
Makes men dance for fair.

REPEAT REFRAIN

—*Lewis F. Muir and Maurice Abrahams*

SECOND HAND ROSE

VERSE 1

Father has a bus'ness,
Strictly second hand.
Ev'rything from toothpicks
To a baby grand.
Stuff in our apartment
Came from Father's store,
Even things I'm wearing
Someone wore before.
It's no wonder that I feel abused.
I never have a thing that ain't been used.

REFRAIN 1

I'm wearing second hand hats,
Second hand clothes,
That's why they call me
Second hand Rose.
Even our piano in the parlor
Father bought for ten cents on the dollar.
Second hand pearls,

I'm wearing second hand curls.
I never get a single thing that's new.
Even Jake the plumber,
He's the man I adore,
Had the nerve to tell me
He's been married before.
Ev'ryone knows
That I'm just second hand Rose
From Second Avenue.

VERSE 2

Each one in the fam'ly
Kicks the whole day long.
Ev'ryone's disgusted,
Ev'rything is wrong.
Second handed doggie,
Second handed cat,
Second handed welcome,
Second handed mat.
I think father's head is made of wood.
He brings home lots of things that ain't
   no good.

REFRAIN 2

I'm wearing second hand shoes,
Second hand hose,
All the girls hand me
Their second hand beaux.
Even my pajamas when I don 'em
Have somebody else's initials on 'em.
Second hand rings,
I'm sick of second hand things,
I never get what other girlies do.
Once while strolling through the Ritz
A girl got my goat,
She nudged her friend and said,
   "Oh! look,
There's my old fur coat."
Ev'ryone knows
That I'm just second hand Rose
From Second Avenue.

—*James F. Hanley*

Cole Porter (1891–1964)

ALONG WITH George M. Cohan, Irving Berlin, Frank Loesser, Harold Rome, and Stephen Sondheim, Cole Porter is one of the few top lyricists who composed his own music. A rich young man from Peru, Indiana, Porter began his professional writing career while still at Yale, and quickly had shows on Broadway. His first successes came in the late twenties ("Let's Do It," "What Is This Thing Called Love?"), but his quintessential work came in the thirties with a series of shows that included *Gay Divorce, Anything Goes, Jubilee, Red Hot and Blue,* and *DuBarry Was a Lady.* His most frequent collaborator was Ethel Merman, and their partnership extended into the forties with *Panama Hattie* and *Something for the Boys.* His most famous score— and biggest hit—was *Kiss Me, Kate* in 1948, which reestablished him as a major force in the American musical theater and prepared the way for his successes of the fifties, *Can-Can* and *Silk Stockings. The Gay Divorcée,* the Astaire/Rogers film version of *Gay Divorce,* used only one song from the show, but that song was "Night and Day." Other films included *Rosalie, Born to Dance, Broadway Melody of 1940, You'll Never Get Rich, The Pirate, High Society,* and *Les Girls.* And then there was the movie *Night and Day,* a ludicrous travesty of Porter's sophisticated life and elegant lifestyle, starring an embarrassed (one hopes) Cary Grant and of course featuring the cream of Porter's life-work, a unique blend of the passionate and the witty.

ALL OF YOU

VERSE

After watching your appeal from ev'ry
   angle,
There's a big romantic deal I've got to
   wangle,
For I've fallen for a certain luscious lass,
And it's not a passing fancy or a fancy pass.

REFRAIN

I love the looks of you, the lure of you,
I'd love to make a tour of you,
The eyes, the arms, the mouth of you,
The east, west, north, and the south
   of you.

I'd love to gain complete control of you,
And handle even the heart and soul
   of you.
So love, at least, a small percent of me, do,
For I love all of you.

ALWAYS TRUE TO YOU IN MY FASHION

VERSE

Oh, Bill,
Why can't you behave,
Why can't you behave?
How in hell can you be jealous
When you know, baby, I'm your slave?

I'm just mad for you,
And I'll always be,
But naturally. . . .

REFRAIN I

If a custom-tailored vet
Asks me out for something wet,
When the vet begins to pet, I cry,
    "Hooray!"
But I'm always true to you, darlin', in my
    fashion,
Yes, I'm always true to you, darlin', in
    my way.
I enjoy a tender pass
By the boss of Boston, Mass.,
Though his pass is middle-class and notta
    Backa Bay.
But I'm always true to you, darlin', in my
    fashion,
Yes, I'm always true to you, darlin', in
    my way.
There's a madman known as Mack
Who is planning to attack,
If his mad attack means a Cadillac, okay!
But I'm always true to you, darlin', in my
    fashion,
Yes, I'm always true to you, darlin', in
    my way.

REFRAIN 2

I've been asked to have a meal
By a big tycoon in steel,
If the meal includes a deal, accept I may.
But I'm always true to you, darlin', in my
    fashion,
Yes, I'm always true to you, darlin', in
    my way.
I could never curl my lip
To a dazzlin' diamond clip,
Though the clip meant "Let 'er rip," I'd
    not say "Nay!"
But I'm always true to you, darlin', in my
    fashion,

Yes, I'm always true to you, darlin', in
    my way.
There's an oil man known as Tex
Who is keen to give me checks,
And his checks, I fear, mean that sex is
    here to stay!
But I'm always true to you, darlin', in my
    fashion,
Yes, I'm always true to you, darlin', in
    my way.

REFRAIN 3

There's a wealthy Hindu priest
Who's a wolf, to say the least,
When the priest goes too far east, I also
    stray.
But I'm always true to you, darlin', in my
    fashion,
Yes, I'm always true to you, darlin', in
    my way.
There's a lush from Portland, Ore.,
Who is rich but sich a bore,
When the bore falls on the floor, I let
    him lay.
But I'm always true to you, darlin', in my
    fashion,
Yes, I'm always true to you, darlin', in
    my way.
Mister Harris, plutocrat,
Wants to give my cheek a pat.
If the Harris pat
Means a Paris hat,
Bébé, Oo-la-la!
Mais je suis toujours fidèle, darlin', in my
    fashion,
Oui, je suis toujours fidèle, darlin', in
    my way.

REFRAIN 4

From Ohio, Mister Thorne
Calls me up from night 'til morn,
Mister Thorne once cornered corn and
    that ain't hay.

But I'm always true to you, darlin', in my
    fashion,
Yes, I'm always true to you, darlin', in
    my way.
From Milwaukee, Mister Fritz
Often moves me to the Ritz,
Mister Fritz is full of Schlitz and full
    of play.
But I'm always true to you, darlin', in my
    fashion,
Yes, I'm always true to you, darlin', in
    my way.
Mister Gable, I mean Clark,
Wants me on his boat to park,
If the Gable boat
Means a sable coat,
Anchors aweigh!
But I'm always true to you, darlin', in my
    fashion,
Yes, I'm always true to you, darlin', in
    my way.

ANYTHING GOES

VERSE
Times have changed,
And we've often rewound the clock
Since the Puritans got a shock
When they landed on Plymouth Rock.
If today
Any shock they should try to stem,
'Stead of landing on Plymouth Rock,
Plymouth Rock would land on them.

REFRAIN I
In olden days, a glimpse of stocking
Was looked on as something shocking,
But now, God knows,
Anything goes.
Good authors, too, who once knew better
    words
Now only use four-letter words

Writing prose,
Anything goes.
If driving fast cars you like,
If low bars you like,
If old hymns you like,
If bare limbs you like,
If Mae West you like,
Or me undressed you like,
Why, nobody will oppose.
When ev'ry night, the set that's smart is in-
Truding in nudist parties in
Studios,
Anything goes.

REFRAIN 2
When Missus Ned McLean (God
    bless her)
Can get Russian reds to "yes" her,
Then I suppose
Anything goes.
When Rockefeller still can hoard en-
Ough money to let Max Gordon
Produce his shows,
Anything goes.
The world has gone mad today,
And good's bad today,
And black's white today,
And day's night today,
And that gent today
You gave a cent today
Once had several châteaux.
When folks who still can ride in jitneys
Find out Vanderbilts and Whitneys
Lack baby clo'es,
Anything goes.

REFRAIN 3
If Sam Goldwyn can with great conviction
Instruct Anna Sten in diction,
Then Anna shows
Anything goes.
When you hear that Lady Mendl
    standing up

Now turns a handspring landing up-
On her toes,
Anything goes.
Just think of those shocks you've got,
And those knocks you've got,
And those blues you've got,
From that news you've got,
And those pains you've got
(If any brains you've got)
From those little radios.
So Missus R., with all her trimmin's,
Can broadcast a bed from Simmons,
'Cause Franklin knows
Anything goes.

At Long Last Love

VERSE
I'm so in love,
And though it gives me joy intense,
I can't decipher
If I'm a lifer,
Or if it's just a first offense.
I'm so in love,
I've no sense of values left at all.
Is this a playtime,
Affair of Maytime,
Or is it a windfall?

REFRAIN I
Is it an earthquake or simply a shock?
Is it the good turtle soup or merely
    the mock?
Is it a cocktail, this feeling of joy,
Or is what I feel the real McCoy?
Have I the right hunch or have I the
    wrong?
Will it be Bach I shall hear or just a Cole
    Porter song?
Is it a fancy not worth thinking of?
Or is it at long last love?

REFRAIN 2
Is it the rainbow or just a mirage?
Will it be tender and sweet or merely
    massage?
Is it a brainstorm in one of its quirks,
Or is it the best, the crest, the works?
Is it for all time or simply a lark?
Is it the Lido I see or only Asbury Park?
Should I say "Thumbs down" and give it a
    shove,
Or is it at long last love?

REFRAIN 3
Is it a breakdown or is it a break?
Is it a real Porterhouse or only a steak?
What can account for these strange
    pitter-pats?
Could this be the dream, the cream, the
    cat's?
Is it to rescue or is it to wreck?
Is it an ache in the heart or just a pain in
    the neck?
Is it the ivy you touch with a glove,
Or is it at long last love?

Begin the Beguine

When they begin the beguine
It brings back the sound of music so
    tender,
It brings back a night of tropical splendor,
It brings back a memory ever green.
I'm with you once more under the stars,
And down by the shore an orchestra's
    playing,
And even the palms seem to be swaying
When they begin the beguine.
To live it again is past all endeavor
Except when that tune clutches my
    heart.
And there we are, swearing to love forever,
And promising never,

Never to part.
What moments divine, what rapture
serene,
Till clouds came along to disperse the joys
we had tasted,
And now when I hear people curse the
chance that was wasted,
I know but too well what they mean.
So don't let them begin the beguine!
Let the love that was once a fire remain an
ember.
Let it sleep like the dead desire I only
remember
When they begin the beguine.
Oh yes, let them begin the beguine, make
them play!
Till the stars that were there before return
above you,
Till you whisper to me once more,
"Darling, I love you!"
And we suddenly know what heaven
we're in
When they begin the beguine.

Brush Up Your Shakespeare

The girls today in society
Go for classical poetry,
So to win their hearts one must quote
with ease
Aeschylus and Euripides.
One must know Homer and, b'lieve
me, Bo,
Sophocles, also Sappho-ho.
Unless you know Shelley and Keats
and Pope,
Dainty debbies will call you a dope.
But the poet of them all
Who will start 'em simply ravin'
Is the poet people call
The Bard of Stratford-on-Avon.

REFRAIN 1
Brush up your Shakespeare,
Start quoting him now.
Brush up your Shakespeare
And the women you will wow.
Just declaim a few lines from "Othella"
And they'll think you're a helluva fella.
If your blonde won't respond when you
flatter 'er,
Tell her what Tony told Cleopatterer.
If she fights when her clothes you are
mussing,
What are clothes? "Much Ado About
Nussing."
Brush up your Shakespeare
And they'll all kowtow.

REFRAIN 2
Brush up your Shakespeare,
Start quoting him now.
Brush up your Shakespeare
And the women you will wow.
With the wife of the British embessida
Try a crack out of "Troilus and
Cressida,"
If she says she won't buy it or tike it
Make her tike it, what's more, "As You
Like It."
If she says your behavior is heinous,
Kick her right in the "Coriolanus."
Brush up your Shakespeare
And they'll all kowtow.

REFRAIN 3
Brush up your Shakespeare,
Start quoting him now.
Brush up your Shakespeare
And the women you will wow.
If you can't be a ham and do "Hamlet,"
They will not give a damn or a damnlet.
Just recite an occasional sonnet
And your lap'll have "Honey" upon it.
When your baby is pleading for pleasure

Let her sample your "Measure for
    Measure."
Brush up your Shakespeare
And they'll all kowtow.

REFRAIN 4

Brush up your Shakespeare,
Start quoting him now.
Brush up your Shakespeare
And the women you will wow.
Better mention "The Merchant of
    Venice"
When her sweet pound o' flesh you would
    menace.
If her virtue, at first, she defends—well,
Just remind her that "All's Well That
    Ends Well."
And if still she won't give you a bonus,
You know what Venus got from Adonis!
Brush up your Shakespeare
And they'll all kowtow.

REFRAIN 5

Brush up your Shakespeare,
Start quoting him now.
Brush up your Shakespeare
And the women you will wow.
If your goil is a Washington Heights
    dream,
Treat the kid to "A Midsummer Night's
    Dream."
If she then wants an all-by-herself night,
Let her rest ev'ry 'leventh or "Twelfth
    Night."
If because of your heat she gets huffy,
Simply play on and "Lay on, Macduffy!"
Brush up your Shakespeare
And they'll all kowtow.
We trow, and they'll all kowtow.

GRAND FINALE

Brush up your Shakespeare,
Start quoting him now.

Brush up your Shakespeare
And the women you will wow.
So tonight just recite to your matey,
"Kiss me, Kate, kiss me, Kate, kiss me,
    Katey."
Brush up your Shakespeare
And they'll all kowtow.

DOWN IN THE DEPTHS

VERSE

Manhattan—
I'm up a tree.
The one I've most adored
Is bored
With me.
Manhattan—
I'm awf'lly nice,
Nice people dine with me,
And even twice.
Yet the only one in the world I'm mad
    about
Talks of somebody else
And walks out.

REFRAIN

With a million neon rainbows burning
    below me
And a million blazing taxis raising a roar,
Here I sit, above the town,
In my pet pailletted gown
Down in the depths on the ninetieth
    floor.
While the crowds at El Morocco punish
    the parquet
And at "21" the couples clamor for more,
I'm deserted and depressed
In my regal eagle nest,
Down in the depths on the ninetieth
    floor.
When the only one you wanted wants
    another,

What's the use of swank and cash in the
  bank galore?
Why, even the janitor's wife
Has a perfectly good love life,
And here am I
Facing tomorrow
Alone with my sorrow,
Down in the depths on the ninetieth
  floor.

Ev'ry Time We Say Good-bye

VERSE

We love each other so deeply
That I ask you this, sweetheart,
Why should we quarrel ever,
Why can't we be enough clever
Never to part?

REFRAIN

Ev'ry time we say good-bye
I die a little.
Ev'ry time we say good-bye
I wonder why a little.
Why the gods above me
Who must be in the know
Think so little of me
They allow you to go.
When you're near there's such an air
Of Spring about it,
I can hear a lark somewhere
Begin to sing about it.
There's no love song finer,
But how strange
The change
From major to minor
Ev'ry time we say good-bye,
Ev'ry single time we say good-bye.

Friendship

REFRAIN 1

HE: If you're ever in a jam, here I am.
SHE: If you ever need a pal, I'm your gal.
HE: If you ever feel so happy you land
  in jail,
  I'm your bail.
BOTH: It's friendship, friendship,
  Just a perfect blendship.
  When other friendships have been
    forgot,
  Ours will still be hot.
  Lahdle–ahdle–ahdle–dig, dig, dig.

REFRAIN 2

SHE: If you ever lose your way, come
  to May.
HE: If you ever make a flop, call for Pop.
SHE: If you ever take a boat and get lost
  at sea,
  Write to me.
BOTH: It's friendship, friendship,
  Just a perfect blendship.
  When other friendships have been
    forgit,
  Ours will still be it,
  Lahdle–ahdle–ahdle–chuck,
    chuck, chuck.

REFRAIN 3

HE: If you're ever down a well, ring
  my bell.
SHE: If you ever catch on fire, send
  a wire.
HE: If you ever lose your teeth and
  you're out to dine,
  Borrow mine.
BOTH: It's friendship, friendship,
  Just a perfect blendship.
  When other friendships have
    ceased to jell,

Ours will still be swell.
Lahdle–ahdle–ahdle–hep,
   hep, hep.

REFRAIN 4

SHE: If they ever black your eyes, put
   me wise.
HE: If they ever cook your goose, turn
   me loose.
SHE: If they ever put a bullet through
   your brr-ain,
   I'll complain.
BOTH: It's friendship, friendship,
   Just a perfect blendship.
   When other friendships go up in
   smoke,
   Ours will still be oke.
   Lahdle–ahdle–ahdle–chuck,
   chuck, chuck,
   Quack, quack, quack,
   Tweet, tweet, tweet,
   Push, push, push,
   Give, give, give,
   Gong, gong, gong,
   Cluck, cluck, cluck,
   Woof, woof, woof,
   Peck, peck, peck,
   Put, put, put,
   Hip, hip, hip.

REFRAIN 5

HE: If you ever lose your mind, I'll
   be kind.
SHE: If you ever lose your shirt, I'll
   be hurt.
HE: If you're ever in a mill and get
   sawed in half,
   I won't laugh.
BOTH: It's friendship, friendship,
   Just a perfect blendship.
   When other friendships have been
   forgate,
   Ours will still be great.

Lahdle–ahdle–ahdle–goof,
   goof, goof.

REFRAIN 6

SHE: If they ever hang you, pard, send
   a card.
HE: If they ever cut your throat, write
   a note.
SHE: If they ever make a cannibal stew
   of you,
   Invite me too.
BOTH: It's friendship, friendship,
   Just a perfect blendship.
   When other friendships are up the
   crick,
   Ours will still be slick,
   Lahdle–ahdle–ahdle–zip,
   zip, zip.

FROM THIS MOMENT ON

VERSE

Now that we are close,
No more nights morose.
Now that we are one,
The beguine has just begun.
Now that we're side by side,
The future looks so gay.
Now we are alibi-ed
When we say:

REFRAIN

From this moment on,
You for me, dear,
Only two for tea, dear,
From this moment on.
From this happy day,
No more blue songs,
Only whoop-dee-doo songs,
From this moment on.
For you've got the love I need so much,
Got the skin I love to touch,

Got the arms to hold me tight,
Got the sweet lips to kiss me good
  night.
From this moment on,
You and I, babe,
We'll be ridin' high, babe,
Ev'ry care is gone
From this moment on.

GET OUT OF TOWN

VERSE

The farce was ended,
The curtain drawn,
And I at least pretended
That love was dead and gone.
But now from nowhere
You come to me as before,
To take my heart
And break my heart
Once more.

REFRAIN

Get out of town
Before it's too late, my love.
Get out of town,
Be good to me, please.
Why wish me harm?
Why not retire to a farm
And be contented to charm
The birds off the trees?
Just disappear,
I care for you much too much,
And when you are near,
Close to me, dear,
We touch too much.
The thrill when we meet
Is so bittersweet
That, darling, it's getting me down,
So on your mark, get set,
Get out of town.

I CONCENTRATE ON YOU

Whenever skies look gray to me
And trouble begins to brew,
Whenever the winter winds become too
  strong,
I concentrate on you.
When Fortune cries, "Nay, nay!" to me
And people declare, "You're through,"
Whenever the blues become my only song,
I concentrate on you,
On your smile so sweet, so tender,
When at first my kiss you decline,
On the light in your eyes when you
  surrender
And once again our arms intertwine.
And so when wise men say to me
That love's young dream never
  comes true,
To prove that even wise men can be
  wrong,
I concentrate on you,
I concentrate
And concentrate
On you.

I GET A KICK OUT OF YOU

VERSE

My story is much too sad to be told,
But practically ev'rything leaves me
  totally cold.
The only exception I know is the case
Where I'm out on a quiet spree,
Fighting vainly the old ennui,
And I suddenly turn and see
Your fabulous face.

REFRAIN

I get no kick from champagne.
Mere alcohol doesn't thrill me at all,

So tell me why should it be true
That I get a kick out of you?
Some get a kick from cocaine.
I'm sure that if I took even one sniff
That would bore me terrific'ly, too,
Yet I get a kick out of you.
I get a kick ev'ry time I see
You're standing there before me.
I get a kick though it's clear to me
You obviously don't adore me.
I get no kick in a plane.
Flying too high with some guy in
    the sky
Is my idea of nothing to do,
Yet I get a kick out of you.

I'm a Gigolo

VERSE
I should like you all to know
I'm a famous gigolo,
And of lavender, my nature's got just a
    dash in it.
As I'm slightly undersexed,
You will always find me next
To some dowager who's wealthy rather
    than passionate.
Go to one of those night club places
And you'll find me stretching my
    braces
Pushing ladies with lifted faces 'round
    the floor.
But I must confess to you
There are moments when I'm blue,
And I ask myself whatever I do it for.

REFRAIN
I'm a flower that blooms in the
    winter,
Sinking deeper and deeper in "snow."
I'm a baby who has
No mother but jazz,

I'm a gigolo.
Ev'ry morning, when labor is over,
To my sweet-scented lodgings I go,
Take the glass from the shelf
And look at myself,
I'm a gigolo.
I get stocks and bonds
From faded blondes
Ev'ry twenty-fifth of December.
Still I'm just a pet
That men forget
And only tailors remember.
Yet when I see the way all the ladies
Treat their husbands who put up the
    dough,
You cannot think me odd
If then I thank God
I'm a gigolo.

In the Still of the Night

In the still of the night,
As I gaze from my window
At the moon in its flight,
My thoughts all stray to you.
In the still of the night,
While the world is in slumber,
Oh, the times without number,
Darling, when I say to you,
"Do you love me as I love you?
Are you my life-to-be, my dream
    come true?"
Or will this dream of mine
Fade out of sight
Like the moon
Growing dim
On the rim
Of the hill
In the chill,
Still
Of the night?

IT's All Right with Me

It's the wrong time and the wrong place,
Though your face is charming, it's the
    wrong face,
It's not her face but such a charming face
That it's all right with me.
It's the wrong song in the wrong style,
Though your smile is lovely, it's the wrong
    smile,
It's not her smile but such a lovely smile
That it's all right with me.
You can't know how happy I am that
    we met,
I'm strangely attracted to you.
There's someone I'm trying so hard to
    forget,
Don't you want to forget someone too?
It's the wrong game with the wrong chips,
Though your lips are tempting, they're the
    wrong lips,
They're not her lips but they're such
    tempting lips
That if some night you're free,
Dear, it's all right,
It's all right
With me.

IT's De-Lovely

VERSE I

HE: I feel a sudden urge to sing
    The kind of ditty that invokes the
        Spring,
    So control your desire to curse
    While I crucify the verse.
SHE: This verse you've started seems to me
    The Tin-Pantithesis of melody,
    So spare me, please, the pain,
    Just skip the damn thing and sing the
        refrain.

HE: Mi, mi, mi, mi,
    Re, re, re, re,
    Do, sol, mi, do, la, si.
SHE: Take it away.

REFRAIN I

The night is young, the skies are clear,
So if you want to go walking, dear,
It's delightful, it's delicious, it's
    de-lovely.
I understand the reason why
You're sentimental, 'cause so am I,
It's delightful, it's delicious, it's
    de-lovely.
You can tell at a glance
What a swell night this is for romance,
You can hear dear Mother Nature
    murmuring low,
"Let yourself go."
So please be sweet, my chickadee,
And when I kiss you, just say to me,
"It's delightful, it's delicious,
It's delectable, it's delirious,
It's dilemma, it's delimit, it's deluxe,
It's de-lovely."

VERSE 2

SHE: Oh, charming sir, the way you sing
    Would break the heart of Missus
        Crosby's Bing,
    For the tone of your tra la la
    Has that certain je ne sais quoi.
HE: Oh, thank thee kindly, winsome
        wench,
    But 'stead of falling into Berlitz
        French
    Just warble to me, please,
    This beautiful strain in plain
        Brooklynese.
SHE: Mi, mi, mi, mi,
    Re, re, re, re,
    Do, sol, mi, do, la, si.
HE: Take it away.

REFRAIN 2

Time marches on and soon it's plain
You've won my heart and I've lost my
	brain,
It's delightful, it's delicious, it's de-lovely.
Life seems so sweet that we decide
It's in the bag to get unified,
It's delightful, it's delicious, it's de-lovely.
See the crowd in that church,
See the proud parson plopped on his perch,
Get the sweet beat of that organ, sealing
	our doom,
"Here goes the groom, boom!"
How they cheer and how they smile
As we go galloping down that aisle.
It's divine, dear, it's diveen, dear,
It's de-wunderbar, it's de victory,
It's de vallop, it's de vinner, it's de voiks,
It's de-lovely.

REFRAIN 3

The knot is tied and so we take
A few hours off to eat wedding cake,
It's delightful, it's delicious, it's de-lovely.
It feels so fine to be a bride,
And how's the groom? Why, he's slightly
	fried,
It's delightful, it's delicious, it's de-lovely.
To the pop of champagne,
Off we hop in our plush little plane
Till a bright light through the darkness
	cozily calls,
"Niag'ra Falls."
All's well, my love, our day's complete,
And what a beautiful bridal suite,
It's de-reamy, it's de-rowsy,
It's de-reverie, it's de-rhapsody,
It's de-regal, it's de-royal, it's de-Ritz,
It's de-lovely.

REFRAIN 4

We settle down as man and wife
To solve the riddle called "married life,"

It's delightful, it's delicious, it's de-lovely.
We're on the crest, we have no cares,
We're just a couple of honey bears,
It's delightful, it's delicious, it's de-lovely.
All's as right as can be
Till, one night, at my window I see
An absurd bird with a bundle hung on
	his nose—
"Get baby clo'es."
Those eyes of yours are filled with joy
When Nurse appears and cries, "It's a boy,"
He's appalling, he's appealing,
He's a pollywog, he's a paragon,
He's a Popeye, he's a panic, he's a pip,
He's de-lovely.

REFRAIN 5

Our boy grows up, he's six feet three,
He's so good-looking, he looks like me,
It's delightful, it's delicious, it's de-lovely.
He's such a hit, this son of ours,
That all the dowagers send him flowers,
It's delightful, it's delicious, it's de-lovely.
So sublime is his press
That in time L. B. Mayer, no less,
Makes a night flight to New York and tells
	him he should
Go Hollywood.
Good God! Today, he gets such pay
That Elaine Barrie's his fiancée,
It's delightful, it's delicious,
It's delectable, it's delirious,
It's dilemma, it's delimit, it's deluxe,
It's de-lovely.

I'VE GOT YOU UNDER MY SKIN

I've got you under my skin,
I've got you deep in the heart of me,
So deep in my heart, you're really a part
	of me,
I've got you under my skin.

I tried so not to give in,
I said to myself, "This affair never will go
   so well."
But why should I try to resist when,
   darling, I know so well
I've got you under my skin.
I'd sacrifice anything, come what might,
For the sake of having you near,
In spite of a warning voice that comes in
   the night,
And repeats and repeats in my ear,
"Don't you know, little fool, you never
   can win,
Use your mentality,
Wake up to reality."
But each time I do, just the thought
   of you
Makes me stop, before I begin,
'Cause I've got you under my skin.

JUST ONE OF THOSE THINGS

VERSE
As Dorothy Parker once said to her
   boyfriend,
"Fare thee well."
As Columbus announced when he knew he
   was bounced,
"It was swell, Isabelle, swell."
As Abélard said to Héloïse,
"Don't forget to drop a line to me, please."
As Juliet cried in her Romeo's ear,
"Romeo, why not face the fact,
   my dear?"

REFRAIN
It was just one of those things,
Just one of those crazy flings,
One of those bells that now and then
   rings,
Just one of those things.
It was just one of those nights,

Just one of those fabulous flights,
A trip to the moon on gossamer wings,
Just one of those things.
If we'd thought a bit
Of the end of it
When we started painting the town,
We'd have been aware
That our love affair
Was too hot not to cool down.
So good-bye, dear, and amen,
Here's hoping we meet now and then.
It was great fun,
But it was just one of those things.

KATIE WENT TO HAITI

REFRAIN 1
Katie went to Haiti,
Stopped off for a rest.
Katie met a natie,
Katie was impressed.
After a week in Haiti
She started to go away,
Then Katie met another natie,
So Katie prolonged her stay.
After a month in Haiti
She decided to resume her trip,
But Katie met still another natie
And Katie missed the ship.
So Katie lived in Haiti,
Her life there, it was great,
'Cause Katie knew her Haiti
And practically all Haiti
Knew Katie.

REFRAIN 2
Katie stayed in Haiti,
Spending all her pay.
Katie met a natie
Ev'ry other day.
Katie would tell the natie
That Katie was out for thrills.

Each natie got a few for Katie
And Katie, she got the bills.
After a year in Haiti
She decided she should really go,
But Katie had lived at such a ratie
That Katie had no dough.
So Katie stuck to Haiti
Delighted with her fate,
'Cause Katie still had Haiti
And practically all Haiti
Had Katie.

REFRAIN 3

Katie looked at Haiti
Feeling rather tired.
Katie met a natie,
Katie was inspired.
After another natie
She sat down and wrote a book,
A guidebook for visitors to Haiti
Called "Listen, Stop and Look!"
After the book by Katie
Had been published in the U.S.A.,
The ratio of tourist trade in Haiti
Got bigger ev'ry day.
When Katie died at eighty
They buried her in state,
For Katie made her Haiti
And practically all Haiti
Made Katie.

THE LAZIEST GAL IN TOWN

VERSE

I've a beau, his name is Jim,
He loves me and I love him,
But he tells me I'm too prim,
That means I'm too slow.
I let him rant, I let him rave,
I let him muss my permanent wave,
But when he says "Let's misbehave,"
My reply is "No!"

REFRAIN

It's not 'cause I wouldn't,
It's not 'cause I shouldn't,
And, Lord knows, it's not 'cause I
    couldn't,
It's simply because I'm the laziest gal
    in town.
My poor heart is achin'
To bring home the bacon,
And if I'm alone and forsaken,
It's simply because I'm the laziest gal
    in town.
Though I'm more than willing to learn
How these gals get money to burn,
Ev'ry proposition I turn down,
'Way down.
It's not 'cause I wouldn't,
It's not 'cause I shouldn't,
And, Lord knows, it's not 'cause I
    couldn't,
It's simply because I'm the laziest gal
    in town.

VERSE SUNG BY MARLENE DIETRICH

Nothing ever worries me,
Nothing ever hurries me,
I take pleasure leisurely
Even when I kiss.
But when I kiss they want some more,
And wanting more becomes a bore,
It isn't worth the fighting for,
So I tell them this:

REFRAIN

LET'S DO IT, LET'S FALL IN LOVE

VERSE

When the little bluebird,
Who has never said a word,
Starts to sing "Spring, spring,"
When the little bluebell,

In the bottom of the dell,
Starts to ring "Ding, ding,"
When the little blue clerk,
In the middle of his work,
Starts a tune to the moon up above,
It is nature, that's all,
Simply telling us to fall
In love.

REFRAIN 1

And that's why Chinks do it, Japs do it,
Up in Lapland, little Lapps do it,
Let's do it, let's fall in love.
In Spain, the best upper sets do it,
Lithuanians and Letts do it,
Let's do it, let's fall in love.
The Dutch in old Amsterdam do it,
Not to mention the Finns,
Folks in Siam do it,
Think of Siamese twins.
Some Argentines, without means, do it,
People say, in Boston, even beans do it,
Let's do it, let's fall in love.

REFRAIN 2

The nightingales, in the dark, do it,
Larks, k-razy for a lark, do it,
Let's do it, let's fall in love.
Canaries, caged in the house, do it,
When they're out of season, grouse do it,
Let's do it, let's fall in love.
The most sedate barnyard fowls do it,
When a chanticleer cries.
High-browed old owls do it,
They're supposed to be wise.
Penguins in flocks, on the rocks, do it,
Even little cuckoos, in their clocks, do it,
Let's do it, let's fall in love.

REFRAIN 3

Romantic sponges, they say, do it,
Oysters, down in Oyster Bay, do it,
Let's do it, let's fall in love.

Cold Cape Cod clams, 'gainst their wish,
    do it,
Even lazy jellyfish do it,
Let's do it, let's fall in love.
Electric eels, I might add, do it,
Though it shocks 'em, I know.
Why ask if shad do it?
Waiter, bring me shad roe.
In shallow shoals, English soles do it,
Goldfish, in the privacy of bowls, do it,
Let's do it, let's fall in love.

REFRAIN 3 (ENGLISH PRODUCTION)

Young whelks and winkles in pubs
    do it,
Little sponges, in their tubs, do it,
Let's do it, let's fall in love.
Cold salmon, quite 'gainst their wish,
    do it,
Even lazy jellyfish do it,
Let's do it, let's fall in love.
The most select schools of cod do it,
Though it shocks 'em, I fear.
Sturgeon, thank God, do it,
Have some caviar, dear.
In shady shoals, English soles do it,
Goldfish, in the privacy of bowls, do it,
Let's do it, let's fall in love.

REFRAIN 4

The dragonflies, in the reeds, do it,
Sentimental centipedes do it,
Let's do it, let's fall in love.
Mosquitoes, heaven forbid, do it,
So does ev'ry katydid, do it,
Let's do it, let's fall in love.
The most refined ladybugs do it,
When a gentleman calls.
Moths, in your rugs, do it.
What's the use of mothballs?
Locusts in trees do it, bees do it,
Even overeducated fleas do it,
Let's do it, let's fall in love.

The chimpanzees, in the zoos, do it,
Some courageous kangaroos do it,
Let's do it, let's fall in love.
I'm sure giraffes, on the sly, do it,
Heavy hippopotami do it,
Let's do it, let's fall in love.
Old sloths who hang down from twigs
    do it,
Though the effort is great.
Sweet guinea pigs do it,
Buy a couple and wait.
The world admits bears in pits do it,
Even pekineses in the Ritz, do it,
Let's do it, let's fall in love.

LET'S NOT TALK ABOUT LOVE

SHE: Relax for one moment, my Jerry,
    Come out of your dark monastery,
    While Venus is beaming above.
    Darling, let's talk about love.

Let's talk about love, that wonderful
    thing,
Let's blend the scent of Venice with Paris
    in spring,
Let's gaze at that moon and try to believe
We're Venus and Adonis, or Adam and Eve.
Let's throw away anxiety, let's quite forget
    propriety,
Respectable society, the rector and his
    piety,
And contemplate l'amour in all its infinite
    variety,
My dear, let's talk about love.
Pretend you're Chopin and I'll be
    George Sand.
We're on the Grand Canal and, oh, baby,
    it's grand!

Let's mention Walküres and helmeted
    knights,
I'm beautiful Brünnhilde, you're Siegfried
    in tights,
Let's curse the asininity of trivial
    consanguinity,
Let's praise the masculinity of Dietrich's
    new affinity,
Let's picture Cleopatra saying "Scram" to
    her virginity,
My dear, let's talk about love.
The weather's so warm and you are
    so cute,
Let's dream about Tahiti and tropical
    fruit.
I've always said men were simply deevine.
(Did you know that Peggy Joyce was once a
    pupil of mine?)
Let's gather miscellanea on Oberon's
    Titania,
Or ladies even brainier who've moved to
    Pennsylvania
(Bucks County, so I hear, is just a nest of
    nymphomania),
My dear, let's talk about love.

HE: My buddies all tell me selectees
    Are expected by ladies to neck-
        tease,
    I could talk about love and
        why not?
    But believe me, it wouldn't be
        so hot,
    So—

Let's talk about frogs, let's talk about
    toads,
Let's try to solve the riddle why chickens
    cross roads,
Let's talk about games, let's talk about
    sports,

Let's have a big debate about ladies in
    shorts.
Let's question the synonymy of freedom
    and autonomy,
Let's delve into astronomy, political
    economy,
Or if you're feeling biblical, the book of
    Deuteronomy,
But let's not talk about love.
Let's ride the New Deal, like Senator
    Glass,
Let's telephone to Ickes and order
    more gas,
Let's curse the Old Guard and
    Hamilton Fish,
Forgive me, dear, if Fish is your
    favorite dish.
Let's heap some hot profanities on Hitler's
    inhumanities,
Let's argue if insanity's the cause of his
    inanities,
Let's weigh the Shubert Follies with the
    Ear-rl Carroll Vanities,
But let's not talk about love.
Let's talk about drugs, let's talk
    about dope,
Let's try to picture Paramount minus
    Bob Hope,
Let's start a new dance, let's try a
    new step,
Or investigate the cause of Missus
    Roosevelt's pep.
Why not discuss, my dee-arie,
The life of Wallace Bee-ery
Or bring a jeroboam on
And write a drunken poem on
Astrology, mythology,
Geology, philology,
Pathology, psychology,
Electro-physiology,
Spermology, phrenology?
I owe you an apology,
But let's not talk about love.

REFRAIN 3

Let's speak of Lamarr, that Hedy so fair,
Why does she let Joan Bennett wear all her
    old hair?
If you know Garbo, then tell me this news,
Is it a fact the Navy's launched all her old
    shoes?
Let's check on the veracity of Barrymore's
    bibacity
And why his drink capacity should get so
    much publacity,
Let's even have a huddle over Ha'vard
    Univassity,
But let's not talk about love.
Let's wish him good luck, let's wish him
    more pow'r,
That Fiorella fella, my favorite flow'r,
Let's get some champagne from over
    the seas,
And drink to Sammy Goldwyn,
Include me out please.
Let's write a tune that's playable, a ditty
    swing-and-swayable
Or say whatever's sayable about the Tow'r
    of Ba-abel,
Let's cheer for the career of itty-bitty Betty
    Gra-abel,
But let's not talk about love.
In case you play cards, I've got some
    right here,
So how about a game o' gin rummy,
    my dear?
Or if you feel warm and bathin's
    your whim,
Let's get in the all-together and enjoy a
    short swim.
No, honey, ah suspect you-all
Of bein' intellectual
And so, instead of gushin' on,
Let's have a big discussion on
Timidity, stupidity, solidity, frigidity,
Avidity, turbidity, Manhattan, and
    viscidity,

Fatality, morality, legality, finality,
Neutrality, reality, or Southern
    hospitality,
Pomposity, verbosity,
You're losing your velocity,
But let's not talk about love.

LOVE FOR SALE

VERSE

When the only sound in the empty
    street
Is the heavy tread of the heavy feet
That belong to a lonesome cop,
I open shop.
When the moon so long has been
    gazing down
On the wayward ways of this
    wayward town
That her smile becomes a smirk,
I go to work.

REFRAIN

Love for sale,
Appetizing young love for sale.
Love that's fresh and still unspoiled,
Love that's only slightly soiled,
Love for sale.
Who will buy?
Who would like to sample my
    supply?
Who's prepared to pay the price
For a trip to paradise?
Love for sale.
Let the poets pipe of love
In their childish way,
I know ev'ry type of love
Better far than they.
If you want the thrill of love,
I've been through the mill of love,
Old love, new love,
Ev'ry love but true love.

Love for sale,
Appetizing young love for sale.
If you want to buy my wares,
Follow me and climb the stairs,
Love for sale.

MISS OTIS REGRETS

Miss Otis regrets she's unable to lunch
    today,
Madam,
Miss Otis regrets she's unable to lunch
    today.
She is sorry to be delayed,
But last evening down in lovers' lane she
    strayed,
Madam,
Miss Otis regrets she's unable to lunch
    today.
When she woke up and found
That her dream of love was gone,
Madam,
She ran to the man
Who had led her so far astray,
And from under her velvet gown
She drew a gun and shot her
    lover down,
Madam,
Miss Otis regrets she's unable to lunch
    today.
When the mob came and got her
And dragged her from the jail,
Madam,
They strung her upon
The old willow across the way,
And the moment before she died
She lifted up her lovely head and
    cried,
Madam,
"Miss Otis regrets she's unable to lunch
    today."

My Heart Belongs to Daddy

VERSE

I used to fall
In love with all
Those boys who maul
Refined ladies.
But now I tell
Each young gazelle
To go to hell–
I mean, Hades.
For since I've come to care
For such a sweet millionaire . . .

REFRAIN I

While tearing off
A game of golf
I may make a play for the caddy.
But when I do
I don't follow through,
'Cause my heart belongs to Daddy.
If I invite
A boy, some night,
To dine on my fine finnan haddie,
I just adore
His asking for more,
But my heart belongs to Daddy.
Yes, my heart belongs to Daddy,
So I simply couldn't be bad.
Yes, my heart belongs to Daddy,
Da-da, da-da-da, da-da-da, dad!
So I want to warn you, laddie,
Tho' I know you're perfectly swell,
That my heart belongs to Daddy,
'Cause my Daddy, he treats me so well.
He treats it and treats it,
And then he repeats it,
Yes, Daddy, he treats it so well.

REFRAIN 2

Saint Patrick's Day,
Although I may

Be seen wearing green with a paddy,
I'm always sharp
When playing the harp,
'Cause my heart belongs to Daddy.
Though other dames
At football games
May long for a strong undergraddy,
I never dream
Of making the team,
'Cause my heart belongs to Daddy.
Yes, my heart belongs to Daddy,
So I simply couldn't be bad.
Yes, my heart belongs to Daddy,
Da-da, da-da-da, da-da-da, dad!
So I want to warn you, laddie,
Tho' I simply hate to be frank,
That I can't be mean to Daddy
'Cause my Da-da-da-daddy might spank.
In matters artistic
He's not modernistic,
So Da-da-da-daddy might spank.

Night and Day

VERSE

Like the beat beat beat of the tom-tom
When the jungle shadows fall,
Like the tick tick tock of the stately clock
As it stands against the wall,
Like the drip drip drip of the raindrops
When the summ'r show'r is through,
So a voice within me keeps repeating
You–you–you.

REFRAIN

Night and day you are the one,
Only you beneath the moon and under
    the sun,
Whether near to me or far
It's no matter, darling, where you are,
I think of you, night and day.
Day and night, why is it so

That this longing for you follows wherever
    I go?
In the roaring traffic's boom,
In the silence of my lonely room,
I think of you, night and day.
Night and day under the hide of me
There's an, oh, such a hungry yearning
    burning inside of me,
And its torment won't be through
Till you let me spend my life making love
    to you
Day and night, night and day.

RED, HOT AND BLUE

VERSE

Due to the tragic lowness of my brow,
All music that's highbrow
Gets me upset.
Each time I hear a strain of Stravinsky's,
I hurry to Minsky's
And try to forget.
I don't like Schubert's music or
    Schumann's,
I'm one of those humans
Who only goes in for Berlin and Vincent
    Youmans.
I'm for the guy that eludes
Bach sonatas and Chopin preludes.
So when some nice man I meet,
I always murmur tout d'suite:

REFRAIN I

"If you want to thrill me
And drill me
For your crew,
Sing me a melody that's red, hot and blue.
Before you expand on that grand cottage
    for two,
Sing me a melody that's red, hot and blue.
I can't take Sibelius,
Or Delius,

But I swear I'd throw my best pal away
For Calloway.
So when we're all set and I get married
    to you,
Don't let that violin
Start playing *Lohengrin,*
It may be sweet as sin
But it's not
Red, hot
And blue."

REFRAIN 2

"If you ask me, toots,
Just what puts
Me in a stew,
Sing me a melody that's red, hot and blue.
If I'm quite correct,
You expect
Me to come through,
Sing me a melody that's red, hot and blue.
This craze that's pursuin' me
May ruin me,
But my Waterloo won't be Wellington
But Ellington.
So if you feel tonight
Like a light
Ev'ning for two,
I've no desire to hear
Flagstad's Brünnhilde, dear,
She waves a pretty spear,
But she's not
Red, hot
And blue."

RIDIN' HIGH

VERSE

Love had socked me,
Simply knocked me
For a loop.
Luck had dished me
Till you fished me

From the soup.
Now, together,
We can weather
Anything.
So please don't sputter
If I should mutter:

REFRAIN
"Life's great, life's grand,
Future all planned,
No more clouds in the sky.
How'm I ridin'?
I'm ridin' high.
Someone I love,
Mad for my love,
So long, Jonah, good-bye.
How'm I ridin'?
I'm ridin' high."
Floating on a starlit ceiling,
Doting on the cards I'm dealing,
Gloating, because I'm feeling
So hap-hap-happy,
I'm slap-happy.
So ring bells, sing songs,
Blow horns, beat gongs,
Our love never will die.
How'm I ridin'? I'm ridin' high.

PATTER 1
What do I care
If Missus Harrison Williams is the best-
    dressed woman in town?
What do I care
If Countess Barbara Hutton has a Rolls-
    Royce built for each gown?
Why should I have the vapors
When I read in the papers
That Missus Simpson dined behind the
    throne?
I've got a cute king of my own.
What do I care
If Katie Hepburn is famous for the world's
    most beautiful nose,

Or if I, for my sins,
Don't possess underpins
Like the pegs "Legs" Dietrich shows?
I'm feeling swell,
In fact so well
It's time some noise began,
For although I'm not
A big shot,
Still, I've got my man.

So ring bells, sing songs,
Blow horns, beat gongs,
Our love never will die.
How'm I ridin'?
I'm ridin' high.

PATTER 2
What do I care
If Missus Dorothy Parker has the
    country's wittiest brain?
What do I care
If little Eleanor Jarrett only swims in
    vintage champagne?
Why should I be a-flutter
When Republicans mutter
That Missus R. gets pay to write her day,
If I could write my nights, hey, hey!
What do I care
If fair Tallulah possesses tons and tons of
    jewels from gents?
Or if someone observes
That I haven't the curves
That Simone Simon presents?
I'm doin' fine,
My life's divine,
I'm living in the sun
'Cause I've a big date
With my fate,
So I rate
A-1.

So ring bells, sing songs,
Blow horns, beat gongs,

Our love never will die.
How'm I ridin'? I'm ridin' high.

So in Love

Strange, dear, but true, dear,
When I'm close to you, dear,
The stars fill the sky,
So in love with you am I.
Even without you
My arms fold about you.
You know, darling, why,
So in love with you am I.
In love with the night mysterious,
The night when you first were there,
In love with my joy delirious
When I knew that you could care.
So taunt me and hurt me,
Deceive me, desert me,
I'm yours 'til I die,
So in love,
So in love,
So in love with you, my love,
Am I.

The Tale of the Oyster

Down by the sea lived a lonesome oyster,
Ev'ry day getting sadder and moister.
He found his homelife awf'lly wet,
And longed to travel with the upper set.
Poor little oyster.
Fate was kind to that oyster we know,
When one day the chef from the Park
    Casino
Saw that oyster lying there,
And said, "I'll put you on my bill of fare."
Lucky little oyster.
See him on his silver platter
Watching the queens of fashion chatter,
Hearing the wives of millionaires
Discuss their marriages and their love
    affairs.
Thrilled little oyster.
See that bivalve social climber
Feeding the rich Mrs. Hoggenheimer,
Think of his joy as he gaily glides
Down to the middle of her gilded
    insides.
Proud little oyster.
After lunch, Mrs. H. complains,
And says to her hostess, "I've got such
    pains.
I came to town on my yacht today,
But I think I'd better hurry back to Oyster
    Bay."
Scared little oyster.
Off they go through the troubled tide,
The yacht rolling madly from side
    to side.
They're tossed about till that poor young
    oyster
Finds that it's time he should quit his
    cloister.
Up comes the oyster.
Back once more where he started from,
He murmured, "I haven't a single qualm,
For I've had a taste of society,
And society has had a taste of me."
Wise little oyster.

They Couldn't Compare to You

VERSE
Oh, what a bevy of beauties,
Oh, what a school of fish,
Oh, what a covey of cuties,
Oh, what a dish delish!
I've known but litters of minxes,
All of 'em fun for a while,
Yet now, for the nonce, what methinks is,
You've got 'em
Beat a mile.

REFRAIN I

They couldn't compare to you,
They couldn't compare to you,
Although I've played
Many, many a maid,
They couldn't compare to you.
I've thoroughly pitched the woo
From the heights of Valhalla to
     Kalamazoo,
And though they all
Had a lot on the ball,
They couldn't compare to you.
Of ladies fair
I've loved more than my share,
And strange but true,
I hereby declare,
From tiptoe to hair,
They could not compare
To you.

PATTER

After playing the local sirens
Who resided in my environs,
I decided to learn the art of Cupid's
     trickery,
So, at once, I started cruising,
Found the Muses so amusing
That I even got a kick outa Terpsichore.
After her, I met Calypso,
Who was definitely a dipso,
Then I fled to Big Brünnhilde, she was
     German.
After snitching Eve from Adam,
I attended *Call Me Madam*
And shortly began to nestle Essel
     Merman.
I admired the silken body
Of the chic Scheherazade,
Then of Lady Godiva I became the lord.
After that I staged an orgy
For some friends o' Lucretia Borgie,
And ended up at the Stork with
     Fanny Ward.

After having had a party
With Phoenicia's goddess Astarte,
Well, I raised a bit of hell with Penelope.
After quieting all my urgin's
For several Vestal Virgins,
I put on a strip for Gypsy Rose Lee.
Though I liked the Queen of Sheba,
She was mentally an amoeba.
As for Beatrice d'Este,
She was a pest and far too chesty.
As for the passionate wife of Nero,
My reaction was frankly zero.
As for that sorceress known as Circe,
She was so hot I hollered for mercy!
There was Galatea,
And mean Medea,
And Sappho, one of the best.
There was Nefertiti,
A perfect sweetie,
And gay Mae West.
I was a helluva fella
With Cinderella
And Isabella of Spain.
And I used to caress
Both Lola Montez
And that damn Calamity Jane.
When betwixt Nell Gwyn
And Anne Boleyn
I was forced to make my choice,
I became so confused
I was even amused
And abused by Peggy Joyce.
There was Mélisande,
A platinum blonde
(How I loved to ruffle her locks).
There was bright Aurora,
Then Pandora,
Who let me open her box!

REFRAIN 2

They couldn't compare to you,
They couldn't compare to you,
Although I've played

Many, many a maid
They couldn't compare to you.
I've thoroughly pitched the woo
From Galli-pippo-lippy to Tippecanoe.
And though they all
Had a lot on the ball,
They couldn't compare to you.
Of ladies fair,
I've loved more than my share,
And strange but true,
I hereby declare,
From tiptoe to hair,
From hep cat to square,
From dressed-up to bare,
They could not compare
To you.

Too Darn Hot

VERSE 1

It's too darn hot,
It's too darn hot.
I'd like to sup with my baby tonight,
And play the pup with my baby tonight.
I'd like to sup with my baby tonight,
And play the pup with my baby tonight,
But I ain't up to my baby tonight,
'Cause it's too darn hot.
It's too darn hot,
It's too darn hot.
I'd like to stop for my baby tonight,
And blow my top with my baby tonight.
I'd like to stop for my baby tonight,
And blow my top with my baby tonight.
But I'd be a flop with my baby tonight,
'Cause it's too darn hot.
It's too darn hot,
It's too darn hot.
I'd like to fool with my baby tonight,
Break ev'ry rule with my baby tonight.
I'd like to fool with my baby tonight,
Break ev'ry rule with my baby tonight,

But, pillow, you'll be my baby tonight,
'Cause it's too darn hot.

REFRAIN 1

According to the Kinsey Report
Ev'ry average man you know
Much prefers to play his favorite sport
When the temperature is low.
But when the thermometer goes way up
And the weather is sizzling hot,
Mister Adam
For his madam
Is not.
'Cause it's too, too,
Too darn hot,
It's too darn hot,
It's too darn hot.

VERSE 2

It's too darn hot,
It's too darn hot.
I'd like to call on my baby tonight,
And give my all to my baby tonight,
I'd like to call on my baby tonight,
And give my all to my baby tonight,
But I can't play ball with my baby tonight,
'Cause it's too darn hot.
It's too darn hot,
It's too darn hot.
I'd like to meet with my baby tonight,
Get off my feet with my baby tonight,
I'd like to meet with my baby tonight,
Get off my feet with my baby tonight,
But no repeat with my baby tonight,
'Cause it's too darn hot.
It's too darn hot,
It's too darn hot.
I'd like to coo with my baby tonight,
And pitch some woo with my baby tonight,
I'd like to coo with my baby tonight,
And pitch some woo with my baby tonight,
But, brother, you bite my baby tonight,
'Cause it's too darn hot.

REFRAIN 2

According to the Kinsey Report
Ev'ry average man you know
Much prefers to play his favorite sport
When the temperature is low,
But when the thermometer goes way up
And the weather is sizzling hot,
Mister Gob
For his squab,
A marine
For his queen,
A G.I.
For his cutie-pie
Is not,
'Cause it's too, too,
Too darn hot,
It's too darn hot.
It's too, too, too, too darn hot.

WHAT IS THIS THING CALLED LOVE?

VERSE I

I was a humdrum person
Leading a life apart,
When love flew in through my
     window wide
And quickened my humdrum heart.
Love flew in through my window,
I was so happy then.
But after love had stayed a little while,
Love flew out again.

REFRAIN

What is this thing called love?
This funny thing called love?
Just who can solve its mystery?
Why should it make a fool of me?
I saw you there one wonderful day.
You took my heart and threw it away.
That's why I ask the Lord in heaven above,
What is this thing called love?

VERSE 2

You gave me days of sunshine,
You gave me nights of cheer,
You made my life an enchanted dream
Till somebody else came near.
Somebody else came near you,
I felt the winter's chill,
And now I sit and wonder night and day
Why I love you still.

REPEAT REFRAIN

WHERE IS THE LIFE THAT LATE I LED?

VERSE

Since I reached the charming age of
     puberty
And began to finger feminine curls,
Like a show that's typically Shuberty
I have always had a multitude of girls.
But now that a married man, at last, am I,
How aware of my dear, departed past
     am I!

REFRAIN I

Where is the life that late I led?
Where is it now? Totally dead.
Where is the fun I used to find?
Where has it gone? Gone with the wind.
A married life may all be well,
But raising an heir
Could never compare
With raising a bit of hell.
So I repeat what first I said,
Where is the life that late I led?

PATTER I

In dear Milano, where are you, Momo,
Still selling those pictures of the
     Scriptures in the Duomo?
And, Carolina, where are you, Lina,

Still peddling your pizza in the streets o'
 Taormina?
And in Firenze, where are you, Alice,
Still there in your pretty, itty-bitty Pitti
 Palace?
And sweet Lucretia, so young and
 gay-ee?
What scandalous doin's in the ruins of
 Pompeii?

REFRAIN 2

Where is the life that late I led?
Where is it now? Totally dead.
Where is the fun I used to find?
Where has it gone? Gone with the wind.
The marriage game is quite all right,
Yes, during the day
It's easy to play,
But, oh, what a bore at night.
So I repeat what first I said,
Where is the life that late I led?

PATTER 2

Where is Rebecca, my Becki-weckio,
Again is she cruising that amusing Ponte
 Vecchio?
Where is Fedora, the wild virago?
It's lucky I missed her gangster sister from
 Chicago.
Where is Venetia, who loved to chat so,
Could still she be drinkin' in her stinkin'
 pink palazzo?
And lovely Lisa, where are you, Lisa?
You gave a new meaning to the leaning
 tow'r of Pisa.

REFRAIN 3

Where is the life that late I led?
Where is it now? Totally dead.
Where is the fun I used to find?
Where has it gone? Gone with the wind.
I've oft been told of nuptial bliss,
But what do you do,

A quarter to two,
With only a shrew to kiss?
So I repeat what first I said,
Where is the life that late I led?

YOU DON'T KNOW PAREE

VERSE

You come to Paris, you come to play;
You have a wonderful time, you go away.
And, from then on, you talk of Paris
 knowingly;
You may know Paris, you don't know
 Paree.

REFRAIN

Though you've been around a lot,
And danced a lot, and laughed a lot,
You don't know Paree.
You may say you've seen a lot,
And heard a lot, and learned a lot;
You don't know Paree.
Paree will still be laughing after
Ev'ry one of us disappears,
But never once forget, her laughter
Is the laughter that hides the tears.
And until you've lived a lot,
And loved a lot, and lost a lot,
You don't know Paree,
You don't know Paree.

YOU'RE THE TOP

VERSE 1

At words poetic, I'm so pathetic
That I always have found it best,
Instead of getting 'em off my chest,
To let 'em rest
Unexpressed.
I hate parading
My serenading,

As I'll probably miss a bar,
But if this ditty
Is not so pretty,
At least it'll tell you
How great you are.

REFRAIN 1
You're the top!
You're the Colosseum.
You're the top!
You're the Louvre Museum.
You're a melody from a symphony by
    Strauss,
You're a Bendel bonnet,
A Shakespeare sonnet,
You're Mickey Mouse.
You're the Nile,
You're the Tow'r of Pisa,
You're the smile
On the Mona Lisa.
I'm a worthless check, a total wreck,
    a flop,
But if, baby, I'm the bottom
You're the top!

VERSE 2
Your words poetic are not pathetic.
On the other hand, boy, you shine,
And I can feel after every line
A thrill divine
Down my spine.
Now gifted humans
Like Vincent Youmans
Might think that your song is bad,
But for a person
Who's just rehearsin',
Well, I gotta say this, my lad:

REFRAIN 2
You're the top!
You're Mahatma Gandhi.
You're the top!
You're Napoleon brandy.

You're the purple light of a summer night
    in Spain,
You're the National Gall'ry,
You're Garbo's sal'ry,
You're cellophane.
You're sublime,
You're a turkey dinner,
You're the time
Of the Derby winner.
I'm a toy balloon that is fated soon
    to pop,
But if, baby, I'm the bottom
You're the top!

REFRAIN 3
You're the top!
You're a Ritz hot toddy.
You're the top!
You're a Brewster body.
You're the boats that glide on the sleepy
    Zuider Zee,
You're a Nathan panning,
You're Bishop Manning,
You're broccoli.
You're a prize,
You're a night at Coney,
You're the eyes
Of Irene Bordoni.
I'm a broken doll, a fol-de-rol, a blop,
But if, baby, I'm the bottom
You're the top!

REFRAIN 4
You're the top!
You're an Arrow collar.
You're the top!
You're a Coolidge dollar.
You're the nimble tread of the feet of Fred
    Astaire,
You're an O'Neill drama,
You're Whistler's mama,
You're Camembert.
You're a rose,

You're Inferno's Dante,
You're the nose
On the great Durante.
I'm just in the way, as the French
    would say
"De trop,"
But if, baby, I'm the bottom
You're the top!

REFRAIN 5
You're the top!
You're a Waldorf salad.
You're the top!
You're a Berlin ballad.
You're a baby grand of a lady and a gent,
You're an old Dutch master,
You're Mrs. Astor,
You're Pepsodent.
You're romance,
You're the steppes of Russia,
You're the pants on a Roxy usher.
I'm a lazy lout that's just about
    to stop,
But if, baby, I'm the bottom
You're the top!

REFRAIN 6
You're the top!
You're a dance in Bali.
You're the top!
You're a hot tamale.

You're an angel, you, simply too, too, too
    diveen,
You're a Botticelli,
You're Keats, you're Shelley,
You're Ovaltine.
You're a boon,
You're the dam at Boulder,
You're the moon
Over Mae West's shoulder.
I'm a nominee of the G.O.P. or GOP,
But if, baby, I'm the bottom
You're the top!

REFRAIN 7
You're the top!
You're the Tower of Babel.
You're the top!
You're the Whitney stable.
By the river Rhine,
You're a sturdy stein of beer.
You're a dress from Saks's,
You're next year's taxes,
You're stratosphere.
You're my thoist,
You're a Drumstick Lipstick,
You're da foist
In da Irish Svipstick.
I'm a frightened frog
That can find no log to hop,
But if, baby, I'm the bottom
You're the top!

Al Dubin (1891–1945)

BORN IN ZURICH and brought to America when he was two, Al Dubin took some time—and service in World War I—to get his career in gear. But with his easy vernacular style, he was already a success when he went to Hollywood in 1929, and he became (deservedly) one of its most consistently successful lyricists until the mid-forties, when he died, too young, after a life of too much food and drink. His first assignment for Warners was to write, with Joe Burke, the score for *Gold Diggers of Broadway* ("Tip Toe Through the Tulips"). It was a big hit, and he and Burke worked together until his great partnership with Harry Warren began in 1932, when Warners paired them to write the score for *42nd Street.* Together, Warren and Dubin turned out dozens of snappy hits for the *Gold Diggers* series (the Oscar-winning "Lullaby of Broadway" appeared in the 1935 edition), *Footlight Parade, Dames,* and other typical Warners musicals. But Dubin's career featured hits both before and after Warren—from "A Cup of Coffee, a Sandwich, and You," sung by Gertrude Lawrence and Jack Buchanan in *Charlot's Revue of 1926,* to "Feudin' and Fightin'," which became a hit for Dorothy Shay, "The Park Avenue Hillbilly," two years after his death. (It's now thought that "Feudin' and Fightin' " may have been written by Frank Loesser, a former partner.)

A CUP OF COFFEE, A SANDWICH, AND YOU

(with Billy Rose)

VERSE

In the movie plays
Of nowadays,
A romance always must begin in June.
Tales in magazines
Have all their scenes
Of love laid in a garden 'neath the moon.
But I don't miss
That kind of bliss.
What I want is this:

REFRAIN

A cup of coffee, a sandwich, and you,
A cozy corner, a table for two,
A chance to whisper and cuddle and coo,
With lots of huggin' and kissin' in view.
I don't need music, lobster, or wine
Whenever your eyes look into mine.
The things I long for are simple and few:
A cup of coffee, a sandwich, and you!

—*Joseph Meyer*

DAMES

VERSE

Who writes the words and music
For all the girly shows?
No one cares,
And no one knows.
Who is the handsome hero

Some villain always frames?
But who cares
If there's a plot or not,
When they've got a lot of dames!

REFRAIN
What do you go for,
Go see a show for?
Tell the truth,
You go to see those beautiful dames.
You spend your dough for
Bouquets that grow for
All those cute and cunning,
Young and beautiful dames.
Oh! Dames
Are temporary flames
To you.
Dames,
You don't recall their names,
Do you?
But their caresses
And home addresses
Linger in your mem'ry of
Those beautiful dames.

—*Harry Warren*

FORTY-SECOND STREET

VERSE
In the heart of little old New York,
You'll find a thoroughfare.
It's the part of little old New York
That runs into Times Square.
A crazy quilt
That "Wall Street Jack" built,
If you've got a little time to spare,
I want to take you there.

REFRAIN
Come and meet
Those dancing feet

On the avenue
I'm taking you to,
Forty-second Street.
Hear the beat
Of dancing feet,
It's the song I love
The melody of,
Forty-second Street.
Little "nifties"
From the Fifties,
Innocent and sweet;
Sexy ladies
From the Eighties,
Who are indiscreet.
They're side by side,
They're glorified,
Where the underworld can meet the elite,
Forty-second Street.
Naughty, bawdy,
Gawdy, sporty,
Forty-second Street.

—*Harry Warren*

THE GOLD DIGGERS' SONG
(WE'RE IN THE MONEY)

VERSE
Gone are my blues,
And gone are my tears;
I've got good news
To shout in your ears.
The silver dollar has returned to the fold,
With silver you can turn your dreams
    to gold.

REFRAIN
We're in the money,
We're in the money;
We've got a lot of what it takes to get
    along!
We're in the money,

The skies are sunny;
Old man Depression,
You are through, you done us wrong!
We never see a headline
'Bout a breadline, today,
And when we see the landlord,
We can look that guy
Right in the eye.
We're in the money,
Come on, my honey,
Let's spend it, lend it, send it
Rolling along!

—*Harry Warren*

I ONLY HAVE EYES FOR YOU

VERSE

My love must be a kind of blind love,
I can't see anyone but you.
And dear, I wonder if you find love
An optical illusion, too?

REFRAIN

Are the stars out tonight?
I don't know if it's cloudy or bright,
'Cause I only have eyes
For you, dear.
The moon may be high,
But I can't see a thing in the sky,
'Cause I only have eyes
For you.
I don't know if we're in a garden,
Or on a crowded avenue.
You are here, so am I,
Maybe millions of people go by,
But they all disappear
From view,
And I only have eyes for you.

—*Harry Warren*

I'LL STRING ALONG WITH YOU

VERSE

All my life I waited for an angel,
But no angel ever came along.
Then one happy afternoon I met you
And my heart began to sing a song.
Somehow, I mistook you for an angel,
But now I'm glad that I was wrong.

REFRAIN

You may not be an angel,
'Cause angels are so few.
But until the day that one comes along,
I'll string along with you.
I'm looking for an angel
To sing my love song to,
And until the day that one comes along,
I'll sing my song to you.
For ev'ry little fault that you have,
Say! I've got three or four.
The human little faults you do have
Just make me love you more.
You may not be an angel,
But still I'm sure you'll do.
So until the day that one comes along,
I'll string along with you.

—*Harry Warren*

LULLABY OF BROADWAY

VERSE I

Come on along and listen to
The lullaby of Broadway.
The hip hooray and ballyhoo,
The lullaby of Broadway.
The rumble of a subway train,
The rattle of the taxis,
The daffydils who entertain
At Angelo's and Maxie's.

When a Broadway baby says "Good
    night,"
It's early in the morning.
Manhattan babies don't sleep tight
Until the dawn:

REFRAIN
Good night,
Baby,
Good night,
Milkman's on his way.
Sleep tight,
Baby,
Sleep tight,
Let's call it a day,
Hey! Let's call it a day.
Listen to the lullaby
Of old Broadway.

VERSE 2
Come on along and listen to
The lullaby of Broadway.
The hi-dee-hi and boop-a-doo,
The lullaby of Broadway.
The band begins to go to town,
And ev'ryone goes crazy.
You rock-a-bye your baby 'round
'Til ev'rything gets hazy.
"Hush-a-bye, I'll buy you this and that,"
You hear a daddy saying.
And baby goes home to her flat
To sleep all day:

REPEAT REFRAIN

—Harry Warren

LULU'S BACK IN TOWN

VERSE
Where's that careless chambermaid?
Where'd she put my razor blade?

She mislaid it,
I'm afraid,
It's gotta be foun'.
Ask her when she cleaned my room
What she did with my perfume.
I just can't lose it,
I've gotta use it,
'Cause Lulu's back in town.

REFRAIN
Gotta get my old tuxedo pressed,
Gotta sew a button on my vest,
'Cause tonight I've gotta look my best,
Lulu's back in town.
Gotta get a half a buck somewhere,
Gotta shine my shoes and slick my hair,
Gotta get myself a boutonniere,
Lulu's back in town.
You can tell all my pets,
All my Harlem coquettes,
Mister Otis regrets
That he won't be aroun'.
You can tell the mailman not to call,
I ain't comin' home until the fall
And I might not get back home at all,
Lulu's back in town.

—Harry Warren

REMEMBER ME?

VERSE
Here's a song that I've created,
Nothing too sophisticated,
It's a theme that ev'rybody knows.
Not a hilly-billy ballad
Full of sentimental salad,
Though you'll think it silly,
I suppose.
My own refrain,
Child of my brain,
And my song is dedicated

To the people who are mated,
Listen now for here is how it goes;

REFRAIN
Do you remember one September
    afternoon,
I stood with you and listened to a
    wedding tune,
And didn't I go with you on your
    honeymoon?
Remember me?
Do you recall a cottage small upon a hill,
Where ev'ry day I had to pay
    another bill?
And if I'm not mistaken, dear,
I pay them still,
Remember me?
I can see
That little angel on your knee.
Can't you see,
He kinda sorta looks like me?
For I'm the boy whose only joy is
    loving you,
Who worries till he hurries home when
    day is through.
And I'm the guy you give your good night
    kisses to,
Remember me?

—*Harry Warren*

September in the Rain

VERSE
My daydreams lie buried in autumn
    leaves,
They're covered with autumn rain.
The time is sweet September,
The place, a shady lane.
I'm riding the wings of an autumn
    breeze,
Back to my memories.

REFRAIN
The leaves of brown came
    tumbling down,
Remember?
In September,
In the rain.
The sun went out just like a dying ember,
That September,
In the rain.
To ev'ry word of love I heard you
    whisper,
The raindrops seemed to play a sweet
    refrain.
Though Spring is here,
To me it's still September,
That September,
In the rain.

—*Harry Warren*

She's a Latin from Manhattan

VERSE
Fate
Sent her to me
Over the sea from Spain.
Ah! She's the one in a million
For me.
I found my romance
When she went dancing by;
Ah! She must be a Castilian,
Si si.
Is she from Havana or Madrid?
But something about her is making me
    doubt her,
I think I remember the kid.

REFRAIN
She's a Latin from Manhattan,
You can tell by her "Manyana."
She's a Latin from Manhattan
And not Havana.

Though she does the rhumba for us
And she calls herself Dolores,
She was in a Broadway chorus,
Known as Susie Donahue.
She can take a tambourine and whack it,
But with her it's just a racket,
She's a hoofer from Tenth Avenue.
She's a Latin from Manhattan,
She's a Forty-second Streeter,
She's a Latin from Manhattan,
Señorita Donahue.

—Harry Warren

SHUFFLE OFF TO BUFFALO

VERSE
Now that we have had the rice and
    flowers,
The knot
Is tied.
I can visu'lize such happy hours,
Close by
Your side.
The honeymoon in store
Is one that you'll adore,
I'm gonna take you for a ride.

REFRAIN
I'll go home and get my panties,
You go home and get your scanties,
And away we'll go.
Mm!
Off, we're gonna shuffle,
Shuffle off to Buffalo.
To Niag'ra in a sleeper,
There's no honeymoon that's cheaper,
And the train goes slow.
Ooh!
Off, we're gonna shuffle,
Shuffle off to Buffalo.
Someday, the stork may pay a visit

And leave a little souvenir.
Just a little cute "what is it,"
But we'll discuss that later, dear.
For a little silver quarter,
We can have the Pullman porter
Turn the lights down low.
Ooh!
Off we're gonna shuffle
Shuffle off to Buffalo.

—Harry Warren

YOUNG AND HEALTHY

VERSE
I know a bundle of humanity,
She's about so high.
I'm nearly driven to insanity
When she passes by.
She's a snooty little cutie,
She's been so hard to kiss;
I'll try to overcome her vanity,
And then I'll tell her this:

REFRAIN
"I'm young and healthy,
And you've got charms;
It would really be a sin
Not to have you in
My arms.
I'm young and healthy,
And so are you;
When the moon is in the sky,
Tell me, what am I
To
Do?
If I could hate yuh,
I'd keep away;
But that ain't my nature,
I'm full of vitamin 'A,'
Say!
I'm young and healthy,

So let's be bold;
In a year or two or three,
Maybe we will be
Too
Old."

—*Harry Warren*

YOU'RE GETTING TO BE A HABIT
WITH ME

VERSE

I don't know exactly how it started,
But it started
In fun.
I just wanted someone to be gay with,
To play with
Someone.
But now I realize that
I could never let you go,
And I've come to tell you so.

REFRAIN

Ev'ry kiss, ev'ry hug
Seems to act just like a drug;
You're getting to be a habit with me.
Let me stay in your arms,
I'm addicted to your charms;
You're getting to be a habit with me.
I used to think your love was something
    that I
Could take or leave alone,
But now I couldn't do without my supply,
I need you for my own.
Oh, I can't break away,
I must have you ev'ry day,
As regularly as coffee or tea.
You've got me in your clutches,
And I can't get free;
You're getting to be a habit with me.
(Can't break it!)
You're getting to be a habit with me.

—*Harry Warren*

Clarence Gaskill (1892–1948)

B Y T H E A G E of sixteen, Clarence Gaskill was playing piano in a Philadelphia theater, and at twenty-one he owned a music publishing house. He was a machine gunner in World War I and toured in vaudeville as the Melody Monarch. His song output was sporadic, but he wrote both words and music for Earl Carroll's *Vanities of 1925,* and later worked with such first-rate collaborators as Duke Ellington, Jimmy McHugh, Cab Calloway, and Leo Robin. Since he composed as well as wrote lyrics, it's not always clear what part he played in creating any given song–publishing credits are notoriously vague about such matters–but he certainly had a hand in a number of important songs of his period: "I Can't Believe That You're in Love with Me," "Prisoner of Love," et al.

I CAN'T BELIEVE THAT YOU'RE IN LOVE WITH ME

VERSE I
Yesterday you came my way
And when you smiled at me,
In my heart I felt a thrill.
You see,
That it was love at sight
And I was right to love you as I do.
Still, I never dreamed that you
Could love me, too.

REFRAIN
Your eyes of blue, your kisses, too,
I never knew what they could do,
I can't believe that you're in love with me.
You're telling ev'ryone I know,
I'm on your mind each place you go,
They can't believe that you're in love
    with me.
I have always placed you far above me,
I just can't imagine that you love me.
And after all is said and done,
To think that I'm the lucky one,

I can't believe that you're in love
    with me.

VERSE 2
Skies are gray, I'm blue each day
When you are not around.
Ev'rything goes wrong,
My dear, I've found.
But when you're by my side
I fill with pride, for I'm so proud of you.
It all seems too good to me
To all be true.

REPEAT REFRAIN

–Jimmy McHugh

MINNIE, THE MOOCHER
(with Cab Calloway and Irving Mills)

VERSE I
Now here's a story 'bout Minnie, the
    Moocher,
She was a low-down hoochy coocher,

She was the roughest, toughest frail,
But Minnie had a heart as big as a whale.

REFRAIN 1
Ho de ho de ho (Ho de ho de ho)
Rah de dah de dah (Rah de dah de dah)
Teedle dee de dee (Teedle dee de dee)
Ho de ho de ho (Ho de ho de ho)
Now ho de ho. Poor Min, poor Min,
    poor Min.

VERSE 2
She messed around wid a bloke named
    Smokey,
She loved him though he was a "coke-y."
He took her down to Chinatown,
And showed her how to kick the gong
    around.

REFRAIN 2
Hi de hi de hi (Hi de hi de hi)
Ree de dah de doo (Ree de dah de doo)
Bode dah do dah (Bode dah do dah)
Ho de ho de ho (Ho de ho de ho)
She ho de ho. Poor Min, poor Min,
    poor Min.

VERSE 3
She had a dream 'bout the King of
    Sweden,
He gave her things that she was needin',
Gave her a home built of gold and steel,
A platinum car with diamond-studded
    wheels.

REFRAIN 3
Wah de woo de way, Oh baby,
Doh de dee de doh, Ho de ho de ho.

VERSE 4
He gave her his town house, and racing
    horses,
Each meal she ate was a dozen courses,

She had a million dollars in nickels and
    dimes,
And ev'ry day she counted 'em a million
    times.

REFRAIN 4
Bee de doo de dow, Oh Minnie,
Wa de wa de doo, Ho de ho de ho.

VERSE 5
Now Min' and Smokey, they started
    jaggin',
They got a free ride in a wagon,
She gave him the money to pay her bail,
But he left her flat in the County Jail.

REFRAIN 5
Skee de doo de dee, Skah de dah de dah,
Skow de dow de dow, Ho de ho de ho.

VERSE 6
Poor Minnie met Old Deacon Low-down,
He preached to her she ought to slow down,
But Minnie wiggled her jelly roll,
Deacon Low-down hollered, "Oh save
    my soul."

REFRAIN 6
Yip i yip i ay, Ump i dump i dah,
Yah de dah de do, Ho de ho de ho.

VERSE 7
They took her where they put the crazies,
Now poor old Min' is kickin' up daisies.
You've heard my story, this ends the song,
She was just a good gal, but they done her
    wrong.

REFRAIN 7
Whoop ee doop ee dah, Hi de hi de hi
Skid a ma rinky dee, Ho de ho de ho.

    —*Cab Calloway*

PRISONER OF LOVE

(with Leo Robin)

VERSE

Someone that I belong to
Doesn't belong to me;
Someone who can't be faithful
Knows that I have to be.
Wonder if I am wrong to
Give her my loyalty.
Why should I be a lone soul?
Why can't I own my own soul?

REFRAIN

Alone from night to night, you'll find me,
Too weak to break the chains that
    bind me;

I need no shackles to remind me,
I'm just a prisoner of love.
For one command I stand and wait now,
From one who's master of my Fate now;
I can't escape, for it's too late now,
I'm just a prisoner of love.
What's the good of my caring
If someone is sharing
Those arms with me?
Although she has another,
I can't have another,
For I'm not free.
She's in my dreams, awake or sleeping,
Upon my knees to her I'm creeping;
My very life is in her keeping,
I'm just a prisoner of love.

—Russ Columbo

Mort Dixon (1892–1956)

BEFORE 1923, when Mort Dixon–a native New Yorker–had a hit with his first published song, "That Old Gang of Mine," he had served in World War I and worked as a streetcar conductor, a bank clerk, a waiter and bartender, and on the vaudeville stage. Within the next few years he wrote the words for two of the most successful songs of the twenties, "Bye Bye Blackbird" and "I'm Looking Over a Four-Leaf Clover," which had a second huge success in 1947 in a recording by Art Mooney. There was also the highly popular (and politically dubious) "Nagasaki"–well, at least he didn't call them "Nips." Dixon collaborated several times with Billy Rose, particularly for the show *Sweet and Low,* and wrote successfully for an Ed Wynn show, *The Laugh Parade,* but his career petered out after 1935's "The Lady in Red."

BYE BYE BLACKBIRD

VERSE 1

Blackbird, blackbird,
Singing the blues all day
Right outside of my door.
Blackbird, blackbird,
Why do you sit and say,
"There's no sunshine in store"?
All through the winter you hung around,
Now I begin to feel homeward bound.
Blackbird, blackbird,
Gotta be on my way,
Where there's sunshine galore.

REFRAIN

Pack up all my care and woe,
Here I go,
Singing low,
Bye bye, blackbird.
Where somebody waits for me,
Sugar's sweet,
So is she,
Bye bye, blackbird.

No one here can love and understand me.
Oh, what hard luck stories they all hand me.
Make my bed and light the light,
I'll arrive
Late tonight,
Blackbird,
Bye bye.

VERSE 2

Bluebird, bluebird,
Calling me far away.
I've been longing for you.
Bluebird, bluebird,
What do I hear you say,
"Skies are turning to blue"?
I'm like a flower that's fading here
Where ev'ry hour is one long tear.
Bluebird, bluebird,
This is my lucky day,
Now my dreams will come true.

REPEAT REFRAIN

—Ray Henderson

A GREAT BIG BUNCH OF YOU

VERSE

Say, little honey,
I haven't any money,
But it's grand, it's grand.
It's grand when you haven't any money
To hold your honey's hand.
Say, little honey,
Don't you think my clothes are funny
Being second hand?
And though I'm out of style,
What is it makes my life worthwhile?

REFRAIN

A little walk, a little park,
A little bench, a little dark,
A little who's this, a little what's this,
And a great big bunch of you.
A little kiss, a little sigh,
A little when, a little why,
A little who's this, a little what's this,
And a great big bunch of you.
I'm like a robin in the spring
That wants to sing all day.
I'll pawn my watch and everything
If you'll agree with what I say.
A little house, a little lot,
And what have we got, well you know what.
A little who's this, a little what's this,
And a great big bunch of you.

—Harry Warren

I FOUND A MILLION DOLLAR BABY
(IN A FIVE AND TEN CENT STORE)
(with Billy Rose)

VERSE I

Love comes along like a popular song,
Anytime or anywhere at all.

Rain or sunshine, Spring or Fall,
You never know when it may say hello
In a very unexpected place.
For example, take my case:

REFRAIN

It was a lucky April shower,
It was the most convenient door.
I found a million dollar baby
In a five and ten cent store.
The rain continued for an hour,
I hung around for three or four,
Around a million dollar baby
In a five and ten cent store.
She was selling china
And when she made those eyes,
I kept buying china
Until the crowd got wise.
Incident'ly,
If you should run into a shower,
Just step inside my cottage door
And meet the million dollar baby
From the five and ten cent store!

VERSE 2

Love used to be quite a stranger to me,
Didn't know a sentimental word,
Thoughts of kissing seemed absurd.
Then came a change, and you may think it
    strange,
But the world became a happy tune
Since that April afternoon.

REPEAT REFRAIN

—Harry Warren

THE LADY IN RED

VERSE

Say! Have you ever met the girl who's the
    toast of the town,

A work of art without question,
Who gives your heart a queer congestion?
Say! Have you met the dream in the red
    velvet gown?
If you will pardon my suggestion,
You'd better write her number down.
She's the gay young bird all the magazines
    feature,
'Pon my word, she's the zippiest creature,
    Yeah! Yeah!
She's the valentine all the movies are
    after,
She won't sign cause she really don't hafta.
I declare,

REFRAIN

Oh! The lady in red,
The fellows are crazy for the lady in red.
She's a bit gaudy, but Lawdy, what a
    personality!
Oh! The lady in red
Is fresh as a daisy when the town is in bed,
Dancing and dining and shining with
    originality.
She's very proper, she's nothing more
    than a pal,
But oh me! And oh my!
You'd never stop'er, she'd be a
    dangerous gal
If she should ever meet the right guy.
Oh! The lady in red,
The fellows are crazy for the lady in red.
Is she a study, oh buddy,
What a personality!

—*Allie Wruber*

NAGASAKI

VERSE I

Fellows, if you're on
I will spin a yarn

That was told to me by able-seaman Jones.
Once he had the blues
So he took a cruise
Far away from nightclubs
And from saxophones.
He said "Yo-ho, I made a certain port,
And when you talk about real he-man
    sport. . .

REFRAIN I

Hot ginger and dynamite,
There's nothing but that at night
Back in Nagasaki
Where the fellers chew tobaccy
And the women wicky wacky woo.
The way they can entertain
Would hurry a hurricane
Back in Nagasaki
Where the fellers chew tobaccy
And the women wicky wacky woo.
Oh, Fujiyama,
You get a mommer
And then your troubles increase.
In some pagoda
She orders soda,
The earth shakes milkshakes ten cents
    apiece.
They kissee and huggee nice,
By Jingo! It's worth the price,
Back in Nagasaki
Where the fellers chew tobaccy
And the women wicky wacky woo.

VERSE 2

When the day is warm
You can keep in form
With a bowl of rice beneath a parasol.
Ev'ry gentleman
Has to use a fan
And they only wear suspenders in the fall.
That's where the gals don't think of rings
    and furs.
Gee! It's the grandest place that ever was.

They give you a carriage free,
The horse is a Japanee,
Back in Nagasaki
Where the fellers chew tobaccy
And the women wicky wacky woo.
They sit you upon the floor,
No wonder your pants get sore
Back in Nagasaki
Where the fellers chew tobaccy
And the women wicky wacky woo.
Oh, sweet kimona,
I pulled a boner,
I kept it up at high speed.
I got rheumatics
And then sciatics,
Of halitosis that's guaranteed.
You must have to act your age
Or wind up inside a cage
Back in Nagasaki
Where the fellers chew tobaccy
And the women wicky wacky woo.

PATTER
With an ice cream cone and a bottle
    of tea
You can rest all day by the hickory tree,
But when night comes 'round, Oh gosh!
    Oh gee!
Mother, Mother, Mother pin a rose
    on me."

—*Harry Warren*

River, Stay 'Way from My Door

VERSE 1
You're just a lonely little river,
But I have heard somebody say
That some day you may
Sweep my home away.

So roll along, you lonely river,
And find your way out to the sea.
I don't bother you,
Don't you bother me.

REFRAIN
You keep goin' your way,
I'll keep goin' my way,
River, stay 'way from my door.
I just got a cabin,
You don't need my cabin,
River, stay 'way from my door.
Don't come up any higher,
I'm so all alone.
Leave my bed and my fire,
That's all I own.
I ain't breakin' your heart,
Don't start breakin' my heart,
River, stay 'way from my door.

VERSE 2
There ain't no use in you pretendin'
That you don't hear me, 'cause
    you do.
And you know it's you
That I'm talkin' to.
If you don't stop, 'twill be the endin'.
I'm beggin' you on bended knees,
Just leave me alone.
Won't you listen, please!

REPEAT REFRAIN

PATTER 1
Oh Lord!
Ain't I been faithful,
And ain't I worked,
Ain't I toiled in the sweatin' sun?
Oh! Lord!
Ain't I come to you
And thanked you for all you've
    done? Oh!
Make the river hear my plea:

I ain't breakin' your heart,
Don't start breakin' my heart,
River, stay 'way from my door.

PATTER 2
Oh Lord!
You made the river,
But won't you try to remember
That you made me?
Oh Lord!
Hear me pray to you,
Make the river hear my plea:

I ain't breakin' your heart,
Don't start breakin' my heart,
River, stay 'way from my door.

—Harry Woods

WOULD YOU LIKE TO TAKE A WALK?

(with Billy Rose)

VERSE 1
I saw you strolling by your solitary.
Am I nosey? Very, very.
I'd like to bet a juicy huckleberry
What you're after is a gal.
We're both in luck, for introductions are
    not necessary.

REFRAIN
Mm–mm–mm–Would you like to take
    a walk?
Mm–mm–mm–Do you think it's
    gonna rain?

Mm–mm–mm–How about a sasparilla?
Gee, the moon is yeller;
Sump'n good'll come from that.
Mm–mm–mm–Have you heard the
    latest song?
Mm–mm–mm–It's a very pretty strain.
Mm–mm–mm–Don't you feel a little
    thrilly?
Gee, it's getting chilly;
Sump'n good'll come from that.
When you're strolling through the
    wherezis,
You need a whozis
To lean upon.
But when you have no whozis,
To hug and whatzis,
Gosh darn!
Mm–mm–mm–Would you like to take
    a walk?
Mm–mm–mm–Do you think it's
    gonna rain?
Mm–mm–mm–Ain't you tired of the
    talkies?
I prefer the walkies.
Sump'n good'll come from that.

VERSE 2
My little heart is full of palpitation.
What I need is consolation.
I'd like to stage a little celebration
In the moonlight right away.
I'll feel all pep't if you'll accept my
    friendly invitation.

REPEAT REFRAIN

—Harry Warren

Jack Yellen (1892–1991)

BORN IN Poland and brought to America at the age of five, Jack Yellen got a B.A. at the University of Michigan and wrote and edited for the *Buffalo Courier,* all the while turning out songs. Once he hit, he worked on a number of Broadway shows, including a series of *George White Scandals* and the *Ziegfeld Follies of 1943,* and for a couple of Shirley Temple movies as well as Paul Whiteman's *The King of Jazz.* (He may be the only lyricist who wrote for both Temple and Sophie Tucker–"My Yiddishe Momma.") Of his string of hits, the most famous is probably "Ain't She Sweet," and although he was a Republican, his "Happy Days Are Here Again" became FDR's campaign song. It would seem that early on he worked on such specialty items as "Vitamins, Hormones and Pills" and "My Mother's Sabbath Candles." What can he have made of them at the end of his almost century-long life?

AIN'T SHE SWEET?

VERSE 1

There she is! There she is!
There's what keeps me up at night.
Oh, gee whiz! Oh, gee whiz!
There's why I can't eat a bite.
Those flaming eyes!
That flaming youth!
Oh, Mister, Oh, Sister,
Tell me the truth.

REFRAIN

Ain't she sweet?
See her coming down the street!
Now I ask you very confidentially,
Ain't she sweet?
Ain't she nice?
Look her over once or twice.
Now I ask you very confidentially,
Ain't she sweet?
Just cast an eye

In her direction.
Oh, me! Oh, my!
Ain't that perfection?
I repeat,
Don't you think that's kind of neat?
And I ask you very confidentially,
Ain't she sweet?

VERSE 2

Tell me where, tell me where
Have you seen one just like that?
I declare, I declare,
That sure is worth looking at.
Oh, boy, how sweet
Those lips must be!
Gaze on it! Doggone it,
Now answer me!

REPEAT REFRAIN

—Milton Ager

ARE YOU HAVIN' ANY FUN?

VERSE

Hey, feller, with a million smackers
And nervous indigestion!
Rich feller eatin' milk and crackers!
I'll ask you one question.
You silly so and so!
With all your dough:

REFRAIN

Are you havin' any fun?
What y' gettin' out o' livin'?
What good is what you've got
If you're not havin' any fun?
Are you havin' any laughs?
Are you gettin' any lovin'?
If other people do, so can you
Have a little fun.
After the honey's in the comb
Little bees go out and play;
Even the old gray mare down home
Has got to have hay. Hey!
Better have a little fun,
You ain't gonna live forever;
Before you're old and gray, still okay,
Have your little fun, son!
Have your little fun!
Are you havin' any?
Why do you work and slave and save?
Life is full of ifs and buts.
You know the squirrels save and save,
And what have they got? Nuts!
Better have a little fun,
You ain't gonna live forever.
Before you're old and gray, still okay,
Have your little fun, son!
Have your little fun!
Are you havin' any?

—*Sammy Fain*

GLAD RAG DOLL

VERSE 1

Little painted lady with your lovely
    clothes,
Where are you bound for, may I ask?
What your diamonds cost you,
Ev'rybody knows.
All the world can see behind
    your mask.

REFRAIN

All dolled up
In glad rags,
Tomorrow may turn to sad rags,
They call you glad rag doll.
Admired,
Desired
By lovers who soon grow tired,
Poor little glad rag doll.
You're just a pretty toy
They like to play with;
You're not the kind they choose
To grow old and gray with.
Don't make this
The end, dear,
It's never too late to mend, dear,
Poor little glad rag doll.

VERSE 2

All this glare and glitter, all your
    tinseled toys,
What will they lead to in the end?
Memories so bitter
Of regretted joys,
And a world without a single friend.

REPEAT REFRAIN

—*Dan Dougherty and Milton Ager*

HAPPY DAYS ARE HERE AGAIN

VERSE

So long, sad times!
Go 'long, bad times!
We are rid of you at last.
Howdy, gay times!
Cloudy gray times,
You are now a thing of the past.

REFRAIN

'Cause happy days are here again!
The skies above are clear again.
Let us sing a song of cheer again,
Happy days are here again!
All together shout it now!
There's no one who can doubt it now,
So let's tell the world about it now,
Happy days are here again!
Your cares and troubles are gone,
There'll be no more from now on.
Happy days are here again,
The skies above are clear again,
Let us sing a song of cheer again,
Happy days are here again!

—Milton Ager

HARD-HEARTED HANNAH
(THE VAMP OF SAVANNAH)
(with Bob Bigelow and Charles Bates)

VERSE 1

In old Savannah,
I said, Savannah,
The weather there is nice and warm.
The climate's of the southern brand,
But here's what I don't understand:
They've got a gal there,
A pretty gal there,
Who's colder than an arctic storm.

Got a heart just like a stone;
Even ice men leave her alone.

REFRAIN 1

They call her Hard-Hearted Hannah,
The vamp of Savannah,
The meanest gal in town.
Leather is tough but Hannah's heart is
    tougher;
She's a gal who loves to see men suffer!
To tease 'em and thrill 'em,
To torture and kill 'em,
Is her delight, they say.
I saw her at the seashore with a great
    big pan;
There was Hannah pouring water on a
    drowning man.
She's Hard-Hearted Hannah,
The vamp of Savannah.

VERSE 2

You ought to see her,
You ought to see her,
Outside she's just as soft as silk.
But socially she's hard as nails,
She's just a gal who hates the males!
And when she's nasty,
Oh, when she's nasty,
She's 'bout as sweet as sour milk.
Nothing she likes better than
Feedin' poisoned food to a man.

REFRAIN 2

They call her Hard-Hearted Hannah,
The vamp of Savannah,
The meanest gal in town.
Talk of your cold, refrigerating mammas,
Brother, she's the polar bear's pajamas!
To tease 'em and thrill 'em,
To torture and kill 'em,
Is her delight, they say.
An ev'ning spent with Hannah sitting on
    your knees

Is like trav'ling through Alaska in your
    B.V.D.'s.
She's Hard-Hearted Hannah,
The vamp of Savannah.

    —*Milton Ager*

LOUISVILLE LOU
(THE VAMPIN' LADY)

VERSE 1

Folks, you've heard of scandalous
    vamps;
History is full of lovemakin' champs,
But if you crave a brand-new thrill,
Come and meet the vamp of Louisville.
She's a gal who's nobody's fool;
Got a kiss that's like the kick of a mule.
Until you're vamped by this brunette,
Brother, you ain't had no vampin' yet.

REFRAIN 1

They call the lady Louisville Lou.
Oh, what that vampin' baby can do!
She is the most heartbreakin'est, shimmy-
    shakin'est
That the world ever knew.
She's got the kind of lovin' that holds 'em,
Big, black eyes and she rolls 'em!
Hot lips
That are pips
And no more conscience than a snake
    has hips!
And when she struts her feathers and
    plumes,
The porters drop their mops and their
    brooms.
You oughta see them trailin' her, inhalin'
    her perfumes,
And even Old Black Joes who are old
    and weak

Hang around and want to be her
    sheik.
So, brother, here's my warnin' to you,
Keep far away from Louisville Lou.

VERSE 2

Cullud gals, you'd better look out
If you've got a man you're crazy about,
'Cause he may be the best of men
But he's bound to weaken now and then.
Give him plenty lovin' each night;
Don't you ever leave him out of your
    sight,
'Cause if he meets this high brown doll,
Then you haven't got a chance at all.

REFRAIN 2

They call the lady Louisville Lou.
Oh, what that vampin' baby can do!
She got the meanest pair o' eyes, Theda
    Bara eyes,
That the world ever knew.
She's got a pretty form and she shows it,
She's some gal and she knows it!
What pep!
Does she step?
That's what she don't do nothin' else
    excep'!
And when she struts her feathers and
    plumes,
The porters drop their mops and their
    brooms.
You oughta see them trailin' her, inhalin'
    her perfumes,
And even Deacon Jones, who is old
    and bent,
Sold his crutches just to pay her rent.
So, brother, here's my warnin' to you,
Keep far away from Louisville Lou.

    —*Milton Ager*

Mamma Goes Where Papa Goes

VERSE I
"How come, Henry dear,"
Said Missus Henry Brown,
"You always disappear
When the evenin' sun goes down?
You eat my meat
And drink my chicken soup;
Then I notice that you fly the coop.
You can't pass through that door
Without your mamma any more."

REFRAIN I
'Cause Mamma goes where Papa goes
Or Papa don't go out tonight!
Mamma goes 'cause Mamma knows
You can't be trusted out of her sight.
1. Mamma's got a feelin' that she must
      be near
   Just to help her Papa keep his
      conscience clear.

So Mamma goes where Papa goes
Or Papa don't go out tonight.
No! Papa don't go out tonight.

VERSE 2
"Says which, Daddy mine,"
Continued Missus Brown,
"You got a date at nine
With a business friend downtown?
'Course I don't know,
But, Henry, I suspec's
That your friend is of the female sex.
So Mamma goes along
To see you keep your will pow'r strong."

REFRAIN 2
2. I don't mean to say you've been
      behavin' bad.
   You ain't yet ben gotten, but you can
      be had.

—Milton Ager

Roy Turk (1892–1934)

AN ARCHITECTURE STUDENT who had been born in New York, Roy Turk joined the navy during World War I and started writing special material for stars like Sophie Tucker and Nora Bayes. More than twenty years after his death, his "Are You Lonesome Tonight?" became one of Elvis Presley's greatest hits—an unparalleled (and unlikely) stretch. (Another unlikely contrast: Guy Lombardo on "Gimme a Little Kiss, Will Ya, Huh?" and Bessie Smith on "Aggravatin' Man.") With his chief collaborator, Fred E. Ahlert, Turk wrote torch songs for Ruth Etting and Helen Morgan, and his "Where the Blue of the Night (Meets the Gold of the Day)" became Bing Crosby's theme song. Most of his work, unlike that of so many of his contemporaries, was done neither for Broadway nor for Hollywood; the songs stood alone.

AIN'T THAT THE WAY IT GOES?

VERSE

What a mixup, and what a mess,
Why, you seem to be against the wall.
Yes, and I'm in love with someone
Who can't see me at all.
And I suppose somebody cares
     for you
Whom you cannot stand.
Now here's the thing in a nutshell,
Who says love was grand?

REFRAIN

I'm so in love with Mary,
And I hear you're bored to tears
     with Rose.
Yes, but Rose is the one who always
     loves me,
Ain't that the way it goes?
I suppose you dance your best
     with Mary?
I always step on Rosie's toes.

And yet Rose says you dance divinely.
Ain't that the way it goes?
What a fix, oh gee,
I'm in an awful tight one.
Poor unlucky me,
I'm in wrong with the right one.
I get the air from Mary.
Yeah, you get what's called the
     turned-up nose.
And still I care for my little Mary,
Ain't that the way it goes?
I thought I'd take up golfing,
Took lessons from the pros,
Ten-pound plus-fours don't suit me,
Ain't that the way it goes?
I'm fond of skirts and blouses,
Frillies and furbelows,
All of my pals wear trousers,
Ain't that it the way it goes?
I backed a horse on Tuesday,
It lost by just a nose,
Came back and won on Wednesday,
Ain't that the way it goes?

I get lots of breaks, but every break's a
  bad one,
Oh my, I guess I was born to envy
  someone.
One day I went in swimming,
Somebody stole my clothes.
Up came a Girl Guides picnic,
Ain't that the way it goes?

—Fred E. Ahlert

ARE YOU LONESOME TONIGHT?

VERSE 1
Tonight I'm downhearted,
For though we have parted
I love you, and I always will.
And while I'm so lonely,
I'm writing you only,
To see if you care for me still.

REFRAIN
Are you lonesome tonight,
Do you miss me tonight,
Are you sorry we drifted apart?
Does your memory stray
To a bright summer day,
When I kissed you and called you
  sweetheart?
Do the chairs in your parlor seem empty
  and bare?
Do you gaze at your doorstep and picture
  me there?
Is your heart filled with pain,
Shall I come back again?
Tell me, dear,
Are you lonesome tonight?

VERSE 2
I hold with affection
A fond recollection,

A romance of days now gone by.
And often I wonder
If I made a blunder
By letting you bid me "Good-bye."

REPEAT REFRAIN

—Lou Handman

GIMME A LITTLE KISS
(WILL YA, HUH?)
(with Jack Smith)

VERSE 1
A little boy
Was wild about
A little girl
Who found it out,
She tried to play so "hard to get,"
He hasn't even kissed her yet.
He leaves her when
She turns him down,
Comes back again
And hangs around,
Waiting for one kiss,
While he pleads like this:

REFRAIN 1
BOY: Gimme a little kiss,
  Will ya, huh?
  What are ya gonna miss?
  Will ya, huh?
  Gosh oh gee! Why do you refuse?
  I can't see what you've got to lose.
  Aw, gimme a little squeeze,
  Will ya, huh?
  Why do you wanna make me blue?
  I wouldn't say a word if I were askin'
    for the world,
  But what's a little kiss between a
    feller and his girl?

Aw, gimme a little kiss,
Will ya, huh?
And I'll give it right back to you.

VERSE 2
It's been a year
Since first they met,
He hasn't quite
Succeeded yet.
A month ago he held her hand,
His patience I can't understand.
That they're engaged
Don't mean a thing,
He's in a rage,
Takes back his ring,
Gives it back once more,
While he starts to roar:

REFRAIN 2
BOY: Gimme a little kiss,
Will ya, huh?
Must I go on like this?
Will ya, huh?
Once again a plea I'm
gonna make,
Tell me when do I get a break.
Aw, say that you're givin' in,
Will ya, huh?
Anything that you ask I'll do.
I'll take you for a buggy ride, where
we can be alone,
And once you kiss me, you will never
think of walking home.
Aw, gimme a little kiss,
Will ya, huh?
Or I'll steal about ten from you.

REFRAIN 3
GIRL: Gimme a little coat,
Will ya, huh?
Sable or mink or goat,
Will ya, huh?

My poor hand is bare as anything,
I could stand a bracelet or a ring.
Aw, gimme a little car,
Will ya, huh?
That would be mighty nice to do.
A Packard or a Lincoln or a Cadillac
sedan.
I'll even take a Rolls and you can add
a chauffeur man.
But don't you give me a Ford,
Will ya, huh?
Or I'll give it right back to you.

—*Maceo Pinkard*

I DON'T KNOW WHY
(I JUST DO)

VERSE
All day long you're asking me
What I see in you.
All day long I'm answering,
But what good does it do?
I have nothing to explain,
I just love you, love you,
And I'll tell you once again

REFRAIN
I don't know why
I love you like I do,
I don't know why,
I just do.
I don't know why
You thrill me like you do,
I don't know why,
You just do.
You never seem to want my
romancing,
The only time you hold me
Is when we're dancing.
I don't know why

I love you like I do,
I don't know why,
I just do.

—Fred E. Ahlert

I'll Get By
(As Long As I Have You)

VERSE
I've neither wealth nor power,
But now that you said you're mine
Wherever I go,
Whatever I do,
I'll be doin' fine.
For

REFRAIN
I'll get by
As long as I have you.
Though there be rain
And darkness, too,
I'll not complain,
I'll see it through.
Though I may be far away,
It's true,
Say, what care I,
Dear, I'll get by
As long as I
Have you.
I'll get by
As long as I have you.
Though there be rain
And darkness, too,
I'll not complain,
I'll see it through.
Poverty
May come to me,
That's true.
Say, what care I,
Dear, I'll get by

As long as I
Have you.

—Fred E. Ahlert

Mean to Me

VERSE I
Sweetheart, I love you,
Think the world of you,
But I'm afraid you don't care for me.
You never show it,
Don't let me know it,
Ev'ryone says I'm a fool to be
Pining the whole day through.
Why do you act like you do?

REFRAIN
You're mean to me,
Why must you be mean to me?
Gee, Honey, it seems to me
You love to see me cryin'.
I don't know why I stay home
Each night, when you say you'll phone.
You don't and I'm left alone,
Singin' the blues and sighin'.
You treat me coldly
Each day in the year.
You always scold me
Whenever somebody is near.
Dear, it must be
Great fun to be mean to me.
You shouldn't, for can't you see
What you mean to me?

VERSE 2
I treat you sweetly,
I'm yours completely,
Think of you, dream of you, all day
    through.
I thought I pleased you,

Whatever seized you
That made you treat me the way you do?
Love you, I always will,
Think of you only, and still

REPEAT REFRAIN

—*Fred E. Ahlert*

WALKIN' MY BABY BACK HOME

Gee! It's great, after bein' out late,
Walkin' my baby back home.
Arm in arm, over meadow and farm,
Walkin' my baby back home.
We go 'long harmonizin' a song,
Or I'm reciting a poem.
Owls go by, and they give me the eye,
Walkin' my baby back home.
We stop for a while,

She gives me a smile,
And snuggles her head to my chest.
We start in to pet,
And that's when I get
Her talcum all over my vest.
After I kinda straighten my tie,
She has to borrow my comb.
One kiss, then I continue again,
Walkin' my baby back home.
She's 'fraid of the dark,
So I have to park
Outside of her door till it's light.
She says if I try
To kiss her, she'll cry.
I dry her tears all through the night.
Hand in hand to a barbecue stand
Right from her doorway we roam.
Eats! and then it's a pleasure again,
Walkin' my baby back home.

—*Fred E. Ahlert*

Walter Donaldson (1893–1947)

WHEN WALTER DONALDSON DIED, at the age of fifty-four, he had been turning out hits for more than thirty years. Born the son of a music teacher in Brooklyn, he was composing before he was twenty. During World War I, in the entertainment division of the army, he met Sergeant Irving Berlin, for whose company he went to work after the war. (Later, he was to found his own music publishing company.) Beginning in 1919 he wrote the music for close to a dozen million-copy sellers ("My Blue Heaven" alone is said to have sold five million). His "My Mammy" was immortalized, if that's the word, by Al Jolson in *Sinbad,* and he wrote for Eddie Cantor, too, in *Whoopee.* But by 1929 he had left New York for California, where he mostly worked in film until his death. Donaldson was primarily a composer, enjoying successful collaborations with such lyricists as Gus Kahn, Johnny Mercer, Lewis and Young, and Edgar Leslie, but when he wrote his own lyrics, they were usually good.

BECAUSE MY BABY DON'T MEAN MAYBE NOW

VERSE I

Ev'ry thing seems lovely,
The world is so serene.
When I say things are lovely,
You know just what I mean.
It means that I'll be happy,
No more I'll have to guess.
I feel so, oh! so happy
Since someone answered "Yes."

REFRAIN

Birds are singing merrily,
The sun is shining peacefully,
Because my baby don't mean
    maybe now!
When the preacher questions me
I'll say "Yessir, yes-siree,"
Because my baby don't mean maybe now!

I just got a little letter just
    yesterday,
Now I feel a little better, and so I say:
"Life is short and mighty sweet,
But I know mine is quite complete,
Because my baby don't mean
    maybe now!"

VERSE 2

Ev'rything is rosy,
I feel so so-and-so.
When I say things are rosy,
I know you know I know.
Ev'rything is peaches,
The preacher's on his way.
The way I feel is peaches,
Today's a holiday.

REPEAT REFRAIN

LITTLE WHITE LIES

VERSE

'Twas a night like this,
Filled with bliss.
You led my heart astray.
'Twas just a real sweet chance
To learn romance
In a perfect way.
It was the end of a perfect day,
Say. . .

REFRAIN

The moon was all aglow
And heaven was in your eyes,
The night that you told me
Those little white lies.
The stars all seemed to know
That you didn't mean all those sighs,
The night that you told me,
Those little white lies.
I try,
But there's no forgetting
When ev'ning appears.
I sigh,
But there's no regretting
In spite of my fears.
1. The Devil was in your heart,
   But Heaven was in your eyes
   The night that you told me
   Those little white lies!
2. Who wouldn't believe those lips,
   Who ever could doubt those eyes?
   The night that you told me
   Those little white lies!

YOU'RE DRIVING ME CRAZY
(WHAT DID I DO?)

VERSE I

You left me sad and lonely.
Why did you leave me lonely?
'Cause here's a heart that's only
For nobody but you!
I'm burning like a flame, dear,
I'll never be the same, dear,
I'll always place the blame, dear,
On nobody but you.
Yes!

REFRAIN

You!
You're driving me crazy!
What did I do?
What did I do?
My tears for you
Make ev'rything hazy,
Clouding the skies
Of blue.
How true
Were the friends who were near me
To cheer me,
Believe me, they knew.
But you
Were the kind who would hurt me,
Desert me
When I needed you.
Yes, you!
You're driving me crazy!
What did I do
To you?

VERSE 2

I've tried so hard to find, dear,
What made you change your
    mind, dear.

It's kinda hard to find, dear,
That somebody like you!
Not other heart or hand, dear,
Could make this world seem
    grand, dear,

But you don't understand, dear,
It's nobody but you.
Yes!

REPEAT REFRAIN

Herman Hupfeld (1894–1951)

A S TIME GOES BY," Herman "Dodo" Hupfeld's most famous lyric by far, had a modest success in 1931 as recorded by Rudy Vallee. Eleven years later, it was featured in *Casablanca* and began its career as one of the century's most loved (and recorded) songs. But Hupfeld's range was wider and weirder than "As Time Goes By" would suggest–see "When Yuba Plays the Rumba on the Tuba," as well as such titles as "Savage Serenade" and "My Little Dog Has Ego." He was also a capable pianist, having accompanied Irene Castle and performed his own songs in Ziegfeld's *Midnight Frolic.* Among the musicals he wrote for were *The Little Show* and *Murder at the Vanities.* Hupfeld–who was born and died in Monclair, New Jersey–had come from a musical family and when he was nine years old, was sent to Germany for serious training.

ARE YOU MAKIN' ANY MONEY?

VERSE

You've got to hand it to the fair sex,
They're anything but slow.
They're revolutionizing romance,
Each Romeo should know.
They don't want to hear about the
     moonlight,
Or the flowers, or the Spring.
Here's the little question they will ask you,
When you flash that famous ring.

REFRAIN

You make time and you make love dandy,
You make swell molasses candy,
But, Honey, are you makin' any money,
That's all I want to know.
You make fun and you could make
     trouble,
Make mistakes and that goes double,
But, Honey, are you makin' any money,
That's all I want to know.
You make dates and you make trains,

I can get that through my head.
It's a cinch in a pinch you could make
     breakfast,
Even make the bed.
You make good when you make a
     promise,
No, I'm not a doubting Thomas,
But, Honey, are you makin' any money,
That's all I want to know.

AS TIME GOES BY

VERSE

This day and age we're living in
Gives cause for apprehension,
With speed and new invention
And things like third dimension.
Yet, we get a trifle weary
With Mister Einstein's the'ry,
So we must get down to earth,
At times relax, relieve the tension.
No matter what the progress
Or what may yet be proved,

The simple facts of life are such
They cannot be removed.

REFRAIN

You must remember this,
A kiss is still a kiss,
A sigh is just a sigh;
The fundamental things apply,
As time goes by.
And when two lovers woo,
They still say, "I love you,"
On that you can rely;
No matter what the future brings,
As time goes by.
Moonlight and love songs
Never out of date,
Hearts full of passion,
Jealousy and hate.
Woman needs man
And man must have his mate,
That no one can deny.
It's still the same old story,
A fight for love and glory,
A case of do or die!
The world will always welcome lovers
As time goes by.

LET'S PUT OUT THE LIGHTS AND GO TO SLEEP

VERSE I

Didn't we have a lovely evening?
Our party was a great success.
Oh, didn't Missus Smith look stunning?
Did you notice Missus Jones' new dress?
What did Mister Brown say to Uncle Benny?
Just one of those things, he had a few
    too many.
Sure was a hungry crowd,
They didn't leave a scrap for Rover.
We ought to feel real proud,
And mighty glad the darn thing's over.

REFRAIN

No more company to feed,
No more papers left to read,
What's to do about it?
Let's put out the lights and go to sleep.
No more anything to drink.
Leave those dishes in the sink.
What's to do about it?
Simply nighty-night and so to sleep.
You're waiting now for me to say,
"I love you more and more and more, dear,
You're looking younger ev'ry day,
You never were so sweet before, dear."
No more money in the bank,
No cute baby we can spank.
What's to do about it?
Let's put out the lights and go to sleep.

VERSE 2

Didn't they make an awful mess, though?
There's been a lot of damage done.
Oh, can't we laugh it off? I guess so.
This is what you call expensive fun.
All those little rings made by naughty
    glasses,
Those cigarette burns, remains of
    demitasses.
Now, honey, please don't weep,
It's simply that you're weak from
    laughter.
We better get some sleep,
So we can face the morning after.

REPEAT REFRAIN

WHEN YUBA PLAYS THE RUMBA ON THE TUBA

VERSE

His name was Yuba!
He was homely, he was dumb.
And so was Yuba

Just a big ambitious bum.
He wouldn't do-a
So much as chew a piece of gum.
So this is news to me.
I understand-a
He's an overnight success,
He's in demand-a;
Why, I never could have guessed.
Well, he found a big bass tuba,
Then he bummed his way to Cuba,
And the rest is history.

REFRAIN

Down in Havana there's a funny-lookin'
    booba;
He plays the rumba on the tuba, down
    in Cuba.
Oh, any sap'll sell an apple,
But this chap would rather grapple
With his umpa, umpa, umpa–
They prefer it to a boop-a, doop-a,
    doop-a.
They love the rumba on the tuba down
    in Cuba.
It doesn't take him very long to get a
    tumble,
For all the rumba lovers go into their
    rumble.
Oh, how I'd like to be his double
For, without a bit of trouble,
With his umpa, umpa, umpa
He can knock eleven ladies for a loop-a.

They love the rumba on the tuba down
    in Cuba.
He's not a greenhorn,
He blows a mean horn,
A must-be-seen horn.
Oh, he's a whiz!
Why, all Havana loves this funny-lookin'
    boob-a
Who plays the rumba on the tuba, down
    in Cuba.
1. I can't believe it, but they tell us
   Ev'ry peanut vendor's jealous
   Of his umpa, umpa, umpa,
   They prefer it to the boop-a, doop-a,
       doop-a.
   They love the rumba on the tuba down
       in Cuba.
   They love his umpa, umpa, umpa,
       umpa, ump!
   Down in Ha-ump! ump! ump!

REPEAT REFRAIN

2. He's getting wealthy, strong, and hardy
   Thanks to plenty good Bacardi,
   And his umpa, umpa, umpa.
   Oh, he knocked the boop-a, doop-a for a
       loop-a.
   They love the rumba on the tuba down
       in Cuba.
   They love his umpa, umpa, umpa,
       umpa, ump!
   Down in Ha-ump! ump! ump!

Ted Koehler (1894–1973)

BORN IN WASHINGTON, D.C., Ted Koehler worked as a photo-engraver, a pianist for silent films, and a producer of nightclub shows before starting to write in the early twenties. He hit his stride when he began his successful collaboration with Harold Arlen in 1930, with "Get Happy." The team flourished brilliantly in the following years when they were hired to replace Dorothy Fields and Jimmy McHugh for Harlem's famous Cotton Club Revues. It was there that Ethel Waters first sang their "Stormy Weather" and the sixteen-year-old Lena Horne introduced "As Long As I Live." Arlen, of course, went on to an illustrious career through the following decades, but Koehler, although he had occasional hits after the mid-thirties, never really recaptured the early and large success of his swingy, bluesy lyrics for Arlen.

AS LONG AS I LIVE

VERSE
What's the use,
There is no excuse
To be hiding what's on my mind.
Lovin' you is a secret I can't conceal.
Since we met
I've been all upset,
But I've really made up my mind
To confess just exactly the way I feel.

REFRAIN 1
Maybe I can't live to love you
As long as I want to,
Life isn't long enough, baby,
But I can love you as long as I live.
Maybe I can't give you diamonds and
    things
Like I want to,
But I can promise you, baby,
I'm gonna want to as long as I live.
I never cared,
But now I'm scared,

I won't live long enough.
That's why I wear my rubbers when it rains
And eat an apple ev'ry day,
Then see the doctor anyway.
What if I can't live to love you
As long as I want to?
'Long as I promise you, baby,
I'm gonna love you
As long as I live.

REFRAIN 2
Maybe I can't live to love you
As long as I want to,
Life isn't long enough, baby,
But I can love you as long as I live.
Maybe I can't give you diamonds and
    things
Like I want to,
But I can promise you, baby,
I'm gonna want to as long as I live.
I'll even wear
Long underwear
When winter breezes blow.
I'm gonna take good care of me because

A sneeze or two might mean the flu,
And that would never, never do.
What if I can't live to love you
As long as I want to?
'Long as I promise you, baby,
I'm gonna love you
As long as I live.

—*Harold Arlen*

BETWEEN THE DEVIL AND THE DEEP BLUE SEA

VERSE

Is there anyone around who cannot see
It's the well-known runaround you're
    giving me?
I suppose you'll tell me I'm all wrong.
It's a bitter pill to take, coming from you,
Though I've made a big mistake, what can
    I do?
I don't know what makes me string along.

REFRAIN

I don't want you,
But I'd hate to lose you,
You've got me in between
The devil and the deep blue sea.
I forgive you,
'Cause I can't forget you,
You've got me in between
The devil and the deep blue sea.
I ought to cross you off my list,
But when you come knocking at my door
Fate seems to give my heart a twist,
And I come running back for more.
I should hate you,
But I guess I love you,
You've got me in between
The devil and the deep blue sea.

—*Harold Arlen*

DON'T WORRY 'BOUT ME

VERSE

This is the one moment
That I thought I never could live
    through.
But now somehow that it's here, my dear,
That foolish fear disappears.
And saying good-bye seems sweet.
It's plain that fate didn't want us on a one
    way street.

REFRAIN

Don't worry 'bout me,
I'll get along.
Forget about me,
Be happy, my love.
Let's say that our little show
Is over, and so
The story ends.
Why not call it a day
The sensible way,
And still be friends?
"Look out for yourself"
Should be the rule.
Give your heart and your love
To whomever you love,
Don't be a fool.
Darling, why should you cling
To some fading thing
That used to be?
If you can forget,
Don't worry 'bout me.

—*Rube Bloom*

GOOD FOR NOTHIN' JOE

It's gonna rain any minute,
There's not a star in sight, things are
    mighty slow.

I guess I'll close up shop and go home
    to Joe.
I know he won't be glad to see me
Without a penny to the good,
But I'm not caring much what
    happens,
I've done the best that I could.
He's just good for nothin' Joe,
And though I love him so
I'd be good for nothin', too, I know,
If he'd ever leave me flat,
Oh yeah, I'm certain of that.
Folks I know can't understand
Why I must love that man.
Lord, he sends me like nobody can,
Now ain't a woman just like that?
I wouldn't mind doing what I'm doing,
I'd beat these streets till my feet
    were sore.
But when I'm tired and I go home
    to him,
Instead of sympathy he's just as mean as
    can be.
But there's nothing I can do
Because I love that man so,
I'd be good for nothin', too, I know,
Without good for nothin' Joe.

—Rube Bloom

Happy As the Day Is Long

VERSE

I'm sick of love songs,
Lovey dove songs.
I'm tired of tuning in on crooners
    crooning
'Bout their broken hearts.
I've got a new song,
Not a blue song,
It's just a jingle sets you all a-tingle
Ev'rytime it starts.

The words and the melody
Are full of simplicity.
To me it's a rhapsody when I sing:

REFRAIN

I've got my trousers pressed,
Shoes shined,
I had my coat and vest
Relined.
Take a look at my lapel,
See the flower, can't you tell
I'm as happy as the day is long.
I haven't got a dime
To lend,
I've got a lot of time
To spend.
Just a pocket full of air,
Feelin' like a millionaire,
'Cause I'm happy as the day is long.
Got a heavy affair,
And I'm havin' my fun.
Am I walkin' on air?
Gee, but I'm the lucky one!
I've got my peace of mind,
Knock wood,
I hear that love is blind.
That's good,
'Cause the things I never see
Never seem to worry me,
So I'm happy as the day is long.

—Harold Arlen

I Gotta Right to Sing the Blues

VERSE

I don't care who
Knows I am blue.
My song wouldn't take long
To give my heart away.
I know it's plain
My heart's in pain,

My song
Couldn't belong
To someone feeling gay.

REFRAIN
I gotta right to sing the blues,
I gotta right to feel low down,
I gotta right to hang around
Down around the river.
A certain man in this old town
Keeps draggin' my poor heart around,
All I see for me is misery.
I gotta right to sing the blues,
I gotta right to moan and sigh,
I gotta right to sit and cry
Down around the river.
I know the deep blue sea
Will soon be calling me.
It must be love, say what you choose,
I gotta right to sing the blues.

—Harold Arlen

I've Got the World on a String

VERSE
Merry month of May,
Sunny skies of blue,
Clouds have rolled away
And the sun peeps through,
May express happiness.
Joy you may define
In a thousand ways,
But a case like mine
Needs a "special phrase"
To reveal
How I feel.

REFRAIN
I've got the world on a string,
Sittin' on a rainbow;

Got the string around my finger.
What a world,
What a life,
I'm in love!
I've got a song that I sing,
I can make the rain go
Anytime I move my finger.
Lucky me,
Can't you see,
I'm in love.
Life is a beautiful thing
As long as I hold the string.
I'd be a silly so and so,
If I should ever let go.
I've got the world on a string,
Sittin' on a rainbow,
Got the string around my finger.
What a world,
What a life,
I'm in love!

—Harold Arlen

Ill Wind

Blow,
Ill wind,
Blow away,
Let me rest today.
You're blowin' me no good,
No good.
Go, ill wind,
Go away.
Skies are, oh, so gray
Around my neighborhood,
And that's no good.
You're only misleadin'
The sunshine I'm needin';
Ain't that a shame?
It's so hard to keep up with
The troubles that creep up
From out of nowhere

When love's to blame.
So,
Ill wind,
Blow away,
Let me rest today.
You're blowin' me no good,
No good.

—*Harold Arlen*

LET'S FALL IN LOVE

VERSE

I have a feeling,
It's a feeling
I'm concealing,
I don't know why.
It's just a mental,
Incidental,
Sentimental
Alibi.
But I adore you,
So strong for you.
Why go on stalling?
I am falling,
Love is calling,
Why be shy?

REFRAIN

Let's fall in love,
Why shouldn't we fall in love?
Our hearts are made of it,
Let's take a chance,
Why be afraid of it?
Let's close our eyes,
And make our own Paradise.
Little we know of it,
Still we can try
To make a go of it.
We might have been meant for each
    other,
To be

Or not to be,
Let our hearts discover.
Let's fall in love,
Why shouldn't we fall in love?
Now is the time for it
While we are young,
Let's fall in love.

—*Harold Arlen*

SING, MY HEART

VERSE

Come, don't let us be foolish,
We mustn't be foolish,
Our dream isn't over,
Silly heart of mine.
Come, let's reason together,
We're not certain whether
The sweet or the bitter is in store.
So what are you almost breaking for?

REFRAIN

Go on and sing, my heart,
You know it's Spring, my heart,
So why not show it?
Pretend you're glad, my heart,
Although you're sad, my heart,
He mustn't know it.
Remember, love is not an easy game,
No two hearts ever beat quite the same.
Go on and dance, my heart,
Our only chance, my heart,
Is to forget it.
Should you despair, my heart,
He'll know we care, my heart,
And we'll regret it.
If it's to be
We soon shall see,
And if it's not to be
No pow'r on earth can make it so.
Pretend it's Spring, my heart,

Go on and sing, my heart,
For if you sing he'll never know.

—Harold Arlen

SPREADIN' RHYTHM AROUND

VERSE

There's an island not so tropical,
But a topical spot.
No palm trees sway,
But you'll find it hotter than hot.
Strangers go there to relax a bit
And to wax a bit gay.
When they write home,
Here's what they have to say:

REFRAIN

Music ev'rywhere, feet are pattin',
Puttin' tempo in old Manhatt'n.
Ev'rybody is out high-hattin',
Spreadin' rhythm around.
Ev'rywhere you go, trumpets blarin',
Drums and saxophones rip and tearin',
Ev'rybody you meet is rarin',
Spreadin' rhythm around.
Up in Harlem in any flat
They give it that thing
Which accordin' to one and all
Is what they call swing.
Those who can't afford silks and satin,
Dames with gigolos who are Latin,
Come from Yonkers, the Bronx and
    Stat'n,
Spreadin' rhythm around.

—Jimmy McHugh

STOP! YOU'RE BREAKIN' MY HEART

VERSE

What's the name of this game we're
    playing?
Luck is goin' your way.
You keep winnin' and I keep losin',
Now I'm refusin' to play.

REFRAIN

Stop! You're breakin' my heart.
This joke is goin' too far.
Come out wherever you are.
How come you like to do me like you do?
Stop! You're drivin' me wild.
It's tough to take it and grin.
And how you're rubbin' it in,
Because you know that I'm in love
    with you.
I'm so,
You're so,
Oh, I don't know, I'm just losin' all
    hope.
You're much
Too much,
I'm just about at the end of my rope,
So stop! Upsettin' my cart.
Look out! I'm startin' to burn.
The worm will certainly turn
If you don't
Stop!
Stop!
Stop!
Stop!
Stop! You're breakin' my heart.

—Burton Lane

STORMY WEATHER
(KEEPS RAININ' ALL THE TIME)

REFRAIN
Don't know why
There's no sun up in the sky,
Stormy weather,
Since my man and I ain't together,
Keeps rainin' all the time.
Life is bare,
Gloom and mis'ry ev'rywhere,
Stormy weather,
Just can't get my poor self together,
I'm weary all the time,
The time,
So weary all the time.
When he went away
The blues walked in and met me.
If he stays away
Old rockin' chair will get me.
All I do is pray
The Lord above will let me
Walk in the sun once more.
Can't go on,
Ev'rything I had is gone,
Stormy weather,
Since my man and I ain't together,
Keeps rainin' all the time,
Keeps rainin' all the time.
I walk around, heavy-hearted and sad.
Night comes around and I'm still feelin' bad.
Rain pourin' down, blindin' ev'ry hope
    I had.
This pitterin' patterin',
Beatin' an' splatterin',
Drives me mad.
Love, love, love, love,
This misery is just too much for me.
Can't go on,
Ev'rything I had is gone,
Stormy weather,
Since my man and I ain't together,
Keeps rainin' all the time,
Keeps rainin' all the time.

—Harold Arlen

TESS'S TORCH SONG
(I HAD A MAN)

VERSE
Here is a story
'Bout a gal,
Folks called her Torchy Tess.
Because she trusted,
Her heart got busted,
Love made her life a mess.
It evidently was an awful blow,
For this is word for word poor Tess's tale
    of woe:

REFRAIN
I had a man,
He was a good man,
That is you see what I mean is,
I thought he was a good man.
I had a friend,
She was a good friend,
I told my friend 'bout my man
'Cause I thought she was a good friend.
Life was sweet,
Didn't I have my man?
World complete,
Then the fireworks began.
Ain't got no man,
Ain't got no friend,
I'll bet you can guess just exactly what
    happened.
That was the end,
The end of my friend,
The end of my man,
And almost the end of me.

—Harold Arlen

TRUCKIN'

VERSE

Listen, you rhythm rounders,
Harlem is talkin' now;
You know the truck bug got you,
But you never knew just how.
That's what I wanna tell you,
I've got it figured out.
Now, if you want the lowdown,
Here's how it came about:

REFRAIN

We had to have somethin' new,
A dance to do up here in Harlem,
So, someone started truckin'.
As soon as the news got 'round
The folks downtown came up to Harlem,
Saw ev'rybody truckin'.
It didn't take long
Before the high-hats were doin' it,
Park Avenue-in' it.
All over town,
You'll see them scuffle-in', shuffle-in',
Truckin' along.
It spread like a forest blaze,
Became a craze,
And thanks to Harlem
Now ev'rybody's truckin'.

—Rube Bloom

WHEN THE SUN COMES OUT

When the sun comes out
And that rain stops beatin' on my
    windowpane;
When the sun comes out
There'll be bluebirds 'round my door
Singin' like they did before
That ol' storm broke out

And my man walked off and left me in
    the rain.
Though he's gone,
I doubt if he'll stay away for good,
I'd stop livin' if he should.
Love is funny;
It's not always peaches, cream, and
    honey.
Just when ev'rything looked bright and
    sunny,
Suddenly the cyclone came.
I'll never be the same
'Til that sun comes out,
And the rain stops beatin' on my
    window pane.
If my heart holds out,
Let it rain and let it pour,
It may not be long before
There's a knockin' at my door,
Then you'll know the one I loved walked in
When the sun comes out.

—Harold Arlen

WRAP YOUR TROUBLES IN DREAMS

(with Billy Moll)

VERSE I

What price happiness?
What price happiness?
Who can truthfully say?
But for ev'ry share with tears we pay.
Love is happiness!
I've had happiness,
But it ended one day.
Now I look at life a different way.

REFRAIN

When skies are cloudy and gray,
They're only gray for a day,
So wrap your troubles in dreams,
And dream your troubles away.

Until that sunshine peeps through,
There's only one thing to do,
Just wrap your troubles in dreams,
And dream your troubles away.
Your castles may tumble,
That's Fate, after all,
Life's really funny that way.
No use to grumble,
Just smile as they fall,
Weren't you king for a day?
Say!
Just remember that sunshine
Always follows the rain,
So wrap your troubles in dreams,
And dream your troubles away.

VERSE 2

Sorrow's bound to come,
Teach your heart to hum,
Bid your troubles adieu.
Soon you'll see your bluebird fly
   in view.
You can easily
Learn this melody,
What a wonderful song.
It will cheer you when the day
   is long.

REPEAT REFRAIN

—*Harry Barris*

Arthur Freed (1894–1973)

ARTHUR FREED IS one of the few major songwriters who had an even larger career in another field. Although he went to Hollywood as a lyricist–he and Nacio Herb Brown started at M-G-M with the 1929 Oscar winner, "The Broadway Melody"–he became the associate producer of *The Wizard of Oz* in 1939 and, that same year, the producer of another Judy Garland success, *Babes in Arms*. As head of the famous "Freed Unit," he was responsible for such triumphs as *An American in Paris* and *Gigi*, both Oscar winners, *Cabin in the Sky, Meet Me in St. Louis, Ziegfeld Follies,* and *The Band Wagon. Variety* estimated that his films brought in "a staggering total of $280,000,000 for Metro," and that was in the days when ten million was an enormous gross. But though he won every conceivable award Hollywood had to offer, he may be best remembered for a few of his songs, and for the movie, *Singin' in the Rain,* based on them. (The song itself began its life in *Hollywood Music Box Revue of 1928.*) Freed–born in Charleston, South Carolina, but raised in Seattle–attended the Philips Exeter Academy as a boy, but began in show business from the bottom up–as a piano player in a music-publishing house. He was in vaudeville with the Marx Brothers and the Gus Edwards Revue before starting to produce shows and turn out songs in New York (his first hit was "I Cried For You," in 1923), and even when he was one of Hollywood's top producers, he went on writing. His lyrics weren't elaborate or sophisticated, but they were high-level examples of Tin Pan Alley twenties' and thirties' style transplanted to the movies.

ALL I DO IS DREAM OF YOU

VERSE I

Out of a clear blue sky
Into my heart you came,
Not for a day
But here to stay.
I'll always feel the same.

REFRAIN

All I do is dream of you the whole night
   through.
With the dawn, I still go on and dream
   of you.

You're ev'ry thought, you're ev'rything,
You're ev'ry song I ever sing.
Summer, Winter, Autumn, and Spring,
And were there more
Than twenty-four
Hours a day,
They'd be spent in
Sweet content
Dreaming away.
When skies are gray, when skies
   are blue,
Morning, noon and nighttime, too,
All I do the whole day through is dream
   of you.

When e'vry day begins,
When ev'ry day is done,
Here in my heart,
Never to part,
You'll always be the one.

—*Nacio Herb Brown*

BROADWAY MELODY

There may be streets that have their
    sorrow,
A tear today, a smile tomorrow,
But there's a street that lives in glory,
It always tells the same old story.

Don't bring a frown to old Broadway,
You've got to clown on Broadway.
Your troubles there are out of style,
For Broadway always wears a smile.
A million lights they flicker there,
A million hearts beat quicker there,
No skies of gray on the great
    White Way,
That's the Broadway Melody.

—*Nacio Herb Brown*

FIT AS A FIDDLE

The world is right,
My heart is light,
I'm like a baby,
There is no "maybe,"
I know my fate.

I never knew
What love could do,
My heart is reeling,
The way I'm feeling
Is simply great.

Fit as a fiddle and ready for love,
I could jump over the moon up above,
Fit as a fiddle and ready for love.
Haven't a worry, I haven't a care,
Feel like a feather that's floating
    on air,
Fit as a fiddle and ready for love.
Soon the church bells will be ringing,
And I'll march with Ma and Pa.
How those church bells will be ringing
With a Hey nonny nonny and a
    hot-cha-cha.
Hi diddile diddle, my baby's okay,
Ask me a riddle, oh what did she say?
Fit as a fiddle and ready for love.

This is the day,
My lucky day,
I'm so excited,
I'm so delighted,
With ev'rything.
You're in my heart,
Never to part,
I am so happy,
I feel so happy,
I want to sing:

—*Al Hoffman and Al Goodhart*

Good Morning

VERSE

Here we are together,
A couple of stayer uppers,
Our day is done at breakfast time
And starts in with our suppers.
Here we are together,
But the best of friends must part;
So let me sing this parting song
From the bottom of my heart.

REFRAIN

Good morning, good morning,
We've danced the whole night
    through;
Good morning, good morning to you!
Good morning, good morning,
It's great to stay up late;
Good morning, good morning to you!
When the band began to play,
The stars were shining bright.
Now the milkman's on his way,
It's too late to say good night.
So good morning, good morning,
Sunbeams will soon smile through,
Good morning, good morning to you!

—Nacio Herb Brown

I Cried for You

VERSE I

I remember other days,
How I used to weep
Over things you said to me,
I couldn't even sleep.
You forgot your promises, ev'ry single vow.
All you did was laugh at me, but things are
    different now.

REFRAIN

I cried for you,
Now it's your turn to cry over me.
Ev'ry road has a turning,
That's one thing you're learning.
I cried for you,
What a fool I used to be.
Now I found two eyes just a little bit
    bluer,
I found a heart just a little bit truer.
I cried for you,
Now it's your turn to cry for me.

VERSE 2

How can I forget the hours
That I worried through
Wondering the livelong day
Just what next thing to do?
In those days you never thought anything
    of me.
But the slave that was all yours now at last
    is free.

REPEAT REFRAIN

—Gus Arnheim and Abe Lyman

I've Got a Feelin' You're Foolin'

VERSE

You are a picture no artist could paint,
But you're a mixture of devil and saint.
I just sigh and dream and try
To figure you out!
Love is in season, the moon's up
    above.
Though it be treason to question
    your love,
Ev'ry time I look at you
My heart's in doubt.

REFRAIN

I've got a feelin' you're foolin',
I've got a feelin' you're havin' fun.
I'll get a go-by when you are done
Foolin' with me.
I've got a feelin' you're foolin',
I've got a notion it's make believe.
I think you're laughin' right up your sleeve,
Foolin' with me.
Life is worth living
While you are giving
Moments of paradise.
You're such a standout,
But how you hand out
That hokus, pokus from your eyes.
I've got a feelin' you're foolin',
I've got a feelin' it's all a frame.
It's just the well-known old army game,
Foolin' with you.

—*Nacio Herb Brown*

SINGIN' IN THE RAIN

REFRAIN

Singin' in the rain,
Just singin' in the rain.
What a glorious feeling,
I'm happy again.
I'm laughing at clouds
So dark up above,
The sun's in my heart
And I'm ready for love.
Let the stormy clouds chase
Ev'ry one from the place,
Come on with the rain,
I've a smile on my face.
I'll walk down the lane
With a happy refrain,
And singin'
Just singin' in the rain.

INTERLUDE

Why am I smilin' and why do I sing?
Why does December seem sunny as Spring?
Why do I get up each morning to start
Happy and het up with joy in my heart?
Why is each new task a trifle to do?
Because I am living a life full of you.

REPEAT REFRAIN

—*Nacio Herb Brown*

THIS HEART OF MINE

VERSE

Maybe it was the music
Or a glamorous sky of blue;
Maybe it was the mood I was in,
Or maybe it was really you,
Really you.

REFRAIN

This heart of mine
Was doing very well;
The world was fine
As far as I could tell;
And then quite suddenly I met you,
And I dreamed of gay amours;
At dawn I woke up singing
Sentimental overtures.
This heart of mine
Is gaily dancing now;
I taste the wine
Of real romancing now.
Somehow, this crazy world has
Taken on a wonderful design.
As long as life endures, it's yours,
This heart of mine.

—*Harry Warren*

You Were Meant for Me

VERSE
Life was a song,
You came along,
I've laid awake the whole night through.
If I but dared
To think you cared,
This is what I'd say to you:

REFRAIN
"You were meant for me,
I was meant for you.

Nature patterned you and when she
    was done,
You were all the sweet things rolled up
    in one.
You're like a plaintive melody
That never lets me free.
For I'm content
The angels must have sent you,
And they meant you
Just for me."

—*Nacio Herb Brown*

B. G. (Buddy) DeSylva (1895–1950),
Lew Brown (1893–1958),
and Ray Henderson (1896–1970)

DESYLVA, BROWN, AND HENDERSON" is the name of a famous songwriting trio as well as of their music publishing house, but it's also a symbol for a certain kind of song at a very specific moment—their work epitomizes the jaunty, easy style of the late twenties and early thirties. The partnership lasted only six years, from 1925 to 1930—and all three men had successful careers both before and after it flourished—but we think of them together, which is one reason why Ray Henderson, the composer, is included in this roundup of lyricists. Besides, as he told Robert Kimball late in his life, the three men worked together on everything—he had a hand in the lyrics, too. DeSylva, whose father was in vaudeville, got his professional start writing for Al Jolson—in other words, at the top. (His first hit, written with Gus Kahn, was "I'll Say She Does," introduced, like so many other hits, into Jolson's 1918 *Sinbad.*) He was to write other songs for Jolson—"April Showers," "California, Here I Come"—and would collaborate with George Gershwin and Victor Herbert, among others, before meeting up with Brown and Henderson. Lew Brown, born in Odessa, Russia, was already writing songs at nineteen ("I'm the Lonesomest Gal in Town"); through the late teens and early twenties he had a series of hits with the prolific Albert von Tilzer and wrote for a number of successful shows, including *Hitchy-Koo* and *The Greenwich Village Follies*. Ray Henderson, after completing his formal musical education at the Chicago Conservatory of Music, started out in Tin Pan Alley as a song-plugger, but by 1923 he was turning out smash hits: "That Old Gang of Mine," "Five Foot Two, Eyes of Blue," "Bye Bye Blackbird." When the three men finally got together, their success was immediate, its high point the tremendous Broadway hit *Good News*. Moving to California early in the thirties, DeSylva became an important Hollywood producer and gradually abandoned writing. Brown and Henderson went on together for a while, writing Broadway shows, until Brown eventually followed DeSylva to Hollywood to work with other collaborators into the fifties, still racking up hits, including the Andrews Sisters' blockbuster "Roll Out the Barrel." And Henderson found other lyricists—Irving Caesar, Jack Yellen—to work with. But the quintessential twenties world of DeSylva, Brown, and Henderson—a world of college musicals, raccoon coats, and "Varsity Drags"—was gone forever.

April Showers

(B. G. DeSylva alone)

VERSE

Life is not a highway strewn with
    flowers,
Still it holds a goodly share of bliss.
When the sun gives way to April
    showers
Here's the point that you should
    never miss.

REFRAIN

Though April showers
May come your way,
They bring the flowers
That bloom in May.
So if it's raining,
Have no regrets,
Because it isn't raining rain, you know,
It's raining violets.
And where you see clouds
Upon the hills,
You soon will see crowds
Of daffodils:
So keep on looking for a bluebird
And list'ning for his song,
Whenever April showers come along.

—Louis Silvers

The Best Things in Life Are Free

VERSE

There are so many kinds of riches,
And only one of them is gold.
The wealth you miss,
Remember this,
Worthwhile things cannot be bought
    or sold.

REFRAIN

The moon belongs to ev'ryone,
The best things in life are free.
The stars belong to ev'ryone,
They gleam there for you and me.
The flowers in Spring,
The robins that sing,
The sunbeams that shine,
They're yours, they're mine!
And love can come to ev'ryone,
The best things in life are free.

The Birth of the Blues

VERSE

Oh!
They say some people long ago
Were searching for a diff'rent tune,
One that they could croon
As only they can.
They only had the rhythm
So
They started swaying to and fro.
They didn't know just what to use,
That is how the blues really began:

REFRAIN

They heard the breeze in the trees
Singing weird melodies
And they made that
The start of the blues.
And from a jail came the wail
Of a downhearted frail,
And they played that
As part of the blues.
From a whippoorwill
Out on a hill
They took a new note,
Pushed it through a horn
'Til it was worn
Into a blue note!
And then they nursed it,

Rehearsed it,
And gave out the news
That the Southland
Gave birth to the blues!

(Here Am I) Broken Hearted

(Lew Brown alone)

VERSE 1

Standing alone on the highway,
I met a boy that I knew.
He said, "If you're going my way,
I've got a story for you.
You know of my old girl Mary,
You've heard of my old pal Jim,
Look over there,
I'll show you where,
You'll find her spooning with him."

REFRAIN 1

There she is,
My old gal.
There he is,
My old pal.
And here am I
Broken hearted.
Mine in May,
His in June,
She forgot
Mighty soon,
And here am I,
Broken hearted.
The last time that we said "good-bye"
I knew that she was through.
It's bad enough that I lost her,
I had to lose him, too.
There they go
In their joy,
Happy girl,
Lucky boy,
And here am I,
Broken hearted.

VERSE 2

That is the tale he related,
My heart went out to him there.
He said, "I guess it was fated,
They made a wonderful pair.
You might expect me to hate her,
Say that I'm sorry we met.
I am resigned,
I only mind
'Cause it's so hard to forget."

REPEAT REFRAIN

Button Up Your Overcoat

VERSE 1

Listen, Big Boy!
Now that I've got you made,
Goodness, but I'm afraid
Something's gonna happen to you.
Listen, Big Boy!
You've got me hooked and how!
I would die if I should lose you now.

REFRAIN 1

Button up your overcoat
When the wind is free,
Take good
Care of yourself,
You belong to me!
Eat an apple ev'ry day;
Get to bed by three.
Take good
Care of yourself,
You belong to me!
Be careful crossing streets,
Oo–oo!
Don't eat meats,
Oo–oo!
Cut out sweets,
Oo–oo!
You'll get a pain and ruin your tum-tum!

Keep away from bootleg hooch
When you're on a spree.
Take good
Care of yourself,
You belong to me!

VERSE 2
Listen, girlfriend!
You've knocked me off my feet.
I think you're very sweet
Making such a fuss about me.
Listen, girlfriend!
Now that I'm fond of you,
I'm afraid I'm gonna worry too.

REFRAIN 2
Button up your overcoat
When the wind is free,
Take good
Care of yourself,
You belong to me!
Wear your flannel underwear
When you climb a tree.
Take good
Care of yourself,
You belong to me!
Don't sit on hornets' tails,
Oo–oo!
Or on nails,
Oo–oo!
Or third rails,
Oo–oo!
You'll get a pain and ruin your tum-tum!
Don't go out with college boys
When you're on a spree.
Take good
Care of yourself,
You belong to me!

CALIFORNIA, HERE I COME
(B. G. DeSylva and Al Jolson)

VERSE 1
When the wintry winds are blowing
And the snow is starting in to fall,
Then my eyes turn westward, knowing
That's the place I love the best of all.
California, I've been blue
Since I've been away from you.
I can't wait 'til I get going,
Even now I'm starting in to call
Oh,

REFRAIN
California, here I come,
Right back where I started from.
Where bowers
Of flowers
Bloom in the sun;
Each mornin'
At dawnin'
Birdies sing and ev'rything.
A sun-kissed miss said, "Don't be late."
That's why I can hardly wait.
Open up that Golden Gate,
California, here I come.

VERSE 2
Anyone who likes to wander
Ought to keep this saying in his mind,
"Absence makes the heart grow fonder"
Of the good old place you leave behind.
When you've hit the trail a while,
Seems you rarely see a smile;
That's why I must fly out yonder
Where a frown is mighty hard to find!
Oh,

REPEAT REFRAIN

—Joseph Meyer

Do It Again

(B. G. DeSylva alone)

VERSE
Tell me, tell me,
What did you do to me?
I just got a thrill
That was new to me.
When your two lips
Were pressed to mine.
When you held me,
I wasn't snuggling,
You should know
I really was struggling.
I've only met you,
And I shouldn't let you,
But

REFRAIN
Oh,
Do it again,
I may say, "No, no, no, no, no,"
But do it again.
My lips just ache
To have you take
The kiss that's waiting for you.
You know if you do,
You
Won't regret it,
Come and get it.
Oh,
No one is near,
I may cry, "Oh, oh, oh, oh, oh,"
But no one will hear.
Mama may scold me
'Cause she told me
It is naughty, but then,
Oh, do it again,
Please do it again!

—*George Gershwin*

Don't Bring Lulu

(Lew Brown, with Billy Rose)

VERSE 1
"Your presence is requested,"
Wrote little Johnny White,
But with this invitation
There is a stipulation.
When you attend this party
You'll all be treated right.
But there's a wild and wooly woman
You boys can't invite.

REFRAIN 1
Now you can bring Pearl,
She's a darn nice girl,
But don't bring Lulu.
You can bring Rose
With the turned-up nose,
But don't bring Lulu.
Lulu always wants to do
What we boys don't want her to.
When she struts her stuff around,
London Bridge is falling down.
You can bring cake
Or porterhouse steak,
But don't bring Lulu.
Lulu gets blue
And she goes "coo-coo"
Like the clock upon the shelf.
She's the kind of smarty
Who breaks up every party.
Hullaba loo loo,
Don't bring Lulu,
I'll bring her myself.

VERSE 2
We all went to the party,
A real high-toned affair,
And then along came Lulu
As wild as any Zulu.
She started in to

"Charleston"
And how the boys did stare.
But when she did the hula hula,
Then she got the air.

REFRAIN

Now you can bring Nan
With the old deadpan,
But don't bring Lulu.
You can bring Tess
With her "no" and "yes,"
But don't bring Lulu.
Lulu has the reddest hair,
Redder here and redder there.
How can we boys keep our head?
Bulls go wild when they see red.
You can bring peas
And crullers and cheese,
But don't bring Lulu.
Give her two beers
And she tears portieres
And she throws cups off the shelf.
When she loves with feeling
The boys all hit the ceiling.
Hullaba loo loo,
Don't bring Lulu,
She'll come here herself.

—Ray Henderson

I Want to Be Bad

To be
or not to be,
That is not the question.
I decided long ago to be.
With me
It's what to be.
Make me some suggestion.
Good or bad, which is the best for me?
When you're after

Fun and laughter
This aggravates
You
Some reformer
Says a warmer
Climate awaits
You.

REFRAIN

If it's naughty to rouge your lips,
Shake your shoulders and twist
    your hips,
Let a lady confess,
I want to be bad.
If it's naughty to vamp the men,
Sleep each morning till after ten,
Then the answer is, "Yes, I want to
    be bad."
This thing of being a good little "Goodie"
    is all very well.
What can you do if you're loaded with
    plenty of hell-
Th and vigor?
When you're learning what lips are for,
If it's naughty to ask for more,
Let a lady confess,
I want to be bad.

I'll Say She Does

(B. G. DeSylva, Gus Kahn, Al Jolson)

VERSE I

I've got a brand new sweetie
Better than the one before.
Oh! She's got everything
And a little bit more.
I don't know much about her,
And yet I know a lot.
'Cause what it takes to make me
    love her,
I want to tell you she's got.

REFRAIN

Does she make ev'rybody stare?
I'll say she does.
Does she give 'em that "I don't care"?
I'll say she does.
But is she nicer to me
And does she sit on my knee?
Does she?
I'll say she does.
And does she crave
A wedding 'n' ev'rything?
I'll say she does.
Was she happy to get the ring?
You bet she was.
And can she dance?
Can she twist?
Does she do a lot of things I can't
    resist?
Does she?
I'll say she does.

VERSE 2

It was so hard to get her,
She can never get away.
Because I'm watching her
All the night and all day.
I've always had her picture,
I had it in my mind.
I always knew what kind I wanted,
And she's exactly the kind.

REPEAT REFRAIN

—*B. G. DeSylva*

IF I HAD A TALKING PICTURE
OF YOU

VERSE 1

I talk to your photograph each day.
You should hear the lovely things I say.

But I've thought how happy I would be
If your photograph could talk to me.

REFRAIN

If I had a talking picture of you-oo,
I would run it ev'ry time I felt blue-oo.
I would sit there in the gloom
Of my lonely little room,
And applaud each time you whispered, "I
    love you!
Love you!"
On the screen the moment you came in
    view-oo,
We would talk the whole thing over, we
    two-oo,
I would give ten shows a day,
And a midnight matinee,
If I had a talking picture of you.

VERSE 2

All I have to keep me company
Is the photograph you gave to me.
I propose a thousand plans, but oh,
It don't answer "Yes" or even "No."

REPEAT REFRAIN

IF YOU KNEW SUSIE
(LIKE I KNOW SUSIE)

(B. G. DeSylva alone)

REFRAIN 1

If you knew Susie
Like I know Susie,
Oh, oh, oh what a girl!
There's none so classy
As this fair lassie,
Oh, oh!
Holy Moses, what a chassis!
We went riding,
She didn't balk.

Back from Yonkers
I'm the one who had to walk!
If you knew Susie
Like I know Susie,
Oh, oh what a girl!

REFRAIN 2
If you knew Susie
Like I know Susie,
Oh, oh, oh what a girl!
She wears long tresses
And nice tight dresses,
Oh, oh!
What a future she possesses!
Out in public,
How she can yawn.
In a parlor
You would think the war was on!
If you knew Susie
Like I know Susie,
Oh, oh what a girl!

—Joseph Meyer

It All Depends on You

VERSE 1
Lovers depend on moonlight
For a love affair.
Babies depend on mothers
For their tender care.
Flowers depend on sunshine
And the morning dew.
Each thing depends on something,
And I depend on you.

REFRAIN
I can be happy,
I can be sad,
I can be good or
I can be bad,
It all depends on you.

I can be lonely
Out in a crowd,
I can be humble,
I can be proud,
It all depends on you.
I can save money,
Or spend it,
Go right on living,
Or end it.
You're to blame, honey,
For what I do.
I know that
I can be beggar,
I can be king,
I can be almost any old thing,
It all depends on you.

VERSE 2
Isn't it sweet to know, dear,
You can help me on?
Wouldn't it hurt to know, dear,
All my hopes were gone?
Wouldn't it make you proud, dear,
If I made a name?
But if I failed to win, dear,
Would you want all the blame?

Life Is Just a Bowl of Cherries
(Lew Brown alone)

VERSE
People are queer,
They're always crowing,
Scrambling and rushing about.
Why don't they stop some day,
Address themselves this way?
Why are we here?
Where are we going?
It's time that we found out.
We're not here to stay,
We're on a short holiday.

REFRAIN

Life is just a bowl of cherries.
Don't make it serious,
Life's too mysterious.
You work, you save, you worry so,
But you can't take your dough when you
    go, go, go.
So keep repeating it's the berries,
The strongest oak must fall.
The sweet things in life
To you were just loaned,
So how can you lose
What you've never owned?
Life is just a bowl of cherries,
So live and laugh at it all.

REPEAT REFRAIN

—*Ray Henderson*

LOOK FOR THE SILVER LINING

(B. G. DeSylva alone)

VERSE I

HE: Please don't be offended if I preach
    to you a while,
    Tears are out of place in eyes that
    were meant to smile.
    There's a way to make your very
    biggest troubles small,
    Here's the happy secret of it all:

REFRAIN

Look for the silver lining
Whene'er a cloud
Appears in the blue.
Remember, somewhere
The sun is shining
And so the right thing
To do
Is make it shine for you.
A heart full of joy and gladness

Will always banish sadness
And strife,
So always look for
The silver lining
And try to find the sunny side of life.

VERSE 2

SHE: As I wash my dishes, I'll be following
    your plan,
    Till I see the brightness in ev'ry pot
    and pan.
    I am sure your point of view will ease
    the daily grind,
    So I'll keep repeating in my mind:

REPEAT REFRAIN

—*Jerome Kern*

MAGNOLIA

VERSE I

Lovey Joe, a boy I know, an expert judge
    of gals,
Was speaking of his lady love, ravin' to
    his pals.
He said she's called Magnolia and she'd
    ruin any man,
I just can't describe her, but I'll do the
    best I can.

REFRAIN I

Take some honey from the bee,
Mix it up with TNT,
What have you got?
Magnolia.
Clara Bow, ain't she delish,
Season her with Lillian Gish,
What have you got?
Magnolia.
Listen pal, describing that gal is
    tryin',

When I'm done, it's twenty to one you'll
    say I'm lying.
Take Cleopatra and Camille,
Add some more sex appeal,
Mix the lot and what have you got?
Magnolia.

VERSE 2

Lovey Joe was all aglow to get that off his
    chest.
The boys agreed the gal had speed
    and said
"Let's hear the rest."
Said Joe, "I really hate to, I'd make you
    feel too bad,
But while I'm on the subject, there's a few
    words I might add.

REFRAIN 2

Take your cuties far and near,
Add some Follies atmosphere,
What have you got?
Magnolia.
Juliet and Lulu Belle,
Take 'em both and shake 'em well,
What have you got?
Magnolia.
Man, you know each season they grow
    more sporty.
Close your eyes and picture the prize of
    nineteen-forty.
Take Mother Eve in her cute dress,
Think of that and picture less.
Mix the lot and what have you got?
Magnolia."

Maybe This Is Love

VERSE 1

HE: Many girls I've met,
    A few were sightly.
    I thought them all wet

And bowed politely.
Something's changing me,
Rearranging me.
All I do is dream about you nightly.

REFRAIN

I'm on air,
My head's reeling,
And right there
A strange feeling
From nowhere
Has come stealing,
Maybe, maybe this is love!
My time's through
To think coolly,
My heart, too,
Is unruly.
It's all new
To yours truly,
Maybe this is love.

VERSE 2

SHE: Though for years and years
    I've lived sedately,
    Something, it appears,
    Has changed me lately.
    We've just met, it's true,
    Funny, yet it's true,
    There's something about you thrills
      me greatly.

REPEAT REFRAIN

Never Swat a Fly

VERSE 1

Love has made me tender:
I now appreciate
Ev'ry little creature on this earth that has
    a mate.
Once I hated crickets;
I couldn't stand a bee.

Now here is the motto that I follow
    faithfully:

REFRAIN I

Never swat a fly,
He may love another fly;
He may sit with her and sigh
The way I do with you.
Never harm a flea,
He may have a fav'rite she
That he bounces on his knee,
The way I do with you.
Never stop a bee if he is going
    anywhere;
You may be concluding some terrific love
    affair.
Be careful!
Don't step on an ant
In the middle of a pant;
He may want to but he can't
The way I do with you.

VERSE 2

I'm the same as you are:
The tears come to my eyes
When I see professors chasing helpless
    butterflies.
Fishermen are hateful,
They lead a wicked life:
Ev'ry day they separate some husband
    from his wife.

REFRAIN 2

Never swat a fly,
He may love another fly;
He may sit with her and sigh
The way I do with you.
Never spray a nit
With a great big can of Flit;
He may think some nit has "It,"
The way I do with you.
Never stop a moth if he is gliding through
    the air;

He may have a date in someone's flannel
    underwear.
Be careful!
Don't you dare to slay
Two mosquitoes while they play;
They may want to make "Hey! Hey!"
The way I do with you.

SOMEBODY LOVES ME

(B. G. DeSylva and Ballard MacDonald)

VERSE

When this world began
It was Heaven's plan,
There should be a girl for ev'ry single man.
To my great regret
Someone has upset
Heaven's pretty program,
For we've never met.
I'm clutching at straws,
Just because
I may meet her yet.

REFRAIN

Somebody loves me,
I wonder who,
I wonder who she can be.
Somebody loves me,
I wish I knew,
Who can she be worries me.
For ev'ry girl who passes me
I shout, "Hey! maybe,
You were meant to be my loving baby."
Somebody loves me,
I wonder who.
Maybe it's you.

—George Gershwin

Straw Hat in the Rain

(Lew Brown alone)

VERSE

Is your icebox full of food?
Is your cellar full of coal?
Are you in a gayer mood
Since you've reached that certain goal?
With that high hat on your head,
You're the symbol of success,
And just around the corner
There's a signal of distress.

REFRAIN

Hey! There, high hat,
You're a high and dry hat,
Won't you do a little something
For the straw hat in the rain?
Say! There, high hat,
You'd be a "regular guy" hat,
If you threw a little something
To the straw hat in the rain.
Can't you hear the thunder?
He'll be washed away.
Pull him out from under,
He may still turn out O.K.
This "all in" hat
Was once a Yankee Doodle tin hat,
Won't you do a little something
For the straw hat in the rain?

—Harry Akst

Sunny Side Up

VERSE I

There's one thing to think of when
    you're blue,
There are others much worse off than you.
If a load of trouble should arrive,
Laugh and say, "It's great to be alive!"

REFRAIN

Keep your sunny side up. Up!
Hide the side that gets blue.
If you have nine sons in a row,
Baseball teams make money,
    you know!
Keep your funny side up. Up!
Let your laughter come through. Do!
Stand upon your legs,
Be like two fried eggs,
Keep your sunny side up!

VERSE 2

Life can be a pleasure or a pain,
Good or bad, successful or in vain,
Happiness is just a point of view.
If you'd have it, here's the thing
    to do:

REPEAT REFRAIN

Thank Your Father

VERSE

When I think that you're the one girl I
    adore,
Gratitude inflates my bosom more
    and more.
When I see your slender grace,
Analyze your form and face,
Then I think how much I must be
    thankful for.

REFRAIN I

Oh!
Thank your father,
Thank your mother!
Thank 'em both for meeting up with one
    another!
Thank the horse that pulled the buggy that
    night.
Thank your dad for being just a bit tight.

Thank the June night,
Thank the moonlight
That caressed them from above.
1. And thank goodness for their
        marriage,
    And for that baby carriage!
    Or I'd have no one to love!

REPEAT REFRAIN
2. Though your father's name was
        Stanley,
    Thank goodness he was manly!
    Or I'd have no one to love!

THAT OLD FEELING

(Lew Brown alone)

VERSE
Last night I started out happy,
Last night my heart was so gay,
Last night I found myself dancing
In my fav'rite cabaret.
You were completely forgotten,
Just an affair of the past.
Then suddenly something happened
    to me,
And I found my heart beating, oh so fast.

REFRAIN
I saw you last night
And got that old feeling.
When you came in sight
I got that old feeling.
The moment that you danced by
I felt a thrill,
And when you caught my eye
My heart stood still.
Once again I seemed to feel
That old yearning.
And I knew the spark of love
Was still burning.
There'll be no new romance for me,

It's foolish to start,
For that old feeling
Is still in my heart.

—Sammy Fain

TURN ON THE HEAT

VERSE I
You think the coldest girls in the world are
    Eskimos,
You'll find the hottest girls in the world
    are Eskimos.
They have no steam heat,
But they have dancing feet;
They shake their stuff and melt the ice and
    snows.
All Eskimosey husbands each morning of
    their lives,
Jump out of bed and holler to their wives:

REFRAIN
Turn on the heat!
Start in to strut!
Wiggle and wobble
And warm up the hut.
Oh! Oh!
It's thirty below!
Turn on the heat,
Fifty degrees,
Get hot for Papa
Or Papa will freeze!
Oh! Oh!
Start melting the snow!
If you are good,
My little radiator,
It's understood
You'll get a gumdrop later!
Turn on the heat!
Pour in the oil!
Start in to bubble
And come to a boil.

You put the burn on for Papa
And turn on the heat!

VERSE 2

Up in the Arctic Zone, the land of the
     midnight sun,
They have a dance their own so hot but not
     overdone.
Ev'ry Eskimo,
They're swaying to and fro;
Their dance is what they call the "Hot
     Igloo."
They freeze a step with ease and pep just to
     keep 'em warm.
There's no mistake this dance will "take"
     by storm.

REPEAT REFRAIN

THE VARSITY DRAG

VERSE

We've always thought
Knowledge is naught;
We should be taught
To dance.
Right here at Tait,
We're up to date;
We teach a great
New dance.
Don't think that I brag,
I speak of the Drag.
Why should a Sheik
Learn how to speak
Latin and Greek
Badly?
Give him a neat
Motto complete,
"Say it with feet
Gladly!"
First lesson right now;

You'll love it, and how!
You'll love it!

REFRAIN

Here is the Drag,
See how it goes;
Down on the heels,
Up on the toes.
That's the way to do
The Varsity Drag.
Hotter than hot,
Newer than new!
Meaner than mean,
Bluer than blue,
Gets as much applause
As waving the flag!
You can pass
Many a class,
Whether you're dumb or wise,
If you all
Answer the call,
When your professor cries:
"Ev'rybody,
Down on the heels,
Up on the toes,
Stay after school,
Learn how it goes;
Ev'rybody
Do the Varsity Drag."

YOU'RE AN OLD SMOOTHIE

(B. G. DeSylva alone)

VERSE

You're the smoothest so and so,
Not only that, you're mighty cute.
You're slicker far than the trousers are
Of my last year's blue serge suit.
I'm the softest so and so
That any girlie ever knew.
Oh, I may be dumb

As they ever come,
But at least I'm on to you!

REFRAIN

You're an old smoothie,
I'm an old softie;
I'm just like putty in the hands
Of a girl like you.
You're an old meanie,
I'm a big booby;
I just go nutty in the hands
Of a girl like you.
Poor me,
You played me for a sap;
Poor you,
You thought you'd laid a trap!
Well, dear,
I think it's time you knew
You've done just what I wanted
     you to.
Silly old smoothie,
Crafty old softie,
I'll stick like putty to the hand
Of a girl like you.

—Richard Whiting and
Nacio Herb Brown

YOU'RE THE CREAM IN MY COFFEE

VERSE I

HE: I'm not a poet,
     How well I know it,
     I've never been a raver.
     But when I speak of you
     I rave a bit, it's true.
     I'm wild about you,
     I'm lost without you.
     You give my life its flavor,

What sugar does for tea,
That's what you do for me.

REFRAIN I

You're the cream in my coffee,
You're the salt in my stew,
You will always be
My necessity,
I'd be lost without you.
You're the starch in my collar,
You're the lace in my shoe,
You will always be
My necessity,
I'd be lost without you.

1. Most men tell lovetales
   And each phrase dovetails;
   You've heard each known way.
   This way is my own way.
You're the sail of my loveboat,
You're the captain and crew.
You will always be
My necessity,
I'd be lost without you.

VERSE 2

SHE: You have a great way,
     An up-to-date way,
     Of telling me you love me.
     It gives me such a thrill,
     I know it always will.
     My head is turning,
     And just from learning
     Your estimation of me.
     And as for you, I'll say,
     "I feel the self-same way."

REPEAT REFRAIN

2. You give life savor,
   Bring out its flavor,
   So this is clear, dear,
   You're my Worcestershire, dear.

Leo Robin (1895–1984)

ONE OF THE MOST PROLIFIC and successful Hollywood lyricists (over 115 movies, and ten Oscar nominations; he won for "Thanks for the Memory"), Leo Robin was born in Pittsburgh and went to the University of Pennsylvania law school and Carnegie Tech drama school. His breakthrough came in collaborating with Clifford Grey on the lyrics for Vincent Youmans' *Hit the Deck* ("Hallelujah!"), and a couple of years later he was in California, collaborating with Richard Whiting on "Beyond the Blue Horizon" for Jeanette Macdonald and "Louise" for Maurice Chevalier, but soon he was paired with composer Ralph Rainger. They had a streak of big hits for Bing Crosby in Crosby's Paramount musicals–sentimental numbers like "Love in Bloom," "June in January," and "Blue Hawaii," which Elvis was to sing years later. In 1942 Rainger was killed in an airplane crash, and Robin went to 20th Century Fox–Busby Berkeley's demented *The Gang's All Here* and, with Jerome Kern, "In Love in Vain" for *Centennial Summer.* Capping his career was his one Broadway smash hit, *Gentlemen Prefer Blondes,* in which Carol Channing became a star singing "Diamonds Are a Girl's Best Friend." Later sources give his year of birth as 1900, but *Who's Who* through the sixties and seventies carries him back to 1895.

BEYOND THE BLUE HORIZON

VERSE

Blow, whistle,
Blow away,
Blow 'way the past.
Go, engine,
Anywhere,
I don't care how fast.
On, on
From darkness into dawn,
From rain into the rainbow,
Fly with me.
Gone, gone,
All my grief and woe.
What matter where I go
If I am free?

REFRAIN

Beyond the blue horizon
Waits a beautiful day.
Good-bye to things that bore me,
Joy is waiting for me.
I see a new horizon.
My life has only begun.
Beyond the blue horizon
Lies a rising sun.

*—Richard A. Whiting and
W. Franke Harling*

DIAMONDS ARE A GIRL'S BEST FRIEND

VERSE I

The French are glad to die for love,
They delight in fighting duels.
But I prefer a man who lives,
And gives expensive jewels.

REFRAIN I

A kiss on the hand may be quite
    Continental,
But diamonds are a girl's best friend.
A kiss may be grand,
But it won't pay the rental
On your humble flat
Or help you at the Automat.
Men grow cold
As girls grow old
And we all lose our charms in the end.
But square-cut or pear-shape,
These rocks don't lose their shape,
Diamonds are a girl's best friend.

VERSE 2

A well-conducted rendezvous
Makes a maiden's heart beat quicker,
But when the rendezvous is through,
These stones still keep their flicker.

REFRAIN 2

There may come a time when a lass needs a
    lawyer,
But diamonds are a girl's best friend.
There may come a time
When a hard-boiled employer
Thinks you're awful nice,
But get that "ice" or else no dice.
He's your guy
When stocks are high,
But beware when they start to descend.

It's then that those louses
Go back to their spouses,
Diamonds are a girl's best friend.

—Jule Styne

EASY LIVING

Living for you is easy living,
It's easy to live when you're in love,
And I'm so in love there's nothing in life
    but you.
I never regret the years I'm giving,
They're easy to give when you're
    in love.
I'm happy to do whatever I do for you,
For you.
Maybe I'm a fool, but it's fun.
People say you rule me with one
Wave of your hand,
Darling, it's grand,
They just don't understand.
Living for you is easy living,
It's easy to live when you're in love,
And I'm so in love there's nothing in life
    but you.

—Ralph Rainger

FOR EVERY MAN THERE'S A WOMAN

For ev'ry man there's a woman.
For ev'ry life there's a plan.
And wise men know it was ever so;
Since the world began,
Woman was made for man.
Where is she,
Where is *the*
Woman for me?

For ev'ry prince there's a princess,
For ev'ry Joe there's a Joan.
And if you wait you will meet the mate
Born for you alone,
Happy to be your own.
Where is she,
Where is *the*
Woman for me?
Find the one,
Find the one,
Then together you will find the sun.
For ev'ry heart there's a moment,
For ev'ry hand a glove,
And for ev'ry woman, a man to love.
Where is she?
Where is *the*
One for me?

—Harold Arlen

Hooray for Love

VERSE

Here's to my best romance,
Here's to my worst romance,
Here's to my first romance
Ages ago.
Here's to the girls I've kissed,
And to complete the list,
Here's to the girls who said "No!"

REFRAIN 1

Love! love! Hooray for love!
Who is ever too blasé for love?
Make this a night for love.
If we have to fight let's fight for love.
Some sigh and cry for love.
Ah, but in Paree they die for love.
Some waste away for love.
Just the same, hooray for love!
It's the wonder of the world,
It's a rocket to the moon.

It gets you high,
It gets you low,
But once you get that glow,
Oh! love!

REFRAIN 2

Some trust to fate for love.
Others have to take off weight
for love.
Some go berserk for love.
Loafers even go to work for love.
Sad songs are sobbed for love.
People have their noses bobbed
for love.
Some say we pay for love.
Just the same, hooray for love!
It's the wonder of the world,
It's a rocket to the moon.
It gets you high,
It gets you low,
But once you get that glow,
Oh! love!

—Harold Arlen

In Love in Vain

VERSE

Love can be a blessing
But also most depressing,
And I don't mind confessing
That I feel mighty blue!

REFRAIN

It's only human
For anyone to want to be in love,
But who wants to be in love in vain?
At night you hang around the house and
eat your heart out,
And cry your eyes out,
And wrack your brain.
You sit and wonder

Why anyone as wonderful as he
Should cause you such misery
    and pain.
I thought that I would be in heaven,
But I'm only up a tree,
'Cause it's just my luck
To be in love in vain.

—Jerome Kern

LITTLE GIRL FROM LITTLE ROCK

VERSE

In my Park Avenue penthouse
I'm sophisticated and smart,
But a town down in the Ozarks
Is where I got my start.

REFRAIN I

I'm just a little girl from Little Rock,
We lived on the wrong side of the
    tracks.
But a gentleman took me out one night
And after he taught me wrong from
    right,
We moved to the right side of the
    tracks.
Then someone broke my heart in
    Little Rock,
And I up and left old Arkansas,
Like a little lost lamb I roamed about,
I came to New York and I found out
The one you call Daddy ain't your paw.
1. I was young and determined,
    I was wined and dined and ermined,
    Ev'ry night opportunity would
        knock.
    And some of these days in my fancy
        clothes,
    I'm a-going back home and thumb
        my nose
    At the one who done me wrong,

The one who done me wrong,
The one who done me wrong,
In Little Rock.

REPEAT REFRAIN

2. For a kid from a small street
    I did very well in Wall Street,
    Although I never owned a share of
        stock.
    And now that I'm known in the biggest
        banks,
    I'm a-going back home and give my
        thanks
    To the one who done me wrong,
    The one who done me wrong,
    The one who done me wrong,
    In Little Rock.

—Jule Styne

LOUISE

VERSE 1

Wonderful!
Oh, it's wonderful
To be in love with you.
Beautiful!
You're so beautiful,
You haunt me all day through.

REFRAIN I

Ev'ry little breeze
Seems to whisper "Louise."
Birds in the trees
Seem to twitter "Louise."
Each little rose
Tells me it knows
I love you, love you.
Ev'ry little beat
That I feel in my heart
Seems to repeat
What I felt at the start.

Each little sigh
Tells me that I
Adore you, Louise.
Just to see and hear you
Brings joy I never knew.
But to be so near you
Thrills me through and through.
Anyone can see
Why I wanted your kiss,
It had to be,
But the wonder is this:
Can it be true
Someone like you
Could love me, Louise?

VERSE 2
Innocent!
You're as innocent
And gentle as a dove.
Heaven sent!
You were heaven sent,
An angel from above.

REFRAIN 2
Ev'ry little breeze
Seems to whisper "Louise."
Birds in the trees
Seem to twitter "Louise."
Each little rose
Tells me it knows
I love you, love you.
Ev'ry little beat
That I feel in my heart
Seems to repeat
What I felt at the start.
Each little sigh
Tells me that I
Adore you, Louise.
Often when I'm gloomy
And in my lonely room,
Thoughts of you come to me
Like a sweet perfume.

Anyone can see
Why I wanted your kiss,
It had to be,
But the wonder is this:
Can it be true
Someone like you
Could love me, Louise?

—Richard A. Whiting

LOVE IS JUST AROUND THE CORNER

VERSE
Beautiful miracle,
Pardon my lyrical
Rhapsody,
But can't you see
You've captured me?
Being so glamorous,
Can't you be amorous
Just with me?
Make it soon,
Take a look at the moon, ooh . . .

REFRAIN
Love is just around the corner,
Any cozy little corner,
Love is just around the corner
When I'm around you.
I'm a sentimental mourner,
And I couldn't be forlorner
When you keep me on a corner
Just waiting for you.
Venus de Milo was noted for her
        charms,
But strictly between us,
You're cuter than Venus,
And what's more you got arms.
So let's go cuddle in a corner,
Any cozy little corner.

Love is just around the corner,
And I'm around you.

—Lewis E. Gensler

MY CUTEY'S DUE AT TWO-TO-TWO TODAY

VERSE I

Hey there, taxi, do your stuff,
I can't get there fast enough,
Take me to that train from way
    out West.
I'm just jumping in my shoes,
'Cause there ain't no time to lose,
Got a date one-fifty-eight
With the one that I love best.

REFRAIN

My cutey's due at two-to-two,
She's coming thru on a big
    choo-choo.
She's been away for months.
But I haven't cheated once,
Stayed home nights, didn't dance,
Wasn't taking any chance,
Didn't flirt and though it hurt
I just couldn't do my cutey dirt.
My days were blue, my nights were
    black,
But I just knew that she'd come back,
For I love her and she loves me
    and, say,
Don't think there ain't no Santa
    Claus,
1. I know darn well there is because,
    My cutey's due at two-to-two today.

VERSE 2

No one knows how glad I am
Since I got that telegram,

Sweeter than a message from above.
Seems just like a century
Since she's been away from me,
But you bet I'm gonna get
What I've kept on dreaming of.

REPEAT REFRAIN

2. And when I feel her lips on mine
    I won't let go 'til half past nine,
    My cutey's due at two-to-two
        today.

REPEAT REFRAIN

3. Tonight I'll disconnect my phone
    Because I want to be alone,
    My cutey's due at two-to-two
        today.

—Albert Von Tilzer

MY IDEAL

VERSE

Long ago my heart and mind
Got together and designed
The wonderful girl for me,
Oh what a fantasy.
Though the idol of my heart
Can't be ordered à la carte
I wonder if she will be
Always a fantasy.

REFRAIN

Will I ever find
The girl in my mind
The one who is my ideal?
Maybe she's a dream and yet she
    might be
Just around the corner, waiting for me.
Will I recognize
A light in her eyes

That no other eyes reveal?
Or will I pass her by
And never even know
That she is my ideal?

—*Richard A. Whiting and Newell Chase*

No Love, No Nothin'

VERSE
I'm just about as solitary
As anyone could be.
Of course my life is not so merry,
But that's all right with me.

REFRAIN
No love, no nothin',
Until my baby comes home.
No sir! No nothin',
As long as baby must roam.
I promised him I'd wait for him till even
    Hades froze,
I'm lonesome, Heaven knows,
But what I said still goes.
No love, no nothin',
And that's a promise I'll keep.
No fun with no one,
I'm getting plenty of sleep.
My heart's on strike and though it's like an
    empty honeycomb,
No love, no sir, no nothin'
Till my baby comes home.

—*Harry Warren*

Thanks for the Memory

Thanks for the memory
Of candlelight and wine,
Castles on the Rhine,

The Parthenon and moments on the
    Hudson River Line.
How lovely it was!
Thanks for the memory
Of rainy afternoons,
Swingy Harlem tunes,
And motor trips and burning lips and
    burning toast and prunes.
How lovely it was!
Many's the time that we feasted,
And many's the time that we fasted.
Oh well, it was swell while it lasted;
We did have fun
And no harm done.
And thanks for the memory
Of sunburns at the shore,
Nights in Singapore.
You might have been a headache but you
    never were a bore,
So thank you so much.
Awf'ly glad I met you,
Cheerio and toodle-oo,
And thank you so much!
Thanks for the memory
Of sentimental verse,
Nothing in my purse,
And chuckles when the preacher said
    "For better or for worse."
How lovely it was!
Thanks for the memory
Of lingerie with lace,
Pilsner by the case,
And how I jumped the day you trumped
    my one and only ace.
How lovely it was!
We said good-bye with a highball,
Then I got as high as a steeple.
But we were intelligent people,
No tears, no fuss,
Hurray for us.
So thanks for the memory,
And strictly entre nous,

Darling, how are you?
And how are all the little dreams that
    never did come true?
Awf'ly glad I met you,

Cheerio and toodle-oo,
And thank you so much!

—Ralph Rainger

Lorenz Hart (1895–1943)

THE PARTNERSHIP BETWEEN Lorenz Hart and Richard Rodgers, the only composer Hart worked with after they got their start, lasted some twenty-five years, and produced what is arguably the most brilliant collaborative work of the American musical comedy. Rodgers was a sixteen-year-old undergraduate at Columbia when they met; Hart was doing post-graduate work there, and translating German plays for the Shuberts. From Columbia Varsity shows they went on to the *Garrick Gaieties* and their first hit, "Manhattan," whose ingenious lyrics immediately identified Hart as a new voice on Broadway. Their roster of hit shows included *Jumbo, On Your Toes, Babes in Arms, I Married an Angel, The Boys from Syracuse,* the revolutionary *Pal Joey, By Jupiter,* and *A Connecticut Yankee,* the 1927 show that was revived just a week before Hart's lamentably early death. But the Rodgers and Hart musical had already come to an end when, in 1942, Hart backed away from working on *Oklahoma!* and was replaced with Oscar Hammerstein II. Mid-World War II was clearly no time for the mordancy of the typical Hart lyric; the corn was now as high as an elephant's eye. Hart's lyrics display a unique blend of cynicism, wit, and an underlying sadness. His range can be readily calculated from the hits of a single typical R & H show, *Babes in Arms:* "My Funny Valentine," "Johnny One-Note," "Where or When," "The Lady Is a Tramp." In his later years, Lorenz Hart was not a happy man, nor an easy one to work with: His alcoholism and compulsive lack of punctuality were a torment to Dick Rodgers. As Rodgers once said of the day when he first met Larry Hart, "In one afternoon, I acquired a career, a partner, a best friend—and a source of permanent irritation." Mickey Rooney did a capable job of dramatizing Hart's frustration and self-destructive nature in the M-G-M biopic of the team, *Words and Music.*

BEWITCHED, BOTHERED AND BEWILDERED

VERSE

He's a fool, and don't I know it—
But a fool can have his charms;
I'm in love and don't I show it,
Like a babe in arms.
Men are not a new sensation;
I've done pretty well, I think.
But this half-pint imitation
Put me on the blink.

REFRAIN I

I'm wild again,
Beguiled again,
A simpering, whimpering child again—
Bewitched, bothered and bewildered am I.
Couldn't sleep
And wouldn't sleep

Until I could sleep where I shouldn't sleep–
Bewitched, bothered and bewildered am I.
Lost my heart, but what of it?
My mistake, I agree.
He's a laugh, but I love it
Because the laugh's on me.
A pill he is,
But still he is
All mine and I'll keep him until he is
Bewitched, bothered and bewildered
Like me.

REFRAIN 2
Seen a lot–
I mean a lot–
But now I'm like sweet seventeen a lot–
Bewitched, bothered and bewildered am I.
I'll sing to him,
Each Spring to him,
And worship the trousers that cling
    to him–
Bewitched, bothered and bewildered am I.
When he talks he is seeking
Words to get off his chest.
Horizontally speaking,
He's at his very best.
Vexed again,
Perplexed again,
Thank God I can be oversexed again–
Bewitched, bothered and bewildered am I.

REFRAIN 3
Sweet again,
Petite again,
And on my proverbial seat again–
Bewitched, bothered and bewildered am I.
What am I?
Half shot am I.
To think that he loves me,
So hot am I–
Bewitched, bothered and bewildered am I.
Though at first we said, "No, sir,"
Now we're two little dears.

You might say we are closer
Than Roebuck is to Sears.
I'm dumb again
And numb again,
A rich, ready, ripe little plum again–
Bewitched, bothered and bewildered am I.

ENCORE
You know,
It is really quite funny
Just how quickly he learns
How to spend all the money
That Mr. Simpson earns.
He's kept enough,
He's slept enough,
And yet where it counts
He's adept enough–
Bewitched, bothered and bewildered am I.

REPRISE
Wise at last,
My eyes at last
Are cutting you down to your size at last–
Bewitched, bothered and bewildered
    no more.
Burned a lot,
But learned a lot,
And now you are broke, though you
    earned a lot–
Bewitched, bothered and bewildered
    no more.
Couldn't eat–
Was dyspeptic,
Life was so hard to bear;
Now my heart's antiseptic,
Since you moved out of there.
Romance–finis;
Your chance–finis;
Those ants that invaded my pants–finis–
Bewitched, bothered and bewildered
    no more.

–Richard Rodgers

Blue Moon

VERSE I

Once upon a time,
Before I took up smiling,
I hated the moonlight!
Shadows of the night
That poets find beguiling
Seemed flat as the moonlight.
With no one to stay up for,
I went to sleep at ten.
Life was a bitter cup for
The saddest of all men.

REFRAIN

Blue moon,
You saw me standing alone,
Without a dream in my heart,
Without a love of my own.
Blue moon,
You knew just what I was there for,
You heard me saying a prayer for
Someone I really could care for.
And then there suddenly appeared
    before me
The only one my arms will ever hold.
I heard somebody whisper, "Please
    adore me,"
And when I looked,
The moon had turned to gold!
Blue moon,
Now I'm no longer alone,
Without a dream in my heart,
Without a love of my own.

VERSE 2

Once upon a time,
My heart was just an organ,
My life had no mission.
Now that I have you,
To be as rich as Morgan
Is my one ambition.

Once I awoke at seven,
Hating the morning light.
Now I awake in Heaven
And all the world's all right.

REPEAT REFRAIN

—Richard Rodgers

The Blue Room

VERSE I

All my future plans,
Dear, will suit your plans.
Read the little blueprints.
Here's your mother's room.
Here's your brother's room.
On the wall are two prints.
Here's the kiddies' room,
Here's the biddy's room,
Here's a pantry lined with shelves, dear.
Here I've planned for us
Something grand for us,
Where we two can be ourselves, dear.

REFRAIN

We'll have a blue room,
A new room
For two room,
Where ev'ry day's a holiday
Because you're married to me.
Not like a ballroom,
A small room,
A hall room,
Where I can smoke my pipe away
With your wee head upon my knee.
We will thrive on,
Keep alive on,
Just nothing but kisses,
With Mister and Missus
On little blue chairs.
You sew your trousseau,

And Robinson Crusoe
Is not so far from worldly cares
As our blue room far away upstairs.

VERSE 2
From all visitors
And inquisitors
We'll keep our apartment.
I won't change your plans–
You arrange your plans
Just the way your heart meant.
Here we'll be ourselves
And we'll see ourselves
Doing all the things we're scheming.
Here's a certain place,
Cretonne curtain place,
Where no one can see us dreaming.

REPEAT REFRAIN

—*Richard Rodgers*

DANCING ON THE CEILING

VERSE
The world is lyrical
Because a miracle
Has brought my lover to me!
Though he's some other place,
His face I see.
At night I creep in bed
And never sleep in bed,
But look above in the air.
And to my greatest joy,
My boy is there!
It is my prince who walks
Into my dreams and talks.

REFRAIN
He dances overhead
On the ceiling, near my bed;
In my sight

Through the night.
I try to hide in vain
Underneath my counterpane;
There's my love
Up above.
I whisper, "Go away, my lover,
It's not fair."
But I'm so grateful to discover
He's still there.
I love my ceiling more
Since it is the dancing floor
Just for
My love.

—*Richard Rodgers*

FALLING IN LOVE WITH LOVE

VERSE
I weave with brightly colored strings
To keep my mind off other things;
So, ladies, let your fingers dance,
And keep your hands out of romance.
Lovely witches,
Let the stitches
Keep your fingers under control.
Cut the thread, but leave
The whole heart whole.
Merry maids can sew and sleep;
Wives can only sew and weep!

REFRAIN
Falling in love with love
Is falling for make-believe.
Falling in love with love
Is playing the fool.
Caring too much is such
A juvenile fancy.
Learning to trust is just
For children in school.
I fell in love with love
One night when the moon was full.

I was unwise, with eyes
Unable to see.
I fell in love with love,
With love everlasting,
But love fell out with me.

—Richard Rodgers

GLAD TO BE UNHAPPY

VERSE
Look at yourself.
If you had a sense of humor,
You would laugh to beat the band.
Look at yourself.
Do you still believe the rumor
That romance is simply grand?
Since you took it right
On the chin,
You have lost that bright
Toothpaste grin.
My mental state is all a-jumble.
I sit around and sadly mumble.

REFRAIN
Fools rush in, so here I am,
Very glad to be unhappy.
I can't win, but here I am,
More than glad to be unhappy.
Unrequited love's a bore,
And I've got it pretty bad.
But for someone you adore,
It's a pleasure to be sad.
Like a straying baby lamb
With no mammy and no pappy,
I'm so unhappy,
But oh, so glad.

—Richard Rodgers

HAVE YOU MET MISS JONES?

VERSE
It happened–I felt it happen.
I was awake–I wasn't blind.
I didn't think–I felt it happen,
Now I believe in matter over mind.
And now you see we mustn't wait.
The nearest moment that we marry is
    too late!

REFRAIN
"Have you met Miss Jones?"
Someone said as we shook hands.
She was just Miss Jones to me.
Then I said, "Miss Jones,
You're a girl who understands
I'm a man who must be free."
And all at once I lost my breath,
And all at once was scared to death,
And all at once I owned the earth and sky!
Now I've met Miss Jones,
And we'll keep on meeting till we die,
Miss Jones and I.

—Richard Rodgers

HE WAS TOO GOOD TO ME

VERSE
There goes my young intended.
The thing is ended.
Regrets are vain.
I'll never find another half so sweet.
I was a good sport,
Told him
Good-bye,
Eyes dim,
But why
Complain?

He was too good to me–
How can I get along now?
So close he stood to me–
Ev'rything seems all wrong now!
He would have brought me the sun.
Making me smile–
That was his fun!
When I was mean to him,
He'd never say, "Go 'way now."
I was a queen to him.
Who's goin' to make me gay now?
It's only natural I'm blue.
He was too good to be true.

–Richard Rodgers

I DIDN'T KNOW WHAT TIME IT WAS

VERSE I
Once I was young–
Yesterday, perhaps–
Danced with Jim and Paul
And kissed some other chaps.
Once I was young,
But never was naïve.
I thought I had a trick or two
Up my imaginary sleeve.
And now I know I was naïve.

REFRAIN
I didn't know what time it was,
Then I met you.
Oh, what a lovely time it was,
How sublime it was, too!
I didn't know what day it was.
You held my hand.
Warm like the month of May it was,
And I'll say it was grand.
Grand to be alive, to be young,

To be mad, to be yours alone!
Grand to see your face, feel your
  touch,
Hear your voice say I'm all your own.
I didn't know what year it was.
Life was no prize.
I wanted love and here it was
Shining out of your eyes.
I'm wise,
And I know what time it is now.

VERSE 2
Once I was old–
Twenty years or so–
Rather well preserved:
The wrinkles didn't show.
Once I was old,
But not too old for fun.
I used to hunt for little girls
With my imaginary gun.
But now I aim for only one!

REPEAT REFRAIN

–Richard Rodgers

I WISH I WERE IN LOVE AGAIN

VERSE
You don't know that I felt good
When we up and parted.
You don't know I knocked on wood,
Gladly brokenhearted.
Worrying is through,
I sleep all night,
Appetite and health restored.
You don't know how much I'm bored.

REFRAIN I
The sleepless nights,
The daily fights,

The quick toboggan when you reach the
   heights–
I miss the kisses and I miss the bites.
I wish I were in love again!
The broken dates,
The endless waits,
The lovely loving and the hateful hates,
The conversation with the flying plates–
I wish I were in love again!
No more pain,
No more strain,
Now I'm sane, but . . .
I would rather be gaga!
The pulled-out fur
Of cat and cur,
The fine mismating of a him and her–
I've learned my lesson, but I wish
   I were
In love again!

REFRAIN 2
The furtive sigh,
The blackened eye,
The words "I'll love you till the day I die,"
The self-deception that believes
   the lie–
I wish I were in love again.
When love congeals
It soon reveals
The faint aroma of performing seals,
The double-crossing of a pair of heels.
I wish I were in love again!
No more care.
No despair.
I'm all there now,
But I'd rather be punch-drunk!
Believe me, sir,
I much prefer
The classic battle of a him and her.
I don't like quiet and I wish I were
In love again!

—*Richard Rodgers*

IT NEVER ENTERED MY MIND

VERSE
I don't care if there's powder on my nose.
I don't care if my hairdo is in place.
I've lost the very meaning of repose.
I never put a mud pack on my face.
Oh, who'd have thought
That I'd walk in a daze now?
I never go to shows at night,
But just to matinees now.
I see the show
And home I go.

REFRAIN I
Once I laughed when I heard you saying
That I'd be playing solitaire,
Uneasy in my easy chair.
It never entered my mind.
Once you told me I was mistaken,
That I'd awaken with the sun
And order orange juice for one.
It never entered my mind.
You have what I lack myself,
And now I even have to scratch my back
   myself.
Once you warned me that if you
   scorned me
I'd sing the maiden's prayer again
And wish that you were there again
To get into my hair again.
It never entered my mind.

REFRAIN 2
Once you said in your funny lingo
I'd sit at bingo day and night
And never get the numbers right.
It never entered my mind.
Once you told me I'd stay up Sunday
To read the Monday-morning dirt
And find you're merging with some skirt.
It never entered my mind.

Life is not so sweet alone.
The man who came to dinner lets me eat
    alone.
I confess it–I didn't guess it,
That I would sit and mope again,
And all the while I'd hope again
To see my darling dope again.
It never entered my mind!

—*Richard Rodgers*

IT'S GOT TO BE LOVE

VERSE I
SHE: I love your eyes,
    But I wouldn't know the color.
    Aquamarine
    Or em'rald green?
    And if your hair
    Couldn't possibly be duller,
    The shade I see
    Looks gold to me.
    That's how naïve I've grown to be.
    Mais oui.

REFRAIN I
It's got to be love!
It couldn't be tonsillitis;
It feels like neuritis,
But nevertheless it's love.
Don't tell me the pickles and pie à la mode
They served me,
Unnerved me,
And made my heart a broken-down pump.
It's got to be love!
It isn't the morning after
That makes every rafter
Go spinning around above.
I'm sure that it's fatal, or why do I get
That sinking feeling?
I think that I'm dead,
But nevertheless it's only love.

VERSE 2
HE: It's got to be love!
    It could have been fallen arches
    Or too many starches,
    But nevertheless it's love.
    Don't tell me the lamp in the
        barbershop
    Gave me sunstroke.
    With one stroke
    You made me feel like
        yesterday's hash.

REFRAIN 2
It's got to be love!
It couldn't be indigestion.
Beyond any question
I'm fluttery as a dove.
I've heard people say it's no worse than
    a cold,
But, oh, that fever!
I'm burned to a crisp,
But nevertheless it's only love.

—*Richard Rodgers*

I'VE GOT FIVE DOLLARS

VERSE I
HE: Mister Shylock was stingy;
    I was miserly, too.
    I was more selfish
    And crabby than a shellfish.
    Oh, dear, it's queer
    What love can do!
    I'd give all my possessions
    For you.

REFRAIN I
I've got five dollars;
I'm in good condition;
And I've got ambition–
That belongs to you.

Six shirts and collars;
Debts beyond endurance
On my life insurance–
That belongs to you.
I've got a heart
That must be spurtin'!
Just be certain
I'll be true!
Take my five dollars!
Take my shirts and collars!
Take my heart that hollers,
"Ev'rything I've got belongs to you!"

VERSE 2
SHE: Peggy Joyce has a bus'ness;
     All her husbands have gold.
     And Lilyan Tashman
     Is not kissed by an ashman.
     But now, somehow,
     Wealth leaves me cold.
     Though you're poor as a church
        mouse,
     I'm sold!

REFRAIN 2
I've got five dollars;
Eighty-five relations;
Two lace combinations–
They belong to you!
Two coats with collars;
Ma and Grandma wore 'em;
All the moths adore 'em–
They belong to you!
I've got two lips
That care for mating,
Therefore waiting
Will not do!
Take my five dollars!
Take my coats and collars!
Take my heart that hollers,
"Ev'rything I've got belongs to you!"

—*Richard Rodgers*

JOHNNY ONE-NOTE

VERSE
Johnny could only sing one note
And the note he sang was this:
Ah!

REFRAIN I
Poor Johnny One-Note
Sang out with gusto
And just overlorded the place.
Poor Johnny One-Note
Yelled willy-nilly
Until he was blue in the face–
For holding one note was his ace.
Couldn't hear the brass,
Couldn't hear the drum.
He was in a class
By himself, by gum.
Poor Johnny One-Note
Got in *Aïda*–
Indeed a great chance to be brave.
He took his one note,
Howled like the North Wind–
Brought forth wind that made
     critics rave,
While Verdi turned 'round in his grave!
Couldn't hear the flute
Or the big trombone.
Ev'ryone was mute.
Johnny stood alone.

TRIO
Cats and dogs stopped yapping,
Lions in the zoo
All were jealous of Johnny's big trill.
Thunderclaps stopped clapping,
Traffic ceased its roar,
And they tell us Niag'ra stood still.
He stopped the train whistles,
Boat whistles,
Steam whistles,

Cop whistles,
All whistles bowed to his skill.

REFRAIN 2

Sing, Johnny One-Note,
Sing out with gusto
And just overwhelm all the crowd.
Ah!
So sing, Johnny One-Note, out loud!
Sing, Johnny One-Note!
Sing, Johnny One-Note, out loud!

THE LADY IS A TRAMP

VERSE

I've wined and dined on Mulligan stew
And never wished for turkey
As I hitched and hiked and grifted, too,
From Maine to Albuquerque.
Alas, I missed the Beaux Arts Ball,
And what is twice as sad,
I was never at a party
Where they honored Noël Ca'ad.
But social circles spin too fast for me.
My Hobohemia is the place to be.

REFRAIN 1

I get too hungry for dinner at eight.
I like the theater, but never come late.
I never bother with people I hate.
That's why the lady is a tramp.
I don't like crap games with barons and
    earls.
Won't go to Harlem in ermine and pearls.
Won't dish the dirt with the rest of the
    girls.
That's why the lady is a tramp.
I like the free, fresh wind in my hair,
Life without care.
I'm broke—it's oke.
Hate California—it's cold and it's damp.
That's why the lady is a tramp.

REFRAIN 2

I go to Coney—the beach is divine.
I go to ball games—the bleachers are fine.
I follow Winchell and read ev'ry line.
That's why the lady is a tramp.
I like a prizefight that isn't a fake.
I love the rowing on Central Park Lake.
I go to opera and stay wide awake.
That's why the lady is a tramp.
I like the green grass under my shoes.
What can I lose?
I'm flat! That's that!
I'm all alone when I lower my lamp.
That's why the lady is a tramp.

REFRAIN 3

Don't know the reason for cocktails
    at five.
I don't like flying—I'm glad I'm alive.
I crave affection, but not when I drive.
That's why the lady is a tramp.
Folks go to London and leave me behind.
I'll miss the crowning, Queen Mary
    won't mind.
I don't play Scarlett in *Gone With
    the Wind.*
That's why the lady is a tramp.
I like to hang my hat where I please.
Sail with the breeze.
No dough—heigh-ho!
I love La Guardia and think he's a champ.
That's why the lady is a tramp.

REFRAIN 4

Girls get massages, they cry and
    they moan.
Tell Lizzie Arden to leave me alone.
I'm not so hot, but my shape is my own.
That's why the lady is a tramp!
The food at Sardi's is perfect, no doubt.
I wouldn't know what the Ritz is about.
I drop a nickel and coffee comes out.
That's why the lady is a tramp!

I like the sweet, fresh rain in my face.
Diamonds and lace,
No got—so what?
For Robert Taylor I whistle and stamp.
That's why the lady is a tramp!

—Richard Rodgers

LITTLE GIRL BLUE

REFRAIN
Sit there and count your fingers.
What can you do?
Old girl, you're through.
Sit there and count your little fingers,
Unlucky little girl blue.
Sit there and count the raindrops
Falling on you.
It's time you knew
All you can count on is the raindrops
That fall on little girl blue.
No use, old girl,
You may as well surrender.
Your hope is getting slender.
Why won't somebody send a tender
Blue boy, to cheer a
Little girl blue?

TRIO PATTER
When I was very young
The world was younger than I,
As merry as a carousel.
The circus tent was strung
With ev'ry star in the sky
Above the ring I loved so well.
Now the world has grown old.
Gone are the tinsel and gold.

REPEAT REFRAIN

—Richard Rodgers

MANHATTAN

VERSE
Summer journeys to Niag'ra
And to other places aggra-
Vate all our cares.
We'll save our fares!
I've a cozy little flat in
What is known as old Manhattan,
We'll settle down
Right here in town!

REFRAIN I
We'll have Manhattan,
The Bronx and Staten
Island too.
It's lovely going through
The zoo.
It's very fancy
On old Delancey
Street, you know.
The subway charms us so
When balmy breezes blow
To and fro.
And tell me what street
Compares with Mott Street
In July?
Sweet pushcarts gently gliding by.
The great big city's a wondrous toy
Just made for a girl and boy.
We'll turn Manhattan
Into an isle of joy.

REFRAIN 2
We'll go to Greenwich,
Where modern men itch
To be free;
And Bowling Green you'll see
With me.
We'll bathe at Brighton;
The fish you'll frighten
When you're in.

Your bathing suit so thin
Will make the shellfish grin,
Fin to fin.
I'd like to take a
Sail on Jamaica
Bay with you.
And fair Canarsie's lake
We'll view.
The city's bustle cannot destroy
The dreams of a girl and boy.
We'll turn Manhattan
Into an isle of joy.

REFRAIN 3
We'll go to Yonkers
Where true love conquers
In the wilds.
And starve together, dear,
In Childs.
We'll go to Coney
And eat baloney
On a roll.
In Central Park we'll stroll,
Where our first kiss we stole,
Soul to soul.
Our future babies
We'll take to *Abie's*
Irish Rose.
I hope they'll live to see
It close.
The city's clamor can never spoil
The dreams of a boy and goil.
We'll turn Manhattan
Into an isle of joy.

REFRAIN 4
We'll have Manhattan,
The Bronx and Staten
Island too.
We'll try to cross
Fifth Avenue.
As black as onyx
We'll find the Bronnix

Park Express.
Our Flatbush flat, I guess,
Will be a great success,
More or less.
A short vacation
On Inspiration Point
We'll spend,
And in the station house we'll end.
But Civic Virtue cannot destroy
The dreams of a girl and boy.
We'll turn Manhattan
Into an isle of joy.

—*Richard Rodgers*

THE MOST BEAUTIFUL GIRL IN THE WORLD

VERSE
We used to spend the Spring
  together
Before we learned to walk;
We used to laugh and sing together
Before we learned how to talk.
With no reason for the season,
Spring would end as it would start.
Now the season has a reason
And there's Springtime in my
  heart.

REFRAIN
The most beautiful girl in the world
Picks my ties out,
Eats my candy,
Drinks my brandy—
The most beautiful girl in the world.
The most beautiful girl in the world
Isn't Garbo, isn't Dietrich,
But the sweet trick
Who can make me believe it's a beautiful
  world.
Social—not a bit.

Nat'ral kind of wit.
She'd shine anywhere.
And she hasn't got platinum hair.
The most beautiful house in the world
Has a mortgage–
What do I care?
It's good-bye care
When my slippers are next to the ones
    that belong
To the one and only beautiful girl in the
    world!

    —Richard Rodgers

MOUNTAIN GREENERY

VERSE I

HE: On the first of May
    It is moving day;
    Spring is here, so blow your job–
    Throw your job away.
    Now's the time to trust
    To your wanderlust.
    In the city's dust you wait.
    Must you wait?
    Just you wait:

REFRAIN I

In a mountain greenery
Where God paints the scenery–
Just two crazy people together.
While you love your lover, let
Blue skies be your coverlet–
When it rains we'll laugh at the
    weather.
And if you're good
I'll search for wood,
So you can cook
While I stand looking.
Beans could get no keener re-
Ception in a beanery.
Bless our mountain greenery home!

VERSE 2

SHE: Simple cooking means
    More than French cuisines;
    I've a banquet planned which is
    Sandwiches and beans.
    Coffee's just as grand
    With a little sand.
    Eat and you'll grow fatter, boy.
    S'matter, boy?
    'Atta boy!

REFRAIN 2

In a mountain greenery
Where God paints the scenery–
Just two crazy people together.
How we love sequestering
Where no pests are pestering–
No dear mama holds us in tether!
Mosquitoes here
Won't bite you, dear;
I'll let them sting
Me on the finger.
We could find no cleaner re-
Treat from life's machinery
Than our mountain greenery home!

    —Richard Rodgers

MY FUNNY VALENTINE

VERSE

Behold the way our fine-feathered
    friend
His virtue doth parade.
Thou knowest not, my dim-witted
    friend,
The picture thou hast made.
Thy vacant brow and thy tousled hair
Conceal thy good intent.
Thou noble, upright, truthful,
    sincere,
And slightly dopey gent–you're . . .

REFRAIN

My funny valentine,
Sweet comic valentine,
You make me smile with my heart.
Your looks are laughable,
Unphotographable,
Yet you're my fav'rite work of art.
Is your figure less than Greek?
Is your mouth a little weak?
When you open it to speak
Are you smart?
But don't change a hair for me,
Not if you care for me,
Stay, little valentine, stay!
Each day is Valentine's Day.

—Richard Rodgers

Until the thrill
Of that moment when
My heart stood still.

VERSE 2

SHE: Through all my school days
    I hated boys;
    Those April Fool days
    Brought me loveless joys.
    I read my Plato,
    Love I thought a sin.
    But since your kiss
    I'm reading Missus Glyn!

REPEAT REFRAIN

Richard Rodgers

MY HEART STOOD STILL

VERSE I

HE: I laughed at sweethearts
    I met at schools;
    All indiscreet hearts
    Seemed romantic fools.
    A house in Iceland
    Was my heart's domain.
    I saw your eyes;
    Now castles rise in Spain!

REFRAIN

I took one look at you,
That's all I meant to do,
And then my heart stood still!
My feet could step and walk,
My lips could move and talk,
And yet my heart stood still!
Though not a single word was spoken,
I could tell you knew.
That unfelt clasp of hands
Told me so well you knew.
I never lived at all

MY ROMANCE

VERSE

I won't kiss your hand, madam,
Crazy for you though I am.
I'll never woo you on bended knee,
No, madam, not me.
We don't need that flow'ry fuss.
No, sir, madam, not for us.

REFRAIN

My romance
Doesn't have to have a moon in the sky.
My romance
Doesn't need a blue lagoon standing by.
No month of May,
No twinkling stars.
No hideaway,
No soft guitars.
My romance
Doesn't need a castle rising in Spain,
Nor a dance
To a constantly surprising refrain.
Wide awake,

I can make
My most fantastic dreams come true.
My romance
Doesn't need a thing but you.

—Richard Rodgers

Nobody's Heart

REFRAIN

Nobody's heart belongs to me,
Heigh-ho, who cares?
Nobody writes his songs to me,
No one belongs to me–
That's the least of my cares.
I may be sad at times,
And disinclined to play,
But it's not bad at times
To go your own sweet way.
Nobody's arms belong to me,
No arms feel strong to me.
I admire the moon
As a moon,
Just a moon.
Nobody's heart belongs to me today.

INTERLUDE

Ride, Amazon, ride.
Hunt your stags and bears.
Take life in its stride.
Heigh-ho! Who cares?
Go hunting with pride,
Track bears to their lairs.
Ride, Amazon, ride.
Heigh-ho, who cares?

REPEAT LAST SIX LINES OF REFRAIN

COMIC REPRISE

Nobody's heart belongs to me.
Heigh-ho, that's bad.
Love's never sung her songs to me–

No one belongs to me.
I have never been had.
I've had no trial in the game of man
    and maid.
I'm like a violin that no one's ever played.
Words about love are Greek to me.
Nice girls won't speak to me.
I despise the moon
As a moon,
It's a prune.
Nobody's heart belongs to me today.

—Richard Rodgers

A Ship Without a Sail

VERSE I

I don't know what day it is,
Or if it's dark or fair.
Somehow that's just the way it is,
And I don't really care.
I go to this or that place,
I seem alive and well.
My head is just a hat place,
My breast an empty shell!
And I've a faded dream to sell.

REFRAIN

All alone, all at sea!
Why does nobody care for me?
When there's no love to hold my love,
Why is my heart so frail,
Like a ship without a sail?
Out on the ocean
Sailors can use a chart.
I'm on the ocean
Guided by just a lonely heart.
Still alone, still at sea!
Still there's no one to care for me.
When there's no hand to hold my hand
Life is a loveless tale
For a ship without a sail.

VERSE 2

When love leaves you all alone,
You're living in the past.
Then you feel so small alone,
And oh, the world seems vast.
You tell your grief to no girls;
You never make it known.
Your smile is like a showgirl's,
Your laugh a hollow tone.
And then your little heart's a stone.

REPEAT REFRAIN

—*Richard Rodgers*

Spring Is Here

VERSE

Once there was a thing called Spring,
When the world was writing verses
Like yours and mine.
All the lads and girls would sing
When we sat at little tables
And drank May wine.
Now April, May, and June
Are sadly out of tune.
Life has stuck the pin in the balloon.

REFRAIN

Spring is here!
Why doesn't my heart go dancing?
Spring is here!
Why isn't the waltz entrancing?
No desire,
No ambition leads me.
Maybe it's because
Nobody needs me.
Spring is here!
Why doesn't the breeze delight me?
Stars appear!
Why doesn't the night invite me?
Maybe it's because

Nobody loves me.
Spring is here, I hear!

—*Richard Rodgers*

Ten Cents a Dance

VERSE

I work at the Palace Ballroom,
But gee, that Palace is cheap;
When I get back to my chilly hall room
I'm much too tired to sleep.
I'm one of those lady teachers,
A beautiful hostess, you know,
The kind the Palace features
For only a dime a throw.

REFRAIN

Ten cents a dance—
That's what they pay me;
Gosh, how they weigh me down!
Ten cents a dance—
Pansies and rough guys,
Tough guys who tear my gown!
Seven to midnight, I hear drums.
Loudly the saxophone blows.
Trumpets are tearing my eardrums.
Customers crush my toes.
Sometimes I think
I've found my hero,
But it's a queer romance.
All that you need is a ticket.
Come on, big boy, ten cents a dance!

PATTER

Fighters and sailors and bowlegged
    tailors
Can pay for their tickets and rent me!
Butchers and barbers and rats from the
    harbors
Are sweethearts my good luck has sent me.
Though I've a chorus of elderly beaux,

Stockings are porous with holes at
    the toes.
I'm here till closing time.
Dance and be merry, it's only a dime.

TAG

Sometimes I think
I've found my hero,
But it's a queer romance.
All that you need is a ticket.
Come on, big boy, ten cents a dance!

—Richard Rodgers

THERE'S A SMALL HOTEL

VERSE

I'd like to get away, Junior,
Somewhere alone with you.
It could be oh, so gay, Junior!
You need a laugh or two.
A certain place I know, Frankie,
Where funny people can have fun.
That's where we two will go, darling,
Before you can count up
One, two, three.
For . . .

REFRAIN

There's a small hotel
With a wishing well;
I wish that we were there
Together.
There's a bridal suite,
One room bright and neat,
Complete for us to share
Together.
Looking through the window
You can see a distant steeple.
Not a sign of people.
Who wants people?
When the steeple bell

Says, "Good night, sleep well,"
We'll thank the small hotel
Together.

INTERLUDE

Pretty window curtains made of chintz
In our make-believe land.
On the wall are sev'ral cheerful prints
Of Grant and Grover Cleveland.
Go down into the parlor and feast your
    eyes
On the moose head on the wall.
Perhaps you'd like to play the organ—
They tune it ev'ry other fall.
The garden will be like
Adam and Eve land.
No, they never did go in for carriage trade;
They get what is known as marriage trade.

CODA

Oh, when the steeple bell
Says, "Good night, sleep well,"
We'll thank the small hotel,
We'll creep into our little shell,
And we will thank the small hotel
Together.

—Richard Rodgers

THIS CAN'T BE LOVE

VERSE I

HE: In Verona, my late cousin Romeo
    Was three times as stupid as my
        Dromio.
    For he fell in love
    And then he died of it.
    Poor half-wit!

REFRAIN

This can't be love
Because I feel so well—

No sobs, no sorrows, no sighs.
This can't be love,
I get no dizzy spell,
My head is not in the skies.
My heart does not stand still—
Just hear it beat!
This is too sweet
To
Be
Love.
This can't be love
Because I feel so well,
But still I love to look in your eyes.

VERSE 2
SHE: Though your cousin loved my cousin
          Juliet,
      Loved her with a passion much more
          truly yet,
      Some poor playwright
      Wrote their drama just for fun.
      It won't run!

REPEAT REFRAIN

COMIC REPRISE
This must be love,
For I don't feel so well—
These sobs, these sorrows, these sighs.
This must be love,
Here comes that dizzy spell,
My head is up in the skies.
Just now my heart stood still—
It missed a beat!
Life is not sweet—
This
Is
Love.
This must be love,
For I don't feel so well.
Alas, I love to look in your eyes.

          —Richard Rodgers

THIS FUNNY WORLD

VERSE
A mop! A broom! A pail!
The stuff my dreams are made of!
You hope, you strive, you fail!
The world's a place you're not afraid of.
But soon you are brought down to earth,
And you learn what your dream was worth.

REFRAIN
This funny world
Makes fun of the things that you strive for.
This funny world
Can laugh at the dreams you're alive for.
If you're beaten, conceal it!
There's no pity for you,
For the world cannot feel it.
Just keep to yourself.
Weep to yourself.
This funny world
Can turn right around and forget you.
It's always sure
To roll right along when you're through.
If you are broke you shouldn't mind.
It's all a joke, for you will find
This funny world is making fun of you.

          —Richard Rodgers

THOU SWELL

VERSE I
Babe, we are well met,
As in a spell met—
I lift my helmet.
Sandy,
You're just dandy
For just this here lad.
You're such a fistful,
My eyes are mistful—

Are you too wistful
To care?
Do say you care
To say, "Come near, lad."
You are so graceful–
Have you wings?
You have a face full
Of nice things.
You have no speaking voice, dear.
With ev'ry word it sings.

REFRAIN

Thou swell!
Thou witty!
Thou sweet!
Thou grand!
Wouldst kiss me, pretty?
Wouldst hold my hand?
Both thine eyes are cute, too–
What they do to me.
Hear me holler
I choose a
Sweet lolla-
Palooza
In thee.
I'd feel so rich in
A hut for two.
Two rooms and kitchen
I'm sure would do.
Give me just a plot of,
Not a lot of, land,
And,
Thou swell!
Thou witty!
Thou grand!

VERSE 2

Thy words are queer, sir,
Unto mine ear, sir,
Yet thou'rt a dear, sir,
To me.
Thou couldst woo me.
Now couldst thou try, knight.

I'd murmur, "Swell," too,
And like it well, too.
More thou wilt tell to
Sandy.
Thou art dandy.
Now art thou my knight.
Thine arms are martial,
Thou hast grace.
My cheek is partial
To thy face.
And if thy lips grow weary,
Mine are their resting place.

REPEAT REFRAIN

–*Richard Rodgers*

TO KEEP MY LOVE ALIVE

VERSE

I've been married and married,
And often I've sighed,
I'm never a bridesmaid,
I'm always the bride.
I never divorced them–
I hadn't the heart.
Yet remember these sweet words
"Till death do us part."

REFRAIN 1

I married many men,
A ton of them,
And yet I was untrue to none of them
Because I bumped off ev'ry one of them
To keep my love alive.
Sir Paul was frail;
He looked a wreck to me.
At night he was a horse's neck to me.
So I performed an appendectomy
To keep my love alive.
Sir Thomas had insomnia;
He couldn't sleep at night.

I bought a little arsenic.
He's sleeping now all right.
Sir Philip played the harp;
I cussed the thing.
I crowned him with his harp
To bust the thing.
And now he plays where harps are
Just the thing,
To keep my love alive,
To keep my love alive.

REFRAIN 2

I thought Sir George had possibilities,
But his flirtations made me ill at ease.
And when I'm ill at ease,
I kill at ease
To keep my love alive.
Sir Charles came from a sanatorium
And yelled for drinks
In my emporium.
I mixed one drink—
He's in memoriam
To keep my love alive.
Sir Francis was a singing bird,
A nightingale. That's why
I tossed him off my balcony,
To see if he could fly.
Sir Athelstane indulged in fratricide;
He killed his dad and that was patricide.
One night I stabbed him at my
    mattress side
To keep my love alive,
To keep my love alive.

ENCORE REFRAINS

I caught Sir James with his protectress,
The rector's wife, I mean the rectoress.
His heart stood still—angina pectoris
To keep my love alive.
Sir Frank brought ladies to my palaces.
I poured a mickey in their chalices.
While paralyzed they got paralysis
To keep my love alive.

Sir Alfred worshipped falconry;
He used to hunt at will.
I sent him on a hunting trip.
They're hunting for him still.
Sir Peter had an incongruity,
Collecting girls with promiscuity.
Now I'm collecting his annuity
To keep my love alive,
To keep my love alive.
Sir Ethelbert would use profanity;
His language drove me near insanity.
So once again I served humanity
To keep my love alive.
Sir Curtis made me cook each dish he ate,
And ev'rything his heart could wish
    he ate,
Until I fiddled with the fish he ate
To keep my love alive.
Sir Marmaduke was awf'lly tall;
He didn't fit in bed.
I solved that problem easily—
I just removed his head.
Sir Mark adored me with formality;
He called a kiss an immorality.
And so I gave him immortality
To keep my love alive,
To keep my love alive.

—*Richard Rodgers*

WAIT TILL YOU SEE HER

VERSE

My friends who knew me
Never would know me,
They'd look right through me,
Above and below me,
And ask, "Who's that man?
Who is that man?
That's not my lighthearted friend!"
Meeting one girl
Was the start of the end.

Love is a simple emotion
A friend should comprehend.

REFRAIN
Wait till you see her,
See how she looks,
Wait till you hear her laugh.
Painters of paintings,
Writers of books,
Never could tell the half.
Wait till you feel
The warmth of her glance,
Pensive and sweet and wise.
All of it lovely,
All of it thrilling,
I'll never be willing to free her.
When you see her
You won't believe your eyes.

—*Richard Rodgers*

WHERE OR WHEN

VERSE
When you're awake, the things you think
Come from the dreams you dream.
Thought has wings, and lots of things
Are seldom what they seem.
Sometimes you think you've lived before
All that you live today.
Things you do come back to you,
As though they knew the way.
Oh, the tricks your mind can play!

REFRAIN
It seems we stood and talked like this
    before.
We looked at each other in the same
    way then,
But I can't remember where or when.
The clothes you're wearing are the clothes
    you wore,

The smile you are smiling you were
    smiling then,
But I can't remember where or when.
Some things that happen for the first time
Seem to be happening again.
And so it seems that we have met before,
And laughed before,
And loved before,
But who knows where or when!

—*Richard Rodgers*

WITH A SONG IN MY HEART

VERSE I
Though I know that we meet ev'ry
    night
And we couldn't have changed since the
    last time,
To my joy and delight,
It's a new kind of love at first sight.
Though it's you and it's I all the time,
Ev'ry meeting's a marvelous pastime.
You're increasingly sweet,
So whenever we happen to meet
I greet you . . .

REFRAIN
With a song in my heart
I behold your adorable face.
Just a song at the start,
But it soon is a hymn to your grace.
When the music swells
I'm touching your hand;
It tells that you're standing near, and . . .
At the sound of your voice
Heaven opens its portals to me.
Can I help but rejoice
That a song such as ours came to be?
But I always knew
I would live life through
With a song in my heart for you.

VERSE 2

Oh, the moon's not a moon for a night
And these stars will not twinkle and
    fade out,
And the words in my ears
Will resound for the rest of my years.
In the morning I'll find with delight
Not a note of our music is played out.
It will be just as sweet,
And an air that I'll live to repeat:
I greet you . . .

REPEAT REFRAIN

—Richard Rodgers

You Are Too Beautiful

VERSE

Like all fools, I believed
What I wanted to believe.
My foolish heart conceived
What foolish hearts conceive.
I thought I found a miracle;
I thought that you'd adore me.
But it was not a miracle,
It was merely a mirage before me.

REFRAIN

You are too beautiful, my dear, to be true,
And I am a fool for beauty.
Fooled by a feeling that
Because I had found you,
I could have bound you, too.
You are too beautiful for one man alone,
For one lucky fool to be with,
When there are other men
With eyes of their own to see with.
Love does not stand sharing,
Not if one cares.
Have you been comparing
My ev'ry kiss with theirs?

If, on the other hand,
I'm faithful to you,
It's not through a sense of duty.
You are too beautiful
And I am a fool for beauty.

—Richard Rodgers

You Took Advantage of Me

VERSE I

HE: In the Spring when the feeling was
    chronic
    And my caution was leaving you flat,
    I should have made use of the tonic
    Before you gave me *that*!
    A mental deficient you'll grade me.
    I've given you plenty of data.
    You came, you saw and you
      slayed me,
    And that-a, is that-a!

REFRAIN

I'm a sentimental sap, that's all.
What's the use of trying not to fall?
I have no will,
You've made your kill
'Cause you took advantage of me!
I'm just like an apple on a bough
And you're gonna shake me down
    somehow.
So what's the use,
You've cooked my goose
'Cause you took advantage of me!
I'm so hot and bothered that I don't know
My elbow from my ear.
I suffer something awful each time you go
And much worse when you're near.
Here am I with all my bridges burned,
Just a babe in arms where you're
    concerned,
So lock the doors

And call me yours
'Cause you took advantage of me.

VERSE 2

SHE: When a girl has the heart of a mother
  It must go to someone, of course;
  It can't be a sister or brother,
  And so I loved my horse.
  But horses are frequently silly–
  Mine ran from the beach of Kailua
  And left me alone for a filly,
  So I-a picked you-a.

REPEAT REFRAIN

—*Richard Rodgers*

ZIP

VERSE

I've interviewed Leslie Howard.
I've interviewed Noël Coward.
I've interviewed the great Stravinsky.
But my greatest achievement
Is the interview I had
With a star who worked for Minsky.
I met her at the Yankee Clipper
And she didn't unzip one zipper.
I said, "Miss Lee, you are such an artist.
Tell me why you never miss.
What do you think of while you work?"
And she said, "While I work
My thoughts go something like this."

REFRAIN 1

Zip! Walter Lippmann wasn't brilliant
  today.
Zip! Will Saroyan ever write a great play?
Zip! I was reading Schopenhauer last night.
Zip! And I think that Schopenhauer was
  right.
I don't want to see Zorina.

I don't want to meet Cobina.
Zip! I'm an intellectual.
I don't like a deep contralto,
Or a man whose voice is alto.
Zip! I'm a heterosexual.
Zip! It took intellect to master my art.
Zip! Who the hell is Margie Hart?

REFRAIN 2

Zip! I consider Dalí's paintings passé.
Zip! Can they make the Metropolitan
  pay?
Zip! English people don't say clerk, they
  say clark.
Zip! Anybody who says clark is a jark!
I have read the great Kabala
And I simply worship Allah.
Zip! I am just a mystic.
I don't care for Whistler's Mother,
Charlie's Aunt or Shubert's brother.
Zip! I'm misogynistic.
Zip! My intelligence is guiding my hand.
Zip! Who the hell is Sally Rand?

REFRAIN 3

Zip! Toscanini leads the greatest of
  bands.
Zip! Jergen's Lotion does the trick for his
  hands.
Zip! Rip Van Winkle on the screen would
  be smart.
Zip! Tyrone Power will be cast in the
  part.
I adore the great Confucius
And the lines of luscious Lucius.
Zip! I am so eclectic.
I don't care for either Mickey–
Mouse and Rooney make me sicky!
Zip! I'm a little hectic.
Zip! My artistic taste is classic and dear.
Zip! Who the hell's Lili St. Cyr?

—*Richard Rodgers*

Irving Caesar (1895–1996)

THE ETERNAL AND IRREPRESSIBLE Irving Caesar of New York wrote two of the most famous songs of the twenties, and seventy years later he was still talking about them. In 1919 he collaborated with the pre-Ira George Gershwin on "Swanee," made into a giant hit by Al Jolson when he interpolated it into his show *Sinbad.* Then, in 1925, for Vincent Youmans's *No, No, Nanette,* he wrote "Tea for Two," so deceptively simple yet so charmingly intricate; it may well be the most performed song of its period. Of course, he had other important songs as well: the "happy" songs, "Sometimes I'm Happy" and "I Want to Be Happy"; a Dixie number for Jolson that became a number-one hit for Jimmy Dorsey, "Is It True What They Say About Dixie?"; with Ted Koehler, Shirley Temple's "Animal Crackers in My Soup"; and with Jimmy Durante, Durante's trademark "Umbriago." But he'll always be first and foremost the man who thought up the words "Tea for two and two for tea. . . ." As over the years—the decades—he went on telling the story, the time it took him to write his lyric grew shorter and shorter, until it was down to two minutes . . .

ANIMAL CRACKERS IN MY SOUP

(with Ted Koehler)

VERSE

Once mother said: "My little pet,
You ought to learn the alphabet."
So in my soup I used to get
All the letters of the alphabet.
I learned them all from A to Z,
And now my mother's giving me . . .

REFRAIN

Animal crackers in my soup,
Monkeys and rabbits loop the loop.
Gosh, oh gee, but I have fun,
Swallowin' animals one by one.
In ev'ry bowl of soup I see
Lions and tigers watching me.
I make 'em jump right through a hoop,
Those animal crackers in my soup.

When I get hold of the "Big bad wolf,"
I just push him under to drown.
Then I bite him in a million bits,
And I gobble him right down.
When they're inside me where it's dark,
I walk aroun' like "Noah's ark."
I stuff my tummy like a "Goop,"
With animal crackers in my soup.

—Ray Henderson

CRAZY RHYTHM

VERSE I

I feel like the Emperor Nero
When Rome was a very hot town;
Father Knickerbocker, forgive me,
I play while your city burns down.
Through all its nightlife I fiddle away,

It's not the right life, but think of the pay.
Someday I will bid it good-bye,
I'll put my fiddle away
And I'll say:

REFRAIN

Crazy rhythm, here's the doorway,
I'll go my way, you'll go your way.
Crazy rhythm, from now on
We're through.
Here is where we have a showdown,
I'm too high hat, you're too low down,
Crazy rhythm, here's good-bye
To you.
They say that
When a highbrow meets a lowbrow
Walking along Broadway,
Soon the highbrow,
He has no brow,
Ain't it a shame,
And you're to blame.
What's the use of Prohibition?
You produce the same condition.
Crazy rhythm,
I've gone crazy, too.

VERSE 2

Ev'ry Greek, each Turk and each Latin,
The Russians and Prussians as well;
When they seek the lure of Manhattan,
Are sure to come under your spell.
Their native folk songs they soon throw
    away,
Those Harlem smoke songs, they soon
    learn to play.
Can't you fall for Carnegie Hall?
Oh, Danny, call it a day
And we'll say:

REPEAT REFRAIN

—*Joseph Meyer and Roger Wolfe Kahn*

I WANT TO BE HAPPY

VERSE 1

HE: I'm a very ordinary man,
    Trying to work out life's happy plan,
    Doing unto others as I'd like to have
        them doing unto me.
    When I find a very lonely soul,
    To be kind becomes my only goal,
    I feel so much better when I tell them
        my philosophy.

REFRAIN

I want to be happy,
But I won't be happy
Till I make you happy, too.
Life's really worth living
When we are mirth giving,
Why can't I give some to you?
When skies are gray
And you say you are blue,
I'll send the sun smiling through.
I want to be happy,
But I won't be happy
Till I make you happy, too.

VERSE 2

SHE: No one ever talked like that to me,
    I have never known such sympathy,
    Only in my dreams.
    It really seems to me it's too good to
        be true.
    There are smiling faces ev'rywhere,
    Surely I deserve my little share,
    I'm a lucky girl to know that I can get
        it all from you.

REPEAT REFRAIN

—*Vincent Youmans*

Is It True What They Say About Dixie?

(with Sammy Lerner)

VERSE

People brag,
People boast,
And consistently drink a toast
To a place
That a lot of them place
At the top of the list–
Are they wrong?
Are they right?
Is there reason for their
    delight?
I must live in doubt
Till the day that I find out.

REFRAIN

Is it true
What they say
About Dixie?
Does the sun
Really shine
All the time?
Do the sweet magnolias
    blossom
At ev'rybody's door?
Do folks keep eating possum
Till they can't eat no more?
Is it true
What they say
About Swannee?
Is a dream
By that stream
So sublime?
Do they laugh,
Do they love,
Like they say
In ev'ry song?
If it's true,

That's where I
Belong.

–Gerald Marks

Just a Gigolo

(Original German lyric by
Julius Brammer)

VERSE

'Twas in a Paris café that first I found him.
He was a Frenchman, a hero of the war.
But war was over, and here's how peace
    had crowned him,
A few cheap medals to wear, and
    nothing more.
Now ev'ry night in this same café you'll
    find him,
And as he strolls by, the ladies hear
    him say,
"If you admire me,
Please hire me,
A gigolo who knew a better day.

REFRAIN

Just a gigolo,
Ev'rywhere I go,
People know the part I'm playing.
Paid for ev'ry dance,
Selling each romance,
Ev'ry night some heart betraying.
There will come a day,
Youth will pass away,
Then what will they say
About me?
When the end comes I know
They'll say 'Just a gigolo,'
As life goes on without me."

–Leonello Casucci

SOMETIMES I'M HAPPY

VERSE I

HE: Ev'ry day seems like a year,
   Sweetheart, when you are not near.
SHE: All that you claim must be true
   For I'm just the same as you:

REFRAIN

Sometimes I'm happy,
Sometimes I'm blue,
My disposition
Depends on you.
I never mind
The rain from the skies,
If I can find
The sun in your eyes.
Sometimes I love you,
Sometimes I hate you,
But when I hate you,
It's 'cause I love you.
That's how I am,
So what can I do?
I'm happy when I'm with you.

VERSE 2

HE: Stars are smiling at me from
   your eyes.
SHE: Sunbeams now there will be in the
   skies.
HE: Tell me that you will be true!
SHE: That will all depend on you, dear!

REPEAT REFRAIN

—*Vincent Youmans*

SPANISH JAKE

(with Sammy Lerner)

VERSE

Land of fandangoes,
Where all the gang goes hotcha,
Land of the sweet muchacha
And of the sweet refrain.
There you will find a sort of a kind of
   loafer,
All of the tourists go for,
When they arrive in Spain.

REFRAIN I

In company his manner's grand,
Upon his knee he'll kiss your hand
And when your rings are gone, make no
   mistake,
Blame Spanish Jake.
He sends you flow'rs, you get a thrill;
But with the thrill you get a bill.
And in the zoo you'll never meet a
   snake
Like Spanish Jake.
His reputation's black as ink is,
He and his half-brother Pincus,
They have guns with many notches—
That's from swatting those cucarochas.
What a man and what a life,
He says someday he'll take a wife.
But he forgets to say whose wife
   he'll take,
That's Spanish Jake.

REFRAIN 2

Six feet tall from shoes to hat,
Without a hat he's half of that.
So if you meet a worm, make no
   mistake,
That's Spanish Jake.
A medal hangs upon his chest,

He got it when he bought the rest,
So if you want to meet the
    latest fake,
Meet Spanish Jake.
He is on a rigid diet,
Eats food only when you buy it.
Even bulls refuse to fight him,
They're afraid that he's gonna
    bite 'em.
He would play a steel guitar
If he could steal a steel guitar.
He's got the kind of neck you'd like to
    break,
That's Spanish Jake.

—Gerald Marks

TEA FOR TWO

VERSE I

I'm discontented
With homes that are rented
So I have invented
My own.
Darling, this place is
A lover's oasis,
Where life's weary chase is
Unknown.
Far from the cry of the city,
Where flowers pretty
Caress the streams,
Cozy to hide in,
To live side by side in,
Don't let it abide in
My dreams.

REFRAIN

Picture you upon my knee,
Just tea for two and two for tea,
Just me for you and you for me alone.
Nobody near us to see us or hear us,

No friends or relations on weekend
    vacations,
We won't have it known, dear,
That we own a telephone, dear.
Day will break and you'll awake
And start to bake a sugar cake
For me to take for all the boys to see.
We will raise a family,
A boy for you, a girl for me,
Oh can't you see how happy we would be?

VERSE 2

You are revealing
A plan so appealing
I can't help but feeling
For you.
Darling, I planned;
Can't you understand, it
Is yours to command it,
So do.
All of your schemes I'm admiring,
They're worth desiring;
But can't you see,
I'd like to wait, dear,
For some future date, dear.
It won't be too late, dear,
For me.

REPEAT REFRAIN

—Vincent Youmans

TOO MANY RINGS AROUND ROSIE

VERSE I

In an early childhood day,
When December seemed like May,
Ring around a Rosie with the boys I used
    to play.
Tommy, Andy, Harold, Joe,
Ate my candy, then would go.

I tried to please them all, you know,
That's why not one became my beau.

REFRAIN

REFRAIN

Too many rings around Rosie
Will never get Rosie a ring.
Too many beaux when she should
    have one,
You know will never bring her
A ring around her finger.
One little name to remember
Is better than having a string.
It doesn't hurt to flirt a bit but use it as
    bait.
Make your catch, make your match before
    it's too late.

For too many rings around Rosie
Will never get Rosie a ring.

VERSE 2

Men are only grown-up boys,
Pretty ladies are their toys,
Here today, tomorrow they're in search of
    other joys.
It is nice to have a few
To go loco over you.
Still, one ring to call your own
Is worth a dozen on the phone.

REPEAT REFRAIN

—*Vincent Youmans*

Oscar Hammerstein II (1895–1960)

HIS GRANDFATHER, the first Oscar Hammerstein, was an important New York opera impresario; his uncle was a producer; his father, William, was a well-known theater manager. But Oscar II handily outstripped them both in success, fame, and importance in theatrical history. After attending Columbia College, the young Hammerstein went into the theater and soon was writing lyrics and librettos. His first major success (in collaboration with Otto Harbach, Herbert Stothart, and Vincent Youmans) was *Wildflower,* and there followed a string of successful operettas—*Rose-Marie, The Desert Song, The New Moon.* And, of course, *Show Boat,* in 1927, for which he wrote the book as well as the lyrics (reworking P. G. Wodehouse's "Bill" for Helen Morgan). He had already worked with Jerome Kern on *Sunny,* and after *Show Boat* they went on to *Sweet Adeline* and *Music in the Air,* among others, but his career was in general decline in the thirties. Nineteen forty-three began not only his most successful period but the most commercially successful collaboration in American musical history—the partnership with Richard Rodgers: *Oklahoma!,* as revolutionary as *Show Boat* had been sixteen years earlier; *Carousel, South Pacific, The King and I, The Sound of Music,* et al., plus the movie *State Fair.* Hammerstein's simple and sincere lyrics, carefully wrought, if at times edging toward corniness, reflected the late-war and post-war mood of America and have kept their power over us; through endless revivals and school productions of his shows, through movies and records, Hammerstein's words—for "Ol' Man River," "Oh, What a Beautiful Mornin'!," and all the others—are imprinted on our minds. He is the great transitional figure in the American musical, carrying us from operetta to the integrated musical, and bridging the generations from Romberg and Kern to his extraordinary protégé, Stephen Sondheim.

ALL ER NOTHIN'

VERSE

HE: You'll have to be a little more
    standoffish
    When fellers offer you a
    buggy ride.
SHE: I'll give a imitation of a crawfish
    And dig myself a hole where I
    can hide.

HE: I heard how you was kickin' up some
    capers
    When I was off in Kansas City, Mo.
    I heard some things you couldn't
    print in papers
    From fellers who been talkin' like
    they know!
SHE: Foot!
    I only did the kind of things I orta,
    Sorta.

To you I was as faithful as c'n be,
Fer me.
Them stories 'bout the way I lost my
    bloomers,
Rumors!
A lot of tempest in a pot o' tea!
HE: The whole thing don't sound very
    good to me.
SHE: Well, y' see.

HE: PATTER:
I go and sow my last wild oat!
I cut out all shenanigans!
I save my money, don't gamble or
    drink
In the back room down at
    Flannigans!
I give up lotsa other things
A gentleman never mentions,
But before I give up any more,
I wanta know your intentions!

REFRAIN 1
HE: With me it's all er nuthin'.
Is it all er nuthin' with you?
It cain't be "in between,"
It cain't be "now and then,"
No half-and-half romance will do.
I'm a one-woman man,
Home-lovin' type,
All complete with slippers and pipe.
Take me like I am, er leave me be!
If you cain't give me all, give me
    nuthin',
And nuthin's whut you'll git
    from me!
SHE: Not even sump'n?
HE: Nuthin's whut you'll git from me!

REFRAIN 2
SHE: With you it's all er nuthin'.
All fer you and nuthin' fer me!
But if a wife is wise,

She's gotta realize
That men like you are wild and free.
So I ain't gonna fuss,
Ain't gonna frown,
Have your fun, go out on the town,
Stay up late and don't come home till
    three.
And go right off to sleep if you're
    sleepy,
There's no use waitin' up fer me!
HE: Oh, Ado Annie!
SHE: No use waitin' up fer me.

REFRAIN 3
SHE: It cain't be "in between"?
HE: Uh-uh.
SHE: It cain't be "now and then"?
HE: No half-and-half romance will do!
SHE: Would you build me a house,
    All painted white,
    Cute and clean and purty and
    bright?
HE: Big enough fer two but not fer
    three!
SHE: Supposin' 'at we should have a
    third one?
HE: He better look a lot like me!
SHE: The spit an' image!
HE: He better look a lot like me!

—*Richard Rodgers*

ALL THE THINGS YOU ARE

VERSE
Time and again I've longed for adventure,
Something to make my heart beat the
    faster.
What did I long for?
I never really knew.
Finding your love I've found my
    adventure,

Touching your hand, my heart beats the
    faster.
All that I want in all of this world is you.

REFRAIN

You are the promised kiss of springtime
That makes the lonely winter seem long.
You are the breathless hush of evening
That trembles on the brink of a
    lovely song.
You are the angel glow
That lights a star,
The dearest things I know
Are what you are.
Some day my happy arms will hold you,
And some day I'll know that moment
    divine,
When all the things you are,
Are mine!

—Jerome Kern

CAN'T HELP LOVIN' DAT MAN

VERSE I

Oh, listen, sister,
I love my mister man,
And I can't tell yo' why.
Dere ain't no reason
Why I should love dat man—
It mus' be sumpin' dat de angels
    done plan.

REFRAIN

Fish got to swim, birds got to fly,
I got to love one man till I die—
Can't help lovin' dat man of mine.
Tell me he's lazy, tell me he's slow,
Tell me I'm crazy (maybe I know)—
Can't help lovin' dat man of mine.
When he goes away
Dat's a rainy day,

But when he comes back dat day is fine,
De sun will shine!
He kin come home as late as kin be,
Home widout him ain't no home to me—
Can't help lovin' dat man of mine.

VERSE 2

Mah man is shif'less
An' good for nuthin' too
(He's mah man jes' de same).
He's never round here
When dere is work to do—
He's never round here when dere's
    workin' to do.
De chimbley's smokin',
De roof is leakin' in,
But he don' seem to care.
He kin be happy
Wid jes' a sip of gin—
Ah even love him when his kisses got gin!

REPEAT REFRAIN

Jerome Kern

DAT'S LOVE
(HABANERA)

Love's a baby dat grows up wild,
An' he don' do what you want him to;
Love ain' nobody's angel child,
An' he won' pay any mind to you.
One man gives me his diamon' stud,
An' I won' give him a cigarette.
One man treats me like I was mud—
An' what I got dat man c'n get.
Dat's love!
Dat's love!
Dat's love!
Dat's love!
You go for me
An' I'm taboo,

But if yo're hard to get, I go for you,
An' if I do,
Den you are through, boy,
My baby, dat's de end of you.
So take your cue, boy,
Don' say I didn' tell you true.
I tol' you true,
I tol' you truly,
If I love you dat's de end of you!
When your lovebird decides to fly,
Dere ain' no door dat you c'n close.
She jus' pecks you a quick good-bye
An' flicks de salt from her tail, an' goes.
If you listen, den you'll get taught,
An' here's your lesson for today:
If I chase you, den you'll get caught,
But once I got you I go my way!
Dat's love!
Dat's love!
Dat's love!
Dat's love!

REPEAT REFRAIN

—Georges Bizet

DON'T EVER LEAVE ME

VERSE

I was created for one man alone;
He wasn't easy to find.
Now that I found him, I wonder just how
I could have lived
Right up to now.
Now I am something completed by you,
I am not one,
Just part of two.

REFRAIN

Don't ever leave me,
Now that you're here!
Here is where you belong.

Ev'rything seems so right when
   you're near,
When you're away it's all wrong.
I'm so dependent,
When I need comfort
I always run to you.
Don't ever leave me!
'Cause if you do,
I'll have no one to run to.

—Jerome Kern

THE FOLKS WHO LIVE ON THE HILL

VERSE

Many men with lofty aims
Strive for lofty goals.
Others play at smaller games,
Being simpler souls.
I am of the latter brand;
All I want to do
Is to find a spot of land
And live there with you.

REFRAIN

Someday
We'll build a home on a hilltop high,
You and I,
Shiny and new,
A cottage that two can fill.
And we'll be pleased to be called
"The folks who live on the hill."
Someday
We may be adding a thing or two,
A wing or two—
We will make changes
As any fam'ly will.
But we will always be called
"The folks who live on the hill."
Our veranda
Will command a

View of meadows green,
The sort of view that seems to want to
    be seen.
And when the kids grow up and leave us,
We'll sit and look at that same old view,
Just we two–
Darby and Joan, who used to be Jack
    and Jill,
The folks who like to be called
What they have always been called–
"The folks who live on the hill."

–Jerome Kern

THE GENTLEMAN IS A DOPE

VERSE

The boss gets on my nerves,
I've got a good mind to quit.
I've taken all I can,
It's time to get up and git
And move to another job.
Or maybe another town!
The gentleman burns me up!
The gentleman gets me down!

REFRAIN

The gentleman is a dope–
A man of many faults,
A clumsy Joe
Who wouldn't know
A rumba from a waltz.
The gentleman is a dope,
And not my cup of tea.
Why do I get in a dither?
He doesn't belong to me!
The gentleman isn't bright,
He doesn't know the score.
A cake will come,
He'll take a crumb
And never ask for more!
The gentleman's eyes are blue,

But little do they see.
Why am I beating my brains out?
He doesn't belong to me!
He's somebody else's problem,
She's welcome to the guy!
She'll never understand him
Half as well as I.
The gentleman is a dope–
He isn't very smart,
He's just a lug
You'd like to hug
And hold against your heart.
The gentleman doesn't know
How happy he could be.
Look at me! Crying my eyes out,
As if he belonged to me.
He'll never belong to me!

–Richard Rodgers

HAPPY TALK

REFRAIN I

Happy talk,
Keep talkin' happy talk,
Talk about things you'd like to do.
You gotta have a dream;
If you don't have a dream,
How you gonna have a dream
    come true?

VERSE I

Talk about a moon
Floatin' in de sky,
Lookin' like a lily on a lake.
Talk about a bird
Learnin' how to fly,
Makin' all de music he can make.

REFRAIN 2

Happy talk,
Keep talkin' happy talk,

Talk about things you'd like to do.
You gotta have a dream;
If you don't have a dream,
How you gonna have a dream come true?

VERSE 2
Talk about a star
Lookin' like a toy,
Peekin' t'rough de branches of a tree.
Talk about a girl,
Talk about a boy,
Countin' all de ripples on de sea.

REFRAIN 3
Happy talk,
Keep talkin' happy talk,
Talk about things you'd like to do.
You gotta have a dream;
If you don't have a dream,
How you gonna have a dream come true?

VERSE 3
Talk about a boy
Sayin' to a girl:
"Golly, baby! I'm a lucky cuss!"
Talk about de girl
Sayin' to de boy:
"You an' me is lucky to be us!"

REFRAIN 4
Happy talk,
Keep talkin' happy talk,
Talk about things you'd like to do.
You gotta have a dream;
If you don't have a dream,
How you gonna have a dream come true?
If you don't talk happy
An' you never have a dream,
Den you'll never have a dream
    come true.

—*Richard Rodgers*

HELLO, YOUNG LOVERS

VERSE
When I think of Tom
I think about a night
When the earth smelled of summer
And the sky was streaked with white,
And the soft mist of England
Was sleeping on a hill–
I remember this,
And I always will . . .
There are new lovers now on the same
    silent hill,
Looking on the same blue sea,
And I know Tom and I are a part of them all,
And they're all a part of Tom and me.

REFRAIN
Hello, young lovers, whoever you are,
I hope your troubles are few.
All my good wishes go with you tonight–
I've been in love like you.
Be brave, young lovers, and follow
    your star,
Be brave and faithful and true.
Cling very close to each other tonight–
I've been in love like you.
I know how it feels to have wings on your
    heels,
And to fly down the street in a trance.
You fly down a street on the chance that
    you'll meet,
And you meet–not really by chance.
Don't cry, young lovers, whatever you do,
Don't cry because I'm alone;
All of my memories are happy tonight,
I've had a love of my own,
I've had a love of my own, like yours–
I've had a love of my own.

—*Richard Rodgers*

I Cain't Say No

VERSE

It ain't so much a question of not knowin'
  whut to do,
I knowed whut's right and wrong since I
  been ten.
I heared a lot of stories–and I reckon they
  are true–
About how girls're put upon by men.
I know I mustn't fall into the pit,
But when I'm with a feller–I fergit!

REFRAIN 1

I'm jist a girl who cain't say no,
I'm in a turrible fix.
I always say, "Come on, let's go!"
Jist when I orta say nix!
When a person tries to kiss a girl
I know she orta give his face a smack.
But as soon as someone kisses me,
I somehow sorta wanta kiss him back.
I'm jist a fool when lights are low.
I cain't be prissy and quaint–
I ain't the type thet c'n faint–
How c'n I be whut I ain't?
I cain't say no!

TRIO

Whut you goin' to do when a feller gits flirty
And starts to talk purty?
Whut you goin' to do?
S'posin' 'at he says 'at yer lips're like
  cherries,
Er roses, er berries?
Whut you goin' to do?
S'posin' 'at he says 'at you're sweeter'n
  cream
And he's gotta have cream er die?
Whut you goin' to do when he talks
  thet way?
Spit in his eye?

REFRAIN 2

I'm jist a girl who cain't say no,
Cain't seem to say it at all.
I hate to disserpoint a beau
When he is payin' a call.
Fer a while I ack refined and cool,
A-settin' on the velveteen settee.
Nen I think of thet o' golden rule,
And do fer him whut he would do fer me.
I cain't resist a Romeo
In a sombrero and chaps.
Soon as I sit on their laps
Somethin' inside of me snaps–
I cain't say no!

REFRAIN 3

I'm jist a girl who cain't say no,
Kissin's my favorite food.
With er without the mistletoe
I'm in a holiday mood.
Other girls are coy and hard to catch,
But other girls ain't havin' any fun.
Ev'ry time I lose a wrestlin' match
I have a funny feelin' that I won.
Though I c'n feel the undertow,
I never make a complaint
Till it's too late fer restraint,
Then when I want to I cain't,
I cain't say no!

—Richard Rodgers

I'll Take Romance

I'll take romance,
While my heart is young and eager to fly,
I'll give my heart a try,
I'll take romance.
I'll take romance,
While my arms are strong and eager
  for you,
I'll give my arms their cue,

I'll take romance.
So, my lover, when you want me, call me,
In the hush of the evening.
When you call me,
In the hush of the evening,
I'll rush to my first real romance,
While my heart is young and eager
    and gay,
I'll give my heart away,
I'll take romance.
I'll take my own romance.

—Ben Oakland

IF I LOVED YOU

VERSE I

When I worked in the mill,
Weavin' at the loom,
I'd gaze absentminded at the roof,
And half the time the shuttle 'd tangle in
    the threads,
And the warp 'd get mixed with
    the woof.
If I loved you!
Oh, somehow I can see
Just exackly how I'd be.

REFRAIN

If I loved you,
Time and again I would try to say
All I'd want you to know.
If I loved you,
Words wouldn't come in an easy way,
'Round in circles I'd go.
Longin' to tell you, but afraid and shy,
I'd let my golden chances pass me by!
Soon you'd leave me,
Off you would go in the mist of day,
Never, never to know
How I loved you,
If I loved you.

VERSE 2

Kinda scrawny and pale,
Pickin' at my food
And lovesick like any other guy,
I'd throw away my sweater and dress up
    like a dude
In a dickey and a collar and a tie.
If I loved you!
And I know I would be
Like you said you'd be with me.

REPEAT REFRAIN

—Richard Rodgers

IT MIGHT AS WELL BE SPRING

VERSE

The things I used to like
I don't like anymore,
I want a lot of other things
I've never had before.
It's just like Mother says,
I "sit around and mope"
Pretending I am wonderful
And knowing I'm a dope.

REFRAIN

I'm as restless as a willow in a windstorm,
I'm as jumpy as a puppet on a string!
I'd say that I had Spring fever,
But I know it isn't Spring.
I am starry-eyed and vaguely discontented,
Like a nightingale without a song to sing.
Oh, why should I have Spring fever
When it isn't even Spring?
I keep wishing I were somewhere else,
Walking down a strange new street,
Hearing words that I have never heard
From a man I've yet to meet.
I'm as busy as a spider, spinning
    daydreams,

I'm as giddy as a baby on a swing.
I haven't seen a crocus or a rosebud
Or a robin on the wing,
But I feel so gay—in a melancholy way—
That it might as well be Spring . . .
It might as well be Spring.

—Richard Rodgers

I'VE TOLD EV'RY LITTLE STAR

VERSE
I make up things to say
On my way to you,
On my way to you,
I find things to say.
I can write poems too,
When you're far away,
When you're far away,
I write poems, too.
But when you are near, my lips go dry, ·
When you are near, I only sigh
Oh, dear.

REFRAIN
I've told ev'ry little star
Just how sweet I think you are—
Why haven't I told you?
I've told ripples in a brook,
Made my heart an open book—
Why haven't I told you?
Friends ask me
Am I in love,
I always answer "Yes."
(Might as well confess;
If I don't, they guess.)
Maybe you may know it, too—
Oh, my darling, if you do,
Why haven't you told me, dear?
Why haven't you told me?

—Jerome Kern

JUNE IS BUSTIN' OUT ALL OVER

VERSE
March went out like a lion,
A-whippin' up the water in the bay.
Then April cried
And stepped aside
And along came pretty little May!
May was full of promises,
But she didn't keep 'em quick enough
　　fer some,
And a crowd of doubtin' Thomases
Was predictin' that the Summer'd
　　never come.
But it's comin', by gum,
Y' ken feel it come!
Y' ken feel it in yer heart,
Y' ken see it in the ground.
Y'ken hear it in the trees,
Y' ken smell it in the breeze.
Look around, look around, look around!

REFRAIN I
June is bustin' out all over!
All over the meadow and the hill,
Buds're bustin' outa bushes,
And the rompin' river pushes
Ev'ry little wheel that wheels beside a mill.
June is bustin' out all over!
The feelin' is gettin' so intense
That the young Virginia creepers
Hev been huggin' the bejeepers
Outa all the mornin' glories on the fence.
Because it's June!
June, June, June—
Jest because it's June, June, June!
Fresh and alive and gay and young,
June is a love song sweetly sung.

REFRAIN 2
June is bustin' out all over!
The saplin's are bustin' out with sap!

Love has found my brother, "Junior,"
And my sister's even loonier,
And my ma is gettin' kittenish with Pap.
June is bustin' out all over!
To ladies the men are payin' court.
Lotsa ships are kept at anchor
Jest because the captains hanker
Fer a comfort they ken only get in port!
Because it's June!
June, June, June—
Jest because it's June, June, June!
June makes the bay look bright and new,
Sails gleamin' white on sunlit blue.

REFRAIN 3

June is bustin' out all over!
The ocean is full of Jacks and Jills.
With her little tail a-swishin'
Ev'ry lady fish is wishin'
That a male would come and grab her by
    the gills!
June is bustin' out all over!
The sheep aren't sleepin' any more.
All the rams that chase the ewe sheep
Are determined there'll be new sheep,
And the ewe sheep aren't even keepin'
    score!
On accounta it's June!
June, June, June—
Jest because it's June—June—June!

—Richard Rodgers

THE LAST TIME I SAW PARIS

VERSE 1

A lady known as Paris,
Romantic and charming,
Has left her old companions
And faded from view.
Lonely men with lonely eyes are seeking
    her in vain,

Her streets are where they were,
But there's no sign of her.
She has left the Seine.

REFRAIN

The last time I saw Paris
Her heart was warm and gay,
I heard the laughter of her heart
In ev'ry street café.
The last time I saw Paris
Her trees were dressed for Spring,
And lovers walked beneath those trees,
And birds found songs to sing.
I dodged the same old taxicabs
That I had dodged for years;
The chorus of their squeaky horns
Was music to my ears.
The last time I saw Paris
Her heart was warm and gay.
No matter how they change her,
I'll remember her that way.

VERSE 2

I'll think of happy hours,
And people who shared them:
Old women selling flowers
In markets at dawn,
Children who applauded Punch and Judy
    in the park,
And those who danced at night,
And kept their Paris bright
Till the town went dark.

REPEAT REFRAIN

—Jerome Kern

LOVER, COME BACK TO ME!

VERSE

You went away, I let you,
We broke the ties that bind;

I wanted to forget you
And leave the past behind.
Still, the magic of the night I met you
Seems to stay forever in my mind.

REFRAIN

REFRAIN

The sky was blue,
And high above
The moon was new,
And so was love.
This eager heart of mine was singing:
"Lover, where can you be?"
You came at last,
Love had its day,
That day is past.
You've gone away.
This aching heart of mine is singing:
"Lover, come back to me!"
When I remember
Ev'ry little thing you used to do,
I'm so lonely.
Ev'ry road I walk along
I've walked along with you,
No wonder I am lonely.
The sky is blue,
The night is cold,
The moon is new,
But love is old,
And while I'm waiting here
This heart of mine is singing:
"Lover, come back to me!"

—*Sigmund Romberg*

MAKE BELIEVE

VERSE

The game of "just supposing"
Is the sweetest game I know,
Our dreams are more romantic
Than the world we see.
And if the things we dream about

Don't happen to be so,
That's just an unimportant technicality.

REFRAIN

We could make believe I love you,
Only make believe that you love me.
Others find peace of mind in pretending;
Couldn't you? Couldn't I? Couldn't we
Make believe our lips are blending
In a phantom kiss, or two, or three?
Might as well make believe I love you,
For, to tell the truth, I do.

INTERLUDE

Your pardon I pray,
'Twas too much to say,
The words that betray my heart.
We only pretend,
You do not offend,
In playing a lover's part.

—*Jerome Kern*

MANY A NEW DAY

VERSE

Why should a woman who is healthy and
    strong
Blubber like a baby if her man goes away?
A-weepin' and a-wailin' how he's done her
    wrong—
That's one thing you'll never hear me say!
Never gonna think that the man I lose
Is the only man among men.
I'll snap my fingers to show I don't care.
I'll buy me a brand-new dress to wear.
I'll scrub my neck and I'll brush my hair,
And start all over again!

REFRAIN I

Many a new face will please my eye,
Many a new love will find me.

Never've I once looked back to sigh
Over the romance behind me.
Many a new day will dawn before I do!
Many a light lad may kiss and fly,
A kiss gone by is bygone;
Never've I asked an August sky,
"Where has last July gone?"
Never've I wandered through the rye,
Wonderin' where has some guy gone—
Many a new day will dawn before I do!

REFRAIN 2
Many a new face will please my eye,
Many a new love will find me.
Never've I once looked back to sigh
Over the romance behind me.
Many a new day will dawn before I do!
Never've I chased the honeybee
Who carelessly cajoled me;
Somebody else just as sweet as he
Cheered me and consoled me.
Never've I wept into my tea
Over the deal someone doled me—
Many a new day will dawn,
Many a red sun will set,
Many a blue moon will shine before
    I do!

—*Richard Rodgers*

MISTER SNOW

VERSE
His name is Mister Snow,
And an upstandin' man is he.
He comes home ev'ry night in his round-
    bottomed boat
With a net full of herring from the sea.
An almost perfect beau,
As refined as a girl could wish,
But he spends so much time in his round-
    bottomed boat

That he can't seem to lose the smell
    of fish.
The fust time he kissed me, the whiff of
    his clo'es
Knocked me flat on the floor of the room.
But now that I love him, my heart's in
    my nose,
And fish is my fav'rite perfume.
Last night he spoke quite low,
And a fair-spoken man is he,
And he said, "Miss Pipperidge, I'd like
    it fine
If I could be wed with a wife.
And, indeed, Miss Pipperidge, if you'll
    be mine,
I'll be yours fer the rest of my life."
Next moment we were promised
And now my mind's in a maze,
Fer all I ken do is look forward to
That wonderful day of days . . .

REFRAIN
When I marry Mister Snow,
The flowers'll be buzzin' with the hum
    of bees,
The birds'll make a racket in the
    churchyard trees,
When I marry Mister Snow.
Then it's off to home we'll go,
And both of us'll look a little dreamy-eyed,
A-drivin' to a cottage by the oceanside
Where the salty breezes blow.
He'll carry me 'cross the threshold,
And I'll be as meek as a lamb.
Then he'll set me on my feet,
And I'll say, kinda sweet:
"Well, Mister Snow, here I am!"
Then I'll kiss him so he'll know
That ev'rythin'll be as right as right
    ken be,
A-livin' in a cottage by the sea with me,
For I love that Mister Snow—
That young, seafarin', bold and darin',

Big, bewhiskered, overbearin' darlin',
   Mister Snow!

    —Richard Rodgers

My Favorite Things

Raindrops on roses and whiskers on
   kittens,
Bright copper kettles and warm woolen
   mittens,
Brown paper packages tied up with
   strings—
These are a few of my favorite things.
Cream-colored ponies and crisp apple
   strudels,
Doorbells and sleigh bells and schnitzel
   with noodles,
Wild geese that fly with the moon on their
   wings—
These are a few of my favorite things.
Girls in white dresses with blue satin
   sashes,
Snowflakes that stay on my nose and
   eyelashes,
Silver-white winters that melt into
   springs—
These are a few of my favorite things.
When the dog bites,
When the bee stings,
When I'm feeling sad,
I simply remember my favorite things
And then I don't feel so bad!

    —Richard Rodgers

Oh, What a Beautiful Mornin'!

VERSE 1

There's a bright, golden haze on the
   meadow,

There's a bright, golden haze on the
   meadow.
The corn is as high as a elephant's eye,
An' it looks like it's climbin' clear up to
   the sky.

REFRAIN

Oh, what a beautiful mornin'!
Oh, what a beautiful day!
I got a beautiful feelin'
Ev'rythin's goin' my way.

VERSE 2

All the cattle are standin' like statues,
All the cattle are standin' like statues.
They don't turn their heads as they see me
   ride by,
But a little brown mav'rick is winkin'
   her eye.

REPEAT REFRAIN

VERSE 3

All the sounds of the earth are like
   music—
All the sounds of the earth are like
   music.
The breeze is so busy it don't miss a tree,
And a ol' weepin' willer is laughin' at me.

REPEAT REFRAIN

    —Richard Rodgers

Ol' Man River

VERSE 1

Dere's an ol' man called de Mississippi;
Dat's de ol' man dat I'd like to be!
What does he care if de world's got
   troubles?
What does he care if de land ain't free?

REFRAIN

Ol' Man River,
Dat Ol' Man River,
He mus' know sumpin'
But don' say nuthin',
He jes' keeps rollin',
He keeps on rollin' along.
He don' plant taters,
He don' plant cotton,
An' dem dat plants 'em
Is soon forgotten.
But Ol' Man River,
He jes' keeps rollin' along.
You an' me, we sweat an' strain,
Body all achin' an' racked wid pain—
Tote dat barge!
Lif' dat bale!
Git a little drunk,
An' you land in jail . . .
Ah gits weary
An' sick of tryin';
Ah'm tired of livin'
An' skeered of dyin',
But Ol' Man River,
He jes' keeps rollin' along.

VERSE 2

Colored folks work on de Mississippi,
Colored folks work while de white
    folks play,
Pullin' dem boats from de dawn to
    sunset,
Gittin' no rest till de Judgment Day—

Don' look up
An' don' look down—
You don' dast make
De white boss frown.
Bend your knees
An' bow your head,
An' pull dat rope
Until yo' dead.

Let me go 'way from de Mississippi,
Let me go 'way from de white man boss;
Show me dat stream called de river
    Jordan,
Dat's de ol' stream dat I long to cross.

REPEAT REFRAIN

—*Jerome Kern*

PEOPLE WILL SAY WE'RE IN LOVE

VERSE I

Why do they think up stories that link my
    name with yours?
Why do the neighbors chatter all day,
    behind their doors?
I know a way to prove what they say is quite
    untrue.
Here is the gist, a practical list of "don'ts"
    for you.

REFRAIN I

Don't throw bouquets at me.
Don't please my folks too much.
Don't laugh at my jokes too much.
People will say we're in love!
Don't sigh and gaze at me.
Your sighs are so like mine.
Your eyes mustn't glow like mine.
People will say we're in love!
Don't start collecting things.
Give me my rose and my glove.
Sweetheart, they're suspecting things.
People will say we're in love.

VERSE 2

Some people claim that you are to blame
    as much as I.
Why do you take the trouble to bake my
    fav'rite pie?

Grantin' your wish, I carved our initials on
   the tree!
Jist keep a slice of all the advice you give
   so free.

REFRAIN 2
Don't praise my charm too much.
Don't look so vain with me.
Don't stand in the rain with me.
People will say we're in love!
Don't take my arm too much.
Don't keep your hand in mine.
Your hand feels so grand in mine.
People will say we're in love!
Don't dance all night with me
Till the stars fade from above.
They'll see it's all right with me.
People will say we're in love.

—Richard Rodgers

SHALL WE DANCE?

VERSE
We've just been introduced,
I do not know you well.
But when the music started,
Something drew me to your side.
So many men and girls
Are in each other's arms,
It made me think
We might be
Similarly occupied.

REFRAIN
Shall we dance?
On a bright cloud of music shall we fly?
Shall we dance?
Shall we then say "good night" and mean
   "good-bye?"
Or, perchance

When the last little star has left the sky,
Shall we still be together
With our arms around each other,
And shall you be my new romance?
On the clear understanding
That this kind of thing can happen,
Shall we dance?
Shall we dance?
Shall we dance?

—Richard Rodgers

SOLILOQUY

I wonder what he'll think of me!
I guess he'll call me
"The old man."
I guess he'll think I can lick
Ev'ry other feller's father—
Well, I can!
I bet that he'll turn out to be
The spit an' image
Of his dad,
But he'll have more common sense
Than his puddin'-headed father
Ever had.
I'll teach him to wrassle,
And dive through a wave,
When we go in the mornin's for our swim.
His mother can teach him
The way to behave,
But she won't make a sissy out o' him—
Not him!
Not my boy!
Not Bill . . .
Bill!
My boy, Bill!
(I will see that he's named
After me,
I will!)
My boy, Bill—

He'll be tall
And as tough
As a tree,
Will Bill!
Like a tree he'll grow,
With his head held high
And his feet planted firm on the ground,
And you won't see no-
Body dare to try
To boss him or toss him around!
No pot-bellied, baggy-eyed bully'll toss
    him around!
I don't give a damn what he does
As long as he does what he likes.
He can sit on his tail
Or work on a rail
With a hammer, a-hammerin' spikes.
He can ferry a boat on the river
Or peddle a pack on his back
Or work up and down
The streets of a town
With a whip and a horse and a hack.
He can haul a scow along a canal,
Run a cow around a corral,
Or maybe bark for a carousel–
(Of course it takes talent to do *that* well).
He might be a champ of the
    heavyweights
Or a feller that sells you glue,
Or President of the United States–
That'd be all right, too.
(His mother'd like that. But he
    wouldn't be
President unless he wanted to be!)
Not Bill!
My boy, Bill–
He'll be tall
And as tough
As a tree,
Will Bill!
Like a tree he'll grow,
With his head held high,
And his feet planted firm on the ground,

And you won't see no-
Body dare to try
To boss him or toss him around!
No fat-bottomed, flabby-faced, pot-
    bellied, baggy-eyed bastard'll boss him
    around!
And I'm damned if he'll marry his boss's
    daughter,
A skinny-lipped virgin with blood like
    water,
Who'll give him a peck and call it a kiss
And look in his eyes through a
    lorgnette . . .
Say!
Why am I takin' on like this?
My kid ain't even been born yet! . . .
I can see him
When he's seventeen or so
And startin' in to go
With a girl.
I can give him
Lots o' pointers, very sound,
On the way to get around
Any girl.
I can tell him–
Wait a minute! Could it be?
What the hell! What if he
Is a girl! . . .
Bill!
Oh, Bill! . . .

(What would I do with her? What could I
    do *for* her?
A bum–with no money!)
You can have fun with a son,
But you got to be a *father*
To a girl! . . .
She mightn't be so bad at that–
A kid with ribbons
In her hair,
A kind o' sweet and petite
Little tintype of her mother–
What a pair!

(I can just hear myself braggin'
    about her!)
My little girl,
Pink and white
As peaches and cream is she.
My little girl
Is half again as bright
As girls are meant to be!
Dozens of boys pursue her,
Many a likely lad
Does what he can to woo her
From her faithful dad.
She has a few
Pink and white young fellers of two or
    three–
But my little girl
Gets hungry ev'ry night
And she comes home to me . . .
My little girl!
My little girl!
I got to get ready before she comes,
I got to make certain that she
Won't be dragged up in slums
With a lot o' bums–
Like me!
She's got to be sheltered and fed, and
    dressed
In the best that money can buy!
I never knew how to get money,
But I'll try–
By God! I'll try!
I'll go out and make it
Or steal it or take it
Or die!

—*Richard Rodgers*

SOME ENCHANTED EVENING

Some enchanted evening,
You may see a stranger,
You may see a stranger

Across a crowded room.
And somehow you know,
You know even then,
That somewhere you'll see her again and
    again.
Some enchanted evening
Someone may be laughing,
You may hear her laughing
Across a crowded room–
And night after night,
As strange as it seems,
The sound of her laughter will sing in your
    dreams.
Who can explain it?
Who can tell you why?
Fools give you reasons–
Wise men never try.
Some enchanted evening,
When you find your true love,
When you feel her call you
Across a crowded room–
Then fly to her side
And make her your own,
Or all through your life you may dream all
    alone.
Once you have found her,
Never let her go.
Once you have found her,
Never let her go!

—*Richard Rodgers*

THE SONG IS YOU

I hear music when I look at you,
A beautiful theme of ev'ry dream I
    ever knew.
Down deep in my heart
I hear it play,
I feel it start,
Then melt away.
I hear music when I touch your hand,

A beautiful melody from some
    enchanted land.
Down deep in my heart
I hear it say:
Is this the day?
I alone
Have heard this lovely strain,
I alone
Have heard this glad refrain.
Must it be
Forever inside of me?
Why can't I let it go?
Why can't I let you know?
Why can't I let you know
The song my heart would sing—
That beautiful rhapsody
Of love and youth and spring?
The music is sweet,
The words are true,
The song is you.

—Jerome Kern

THE SOUND OF MUSIC

VERSE

My day in the hills
Has come to an end, I know.
A star has come out
To tell me it's time to go.
But deep in the dark-green shadows
Are voices that urge me to stay.
So I pause and I wait and I listen
For one more sound,
For one more lovely thing
That the hills might say . . .

REFRAIN

The hills are alive
With the sound of music,
With songs they have sung
For a thousand years.

The hills fill my heart
With the sound of music—
My heart wants to sing
Every song it hears.
My heart wants to beat
Like the wings
Of the birds that rise
From the lake to the trees.
My heart wants to sigh
Like a chime that flies
From a church on a breeze,
To laugh like a brook
When it trips and falls
Over stones in its way,
To sing through the night
Like a lark who is learning to pray.
I go to the hills
When my heart is lonely,
I know I will hear
What I've heard before.
My heart will be blessed
With the sound of music
And I'll sing once more.

—Richard Rodgers

THE SURREY WITH THE FRINGE ON TOP

VERSE I

When I take you out tonight with me,
Honey, here's the way it's goin' to be:
You will set behind a team of snow-white
    horses
In the slickest gig you ever see!

REFRAIN I

Chicks and ducks and geese better
    scurry
When I take you out in the surrey,
When I take you out in the surrey with the
    fringe on top.

Watch thet fringe and see how it flutters
When I drive them high-steppin'
    strutters–
Nosey-pokes'll peek through their
    shutters and their eyes will pop!
The wheels are yeller, the upholstery's
    brown,
The dashboard's genuine leather,
With isinglass curtains y' c'n roll
    right down
In case there's a change in the weather.
Two bright side lights winkin' and
    blinkin',
Ain't no finer rig, I'm a-thinkin';
You c'n keep yer rig if you're thinkin' 'at
    I'd keer to swap
Fer that shiny little surrey with the fringe
    on the top.

VERSE 2

Would y' say the fringe was made
    of silk?
Wouldn't have no other kind but silk.
Has it really got a team of snow-white
    horses?
One's like snow–the other's more
    like milk.

REFRAIN 2

All the world'll fly in a flurry
When I take you out in the surrey,
When I take you out in the surrey with the
    fringe on top.
When we hit that road, hell fer leather,
Cats and dogs'll dance in the heather,
Birds and frogs'll sing all together, and the
    toads will hop!
The wind'll whistle as we rattle along,
The cows'll moo in the clover,
The river will ripple out a whispered song,
And whisper it over and over.
Don't you wisht y'd go on ferever?
Don't you wisht y'd go on ferever?

Don't you wisht y'd go on ferever and ud
    never stop?
In that shiny little surrey with the fringe
    on the top.

REFRAIN 3

I can see the stars gittin' blurry
When we ride back home in the surrey,
Ridin' slowly home in the surrey with the
    fringe on top.
I can feel the day gittin' older,
Feel a sleepy head on my shoulder,
Noddin', droppin' close to my shoulder till
    it falls, kerplop!
The sun is swimmin' on the rim of a hill,
The moon is takin' a header,
And jist as I'm thinkin' all the earth is
    still,
A lark'll wake up in the medder . . .
Hush! You bird, my baby's a-sleepin',
Maybe got a dream worth a-keepin'.
Whoa! you team, and jist keep a-creepin'
    at a slow clip-clop;
Don't you hurry with the surrey with the
    fringe on the top.

–Richard Rodgers

THERE IS NOTHIN' LIKE A DAME

VERSE I

We got sunlight on the sand,
We got moonlight on the sea,
We got mangoes and bananas
You can pick right off a tree,
We got volleyball and Ping-Pong
And a lot of dandy games–
What ain't we got?
We ain't got dames!
We get packages from home,
We get movies, we get shows,
We get speeches from our skipper

And advice from Tokyo Rose,
We get letters doused wit' poifume,
We get dizzy from the smell—
What don't we get?
You know damn well!
We have nothin' to put on a clean white
  suit for.
What we need is what there ain't no
  substitute for.

REFRAIN

There is nothin' like a dame—
Nothin' in the world!
There is nothin' you can name
That is anythin' like a dame.

VERSE 2

We feel restless, we feel blue,
We feel lonely and, in brief,
We feel every kind of feelin'
But the feelin' of relief.
We felt hungry as the wolf felt
When he met Red Riding Hood—
What don't we feel?
We don't feel good!
Lots of things in life are beautiful, but
  brother,
There is one particular thing that is
  nothin' whatsoever in any way, shape,
  or form like any other.

REPEAT REFRAIN

VERSE 3

Nothin' else is built the same!
Nothin' in the world
Has a soft and wavy frame
Like the silhouette of a dame.
There is absolutely nothin' like the frame
  of a dame!
So suppose a dame ain't bright,
Or completely free from flaws,
Or as faithful as a bird dog,

Or as kind as Santa Claus—
It's a waste of time to worry
Over things that they have not;
Be thankful for
The things they got!

REPEAT REFRAIN

TAG

There are no books like a dame
And nothin' looks like a dame.
There are no drinks like a dame
And nothin' thinks like a dame.
Nothin' acts like a dame
Or attracts like a dame.
There ain't a thing that's wrong with any
  man here
That can't be cured by puttin' him near
A girly, womanly, female, feminine dame!

—*Richard Rodgers*

WHO?

(with Otto Harbach)

VERSE I

HE: When a girl's in love with someone,
  He must be indeed a dumb one
  If her secret he cannot unmask.
SHE: Then if I'm in love with someone,
  I must wait until there'll come one
  Boy, who'll know the answer when
    I ask:

REFRAIN

Who
Stole my heart away?
Who
Makes me dream all day?
Dreams, I know, can never be true.
Seems as tho' I'll ever be blue.
Who

Means my happiness?
Who
Would I answer "Yes" to?
Well you ought to guess who,
No one but you.

VERSE 2

HE: Can't say that I'm sure that I know
     What you're driving at. Deny no
     Further if you choose to feel
          that way.
SHE: Make your mind up, don't be shy,
     No game of eenie, meenie, mino
     Can be played with ladies when
          they say:

REPEAT REFRAIN

—Jerome Kern

WHY WAS I BORN?

VERSE

Spending these lonesome evenings
With nothing to do but to live
In dreams that I make up,
All by myself;
Dreaming that you're beside me,
I picture the prettiest stories
Only to wake up,
All by myself.
What is the good of me,
By myself?

REFRAIN

Why was I born?
Why am I living?
What do I get?
What am I giving?
Why do I want a thing I daren't hope for?
What can I hope for?
I wish I knew!

Why do I try
To draw you near me?
Why do I cry?
You never hear me.
I'm a poor fool,
But what can I do?
Why was I born
To love you?

—Jerome Kern

A WONDERFUL GUY

VERSE

I expect every one
Of my crowd to make fun
Of my proud protestations of faith in
     romance,
And they'll say I'm naïve
As a babe to believe
Any fable I hear from a person in pants.
Fearlessly I'll face them and argue their
     doubts away.
Loudly I'll sing about flowers and spring.
Flatly I'll stand on my little flat feet
     and say,
Love is a grand and a beautiful thing!
I'm not ashamed to reveal
The world-famous feeling I feel.

REFRAIN

I'm as corny as Kansas in August,
I'm as normal as blueberry pie.
No more a smart
Little girl with no heart,
I have found me a wonderful guy.
I am in a conventional dither
With a conventional star in my eye,
And you will note
There's a lump in my throat
When I speak of that wonderful guy.
I'm as trite and as gay

As a daisy in May,
A cliché coming true!
I'm bromidic and bright
As a moon-happy night
Pouring light on the dew.
I'm as corny as Kansas in August,
High as a flag on the Fourth of July!
If you'll excuse
An expression I use,
I'm in love,
I'm in love,
I'm in love,
I'm in love,
I'm in love with a wonderful guy!

—*Richard Rodgers*

You'll Never Walk Alone

When you walk through a storm
Keep your head up high
And don't be afraid of the dark.
At the end of the storm
Is a golden sky
And the sweet, silver song of a lark.
Walk on through the wind,
Walk on through the rain,
Though your dreams be tossed and blown.
Walk on, walk on with hope in your heart,
And you'll never walk alone!
You'll never walk alone.

—*Richard Rodgers*

Younger Than Springtime

VERSE
I touch your hand
And my arms grow strong,
Like a pair of birds
That burst with song.
My eyes look down
At your lovely face,
And I hold the world
In my embrace.

REFRAIN
Younger than springtime are you,
Softer than starlight are you;
Warmer than winds of June
Are the gentle lips you gave me.
Gayer than laughter are you,
Sweeter than music are you;
Angel and lover, heaven and earth,
Are you to me.
And when your youth and joy invade
    my arms
And fill my heart, as now they do,
Then, younger than springtime am I,
Gayer than laughter am I,
Angel and lover, heaven and earth,
Am I with you.

—*Richard Rodgers*

Andy Razaf (1895–1973)

ANDY RAZAF UNQUESTIONABLY had the most unusual background of any American lyricist. His maternal grandfather is thought to have been the first black member of the American diplomatic corps–he was U.S. Consul in Madagascar–and his father was the nephew of Madagascar's ruling queen. In fact, his full name was Andreamenentania Paul Razafinkerierfo (it got abbreviated to Razaf in Washington, D.C., where he grew up). Although Razaf was also a composer, his great success came from his lyrics, and particularly those he wrote to Fats Waller music–"Ain't Misbehavin'," "Honeysuckle Rose," etc. His lyrics range from these bouncy hits to the starkly outspoken "Black and Blue" to the swinging "Stompin' at the Savoy" to a series of pungent double-entendre numbers. He wrote for nightclub revues and Broadway shows–*Blackbirds of 1930, Keep Shufflin'*–and he wrote (and published) poetry. Although he is certainly the finest of all black lyricists, to pigeonhole him that way is limiting, even though so much of his material reflects the life of blacks in America. It would be fairer just to say that the astoundingly productive and talented Razaf is one of America's best songwriters. His reputation, which had sadly diminished, was revived with the great success of the 1978 Fats Waller show, *Ain't Misbehavin',* which featured more than half a dozen Razaf lyrics and ended movingly with the cast of five quietly singing, "My only sin is in my skin. What did I do to be so black and blue?"

AIN'T MISBEHAVIN'

VERSE I
Though it's a fickle age,
With flirting all the rage,
Here is one bird with self-control,
Happy inside my cage.
I know who I love best,
Thumbs down on all the rest,
My love was given heart and soul,
So it can stand the test.

REFRAIN
No one to talk with,
All by myself,
No one to walk with
But I'm happy on the shelf,
Ain't misbehavin',
I'm savin' my love for you.
I know for certain
The one I love,
I'm through with flirtin',
It's just you I'm thinkin' of,
Ain't misbehavin',
I'm savin' my love for you.
Like Jack Horner
In the corner,
Don't go nowhere,
What do I care,
Your kisses are worth waitin' for,

Believe me.
I don't stay out late,
Don't care to go,
I'm home about eight,
Just me and my radio,
Ain't misbehavin',
I'm savin' my love for you.

VERSE 2

Your type of man is rare,
I know you really care,
That's why my conscience never
    sleeps
When you're away somewhere.
Sure was a lucky day
When fate sent you my way,
And made you mine alone for keeps,
Ditto to all you say.

REPEAT REFRAIN

    —*Thomas "Fats" Waller and*
      Harry Brooks

BLACK AND BLUE
(WHAT DID I DO TO BE SO BLACK AND BLUE?)

VERSE

Out in the street,
Shufflin' feet,
Couples passin' two by two,
While here am I,
Left high and dry,
Black, and 'cause I'm black I'm blue.
Browns and yellers
All have fellers,
Gentlemen prefer them light.
Wish I could fade,
Can't make the grade,
Nothin' but dark days in sight.

REFRAIN I

Cold empty bed,
Springs hard as lead,
Pains in my head,
Feels like old Ned,
What did I do
To be so black and blue?
No joys for me,
No company,
Even the mouse
Ran from my house,
All my life through
I've been so black and blue.
I'm white
Inside,
It don't help my case,
'Cause I
Can't hide
What is on my face, ooh!
I'm so forlorn,
Life's just a thorn,
My heart is torn,
Why was I born?
What did I do
To be so black and blue?

REFRAIN 2

Just 'cause you're black,
Folks think you lack,
They laugh at you
And scorn you too,
What did I do
To be so black and blue?
When you are near,
They laugh and sneer,
Set you aside
And you're denied;
What did I do
To be so black and blue?
How sad I am,
Each day I feel worse,
My mark of Ham
Seems to be a curse, ooh!

How will it end?
Ain't got a friend,
My only sin
Is in my skin,
What did I do
To be so black and blue?

—Thomas "Fats" Waller

GUESS WHO'S IN TOWN?
(NOBODY BUT THAT GAL OF MINE)

VERSE I
Call in your reporters
If they want some news;
Got a headline story
They are free to use.
Something great has happened,
I got a break and how,
You can bet
I'm all set,
Gonna meet her now.

REFRAIN I
Guess who's in town?
I'm happy when I mention
Nobody but that gal of mine.
Guess who's aroun',
And gets all my attention?
Nobody but that gal of mine.
When she goes by
Weak eyes cry out for glasses
Who can deny
She really knows her molasses?
Oh me, oh my,
Who shows the world what class is?
Nobody but that gal of mine.
Guess who's in town
And is the main attraction?
Nobody but that gal of mine.
Guess who's aroun',
And gettin' plenty action?

Nobody but that gal of mine.
Some honey child,
I want you all to meet her.
I'll put it mild,
When she's around, don't need a heater.
Who's got me wild,
And keeps on getting sweeter?
Nobody but that gal of mine.

VERSE 2
Never like to talk much,
Never like to rave;
But here's one occasion
My tongue won't behave.
Gonna start broadcastin',
I've got a sweet program,
I'm in high,
Please stand by,
See how good I am.

REFRAIN 2
Guess who's in town,
Who do they say is clever?
Nobody but that gal of mine.
Guess who's in town
And lookin' hot as ever?
Nobody but that gal of mine.
She's mine and how,
Tell ev'ryone you've seen us.
We've made a vow,
Devil himself can't come between us.
I'm yellin' now,
Who is a perfect Venus?
Nobody but that gal of mine.
Guess who's in town,
Who do they say is clever?
Nobody but that gal of mine.
Guess who's in town
And fills my life with honey?
Nobody but that gal of mine.
Listen to this,
We've got a date at seven.
Oh what a kiss,

I'll keep her busy until 'leven.
Speakin' of bliss,
Who has the key to Heaven?
Nobody but that gal of mine.

—J. C. Johnson

HONEYSUCKLE ROSE

VERSE

Have no use for any sweets of any kind
Since the day you came around,
From the start I instantly made up
    my mind
Sweeter sweetness can't be found.
You're so sweet,
Can't be beat,
Nothing sweeter ever stood on feet.

REFRAIN

Every honeybee
Fills with jealousy
When they see you out with me.
I don't blame them, goodness knows,
Honeysuckle Rose.
When you're passing by,
Flowers droop and sigh,
And I know the reason why.
You're much sweeter, goodness knows,
Honeysuckle Rose.
Don't buy sugar,
You just have to touch my cup.
You're my sugar,
It's sweet when you stir it up.
When I'm taking sips
From your tasty lips,
Seems the honey fairly drips,
You're confection, goodness knows,
Honeysuckle Rose.

—Thomas "Fats" Waller

I'D GIVE A DOLLAR FOR A DIME

VERSE

That little jukebox right over there
Is like a magic key,
For it can take me anywhere
On wings of memory.

REFRAIN

I'd give a dollar for a dime;
I've got to hear that record play again,
Turn love's December into May again,
Bring me a thrill just one more time.
I'd give a dollar for a dime
So I can hear that sweet refrain again
That carries me down lovers' lane
    again
Back when the world was all in rhyme.
Seems that song was written for us;
Every word and note has charms.
Our two hearts would sing the chorus
As you held me in your arms.
I'd give a dollar for a dime;
My aching heart is on my sleeve again.
To close my eyes and make believe
    again
I'd give a dollar for a dime
To play that record one more time.

—Eubie Blake

THE JOINT IS JUMPIN'
(with A. R. and J. C. Johnson)

REFRAIN I

The joint is jumpin',
It's really jumpin',
Come in, cats, and check your hats,
I mean this joint is jumpin'.
The piano's thumpin',
The dancers are bumpin',

This here spot is more than hot,
In fact, the joint is jumpin'.
Check your weapons at the door,
Be sure to pay your quarter.
Burn your leather on the floor,
Grab anybody's daughter.
The roof is rockin',
The neighbors are knockin',
We're all bums when the wagon comes,
I mean this joint is jumpin'.

VERSE

They have a new expression
Along old Harlem way,
That tells you when a party
Is ten times more than gay.
To say that things are "jumpin' "
Leaves not a single doubt
That everything is in full swing
When you hear somebody shout:

REFRAIN 2

"The joint is jumpin',
It's really jumpin',
Ev'ry Mose is on his toes,
I mean, this joint is jumpin'.
No time for talkin',
This place is walkin',
Hit the jug and cut a rug,
I've said, the joint is jumpin'.
Get your pig feet, beer, and gin,
There's plenty in the kitchen.
What is that who just came in?
Just see the way he's switchin'.
Don't mind the hour,
'Cause I'm in power,
I've got bail if we go to jail,
So keep this joint-a-jumpin'."

—*Thomas "Fats" Waller*

KEEPIN' OUT OF MISCHIEF NOW

VERSE 1

Don't even go to a movie show
If you are not by my side;
I just stay home by my radio,
But I am satisfied.
All my flirting days are gone,
On the level from now on!

REFRAIN

Keepin' out of mischief now,
Really am in love and how!
I'm through playin' with fire,
It's you whom I desire.
All the world can plainly see
You're the only one for me.
I have told them in advance,
They can't break up our romance
Livin' up to ev'ry vow,
Keepin' out of mischief now.

VERSE 2

Don't go for any excitement now,
Books are my best company.
All my opinions have changed somehow,
Old-fashioned as can be.
When you really learn to care
There's a thrill in solitaire.

REPEAT REFRAIN

—*Thomas "Fats" Waller*

MEMORIES OF YOU

VERSE 1

Why can't I forget like I should?
Heaven knows I would if I could
But I just can't keep you off my mind.
Though you're gone and love was in vain,

All around me you still remain.
Wonder why fate should be so unkind.

REFRAIN
Waking skies
At sunrise,
Ev'ry sunset, too,
Seems to be
Bringing me
Memories of you.
Here and there,
Ev'rywhere,
Scenes that we once knew,
And they all
Just recall
Memories of you.
How I wish I could forget those
Happy yesteryears
That have left a rosary of tears.
Your face beams
In my dreams,
'Spite of all I do,
Ev'rything
Seems to bring
Memories of you.

VERSE 2
Though for years we've been apart,
Time heals ev'rything but my heart
That still aches for you the same old way.
Seems I can't escape from the past,
And your spell keeps holding me fast,
Each tomorrow is like yesterday.

REPEAT REFRAIN

—Eubie Blake

MY HANDY MAN

Whoever said a good man was hard to find,
Positively, absolutely, sure was blind.

I've found the best that ever was,
Here's just some of the things he does:
He shakes my ashes,
Greases my griddle,
Churns my butter,
Strokes my fiddle;
My man is such a handy man.
He threads my needle,
Creams my wheat,
Heats my heater,
Chops my meat;
My man is such a handy man.
Don't care if you believe or not,
He sure is good to have around,
Why, when my burners get too hot,
He's there to turn my damper down.
For everything he's got a scheme,
You oughta see the sodder he uses on my
        machine;
My man is such a handy man.
He flaps my flapjacks,
Cleans off the table,
Feeds the horses in my stable;
My man is such a handy man.
Sometimes he's up long before dawn,
Trimming the rough edges off my lawn,
My man is such a handy man.
Never has a single thing to say
While he's working hard,
I wish that you could see the way
He handles my front yard.
My ice don't get a chance to melt away,
He sees that I get a nice, fresh piece
        every day.
My man is such a handy man.

MY HANDY MAN AIN'T HANDY NO MORE

VERSE
Once I used to brag about my handy man,
But I ain't braggin' no more.

Somethin' strange has happened to my
    handy man,
He's not the man he was before.
I wish somebody would explain to me
About this dual personality.

REFRAIN 1

He don't perform his duties like he used
    to do,
He never hauls the ashes 'less I tell him to,
Before he hardly gets to work he says he's
    through;
My handy man ain't handy no more.
The way he used to handle things was
    "Too bad, Jim,"
That man was so efficient, full of pep
    and vim.
Although he looks the same, I know it
    isn't him;
My handy man ain't handy no more.
He's forgotten his domestic science
And he's lost all of his self-reliance.
He won't make a single move unless
    he's told,
He says he isn't lazy, claims that he
    ain't old,
But still he sits around and lets my stove
    get cold;
My handy man ain't handy no more.

REFRAIN 2

Time after time if I'm not right there at
    his heels
He lets that poor horse in my stable miss
    his meals.
There's got to be some changes 'cause
    each day he reveals
My handy man ain't handy no more.
He used to turn in early and get up at dawn,
All full of new ambitions he would trim
    the lawn.
Now when he isn't sleeping all he does
    is yawn;

My handy man ain't handy no more.
Once he used to have so much
    endurance,
Now it looks like he needs life insurance.
I used to brag about my handy man's
    technique,
But now "The spirit's willing but the flesh
    is weak."

CODA

So now I'm gonna get myself a strong
    young sheik,
And tell him that it's solid action that
    I seek.
I'm gonna put that cat on notice it's a
    seven-day week;
My handy man ain't handy no more.

—Eubie Blake

My Man o' War

VERSE

I got myself a military man
And now I'm almost in hysterics.
He has me living on the army plan,
You'd think my parlor was a barracks.
It's so peaceful when he's gone,
But when he's home, the war is on.

REFRAIN 1

My flat looks more like an armory,
Takes out his bugle when he sees me,
At night he's drilling me constantly,
He's my man o'war.
When he advances, can't keep him back,
So systematic in his attack,
All my resistance is bound to crack,
For he's my man o'war.
He never misses when he brings up
His big artillery.
Bullets like kisses that hit the mark

With such rapidity.
His operations always increase,
It seems his movements will never cease,
At night he always disturbs the peace,
He's my man o'war.

REFRAIN 2

I'm always bearing the battle's brunt,
Crazy for action, he's on the hunt,
You're sure to find him right at the
        front,
He's my man o'war.
He storms my trench and he's not dead,
His bayonet makes me cry for aid,
Oh, how he handles his hand grenade,
He's my man o'war.
If I'm retreatin' he goes around
And gets me in the rear.
He keeps repeatin' a flank attack
'Til victory is near.
Now when he turns his machine gun loose,
Then I surrender, for there's no use,
He makes me put up my flag of truce,
He's my man o'war.

                    —Spencer Williams

MY SPECIAL FRIEND

(IS BACK IN TOWN)

(with Bob Schafer)

It can rain, it can snow, it can sleet, it
        can blow,
Doggone it, I don't give a hang.
You can read in my face something soon
        will take place,
I'm saying good-bye to the gang.
I'm acting like a nut,
No, I'm not crazy, but
My special friend is back in town.
I've not been treated right,

But I'll make up tonight,
My special friend is back in town.
Now don't stand in my hall
Or I'll call you down,
From today keep away
'Cause I'm true when he's around.
Take care, don't talk too much
Or we'll both get in dutch,
My special friend is back in town.
Don't phone me at the store,
No, you can't write me anymore,
My special friend is back in town.
Of course, when we meet on the street
Merely stop to say,
"Howdy do. How are you?"
After that you be on your way.
Go on and tell what you know,
I'll swear it isn't so,
My special friend is back in town.
No parties from tonight,
My poker games are tight,
My special friend is back in town.
Take back your jewelry,
It can't be seen on me,
My special friend is back in town.
Take back this, take back that—
After all, they're yours—
Take your dog, take your cat,
Or he'll think you're Santa Claus.
Excuse me while I laugh
But I just hid your photograph,
My special friend is back in town.
First we'll go to a show,
Later on we'll dine,
After that, to my flat,
Can't you guess what's on my mind?
If you don't see no lights,
Don't you ring my bell tonight,
My special friend is back in town.

                    —J. C. Johnson

A Porter's Love Song to a Chambermaid

VERSE

Though my position is of low degree
And all the others may look down on me,
I'll go smiling through,
That's if I have you.
I am the happiest of troubadours
Thinking of you while I'm massaging
    floors,
At my leisure time,
I made up this rhyme:

REFRAIN 1

I will be the oil mop
If you'll be the oil,
Then we both could mingle
Ev'ry time we toil.
I will be the washboard
If you'll be the tub,
Think of all the Mondays,
We can rub-a-dub.
I will be the shoe-brush
If you'll be my shoe,
Then I'll keep you bright, dear,
Feeling good as new.
If you'll be my razor,
I will be your blade,
That's a porter's love song
To a chambermaid.

REFRAIN 2

I will be the dustpan
If you'll be my broom,
Then we could work together
All around the room.
I will be your clothespin,
Be my pulley line,
We'll hang out together,
Wouldn't that be fine?

I will be your dishpan
If you'll be my dish,
We'll meet after meals, dear,
What more could you wish?
If I'll be your window,
Be my window shade,
That's a porter's love song
To a chambermaid.

—James P. Johnson

S'posin'

VERSE 1

I know something
But I can't express it,
Though there is no better time than now.
I have waited
Hoping you would guess it;
Got to make my feelings known
    somehow.

REFRAIN

S'posin' I should fall in love with you,
Do you think that you could love me too?
S'posin' I should hold you and
    caress you,
Would it impress you
Or distress you?
S'posin' I should say, "For you I yearn,"
Would you think I'm speaking out
    of turn?
And s'posin' I declare it,
Would you take my love and share it?
I'm not s'posin' I'm in love with you.

VERSE 2

Always thought that
I was up in grammar
Till the happy day you came my way.
When you're near, all

I can do is stammer;
Hope you'll understand me when I say:

REPEAT REFRAIN

—Paul Denniker

Stompin' at the Savoy

Savoy,
The home of sweet romance–
Savoy,
It wins you at a glance–
Savoy,
Gives happy feet a chance
To dance.
Your form–
Just like a clingin' vine,
Your lips–
So warm and sweet as wine,
Your cheek–
So soft and close to mine,
Divine.
How my heart is singin'
While the band is swingin',
Never tired of rompin'
And stompin' with you.
At the Savoy,
What joy–
A perfect holiday,
Savoy–
Where we can glide and sway,
Savoy–
There let me stomp away,
With you.

—Benny Goodman, Chick Webb,
    and Edgar Sampson

Tan Manhattan

VERSE
When you seek variety
You don't have to sail the sea,
So why cross the foam
When it's right here at home?
For originality
Rhythm, dance, and gaiety,
A symphony of races,
I'll guarantee the place is–

REFRAIN
Tan Manhattan, tan Manhattan
Where the south is north of
    Central Park.
Tan Manhattan, tan Manhattan
Where the sun is brightest after dark.
It's the center of a thousand topics,
You will think that you are in the
    tropics.
Hang your hat in tan Manhattan,
It's the magic town, within a town, done
    up brown.

PATTER
Red-hot gals from Dixieanna,
Señoritas from Havana,
Babies from the Philippines,
Cuties from the Argentines,
Graceful maids from fair Antigua,
Trinidad and Porto Rica,
Panama and Martinique,
Ev'ry kind of type you seek, in

REPEAT REFRAIN

—Eubie Blake

You're Lucky to Me

VERSE 1

BOY: Never since a child,
  Was I reconciled
  By the folks who laugh at bug-a-boos.
  Hoodoos haunted me,
  Trailed me constantly
  Till the day you come my way, like
    good news.

REFRAIN

Whenever you're near,
All my fears disappear,
Dear, it's plain as can be,
You're lucky to me.
My only luck charms
Are your two loving arms,
Anybody can see,
You're lucky to me.
No harm can happen to me anymore,
I'm writing "Thirteens" all over
  my door.
  1. My Mother and Dad
    Thought that my luck was bad,
    Now like me, they agree
    You're lucky to me.

VERSE 2

GIRL: I was just like you,
  Superstitious, too,

Thought myself unlucky all life
  through.
Things are diff'rent now,
Not afraid, somehow,
Since you came, I feel the same as
  you do.

REPEAT REFRAIN

2. I feel "Aces High,"
  For you love me, that's why
  All the world must agree
  You're lucky to me.

PATTER

When I break a looking glass
I never mind a bit,
And I walk under ladders ev'ry day.
When a black cat wants to pass
I fail to throw a fit,
But cheerfully I let it go its way.
Four-leaf clover is passé,
A rabbit foot's a joke,
Ouija boards, to me, are out of
  date.
All that fortune-tellers say
To me is only smoke,
With you, dear, at my side, I laugh
  at fate.

REPEAT REFRAIN

—Eubie Blake

E. Y. Harburg (1896–1981)

RAISED ON New York's tough Lower East Side and educated at City College (where he sat next to Ira Gershwin in classes), E. Y. (Yip) Harburg had a three-year stint as a journalist in South America, wrote light verse for newspapers, and ran an electrical appliance business before starting out as a lyricist in the late twenties. (When he was a kid, he had made a few bucks lighting street lamps for Consolidated Edison.) His long and happy career had two great high spots. The first was *The Wizard of Oz,* in 1939, which amply demonstrated the stretch of his talent: from the classic ballad "Over the Rainbow" to the patter songs of the Munchkins. He had a Broadway success, *Bloomer Girl,* with Harold Arlen, the composer of *Oz,* but his real theatrical smash, written in 1947 with composer Burton Lane, was *Finian's Rainbow,* a show with half a dozen classic songs, also highly various. And consider the range of three of his most famous songs: the Depression anthem "Brother, Can You Spare a Dime?," Vernon Duke's nostalgic ballad "April in Paris," and the jaunty "It's Only a Paper Moon." As he grew older, Harburg's social conscience–and satirical streak–grew stronger. His great early influence was W. S. Gilbert, both for Gilbert's wit and his jaundiced view of society. By the time of the unsuccessful *Flahooley,* Harburg was making his anti-capitalist views resoundingly clear. "For me," he told Max Wilk, "satire has become a weapon. . . . I am stirred when I can tackle a problem that has profundity, depth, and real danger . . . by destroying it with laughter." Fortunately, his strong political convictions didn't keep him from receiving and fully enjoying much honor and attention in his later years.

APRIL IN PARIS

VERSE

April's in the air,
But here in Paris
April wears a diff'rent gown.
You can see her waltzing
Down the street.
The tang of wine is in the air,
I'm drunk with all the happiness
That Spring can give.

Never dreamed it could be so
Exciting to live.

REFRAIN

April in Paris,
Chestnuts in blossom,
Holiday tables under the trees.
April in Paris,
This is a feeling
No one can ever reprise.
I never knew the charm of Spring,

Never met it face to face.
I never knew my heart could sing,
Never missed a warm embrace,
Till,
April in Paris,
Whom can I run to?
What have you done to
My heart?

—Vernon Duke

BROTHER, CAN YOU SPARE A DIME?

VERSE

They used to tell me
I was building a dream,
And so I followed the mob.
When there was earth to plow
Or guns to bear,
I was always there
Right on the job.
They used to tell me
I was building a dream,
With peace and glory ahead.
Why should I be standing in line
Just waiting for bread?

REFRAIN

Once I built a railroad,
Made it run,
Made it race against time.
Once I built a railroad,
Now it's done,
Brother, can you spare a dime?
Once I built a tower
To the sun,
Brick and rivet and lime.
Once I built a tower,
Now it's done,
Brother, can you spare a dime?

Once in khaki suits
Gee, we looked swell,
Full of that Yankee Doodle-de-dum.
Half a million boots went sloggin'
    through hell,
I was the kid with the drum.
Say, don't you remember?
They called me "Al,"
It was "Al" all the time.
Say, don't you remember
I'm your pal?
Buddy, can you spare a dime?

—Jay Gorney

DOWN WITH LOVE

VERSE

You, sons of Adam,
You, daughters of Eve,
The time has come
To take your love-torn hearts
Off your sleeve.
Look, look about you,
What do you see?
Love-sick, love-lorn,
Love-wrecked, love-worn
Boo-hoo-manity.
There'll be no peace on earth
Until this curse
Is wiped off from this love-mad
    universe.
Are we mice or men?
Can't you see the light?
Come you fellow victims,
Let's unite.

REFRAIN

Down with love,
The flowers and rice and shoes.
Down with love,

The root of all midnight blues.
Down with things
That give you that well-known pain.
Take that moon
And wrap it in cellophane.
Down with love,
Let's liquidate all its friends.
Moon and June and roses
And rainbow's ends.
Down with songs
That moan about night and day.
Down with love,
Yes, take it away, away.
Away,
Take it away.
Give it back to the birds and the bees,
And the Viennese.
Down with eyes romantic and
    stupid,
Down with sighs,
Down with Cupid.
Brother, let's stuff that dove,
Down with love!

—Harold Arlen

THE EAGLE AND ME

VERSE

What makes the gopher leave his hole,
Tremblin' with fear and fright?
Maybe the gopher's got a soul?
Wantin' to see the light.
That's it!
Oh yea, oh yea, that's it.
The scripture has it write.
Betcha life that's it.
Nobody like hole.
Nobody like chain.
Don't the good Lord all aroun' you make it
    plain?

REFRAIN

River it like to flow;
Eagle it like to fly.
Eagle it like to feel its wings against
    the sky.
Possum it like to run;
Ivy it like to climb.
Bird in the tree and bumblebee want
    freedom
In Autumn or Summertime.
Ever since that day
When the world was an onion
'Twas natch'ral for the spirit to soar
    and play
The way the Lawd 'awanted it.
Free as the sun is free.
That's how it's gotta be.
Whatever is right for bumblebee and
    river,
And eagle, is right for me.
We gotta be free
The eagle and me.

—Harold Arlen

FUN TO BE FOOLED

(with Ira Gershwin)

VERSE

Spring is here,
I'm a fool if I fall again,
And yet I'm enthralled
By its call again.
You say you love me—
I know from the past
You mean to love me,
But these things don't last.
Fools rush in
To begin new love affairs.
But tonight,
Tonight, my dear, who cares?

REFRAIN
Fun to be fooled,
Fun to pretend,
Fun to believe
Love is unending.
Thought I was done,
Still it is fun
Being fooled again.
Nice when you tell
All that you feel,
Nice to be told
This is the real thing.
Fun to be kissed,
Fun to exist,
To be fooled again.
It's that old devil moon
Having its fling once more,
Selling me Spring once more,
I'm afraid love is king once more.
Fun to be fooled,
Fun to pretend,
This little dream
Won't end.

—Harold Arlen

HAPPINESS IS JUST A THING CALLED JOE

VERSE
Skies ain't gonna cloud no mo',
The crops ain't gonna fail.
Caught a bluebird by the toe,
A rainbow by the tail.
A certain man with eyes that
    shine
Voodoo'd up this heart of mine.

REFRAIN
It seem like happiness is jes' a thing
    called Joe.

He's got a smile that makes the lilac
    wanna grow.
He's got a way that makes the angels heave
    a sigh
When they know little Joe's
Passing by.
Sometime the cabin's gloomy an' the
    table bare,
Then he'll kiss me an' it's Christmas
    ev'rywhere.
Troubles fly away an' life is easy go.
Does he love me good,
That's all I need to know.
Seem like happiness is jes' a thing
    called Joe.
Little Joe,
Mm, mm, mm,
Little Joe.

—Harold Arlen

HOW ARE THINGS IN GLOCCA MORRA?

VERSE
I hear a bird,
A Londonderry bird,
It well may be
He's bringing me
A cheering word.
I hear a breeze,
A River Shannon breeze,
It well may be
It's followed me
Across the seas.
Then tell me, please,

REFRAIN
How are things in Glocca Morra?
Is that little brook still leaping there?
Does it still run down to Donny Cove?

Through Killybegs, Kilkerry and
    Kildare?
How are things in Glocca Morra?
Is that willow tree still weeping there?
Does that laddie with the twinklin' eye
Come whistlin' by,
And does he walk away
Sad and dreamy there,
Not to see me there?
So I ask each weepin' willow
And each brook along the way
And each lad that comes a-whistlin'
Tooralay,
How are things in Glocca Morra
This fine day?

—Burton Lane

I LIKE THE LIKES OF YOU

VERSE

Lady, last Saturday,
Or was it yesterday?
I was rehearsing a speech,
Really, I think it's a peach,
Hope you don't think it a breach
Of recognized etiquette.
I'm from Connecticut.
You see the state that I'm in,
I mean I'm in a mess,
What was that speech
Oh yes . . . yes . . .

REFRAIN

I like the likes of you,
I like the things you do,
I mean, I like the likes of you.
I like your eyes of blue,
I think they're blue, don't you?
I mean, I like your eyes of blue.
Oh dear, if I could only say what I mean,

I mean, if I could mean what I say,
That is, I mean to say
That I mean to say that
I like the likes of you,
Your looks are pure deluxe,
Looks like I like the likes of you.

—Vernon Duke

IF I ONLY HAD A BRAIN
(IF I ONLY HAD A HEART)
(IF I ONLY HAD THE NERVE)

SCARECROW

VERSE

Said a scarecrow swingin' on a pole
To a blackbird sittin' on a fence,
"Oh! the Lord gave me a soul
But forgot to give me common sense.
If I had an ounce of common sense."

REFRAIN

I could while away the hours
Conferrin' with the flow'rs,
Consultin' with the rain.
And my head, I'd be scratchin'
While my thoughts were busy hatchin',
If I only had a brain.
I'd unravel ev'ry riddle
For any individle
In trouble or in pain.
With the thoughts I'd be thinkin'
I could be another Lincoln,
If I only had a brain.
Oh, I could tell you why
The ocean's near the shore,
I could think of things I never thunk
    before,
And then I'd sit
And think some more.

I would not be just a nuffin',
My head all full of stuffin',
My heart all full of pain.
And perhaps I'd deserve you
And be even worthy erv you
If I only had a brain.
Only had a brain.

TIN WOODMAN

VERSE

Said a tinman rattlin' his gibs
To a strawman sad and weary-eyed,
"Oh! the Lord gave me tin ribs,
But forgot to put a heart inside."
Then he banged his hollow chest and
    cried.

REFRAIN

When a man's an empty kettle
He should be on his mettle
And yet I'm torn apart.
Just because I'm presumin'
That I could be kinda human
If I only had a heart.
I'd be tender, I'd be gentle
And awful sentimental
Regarding love and art.
I'd be friends with the sparrows
And the boy that shoots the arrows,
If I only had a heart.
Picture me,
A balcony,
Above a voice sings low,
"Wherefore art thou, Romeo?"
I hear a beat.
Now sweet!
Just to register emotion,
"Jealousy," "Devotion,"
And really feel the part.
I would stay young and chipper
And I'd lock it with a zipper

If I only had a heart.
Only had a heart.

COWARDLY LION

VERSE

Said a lion, poor neurotic lion,
To a miss who listened to him rave,
"Oh! the Lord made me a lion
But the Lord forgot to make me brave."
Then his tail began to curl and wave.

REFRAIN

Life is sad, believe me, Missy, when
You're born to be a sissy,
Without the vim and verve.
But I could change my habits,
Never more be scared of rabbits
If I only had the nerve.
I'm afraid there's no denyin'
I'm just a dandy lion,
A fate I don't deserve.
But I could show my prowess,
Be a lion, not a mowess,
If I only had the nerve.
Oh, I'd
Be in my stride,
A king down to the core.
Oh, I'd roar the way I never roared
    before,
And then I'd rrrwoof,
And roar some more.
I would show the dinosaurus
Who's king around the forres',
A king they better serve.
Why, with my regal beezer
I could be another Caesar
If I only had the nerve.
Only had the nerve.

—Harold Arlen

If This Isn't Love

VERSE

HE: A secret, a secret,
   She says she's got a secret,
   A secret, a secret,
   A secret kind of secret.
   She's achin' for to shout it
   To every daffodil
   And tell the world about it,
   In fact, she says she will.

CHORUS: She says . . .

REFRAIN

HE: She says . . .
   If this isn't love,
   The whole world is crazy.
   If this isn't love,
   I'm daft as a daisy.
   With moons all around
   And cows jumping over,
   There's something amiss
   And I'll eat my hat if this
      isn't love.

   I'm feelin' like the apple
   On top of William Tell,
   With this I cannot grapple
   Because . . .

CHORUS: Because . . .
   HE: You're so adora-bel!
      If this isn't love,
      Then winter is summer.
      If this isn't love,
      My heart needs a plumber.
      I'm swingin' on stars,
      I'm ridin' on rainbows,
      I'm bustin' with bliss
      And I'll kiss your hand if this
         isn't love.

SHE: If this isn't love,
   I'm Carmen Miranda.
   If this isn't love,
   It's red propaganda.
   If this is a dream
   And if I should wake up,
   Will you hear a hiss,
   Will my face be red if this
      isn't love.
HE: I'm gettin' tired of waitin'
   And stickin' to the rules,
   This feelin' calls for matin',
   Like birds and bees and other
      animules.

CHORUS: If this isn't love,
   We're all seeing double,
   If this isn't love,
   HE: I'm really in trouble.
   SHE: If I'm not the girl,
   HE: And I'm not the hero,

CHORUS: A kiss ain't a kiss,
   It's a crisis, man, if this
      isn't love.
   If this isn't love,
   If this isn't love,
   If this isn't love!

—*Burton Lane*

It's Only a Paper Moon

(with Billy Rose)

VERSE

I never feel a thing is real
When I'm away from you.
Out of your embrace,
The world's a temporary parking place.
Mm, mm, mm, mm,
A bubble for a minute,
Mm, mm,

You smile,
The bubble has a rainbow in it.

REFRAIN

Say, it's only a paper moon,
Sailing over a cardboard sea,
But it wouldn't be make-believe
If you believed in me.
Yes, it's only a canvas sky,
Hanging over a muslin tree,
But it wouldn't be make-believe
If you believed in me.
Without your love,
It's a honky-tonk parade.
Without your love,
It's a melody played
In a penny arcade.
It's a Barnum and Bailey world,
Just as phony as it can be,
But it wouldn't be make-believe
If you believed in me.

—*Harold Arlen*

LAST NIGHT WHEN WE WERE YOUNG

Last night
When we were young
Love was a star,
A song unsung,
Life was so new,
So real, so right,
Ages ago,
Last night.
Today,
The world is old.
You went away
And time grew cold.
Where is that star
That seemed so bright
Ages ago,

Last night?
To think
That Spring had depended
On merely this,
A look, a kiss.
To think
That something so splendid
Could slip away
In one little daybreak.
So now
Let's reminisce,
And recollect
The sighs and the kisses,
The arms that clung
When we were young,
Last night.

—*Harold Arlen*

LET'S TAKE A WALK AROUND THE BLOCK

(with Ira Gershwin)

VERSE

I never travel'd further north
Than old Van Cortlandt Park,
And never further south than the
    Aquarium.
I've seen the charm of Jersey City,
But first let me remark
I saw it from the Empire State Solarium.
But I've been putting nickels
In the Postal Savings Bank,
And when those nickels pile up,
We can toddle off in swank,
And I don't mean an ordinary
    Cook's tour,
I mean a "Cabin De Luxe" Tour.

REFRAIN I

HE: Some day we'll go places,
    New lands and new faces,

The day we quit punching the clock.
The future looks pleasant,
But, at present,
Let's take a walk around the block.
You're just the companion
I want at Grand Canyon
For throwing old blades down
    the rock.
The money we have'll
Go for travel,
Meantime, let's walk around the
    block.
Gangway! We'll begin
When our ship comes in.
You'll sit on my lap
All over the map.
To London in Maytime,
To Venice in playtime,
To Paris in time for a frock.
To Boston in bean-time,
Darling, meantime,
Let's take a walk around the block.

REFRAIN 2
In winter at Christmas
We'll visit the isthmus
And see how they lock up a lock.
And then in Caracas,
On a jackass
We'll take a ride around the block.
I give you my promise
We'll visit St. Thomas
And then at the Virgins we'll dock.
SHE: The Virgins can wait, sir,
It grows late, sir,
Let's take a walk around the
    block.
BOTH: Onward to Cathay,
Then to Mandalay,
Then Vladivostok
Where Bolsheviks flock.
We'll send the folks cables,
Accumulate labels,

Buy souvenirs till we're in hock.
Right now we are flat in
Old Manhattan,
Let's take a walk around the block.

—Harold Arlen

LYDIA, THE TATTOOED LADY

Lydia, oh, Lydia,
Say, have you met Lydia?
Oh, Lydia, the tattooed lady.
She has eyes that folks adore so,
And a torso even more so.
Lydia, oh, Lydia,
That "encyclopidia."
Oh, Lydia, the queen of tattoo.
On her back is the battle of Waterloo,
Beside it the wreck of the Hesperus, too,
And proudly above the waves the red,
    white and blue,
You can learn a lot from Lydia.
La la la, la la la
La la la, la la la
She can give you a view of the world in
    tattoo
If you step up and tell her where.
For a dime you can see Kankakee or
    Paree
Or Washington crossing the Delaware.
Oh, Lydia, oh, Lydia,
Say, have you met Lydia?
Oh, Lydia, the tattooed lady.
When her muscles start relaxin',
Up the hill comes Andrew Jackson.
Lydia, oh, Lydia,
That "encyclopidia."
Oh, Lydia, the champ of them all.
For two bits she will do a mazurka in jazz
With a view of Niag'ra that no artist has,
And on a clear day you can see Alcatraz.
You can learn a lot from Lydia.

La la la, la la la
La la la, la la la
Come along and see Buff'lo Bill with his
	lasso,
Just a little classic by Mendel Picasso.
Here is Captain Spaulding exploring the
	Amazon
And Godiva, but with her pajamas on.
La la la, la la la
La la la, la la la
Here is Grover Whalen unveilin' the
	Trylon,
Over on the West Coast we have Treasure
	Islan'.
Here's Nijinsky a doin' the rumba,
Here's her social security numba.
La la la, la la la
La la la, la la la
Oh, Lydia, oh, Lydia,
Say, have you met Lydia,
Oh, Lydia, the champ of them all?
She once swept an admiral clear off
	his feet,
The ships on her hips made his heart skip
	a beat,
And now the old boy's in command of the
	fleet,
For he went and *married* Lydia.

—Harold Arlen

Moon About Town

VERSE

Manhattan is really as grand as it's
	painted,
But tell me, you moon in the clouds,
How does a stranger in town get
	acquainted
Among all these nonchalant crowds?
You know each corner and hideaway,
You know your way about.

I guess I'll just throw my pride away
And ask you to help me out.

REFRAIN

Moon, what's your program,
You moon about town?
Moon, be my escort
And show me around.
Where does one go, moon,
What does one do?
When one's alone, moon,
I'm asking you.
Moon, in this city of millions of lights,
Moon, is there someone else wasting his
	nights?
Tell him about me
And my new gown.
Moon, introduce us,
You moon about town.

PATTER

Maybe somewhere in the city
There's a welcoming committee of one.
Throw your spotlight on some neighbor
Who is lonesome when his labor is done.
Through the windows of the Plaza where
	perhaps my lonely Casanova sits,
For if we keep him on the job he may be
	sighted in the lobby of the Ritz.
Through the windows of the Astor where
	perhaps my lord and master waits
	for me.
Maybe due to matrimony he is all alone at
	Tony's sipping tea,
Or if his wife's in Reno he's alone at the
	casino, glass in hand.
Mr. Moon, don't be contrary, come now,
	let us try to share in neverland.

Moon, in this city of millions of
	lights,
Moon, is there someone else wasting his
	nights?

Tell him about me,
Don't turn me down,
Moon, introduce us, you moon
    about town.

    —Dana Suesse

Necessity

verse

What is the curse
That makes the universe
So all bewilderin'?
What is the hoax
That just provokes
The folks
They call God's childerin?
What is the jinx
That gives a body
And his brother
And ev'ryone aroun'
The runaroun'?

refrain 1

Necessity,
Necessity,
That most unnecessary thing,
Necessity.
What throws a monkey wrench in
A fellow's good intention?
That nasty old invention,
Necessity.
My feet wanna dance in the sun,
My head wants to rest in the shade,
The Lord says, "Go out and have fun,"
But the landlord says,
"Your rent ain't paid."
Necessity,
It's plain to see
What a lovely old world
This silly old world could be.

But man, it's all in a mess
Account of necessity.

refrain 2

Necessity,
Necessity,
There ought to be a law against
Necessity.
The jail would never been there
Except for folks who sin there.
Well, how did I get in there?
Necessity.
Oh, Satan's the father of sin,
And Cupid's the father of love,
Oh, hell is the father of gin,
But no one knows the father of . . .

You mean he's a—

Uh-huh
Necessity,
Necessity,
That's the maximum that
A minimum thing could be.
There's nothing lower than less,
Unless it's necessity.

    —Burton Lane

Old Devil Moon

I
Look at you and suddenly
Something in your eyes I see
Soon begins bewitching me.
It's that old devil moon
That you stole from the skies.
It's that old devil moon in your eyes.
You and your glance
Make this romance
Too hot to handle.

Stars in the night
Blazing their light
Can't hold a candle
To your razzle dazzle.
You've
Got me flyin' high and wide
On a magic carpet ride
Full of butterflies inside.
Wanna cry, wanna croon,
Wanna laugh like a loon.
It's that old devil moon
In your eyes.
Just when I think I'm
Free as a dove,
Old devil moon,
Deep in your eyes,
Blinds me with love.

—Burton Lane

OVER THE RAINBOW

VERSE [NOT SUNG IN *THE WIZARD OF OZ*]
When all the world is a hopeless
    jumble
And the raindrops tumble all around,
Heaven opens a magic lane.
When all the clouds darken up the skyway
There's a rainbow highway to be found
Leading from your windowpane
To a place behind the sun
Just a step beyond the rain.

REFRAIN
Somewhere over the rainbow
Way up high,
There's a land that I heard of
Once in a lullaby.
Somewhere over the rainbow
Skies are blue,

And the dreams that you dare to dream
Really do come true.
Someday I'll wish upon a star
And wake up where the clouds are far
    behind me,
Where troubles melt like lemon drops
Away above the chimney tops,
That's where you'll find me.
Somewhere over the rainbow
Bluebirds fly,
Birds fly over the rainbow
Why then oh why can't I?
If happy little bluebirds fly
Beyond the rainbow,
Why oh why can't I?

—Harold Arlen

THE SPRINGTIME COMETH

The Springtime cometh,
Hummingbird hummeth,
Little brook rusheth,
Merry maiden blusheth,
Ice man goeth,
For thy beauty bloweth
Spring to me.
The bright world shineth,
Tender arm twineth,
Starry eye gloweth,
For they knoweth
That without thee,
Spring could never be.
Daffodil . . . he can't stand still,
Cap he flingeth,
Cane he swingeth,
Song he singeth,
Ding dong day. . . .
Which is to say
The Springtime cometh,
Hummingbird hummeth,

Sugarplum plummeth,
Heart, it humpty-dummeth,
And to summeth up,
The Springtime cometh for the love
    of thee.
Lad and lass
In tall green grass
Gaily skippeth,
Nylon rippeth,
Zipper zippeth,
Ding dong day. . . .
Which is to say
The Springtime cometh,
Hummingbird hummeth,
Geranee-yummeth,
Chrysanthe-mummeth,
Bubble gum gummeth,
And the Springtime cometh for the love
    of thee.

—Sammy Fain

Then I'll Be Tired of You

REFRAIN
I'll be tired of you
When stars are tired of gleaming.
When I am tired of dreaming,
Then I'll be tired of you.
This I know is true:
When winds are tired of blowing,
When grass is tired of growing,
Then I'll be tired of you.
Beyond the years,
Till day is night,
Till wrong is right,
Till birds refuse to sing;
Beyond the years,
The echo of my only love
Will still be whispering,
Whispering.
If my throbbing heart

Should ever start repeating
That it is tired of beating,
Then I'll be tired of you.

—Arthur Schwartz

We're Off to See the Wizard
(The Wonderful Wizard of Oz)

VERSE
Follow the yellow brick road,
Follow the yellow brick road,
Follow, follow, follow, follow,
Follow the yellow brick road.
Follow the rainbow over the stream,
Follow the fellow who follows a
    dream,
Follow, follow, follow, follow,
Follow the yellow brick road.

REFRAIN
We're off to see the wizard,
The wonderful Wizard of Oz.
We hear he is
A whiz of a Wiz
If ever a Wiz there was.
If ever, oh ever a Wiz there was,
The Wizard of Oz is one becoz,
Becoz, becoz, becoz, becoz, becoz–
Becoz of the wonderful things he does.
(Whistle)
We're off to see the wizard,
The wonderful Wizard of Oz.

—Harold Arlen

What Is There to Say?

VERSE
Darling, pardon my confusion,
But are you an optical illusion,

And if not, then what on earth
Are you doing to me?
If my speech is willy nilly,
It's because I cannot gild the lily.
I should love to sing your praises
But phrases and words are silly. . . .

REFRAIN
What is there to say?
And what is there to do?
The dream I've been seeking
Has practic'lly speaking
Come true.
What is there to say?
And how will I pull through?
I knew in a moment
Contentment and home meant
Just you.
You are so lovable,
So liveable,
Your beauty is just unforgivable.
You're made to marvel at
And words to that
Effect
So,
What is there to say?
And what is there to do?
My heart's in a deadlock,
I'd even face wedlock
With you.

—Vernon Duke

WHEN I'M NOT NEAR THE GIRL I LOVE

Oh, my heart is beating wildly
And it's all because you're here.
When I'm not near the girl I love,
I love the girl I'm near.
Ev'ry femme that flutters by me
Is a flame that must be fanned.
When I can't fondle the hand I'm fond of,
I fondle the hand at hand.
My heart's in a pickle, it's constantly
    fickle,
And not too partickle, I fear.
When I'm not near the girl I love,
I love the girl I'm near.
I'm confessing a confession,
And I hope I'm not verbose.
When I'm not close to the kiss that I
    cling to,
I cling to the kiss that's close.
As I'm more and more a mortal,
I am more and more a case.
When I'm not facing the face that I fancy,
I fancy the face I face.
For Sharon I'm carin', but Susan I'm
    choosin',
I'm faithful to whos'n is here.
When I'm not near the girl I love,
I love the girl I'm near.

—Burton Lane

Paul James (1896–1969)

THE TITLE SONGS from *Fine and Dandy* and *Can't We Be Friends?* are the most famous work of the short-lived collaboration of the husband-and-wife team Paul James and Kay Swift. "Paul James" was the pseudonym of James Paul Warburg, from the international banking family; his then wife was a protégée of George Gershwin's, for whom she was to leave Warburg in the early thirties.

CAN THIS BE LOVE?

VERSE

Who knows why the sea
Or why the sky is blue?
Why should you love me,
Or I love you?
Who knows how love starts
Or where its course will run?
Who knows why two hearts
Will beat as one?

REFRAIN

I'm all at sea,
Can this be love?
This mystery,
Can this be love?
I'm in a blue haze
Where nothing seems quite real.
I wander through days
With this crazy feeling.
What can it be,
Can this be love?
This thing that I
Keep dreaming of
All through the night till
I wake at early dawn?
Tell me, can this be love?

—Kay Swift

CAN'T WE BE FRIENDS?

VERSE

I took each word he said as gospel truth,
The way a silly little child would.
I can't excuse it on the grounds of
        youth,
I was no babe in the wild wood.
He didn't mean it,
I should have seen it,
Now it's too late!

REFRAIN I

I thought I'd found the man of my
        dreams.
Now it seems
This is how the story ends:
He's goin' to turn me down and say,
"Can't we be friends?"
I thought for once it couldn't go
        wrong,
Not for long!
I can see the way this ends:
He's goin' to turn me down and say,
"Can't we be friends?"
Never again!
Through with love,
Through with men!
They play their game
Without shame,

And who's to blame?
I thought I'd found a man I could trust,
What a bust!
This is how the story ends:
He's goin' to turn me down and say,
"Can't we be friends?"

REFRAIN 2

I thought I knew the wheat from the
    chaff,
What a laugh!
This is how the story ends:
I let him turn me down and say,
"Can't we be friends?"
I acted like a kid out of school,
What a fool!
Now I see the way this ends:
I let him turn me down and say,
"Can't we be friends?"
Why should I care,
Though he gave me the air?
Why should I cry,
Heave a sigh,
And wonder why?
I should have seen the signal to stop,
What a flop!
This is how the story ends:
I let him turn me down and say,
"Can't we be friends?"

—*Kay Swift*

FINE AND DANDY

VERSE

Please forgive this platitude,
But I like your attitude;
You are just the kind
I've had in mind,
Never could find.
Honey, I'm so keen on you,
I could come to lean on you;
Honor and obey,
Give you your way,
Do what you say.

REFRAIN

Gee, it's all
Fine and dandy,
Sugar candy,
When I've got you.
Then I only see the sunny side,
Even trouble has its funny side.
When you're gone,
Sugar candy,
I get lonesome,
I get so blue.
When you're handy
It's fine and dandy,
But when you're gone
What can I do?

—*Kay Swift*

Howard Dietz (1896–1983)

LIKE ARTHUR FREED, Howard Dietz had a split career: as songwriter and as M-G-M executive. A New Yorker, he was a fellow student of George Gershwin's in high school and a close friend of Larry Hart's and Oscar Hammerstein's at Columbia College. As early as 1924, he did a show with Jerome Kern *(Dear Sir),* and by 1929 he was working with his chief collaborator, Arthur Schwartz. Over the next decade they did nine shows together, including the two *Little Shows, Three's a Crowd,* and *The Band Wagon;* then *Inside U.S.A.* in 1948 and two flops *d'estime* in the sixties, *Jennie* and *The Gay Life.* Whereas their book musicals weren't successful, no one wrote more or better hit revues. Dietz turned out lots of terrific cheerful numbers–"I Love Louisa," "A Shine on Your Shoes," and the ubiquitous "That's Entertainment"–but his real bent lay in highly romantic, some might say high-flown, ballads: "Dancing in the Dark," "You and the Night and the Music," "I See Your Face Before Me." In other words, he was both very clever and very emotional. Not only did Dietz hold a powerful position at Metro (he was head of publicity, then a vice president of Loews), he was a top bridge player, a successful writer of light verse, and an opera librettist, or at least translator: He wrote the famous English-language version of *Die Fledermaus* that Alfred Lunt directed at the Met. He was also the author of many famous mots–"A day away from Tallulah Bankhead is like a month in the country"–and of an entertaining autobiography, *Dancing in the Dark.* To *Variety,* at his death, he was a "Renaissance Man for All Media."

ALONE TOGETHER

Alone together,
Beyond the crowd,
Above the world,
We're not too proud
To cling together,
We're strong
As long as we're
Together.
Alone together,
The blinding rain,
The starless night,
We're not in vain;

For we're together,
And what is there to fear
Together?
Our love
Is as deep as the sea.
Our love
Is as great as a love can be.
And we can weather
The great unknown,
If we're alone together.

—Arthur Schwartz

BLUE GRASS

VERSE

Down in Kentucky
The horses devil a man.
A lady in Louisville
Is only an also-ran.
I got a forehead full of frowns
Since I came to Churchill Downs.

REFRAIN I

Blue grass, blue grass,
Lost my lover in the blue grass,
Blame the ponies in the blue grass.
Hard to compete
With gallopin' feet.
Blue dawn, blue noon,
Only see him in a blue moon,
Lost my lover in the blue, blue grass.
In the cold
When I should be warm,
He can't keep me warm
With a Racing Form.
In the cold
Guess I lost my hold,
Ain't as frisky as a three-year-old.
Nightmare, day mare,
Feelin' older than the gray mare,
Lost my lover in the blue, blue grass.

REFRAIN 2

Blue grass, blue grass,
Lost my lover in the blue grass,
Blame the ponies in the blue grass.
They get the rush,
I get the brush.
Rides 'em, walks 'em,
In his sleep he even talks 'em,
Found my rival in the blue, blue
    grass.
In the cold,
And it looks as though

I ain't in the dough,
Even place or show.
In the cold,
I would give my all,
Even move my bed into a stall.
Might be lucky
Far away from old Kentucky.
Lost my lover in the blue, blue grass.

—Arthur Schwartz

DANCING IN THE DARK

REFRAIN

Dancing in the dark,
Till the tune ends
We're dancing in the dark,
And it soon ends.
We're waltzing in the wonder
Of why we're here.
Time hurries by, we're here
And gone,
Looking for the light
Of a new love
To brighten up the night.
I have you, love,
And we can face the music together,
Dancing in the dark.

INTERLUDE

What though love is old?
What though song is old?
Through them we can be young!
Hear this heart of mine
Make yours part of mine!
Dear one,
Tell me that we're one!

REPEAT REFRAIN

—Arthur Schwartz

Haunted Heart

In the night
Though we're apart,
There's a ghost of you
Within my haunted heart;
Ghost of you,
My lost romance.
Lips that laugh,
Eyes that dance.
Haunted heart
Won't let me be,
In the night,
Though we're apart,
Dreams repeat a sweet but lonely song
    to me.
Dreams are dust,
It's you who must
Belong to me
And thrill
My haunted heart.
Be still,
My haunted heart.
Time rolls on
Trying in vain to cure me,
You are gone,
But you remain to lure me.
You're there in the dark and I call,
You're there but you're not there at all.
Oh, what will I do
Without you,
Without you.

—Arthur Schwartz

I Guess I'll Have to Change My Plan

VERSE

I beheld her and was conquered at the
    start,
And placed her on a pedestal apart.
I planned the little hideaway
That we would share some day.
When I met her I unfolded all my dream,
And told her how she'd fit into my scheme
Of what bliss is.
Then the blow came,
When she gave her name as
"Missus."

REFRAIN 1

I guess I'll have to change my plan,
I should have realized there'd be
    another man!
I overlooked that point completely
Until the big affair began.
Before I knew where I was at
I found myself upon the shelf, and that
    was that.
I tried to reach the moon, but when I got
    there,
All that I could get was the air.
My feet are back upon the ground,
I've lost the one girl I found.

REFRAIN 2

I guess I'll have to change my plan,
I should have realized there'd be
    another man!
Why did I buy those blue pajamas
Before the big affair began?
My boiling point is much too low
For me to try to be a fly Lothario!
I think I'll crawl right back and into my
    shell,
Dwelling in my personal Hell.
I'll have to change my plan around,
I've lost the one girl I found.

—Arthur Schwartz

I See Your Face Before Me

VERSE

In a word of glitter and glow,
In a world of tinsel and show,
The unreal from the real thing is hard
    to know.
I discovered somebody who
Could be truly worthy and true,
Yes, I met my ideal thing
When I met you.

REFRAIN

I see your face before me
Crowding my ev'ry dream.
There is your face before me,
You are my only theme.
It doesn't matter where you are,
I can see how fair you are,
I close my eyes and there you are,
Always.
If you could share the magic,
If you could see me too,
There would be nothing tragic
In all my dreams of you.
Would that my love could haunt you so,
Knowing I want you so,
I can't erase
Your beautiful face
Before me.

—*Arthur Schwartz*

If There Is Someone Lovelier Than You

VERSE

Ev'ry day is a brand new day
When you are mine.
But the moment that you go away,
No sun will shine.
Your love is my reward;
Each night I thank the Lord.
Tell me till time is done,
We'll be one.

REFRAIN

If there is someone lovelier than you,
Then I am blind.
A man without a mind,
If there is someone lovelier than you.
But no, I am not blind,
My eyes have travelled ev'rywhere
In hope that I might find
A creature half so fair.
If there is someone lovelier than you,
By all that's beautiful,
Such beauty can't be true.

—*Arthur Schwartz*

Rhode Island Is Famous for You

VERSE

Ev'ry state has something
Its Rotary Club can boast of;
Some product that the state
Produces the most of.
Rhode Island is little, but oh my,
It has a product anyone would buy.

REFRAIN I

Copper comes from Arizona,
Peaches come from Georgia,
And lobsters come from Maine.
The
Wheat fields
Are the sweet fields
Of Nebraska,
And Kansas
Gets bonanzas
From the grain.
Old whiskey

Comes from old Kentucky,
Ain't the country lucky?
New Jersey gives us glue.
And you,
You come from Rhode Island,
And little old
Rhode Island
Is famous for you!

REFRAIN 2

Cotton comes from Loosiana,
Gophers from Montana,
And spuds from Idaho.
They plow land
In the cow land
Of Missoura,
Where most beef
Meant for roast beef
Seems to grow.
Grand Canyons
Come from Colorada,
Gold comes from Nevada,
Divorces also do.
And you,
You come from Rhode Island,
And little old
Rhode Island
Is famous for you!

REFRAIN 3

Pencils
Come from Pencilvania,
Vests from Vest Virginia
And tents from Tentasee.
They know mink
Where they grow mink
In Wyomink.
A camp chair
In New Hampchair,
That's for me.
And minnows
Come from Minnowsota,
Coats come from Dacoata,

But why should you be blue?
For you,
You come from Rhode Island,
Don't let them ride Rhode Island;
It's famous for you!

—*Arthur Schwartz*

SOMETHING TO REMEMBER YOU BY

VERSE

You are leaving me,
And I will try
To face the world
Alone.
What will be will be,
But time cannot
Erase the love
We've known.
Let me but have a token
Through which your love is spoken,
You are leaving me,
But it will say
You're my own.

REFRAIN

Oh, give me something to remember
    you by,
When you are far away from me,
Dear;
Some little something, meaning love
    cannot die,
No matter where you chance to be.
Though I'll pray for you,
Night and day for you,
It will see me through
Like a charm,
Till you're returning.
So give me something to remember you by,
When you are far away from me.

—*Arthur Schwartz*

That's Entertainment

VERSE

Ev'rything that happens in life
Can happen in a show.
You can make them laugh,
You can make them cry;
Anything, anything can go.

REFRAIN 1

The clown
With his pants falling down,
Or the dance
That's a dream of romance,
Or the scene
Where the villain is mean;
That's entertainment!
The lights
On the lady in tights,
Or the bride
With a guy on the side,
Or the ball
Where she gives him her all,
That's entertainment!
The plot can be hot,
Simply teeming with sex,
A gay divorcée
Who is after her "ex."
It can be *Oedipus Rex*
Where a chap kills his father
And causes a lot of bother.
The clerk who is thrown out of work
By the boss
Who is thrown for a loss
By the skirt
Who is doing him dirt;
The world is a stage,
The stage is a world of entertainment!

REFRAIN 2

The doubt
While the jury is out,
Or the thrill
When they're reading the will,
Or the chase
For the man with the face;
That's entertainment!
The dame
Who is known as the flame
Of the king
Of an underworld ring,
He's an ape
Who won't let her escape,
That's entertainment!
It might be a fight
Like you see on the screen,
A swain getting slain
For the love of a queen.
Some great Shakespearean scene
Where a ghost and a prince meet
And ev'ryone ends in mincemeat.
The gag
May be waving the flag
That began
With a Mister Cohan,
Hip hurray,
The American way;
The world is a stage,
The stage is a world of entertainment!

REFRAIN 3

A show
That is really a show
Sends you out
With a kind of glow
And you say
As you go on your way
"That's entertainment."
A song
That is winging along
Or a dance
With a touch of romance
Is the art
That appeals to the heart,
That's entertainment!

Admit
We're a hit
And we'll go on from there.
We played a charade
That was lighter than air,
A good old-fashioned affair,
As we sing this finale,
We hope it was up your alley.
No death
Like you get in *Macbeth,*
No ordeal
Like the end of *Camille,*
This good-bye
Brings a tear to the eye.
The world is a stage,
The stage is a world of entertainment!

—*Arthur Schwartz*

TRIPLETS

VERSE

Three little unexpected children,
Simultaneously the doctor brought us
And you can see that we'll be
Three forever and aye, ee-i-o.
You wouldn't know how agonizing
Being triple can be.
Each one is individually
The victim of the clinical day,
Ee-i-o.
Ev'ry summer we go away to Baden Baden
    Baden.
Ev'ry winter we come back home to Walla
    Walla Walla.

REFRAIN

We do ev'rything alike;
We look alike, we dress alike,
We walk alike, we talk alike,
And what is more

We hate each other very much.
We hate our folks,
We're sick of jokes on what an art it is to
    tell us apart.
If one of us gets the measles,
Another one gets the measles,
Then all of us gets the measles,
And mumps and croup.
How I wish I had a gun,
A little gun,
It would be fun to shoot the other two
And be only one.

PATTER

Missus Whiffle Poofer loves to talk to
    Missus Hildendorfer
Of the fatal natal day she had her silly
    Willie.
Missus Hassencooper loves to talk to
    Missus Goldenwasser
Of her major operation when she had her
    twins.
But when Mother comes along, she
    silences the others;
She accomplished something that is very
    rare in mothers.
People who disparage marriage, burdened
    with a baby carriage,
Cater to the mater and her large
    perambulator.
M-G-M has got a Leo,
But Mama has got a trio.
She is proud, but says three is a crowd.

AFTER PATTER

We eat the same kind of vittels,
We drink the same kind of bottles,
We sit in the same kind of high chair
(Hi chair, hi chair).
How I wish I had a gun,
A little gun,
It would be fun

To shoot the other two
And be only one.

        —Arthur Schwartz

You and the Night and the Music

VERSE

Song is in the air,
Telling us romance is ours to share.
Now at last we've found one another alone.
Love like yours and mine
Has the thrilling glow of sparkling wine,
Make the most of time ere it has flown.

REFRAIN

You and the night and the music
Fill me with flaming desire,

Setting my being completely
On fire!
You and the night and the music
Thrill me, but will we be one,
After the night and the music
Are done?
Until the pale light of dawning and
    daylight
Our hearts will be throbbing guitars.
Morning may come without
    warning,
And take away the stars.
If we must live for the moment,
Love till the moment is through!
After the night and the music die
Will I
Have you?

        —Arthur Schwartz

Harry Woods (1896–1970)

H ARRY WOODS WAS a quintessential hit-maker of the twenties and early thirties, yet three of his most famous songs had equally great success when they were rediscovered decades later. Three different recordings of "Side by Side" made it into the top ten in 1927, and Kay Starr did it again in 1953; three versions of "I'm Looking over a Four-Leaf Clover" were top ten, also in 1927, while Art Mooney's ukulele treatment was number one for weeks in 1948; and the 1933 hit "Try a Little Tenderness" was rediscovered by Aretha Franklin (1962), Otis Redding (1967), and Three Dog Night (1969). Woods, born with no fingers on his left hand yet a capable piano player, went to Harvard and afterward preferred living on his Massachusetts farm until well into his songwriting career. Among the performers for whom he wrote signature songs were Kate Smith ("When the Moon Comes over the Mountain") and Jessie Matthews ("Over My Shoulder"). Woods was known more for independent songs than for shows, but he also wrote several excellent scores for shows and films, enjoying dual careers in New York and London.

OVER MY SHOULDER

VERSE
I've been a pris'ner, locked in a jail,
Love held the only key;
Love heard me crying, locked in a jail,
Came to the help of me.
Oh! what a wonderful feeling,
To be free, really free!

REFRAIN
So, over my shoulder goes one care,
Over my shoulder go two cares.
Why should I cry? It's blue above.
I'm free at last, and I'm in love.
Over my shoulder go three cares,
Over my shoulder go four cares.
Bye-bye to trouble, it's gone beyond recall;
Over my shoulder goes it all.

PADDLIN' MADELIN' HOME

VERSE I
I love a girl named Madelin',
I know she loves me, too,
For ev'ry night the moon is bright
She rides in my canoe.
At midnight on the river
I heard her father call,
But she don't care and I don't care
If we get back at all.

REFRAIN I
'Cause when I'm paddlin'
    Madelin' home,
Gee! when I'm paddlin' Madelin' home,
First I drift with the tide,
Then pull for the shore,
I hug her and kiss her
And paddle some more.

Then I keep paddlin' Madelin' home
Until I find a spot where we're alone.
Oh! she never says "No,"
So I kiss her and go
Paddlin' Madelin',
Sweet, sweet Madelin',
Paddlin' Madelin' home.

VERSE 2

The moon comes up at six o'clock
And I come up at eight.
She's always waitin' for my call
And meets me at the gate.
I've petted in the parlor
And hugged her in the hall,
But when she's out in my canoe
I love her best of all.

REFRAIN 2

'Cause when I'm paddlin'
    Madelin' home,
Gee! when I'm paddlin' Madelin' home,
First I kiss her awhile,
And when I get through
I paddle for one mile
And drift back for two.
Then I keep paddlin' Madelin' home
Until I find a spot where we're alone.
Oh! if she'd only say,
"Throw your paddles away."
Paddlin' Madelin',
Sweet, sweet Madelin',
Paddlin' Madelin' home.

SIDE BY SIDE

VERSE I

See that sun in the morning
Peeking over the hill?
I'll bet you're sure it always has
And sure it always will.
That's how I feel about someone,

How somebody feels about me.
We're sure we love each other,
That's the way we'll always be.

REFRAIN

Oh! we ain't got a barrel of money,
Maybe we're ragged and funny,
But we'll travel along,
Singin' a song,
Side by side.
Don't know what's comin' tomorrow,
Maybe it's trouble and sorrow,
But we'll travel the road,
Sharin' our load,
Side by side.
Through all kinds of weather,
What if the sky should fall?
Just as long as we're together,
It doesn't matter at all.
When they've all had their quarrels and
    parted,
We'll be the same as we started,
Just trav'lin' along,
Singin' a song,
Side by side.

VERSE 2

We're all hunting for something,
Something we don't know what.
'Cause none of us are satisfied
With things we know we've got.
We all forget about moonlight
As soon as we've given our vow,
But we'd all be so happy
If we'd start and sing right now:

REPEAT REFRAIN

TRY A LITTLE TENDERNESS

(with Jimmy Campbell and
Reginald Connelly)

Oh, she may be weary,
And young girls, they do get weary
Wearin' that same shaggy dress.
But when she gets weary,
Try a little tenderness.
You know she's waiting,
Just anticipatin'
The things that she never did
    possess.
But while she's there waiting,
Try a little tenderness.
That's all you gotta do.
It's not just sentimental, no.
She had her grief and her care.
But for soft words
We all spoke so gentle,
It makes it easier to bear.
You won't regret it,
Young girls, they don't forget it.
Love is their only happiness.
It's all so easy,
Just try a little tenderness.

WE JUST COULDN'T SAY GOOD-BYE

REFRAIN

We thought that love was over,
That we were really through.
I said I didn't love her,
That we'd begin anew.
And you can all believe me,
We sure intended to,
But we just couldn't say good-bye.
The chair and then the sofa,
They broke right down and cried.
The curtains started wavin'

For me to come inside.
I tell you confidentially,
The tears were hard to hide,
And we just couldn't say good-bye.
The clock was striking twelve
    o'clock,
It smiled on us below.
With folded hands it seemed to say,
We'll miss you if you go.
So I went back and kissed her
And when I looked around,
The room was singin' love songs
And dancin' up and down.
And now we're both so happy,
Because at last we've found
That we just couldn't say good-bye.

WHEN THE RED, RED ROBIN COMES BOB, BOB, BOBBIN' ALONG

When the red, red robin
Comes bob, bob, bobbin' along,
    along,
There'll be no more sobbin'
When he starts throbbin' his old, sweet
    song.
Wake up, wake up you sleepy head.
Get up, get up, get out of bed.
Cheer up, cheer up, the sun is red.
Live, love, laugh and be happy.
What if I've been blue?
Now I'm walkin' through fields of
    flow'rs.
Rain may glisten but
Still I listen for hours and hours.
I'm just a kid again,
Doin' what I did again,
Singin' a song,
When the red, red robin
Comes bob, bob, bobbin' along.

Ira Gershwin (1896–1983)

OLDER BROTHER OF the great George Gershwin, the soft-spoken and self-effacing Ira outlived the composer by more than forty-five years. His career started out with a variety of odd jobs: cashier in a Turkish bath, assistant photographer, employee at Altmans department store; he was all the while trying his hand at lyrics and light verse. For some of his early efforts he used the pseudonym "Arthur Francis," to avoid taking advantage of George's growing fame; under this name, he worked successfully with several composers, notably Vincent Youmans ("Oh Me, Oh My, Oh You"). By 1924 he was firmly linked to George–between then and 1937 they worked together on more than a dozen Broadway musicals, from *Lady Be Good* and *Funny Face,* both with the Astaires, to *Girl Crazy* (Ethel Merman's Broadway debut) and *Of Thee I Sing,* for which Ira won the first Pulitzer Prize awarded to a lyricist, to *Porgy and Bess.* Yet even while working with George, Ira took time off to write with Harold Arlen and Yip Harburg for the revue *Life Begins at 8:40*–"Fun to Be Fooled," "Let's Take a Walk Around the Block"–and with Vernon Duke, *The Ziegfeld Follies of 1936* ("I Can't Get Started"). George and Ira wrote several film scores together: "Delicious," for Janet Gaynor; "Shall We Dance," for Astaire and Rogers; and their final collaborations, "A Damsel in Distress," also for Astaire, and "The Goldwyn Follies," both released after George's death. After a two-year lay-off, Ira returned to work with a tremendous Broadway hit–the Kurt Weill/Moss Hart/Gertrude Lawrence *Lady in the Dark*–and then went on with Weill, Jerome Kern, Harry Warren, and others; and, for a grand finale, the Judy Garland *A Star Is Born,* with his old partner Harold Arlen. His book *Lyrics on Several Occasions* is a classic exploration of his art in general and his own clever, good-natured, and highly original art in particular.

THE BABBITT AND THE BROMIDE

VERSE I

A Babbitt met a Bromide on the avenue
  one day,
They held a conversation in their own
  peculiar way.
They both were solid citizens–they both
  had been around.

And as they spoke you clearly saw their
  feet were on the ground.

REFRAIN I

Hello! How are you?
Howza folks? What's new?
I'm great! That's good!
Ha! Ha! Knock wood!
Well! Well! What say?

Howya been? Nice day!

How's tricks? What's new?

That's fine! How are you?

Nice weather we are having but it gives me such a pain:

I've taken my umbrella, so of course it doesn't rain.

Heigh ho! That's life!

What's new? Howza wife?

Gotta run! Oh, my!

Ta! Ta! Olive oil! Good-bye!

VERSE 2

Ten years went quickly by for both these sub-sti-an-tial men,

Then history records one day they chanced to meet again.

That they had both developed in ten years there was no doubt,

And so of course they had an awful lot to talk about:

REFRAIN 2

Hello! How are you?

Howza folks? What's new?

I'm great! That's good!

Ha! Ha! Knock wood!

Well! Well! What say?

Howya been? Nice day!

How's tricks? What's new?

That's fine! How are you?

I'm sure I know your face, but I just can't recall your name.

Well, how've you been, old boy? You're looking just about the same.

Heigh ho! That's life!

What's new? Howza wife?

Gotta run! Oh, my!

Ta! Ta! Olive oil! Good-bye!

VERSE 3

Before they met again some twenty years they had to wait.

This time it happened up above, inside St. Peter's gate.

A harp each one was carrying and both were wearing wings,

And this is what they sang as they kept strumming on the strings:

REFRAIN 3

Hello! How are you?

Howza folks? What's new?

I'm great! That's good!

Ha! Ha! Knock wood!

Well! Well! What say?

Howya been? Nice day!

How's tricks? What's new?

That's fine! How are you?

You've grown a little stouter since I saw you last, I think.

Come up and see me sometime and we'll have a little drink.

Heigh ho! That's life!

What's new? Howza wife?

Gotta run! Oh, my!

Ta! Ta! Olive oil! Good-bye!

—George Gershwin

BIDIN' MY TIME

VERSE 1

Some fellers love to Tip-Toe Through the Tulips;

Some fellers go on Singin' in the Rain;

Some fellers keep on Paintin' Skies with Sunshine;

Some fellers keep on Swingin' Down the Lane–

But–

REFRAIN 1

I'm bidin' my time,

'Cause that's the kinda guy I'm.

While other folks grow dizzy,
I keep busy–
Bidin' my time.
Next year, next year,
Somethin's bound to happen;
This year, this year,
I'll just keep on nappin'–
And–bidin' my time,
'Cause that's the kinda guy I'm.
There's no regrettin'
When I'm settin'–
Bidin' my time.

VERSE 2
Some fellers love to Tell It to the
      Daisies;
Some stroll Beneath the Honeysuckle
      Vines;
Some fellers when they've Climbed the
      Highest Mountain
Still keep a-Cryin' for the Carolines–
But–

REFRAIN 2
I'm bidin' my time,
'Cause that's the kinda guy I'm–
Beginnin' on a Mond'y
Right through Sund'y,
Bidin' my time.
Give me, give me
A glass that's full of tinkle;
Let me, let me
Dream like Rip Van Winkle.
He bided his time,
And like that Winkle guy I'm.
Chasin' way flies,
How the day flies–
Bidin' my time!

TAG
I'm bidin' my time,
'Cause that's the kinda guy I'm–
Stranger, so long,

I'll just go 'long
Bidin' my time.

—George Gershwin

BLAH, BLAH, BLAH

VERSE
I've written you a song,
A beautiful routine.
(I hope you like it.)
My technique can't be wrong:
I learned it from the screen.
(I hope you like it.)
I studied all the rhymes that all the
      lovers sing;
Then just for you I wrote this little thing:

REFRAIN
Blah, blah, blah, blah, moon,
Blah, blah, blah, above;
Blah, blah, blah, blah, croon,
Blah, blah, blah, blah, love.
Tra la la la, tra la la la la, merry month of May;
Tra la la la, tra la la la la, 'neath the clouds
      of gray.
Blah, blah, blah, your hair,
Blah, blah, blah, your eyes;
Blah, blah, blah, blah, care,
Blah, blah, blah, blah, skies.
Tra la la la, tra la la la la, cottage for two–
Blah, blah, blah, blah, darling, with you!

—George Gershwin

BUT NOT FOR ME

VERSE
Old Man Sunshine–listen, you!
Never tell me dreams come true!
Just try it–

And I'll start a riot.
Beatrice Fairfax–don't you dare
Ever tell me he will care;
I'm certain
It's the final curtain.
I never want to hear
From any cheer-
Ful Pollyannas,
Who tell you Fate
Supplies a mate–
It's all bananas!

REFRAIN I
They're writing songs of love,
But not for me;
A lucky star's above,
But not for me.
With love to lead the way,
I've found more clouds of gray
Than any Russian play
Could guarantee.
I was a fool to fall
And get that way;
Heigh ho! Alas! and al-
So lackaday!
Love ain't done right by Nell;
However–what the hell!
I guess he's not for me.

REFRAIN 2
He's knocking on a door,
But not for me;
He'll plan a two by four,
But not for me.
I've heard that love's a game;
I'm puzzled, just the same–
Was I the moth or flame . . . ?
I'm all at sea.
It started off so swell,
This "Let's Pretend";
It all began so well;
But what an end!
The climax of a plot

Should be the marriage knot,
But there's no knot for me.

—*George Gershwin*

Do, Do, Do

VERSE I
HE: I remember the bliss
Of that wonderful kiss.
I know that a boy
Could never have more joy
From any little miss.
SHE: I remember it quite;
'Twas a wonderful night.
HE: Oh, how I'd adore it
If you would encore it. Oh–

REFRAIN I
Do, do, do
What you've done, done, done
Before,
Baby.
Do, do, do
What I do, do, do
Adore,
Baby.
Let's try again,
Sigh again,
Fly again to heaven.
Baby, see
It's A B C–
I love you and you love me.
I know, know, know
What a beau, beau, beau
Should do,
Baby;
So, don't, don't, don't
Say it won't, won't, won't
Come true,
Baby.
My heart begins to hum–

Dum de dum de dum-dum-dum,
So do, do, do,
What you've done, done, done
Before.

VERSE 2

SHE: Sweets we've tasted before
Cannot stand an encore.
You know that a miss
Who always gives a kiss
Would soon become a bore.
HE: I can't see that at all;
True love never should pall.
SHE: I was only teasing;
What you did was pleasing. Oh–

REFRAIN 2

Do, do, do
What you've done, done, done
Before,
Baby.
Do, do, do
What I do, do, do
Adore,
Baby.
Let's try again,
Sigh again,
Fly again to heaven.
Baby, see
It's A B C–
I love you and you love me.

HE: You dear, dear, dear
Little dear, dear, dear,
Come here,
Snappy!
And see, see, see
Little me, me, me
Make you
Happy.

SHE: My heart begins to sigh–
Di de di de di-di-di,

So do, do, do
What you've done, done, done
Before.

—George Gershwin

EMBRACEABLE YOU

VERSE 1

HE: Dozens of girls would storm up;
I had to lock my door.
Somehow I couldn't warm up
To one before.
What was it that controlled me?
What kept my love life lean?
My intuition told me
You'd come on the scene.
Lady, listen to the rhythm of my
heartbeat,
And you'll get just what I mean.

REFRAIN 1

Embrace me,
My sweet embraceable you.
Embrace me,
You irreplaceable you.
Just one look at you–my heart grew tipsy
in me;
You and you alone bring out the gypsy
in me.
I love all
The many charms about you;
Above all,
I want my arms about you.
Don't be a naughty baby,
Come to Papa–come to Papa–do!
My sweet embraceable you.

VERSE 2

SHE: I went about reciting,
"Here's one who'll never fall!"
But I'm afraid the writing

Is on the wall.
My nose I used to turn up
When you'd besiege my heart;
Now I completely burn up
When you're slow to start.
I'm afraid you'll have to take the
    consequences;
You upset the apple cart.

REFRAIN 2

Embrace me,
My sweet embraceable you.
Embrace me,
You irreplaceable you.
In your arms I find love so
    delectable, dear,
I'm afraid it isn't quite respectable, dear.
But hang it!
Come on, let's glorify love!
Ding dang it!
You'll shout "Encore!" if I love.
Don't be a naughty Papa,
Come to baby—come to baby—do!
My sweet embraceable you.

ENCORE REFRAIN

HE: Dear lady,
    My silk-and-lace-able you;
    Dear lady,
    Be my embraceable you.
    You're the only one I love, yes,
        verily so!
    But you're much too shy,
        unnecessarily so!
SHE: I'll try not
    To be so formal, my dear.
HE: Am I not
    A man who's normal, my dear?
    There's just one way to cheer me;
    Come to Papa—come to Papa—do!
    My sweet embraceable you.

—George Gershwin

FASCINATING RHYTHM

VERSE

Got a little rhythm, a rhythm, a rhythm
That pit-a-pats through my brain;
So darn persistent,
The day isn't distant
When it'll drive me insane.
Comes in the morning
Without any warning,
And hangs around me all day.
I'll have to sneak up to it
Someday, and speak up to it.
I hope it listens when I say:

REFRAIN

Fascinating rhythm,
You've got me on the go!
Fascinating rhythm,
I'm all a-quiver.
What a mess you're making!
The neighbors want to know
Why I'm always shaking
Just like a flivver.
Each morning I get up with the sun—
Start a-hopping,
Never stopping—
To find at night no work has been done.
I know that
Once it didn't matter—
But now you're doing wrong;
When you start to patter
I'm so unhappy.
Won't you take a day off?
Decide to run along
Somewhere far away off—
And make it snappy!
Oh, how I long to be the man I used to be!
Fascinating rhythm,
Oh, won't you stop picking on me?

—George Gershwin

A Foggy Day (in London Town)

I was a stranger in the city.
Out of town were the people I knew.
I had that feeling of self-pity:
What to do? What to do? What to do?
The outlook was decidedly blue.
But as I walked through the foggy streets
    alone,
It turned out to be the luckiest day I've
    known.

A foggy day in London Town
Had me low and had me down.
I viewed the morning with alarm.
The British Museum had lost its
    charm.
How long, I wondered, could this
    thing last?
But the age of miracles hadn't passed,
For, suddenly, I saw you there—
And through foggy London Town
The sun was shining ev'rywhere.

—George Gershwin

How Long Has This Been Going On?

HE: As a tot,
    When I trot-
    Ted in little velvet panties,
    I was kissed
    By my sist-
    Ers, my cousins, and my aunties.
    Sad to tell,
    It was hell—
    An Inferno worse than Dante's.

So, my dear, I swore,
"Never, nevermore!"
On my list,

I could cry
Salty tears;
Where have I
Been all these years?
Little wow,
Tell me now:
How long has this been going on?
There were chills
Up my spine,
And some thrills
I can't define.
Listen, sweet,
I repeat:
How long has this been going on?
Oh, I feel that I could melt;
Into heaven I'm hurled.
I know how Columbus felt
Finding another world.
Kiss me once,
Then once more.
What a dunce
I was before!
What a break—
For heaven's sake!
How long has this been going on?

SHE: 'Neath the stars,
    At bazaars,
    Often I've had to caress men.
    Five or ten
    Dollars, then,
    I'd collect from all those yes-men.
    Don't be sad;
    I must add
    That they meant no more than
        chessmen.
    Darling, can't you see—

'Twas for charity?
Though these lips
Have made slips,
I was never really serious.
Who'd 'a' thought
I'd be brought
To a state that's so delirious?

REFRAIN 2

I could cry
Salty tears;
Where have I
Been all these years?
Listen, you–
Tell me, do:
How long has this been going on?
What a kick–
How I buzz!
Boy, you click
As no one does!
Hear me, sweet,
I repeat:
How long has this been going on?
Dear, when in your arms I creep–
That divine rendezvous–
Don't wake me if I'm asleep,
Let me dream that it's true.
Kiss me twice,
Then once more–
That makes thrice;
Let's make it four!
What a break–
For heaven's sake!
How long has this been going on?

REPRISE

Dear, oh dear!
Is that nice!
Listen here,
I smell a mice!
What's the mess?
Come, confess!

How long has this been going on?
Goodness' sake!
My, what brass!
Just a big snake
In the grass!
I must know,
You so-and-so,
How long has this been going on?

—George Gershwin

I CAN'T GET STARTED

VERSE

I'm a glum one; it's explainable:
I met someone unattainable;
Life's a bore,
The world is my oyster no more.
All the papers, where I led the news
With my capers, now will spread the news:
"Superman
Turns Out to Be Flash in the Pan."

REFRAIN I

I've flown around the world in a plane;
I won the race from Newport to Maine;
The North Pole I have charted,
But I can't get started with you.
Around a golf course I'm under par;
The Theatre Guilders want me to star;
I've got a house–a showplace–
But I get no place with you.
You're so supreme,
Lyrics I write of you;
Scheme
Just for a sight of you;
Dream
Both day and night of you,
And what good does it do?
I've been consulted by Franklin D.;
And Greta Garbo's asked me to tea;

And yet I'm brokenhearted
'Cause I can't get started with you.

REFRAIN 2
I do a hundred yards in ten flat;
The Duke of Kent has copied my hat;
With queens I've à la carted,
But I can't get started with you.
When Democrats are all in a mess,
I hear Jim Farley's call of distress,
And I help him maneuver,
But I'm just Hoover to you.
When first we met—
How you elated me!
Pet!
You devastated me!
Yet,
Now you've deflated me
Till you're my Waterloo.
When J. P. Morgan bows, I just nod;
Green Pastures wanted me to play God.
The Siamese Twins I've parted,
But I can't get started with you.

REFRAIN 3
The Himalaya Mountains I climb;
I'm written up in *Fortune* and *Time;*
New Yorker did my profile [*pro-feel*]
But I've had no feel from you.
There's always "Best regards and
    much love"
From Mr. Lehman—you know, the Gov;
I go to ev'ry state ball,
But I'm just behind the eight ball
    with you.
Oh, tell me why
Am I no kick to you?
I,
Who'd always stick to you?
Fly
Through thin and thick to you?
Tell me why I'm taboo!

Oh, what a man you're keeping at bay;
I use a pound of Lifebuoy each day;
But you've got me downhearted
'Cause I can't, I can't, I can't, I can't,
I can't get started with you.

—*Vernon Duke*

I Got Plenty o' Nuthin'

Oh, I got plenty o' nuthin',
An' nuthin's plenty for me.
I got no car, got no mule, I got no
    misery.
De folks wid plenty o' plenty
Got a lock on dey door,
'Fraid somebody's a-goin' to rob 'em
While dey's out a-makin' more.
What for?
I got no lock on de door.
(Dat's no way to be.)
Dey can steal de rug from the floor,
Dat's O.K. wid me,
'Cause de things dat I prize,
Like de stars in de skies,
All are free.
Oh, I got plenty o' nuthin',
An' nuthin's plenty for me.
I got my gal, got my song,
Got Hebben de whole day long.
(No use complainin'!)
Got my gal, got my Lawd, got my song.
I got plenty o' nuthin',
An' nuthin's plenty fo' me.
I got de sun, got de moon, got de deep
    blue sea.
De folks wid plenty o' plenty,
Got to pray all de day.
Seems wid plenty you sure got to worry
How to keep the Debble way,
A-way.

I ain't a-frettin' 'bout Hell
Till de time arrive.
Never worry long as I'm well,
Never one to strive
To be good, to be bad—
What the hell! I is glad
I's alive.
Oh, I got plenty o' nuthin'
An nuthin's plenty fo' me.
I got my gal, got my song,
Got Hebben de whole day long.
(No use complainin'!)
Got my gal,
Got my Lawd,
Got my song!

—George Gershwin

I Got Rhythm

VERSE

Days can be sunny,
With never a sigh;
Don't need what money
Can buy.
Birds in the tree sing
Their dayful of song.
Why shouldn't we sing
Along?
I'm chipper all the day,
Happy with my lot.
How do I get that way?
Look at what I've got:

REFRAIN

I got rhythm,
I got music,
I got my man—
Who could ask for anything more?
I got daisies
In green pastures,
I got my man—

Who could ask for anything more?
Old Man Trouble,
I don't mind him—
You won't find him
'Round my door.
I got starlight,
I got sweet dreams,
I got my man—
Who could ask for anything more—
Who could ask for anything more?

—George Gershwin

Isn't It a Pity?

VERSE I

HE: Why did I wander
Here and there and yonder,
Wasting precious time
For no reason or rhyme?
Isn't it a pity?
Isn't it a crime?
My journey's ended;
Ev'rything is splendid.
Meeting you today
Has given me a
Wonderful idea;
Here I stay!

REFRAIN I

It's a funny thing;
I look at you—
I get a thrill
I never knew;
Isn't it a pity
We never met before?
Here we are at last!
It's like a dream!
The two of us—
A perfect team!
Isn't it a pity
We never met before?

Imagine all the lonely years we've
    wasted:
You, with the neighbors–
I, at silly labors;
What joys untasted!
You, reading Heine,
I, somewhere in China.
Happiest of men
I'm sure to be
If only you
Will say to me,
"It's an awful pity,
We never, never met before!"

VERSE 2

SHE: While you were flitting,
    I was busy knitting.
HE: How did you survive
    Waiting till I'd arrive?
SHE: All my Dresden boyfriends
    Were only half-alive.
    Sleepy was Hermann,
    Fritz was like a sermon,
    Hans was such a bore!
HE: How well I planned it!
SHE: I couldn't stand it
    Anymore!

REFRAIN 2

It's a funny thing;
I look at you–
I get a thrill
I never knew;
Isn't it a pity
We never met before?
Here we are at last!
It's like a dream!
The two of us–
A perfect team–
    HE: For you're more than pretty,
       And I have charm galore!
    SHE: Imagine all the lonely years
       we've wasted:

You, up in Norway–
I, around my doorway.
What joys untasted!
If you'd been handy,
'Twould have been just
    dandy!
Isn't it a shame
We had to wait?
HE: But thank the Lord
    It's not too late!
TOGETHER: Still, it's such a pity
    We never, never met before!

REFRAIN 3

SHE: Love your funny smile,
    Your twinkling eye.
HE: That's very nice–
    For–so do I!
TOGETHER: Isn't it a pity
    We never met before?
HE: Put your hand in mine–
    A perfect fit!
    We never knew–
    Just think of it!
TOGETHER: Isn't it a pity
    We never met before?
HE: Imagine all the lonely years
    I've wasted:
    Fishing for salmon,
    Losing at backgammon.
SHE: What joys untasted!
    My nights were sour
    Spent with Schopenhauer.
TOGETHER: Let's forget the past!
    Let's both agree
    That I'm for you
    And you're for me–
    And it's such a pity
    We never, never met before!

—George Gershwin

IT AIN'T NECESSARILY SO

It ain't necessarily so.
It ain't necessarily so.
De t'ings dat you li'ble
To read in de Bible—
It ain't necessarily so.
Li'l' David was small, but—oh my!
Li'l' David was small, but—oh my!
He fought Big Goliath
Who lay down and dieth—
Li'l' David was small, but—oh my!
Wadoo
Wadoo!
Zim bam boddle-oo!
Zim bam boddle-oo!
Hoodle ah da wah da!
Hoodle ah da wah da!
Scatty wah!
Scatty wah!
Yeah!
Oh, Jonah, he lived in de whale.
Oh, Jonah, he lived in de whale.
Fo' he made his home in
Dat fish's abdomen—
Oh, Jonah, he lived in de whale.
Li'l' Moses was found in a stream.
Li'l' Moses was found in a stream.
He floated on water
Till Ole Pharoah's daughter
She fished him, she *says,* from dat stream.
Wadoo!
Wadoo!
Zim bam boddle-oo!
Zim bam boddle-oo!
Hoodle ah da wah da!
Hoodle ah da wah da!
Scatty wah!
Scatty wah!
Yeah!
It ain't necessarily so,
It ain't necessarily so.

Dey tell all you chillun
De Debble's a villun,
But 'tain't necessarily so.
To get into Hebben
Don't snap fo' a sebben—
Don' have no fault!
Live clean!
Oh, I takes dat gospel
Whenever it's pos'ble—
But wid a grain of salt!
Methus'lah lived nine hundred years.
Methus'lah lived nine hundred years.
But who calls dat livin'
When no gal'll give in
To no man what's nine hundred years?
I'm preachin' dis sermon to show
It ain't nessa, ain't nessa,
Ain't nessa, ain't nessa—
Ain't necessarily so!

—*George Gershwin*

LET'S CALL THE WHOLE THING OFF

VERSE
Things have come to a pretty pass—
Our romance is growing flat,
For you like this and the other,
While I go for this and that.
Goodness knows what the end will be;
Oh, I don't know where I'm at. . . .
It looks as if we two will never be one.
Something must be done.

REFRAIN I
You say eether and I say eyether,
You say neether and I say nyther;
Eether, eyether, neether, nyther—
Let's call the whole thing off!
You like potato and I like po-tah-to;
You like tomato and I like to-mah-to;

Potato, po-tah-to, tomato, to-mah-to–
Let's call the whole thing off!
But oh, if we call the whole thing off, then
    we must part.
And oh, if we ever part, then that might
    break my heart.
So, if you like pajamas and I like
    pa-jah-mas,
I'll wear pajamas and give up pa-jah-mas.
For we know we
Need each other, so we
Better call the calling off off.
Let's call the whole thing off!

REFRAIN 2
You say laughter and I saw lawfter,
You say after and I say awfter;
Laughter, lawfter, after, awfter–
Let's call the whole thing off!
You like vanilla and I like vanella,
You, sa's'parilla and I sa's'parella;
Vanilla, vanella, choc'late, strawb'ry–
Let's call the whole thing off!
But oh, if we call the whole thing off, then
    we must part.
And oh, if we ever part, then that might
    break my heart.
So, if you go for oysters and I go for
    ersters,
I'll order oysters and cancel the ersters.
For we know we
Need each other, so we
Better call the calling off off.
Let's call the whole thing off!

–George Gershwin

LONG AGO (AND FAR AWAY)

VERSE
Dreary days are over,
Life's a four-leaf clover.

Sessions of depressions are through:
Ev'ry hope I longed for long ago
    comes true.

REFRAIN
Long ago and far away
I dreamed a dream one day–
And now that dream is here beside me.
Long the skies were overcast,
But now the clouds have passed:
You're here at last!
Chills run up and down my spine,
Aladdin's lamp is mine:
The dream I dreamed was not denied me.
Just one look and then I knew
That all I longed for long ago was you.

–Jerome Kern

LOVE IS HERE TO STAY

VERSE
The more I read the papers,
The less I comprehend
The world and all its capers
And how it all will end.
Nothing seems to be lasting,
But that isn't our affair;
We've got something permanent–
I mean, in the way we care.

REFRAIN
It's very clear
Our love is here to stay;
Not for a year,
But ever and a day.
The radio and the telephone
And the movies that we know
May just be passing fancies–
And in time may go.
But oh, my dear,
Our love is here to stay.

Together we're
Going a long, long way.
In time the Rockies may crumble,
Gibraltar may tumble
(They're only made of clay),
But–our love is here to stay.

But, oh my dear, our love is here to stay.

—George Gershwin

LOVE IS SWEEPING THE COUNTRY

VERSE

Why are people gay
All the night and day,
Feeling as they never felt before?
What is the thing
That makes them sing?
Rich man, poor man, thief,
Doctor, lawyer, chief,
Feel a feeling that they can't ignore;
It plays a part
In ev'ry heart,
And ev'ry heart is shouting "Encore!"

REFRAIN

Love is sweeping the country;
Waves are hugging the shore;
All the sexes
From Maine to Texas
Have never known such love before.
See them billing and cooing
Like the birdies above!
Each girl and boy alike,
Sharing joy alike,
Feels that passion'll
Soon be national.
Love is sweeping the country–
There never was so much love!

PATTER

Spring is in the air–
Each mortal loves his neighbor.

Who's that loving pair?
That's Capital and Labor.
Chevrolet and Ford
Have felt this cosmic urging;
They, with one accord,
Have kissed and now are merging.
Florida and Cal-
Ifornia get together
In a festi*val*
Of oranges and weather.
Boston's upper zones
Are changing all their habits,
And I hear the Cohns
Are taking up the Cabots.
Taximen take dimes
And never curse the traffic,
While the New York *Times*
Adores the New York *Graphic.*

REPEAT REFRAIN

—George Gershwin

THE MAN I LOVE

VERSE

When the mellow moon begins to beam,
Ev'ry night I dream a little dream;
And of course Prince Charming is the
    theme:
The he
For me.
Although I realize as well as you
It is seldom that a dream comes true,
To me it's clear
That he'll appear.

REFRAIN

Some day he'll come along,
The man I love;
And he'll be big and strong,
The man I love;

And when he comes my way,
I'll do my best to make him stay.
He'll look at me and smile—
I'll understand;
And in a little while
He'll take my hand;
And though it seems absurd,
I know we both won't say a word.
Maybe I shall meet him Sunday,
Maybe Monday—maybe not;
Still I'm sure to meet him one day—
Maybe Tuesday
Will be my good news day.
He'll build a little home
Just meant for two;
From which I'll never roam—
Who would? Would you?
And so, all else above,
I'm waiting for the man I love.

—George Gershwin

THE MAN THAT GOT AWAY

The night is bitter,
The stars have lost their glitter;
The winds grow colder
And suddenly you're older—
And all because of the man that got away.
No more his eager call,
The writing's on the wall;
The dreams you've dreamed have all
Gone astray.
The man that won you
Has run off and undone you,
That great beginning
Has seen the final inning.
Don't know what happened. It's all a
    crazy game.
No more that all-time thrill,
For you've been through the mill—
And never a new love will

Be the same.
Good riddance, good-bye!
Ev'ry trick of his you're on to.
But, fools will be fools—
And where's he gone to?
The road gets rougher,
It's lonelier and tougher.
With hope you burn up—
Tomorrow he may turn up.
There's just no letup the livelong night
    and day.
Ever since this world began
There is nothing sadder than
A one-man woman looking for
The man that got away . . .
The man that got away.

—Harold Arlen

MY SHIP

My ship has sails that are made of silk—
The decks are trimmed with gold—
And of jam and spice
There's a paradise
In the hold.
My ship's aglow with a million pearls,
And rubies fill each bin;
The sun sits high
In a sapphire sky
When my ship comes in.
I can wait the years
Till it appears—
One fine day one Spring.
But the pearls and such,
They won't mean much
If there's missing just one thing:
I do not care if that day arrives—
That dream need never be—
If the ship I sing
Doesn't also bring
My own true love to me—

If the ship I sing
Doesn't also bring
My own true love to me.

—Kurt Weill

Nice Work If You Can Get It

VERSE
VERSE

The man who lives for only making money
Lives a life that isn't necessarily sunny;
Likewise the man who works for fame–
There's no guarantee that time won't
    erase his name.
The fact is
The only work that really brings
    enjoyment
Is the kind that is for girl and boy meant.
Fall in love–you won't regret it.
That's the best work of all–if you can
    get it.

REFRAIN

Holding hands at midnight
'Neath a starry sky . . .
Nice work if you can get it,
And you can get it–if you try.
Strolling with the one girl,
Sighing sigh after sigh . . .
Nice work if you can get it,
And you can get it–if you try.
Just imagine someone
Waiting at the cottage door,
Where two hearts become one . . .
Who could ask for anything more?
Loving one who loves you,
And then taking that vow . . .
Nice work if you can get it,
And if you get it–won't you tell me how?

—George Gershwin

Of Thee I Sing

VERSE

From the Island of Manhattan to the Coast
    of Gold,
From North to South, from East to West,
You are the love I love the best.
You're the dream girl of the sweetest story
    ever told;
A dream I've sought both night and day
For years through all the U.S.A.
The star I've hitched my wagon to
Is very obviously you.

REFRAIN

Of thee I sing, baby–
Summer, Autumn, Winter, Spring, baby.
You're my silver lining,
You're my sky of blue;
There's a love-light shining
Just because of you.
Of thee I sing, baby–
You have got that certain thing, baby!
Shining star and inspiration,
Worthy of a mighty nation–
Of thee I sing!

—George Gershwin

Oh, Lady, Be Good!

VERSE I

Listen to my tale of woe,
It's terribly sad, but true:
All dressed up, no place to go,
Each ev'ning I'm awf'ly blue.
I must win some winsome miss;
Can't go on like this.
I could blossom out, I know,
With somebody just like you.
So–

REFRAIN I

Oh, sweet and lovely lady, be good.
Oh, lady, be good to me!
I am so awf'ly misunderstood,
So, lady, be good to me.
Oh, please have some pity–
I'm all alone in this big city.
I tell you
I'm just a lonesome babe in the wood,
So, lady, be good to me.

VERSE 2

Auburn and brunette and blonde:
I love 'em all, tall or small.
But somehow they don't grow fond;
They stagger but never fall.
Winter's gone, and now it's Spring!
Love! where is thy sting?
If somebody won't respond,
I'm going to end it all.
So–

REFRAIN 2

Oh, sweet and lovely lady, be good.
Oh lady, be good to me!
I am so awf'ly misunderstood,
So, lady, be good to me.
This is tulip weather–
So let's put two and two together.
I tell you
I'm just a lonesome babe in the wood,
So, lady, be good to me.

—George Gershwin

ONE LIFE TO LIVE

VERSE

There are many minds in circulation
Believing in reincarnation.
In me you see
One who doesn't agree.

Challenging possible affronts,
I believe I'll only live once,
And I want to make the most of it;
If there's a party, I want to be the host
    of it;
If there's a haunted house, I want to be the
    ghost of it;
If I'm in town, I want to be the toast
    of it.

REFRAIN

I say to me ev'ry morning:
You've only one life to live.
So why be done in?
Let's let the sun in,
And gloom can jump in the riv'!
No use to beat on the doldrums;
Let's be imaginative.
Each day is numbered–
No good when slumbered–
With only one life to live.
Why let the goblins upset you?
One smile and see how they run!
And what does worrying net you?
Nothing!
The thing
Is to have fun!
All this may sound kind of hackneyed,
But it's the best I can give.
Soon comes December,
So, please remember
You've only one life to live–
Just one life to live.

—Kurt Weill

THE SAGA OF JENNY

VERSE

There once was a girl named Jenny,
Whose virtues were varied and many–
Excepting that she was inclined

Always to make up her mind;
And Jenny points a moral
With which you cannot quarrel–
As you will find.
Who's Jenny?
Never heard of Jenny!
Jenny is out of place!
But I am sure the court'll
Find Jenny is immortal
And has a bearing on this case!
As, for instance?
Well, for instance–

REFRAIN
Jenny made up her mind when she was
    three
She, herself, was going to trim the
    Christmas tree.
Christmas Eve she lit the candles–tossed
    the taper away.
Little Jenny was an orphan on
    Christmas Day.
Poor Jenny! Bright as a penny!
Her equal would be hard to find.
She lost one dad and mother,
A sister and a brother–
But she would make up her mind.
Jenny made up her mind when she was
    twelve
That into foreign languages she would
    delve;
But at seventeen to Vassar it was quite a
    blow
That in twenty-seven languages she
    couldn't say no.
Poor Jenny! Bright as a penny!
Her equal would be hard to find.
To Jenny I'm beholden,
Her heart was big and golden–
But she would make up her mind.
Jenny made her mind up at twenty-two
To get herself a husband was the thing
    to do.

She got herself all dolled up in her satins
    and furs
And she got herself a husband–but he
    wasn't hers.
Poor Jenny! Bright as a penny!
Her equal would be hard to find.
Deserved a bed of roses,
But history discloses
That she would make up her mind.
Jenny made her mind up at thirty-nine
She would take a trip to the Argentine.
She was only on vacation, but the Latins
    agree
Jenny was the one who started the Good
    Neighbor Policy.
Poor Jenny! Bright as a penny!
Her equal would be hard to find.
Oh, passion doesn't vanish
In Portuguese or Spanish–
But she would make up her mind.
Jenny made up her mind at fifty-one
She would write her memoirs before she
    was done.
The very day her book was published,
    hist'ry relates,
There were wives who shot their husbands
    in some thirty-three states.
Poor Jenny! Bright as a penny!
Her equal would be hard to find.
She could give cards and spade-ies
To many other ladies–
But she would make up her mind.
Jenny made her mind up at seventy-five
She would live to be the oldest woman
    alive.
But gin and rum and destiny play funny
    tricks,
And poor Jenny kicked the bucket at
    seventy-six.

Jenny points a moral
With which we cannot quarrel.
Makes a lot of common sense!

Jenny and her saga
Prove that you are gaga
If you don't keep sitting on the fence.
Jenny and her story
Point the way to glory
To all man- and womankind.
Anyone with vision
Comes to this decision:
Don't make up–
You shouldn't make up–
You mustn't make up–
Oh, never make up–
Anyone with vision
Comes to this decision:
Don't make up your mind!

—Kurt Weill

SOMEONE TO WATCH OVER ME

VERSE

There's a saying old
Says that love is blind.
Still, we're often told
"Seek and ye shall find."
So I'm going to seek a certain lad I've had
    in mind.
Looking ev'rywhere,
Haven't found him yet;
He's the big affair
I cannot forget–
Only man I ever think of with regret.
I'd like to add his initial to my
    monogram.
Tell me, where is the shepherd for this
    lost lamb?

REFRAIN

There's a somebody I'm longing to see:
I hope that he
Turns out to be
Someone who'll watch over me.

I'm a little lamb who's lost in the wood;
I know I could
Always be good
To one who'll watch over me.
Although he may not be the man some
Girls think of as handsome,
To my heart he'll carry the key.
Won't you tell him, please, to put on some
    speed,
Follow my lead?
Oh, how I need
Someone to watch over me.

—George Gershwin

STRIKE UP THE BAND

VERSE

We fought in 1917,
Rum-ta-ta tum-tum-tum!
And drove the tyrant from the scene,
Rum-ta-ta tum-tum-tum!
We're in a bigger, better war
For your patriotic pastime.
We don't know what we're fighting for–
But we didn't know the last time!
So load the cannon! Draw the blade!
Rum-ta-ta tum-tum-tum!
Come on, and join the Big Parade!
Rum-ta-ta tum-tum,
Rum-ta-ta tum-tum,
Rum-ta-ta tum-tum-tum!

REFRAIN I

Let the drums roll out!
(Boom-boom-boom!)
Let the trumpet call!
(Ta-ta-ra-ta-ta-ta-ta!)
While the people shout–
(Hooray!)
Strike up the band!
Hear the cymbals ring!

(Tszing-tszing-tszing!)
Calling one and all
(Ta-ta-ra-ta-ta-ta-ta!)
To the martial swing,
(Left, right!)
Strike up the band!

1. There is work to be done, to be done–
There's a war to be won, to be won–
Come, you son of a son of a gun–
Take your stand!
Fall in line, yea Bo–
Come along, let's go!
Hey, leader, strike up the band!

REFRAIN 2

2. Yankee doo doodle-oo doodle-oo,
We'll come through, doodle-oo
doodle-oo,
For the red, white and blue doodle-oo,
Lend a hand.
With our flag unfurled,
We can lick the world!
Hey, leader, strike up the band!

—*George Gershwin*

SUNNY DISPOSISH

VERSE 1

Anytime the thunder starts to
rumble down,
Don't let hope tumble down
Or castles crumble down.
If the blues appear, just make the best
of them;
Just make a jest of them;
Don't be possessed of them.
At the risk of sounding rather
platitudinous–
Here's what I believe should be the
attitude in us:

REFRAIN

A sunny disposish
Will always see you through–
When up above the skies are blah
'Stead of being blue.
Mister Trouble makes our faces
grow long,
But a smile will have him saying,
"So long!'
It really doesn't pay
To be a gloomy pill–
It's absolutely most ridic',
Positively sil'.
The rain may pitter-patter–
It really doesn't matter–
For life can be delish
With a sunny disposish.

VERSE 2

Must confess I like your way of
viewing it–
No use in ruing it
When gloom is blueing it.
Taking your advice, the sad and weary'll
Have no material
To be funereal.
It's a thought that they should be
swallowing, my dear,
Look at me, already you've a following,
my dear.

REPEAT REFRAIN

—*Philip Charig*

'S WONDERFUL

VERSE 1

Life has just begun:
Jack has found his Jill.
Don't know what you've done,
But I'm all a-thrill.

How can words express
Your divine appeal?
You could never guess
All the love I feel.
From now on, lady, I insist,
For me no other girls exist.

REFRAIN 1

'S wonderful! 'S marvelous—
You should care for me!
'S awful nice! 'S paradise—
'S what I love to see!
You've made my life so glamorous,
You can't blame me for feeling
    amorous.
Oh, 's wonderful! 'S marvelous—
That you should care for me!

VERSE 2

Don't mind telling you
In my humble fash
That you thrill me through
With a tender pash.
When you said you care,
'Magine my emosh;
I swore, then and there,
Permanent devosh.
You made all other boys seem blah;
Just you alone filled me with AAH!

REFRAIN 2

'S wonderful! 'S marvelous—
You should care for me!
'S awful nice! 'S Paradise—
'S what I love to see!
My dear, it's four-leaf-clover time;
From now on my heart's working
    overtime.
Oh, 's wonderful! 'S marvelous—
That you should care for me!

—*George Gershwin*

TCHAIKOWSKY (AND OTHER RUSSIANS)

There's Malichevsky, Rubinstein,
    Arensky, and Tchaikowsky,
Sapelnikoff, Dimitrieff, Tscherepnin,
    Kryjanowsky,
Godowsky, Arteiboucheff, Moniuszko,
    Akimenko,
Solovieff, Prokofieff, Tiomkin,
    Korestchenko.
There's Glinka, Winkler, Bortniansky,
    Rebikoff, Ilyinsky;
There's Medtner, Balakireff, Zolotareff,
    and Kvoschinsky.
And Sokoloff and Kopyloff, Dukelsky, and
    Klenowsky,
And Shostakovitsch, Borodine, Glière,
    and Nowakofski.
There's Liadoff and Karaganoff,
    Markievitch, Pantschenko,
And Dargomyzski, Stcherbatcheff,
    Scriabine, Vassilenko,
Stravinsky, Rimsky-Korsakoff,
    Mussorgsky, and Gretchaninoff
And Glazounoff and Caesar Cui,
    Kalinikoff, Rachmaninoff,
Stravinsky and Gretchaninoff,
Rumshinsky and Rachmaninoff,
I really have to stop, the subject has been
    dwelt
Upon enough!
Stravinsky!
Gretchaninoff!
Rumshinsky!
Rachmaninoff!
He'd *better* stop because we feel we all
    have under-
Gone enough!

—*Kurt Weill*

They All Laughed

The odds were a hundred to one against me,
The world thought the heights were too
   high to climb.
But people from Missouri never
   incensed me:
Oh, I wasn't a bit concerned,
For from hist'ry I had learned
How many, many times the worm had
   turned.

REFRAIN I

They all laughed at Christopher Columbus
When he said the world was round;
They all laughed when Edison recorded
   sound.
They all laughed at Wilbur and his
   brother
When they said that man could fly;
They told Marconi
Wireless was a phony–
It's the same old cry!
They laughed at me wanting you,
Said I was reaching for the moon;
But oh, you came through–
Now they'll have to change their tune.
They all said we never could be happy,
They laughed at us–and how!
But ho, ho, ho–
Who's got the last laugh now!

REFRAIN 2

They all laughed at Rockefeller
   Center–
Now they're fighting to get in;
They all laughed at Whitney and his
   cotton gin.
They all laughed at Fulton and his
   steamboat,
Hershey and his choc'late bar.

Ford and his Lizzie
Kept the laughers busy–
That's how people are!
They laughed at me wanting you–
Said it would be Hello! Good-bye!
But oh, you came through–
Now they're eating humble pie.
They all said we'd never get together–
Darling, let's take a bow,
For ho, ho, ho–
Who's got the last laugh–
He, he, he–
Let's at the past laugh–
Ha, ha, ha–
Who's got the last laugh now?

—George Gershwin

They Can't Take That Away from Me

VERSE

Our romance won't end on a sorrowful note,
Though by tomorrow you're gone;
The song is ended, but as the songwriter
   wrote,
"The melody lingers on."
They may take you from me,
I'll miss your fond caress.
But though they take you from me,
I'll still possess:

REFRAIN

The way you wear your hat,
The way you sip your tea,
The mem'ry of all that–
No, no! They can't take that away from me!
The way your smile just beams,
The way you sing off-key,
The way you haunt my dreams–
No, no! They can't take that away from me!
We may never, never meet again

On the bumpy road to love,
Still I'll always, always keep
The mem'ry of—
The way you hold your knife,
The way we danced till three,
The way you've changed my life—
No, no! They can't take that away from me!
No! They can't take that away from me!

—*George Gershwin*

Things Are Looking Up

VERSE

If I should suddenly start to sing
Or stand on my head—or anything,
Don't think that I've lost my senses;
It's just that my happiness finally
    commences.
The long, long ages of dull despair
Are turning into thin air,
And it seems that suddenly I've
Become the happiest man alive.

REFRAIN

Things are looking up!
I've been looking the landscape over
And it's covered with four-leaf clover.
Oh, things are looking up
Since love looked up at me.
Bitter was my cup—
But no more will I be the mourner,
For I've certainly turned the corner.
Oh, things are looking up
Since love looked up at me.
See the sunbeams—
Ev'ry one beams

Just because of you.
Love's in session,
And my depression
Is unmistakably through.
Things are looking up!
It's a great little world we live in!
Oh, I'm happy as a pup
Since love looked up
At me.

—*George Gershwin*

Who Cares?

VERSE

Let it rain and thunder!
Let a million firms go under!
I am not concerned with
Stocks and bonds that I've been
    burned with.
I love you and you love me,
And that's how it will always be.
And nothing else can ever mean a thing.
Who cares what the public chatters?
Love's the only thing that matters.

REFRAIN

Who cares
If the sky cares to fall in the sea?
Who cares what banks fail in Yonkers,
Long as you've got a kiss that conquers?
Why should I care?
Life is one long jubilee,
So long as I care for you—
And you care for me.

—*George Gershwin*

Mann Holiner (1897–1958)

BORN IN BROOKLYN and educated at Cornell, Mann Holiner became an actor in stock, vaudeville, and on Broadway before eventually establishing himself as an important executive in radio, producing for, among others, both Crosby and Sinatra. With his wife, the composer Alberta Nichols, he wrote for the shows *Rhapsody in Black* and *Blackbirds of 1933,* and several of their songs were sung by Ethel Waters in the early thirties. Later, his "Why Shouldn't It Happen to Us?" was taken up by Frank Sinatra. His most famous song, "Until the Real Thing Comes Along," was introduced by Ethel Waters under the title "Till the Real Thing Comes Along." In 1936 it was adapted by Sammy Cahn, Saul Chaplin, and L. E. Freeman, and became a number-one hit for Andy Kirk and His Twelve Clouds of Joy, and a favorite with jazz musicians from Fats Waller to Dexter Gordon to Carmen McCrae.

UNTIL THE REAL THING COMES ALONG

(with Sammy Cahn)

VERSE 1

I've tried to explain that you are my
    Heaven on earth.
Still, I've tried in vain, since words can't
    explain my love and its worth.
This much I know is true,
There'll never be another you.
That's why

REFRAIN

I'd work for you,
I'd slave for you,
I'd be a beggar or a knave for you.
If that isn't love
It will have to do
Until the real thing comes along.
I'd gladly move the earth for you
To prove my love, dear, and its worth
    for you.

If that isn't love
It will have to do
Until the real thing comes along.
With all the words, dear, at my command
I just can't make you understand.
I'll always love you, darling,
Come what may.
My heart is yours,
What more can I say?
I'd sigh for you,
I'd cry for you,
I'd tear the stars down from the sky
    for you.
If that isn't love
It will have to do
Until the real thing comes along.

VERSE 2

I've read all the plays from Shakespeare to
    Eugene O'Neill
To find just one phrase that somewhat
    conveys the way I feel.
I met with no success;

I'm strictly on my own, I guess,
And so

REPEAT REFRAIN

—*Alberta Nichols and Saul Chaplin*

WHY SHOULDN'T IT HAPPEN TO US?

VERSE

Never argue with your heart,
It isn't smart, it isn't sound.
Love don't know from season,
Logic, rhyme, or reason,
Love can be found in every port,
Love gets around, in short.

REFRAIN I

It has happened to a cricket in a
    thicket,
It has happened on a streetcar and
    a bus,
There has even been a rumor
It has happened to a puma,
Why shouldn't it happen to us?
It has happened to the mama of a
    llama,
To a pelican and to an octopus,
Since it happened to the swordfish
It no longer is a bored fish,
Why shouldn't it happen to us?
It's elusive, profusive,
Nobody has an exclusive on love,
Man, beast, or a dove.
Take the regal old eagle,
The porcupine and the beagle,
Yes, and kangaroo
All pitch woo.
It has happened to a tuna at Laguna,
To a girl named Myrtle and a guy
    named Gus,

Hiawatha said "Come to me"
By the shores of Gitcheegoomee.
Why shouldn't it happen to us?

REFRAIN 2

Oh, the busy little hornet doesn't
    scorn it,
To ignore it really is ridiculous.
It's a ritual in Turkey,
Martinique, and Albuquerque,
Why shouldn't it happen to us?
There's no ration on passion,
L'amour is always in fashion,
It wings beggars and kings.
Take the Cheetah, anteater,
The halibut and the mosquitah,
Yes, and billy goats
Feel their oats.
Oh, it thrills the tiny sparrow to its
    marrow,
And the armadillo deems it superplus.
Why our ancient barnyard rooster
Finds it quite a morale booster,
Why shouldn't it happen to us?
I have even heard a reindeer whisper,
"Please say that again, dear."
Why shouldn't it happen to us?

—*Alberta Nichols*

YOU CAN'T STOP ME FROM LOVIN' YOU

VERSE

Oh! you great big brute,
How you mistreat me.
Oh! you great big brute,
You can't defeat me.
You can shower me with abuse,
You'll never shake me loose.
Oh! you great big brute,
You can browbeat me,

But I'm tellin' you it's no use.
Say I get in your hair,
But, baby, I don't care.

REFRAIN 1

You can throw bricks at my window,
You can put tacks in my shoe.
You can sprinkle ground glass on my
    apple "sass,"
 But you can't stop me from lovin' you.
You can put rocks in my pillow,
You can put sand in my stew,
You can be as aloof as the Chrysler roof,
But you can't stop me from lovin' you.
You can sneer at my devotion,
Be as mean as you can be,
Ridicule my great emotion,
But you're never gonna discourage me.
You can put Lux in my cornflakes,
Tell me my brain's good as new,
You can laugh in my face as you trump
    my ace,
But you can't stop me from lovin' you.

REFRAIN 2

You can put Flit in my gargle,
Seal up your pockets with glue,
You can even throw fleas on my
    Pekinese,
But you can't stop me from lovin' you.
You can go tell Walter Winchell
Ev'ry darn thing that I do.
You can tear me to rags
Just to give him gags,
But you can't stop me from lovin' you.
You can cut up my umbrella,
Put a thistle where I sit,
Even make me take "vanella"
When you know I'm crazy 'bout
    "cholk-a-lit."
You can wear socks without garters,
Carry lace handkerchiefs, too.
You can smell of Chanel on your coat
    lapel,
But you can't stop me from lovin' you.

—Alberta Nichols

Noel Gay (1898–1954)

NOEL GAY WAS BORN Richard Armitage, a name he either was keeping in reserve for "serious" music or kept private so as not to embarrass church officials when he went into popular music; educated at the Royal College of Music, he was playing the organ for Wakefield Cathedral when he was fourteen, and subsequently for the Chapel Royal. While at Cambridge, he wrote songs and did arrangements for a band run by the young Lord Louis Mountbatten. Soon he was writing for *The Charlot Revue of 1926,* and there followed an endless string of musical comedies in the West End, the most famous of which is *Me and My Girl* (with its "Lambeth Walk"), originally a hit in 1937 and revived with worldwide success in the early 1980s. Gay wrote for just about everyone of importance on the British musical stage: Jessie Matthews, Lupino Lane, Evelyn Laye, Cicely Courtneidge, Gracie Fields, Jack Hulbert, George Formby ("Leaning on a Lamppost"). His last hit, in 1950, was for Vera Lynn, rounding off an exceptionally happy career that lasted twenty-five years.

LAMBETH WALK

(with Douglas Furber)

VERSE

Lambeth you've never seen,
The skies ain't blue, the grass ain't
    green.
It hasn't got the Mayfair touch,
But that don't matter very much.
We play the Lambeth way,
Not like you but a bit more gay.
And when we have a bit of fun,
Oh, boy.

REFRAIN

Any time you're Lambeth way,
Any evening, any day,
You'll find us all
Doin' the Lambeth walk.
Ev'ry little Lambeth gal

With her little Lambeth pal,
You'll find 'em all
Doin' the Lambeth walk.
Ev'rything free and easy,
Do as you darn well pleasey,
Why don't you make your way
    there,
Go there, stay there.
Once you get down Lambeth way,
Ev'ry evening, ev'ry day,
You'll find yourself
Doin' the Lambeth walk.

LEANING ON A LAMPPOST

VERSE

Leaning on a lamp,
Maybe you think
I look a tramp,

Or you may think I'm hanging 'round to
    steal a car;
But no,
I'm not a crook,
And if you think
That's what I look,
I'll tell you why I'm here and what my
    motives are.

REFRAIN

I'm leaning on a lamppost at the corner of
    the street,
In case a certain little lady comes by.
Oh me, oh my,
I hope the little lady comes by.
I don't know if she'll get away,
She doesn't always get away,
But anyway I know that she'll try.
Oh me, oh my,
I hope the little lady comes by.
There's no other girl I could wait for,
But this one I'd break any date for.
I won't have to ask what she's late for,
She'd never leave me flat,
She's not a girl like that.
She's absolutely wonderful and marvelous
    and beautiful,
And anyone can understand why
I'm leaning on a lamppost at the corner of
    the street,
In case a certain little lady comes by.

ME AND MY GIRL

(with Douglas Furber)

VERSE

Life's an empty thing,
Life can be so awful lonesome.
If you're always on your ownsome,
Life's an empty thing.
Life's a diff'rent thing.
When you've found the one and only,
Then you feel no longer lonely,
Life's a happy thing.
Ev'rything was topsy-turvy,
Life seemed all wrong,
But it came all right as soon as she came
    along.

REFRAIN

Me and my girl,
Meant for each other,
Sent for each other,
And liking it so.
Me and my girl,
'Sno use pretending,
We knew the ending
Some ages ago.
Some little church
With a big steeple,
Just a few people
That both of us know.
And we'll have love, laughter,
Be happy ever after,
Me and my girl.

Hoagy Carmichael (1899–1981)

HOAGY (Hoagland Howard) Carmichael was born in Indiana and educated there, taking a law degree from Indiana University. But he had learned piano from his mother, who played music for silent movies, and found that he had a talent for composition. The great friendship (and influence) of his early life was with the brilliant and doomed Bix Beiderbecke, whose Wolverines recorded Hoagy's first serious effort, "Riverboat Shuffle," in 1924. His most famous song, of course, was "Star Dust," originally written as an instrumental in 1927. Three years later, with lyrics added by Mitchell Parish, it began its career of more than one thousand recordings (the biggest hits were by Isham Jones in 1931, Benny Goodman in 1936, and—biggest of all—Artie Shaw in 1941: two million copies sold). Carmichael wrote only the music for most of his most famous songs—"Lazybones," "Georgia on My Mind," "Skylark," "How Little We Know," et al.—but he had a voice of his own as a lyricist, and was also a big success as a singer and personality, appearing in numerous movies (*To Have and Have Not, Young Man with a Horn, The Best Years of Our Lives,* and others), often as a wry singing piano player; well, he *was* a wry singing piano player. His recording of his own "Ole Buttermilk Sky," which he sang in the movie *Canyon Passage,* was a number-two hit. It would have been number one, but Kay Kyser's version beat it out.

DON'T FORGET TO SAY NO, BABY

Don't forget to say no, baby, while I'm
    with your Uncle Sam.
I'll be missing you so, baby, that's the kind
    of guy I am.
The boys may call your number, but if they
    take you to tea,
Don't be thrilling while I'm drilling,
Remember you belong to me.
Don't forget to say no, baby, if they want a
    kiss goodnight . . .
Just remember it's no, baby, if they want
    to hold you tight.
While I'm out to train don't you entertain,

Remember you're not the USO.
Till I return, baby, don't forget to say no.
The boys may call your number but if they
    take you to tea,
Don't be charming while I'm arming,
Remember you belong to me.
Don't forget to say no, baby, if they want a
    kiss goodnight.
Just remember it's no, baby, if they want
    to hold you tight.
And if you want to please while I'm
    overseas,
Do a blackout from head to toe,
Till I return, baby, don't forget to say no.

Hong Kong Blues

VERSE

It's the story of a very unfortunate
    Memphis man
Who got 'rrested down in old Hong Kong.
He got twenty years privilege taken away
    from him
When he kicked old Buddha's gong.
And now he's bobbin' the piano
Just to raise the price
Of a ticket to the land of the free.
Well, he say his home's in Frisco
Where they ship the rice,
But it's really in Tennessee.
That's why he say

REFRAIN

I need someone to love me,
Need somebody to carry me home to San
    Francisco
And bury my body there.
I need someone to lend me a fifty
    dolla' bill,
And then I'll leave Hong Kong far
    behind me,
For happiness once again.
Won't someone believe
I've a yen to see that bay again?
But when I try to leave,
Old loco man won't let me fly away.
I need someone to love me,
Need somebody to carry me home to San
    Francisco
And bury my body there.

That's the story of a very unfortunate
    Memphis man
Who got 'rrested down in old Hong Kong.
He got twenty years privilege taken away
    from him
When he kicked old Buddha's gong.

I Get Along Without You Very Well

I get along without you very well,
Of course I do,
Except when soft rains fall
And drip from leaves,
Then I recall
The thrill of being sheltered in
    your arms,
Of course I do.
But I get along without you very well.
I've forgotten you, just like I should,
Of course I have,
Except to hear your name
Or someone's laugh that is the same,
But I've forgotten you just like I should.
What a guy!
What a fool am I
To think my breaking heart could kid
    the moon.
What's in store?
Should I 'phone once more?
No, it's best that I stick to my tune.
I get along without you very well,
Of course I do,
Except perhaps in Spring,
But I should never think of Spring,
For that would surely break my heart
    in two.

Lazy River

(with Sidney Arodin)

VERSE

I like lazy weather,
I like lazy days,
Can't be blamed for having lazy ways.
Some old lazy river
Sleeps beside my door,
Whisp'ring to the sunlit shore.

Up a lazy river
By the old mill run,
That lazy, lazy river
In the noonday sun.
Linger in the shade
Of a kind old tree;
Throw away your troubles,
Dream a dream with me.
Up a lazy river
Where the robin's song
Awakes a bright new morning,
We can loaf along.
Blue skies up above,
Ev'ryone's in love,
Up a lazy river,
How happy you can be,
Up a lazy river with me.

ROCKIN' CHAIR

VERSE
Moonlight
On Swanee's muddy shore

By my door.
Music
I've often heard before,
Hear't no more.
Years have slipped away
And left me longin'
For the days of happiness
I'll see no more.

REFRAIN
Old rockin' chair's got me,
Cane by my side;
Fetch me that gin, son,
'Fore I tan your hide.
Can't get from this cabin,
Goin' nowhere;
Just sit me here grabbin'
At the flies 'round this rockin' chair.
My dear old Aunt Harriet
In heaven she be,
Send me sweet chariot,
For the end of these troubles I see.
Old rockin' chair gits it,
Judgment day is here,
Chained to my rockin' chair.

Noël Coward (1899–1973)

S<small>IR NOËL COWARD ENJOYED</small> one of the greatest show business careers of the twentieth century. He began performing at the age of ten–in a "fairy play" called *The Goldfish* with a "star cast of wonder children," of whom he was certainly the most wondrous. He made his mark very young as a playwright–*The Vortex, Private Lives, Design for Living, Hay Fever, Tonight at 8:30, Blithe Spirit*–in most of which he also starred, often with his friend Gertrude Lawrence. But he was also a formidably successful composer/lyricist of revues, musicals, and operettas: *London Calling, Bitter Sweet, Conversation Piece.* He was a filmmaker, an actor, a nightclub performer, a director, a short-story writer, a novelist, but perhaps most of all he was a leading symbol of twenties' and thirties' sophistication and wit; more than anything else, he was a *figure,* central both to the theater of his day and to the idea of camp. Somehow, no one ever seemed to mind that he was conspicuously, if not assertively, homosexual, long before it was politically (or legally) acceptable to be gay. His songs divide into several kinds: the brilliant, scathing satires for which he is best known–"Mad Dogs and Englishmen," "Mrs. Worthington," "Don't Let's Be Beastly to the Germans"; the high-flown operetta arias–"I'll Follow My Secret Heart," "Someday I'll Find You," "I'll See You Again"; the mordant little set pieces–"Poor Little Rich Girl," "Weary of It All." The more sentimental songs wear better musically than verbally, but when Coward is in his W. S. Gilbert vein (which is frequently), nobody's done it better.

A BAR ON THE PICCOLA MARINA

VERSE

In a "bijou" abode
In St. Barnabas Road
Not far from the Esher bypass
Lived a mother and wife
Who, most of her life,
Let every adventure fly past.
She had two strapping daughters and a
    rather dull son
And a much duller husband who at
    sixty-one
Elected to retire

And, later on, expire,
Sing Hallelujah, Hey nonny-no, Hey
    nonny-no, Hey nonny-no!
He joined the feathered choir.
On a wet afternoon
In the middle of June
They all of them came home soaking
Having laid him to rest
By special request
In the family vault at Woking,
And then in the middle of the
    funeral wake
With her mouth full of excellent
    Madeira cake

His widow cried, "That's done,
My life's at last begun,
Sing Hallelujah, Hey nonny-no, Hey
    nonny-no, Hey nonny-no!
It's time I had some fun.
Today, though hardly a jolly day,
At least has set me free,
We'll all have a lovely holiday
On the island of Capri!"

REFRAIN I

In a bar on the Piccola Marina
Life called to Mrs. Wentworth-Brewster,
Fate beckoned her and introduced her
Into a rather queer
Unfamiliar atmosphere.
She'd just sit there, propping up the bar
Beside a fisherman who sang to a guitar.
When accused of having gone too far
She merely cried, "Funiculi,
Just fancy me!
Funicula!"
When he bellowed "Che bella signorina!"
Sheer ecstasy at once produced a
Wild shriek from Mrs. Wentworth-
    Brewster,
Changing her whole demeanor.
When both her daughters and her
    son said,
"Please come home, Mama,"
She murmured rather bibulously, "Who
    d'you think you are?"
Nobody can afford to be so lahdy-bloody-da
In a bar on the Piccola Marina.

INTERLUDE

Every fisherman cried,
"Viva viva" and "Che ragazza."
When she sat in the Grand Piazza
Everybody would rise,
Every fisherman sighed, "Viva viva che
    bella' Inglesi,"
Someone even said, "Whoops-adaisy!"

Which was quite a surprise.
Each night she'd make some gay excuse
And beaming with goodwill
She'd just slip into something loose
And totter down the hill.

REFRAIN 2

To the bar on the Piccola Marina
Where love came to Mrs. Wentworth-
    Brewster,
Hot flushes of delight suffused her,
Right 'round the bend she went,
Picture her astonishment,
Day in, day out she would gad about
Because she felt she was no longer on the
    shelf.
Night out, night in, knocking back the gin
She'd cry, "Hurrah!
Funicula
Funiculi
Funic yourself!"
Just for fun three young sailors from
    Messina
Bowed low to Mrs. Wentworth-Brewster,
Said "Scusi" and politely goosed her.
Then there was quite a scena.
Her family, in floods of tears, cried,
"Leave these men, Mama."
She said, "They're just high-spirited, like
    all Italians are,
And most of them have a great deal more
    to offer than Papa
In a bar on the Piccola Marina."

DON'T LET'S BE BEASTLY TO THE GERMANS

VERSE I

We must be kind
And with an open mind
We must endeavor to find
A way

To let the Germans know that when the
    war is over
They are not the ones who'll have to pay.
We must be sweet
And tactful and discreet
And when they've suffered defeat
We mustn't let
Them feel upset
Or ever get
The feeling that we're cross with them or
    hate them,
Our future policy must be to reinstate
    them.

REFRAIN I

Don't let's be beastly to the Germans
When our victory is ultimately won.
It was just those nasty Nazis who
    persuaded them to fight,
And their Beethoven and Bach are really
    far worse than their bite.
Let's be meek to them,
And turn the other cheek to them,
And try to bring out their latent sense
    of fun.
Let's give them full air parity
And treat the rats with charity,
But don't let's be beastly to the Hun.

VERSE 2

We must be just,
And win their love and trust,
And in addition we must
Be wise
And ask the conquered lands to join our
    hands to aid them.
That would be a wonderful surprise.
For many years
They've been in floods of tears
Because the poor little dears
Have been so wronged and only longed
To cheat the world,
Deplete the world,

And beat
The world to blazes.
This is the moment when we ought to sing
    their praises.

REFRAIN 2

Don't let's be beastly to the Germans
When we've definitely got them on the run.
Let us treat them very kindly as we would a
    valued friend.
We might send them out some bishops as a
    form of lease and lend.
Let's be sweet to them,
And day by day repeat to them
That "sterilization" simply isn't done.
Let's help the dirty swine again
To occupy the Rhine again,
But don't let's be beastly to the Hun.

REFRAIN 3

Don't let's be beastly to the Germans
When the age of peace and plenty has
    begun.
We must send them steel and oil and coal
    and everything they need,
For their peaceable intentions can be
    always guaranteed.
Let's employ with them
A sort of "strength through joy" with them,
They're better than us at honest manly fun.
Let's let them feel they're swell again
And bomb us all to hell again,
But don't let's be beastly to the Hun.

REFRAIN 4

Don't let's be beastly to the Germans,
For you can't deprive a gangster of his gun.
Though they've been a little naughty to
    the Czechs and Poles and Dutch,
But I don't suppose those countries really
    minded very much.
Let's be free with them
And share the BBC with them.

We mustn't prevent them basking in
    the sun.
Let's soften their defeat again
And build their bloody fleet again,
But don't let's be beastly to the Hun.

I've Been to a Marvelous Party

VERSE 1
Quite for no reason
I'm here for the Season
And high as a kite,
Living in error
With Maud at Cap Ferrat
Which couldn't be right.
Everyone's here and frightfully gay,
Nobody cares what people say,
Though the Riviera
Seems really much queerer
Than Rome at its height,
Yesterday night–

REFRAIN 1
I've been to a marvelous party
With Nounou and Nada and Nell,
It was in the fresh air
And we went as we were
And we stayed as we were
Which was Hell.
Poor Grace started singing at midnight
And didn't stop singing till four;
We knew the excitement was bound to
    begin
When Laura got blind on Dubonnet
    and gin
And scratched her veneer with a
    Cartier pin,
I couldn't have liked it more.

REFRAIN 2
I've been to a marvelous party,
I must say the fun was intense,

We all had to do
What the people we knew
Would be doing a hundred years
    hence.
Dear Cecil arrived wearing armor,
Some shells and a black feather boa,
Poor Millicent wore a
    surrealist comb
Made of bits of mosaic from St. Peter's
    in Rome,
But the weight was so great that she
    had to go home,
I couldn't have liked it more!

VERSE 2
People's behavior
Away from Belgravia
Would make you aghast,
So much variety
Watching Society
Scampering past.
If you have any mind at all
Gibbon's divine *Decline and Fall*
Seems pretty flimsy,
No more than whimsy,
By way of contrast.
On Saturday last–

REFRAIN 3
I've been to a marvelous party,
We didn't start dinner till ten,
And young Bobby Carr
Did a stunt at the bar
With a lot of extraordinary men.
Dear Baba arrived with a turtle
Which shattered us all to the core,
The Grand Duke was dancing a fox-trot
    with me
When suddenly Cyril screamed
    "Fiddledidee"
And ripped off his trousers and
    jumped in the sea,
I couldn't have liked it more.

REFRAIN 4

I've been to a marvelous party,
Elise made an entrance with May.
You'd never have guessed
From her fisherman's vest
That her bust had been whittled away.
Poor Lulu got fried on Chianti
And talked about esprit de corps.
Maurice made a couple of passes at Gus,
And Freddie, who hates any kind of a fuss,
Did half the Big Apple and twisted his
    truss,
I couldn't have liked it more.

REFRAIN 5

I've been to a marvelous party,
We played the most wonderful game.
Maureen disappeared
And came back in a beard
And we all had to guess at her name!
We talked about growing old gracefully,
And Elsie who's seventy-four
Said, "A, it's a question of being sincere,
And B, if you're supple you've nothing to
    fear."
Then she swung upside down from a glass
    chandelier,
I couldn't have liked it more.

I Wonder What Happened to Him

VERSE I

The India that one read about
And may have been misled about
In one respect has kept itself intact.
Though "Pukka Sahib" traditions may
    have cracked
And thinned,
The good old Indian army's still a fact.
That famous monumental man
The Officer and Gentleman
Still lives and breathes and functions from
    Bombay to Katmandu.
At any moment one can glimpse
Matured or embryonic "Blimps"
Vivaciously speculating as to what became
    of who.
Though Eastern sounds may fascinate
    your ear,
When West meets West you're always sure
    to hear—

REFRAIN I

Whatever became of old Bagot?
I haven't seen him for a year.
Is it true that young Forbes had to marry
    that faggot
He met in the Vale of Kashmir?
Have you had any news
Of that chap in the "Blues,"
Was it Prosser or Pyecroft or Pym?
He was stationed in Simla, or was it
    Bengal?
I know he got tight at a ball in Nepal
And wrote several four-letter words on
    the wall.
I wonder what happened to him!

REFRAIN 2

Whatever became of old Shelley?
Is it true that young Briggs was cashiered
For riding quite nude on a push-bike
    through Delhi
The day the new Viceroy appeared?
Have you had any word
Of that bloke in the "Third,"
Was it Southerby, Sedgwick, or Sim?
They had him thrown out of the club in
    Bombay
For, apart from his mess bills exceeding
    his pay,
He took to pig-sticking in quite the
    wrong way.
I wonder what happened to him!

VERSE 2

One must admit that by and large
Upholders of the British Raj
Don't shine in conversation as a breed.
Though Indian army officers can read
A bit,
Their verbal wit has rather run to seed.
Their splendid insularity
And roguish jocularity
Was echoing through when Victoria was
    Queen.
In restaurants and dining cars,
In messes, clubs, and hotel bars
They try to maintain tradition in the way
    it's always been.
Though worlds may change and nations
    disappear,
Above the shrieking chaos you will hear—

REFRAIN 3

Whatever became of old Tucker?
Have you heard any word of young Mills
Who ruptured himself at the end of a
    chukka
And had to be sent to the hills?
They say that young Lees
Had a go of "D.T.s"
And his hopes of promotion are slim.
According to Stubbs, who's a bit of a
    louse,
The silly young blighter went out on a
    "souse,"
And took two old tarts into Government
    House.
I wonder what happened to him!

REFRAIN 4

Whatever became of old Keeling?
I hear that he got back from France
And frightened three nuns in a train in
    Darjeeling
By stripping and waving his lance!
D'you remember Munroe,

In the P.A.V.O.?
He was tallish and mentally dim.
The talk of heredity can't be quite true,
He was dropped on his head by his ayah
    at two,
I presume that by now he'll have reached
    G.H.Q.
I'm sure that's what happened to him!

REFRAIN 5

Whatever became of old Archie?
I hear he departed this life
After rounding up ten sacred cows in
    Karachi
To welcome the Governor's wife.
D'you remember young Phipps
Who had *very* large hips
And whose waist was excessively slim?
Well, it seems that some doctor in
    Grosvenor Square
Gave him hormone injections for growing
    his hair
And he grew something here, and he grew
    something there.
I wonder what happened to her—him?

I'LL SEE YOU AGAIN

HE: Now Miss Sarah, if you please,
    Sing a scale for me . . .
    Take a breath and then reprise
    In a different key.
    All my life I shall remember
        knowing you,
    All the pleasure I have found in
        showing you
    The different ways
    That one may phrase
    The changing light, and changing
        shade;
    Happiness that must die,
    Melodies that must fly,

Memories that must fade,
Dusty and forgotten by and by.
SHE: Learning scales will never seem so
    sweet again
Till our Destiny shall let us meet
    again.
HE: The will of Fate
May come too late.
SHE: When I'm recalling these hours
    we've had,
Why will the foolish tears
Tremble across the years,
Why shall I feel so sad,
Treasuring the memory of these days
Always?

I'll see you again,
Whenever Spring breaks through
    again;
Time may lie heavy between,
But what has been
Is past forgetting.
This sweet memory
Across the years will come to me;
Though my world may go awry,
In my heart will ever lie
Just the echo of a sigh,
Good-bye.

LET'S DO IT

(with acknowledgments to Cole Porter)

VERSE I

Mr. Irving Berlin
Often emphasizes sin
In a charming way.
Mr. Coward, we know,
Wrote a song or two to show
Sex was here to stay.
Richard Rodgers, it's true,
Took a more romantic view
Of this sly biological urge.

But it really was Cole
Who contrived to make the whole
Thing merge.

REFRAIN I

He said the Belgians and Greeks do it,
Nice young men who sell antiques do it,
Let's do it, let's fall in love.
Monkeys whenever you look do it,
Aly Khan and King Farouk do it,
Let's do it, let's fall in love.
Louella Parsons can't *quite* do it,
For she's so highly strung,
Marlene *might* do it,
But she looks far too young.
Each man out there shooting crap does it,
Davy Crockett in that dreadful cap does it,
Let's do it, let's fall in love.

REFRAIN 2

Our famous writers in swarms do it,
Somerset and all the Maughams do it,
Let's do it, let's fall in love.
The Brontës felt that they *must* do it,
Ernest Hemingway could–*just*–do it,
Let's do it, let's fall in love.
E. Allan Poe–ho! ho! ho!–did it,
But he did it in verse.
H. Beecher Stowe did it,
But she had to rehearse.
Tennessee Williams, self-taught, does it,
Kinsey with a deafening report does it.
Let's do it, let's fall in love.

VERSE 2

In the Spring of the year
Inhibitions disappear
And our hearts beat high.
We had better face facts:
Every gland that overacts
Has an alibi.
For each bird and each bee,
Each slap-happy sappy tree,

Each temptation that lures us along
Is just Nature *elle-même*
Merely singing us the same
Old song.

REFRAIN 3
In Texas some of the men do it,
Others drill a hole–and then do it,
Let's do it, let's fall in love.
West Point cadets forming fours do it,
People say all those Gabors do it,
Let's do it, let's fall in love.
My kith and kin, more or less, do it,
Every uncle and aunt.
But I confess to it–
I've one cousin that *can't*.
Teenagers squeezed into jeans do it,
Probably we'll live to see machines do it,
Let's do it, let's fall in love.

REFRAIN 4
Girls from the RADA do it,
BBC announcers may do it,
Let's do it, let's fall in love.
The Ballet Jooss to a man do it,
Alfred Lunt and Lynn Fontanne do it,
Let's do it, let's fall in love.
My kith and kin, more or less, do it,
Every uncle and aunt,
But I confess to it,
I've one cousin who can't.
Some mystics, as a routine do it,
Even Evelyn Waugh and Graham Greene
    do it,
Let's do it, let's fall in love.

REFRAIN 5
Each baby bat after dark does it,
In the desert Wilbur Clark does it,
Let's do it, let's fall in love.
We're told that every hormone does it,
Victor Borge all alone does it,
Let's do it, let's fall in love.

Each tiny clam you consume does it,
Even Liberace–we assume–does it,
Let's do it, let's fall in love.

—Cole Porter

LONDON PRIDE

VERSE 1
London Pride has been handed down
    to us.
London Pride is a flower that's free.
London Pride means our own dear
    town to us,
And our pride it forever will be.
Woa, Liza,
See the coster barrows,
Vegetable marrows
And the fruit piled high.
Woa, Liza,
Little London sparrows,
Covent Garden market where the
    costers cry.
Cockney feet
Mark the beat of history.
Every street
Pins a memory down.
Nothing ever can quite replace
The grace of London Town.

INTERLUDE
There's a little city flower every spring
    unfailing
Growing in the crevices by some London
    railing,
Though it has a Latin name, in town and
    countryside
We in England call it London Pride.

VERSE 2
London Pride has been handed down to us.
London Pride is a flower that's free.

London Pride means our own dear town
    to us,
And our pride it forever will be.
Hey, lady,
When the day is dawning
See the policeman yawning
On his lonely beat.
Gay lady,
Mayfair in the morning,
Hear your footsteps echo in the empty
    street.
Early rain
And the pavement's glistening.
All Park Lane
In a shimmering gown.
Nothing ever could break or harm
The charm of London Town.

INTERLUDE

In our city darkened now, street and
    square and crescent,
We can feel our living past in our
    shadowed present,
Ghosts beside our starlit Thames
Who lived and loved and died
Keep throughout the ages London Pride.

VERSE 3

London Pride has been handed down to us.
London Pride is a flower that's free.
London Pride means our own dear town
    to us,
And our pride it forever will be.
Gray city
Stubbornly implanted,
Taken so for granted
For a thousand years.
Stay, city,
Smokily enchanted,
Cradle of our memories and hopes and
    fears.
Every Blitz
Your resistance

Toughening,
From the Ritz
To the Anchor and Crown,
Nothing ever could override
The pride of London Town.

MAD ABOUT THE BOY

VERSE I
SOCIETY WOMAN:
I met him at a party just a couple of
    years ago,
He was rather over-hearty and ridiculous,
But as I'd seen him on the Screen
He cast a certain spell.
I basked in his attraction for a couple of
    hours or so,
His manners were a fraction too
    meticulous,
If he was real or not I couldn't tell,
But like a silly fool, I fell.

REFRAIN I
Mad about the boy,
I know it's stupid to be mad about the boy,
I'm so ashamed of it
But must admit
The sleepless nights I've had about
    the boy.
On the Silver Screen
He melts my foolish heart in every single
    scene.
Although I'm quite aware
That here and there
Are traces of the cad about the boy,
Lord knows I'm not a fool girl,
I really shouldn't care,
Lord knows I'm not a schoolgirl
In the flurry of her first affair.
Will it ever cloy,
This odd diversity of misery and joy?
I'm feeling quite insane

And young again
And all because I'm mad about the boy.

VERSE 2
SCHOOLGIRL:
Homework, homework,
Every night there's homework,
While Elsie practices, the gas goes pop,
I wish, I wish she'd stop.
Oh dear, oh dear,
Here it's always "No, dear,
You can't go out again, you must
    stay home,
You waste your money on that common
    Picturedrome,
Don't shirk—stay here and do your work."
Yearning, yearning,
How my heart is burning.
I'll see him Saturday in *Strong Man's Pain*
And then on Monday and on Friday week
    again.
To me he is the sole man
Who can kiss as well as Colman,
I could faint whenever there's a close-up
    of his lips.
Though John Barrymore is larger,
When my hero's on his charger
Even Douglas Fairbanks, Junior, hasn't
    smaller hips.
If only he could know
That I adore him so.

REFRAIN 2
Mad about the boy,
It's simply scrumptious to be mad about
    the boy,
I know that quite sincerely
Housman really
Wrote *The Shropshire Lad* about
    the boy.
In my English Prose
I've done a tracing of his forehead and
    his nose

And there is, honor bright,
A certain slight
Effect of Galahad about the boy.
I've talked to Rosie Hooper,
She feels the same as me,
She says that Gary Cooper
Doesn't thrill her to the same degree.
In *Can Love Destroy?*
When he meets Garbo in a suit of
    corduroy,
He gives a little frown
And knocks her down.
Oh dear, oh dear, I'm mad about
    the boy.

VERSE 3
COCKNEY:
Every Wednesday afternoon
I get a little time off from three to
    eleven,
Then I go to the Picture House
And taste a little of my particular
    heaven.
He appears
In a little while,
Through a mist of tears
I can see him smiling
Above me.
Every picture I see him in,
Every lover's caress,
Makes my wonderful dreams begin,
Makes me long to confess
That if ever he looked at me
And thought perhaps it was worth the
    trouble to
Love me,
I'd give in and I wouldn't care
However far from the path of virtue he'd
Shove me.
Just supposing our love was brief,
If he treated me rough
I'd be happy beyond belief,
Once would be enough.

REFRAIN 3

Mad about the boy,
I know I'm potty, but I'm mad about
the boy.
He sets me 'eart on fire
With love's desire,
In fact I've got it bad about the boy.
When I do the rooms
I see 'is face in all the brushes and the
brooms.
Last week I strained me back
And got the sack
And 'ad a row with Dad about the boy.
I'm finished with Navarro,
I'm tired of Richard Dix,
I'm pierced by Cupid's arrow
Every Wednesday from four till six.
'Ow I should enjoy
To let 'im treat me like a plaything or a toy,
I'd give my all to him
And crawl to him,
So 'elp me Gawd, I'm mad about the boy.

VERSE 4
TART:

It seems a little silly
For a girl of my age and weight
To walk down Piccadilly
In a haze of love.
It ought to take a good deal more to get a
bad girl down,
I should have been exempt, for
My particular kind of fate
Has taught me such contempt for
Every phase of love,
And now I've been and spent my last half-
crown
To weep about a painted clown.

REFRAIN 4

Mad about the boy,
It's pretty funny, but I'm mad about
the boy.

He has a gay appeal
That makes me feel
There's maybe something sad about
the boy.
Walking down the street,
His eyes look out at me from people that
I meet.
I can't believe it's true,
But when I'm blue
In some strange way I'm glad about the boy.
I'm hardly sentimental,
Love isn't so sublime,
I have to pay my rental
And I can't afford to waste much time.
If I could employ
A little magic that would finally destroy
This dream that pains me
And enchains me,
But I can't because I'm mad about
the boy.

REFRAIN 5

Mad about the boy,
I know it's silly but I'm mad about
the boy,
And even Doctor Freud
Cannot explain
Those vexing dreams I've had about
the boy.
When I told my wife,
She said: "I've never heard such nonsense
in my life!"
Her lack of sympathy
Embarrassed me
And made me frankly *glad* about the boy.
My doctor can't advise me,
He'd help me if he could;
Three times he's tried to
psychoanalyze me,
But it's just no good.
People I employ
Have the impertinence to call me
Myrna Loy.

I rise above it,
Frankly love it,
'Cos I'm absolutely mad about the boy!

MAD DOGS AND ENGLISHMEN

VERSE 1

In tropical climes there are certain times
  of day
When all the citizens retire
To tear their clothes off and perspire.
It's one of those rules that the greatest
  fools obey,
Because the sun is much too sultry
And one must avoid its ultry-violet ray.
    Papalaka papalaka papalaka boo,
    Papalaka papalaka papalaka boo,
    Digariga digariga digariga doo,
    Digariga digariga digariga doo.
The natives grieve when the white men
  leave their huts,
Because they're obviously definitely nuts!

REFRAIN 1

Mad dogs and Englishmen
Go out in the midday sun.
The Japanese don't care to,
The Chinese wouldn't dare to,
Hindoos and Argentines sleep firmly from
  twelve to one.
But Englishmen detest a siesta.
In the Philippines
There are lovely screens
To protect you from the glare.
In the Malay States
There are hats like plates
Which the Britishers won't wear.
At twelve noon
The natives swoon
And no further work is done.
But mad dogs and Englishmen
Go out in the midday sun.

VERSE 2

It's such a surprise for the Eastern eyes
  to see
That though the English are effete,
They're quite impervious to heat.
When the white man rides every native
  hides in glee,
Because the simple creatures hope he
Will impale his solar topee on a tree.
    Bolyboly bolyboly bolyboly baa,
    Bolyboly bolyboly bolyboly baa,
    Habaninny habaninny habaninny haa,
    Habaninny habaninny habaninny haa.
It seems such a shame when the English
  claim the earth
That they give rise to such hilarity and
  mirth.

REFRAIN 2

Mad dogs and Englishmen
Go out in the midday sun.
The toughest Burmese bandit
Can never understand it.
In Rangoon the heat of noon
Is just what the natives shun.
They put their Scotch or Rye down
And lie down
In a jungle town
Where the sun beats down.
To the rage of man and beast,
The English garb
Of the English sahib
Merely gets a bit more creased.
In Bangkok
At twelve o'clock
They foam at the mouth and run.
But mad dogs and Englishmen
Go out in the midday sun.

REFRAIN 3

Mad dogs and Englishmen
Go out in the midday sun.
The smallest Malay rabbit

Deplores this stupid habit.
In Hong Kong
They strike a gong
And fire off a noonday gun
To reprimand each inmate
Who's in late.
In the mangrove swamps
Where the python romps
There is peace from twelve till two.
Even caribous
Lie around and snooze,
For there's nothing else to do.
In Bengal
To move at all
Is seldom, if ever, done.
But mad dogs and Englishmen
Go out in the midday sun.

MRS. WORTHINGTON

Regarding yours, dear Mrs. Worthington,
Of Wednesday the 23rd,
Although your baby
May be
Keen on a stage career,
How can I make it clear
That this is not a good idea?
For her to hope,
Dear Mrs. Worthington,
Is on the face of it absurd.
Her personality
Is not in reality
Inviting enough,
Exciting enough,
For this particular sphere.

REFRAIN I
Don't put your daughter on the stage,
    Mrs. Worthington,
Don't put your daughter on the stage.
The profession is overcrowded

And the struggle's pretty tough,
And admitting the fact
She's burning to act,
That isn't quite enough.
She has nice hands, to give the wretched
    girl her due.
But don't you think her bust is too
Developed for her age?
I repeat,
Mrs. Worthington,
Sweet
Mrs. Worthington,
Don't put your daughter on the stage.

REFRAIN 2
Don't put your daughter on the stage,
    Mrs. Worthington,
Don't put your daughter on the stage.
She's a bit of an ugly duckling
You must honestly confess,
And the width of her seat
Would surely defeat
Her chances of success.
It's a loud voice, and though it's not
    exactly flat,
She'll need a little more than that
To earn a living wage.
On my knees,
Mrs. Worthington,
Please,
Mrs. Worthington,
Don't put your daughter on the stage.

REFRAIN 3
Don't put your daughter on the stage,
    Mrs. Worthington,
Don't put your daughter on the stage.
Though they said at the school of acting
She was lovely as Peer Gynt,
I'm afraid on the whole
An ingénue role
Would emphasize her squint.

She's a big girl, and though her teeth are
  fairly good
She's not the type I ever would
Be eager to engage.
No more buts,
Mrs. Worthington,
NUTS,
Mrs. Worthington,
Don't put your daughter on the stage.

REFRAIN 4
Don't put your daughter on the stage, Mrs.
  Worthington,
Don't put your daughter on the stage.
One look at her bandy legs should prove
She hasn't got a chance,
In addition to which
The son of a bitch
Can neither sing nor dance.
She's a *vile* girl and uglier than
  mortal sin,
One look at her has put me in
A tearing bloody rage,
That sufficed,
Mrs. Worthington,
Christ!
Mrs. Worthington,
Don't put your daughter on the stage.

NEVER AGAIN

Over now,
The dream is over now,
Maybe it really wasn't so important
  anyhow.
What's been can't be again
Reluctantly I see.
My heart is free again,
Belongs to me again,
The brief illusion I lived for has gone.
No more confusion and tears from now on;

To start again
And break my heart again
If you should ask me to,
I'd say, "To hell with you!
Away with you!"

REFRAIN
No, never again,
Never the strange unthinking joy,
Never the pain;
Let me be wise,
Let me learn to doubt romance.
Try to live without romance,
Let me be sane.
Time changes the tune,
Changes the pale unwinking stars,
Even the moon.
Let me be soon
Strong enough to flout romance–
And say "You're out, romance,"
Never again!

NINA

REFRAIN I
Señorita Nina
From Argentina
Knew all the answers.
Although her relatives and friends were
  perfect dancers,
She swore she'd never dance a step until
  she died.
She said, "I've seen too many movies
And all they prove is
Too idiotic,
They all insist that South America's exotic,
Whereas it couldn't be more boring if it
  tried."
She added firmly that she hated
The sound of soft guitars beside a still
  lagoon,

She also positively stated
That she could not abide a
    Southern Moon.
She said with most refreshing candor
That she thought Carmen Miranda
Was subversive propaganda
And should rapidly be shot,
She said she didn't care a jot
If people quoted her or not.
She refused to begin the Beguine
When they requested it,
And she made an embarrassing scene
If anyone suggested it,
For she detested it.
Though no one ever could be keener
Than little Nina
On quite a number
Of very eligible men who did the Rumba,
When they proposed to her she simply left
    them flat.
She said that love should be impulsive
But not convulsive,
And syncopation
Has a discouraging effect on procreation,
And that she'd rather read a book—and
    that was that!

REFRAIN 2

Señorita Nina
From Argentina
Despised the Tango,
And though she never was a girl to let a
    man go,
She wouldn't sacrifice her principles
    for sex.
She looked with scorn on the gyrations
Of her relations
Who danced the Conga,
And swore that if she had to stand it any
    longer
She'd lose all dignity and wring their silly
    necks!

She said that frankly she was blinded
To all their over-advertised romantic
    charms,
And then she got more bloody-minded
And told them where to put their Tropic
    Palms.
She said I hate to be pedantic
But it drives me nearly frantic
When I see that unromantic
Sycophantic
Lot of sluts
Forever wriggling their guts,
It drives me absolutely nuts!
She declined to begin the Beguine
Though they besought her to,
And in language profane and obscene
She cursed the man who taught her to,
She cursed Cole Porter too!
From this it's fairly clear that Nina
In her demeanor
Was so offensive
That when the hatred of her friends grew
    too intensive
She thought she'd better beat it while she
    had the chance.
After some trial and tribulation
She reached the station
And met a sailor
Who had acquired a wooden leg in
    Venezuela,
And so she married him because he
    couldn't dance!

CODA

There surely never could have been a
More irritating girl than Nina,
They never speak in Argentina
Of this degenerate bambina
Who had the luck to find romance
But resolutely wouldn't dance!
She wouldn't dance!—Hola!!

Poor Little Rich Girl

VERSE 1

You're only
A baby,
You're lonely,
And maybe
Someday soon you'll know
The tears
You are tasting
Are years
You are wasting,
Life's a bitter foe.
With fate it's no use competing,
Youth is so terribly fleeting;
By dancing
Much faster,
You're chancing
Disaster,
Time alone will show.

REFRAIN

Poor little rich girl,
You're a bewitched girl,
Better beware!
Laughing at danger,
Virtue a stranger,
Better take care!
The life you lead sets all your nerves a-
jangle,
Your love affairs are in a hopeless tangle,
Though you're a child, dear,
Your life's a wild typhoon.
In lives of leisure
The craze for pleasure
Steadily grows.
Cocktails and laughter,
But what comes after?
Nobody knows.
You're weaving love into a mad jazz
pattern,

Ruled by Pantaloon.
Poor little rich girl, don't drop a stitch
too soon.

VERSE 2

The role you are acting,
The toll is exacting,
Soon you'll have to pay.
The music of living
You lose in the giving,
False things soon decay.
These words from me may surprise you,
I've got no right to advise you,
I've known Life too well, dear,
Your own Life must tell, dear,
Please don't turn away.

REPEAT REFRAIN

Sail Away

VERSE

A different sky,
New worlds to gaze upon,
The strange excitement of an unfamiliar
shore.
One more good-bye,
One more illusion gone,
Just cut your losses and begin
once more.

REFRAIN 1

When the storm clouds are riding through
a winter sky,
Sail away—sail away.
When the love-light is fading in your
sweetheart's eye,
Sail away—sail away.
When you feel your song is orchestrated
wrong,
Why should you prolong your stay?

When the wind and the weather blow your
    dreams sky-high,
Sail away–sail away.

REFRAIN 2
When you can't bear the clamor of the
    noisy town,
Sail away–sail away.
When the friend that you counted on has
    let you down,
Sail away–sail away.
But when, soon or late,
You recognize your fate,
That will be your great, great day.
On the wings of the morning with your
    own true love,
Sail away–sail away.

(I'M So) WEARY OF IT ALL

VERSE
People that I sing to
Bring a breath of Spring to
Envy me my gay career.
No one in the city
Has much time for pity;
Nobody can be sincere.
Thousands cheer me and applaud me,
Everyone stares.
If they've wounded me and bored me,
Nobody cares;
Women at the tables,
Loosening their sables,
Look at me with cruel eyes.
Then a little something in me dies
And cries.

REFRAIN
Weary of it all,
This getting and spending,
This futile unending
Refrain,

It's driving me insane;
I'm so weary of it all.
Other voices call–
The cattle at twilight,
The birds in the sky light
Of dawn–
Yet here am I forlorn,
And so weary of it all.
I miss the wildwood
I wandered through in childhood
With a heart as light as air,
What would I give once again to be there
With my old, deaf mother!
Night begins to fall,
By memory tortured
I dream of an orchard
In Spring,
The songs I used to sing,
Now I have to swing,
I'm so weary of it all.

PATTER
Wake up in the morning
'Round about noon,
A little lunch on a tray,
Shopping without stopping till my senses
    swoon,
Or else some dreary matinée.
Home at five,
More dead than alive,
Another day nearly gone.
Cocktails to mix,
My face and hair to fix,
The weary round goes on.
Eight or nine,
I have to go and dine
With this or that rich man about town,
Caviar and grouse
In an overheated house,
God, how it gets me down!
Home I go defeated and depressed again,
Only time for just one hour of rest again.
Bright lights,

White lights,
Waiters leering,
Faces sneering,
Laughing, chaffing,
Shouting, cheering.
Weary of it all,
This giving and giving,
This life that I'm living in hell.
With broken dreams to sell,
Just an empty shell,
Weary, weary, weary of it all!

WHY MUST THE SHOW GO ON?

VERSE 1

The world for some years
Has been sodden with tears
On behalf of the Acting profession.
Each star playing a part
Seems to expect the Purple Heart.
It's unorthodox
To be born in a box,
But it needn't become an obsession.
Let's hope we have no worse to plague us
Than two shows a night at Las Vegas.
When I think of physicians
And mathematicians
Who don't earn a quarter the dough,
When I look at the faces
Of people in Macy's
There's one thing I'm burning to know:

REFRAIN 1

Why must the show go on?
It can't be all that indispensable,
To me it really isn't sensible,
On the whole,
To play a leading role
While fighting those tears you can't
    control.
Why kick up your legs
When draining the dregs
Of sorrow's bitter cup?
Because you have read
Some idiot has said,
"The curtain must go up!"
I'd like to know why a star takes bows
Having just returned from burying her
    spouse.
Brave boop-a-doopers,
Go home and dry your tears,
Gallant old troupers,
You've bored us all for years,
And when you're so blue,
Wet through
And thoroughly woebegone,
Why must the show go on?
O Mammy!
Why must the show go on?

VERSE 2

We're asked to condole
With each tremulous soul
Who steps out to be loudly applauded.
Stars on opening nights
Sob when they see their names in lights.
Though people who act,
As a matter of fact,
Are financially amply rewarded,
It seems, while pursuing their calling,
Their suffering's simply appalling!
But butchers and bakers
And candlestick makers
Get little applause for their pains,
And when I think of miners
And waiters in diners
One query for ever remains:

REFRAIN 2

Why must the show go on?
The rule is surely not immutable.
It might be wiser and more suitable
Just to close
If you are in the throes
Of personal grief and private woes.

Why stifle a sob
While doing your job
When if you use your head
You'd go out and grab
A comfortable cab
And go right home to bed?
Because you're not giving us much fun,
This "Laugh Clown, Laugh" routine's
    been overdone.
Hats off to Show Folks
For smiling when they're blue,
But more *comme-il-faut* folks
Are sick of smiling through.
And if you're out cold,
Too old,
And most of your teeth have gone,
Why must the show go on?
I sometimes wonder
Why must the show go on?

REFRAIN 3
Why must the show go on?
Why not announce the closing night of it?

The public seem to hate the sight of it,
Dear, and so
Why you should undergo
This terrible strain we'll never know.
We know that you're sad,
We know that you've had
A lot of storm and strife.
But is it quite fair
To ask us to share
Your dreary private life?
We know you're trapped in a gilded cage,
But for Heaven's sake relax and be
    your age.
Stop being gallant
And don't be such a bore,
Pack up your talent,
There's always plenty more,
And if you lose hope
Take dope
And lock yourself in the john.
Why must the show go on?
I'm merely asking
Why must the show go on?

Mitchell Parish (1900–1993)

ACCORDING TO which source you believe, Mitchell Parish was born in New York City; Shreveport, Louisiana; or Lithuania. But wherever he was born, it was certainly he who supplied the words to what is very likely the most popular (and most recorded) of all twentieth-century songs, Hoagy Carmichael's "Star Dust." In fact, supplying words to already successful jazz and other instrumentals, foreign songs, etc., was Parish's chief métier. After an interrupted education in New York, he became a staff lyricist for the Mills music-publishing firm, and since Irving Mills handled Duke Ellington, Parish was employed to turn great Ellington tunes into commercial hits: "Sophisticated Lady" and "Mood Indigo," although credit for the latter was taken by Mills, an all-time credit-taker. Parish's first big hit was the jolly "Sweet Lorraine," in 1928, but his greatest success after "Star Dust" was the almost as highfalutin "Deep Purple." Yet the fancy kind of writing he did for "Star Dust" and "Deep Purple" is so aptly matched to their music that it prevails. Parish was still turning out hits in the rock era—most conspicuously his English version, in 1960, of Domenico Modugno's "Volare." Of all the major non-composing lyricists, he is by far the most important non-collaborator: They handed him a tune, new or old, and he made a song out of it. (As for that interrupted education, apparently he went back to college [NYU] in his late forties and, as a fifty-year-old grandfather, not only got his degree in English literature but was elected to Phi Beta Kappa in his junior year.)

DEEP PURPLE

VERSE

The sun is sinking low
Behind the hill,
I loved you long ago,
I love you still.
Across the years
You come to me at twilight
To bring me love's
Old thrill.

REFRAIN

When the deep purple falls
Over sleepy garden walls,
And the stars begin to flicker in
the sky,
Thru the mist of a memory
You wander back to me,
Breathing my name with a sigh.
In the still of the night
Once again I hold you tight,
Tho' you're gone, your love lives on when
moonlight beams.
And as long as my heart will beat,
Lover, we'll always meet
Here in my deep purple dreams.

—*Peter De Rose*

SOPHISTICATED LADY

   (with Irving Mills)

They say
Into your early life romance came,
And in this heart of yours burned a flame,
A flame that flickered one day
And died away.
Then,
With disillusion deep in your eyes,
You learned that fools in love soon
      grow wise.
The years have changed you, somehow;
I see you now . . .
Smoking, drinking,
Never thinking of tomorrow,
Nonchalant.
Diamonds shining,
Dancing, dining with some man in a
      restaurant.
Is that all you really want?
No,
Sophisticated lady, I know,
You miss the love you lost long ago,
And when nobody is nigh
You cry.

   —Duke Ellington

STAR DUST

   VERSE

And now the purple dusk of twilight time
Steals across the meadows of my heart.
High up in the sky the little stars climb,
Always reminding me that we're apart.
You wandered down the lane and far away,
Leaving me a song that will not die.
Love is now the star dust of yesterday,
The music of the years gone by.

   REFRAIN

Sometimes I wonder why I spend the
      lonely night
Dreaming of a song.
The melody
Haunts my reverie,
And I am once again with you
When our love was new,
And each kiss an inspiration.
But that was long ago:
Now my consolation
Is in the star dust of a song.
Beside a garden wall when stars are bright,
You are in my arms,
The nightingale
Tells his fairy tale
Of paradise, where roses grew.
Tho' I dream in vain,
In my heart it will remain,
My star dust melody,
The memory of love's refrain.

   —Hoagy Carmichael

STARS FELL ON ALABAMA

We lived our little drama,
We kissed in a field of white.
And stars fell on Alabama
Last night.
I can't forget the glamour,
Your eyes held a tender light.
And stars fell on Alabama
Last night.
I never planned in my imagination
A situation so heavenly,
A fairyland where no one else could enter
And in the center
Just you and me,
Dear.
My heart beat like a hammer;

My arms wound around you tight.
And stars fell on Alabama
Last night.

—Frank Perkins

SWEET LORRAINE

I've just found joy,
I'm as happy as a baby boy
With another brand-new choo-choo toy
When I'm with my sweet Lorraine.
A pair of eyes
That are bluer than the summer
    skies,

When you see them you will realize
Why I love my sweet Lorraine.
(I'm so happy)
When it's raining
I don't miss the sun;
For it's in my sweetie's smile.
Just to think that
I'm the lucky one
Who will lead her
Down the aisle.
Each night I pray
That nobody steals her heart away,
Just can't wait until that happy day
When I marry sweet Lorraine.

—Cliff Burwell

Kim Gannon (1900–1974)

Brooklyn born, Kim (James Kimball) Gannon was trained as a lawyer before making his mark as a lyricist, most famously as the writer of Glenn Miller's huge 1942 hit, "Moonlight Cocktail"–ten weeks at number one and over one million copies sold. In 1951, in the wake of Rodgers and Hammerstein, Gannon collaborated on a pleasing if mild musical comedy version of Booth Tarkington's classic piece of Americana, *Seventeen*, which ran almost half a year on Broadway. Half a century later, its score retains its charm.

A Dreamer's Holiday

Climb aboard a butterfly and take off on
    the breeze.
Let your worries flutter by and do the
    things you please,
In the land where dollar bills are falling off
    the trees
On a dreamer's holiday.
Ev'ry day for breakfast there's a dish of
    scrambled stars,
And for luncheon you'll be munchin'
    rainbow candy bars.
You'll be livin' à la mode on Jupiter or Mars,
On a dreamer's holiday.
Make it a long vacation,
Time there is plenty of.
You need no reservation,
Just bring along the one you love.
Help yourself to happiness and sprinkle it
    with mirth,
Close your eyes and concentrate
    and dream for all you're worth.
You will feel terrific when you get back
    down to earth,
From a dreamer's holiday.

—Mabel Wayne

Moonlight Cocktail

Coupl'a jiggers of moonlight and add a star,
Pour in the blue of a June night and one
    guitar,
Mix in a coupl'a dreamers and there
    you are,
Lovers hail the moonlight cocktail.
Now add a coupl'a flowers, a drop of dew.
Stir for a coupl'a hours till dreams
    come true,
As to the number of kisses, it's up to you,
Moonlight cocktails need a few.
Cool it in the summer breeze,
Serve it in the starlight underneath the
    trees.
You'll discover tricks like these
Are sure to make your moonlight cocktail
    please.
Follow the simple directions and they will
    bring
Life of another complexion, where you'll
    be king.
You will awake in the morning and start
    to sing,
Moonlight cocktails are the thing.

—Lucky Roberts

RECIPROCITY

VERSE

I learned it from my teacher way back in
    Sunday School,
The only way to get along is by the
    Golden Rule.
Although the rule is ancient, it still is up
    to date.
It means be nice to others, it means
    reciprocate.

REFRAIN

So if a fellow seems romantic,
It's romantic you should be.
It's only fair to do your share,
It's reciprocity.
And suppose he tries to hug you,
Should you climb the nearest tree?
Oh no, oh no, you've got to show
Some reciprocity.
You look on your porch and there's the boy
    next door.

You can't chase him home, 'cause what's a
    porch for?
So if a fellow wants to kiss me,
I'm full of sympathy.
I'm more than glad to help the lad,
It's reciprocity.
Supposin' he's shy? He needs your help
    much more.
At least you should try, for what are little
    girls for?
When I meet that certain fellow
And he wants to marry me,
I can't do less than answer yes,
It's reciprocity.
We made up our minds the only way
    to live
Is always be kind and even if it
    hurts, give.
So if a fellow wants to kiss me,
I react quite naturally.
I'm not naïve, I just believe
In reciprocity.

—*Walter Kent*

Edward Eliscu (1901–1998)

E DWARD ELISCU WAS a jack-of-all-trades around the Broadway theater–actor (when young), director, producer, writer–and had an equally diverse career in Hollywood. A lifelong outspoken liberal, he was blacklisted in the fifties but was able to go on working in television and the theater. As a lyricist he had two important moments. The first was when he collaborated with Billy Rose on the words for the Vincent Youmans show *Great Day!* It only ran about a month, but it produced three standards: the title song, "More Than You Know," and "Without a Song." Then, also for Youmans, he collaborated with Gus Kahn on the songs for the first Astaire/Rogers musical, *Flying Down to Rio* ("The Carioca"). Among his less-distinguished efforts: "Damn the Torpedoes!" and "Ankle Up the Altar with Me."

FLYING DOWN TO RIO

(with Gus Kahn)

VERSE

An old sailor in old times
Would sing an old song,
Rolling down to Rio by the sea.
A young sailor in these times
Will sing a new song,
Flying down to Rio; come with me,
Where the lovely Brazilian ladies will
    catch your eye
By the light of a million stars in the
    evening sky.

REFRAIN

My Rio, Rio by the sea-o,
Flying down to Rio,
Where there's rhythm and rhyme.
Hey, feller,
Twirl that old propeller,
Got to get to Rio
And we've got to make time.

You'll love it,
Soaring high above it,
Looking down on Rio
From a heaven of blue.
Send a radio to Rio de Janeiro,
With a big hello
Just so they'll know
And stand by there,
We'll fly there.
Hey, Rio,
Ev'rything will be okay,
We're singing and winging
Our way to you.

—Vincent Youmans

GREAT DAY

(with Billy Rose)

VERSE

When skies were dark
Came Noah's ark

(Amen).
When lions roared
Came Daniel's Lord
(Amen).
Lord helps those who pray,
And on Judgment Day,
If you believe,
He shall receive you
(Amen).

REFRAIN

When you're down and out,
Lift up your head and shout,
"There's gonna be a great day."
Angels in the sky
Promise that by and by
There's gonna be a great day.
Gabriel will warn you,
Some early morn you
Will hear his horn
Rooty tootin'.
It's not far away.
Hold up your hands and say,
"There's gonna be a great day."

—*Vincent Youmans*

More Than You Know

(with Billy Rose)

VERSE

Whether you are here or yonder,
Whether you are false or true,
Whether you remain or wander,
I'm growing fonder of you.
Even though your friends
    forsake you,
Even though you don't succeed,
Wouldn't I be glad to take you,
Give you the break you need?

REFRAIN

More than you know,
More than you know,
Man o' my heart, I love you so.
Lately I find
You're on my mind,
More than you know.
Whether you're right,
Whether you're wrong,
Man o' my heart, I'll string along.
You need me so,
More than you'll ever know.
Loving you the way I do,
There's nothing I can do about it.
Loving may be all you can give,
But honey, I can't live without it.
Oh, how I'd cry,
Oh, how I'd cry,
If you got tired and said "good-bye."
More than I'd show,
More than you'd ever know.

—*Vincent Youmans*

Without a Song

(with Billy Rose)

REFRAIN

Without a song
The day would never end;
Without a song
The road would never bend;
When things go wrong,
A man ain't got a friend
Without a song.
That field of corn
Would never see a plow;
That field of corn
Would be deserted now;
A darky's born,
But he's no good nohow

Without a song.
I got my trouble and woe,
But sure as I know
The Jordan will roll,
I'll get along
As long as a song
Is strong in my soul.
I'll never know

What makes the rain to fall;
I'll never know
What makes the grass so tall;
I only know
There ain't no love at all
Without a song.

—Vincent Youmans

Eric Maschwitz (1901–1969)

T HE NAME ON the original credits for "These Foolish Things" and "A Nightingale Sang in Berkeley Square" was "Holt Marvell," but it was Eric Maschwitz
who wrote them. Born in Birmingham, England, Maschwitz had a full and successful
career in British show business. He wrote the librettos and lyrics for a number of hit
musicals—three of them ran in London for more than five hundred performances—and
was a longtime executive with the BBC. The title of his autobiography, *No Chip on My
Shoulder,* no doubt refers to the fact that among the screenplays he wrote was that for
the Robert Donat *Goodbye, Mr. Chips.* His first wife was Hermione Gingold. Could all
those "foolish things" have reminded him of her?

A NIGHTINGALE SANG IN BERKELEY SQUARE

VERSE

When true lovers meet in Mayfair, so the
    legends tell,
Songbirds sing,
Winter turns to spring,
Ev'ry winding street in Mayfair falls
    beneath the spell.
I know such enchantment can be,
'Cause it happened one evening to me.

REFRAIN I

That certain night,
The night we met,
There was magic abroad in the air.
There were angels dining at the Ritz,
And a nightingale sang in Berkeley
    Square.
I may be right,
I may be wrong,
But I'm perfectly willing to swear
That when you turned and smiled at me,
A nightingale sang in Berkeley Square.

The moon that lingered over
    London town,
Poor puzzled moon,
He wore a frown.
How could he know we two were so
    in love?
The whole darn world
Seemed upside down.
The streets of town
Were paved with stars;
It was such a romantic affair.
And as we kissed and said "good night,"
A nightingale sang in Berkeley Square.

REFRAIN 2

Strange it was,
How sweet and strange,
There was never a dream to compare
With that hazy, crazy night we met,
When a nightingale sang in Berkeley
    Square.
This heart of mine
Beat loud and fast
Like a merry-go-round in a fair,
For we were dancing cheek to cheek

And a nightingale sang in Berkeley
    Square.
When dawn came stealing up all gold
    and blue
To interrupt
Our rendezvous,
I still remember how you smiled and said,
"Was that a dream
Or was it true?"
Our homeward step
Was just as light
As the tap-dancing feet of Astaire.
And like an echo far away,
A nightingale sang in Berkeley Square.
I know 'cause I was there,
That night in Berkeley Square.

    —*Manning Sherwin*

PARIS IS NOT THE SAME

VERSE

Haunting the page of my passport,
Faint as a ghost of the past,
Are the day and the hour of my heart's one
    adventure,
The sweetest, the first, and the last.
One precious moment of madness,
Something too sweet to explain,
When my heart kept repeating, "I love
    you, I love you,"
In time with the wheels of the train.

REFRAIN

When I return to Paris in the Spring,
My foolish heart must be aflame.
Why has the magic gone from everything?
Paris is not the same.
Though there are chestnut blossoms in
    the bois,
Like Easter candles all aflame,

And yet somehow in spite of the beauty of
    April,
Paris is not the same.
Lonely and sad in the room on the
    courtyard
Away from the sound of the street,
Haunted at night by the ghost of a
    memory,
Impossibly lonely and heavenly sweet.
Among the voices on the boulevard
There's one that seems to call my name.
But I never look 'round, for I know there's
    no one,
No one to call my name.
Paris is not the same.

    —*James Strachey*

THESE FOOLISH THINGS
  (REMIND ME OF YOU)

VERSE

Oh! will you never let me be?
Oh! will you never set me free?
The ties that bound us
Are still around us,
There's no escape that I can see.
And still those little things remain,
That bring me happiness or pain.

REFRAIN I

A cigarette that bears a lipstick's traces,
An airline ticket to romantic places,
And still my heart has wings.
These foolish things
Remind me of you.
A tinkling piano in the next apartment,
Those stumbling words that told you what
    my heart meant,
A fairground's painted swings,
These foolish things

Remind me of you.
You came, you saw, you conquer'd me;
When you did that to me,
I knew somehow this had to be.
The winds of March that make my heart a
    dancer,
A telephone that rings, but who's to
    answer?
Oh, how the ghost of you clings!
These foolish things
Remind me of you.

REFRAIN 2
First daffodils and long excited cables,
And candle lights on little corner tables,
And still my heart has wings.
These foolish things
Remind me of you.
The park at evening when the bell has
    sounded,
The "Ile de France" with all the gulls
    around it,
The beauty that is Spring's,
These foolish things
Remind me of you.
How strange, how sweet,
To find you still;
These things are dear to me,
They seem to bring you near to me.
The sigh of midnight trains in empty
    stations,

Silk stockings thrown aside, dance
    invitations.
Oh, how the ghost of you clings!
These foolish things
Remind me of you.

REFRAIN 3
Gardenia perfume ling'ring on a pillow,
Wild strawb'ries only seven francs a kilo,
And still my heart has wings.
These foolish things
Remind me of you.
The smile of Garbo and the scent of roses,
The waiters whistling as the last bar
    closes,
The song that Crosby sings,
These foolish things
Remind me of you.
How strange, how sweet,
To find you still;
These things are dear to me,
They seem to bring you near to me.
The scent of smold'ring leaves, the wail of
    steamers,
Two lovers on the street who walk like
    dreamers.
Oh, how the ghost of you clings!
These foolish things
Remind me of you.

—James Strachey and Harry Link

Ned Washington (1901–1976)

NED WASHINGTON WILL NO DOUBT be longest remembered as the man who wrote "When You Wish Upon a Star," the Oscar-winning song from Disney's *Pinocchio,* but his claim to fame rests on a solid mantle of almost forty other film-title songs, from "My Foolish Heart" and "Green Dolphin Street" to "The High and the Mighty" and "High Noon," which won him another Oscar. (He received yet another Oscar for the film score of *Pinocchio,* bringing his total to three.) He contributed many songs to a variety of Broadway shows, and his "I'm Getting Sentimental Over You" was Tommy Dorsey's theme song. But his ingenuity at finding appropriate words for film music remained his strongest point, as with the haunting lyric for "Stella by Starlight," a song that quickly eclipsed the movie it came from, the tame Ray Milland thriller *The Uninvited.*

GIVE ME A HEART TO SING TO

VERSE

There's something inside of my heart that
　　cries,
It cries, for it wants to live.
A song of devotion, a song that speaks of
　　love.
It's hard to believe that you can't
　　surmise
The treasure I have to give.
Is love out of fashion, the thing that I'm
　　dreaming of?

REFRAIN

Give me a heart to sing to,
Or my song you'll never hear.
For I must have a heart to sing to,
Or my song wouldn't be sincere.
Give me your love to guide me,
Let us find a world apart.
And as long as you're there beside me,
There'll be melody in my heart.

I'm in your hands to take and
　　hold me,
To make or mold me,
If you but knew.
In you I find my consolation,
My destination
Depends on you.
Love must have love to cling to,
As a leaf clings to a tree.
So I must have a song to sing to,
And a heart that will sing to me.

—Victor Young

A HUNDRED YEARS FROM TODAY

(with Joseph Young)

VERSE

Life is such a great adventure,
Learn to live it as you go.
No one in the world can censure
What we do here below.

Don't save your kisses, just pass them
    around,
You'll find my reason is logic'lly sound.
Who's going to know that you passed them
    around,
A hundred years from today!
Why crave a penthouse that's fit for a
    queen,
You're nearer Heaven on Mother Earth's
    green.
If you had millions, what would they all
    mean,
A hundred years from today?
So laugh and sing,
Make love the thing,
Be happy while you may.
There's always one
Beneath the sun
Who's bound to make you feel that way.
The moon is shining, and that's a
    good sign.
Cling to me closer and say you'll be mine.
Remember, darling, we won't see it shine
A hundred years from today.

—*Victor Young*

LOVE IS THE THING

VERSE

My darling, all around us people clamor,
They're striving for the things they'll
    never own.
The only thing that hasn't lost its
    glamour
Is love and love alone.

REFRAIN

What does it matter if we're rich or
    we're poor?
Fortune and fame, they never endure.

Oh, love is the thing,
Love is the thing!
What good is money if your heart isn't
    light?
Here in your arms, I'm wealthy tonight.
When youth has its fling,
Love is the thing!
While others fight for pow'r,
We can walk among the flow'rs,
Knowing that the best thing in life is a
    thing that's free,
Love for you and me.
And even tho' our castles crumble and fall,
We have the right to laugh at them all,
For love is still King,
Love is the thing!

—*Victor Young*

MY FOOLISH HEART

VERSE

The scene is set for dreaming,
Love's knocking at the door.
But oh, my heart,
I'm reluctant to start,
For we've been fooled before.

REFRAIN

The night is like a lovely tune,
Beware my foolish heart!
How white the ever constant moon;
Take care my foolish heart!
There's a line between love and
    fascination
That's hard to see on an evening such
    as this,
For they both give the very same sensation
When you're lost in the magic of a kiss.
Her lips are much too close to mine,
Beware my foolish heart.
But should our eager lips combine

Then let the fire start.
For this time it isn't fascination,
Or a dream that will fade and fall apart.
It's love, this time, it's love,
My foolish heart.

—Victor Young

THE NEARNESS OF YOU

VERSE

Why do I just wither and forget all
    resistance
When you and your magic pass by?
My heart's in a dither, dear, when you're at
    a distance,
But when you are near, Oh, my!

REFRAIN

It's not the pale moon that excites me,
That thrills and delights me.
Oh, no,
It's just the nearness of you.
It isn't your sweet conversation
That brings this sensation.
Oh, no,
It's just the nearness of you.
When you're in my arms
And I feel you so close to me,
All my wildest dreams come true.
I need no soft lights to enchant me
If you'll only grant me
The right
To hold you ever so tight,
And to feel in the night
The nearness of you.

—Hoagy Carmichael

A WOMAN'S INTUITION

VERSE

Sizing up our present situation,
It's as crazy as a crazy quilt.
It's just a routine,
It's a pinball machine,
And the lights are saying "tilt."

REFRAIN

You go along in your quiet way,
Act more strange ev'ry day,
In this position
A woman's intuition
Will tell her all there is to know.
It's very clear that there's
    someone new
Hurting me, charming you,
That great magician,
A woman's intuition,
Has told me all these things are so.
You haven't held me in your arms
    lately,
You haven't kissed me in the tender way
    you should.
It's rather obvious you've changed
    greatly,
But I wouldn't say the change was for
    the good.
To give you up, what a fool I'd be,
Not a chance, no sirree!
On no condition,
For my woman's intuition
Says you're the only one for me.

—Victor Young

Meredith Willson (1902–1984)

Meredith willson (from Iowa, of course) studied at the Walter Damrosch Institute and became a lead flautist for the John Philip Sousa band and then for the New York Philharmonic. In the thirties he was in Hollywood, making a big name for himself in radio and a small name as a songwriter–an early hit was "You and I." It took him eight years to get *The Music Man* to Broadway, but after it opened late in 1957, it ran for more than three years before spawning an equally successful movie version. The modestly appealing *The Unsinkable Molly Brown* followed, then the unappealing *Here's Love* and a show (about Christopher Columbus) that never made it into town. Willson's large reputation is based on one terrific piece of work, but it got him on a U.S. postage stamp!

Seventy-six Trombones

Seventy-six trombones led the big parade,
With a hundred and ten cornets close
    at hand.
They were followed by rows and rows
Of the finest virtuosos,
The cream of ev'ry famous band.
Seventy-six trombones caught the
    morning sun,
With a hundred and ten cornets right
    behind.
There were more than a thousand reeds
Springing up like weeds,
There were horns of ev'ry shape
    and kind.
There were copper-bottom tympani in
    horse platoons,
Thundering, thundering, all along
    the way.
Double-bell euphoniums and big
    bassoons,
Each bassoon having his big fat say.

There were fifty mounted cannon in the
    battery,
Thundering, thundering, louder than
    before.
Clarinets of ev'ry size and trumpeters
    who'd improvise
A full octave higher than the score.
Seventy-six trombones led the big
    parade,
When the order to march rang out loud
    and clear.
Starting off with a big bang bong
On a Chinese gong,
By a big bang bonger at the rear.
Seventy-six trombones hit the
    counterpoint,
While a hundred and ten cornets played
    the air.
Then I modestly took my place
As the one and only bass,
And I oompahed up and down the
    square.

TILL THERE WAS YOU

There were bells on the hill,
But I never heard them ringing,
No, I never heard them at all
Till there was you.
There were birds in the sky,
But I never saw them winging,
No, I never saw them at all
Till there was you.
And there was music,
And there were wonderful roses,
They tell me,
In sweet fragrant meadows of dawn,
And dew.
There was love all around,
But I never heard it singing,
No, I never heard it at all
Till there was you.

YA GOT TROUBLE

Well ya got trouble, my friend, right here,
I say trouble right here in River City.
Why sure, I'm a billiard player, certainly
    mighty proud,
I say I'm always mighty proud to say it.
I consider that the hours I spend with a
    cue in my hand are golden.
Help you cultivate horse sense and a cool
    head and a keen eye.
'Jever take'n try to give an ironclad
    leave to yourself from a three-rail
    billiard shot?
But just, as I say, it takes judgment,
    brains, and maturity to score in a balk-
    line game,
I say that any boob kin take'n shove a ball
    in a pocket,
And I call that sloth!

The first big step on the road to the depths
    of degrada . . .
I say, first it's a little ah, medicinal wine
    from a teaspoon;
Then beer from a bottle.
And the next thing you know, your son is
    playin' fer money in a pinchback suit,
And list'nin' to some big out-a-town jasper
    hearin' him tell about horse-race
    gamblin'.
Not a wholesome trottin' race, no! But a
    race where they se' down right on a
    horse!
Like to see some stuck-up jockey boy
    settin' on Dan Patch?
Make your blood boil?
Well I should say.
Now friends, lemme tell you what I mean.

Ya got one, two, three, four, five, six
    pockets in a table!
Pockets that mark the diff'rence between a
    gentleman and a bum,
With a capital "B," and that rhymes
    with "P,"
And that stands for pool.
And all week long your River City youth'll
    be frittern away,
I say, your young men'll be frittern.
Frittern away their noontime,
    suppertime, choretime too!
Get the ball in the pocket!
Never mind gettin' dandelions pulled or
    the screen door patched or the
    beefsteak pounded.
Never mind pumpin' any water 'til your
    parents are caught with the cistern
    empty on a Saturday night.
And that's trouble,
Oh, yes, ya got lots 'n' lots 'a trouble.
I'm thinkin' of the kids in the
    knickerbockers, shirttails, young

ones, peekin' in the pool-hall window after school,

Ya got trouble, folks, right here in River City. Trouble, with a capital "T" and that rhymes with "P" and that stands for pool!

Now I know all you folks are the right kind of parents.

I'm gonna be perfectly frank.

Would ya like to know what kinda conversation goes on while they're loafin' around the hall?

They'll be tryin' out Bevo; tryin' out Cubebs; tryin' out Tailor Mades, like cigarette fiends,

And braggin' all about how they're gonna cover up a telltale breath with Sen-Sen.

One fine night they leave the pool hall headin' for the dance at the Arm'ry.

Libertine men and scarlet women and ragtime,

Shameless music that'll drag your son and your daughter

To the arms of a jungle animal instinct mass-steria!

Friends, the idle brain is the devil's playground,

Trouble!

Right here in River City!

With a capital "T" and that rhymes with "P" and that stands for pool.

We've surely got trouble!

Right here in River City!

Gotta figger out a way to keep the young ones moral after school.

Our children's children gonna have trouble.

Oh, we got trouble.

We're in terrible, terrible trouble.

That game with the fifteen numbered balls is the Devil's tool!

Oh, yes, we've got trouble, trouble, trouble.

Yes, we got trouble here,

We got big, big trouble with a "T," gotta rhyme it with "P," and that stands for pool!

Ogden Nash (1902–1971)

H ARVARD-EDUCATED Ogden Nash was, needless to say, America's most brilliant and successful writer of light verse, but he hoped to establish himself as a Broadway lyricist, too. Despite first-rate collaborators (Vernon Duke, Jerome Robbins, Bette Davis) on "Two's Company," and S. J. Perelman, Al Hirschfeld, and Dolores Gray on "Sweet Bye and Bye," his only considerable success came with "One Touch of Venus," music by Kurt Weill, book by Nash himself with Perelman, choreography by Agnes de Mille, and starring Mary Martin.

I'M A STRANGER HERE MYSELF

REFRAIN 1

Tell me, is love still a popular suggestion,
Or merely an obsolete art?
Forgive me for asking this simple
    question,
I'm unfamiliar with his heart,
I'm a stranger here myself.
Why is it wrong to murmur, I adore him,
When it's shamefully obvious, I do?
Does love embarrass him, or does it
    bore him?
I'm only waiting for my cue,
I'm a stranger here myself.

VERSE 1

I dream of a day, of a gay warm day,
With my fate between his hands.
Have I missed the path, have I gone
    astray?
I ask, and no one understands.

REFRAIN 2

Love me or leave me, that seems to be the
    question;
I don't know the tactics to use.

But if he should offer a personal
    suggestion,
How could I possibly refuse, when
I'm a stranger here myself?

VERSE 3

Please tell me, tell a stranger by curiosity
    goaded,
Is there really any danger that love is now
    outmoded?
I'm int'rested especially in knowing why
    you waste it;
True romance is so fleshly, with what have
    you replaced it?
What is your latest foible?
Is gin rummy more exquisite?
Is skiing more enjoy'ble?
For heaven's sake, what is it?

REFRAIN 3

I can't believe that love has lost its glamor,
That passion is really passé.
If gender is just a term in grammar,
How can I ever find my way, since
I'm a stranger here myself?

REPEAT VERSE 2

CODA

How can he ignore my available
    condition?
Why these Victorian views?
You see here before you a woman with a
    mission;
I must discover the key to his ignition,
And then if he should make a diplomatic
    proposition,
How could I possibly refuse,
When I'm a stranger here myself?

—Kurt Weill

ROUND ABOUT

VERSE

When you look life in the face
There's too much time, there's too much
    space.
There's too much future, too much past.
Man is so little, and the world so vast;
You may fancy yourself as an immortal
    creature,
But you're just a cartoon between a double
    feature.

REFRAIN

You go round about
And round about
And round about you go.
For an olden spell is wound about
    the game.
Then it's ring around
And swing around
Your partners as you go,
But the more they change, the more they
    are the same.
When the dancing is done,
You are back where you started;
1. When the music begins, it plays the
    same old tune.

Then it's round about
And round about
And round about again
As you pray again
Each day again to soar;
On your way again,
It's round about once more.

INTERLUDE

You wake each morning alive and gay.
You think today is another day.
Your future seems a primrose path.
You hum to your pillow and you sing in
    your bath.
Your stockings hug you along the seam.
Your girdle fits like a sophomore's dream.
You roam the world like a romantic rover.
You find today is just yesterday
    warmed over.
You meet a man and you're on the crest.
You think he is diff'rent from all the rest.
You start to dream of a cozy flat
With milk for the kids and cream for
    the cat,
And that's the moment not to be
    astounded
To find that you've been merry-go-
    rounded.

REPEAT REFRAIN

2. Each tomorrow the sun shines through
    your vacant heart.
Then it's round about
And round about
And round about again
As you grope again
And hope again to soar;
It's no soap again,
It's round about once more.

—Vernon Duke

The Sea-Gull and the Ea-Gull

A sea-gull met an ea-gull
In an ea-gloo way up North.
The sea-gull eyed the ea-gull
And the following words came forth:
"I'm a sea-gull, you're an ea-gull,
You are re-gull, like a king,
You are royal like Standard Oyal,
So how about a royal fling?
I'm a sea-gull, you're an ea-gull,
It's ille-gull, but sublime.
I'm a she-gull without a he-gull,
So why are we wasting time?"
Said the sea-gull to the ea-gull:
"My feathers you can see.
A duck has down, but I got no down,
You can never get down off me.
If the wee gull is half an ea-gull
Don't imagine that I will fret,
Once I had one by a bea-gull
And I haven't stopped laughing yet."
Said the ea-gull to the sea-gull
As he doffed his re-gull crown:
You're a bad bird, you're a bad,
    bad bird,
But you're the only bird in town.

—Vernon Duke

Speak Low

REFRAIN
Speak low
When you speak love,
Our summer day
Withers away
Too soon, too soon.
Speak low
When you speak love,

Our moment is swift,
Like ships adrift
We're swept apart
Too soon.
Speak low,
Darling, speak low,
Love is a spark
Lost in the dark
Too soon, too soon.
I feel
Wherever I go
That tomorrow is near,
Tomorrow is here
And always too soon.
Time is so old
And love so brief.
Love is pure gold
And time a thief.
We're late,
Darling, we're late.
The curtain descends,
Ev'rything ends
Too soon, too soon.
I wait,
Darling, I wait.
Will you speak low to me,
Speak love to me, and soon?

—Kurt Weill

Sweet Bye and Bye

VERSE
What's the news?
What's the word?
What's the time?
Haven't you heard?
The future is just terrific and thanks to
    Grover Whalen
Mankind will move from the Y-M-C-A to
    the Weylin.

REFRAIN
Sweet bye and bye,
Sweet land of milk and honey,
Let's you and I
Hold out for apple pie in the sky,
It's the sweet bye and bye.
Clouds roll away,
Let's grab the silver lining.
Here's your bouquet,
Our ship is sailing home up the bay.
Christmas comes ev'ry day,

Fool ev'ry clock in town,
Turn the calendar upside down,
Eat our cake and have it too,
Do it up brown.
Sweet bye and bye,
We're knee-deep in confetti,
Rain turns to rye,
There's caviar for all in the street,
In the sweet bye and bye.

—Vernon Duke

Sam Coslow (1902–1983)

S AM COSLOW, sometimes lyricist, sometimes composer, sometimes both, was around forever. His first hit, "Grieving for You," was written when he was seventeen; in the early twenties he was writing for Al Jolson; and he was still turning out hits thirty-odd years later. Along the way, he made a few records himself, worked for *Variety,* produced a few movies, teamed up with Colonel James Roosevelt to make coin-operated movie machines ("Soundies"), made a fortune in investments, and founded an investment newsletter as well as a music publishing firm. He was very busy in Hollywood, where he wrote for stars like Lillian Roth, Bing Crosby, Maurice Chevalier, and Mae West. One of his most famous songs, "Cocktails for Two," was a number-one hit for Duke Ellington in 1934; it was given a very different treatment by Spike Jones eleven years later. Probably his most performed song today is "My Old Flame."

COCKTAILS FOR TWO

Oh, what delight
To be given the right
To be carefree and gay once again.
No longer slinking,
Respectably drinking
Like civilized ladies and men.
No longer need we miss
A charming scene like this.
In some secluded rendezvous
That overlooks the avenue,
With someone sharing a delightful chat
Of this and that,
And cocktails for two.
As we enjoy a cigarette
To some exquisite chansonnette,
Two hands are sure to slyly meet beneath
A serviette
With cocktails for two.
My head may go reeling,
But my heart will be obedient,
With intoxicating kisses
For the principal ingredient.
Most any afternoon at five
We'll be so glad we're both alive.
Then maybe fortune will complete her plan
That all began
With cocktails for two.

—Arthur Johnston

(I'M IN LOVE WITH)
THE HONORABLE MR. SO AND SO

I'm in love with the honorable Mister So
    and So.
I can't mention his name with propriety,
He's a pillar of Gotham society
And the newspaper columnists all would
    love to know
I'm in love with the honorable Mister So
    and So.

He goes out with the fashionable Lady So
   and So.
While they dine and they dance in a swell
   room,
I must wait in a stuffy hotel room
For the moment so rare that's convenient
   for him to spare.
He gets terribly annoyed if he doesn't find
   me there.
Why must I be living in a back street
Just so he can hide me?
I long to shout it from the housetops
Instead of keeping it all inside me.
There are so many fascinating places I
   could go,
Invitations galore I get nightly,
"Awf'lly sorry!" I tell them politely,
I'm in love with the honorable Mister So
   and So.

IT'S LOVE AGAIN

VERSE

I was the type who would laugh at
   romance,
Called it a lot of Chop Suey,
I was finished with that sort of hooey.
But we never learn, do we?
My point of view is completely reversed,
I find that I'm just as "scroo-ey."

REFRAIN

It's love again,
It's love again,
I'll shout it from the housetops up above
   again,
That state of sweet inanity
That borders on insanity
Is love again.
I feel the urge again
To merge again

And melodies of love within me surge
   again.
So if I choose to rest my chin
With passion on a violin,
It's love again.
Love is the thing that makes a bull and
   heifer
Feel just like an airy zephyr breeze.
Love is an effervescent drink
That makes a Cockney coster think he's
   Viennese.
It feels like Spring again,
I'll sing again
And be just like a vine that has to cling
   again.
So if I wax poetic,
Be a little sympathetic,
For it's love again.

MY OLD FLAME

VERSE

The music seemed to be so reminiscent;
I knew I'd heard it somewhere before.
I racked my recollections as I listened–
When suddenly I remembered once more.

REFRAIN

My old flame,
I can't even think of his name,
But it's funny now and then,
How my thoughts go flashing back again
To my old flame.
My old flame,
My new lovers all seem so tame.
For I haven't met a gent
So magnificent or elegant
As my old flame.
I've met so many who had fascinatin' ways,
A fascinatin' gaze in their eyes;
Some who took me up to the skies.

But their attempts at love
Were only imitations of
My old flame.
I can't even think of his name.
But I'll never be the same,
Until I discover what became
Of my old flame.

—*Arthur Johnston*

(Up on Top of a Rainbow)
Sweepin' the Clouds Away

VERSE

Don't go 'round mopin', hopin'
Happiness will come.
That's not the way,
It doesn't pay,
If you want happiness
Just help yourself to some.
Why don't you try to
Take life the way I do?

REFRAIN

Let the whole world sigh or cry,
I'll be high
In the sky,
Up on top of a rainbow,
Sweepin' the clouds away.
I don't care what's down below,
Let it rain,
Let it snow,
I'll be up on a rainbow,
Sweepin' the clouds away.
I have learned life's lesson:
Fighters who always win
Are those who can take it right on the chin
And grin.
And so I shout to ev'ryone,

"Find your place
In the sun
Up on top of a rainbow,
Sweepin' the clouds away."

True Blue Lou
(with Leo Robin)

VERSE

Down in the pool room
Some of the gang were talkin' of gals
 they knew.
"Women are all the same," said Joe.
One dizzy bird said, "Pal, ain't you heard
The story of True Blue Lou?
Listen and get an earful, Bo."

REFRAIN

Say, she was a dame in love with a guy,
She stuck to him but didn't know why.
Ev'ryone blamed her,
Still they all named her
True Blue Lou.
He gave her nothing, she gave him all.
But when he had his back to the wall,
Who fought to save him,
Smiled and forgave him?
True Blue Lou.
He got a break and went away
To get a new start.
But, poor kid, she never got a break,
Except the one way down in her heart.
Maybe somewhere in heaven above
There's a reward for that kind of love.
Angels won't blame her,
They too will name her
True Blue Lou.

—*Richard A. Whiting*

Irving Kahal (1903–1942)

IRVING KAHAL (pronounced "Kale") was born in Houtzdale, Pennsylvania, studied at Cooper Union, and began as a singer with Gus Edwards' Minstrels, but he gave up performing when, in 1927, he began a partnership with composer Sammy Fain that lasted until Kahal's early death. Their first song together was a big hit–"Let a Smile Be Your Umbrella"–and their "By a Waterfall" provided the background for one of Busby Berkeley's most famous extravanganzas, in the Dick Powell/Ruby Keeler *Footlight Parade.* In 1944, during World War II, the evocative "I'll Be Seeing You," written six years earlier, became a number-one hit for Bing Crosby and almost as big a hit for Tommy Dorsey and Frank Sinatra, as well as becoming a signature song for the chanteuse Hildegarde. But Kahal, dead before forty, wasn't there to enjoy what may have been his greatest success.

I Can Dream, Can't I?

VERSE

As we eye the blue horizon's bend,
Earth and sky appear to meet and end,
But it's merely an illusion.
Like your heart and mine,
There is no sweet conclusion.

REFRAIN

I can see,
No matter how near you'll be,
You'll never belong to me,
But I can dream, can't I?
Can't I pretend
That I'm locked in the bend
Of your embrace?
For dreams are just like wine,
And I am drunk with mine.
I'm aware
My heart is a sad affair,
There's much disillusion there,
But I can dream, can't I?

Can't I adore you
Although we are oceans apart?
I can't make you open your heart,
But I can dream, can't I?

—*Sammy Fain*

I'll Be Seeing You

VERSE

Cathedral bells were tolling
And our hearts sang on,
Was it the spell of Paris
Or the April dawn?
Who knows if we shall meet again?
But when the morning chimes ring sweet
    again:

REFRAIN

I'll be seeing you
In all the old familiar places
That this heart of mine embraces

All day through.
In that small café,
The park across the way,
The children's carousel,
The chestnut trees, the wishing well.
I'll be seeing you
In ev'ry lovely summer's day,
In ev'rything that's light and gay,
I'll always think of you that way.
I'll find you in the morning sun,
And when the night is new
I'll be looking at the moon,
But I'll be seeing you.

—*Sammy Fain*

THE NIGHT IS YOUNG AND YOU'RE SO BEAUTIFUL

(with Billy Rose)

VERSE I

So proper and polite,
Upon this lovely night
We sit here making foolish conversation,
Instead of being bright.
Let's be ourselves tonight
And take advantage of the situation:

REFRAIN

The night is young and you're so beautiful,
Here among the shadows, beautiful lady,
Open your heart.
The scene is set, the breezes sing of it;
Can't you get into the swing of it, lady,
When do we start?
When the lady is kissable
And the ev'ning is cool,
Any dream is permissible
In the heart of a fool.
The moon is high and you're so
    glamorous,
And if I seem overamorous, lady,

What can I do?
The night is young and I'm in love with you!

VERSE 2

Instead of making love,
We stand here talking of
The merits of the Fair and Grover
    Cleveland.
Forget the Ferris wheel,
My sugar plum, let's steal
Into the painted realms of
    make-believe land.

REPEAT REFRAIN

—*Dana Suesse*

WEDDING BELLS ARE BREAKING UP THAT OLD GANG OF MINE

(with Willie Raskin)

VERSE I

What a lonely town this is for me,
Things are not just what they used to be.
I see all my pals,
Spooning with their gals,
They don't seem to have much time for me.

REFRAIN

Not a soul down on the corner,
That's a pretty certain sign
That wedding bells are breaking up
That old gang of mine.
All the boys are singing love songs,
They forgot "Sweet Adeline."
Those wedding bells are breaking up
That old gang of mine.
There goes Jack, there goes Jim,
Down to lovers' lane.
Now and then we meet again,
But they don't seem the same.
Gee, I get a lonesome feeling

When I hear the church bells chime,
Those wedding bells are breaking up
That old gang of mine.

VERSE 2

I get invitations all day through,
One by one my buddies say adieu.
Though I knew they'd go,
Still I didn't know
I would miss them all the way I do.

REPEAT REFRAIN

—Sammy Fain

WHEN I TAKE MY SUGAR TO TEA

(with Pierre Norman)

VERSE

I'm just a little "Jackie Horner"
Since I met my sugar cane.
That gang of mine has been revealin'
That they're feelin' sore.
I left the lamplight on the corner,

For the moon in lover's lane;
I'm doing things I never did before.

REFRAIN

When I take my sugar to tea,
All the boys are jealous of me,
'Cause I never take her where the
    gang goes,
When I take my sugar to tea.
I'm rowdy-dowdy, that's me,
She's a high-hat baby, that's she.
So I never take her where the
    gang goes,
When I take my sugar to tea.
Ev'ry Sunday afternoon
We forget about our cares,
Rubbing elbows at the Ritz
With those millionaires.
When I take my sugar to tea,
I'm as Ritzy as I can be,
'Cause I never take her where the
    gang goes,
When I take my sugar to tea.

—Sammy Fain

Ray Noble (1903–1978)

R AY (STANLEY RAYMOND) NOBLE spent his first three decades in England, where–the son of a doctor–he studied to become a surgeon. Switching to music, he quickly became a successful arranger and band conductor (his lead vocalist was Britain's top male singer, Al Bowlly), and by the early thirties he was also a successful songwriter ("Good Night, Sweetheart" was his first substantial hit). In 1934 he was invited to lead a band at the new Rainbow Room in New York's Rockefeller Center, and two years later he was in Hollywood, as musical director for George Burns and Gracie Allen. He also conducted and arranged for Fred Astaire, even playing the bandleader in Astaire's *A Damsel in Distress.* In the late thirties, he began a thirteen-year association with the Edgar Bergen/Charlie McCarthy show. His romantic, relaxed lyrics reflect the kind of swing music he had grown up listening to and playing, and although his output of songs was small, he remains the one important songwriter who also led a top-level band: In America, Ray Noble and His Orchestra had more than twenty-five top-ten hits between 1931 and 1949, and seven of them reached number one, the last being his famous recording of "Linda," with Buddy Clark.

GOOD NIGHT, SWEETHEART

*(with Jimmy Campbell and
Reginald Connelly)*

VERSE I

The day is over and its cares
 and woes
In peaceful sweet repose
Will fade and die.
A dreamy dreamland beckons you
 and me.
How happy life would be,
If we could dream forever!

REFRAIN

Good night, sweetheart,
Till we meet tomorrow.
Good night, sweetheart,
Sleep will banish sorrow.

Tears and parting
May make us forlorn,
But with the dawn
A new day is born.
(So I'll say) Good night, sweetheart,
Tho' I'm not beside you.
Good night, sweetheart,
Still my love will guide you.
Dreams enfold you,
In each one I'll hold you.
Good night, sweetheart, good
 night.

VERSE 2

Let others dread the thought of
 parting time,
No reason or no rhyme
In thinking so.
To us the sweetest hour is parting time,

For then we really find
Love's perfect glow revealing.

REPEAT REFRAIN

I Hadn't Anyone Till You

VERSE

I'll admit an occasional affair,
But somehow they all made me feel
That love wasn't there;
My heart was aware
The whole thing wasn't real.
I never knew what was wrong
Until the day you came along.

REFRAIN

I hadn't anyone
Till you.
I was a lonely one
Till you.
I used to lie awake and wonder
If there could be
A someone in the wide world
Just made for me.
Now I see I had to save my love
For you.
I never gave my love
Till you.
And through my lonely heart
    demanding it,
Cupid took a hand in it.
I hadn't anyone
Till you.

The Touch of Your Lips

VERSE

When troubles get me,
Cares beset me
And won't let me go,

I turn to you
For consolation.
There I find new peace of mind;
To leave behind my woe
I turn to you
As I shall always do.

REFRAIN

The touch of your lips
Upon my brow,
Your lips that are cool
And sweet.
Such tenderness
Lies in their soft caress,
My heart forgets to beat.
The touch of your hands
Upon my head,
The love in your eyes
A-shine.
And now at last
The moment divine,
The touch of your lips
On mine.

The Very Thought of You

VERSE I

I don't need your photograph
To keep by my bed;
Your picture is always in my head.
I don't need your portrait, dear,
To call you to mind,
For sleeping or waking, dear, I find:

REFRAIN

The very thought of you,
And I forget to do
The little ordinary things
That ev'ryone ought to do.
I'm living in a kind of daydream,
I'm happy as a king.
And foolish tho' it may seem,

To me that's ev'rything.
The mere idea of you,
The longing here for you,
You'll never know how slow
The moments go till I'm near to you.
I see your face in ev'ry flower,
Your eyes in stars above.
It's just the thought of you,
The very thought of you, my love.

VERSE 2
I hold you responsible,
I'll take it to law,
I never felt like this before.
I'm suing for damages,
Excuses won't do,
I'll only be satisfied with you.

REPEAT REFRAIN

Eddie DeLange (1904–1949)

H IS MOST DISTINGUISHED collaborator was Duke Ellington, but Eddie DeLange also wrote such hokey stuff as "Along the Navajo Trail" and "Who Threw the Whiskey in the Well?" His mother was a Ziegfeld Follies girl and his father was a playwright, so it was natural for DeLange to go into show business after graduating from the University of Pennsylvania. He went to Hollywood in 1932, as a stunt man, but soon returned to New York, where in the late thirties he co-led the Hudson-DeLange Orchestra, which had a few modest record hits. He collaborated successfully with Jimmy Van Heusen—"Shake Down the Stars" and the "Swing" version of Shakespeare's *A Midsummer Night's Dream;* it was called "Swingin' the Dream," and featured the beautiful "Darn That Dream." By 1944, DeLange was back in Hollywood, where he lived until his early death.

DARN THAT DREAM

VERSE

Love is a strange and powerful thing,
It can bring you down or make you sing.
Love may give you a millionaire's scheme,
But it only gave me one dream.

REFRAIN

Darn that dream
I dream each night,
You say you love me
And you hold me tight,
But when I awake
You're out of sight,
Oh, darn that dream.
Darn your lips
And darn your eyes,
They lift me high
Above the moonlit skies,
Then I tumble out
Of Paradise,
Oh, darn that dream.

Darn that one-track mind of mine,
It can't understand that you
        don't care.
Just to change the mood I'm in,
I'd welcome a nice old nightmare.
Darn that dream
And bless it too,
Without that dream,
I never would have you.
But it haunts me
And it won't come true,
Oh, darn that dream.

—*Jimmy Van Heusen*

SHAKE DOWN THE STARS

VERSE

It's an awful feeling to watch the moon and
        stars above;
It's an awful feeling when you're alone
        without your love.

I wish I had a high stepladder
So I could scatter the stars.

REFRAIN
Shake down the stars,
Pull down the clouds,
Turn off the moon,
Do it soon;
I
Can't enjoy this night without you,
Shake down the stars.
Dry up the streams,
Stop all my dreams,
Cut off the breeze,
Do it please;
I
Never thought I'd cry about you,
Shake down the stars.
I gave you my arms,
My lips, my heart,
My life, my love, my all;
But the best that I had to offer you
I found was all too small.
Crush ev'ry rose,
Hush ev'ry pray'r,

Break ev'ry vow,
Do it now;
I know I can't go on without you,
Shake down the stars.

—*Jimmy Van Heusen*

SOLITUDE

(with Irving Mills)

In my solitude, you'll haunt me
With reveries of days gone by.
In my solitude, you'll taunt me
With memories that never die.
I sit in my chair,
Filled with despair,
No one could be so sad.
With gloom everywhere
I sit and I stare,
I know that I'll soon go mad.
In my solitude, I'm praying,
Dear Lord above, send back my love.

—*Duke Ellington*

Mack Gordon (1904–1959)

ONE OF THE BEST of the Hollywood pros, Mack Gordon had two extended partnerships—with the more formulaic Harry Revel ("Did You Ever See a Dream Walking?") and the master Harry Warren. Having been brought to New York as a young child from Warsaw, Poland, he got his start as a roly-poly comic singer in minstrel shows and vaudeville, but by 1929 he was writing for the movies, and the following year had his first important song, "Time on My Hands," with co-lyricist Harold Adamson. The partnership with Warren produced one of the greatest hits of the forties, "Chattanooga Choo-Choo," as well as a series of successful ballads (their "You'll Never Know" was an Oscar winner). Together, they collaborated on a series of exotic 20th Century Fox musicals featuring Alice Faye, Sonia Henie, Betty Grable, Carmen Miranda: they went "Down Argentine Way" and on a "Weekend in Havana," they enjoyed "That Night in Rio," a "Sun Valley Serenade," and "Springtime in the Rockies." Gordon's last major hit was "Mam'selle," from the movie *The Razor's Edge*, which in 1947 went to number one for both Art Lund and Frank Sinatra and to number three for Dick Haymes.

CHATTANOOGA CHOO-CHOO

Pardon me, boy,
Is that the Chattanooga choo-choo?
Track twenty-nine.
Boy, you can gimme a shine.
I can afford
To board a Chattanooga choo-choo,
I've got my fare
And just a trifle to spare.
You leave the Pennsylvania station 'bout a
    quarter to four,
Read a magazine and then you're in
    Baltimore.
Dinner in the diner,
Nothing could be finer
Than to have your ham'n' eggs in Carolina.
When you hear the whistle blowin' eight to
    the bar,

Then you know that Tennessee is not
    very far.
Shovel all the coal in,
Gotta keep it rollin'.
Woo, woo, Chattanooga, there you are.
There's gonna be
A certain party at the station,
Satin and lace,
I used to call funny face.
She's gonna cry
Until I tell her that I'll never roam,
So Chattanooga choo-choo,
Won't you choo-choo me home.
Chattanooga choo-choo,
Won't you choo-choo me home.

—Harry Warren

HEAD OVER HEELS IN LOVE

VERSE

Oh,
What has happened to me?
I'm the happiest one,
I'm a son of a gun,
And I'm ridin' on high.
Oh,
What has happened to me?
I'm the silliest goose,
I'm a happy papoose,
And I'll tell you just why,
Yes, I'll tell you just why.
I, I, I, I, I, I.

REFRAIN

I sing when I'm talkin',
I dance when I'm walkin',
And oh! how lovely it feels
Just to be, to be, to be,
Head over heels in love.
Can't sleep a wink
And I can't even think,
And I miss about half of my meals.
'Cause I fell, I fell, I fell,
Head over heels in love.
Ev'ry night I'm the mooniest one,
The Juneiest one,
The looniest one;
Love made me the crooniest one,
Spring has sprung, oh,
Tra-la-la.
My heart is a-flutter,
I stammer and stutter,
I sus-sus-suppose it reveals
That I am, I am, I am
High in the heavens above,
Head over heels in love.

—*Harry Revel*

I, YI, YI, YI, YI
(I LIKE YOU VERY MUCH)

VERSE

There's a girl in Rio de Janeiro
Who sings in a café
With a smile that's so entrancing,
So sweet, so cute, so gay.
When you go to Rio de Janeiro,
Say, you'll enjoy your stay,
When she sings an American love song
In a South American way:

REFRAIN

I, yi, yi, yi, yi, I like you very much,
I, yi, yi, yi, yi, I think you're grand.
Why, why, why is it that when I feel your
    touch,
My heart starts to beat, to beat
    the band?
I, yi, yi, yi, yi, like you to hold me tight,
You are too, too, too, too, too divine.
If you want to be in someone's arms
    tonight,
Just be sure the arms you're in
    are mine.
Oh, I like your lips,
And I like your eyes.
Would you like my hips
To hipsnotize you?
Si, si, si, si, si, si, see the moon above,
Way, way, way, way, way up in the blue,
Si, si, si, señor, I think I fall in love,
And when I fall, I think I fall for you.

I, yi, yi, yi,
Si, si, si, si,
I, yi, yi, yi can see, see, see
That you're for me.

—*Harry Warren*

I'VE GOT A GAL IN KALAMAZOO

A B C D E F G H
I got a gal
In Kalamazoo.
Don't wanna boast,
But I know she's the toast
Of Kalamazoo zoo zoo, zoo zoo zoo.
Years have gone by,
My, my, how she grew.
I liked her looks
When I carried her books
In Kalamazoo zoo zoo zoo zoo.
I'm gonna send a wire,
Hoppin' on a flyer,
Leavin' today.
Am I dreamin'
I can hear her screamin',
"Hiya, Mister Jackson,"
Ev'rything's O K
A L A M A Z
O oh, what a gal,
A real pipperoo.
I'll make my bid
For that freckle-faced kid
I'm hurrying to.
I'm goin' to Michigan to
See the sweetest gal
In Kalamazoo.
Zoo zoo zoo zoo,
Zoo!
Kalamazoo!

—*Harry Warren*

LOVE THY NEIGHBOR

VERSE
Never treat others with scorn,
We're only here 'cause we're born.
Although you're "way up"
You may not "stay up."
Stop tooting your horn.
Why boast of the wealth you possess
High on the hill of success?
On friendship you never should
    frown,
You'll need the same friends
On the weary way down!

REFRAIN
So love thy neighbor,
Walk up and say "How be ya!
Gee! but I'm glad to see ya.
Pal, How's tricks? What's new?"
Love thy neighbor,
Offer to share his burden,
Tell him to say the word 'n'
You will see him through,
Especially
If there should be
A beautiful girl next door.
Say to that girl next door,
"Don't think I'm bold,
But my mother told me
To love thy neighbor,"
And you will find your labor
A great deal easier,
Life'll be breezier,
If you love thy neighbor.

—*Harry Revel*

MAM'SELLE

VERSE
It was Montmartre,
It was midnight
Come to think of it,
It was spring.
There was music,
I was list'ning.
Then in the room somewhere

Someone began to sing
This serenade made for remembering:

REFRAIN

A small café, Mam'selle,
Our rendezvous, Mam'selle.
The violins were warm and sweet.
And so were you, Mam'selle.
And as the night danced by
A kiss became a sigh.
Your lovely eyes seemed to sparkle just
    like wine does,
No heart ever yearned the way that
    mine does
For you.
And yet I know too well
Someday you'll say good-bye.
Then violins will cry,
And so will I, Mam'selle.

—Edmund Goulding

MEET THE BEAT OF MY HEART

VERSE

There he goes.
Have you ever seen such perfection?
There he goes,
My one and my only selection.
He can make most any dream come true.
Let me introduce him to you.

REFRAIN

Meet the beat of my heart,
Meet the reason I beam so.
Why I'm happy and seem so
Delighted, excited, and got such a glow on.
Meet the beat of my heart,
Meet the time and the weather,
The tick that holds me together.
Without him beside me I never could
    go on.

Why do birdies sing all the day? (tweet
    tweet tweet?)
What started spring on its way? (tra la la)
Oh! Oh! If you want to know the
    inspiration,
Meet the beat of my heart,
Meet the song I'm rehearsin'.
You're gonna meet heaven in person
When you meet
The beat of my heart.

—Harry Revel

SERENADE IN BLUE

When I hear that serenade in blue,
I'm somewhere in another world alone
    with you,
Sharing all the joys we used to know,
Many moons ago.
Once again your face comes back to me,
Just like the theme of some forgotten
    melody
In the album of my memory,
Serenade in blue.
It seems like only yesterday,
A small café, a crowded floor,
And as we dance the night away,
I hear you say, "Forever more";
And then the song became a sigh,
Forever more became good-bye,
But you remained in my heart.
So tell me, darling, is there still a spark,
Or only lonely ashes of the flame
    we knew?
Should I go on whistling in the dark?
Serenade in blue.

—Harry Warren

There Will Never Be Another You

VERSE

This is our last dance together,
Tonight soon will be long ago.
And in our moment of parting,
This is all
I want you to know:

REFRAIN

There will be many other nights like this,
And I'll be standing here with
    someone new.
There will be other songs to sing,
Another Fall, another Spring,
But there will never be another you.
There will be other lips that I may kiss,
But they won't thrill me like yours used
    to do.
Yes, I may dream a million dreams,
But how can they come true,
If there will never ever be another you?

—Harry Warren

There's a Lull in My Life

VERSE

The stars are still on high,
But they don't twinkle anymore.
Why does it seem
They've lost their gleam?
Somehow the lovely flowers have no
    fragrance anymore.
Where is their bloom,
Their sweet perfume?
Darling, that just shows what your good-
    bye can do.
Until you return there's nothing I
    can do.

REFRAIN

Oh,
There's a lull in my life.
It's just a void and empty space
When you are not in my embrace.
Oh,
There's a lull in my life.
The moment that you go away,
There is no night, there is no day.
The clock stops ticking,
The world stops turning,
Ev'rything stops but that flame in my
    heart that keeps burning,
Burning.
Oh, oh, oh,
There's a lull in my life.
No matter how I may pretend,
I know that you alone can end
The ache in my heart,
The call of my arms,
The lull in my life.

—Harry Revel

You Hit the Spot

VERSE

You're as thrilling as a college cheer,
As sympathetic as a baby's tear,
You're as smooth as a kitten's ear,
I never would trade you for all the money
    in the mint.
It feels like love,
It looks like love,
Or can't you take a hint?

REFRAIN

You hit the spot,
Like a balmy breeze on a night in May.
You hit the spot,
Like a cool mint julep on a summ'ry day.
You hit a new high in my estimation.

I had to fall
'Cause you've got so much on the ball.
Oh! You hit the spot,
Like the first embrace when the knot
    is tied.
You hit the spot,
Like a pipe and slippers by a fireside.
Matter of factly,
Don't know exactly
What it is that you've got.
But ooh-ooh-ooh,
You ooh-ooh hit the spot.

—Harry Revel

You Make Me Feel So Young

VERSE
Do I seem as cheerful
As a schoolboy playing hooky?
Do I seem to gurgle
Like a baby with a cookie?
If I do,
The cause of it all is you.

REFRAIN
You make me feel so young,
You make me feel so spring has
    sprung,
And ev'ry time I see you grin,
I'm such a happy in-dividual.
The moment that you speak,
I wanna go play hide-and-seek,
I wanna go and bounce the moon,
Just like a toy balloon.
You and I
Are just like a couple of tots
Running across a meadow,
Picking up lots of forget-me-nots.
You make me feel so young,
You make me feel there are songs to
    be sung,
Bells to be rung,
And a wonderful fling to be flung.
And even when I'm old and gray,
I'm gonna feel the way I do today,
'Cause you make me feel so
    young.

—Josef Myrow

Allan Roberts (1905–1966)
and Doris Fisher (1915–   )

DORIS FISHER WAS the daughter of composer Fred Fisher and the sister of Marvin and Dan Fisher, both songwriters, too; she went to Juilliard and sang with Eddy Duchin and on her own CBS show. Allan Roberts, from Brooklyn, wrote for burlesque shows and nightclubs, and worked for Mike Todd in the late thirties. He worked with several other lyricists, but his main collaboration was with Fisher. Together, they had a number of successful songs and wrote the songs for several movies for Columbia, chief among them two Rita Hayworth vehicles: *Down to Earth* and the spectacular *Gilda,* in which Hayworth lip-synched and vamped the famous "Put the Blame on Mame," but didn't (because she couldn't) sing it.

PUT THE BLAME ON MAME

VERSE I

When Missus O'Leary's cow kicked the
    lantern
In Chicago town,
They say that started the fire
That burned Chicago down.
That's the story that went around,
But here's the real lowdown:

REFRAIN I

Put the blame on Mame, boys,
Put the blame on Mame.
Mame kissed a buyer from out of town,
That kiss burned Chicago down.
So you can put the blame on
    Mame, boys,
Put the blame on Mame.

VERSE 2

When they had the earthquake in San
    Francisco,
Back in nineteen-six,
They said that ol' mother nature
Was up to her ol' tricks.
That's the story that went around,
But here's the real lowdown:

REFRAIN 2

Put the blame on Mame, boys,
Put the blame on Mame.
One night she started to shim and
    shake,
That brought on the Frisco quake.
So you can put the blame on
    Mame, boys,
Put the blame on Mame.

VERSE 3

When they had the gold rush, folks started
    running to Cal-i-for-ni-ay,
They all had dreams of making a million
    bucks a day.
That's the story that went around,
But here's the real lowdown:

REFRAIN 3

Put the blame on Mame, boys,
Put the blame on Mame.
She caused the gold rush, it's my belief,
Diggin' gold from some guy's teeth.
So you can put the blame on
    Mame, boys,
Put the blame on Mame.

VERSE 4

Remember the blizzard back in
    Manhattan, in eighteen-eighty-six?
They say the traffic was tied up and folks
    were in a fix.
That's the story that went around,
But here's the real lowdown:

REFRAIN 4

Put the blame on Mame, boys,
Put the blame on Mame.
Mame gave a chump such an ice-cold no,
For seven days they shoveled snow.
So you can put the blame on
    Mame, boys,
Put the blame on Mame.

VERSE 5

There was once a shootin' up in the
    Klondike when they got Dan Magrew
Folks were puttin' the blame on the lady
    known as "Lou."
That's the story that went around,
But here's the real lowdown:

REFRAIN 5

Put the blame on Mame, boys,
Put the blame on Mame.
Mame did a dance and she dropped
    her fan,
That's the thing that murdered Dan.
So you can put the blame on Mame, boys,
Put the blame on Mame.

THAT OLD DEVIL CALLED LOVE

It's that old devil called love again,
Gets behind me, keeps giving me that
    shove again,
Putting rain in my eyes, tears in my dreams,
And rocks in my head.
It's that sly son-of-a-gun again,
He keeps telling me that I'm the lucky one
    again,
But I still have that rain, still have those
    tears,
And those rocks in my head.
Suppose I didn't stay–
Ran away, wouldn't play–
That devil, what a potion he would brew.
He'd follow me around, fill me up, tear
    me down,
Till I'd be so bewildered, I wouldn't know
    what to do.
Might as well give up the fight again,
I know darn well he'll convince me that
    he's right again.
When he sings that siren song, I just gotta
    tag along
With that old devil called love.

TIRED

Tired of the life I lead,
Tired of the blues I breathe,
Tired counting things I need,
Gonna cut out wine, and that's the truth,
Get a brand-new guy while I got my youth.
Tired of the clothes I wear,
Tired of the patches bare,
Tired of the crows I scare,
Gonna truck downtown and spend
    my moo,
Get some short-vamped shoes and a new
    guy, too.

A-scrubbin' and a-cleanin' sure leaves my
    glamour with a scar,
A-mendin' and a-moppin',
A-starchin' and a-shoppin'
Don't make me look like no
    Hedy Lamarr.

Tired 'cause the tears I shed,
Tired of living in the red,
Tired of the same old bed.
Gonna lead the life of Cindy Lou,
Gonna do the things I know she'd do.
'Cause I'm tired, mighty tired, of you.

Dorothy Fields (1905–1974)

H ER FATHER WAS half of the famous vaudeville team of Weber and Fields; her brother Joseph was a producer, and another brother, Herbert, was a playwright and her frequent collaborator. But Dorothy, who wasn't supposed to go into show business, turned out to be the most famous Fields of them all. (When her father told her that "ladies don't write lyrics," she countered, "I'm not a lady, I'm your daughter," and later went on to say that she'd write lyrics for the Westchester Kennel Club if invited.) Indisputably America's most brilliant and successful woman lyricist, Dorothy Fields got her start with composer Jimmy McHugh in the unlikely milieu of Harlem's Cotton Club. Soon they were working on *Blackbirds of 1928* ("I Can't Give You Anything but Love"), and went on to produce such masterpieces as "On the Sunny Side of the Street" and "I'm in the Mood for Love," although there have been persistent rumors, fueled by Andy Razaf and Fats Waller, that McHugh bought one or more of these songs from them. By the mid-thirties, Dorothy Fields had made it clear that she didn't need help from anybody: Her partnership with Jerome Kern produced "Lovely to Look At" in *Roberta* and then the entire score for *Swing Time*–"A Fine Romance," "Pick Yourself Up," "Bojangles of Harlem." She and Kern were supposed to write *Annie Get Your Gun,* and when he died suddenly and Irving Berlin took over, she and her brother Herbert wrote the book. She had fruitful collaborations with Sigmund Romberg *(Up in Central Park);* Arthur Schwartz *(Stars in Your Eyes, By the Beautiful Sea, A Tree Grows in Brooklyn);* and Cy Coleman *(Sweet Charity, Seesaw),* as well as writing the libretto, with her brother, for three Cole Porter musicals. She wrote for Ethel Merman, Astaire and Rogers, Shirley Booth, Gwen Verdon, and Bert Lahr. And after a career that spanned forty-five years of hit shows and songs, she ended up on the face of an American postage stamp.

BLUE AGAIN

VERSE

I have learned that love is not a picnic;
Love can do an awful lot of stunts.
Love is like the colic or the measles:
Almost ev'rybody gets it once.
First we fight and argue for an hour,
Then we kiss and sail the sky above;

Just at present life is kinda sour!
What is this thing called love?

REFRAIN

'Cause I'm blue again,
Blue again,
And you know darn well that it's you again,
'Cause you said last night we were through
    again,

And now I'm blue again.
I'm alone again,
'Lone again,
And I'm out around on my own again,
'Cause my mockingbird has flown again,
And I'm alone again.
Though I say I hate you,
I love you more ev'ry day.
Though I aggravate you,
Honest, I'm dyin' to say,
That it's new again!
You again!
And we'll meet today at two again.
But tonight we'll fight and be through
    again,
And I'll be blue again.

—Jimmy McHugh

BOJANGLES OF HARLEM

VERSE
Ask anyone
Up Harlem way
Who that guy Bojangles is.
They may not know
Who's President,
But ask 'em who Bojangles is.
He's in the most entrancin' bus'ness,
It's what they call the "Dancin' bus'ness."
When there's a beat
Upon the street,
Brother, you go
And bet all your dough!
Sister, you know!
That ain't no one but Bo!

REFRAIN
Oh! Bojangles of Harlem,
You dance such hot stuff!
Young folks love you in Harlem,
They say you've got stuff!

Though guys rumba out of pool rooms,
And kids start "truckin' " out of school
    rooms.
Oh! Bojangles of Harlem!
The whole town's at your heels!
Leaving their flats,
Missing their meals!
Running like rats,
Going astray,
Throw those long legs
Away!

—Jerome Kern

DON'T BLAME ME

VERSE I
Ever since the lucky night I found you
I've hung around you, just like a fool.
Falling head and heels in love
Like a kid out of school.
My poor heart is in an awful state now,
But it's too late now to call a halt.
So if I become a nuisance
It's all your fault!

REFRAIN
Don't blame me
For falling in love with you.
I'm under your spell,
But how can I help it!
Don't blame me!
Can't you see
When you do the things you do!
If I can't conceal
The thrill that I'm feeling,
Don't blame me.
I can't help it if that doggoned moon
    above
Makes me need
Someone like you to love!
Blame your kiss,

As sweet as a kiss can be.
And blame all your charms
That melt in my arms,
But don't blame me.

VERSE 2

I like ev'ry single thing about you.
Without a doubt you are like a dream.
In my mind I find a picture
Of us as a team.
Ever since the hour of our meeting
I've been repeating a silly phrase,
Hoping that you'll understand me
One of these days.

REPEAT REFRAIN

—Jimmy McHugh

A Fine Romance

A fine romance, with no kisses!
A fine romance, my friend, this is!
We should be like a couple of hot tomatoes,
But you're as cold as yesterday's mashed
    potatoes.
A fine romance! You won't nestle!
A fine romance! You won't wrestle!
I might as well play bridge with my old
    maid aunts!
I haven't got a chance.
This is a fine romance.
A fine romance, my good fellow!
You take romance! I'll take Jell-O!
You're calmer than the seals in the Arctic
    Ocean,
At least they flap their fins to express
    emotion.
A fine romance! With no quarrels!
With no insults, and all morals!
I've never mussed the crease in your blue
    serge pants,

I never get the chance.
This is a fine romance.
A fine romance, with no kisses!
A fine romance, my friend, this is!
We two should be like clams in a dish of
    chowder;
But we just "fizz" like parts of a Seidlitz
    powder.
A fine romance, with no clinches!
A fine romance, with no pinches!
You're just as hard to land as the "Ile de
    France,"
I haven't got a chance,
This is a fine romance!
A fine romance, my dear Duchess!
Two old fogies who need crutches!
True love should have the thrills that a
    healthy crime has!
We don't have half the thrills that the
    "March of Time" has!
A fine romance, my good woman!
My strong "aged-in-the-wood" woman!
You never give the orchids I send a
    glance!
No! You like cactus plants.
This is a fine romance!

—Jerome Kern

Have Feet, Will Dance

Have feet, will dance,
Have song, will sing,
Have lips, will kiss,
And have arms, will cling.
Have dress, will press,
Have shoes, will shine,
Have date with a gate at nine.
I met this doll-face
He said "Hi" and I flipped,
If he likes dancing,
Boy, am I equipped.

Have lights, will dim,
Have disk, will spin,
Have bet will get him,
Have hunch will win.
All I need is a chance,
Have song, will sing,
Have arms, will cling,
Have feet, will dance.

—Burton Lane

I Can't Give You Anything but Love

VERSE I

Gee, but it's tough to be broke, kid,
It's not a joke, kid, it's a curse.
My luck is changing, it's gotten
From simply rotten to something worse.
Who knows, someday I will win, too.
I'll begin to reach my prime;
Now though I see what our end is,
All I can spend is just my time.

REFRAIN

I can't give you anything but love,
Baby,
That's the only thing I've plenty of,
Baby.
Dream a while, scheme a while,
We're sure to find
Happiness, and I guess
All those things you've always pined for,
Gee, I'd like to see you looking swell,
Baby.
Diamond bracelets Woolworth
    doesn't sell,
Baby.
Till that lucky day, you know
    darned well,
Baby,
I can't give you anything but love.

VERSE 2

Rome wasn't built in a day, kid,
You have to pay, kid,
For what you get.
But I am willing to wait, dear,
Your little mate, dear, will not forget.
You have a lifetime before you,
I'll adore you, come what may;
Please don't be blue for the present,
When it's so pleasant
To hear you say:

REPEAT REFRAIN

—Jimmy McHugh

I Won't Dance

(with Jimmy McHugh, based on an earlier lyric by Oscar Hammerstein II and Otto Harbach)

VERSE

Think of what you're losing
By constantly refusing
To dance with me.
You'd be the idol of France with me!
And yet you stand there and shake your
    foolish head dramatic'lly.
While I wait here so ecstatic'lly
You just look and say emphatic'lly,
Not this season!
There's a reason!

REFRAIN

HE: I won't dance!
    Don't ask me.
    I won't dance!
    Don't ask me.
    I won't dance,
    Madame, with you.
    My heart won't let my feet do things
        they should do!

You know what?
You're lovely.

SHE: And so what? I'm lovely!

HE: But oh! what
You do to me!
I'm like an ocean wave that's bumped
on the shore;
I feel so absolutely stumped on the
floor!

SHE: When you dance you're charming
and you're gentle!
'Spec'lly when you do the
"Continental."

HE: But this feeling isn't purely mental;
For heaven rest us,
I'm not asbestos.
And that's why
I won't dance!
Why should I?
I won't dance!
How could I?
I won't dance!
Merci beaucoup!
I know that music leads the way to
romance.
So if I hold you in my arms,
I won't dance!

—Jerome Kern

I'm in the Mood for Love

VERSE

Lovely interlude,
Most romantic mood,
And your attitude is right, dear.
Sweetheart!
You have me under a spell!
Now my dream is real!
That is why I feel
Such a strong appeal tonight!
Somehow

All my reason takes flight,
Dear.

REFRAIN

I'm in the mood for love
Simply because you're near me.
Funny, but when you're near me,
I'm in the mood for love.
Heaven is in your eyes,
Bright as the stars we're under.
Oh! Is it any wonder
I'm in the mood for love?
Why stop to think of whether
This little dream might fade?
We've put our hearts together,
Now we are one,
I'm not afraid!
If there's a cloud above,
If it should rain we'll let it.
But for tonight, forget it!
I'm in the mood for love.

—Jimmy McHugh

I'm Livin' in a Great Big Way

VERSE

I saw before me
A stormy condition,
But I refused to be blue.
Now I'm relyin'
On my intuition;
Here's my happy point of view:

REFRAIN

Got a snap in my fingers,
Got a rhythm in my walk.
As the elephants say,
I'm livin' in a great big way.
Got a hand full of nothin',
And I watch it like a hawk;
Well, I'm doin' O.K.,

I'm livin' in a great big way.
I'm the salt in the ocean,
I'm the sun in the sky,
I'm a Franklin D. Roosevelt.
I'm a million dollars, long as I
Got a snap in my fingers,
Got a rhythm in my walk,
Got the devil to pay,
I'm livin' in a great big way.

—*Jimmy McHugh*

IT'S ALL YOURS

VERSE
Don't say the daily struggle will get
    you down,
Don't say you're tired fighting it out.
Enter reason, exit doubt.
There's no blessing,
You must do without.

REFRAIN
It's all yours,
Ev'rything you see,
It's all yours,
Absolutely free.
Just leave your cloister,
Baby, stop mopin',
The world's your oyster
Ready to open.
It's all yours,
If it's health you want
To call yours,
All the wealth you want.
The sun, the moon,
The land and the sea, too,
Me, too,
It's all of it yours,
It's all of it yours.

—*Arthur Schwartz*

LOVELY TO LOOK AT

(with Jimmy McHugh)

VERSE 1
Clothes must play a part
To light an eye, to win a heart;
They say a gown can almost speak,
If it is chic.
Should you select the right effect, you
    cannot miss.
You may be sure,
He will tell you this:

REFRAIN
Lovely to look at,
Delightful to know,
And heaven to kiss.
A combination like this
Is quite my most impossible scheme
    come true,
Imagine finding a dream like you!
You're lovely to look at,
It's thrilling to hold you terribly tight.
For we're together, the moon is new,
And oh, it's lovely to look at you
Tonight!

VERSE 2
What appeals to me
Is just your charm and dignity;
Not what you wear, but just an air,
Of great repose.
You are quite perfect from your head down
    to your toes.
Both night and day,
I am moved to say:

REPEAT REFRAIN

—*Jerome Kern*

Make the Man Love Me

VERSE

You kissed me once by mistake,
Thought I was somebody else.
I felt that kiss and I envied that
    somebody else.
I wanted you for myself.
I guess I was shameless and bold.
But I made a plan in my heart,
I've never breathed,
I've never told.

REFRAIN

I must try to make the man love me,
Make the man love me now.
By and by, I'll make the man happy,
I know how.
He must see how badly I want him,
Want him just as he is.
May I say that should the man ask me,
I'll be his.
Can I tell the man just how dearly
Blessed we would be?
All the beauty I see so clearly,
Oh, why can't he?
So, I pray to heaven above me,
Pray until day grows dim,
For a way to make the man love me
As I love him.

—*Arthur Schwartz*

Never Gonna Dance

Though I'm left without a penny,
The wolf was discreet;
He left me my feet,
And so I put them down on anything
But the La Belle,
La perfectly swell romance.

Never gonna dance,
Never gonna dance,
Only gonna love,
Never gonna dance.
Have I a heart that acts like a heart,
Or is it a crazy drum,
Beating the weird tattoos
Of the St. Louis blues?
Have I two eyes to see your two eyes,
Or see myself on my toes,
Dancing to radios
For Major Edward Bowes?
I'll put my shoes on beautiful trees,
I'll give my rhythm back to the breeze,
My dinner clothes may dine where they
    please,
For all I really want is you.
And to Groucho Marx I give my cravat,
To Harpo goes my shiny silk hat,
To heaven I give a vow to adore you.
I'm starting now to be much more
    positive that
Though I'm left without a penny,
The wolf was not smart;
He left me my heart.
And so I'll never go for anything
But the La Belle,
La perfectly swell romance,
Never gonna dance,
Never gonna dance,
Only gonna love you,
Never gonna dance.

—*Jerome Kern*

On the Sunny Side of the Street

VERSE

Walked with no one,
And talked with no one,
And I had nothing but shadows.

Then one morning you passed,
And I brightened at last.
Now I greet the day,
And complete the day,
With the sun in my heart.
All my worry blew away
When you taught me how to say:

Grab your coat, and get your hat,
Leave your worry on the doorstep.
Just direct your feet
To the sunny side of the street.
Can't you hear a pitter pat?
And that happy tune is your step.
Life can be so sweet,
On the sunny side of the street.
I used to walk in the shade
With those blues on parade,
But I'm not afraid,
This rover crossed over.
If I never have a cent,
I'll be rich as Rockefeller.
Gold dust at my feet,
On the sunny side of the street.

—Jimmy McHugh

PICK YOURSELF UP

Please teacher,
Teach me something.
Nice teacher,
Teach me something.
I'm as awkward as a camel,
That's not the worst,
My two feet
Haven't met yet,
But I'll be
Teacher's pet yet,
'Cause I'm gonna learn to dance or burst.

Nothing's impossible I have found,
For when my chin is on the ground,
I pick myself up,
Dust myself off,
Start all over again.
Don't lose your confidence if you slip,
Be grateful for a pleasant trip,
And pick yourself up,
Dust yourself off,
Start all over again.
Work like a soul inspired,
Till the battle of the day is won.
You may be sick and tired,
But you'll be a man, my son!
Will you remember the famous men,
Who had to fall to rise again?
So take a deep breath,
Pick yourself up,
Dust yourself off,
Start all over again.

I'll get some self-assurance
If your endurance is great.
I'll learn by easy stages
If you're courageous and wait.
To feel the strength I want to,
I must hang on to your hand.
Maybe by the time I'm fifty
I'll get up and do a nifty.

—Jerome Kern

REMIND ME

Turn off that charm,
I'm through with love for a while.
I'm through, and yet

You have a fabulous smile.
So if I forget,

REFRAIN
Remind me
Not to find you so attractive,
Remind me
That the world is full of men.
When I start to miss you,
To touch your hand,
To kiss you,
Remind me
To count to ten!
I had a feeling when I met you
You'd drive me crazy, if I'd let you.
But all my efforts to forget you
Remind me, I'm in love again.
I get my heart well in hand,
And I'm certain
That I can take you or leave you alone,
Then you "Begin that Beguine"
    again,
And boom! I give in again.
I have a will made of steel, my friend,
But when it seems about to bend,
Remind me
Not to mention that I love you.
Remind me
To be sorry that we met.
Although I adore you,
Remind me to ignore you,
You're one thing I will regret!
So when your charm begins to
    blind me,
I'll simply tie my hands behind me,
Don't let me kiss you, please
    remind me,
Unless, my darling, you forget.

—Jerome Kern

THERE MUST BE SOMETHIN' BETTER THAN LOVE

VERSE
Give it up!
Give it up!
Too much man,
Too much grief,
No more man,
No more grief,
To be brief,
I got a firm belief.

REFRAIN 1
There must be somethin' better than love,
There must be somethin' better in view,
But if there's somethin' better than love,
Who wants it? Do you?
There jes' must be some practical plan
That don't require de service of man.
Suppose they find that practical plan–
Who wants it? Neither do I!
'A course there's de solitary life,
Sittin' with yo' knittin' an' yo' cat.
O ho! Yo' knittin' an' yo' cat!
You know what you can do with that!
What makes yo' two eyes wetter than love?
What makes you feel "upsetter"
    than love?
But if there's somethin' better than love,
Who's got it?
Who wants it?
Do you?

REFRAIN 2
There must be somethin' better than love,
There must be somethin' better to do,
But if there's somethin' better to do,
Who'd do it? Would you?
There must be some respectable vice,
A small sin at a moderate price.
Suppose there's one respectable vice–

Who'd practice it? Don't look at me!
'A course there's de solitary man
Sleepin' in his solitary bed.
O ho! His solitary bed!
You know that gentleman is dead!
There's nothin' more "goat-getter"
    than love,
There's nothin' "triple-threater"
    than love,
But if there's somethin' better than love
An' you like it! Ho! Ho!
You can keep it! Ho! Ho!
I don't want it! Ho! Ho!
I can't use it! No! No!
There's nothin' better than love.

—Morton Gould

THE WAY YOU LOOK TONIGHT

Some day when I'm awf'ly low,
When the world is cold,
I will feel a glow just thinking of you,
And the way you look tonight.
Oh, but you're lovely
With your smile so warm,
And your cheek so soft,
There is nothing for me but to love you,
Just the way you look tonight.
With each word your tenderness grows,
Tearing my fear apart.
And that laugh that wrinkles your nose
Touches my foolish heart.
Lovely, never, never change,
Keep that breathless charm,
Won't you please arrange it,
'Cause I love you,
Just the way you look tonight,
Mm mm mm mm
Just the way you look tonight.

—Jerome Kern

YOU COULDN'T BE CUTER

VERSE
Your poise!
Your pose!
That cute fantastic nose!
You're mighty like a knockout,
You're mighty like a rose!
I'm sold,
I'm hooked!
The well-known goose is cooked!
You got me, little fella,
I'm sunk!
I'm gone!
I'm hooked!

REFRAIN
You couldn't be cuter,
Plus that you couldn't be smarter,
Plus that intelligent face,
You have a disgraceful charm for me.
You couldn't be keener,
You look so fresh from the cleaner,
You are the little grand slam
I'll bring to my family.
My ma will show you an album
    of me
That'll bore you to tears!
And you'll attract all the relatives we
Have dodged for years and years.
And what'll they tell me?
Exactly what'll they tell me?
They'll say you couldn't be nicer,
Couldn't be sweeter,
Couldn't be better,
Couldn't be smoother,
Couldn't be cuter,
Baby, than you are!

—Jerome Kern

Herb Magidson (1906–1986)

W INNER OF the first Oscar for a song–"The Continental," from *The Gay Divorcée*–
Herb Magidson was a solid lyricist for movies and shows for more than two
decades. One of his most challenging jobs was writing words for a song to be called
"Gone with the Wind" the year after the book was published, and he succeeded so well
that it took on a life of its own, wholly apart from the country's most famous novel and
film. Born in Braddock, Pennsylvania, and trained in journalism at the University of
Pennsylvania, he was imported to New York by Sophie Tucker in 1928, and soon was in
Hollywood–something called "Doin' the Raccoon," from a Warner Bros. college
musical, was a number-five hit for the George Olsen orchestra early in 1929. In 1938
his "Music, Maestro, Please" had three hit records, of which Tommy Dorsey's got to
number one; in 1945, two different recordings of "I'll Buy That Dream" reached number two; and five years later, "Enjoy Yourself" was a hit for Guy Lombardo as well as for
Doris Day. A career that produced successful material for Sophie Tucker, Fred Astaire,
Tommy Dorsey, Deanna Durbin, Harry James, and Doris Day certainly demonstrates
an impressive professional range.

THE CONTINENTAL
(YOU KISS WHILE YOU'RE DANCING)

Beautiful music!
Dangerous rhythm!
It's something daring,
"The Continental."
A way of dancing that's really ultra new;
It's very subtle,
"The Continental,"
Because it does what you want it to do.
It has a passion,
"The Continental,"
An invitation to moonlight and romance;
It's quite the fashion,
"The Continental,"
Because you tell of your love while you
    dance.
Your lips

Whisper, so tenderly,
Her eyes
Answer your song.
Two bodies swaying
"The Continental,
And you are saying just what you're
    thinking of.
So keep on dancing
"The Continental,"
For it's the song of romance and of love.
You kiss
While you're dancing;
It's continental,
It's continental.
You sing
While you're dancing;
Your voice is gentle
And sentimental.
You'll know, before the dance is through,

That you're in love with her
And she's in love with you.
You'll find,
While you're dancing,
That there's a rhythm in your heart
    and soul;
A certain rhythm that you can't control,
And you will do "The Continental"
All the time.
Beautiful music!
Dangerous rhythm!

    —Con Conrad

GONE WITH THE WIND

VERSE

It was only yesterday,
I thought love had come to stay,
But just like a bird in flight
Love has vanished overnight.

REFRAIN

Gone with the wind,
Just like a leaf that has blown away.
Gone with the wind,
My romance has flown away.
Yesterday's kisses are still on my lips,
I had a lifetime of Heaven
At my fingertips.
But now all is gone,
Gone is the rapture that thrilled my
    heart.
Gone with the wind,
The gladness that filled my heart.
Just like a flame,
Love burned brightly, then became
An empty smoke dream that has gone,
Gone with the wind.

    —Allie Wrubel

(I'M AFRAID) THE MASQUERADE IS OVER

Your eyes don't shine like they used to
    shine,
And the thrill is gone when your lips
    meet mine.
I'm afraid the masquerade is over,
And so is love, and so is love.
Your words don't mean what they used
    to mean.
They were once inspired, now they're just
    routine.
I'm afraid the masquerade is over,
And so is love, and so is love.
I guess I'll have to play Pagliacci
And get myself a clown's disguise,
And learn to laugh like Pagliacci
With tears in my eyes.
You look the same, you're a lot the same,
But my heart says, "No, no you are not
    the same."
I'm afraid the masquerade is over,
And so is love, and so is love.

    —Allie Wrubel

MUSIC, MAESTRO, PLEASE!

VERSE

A table near the band,
A small one;
Some cigarettes, a drink,
Yes, a tall one.
And, waiter, I could use
A chaser for my blues.

REFRAIN

Tonight
I mustn't think of her,
Music, Maestro, please!

Tonight,
Tonight I must forget how much I
        need her.
So Mister Leader,
Play your lilting melodies.
Ragtime, jazz-time, swing,
Any old thing,
To help me ease the pain
That solitude can bring.
She used to like waltzes,
So please don't play a waltz.
She danced divinely
And I loved her so.
But there I go.
Tonight I mustn't think of her,
No more memories.
Swing out,
Tonight I must forget,
Music, Maestro, please!

—Allie Wrubel

T'AIN'T NO USE

VERSE
He walked out and left me flat,
He was right and that is that.
Let it rain and let it pour
Cause it don't matter no more.

REFRAIN
T'ain't no use,
T'ain't no use,

Cooked my goose,
T'aint no use.
Played it fast,
Played it loose,
Couldn't last,
T'aint no use.
Here am I,
High and dry,
My, oh my,
He didn't even say good-bye.
T'aint no use,
T'aint no use,
Cooked my goose,
T'aint no use.
T'aint no use,
T'aint no use,
No more love,
T'aint no use.
I've got pains,
Misery.
Got no brains,
Woe is me.
Why did I
Let him go?
Why, oh why,
I'm just a no good so and so.
T'aint no use,
T'aint no use,
Cooked my goose,
T'aint no use.

—Burton Lane

Harold Adamson (1906–1980)

HAROLD ADAMSON WORKED on sixty-five movies, and was nominated for five Oscars; it was a long and useful career. At least two of his songs–"Time on My Hands" (with co-lyricist Mack Gordon) and "Everything I Have Is Yours" (Joan Crawford sang it in *Dancing Lady*)–are important standards, and others, like the wartime "Comin' in on a Wing and a Prayer," were big hits in their day. (In 1940 alone he had two number-one hits: Glenn Miller's "The Woodpecker Song" and the Andrews Sisters' "Ferry Boat Serenade.") Adamson was born in Greenville, New Jersey, and went to Harvard, where he wrote Hasty Pudding shows. Decades later he contributed to several Broadway musicals, including *Banjo Eyes* for Eddie Cantor and *As the Girls Go* for Bobby Clark.

EVERYTHING I HAVE IS YOURS

VERSE

The more I'm with you, the more I can see
My love is yours alone.
You came and captured a heart that
    was free,
Now I've nothing I can call my own.

REFRAIN

Everything I have is yours,
You're part of me.
Everything I have is yours,
My destiny.
I would gladly give the sun to you
If the sun were only mine.
I would gladly give the earth to you
And the stars that shine.
Everything that I possess
I offer you.
Let my dream of happiness
Come true.
I'd be happy just to spend my life
Waiting at your beck and call.

Everything I have is yours,
My life,
My all.

—*Burton Lane*

I JUST FOUND OUT ABOUT LOVE

I just found out about love
And I like it,
I like it;
I like what love has been doing to me.
I hold you close in my arms
And I like it,
I like it;
Oh, what a wonderful future I see.
It's a one-time only,
It's a lifetime deal,
And I know it's real,
I can tell by the way that I feel.
Right now I'm livin' it up
And I like it,
I like it.

Hey, you! Give me a clue,
What's love doin' to you?
Looks like
You could be liking it, too.

—Jimmy McHugh

It's a Most Unusual Day

VERSE

I woke up singing this morning,
Got out of the right side of bed.
I woke up singing this morning
And wondering what was ahead.
I took one good look at the sun
And was I the luckiest one!

REFRAIN

It's a most unusual day,
Feel like throwing my worries away.
As an old native-born Californian
    would say,
It's a most unusual day.
There's a most unusual sky,
Not a sign of a cloud passing by,
And if I want to sing,
Throw my heart in the ring,
It's a most unusual day.
There are people
Meeting people,
There is sunshine
Ev'rywhere.
There are people
Greeting people,
And a feeling of spring in the air.
It's a most unusual time,
I keep feeling my temp'rature climb.
If my heart won't behave in the
    usual way,
Well there's only one thing to say—
It's a most unusual,

Most unusual,
Most unusual day.

—Jimmy McHugh

It's Been So Long

VERSE

I think of things we used to do
And wonder why we had to part.
I think of all the joys we knew,
And there's a longing in my
    heart. . . .

REFRAIN

'Cause it's been
So
Long
Since I held you tight
When we said good night.
It's been
So
Long,
Honey, can't you see
What you've done to me?
I've been in a kind of daze
For days and days and days,
Feelin' blue
Missin' you,
In oh, so many ways.
'Cause it was
So
Long
When we had that date,
Ev'ry night at eight.
It was
So long,
Then we said good-bye,
What a fool was I.
Let me get back in your arms where I
    belong.

'Cause it's been
Oh!
So
Long.

—*Walter Donaldson*

MAKE WITH THE FEET

VERSE
Ev'ryone is on the make for
    something.
Some make hay while some are
    marking time.
Some make mighty mountains out of
    molehills.
Some make money, some
    make love,
Some make a grand concession.
But if you want to make a good
    impression,
Just

REFRAIN
Make with the feet.
When the rhythm is broken,
Be outspoken.
Make with the feet,
Let 'em talk.
Make with the beat.
When the music is airy,
Fred Astairey,
Just put that heat
In your walk.
Your feet should play the part
Of artful dodgers.
If that's the spot you're in,
You'll win a Ginger Rogers.
Swing can be sweet,
But it shouldn't be lacy—
Page Count Basie!

Fake a break and
Make with the feet.

—*Vernon Duke*

TIME ON MY HANDS
(with Mack Gordon)

VERSE
When the day fades away into
    twilight,
The moon is my light of love.
In the night, I am quite a romancer;
I find an answer above.
To bring me consolation,
You're my inspiration,
This is my imagination.

REFRAIN
Time on my hands,
You in my arms,
Nothing but love in view;
Then if you fall,
Once and for all,
I'll see my dreams come true.
Moments to spare for
Someone you care for;
One love affair for two.
With time on my hands
And you in my arms
And love in my heart
All for you.

—*Vincent Youmans*

WHERE ARE YOU?

VERSE
Loving you was all that really
    mattered,

Don't know why you ever went away;
Gone is ev'ry joy and inspiration,
What's the use in trying to be gay?
Even though my ev'ry dream is shattered,
I keep hoping you'll come back
    some day.

REFRAIN
Where are you?
Where have you gone without me?
I thought you cared about me.
Where are you?
Where's my heart?

Where is the dream we started?
I can't believe we're parted.
Where are you?
When we said good-bye, love,
What had we to gain?
When I gave you my love,
Was it all in vain?
All life through
Must I go on pretending?
Where is my happy ending?
Where are you?

—Jimmy McHugh

Alec Wilder (1907–1980)

A LEC WILDER WAS one of the most individual, talented, and eccentric figures in mid-twentieth-century American popular music. Born in Rochester, New York, the son of a bank president, he studied at the Eastman School of Music there, and a large part of his life was spent writing classical music that was often taken as too classical for the jazz world and too jazzy for the classical world. But he also wrote many songs that became standards, though they were far from standard. Sometimes he wrote his own lyrics, sometimes he wrote *only* the lyrics, sometimes other writers—like William Engvick—wrote to his music; sometimes he wrote for specific performers: Frank Sinatra and Mabel Mercer were among his greatest admirers. At their best, his songs are brilliantly artful, at their worse they can be arty. But they're always distinctive, and many of them have lasted. Wilder is also the author (with the assistance of James T. Maher), of *American Popular Song,* generally considered the classic work on the subject. Home was the Algonquin Hotel, where he lived for more than fifty years.

DID YOU EVER CROSS OVER TO SNEDEN'S

Did you go to the school by the river?
Did you spend all your young days there?
Did you ever cross over to Sneden's
With the setting sun blessing your hair?
Did you ever cross over to Sneden's
Where the white houses cling to the hill?
Did you ever cross over to Sneden's?
Do you think that you ever will?
All the wide-branching elms then were
    saplings,
And the soft rolling land did sleep;
And the silent stream flowed in
    contentment,
And it seemed a man never could weep.
Did you ever cross over to Sneden's
Where the white houses cling to the hill?
Did you ever cross over to Sneden's?
Do you think that you ever will?

Is the past like a dream in remembrance?
Can you see now the frock you wore
On the day that you started for
    Sneden's
From the strangely still, faraway shore?
Long I waited that day by the river;
Long I waited, my heart beat fast;
Long I'd planned what I'd say when you
    landed,
And I waited till daylight, daylight had
    passed.
I am still living over at Sneden's,
And I still walk along the shore;
And I gaze at the elms across the river,
And I know that I'll see you no more.
Did you ever cross over to Sneden's
Where the white houses cling to
    the hill?
Did you ever cross over to Sneden's?
Do you think that you ever will?

I'll Be Around

I'll be around,
No matter how
You treat me now,
I'll be around
From now on.
Your latest love
Can never last,
And when it's past,
I'll be around
When he's gone.
Good-bye again,
And if you find a love like mine,
Just now and then
Drop a line
To say you're feeling fine.
And when things go wrong,
Perhaps you'll see
You're meant for me.
So, I'll be around
When he's gone.

It's So Peaceful in the Country

VERSE
The skyline of New York is a splendid sight.
I know Chicago's loop is magical at night.
The natives of Cleveland, of 'Frisco and
    Boston,
And natives of cities a stranger gets lost in,
All of them tell you their city's the best,
From deep in the South and from out in
    the West.
Perhaps it's all true,
But from my point of view:

REFRAIN
It's so peaceful in the country,
It's so simple and quiet,
You really ought to try it.

SHE: You walk about
    And talk about
    The pleasant things in life.
[or]
HE: In rain or shine
    You're feeling fine
    And life is sweet and slow.

It's so restful in the country,
It's the right kind of diet.
You really ought to try it.

SHE: You read a book
    Or try to cook
    Like any good man's wife.
[or]
HE: You lie and dream
    Beside a stream
    While daisies nod "Hello."

City living is a pretty living,
It's so full of unexpected thrills;
But there's too much stone, too much
    telephone,
There's too much of ev'rything but trees
    and hills.
It's so peaceful in the country,
It's so simple and quiet,
Some day you're bound to try it.
The only place to be,
The place for you and me,
Where it's peaceful in the country.

Trouble Is a Man

VERSE
A woman gets all the blame
For everything that happens under
    the sun,
But when it comes to being bad,
A woman's not the only one.

REFRAIN

Trouble is a man,
A man who loves me no more, no more.
Trouble is a man,
A man I'll always adore.
Nothing good to say about him,
Still, I hate the day without him.
Why should he
Happen to be
The one, my only?

Trouble is a man,
A man who's handsome and tall, so tall,
Trouble is a man
Who's for himself and that's all.
After all we planned,
He didn't mean it;
Now I understand,
I should have seen it.
Trouble is a man,
Trouble is a man I love.

Edward Heyman (1907–1981)

WHEN EDWARD HEYMAN—from a midwestern family whose money came from sausage casings—was twenty-three, he co-wrote the lyrics for the great standard "Body and Soul." With its composer, Johnny Green, he was to write several other huge hits of the early and mid-thirties ("Out of Nowhere" was a number-one hit for Bing Crosby in 1931, and "I Wanna Be Loved," written in 1932, went to number one for the Andrews Sisters eighteen years later); he was still writing hits—"When I Fall in Love"—as late as 1952. Along the way, he wrote for eight Broadway shows, ten movies, and productions at Radio City Music Hall. Heyman, born in New York and raised in Chicago, started writing college musicals at the University of Michigan; later, he was to run an English-speaking theater company in Mexico.

BLAME IT ON MY YOUTH

VERSE

You were my adored one,
Then you became the bored one,
And I was like a toy that brought you joy
    one day,
A broken toy that you preferred to
    throw away.

REFRAIN

If I expected love
When first we kissed,
Blame it on my youth.
If only just for you
I did exist,
Blame it on my youth.
I believed ev'rything
Like a child of three.
You meant more than anything,
All the world to me!
If you were on my mind
All night and day,
Blame it on my youth.

If I forgot to eat and sleep and pray,
Blame it on my youth.
If I cried a little bit
When first I learned the truth,
Don't blame it on my heart,
Blame it on my youth.

—*Oscar Levant*

BODY AND SOUL

(with Robert Sour and Frank Eyton)

VERSE

Life's dreary for me,
Days seem to be
Long as years.
I look for the sun,
But I see none
Through my tears.
Your heart must be like a stone
To leave me here all alone
When you could make my life worth living
By simply taking what I'm set on giving.

REFRAIN

My heart is sad and lonely,
For you I sigh, for you, dear, only.
Why haven't you seen it?
I'm all for you, body and soul!
I spend my days in longing
And wond'ring why it's me you're
    wronging.
I tell you I mean it,
I'm all for you, body and soul!
I can't believe it,
It's hard to conceive it
That you'd turn away romance.
Are you pretending,
It looks like the ending
Unless I could have one more chance to
    prove, dear,
My life a wreck you're making,
You know I'm yours for just the taking.
I'd gladly surrender
Myself to you, body and soul!

—Johnny Green

EASY COME, EASY GO

VERSE

Love has fooled us,
It has cooled us,
Once it ruled us,
Now we're free.
We'll be happy
In rememb'ring
That we found love easily.

REFRAIN

Easy come,
Easy go,
That's the way.
If love must have its day,
Then as it came
Let it go.

No remorse,
No regret,
We should part
Exactly as we met,
Just easy come,
Easy go.
We never dreamt of romantic dangers,
But now that it ends let's be friends
And not two strangers.
Easy come,
Easy go,
Here we are,
So darling, "Au revoir,"
It's easy come,
Easy go.

—Johnny Green

HO HUM

VERSE I

Good-bye to Winter, I'll see you next year.
Hello to Springtime, gee I'm glad
    you're here.
Listen you flivver, get yourself outside.
Come on my sweetheart, take me for
    a ride.

REFRAIN I

Ho hum,
Spring is here now.
Ho hum,
Skies are very clear now.
Ho hum,
Love is near now
For you and me.
Ho hum,
April showers.
Ho hum,
Lots of pretty flowers.
Ho hum,
Happy hours

For you and me.
All the world is sweet once again,
Heaven's at my feet once again.
Ho hum,
Lazy weather.
Ho hum,
Feeling like a feather.
Ho hum,
We're together,
And so
Ho hum.
Serenading, ocean wading,
    orange-ading.
Street musicians, great ambitions, great
    conditions,
Ho hum.

VERSE 2

Chocolate bars, milk from dairies,
Motor cars, dawn, and huckleberries,
Twinkling stars, Johns and Marys
Strolling up and down the park.
In the sky, moonlight hovers,
On the bed, soft and downy covers,
On the street lots of lovers
Finding places nice and dark.
There's one thing on which we agree:
Spring is very young, so are we.

REFRAIN 2

Ho hum,
Frogs are groaning.
Ho hum,
Mandolins are moaning.
Ho hum,
Microphoning
From me to you.
Ho hum.

—Dana Suesse

I COVER THE WATERFRONT

VERSE

Away from the city that hurts and mocks,
I'm standing alone by the desolate docks,
In the still and the chill of the night.
I see the horizon, the great unknown,
My heart has an ache; it's as heavy as
    stone.
Will the dawn coming on make it light?

REFRAIN

I cover the waterfront,
I'm watching the sea.
Will the one I love
Be coming back to me?
I cover the waterfront
In search of my love,
And I'm covered by
A starless sky above.
Here am I
Patiently waiting,
Hoping and longing.
Oh! how I yearn!
Where are you?
Are you forgetting?
Do you remember?
Will you return?
I cover the waterfront,
I'm watching the sea.
For the one I love
Must soon come back to me.

—Johnny Green

I WANNA BE LOVED

(with Billy Rose)

VERSE

Man, you funny thing,
Don't you know it's Spring?

Ev'ry bench and swing
Discovers lovers.
Here we sit and sit
While the moon is lit.
Am I feeling happy?
Not a bit.

REFRAIN 1
I wanna be loved with inspiration,
I wanna be loved starting tonight.
Instead of merely holding conversation,
Hold me tight!
I wanna be loved, I crave affection,
Those kisses of yours
I'd gladly share.
I want your eyes to shine in my direction.
Make me care!
I want the kind of romance
That should be strong and equally as tender.
I only ask for the chance
To know the meaning of the word
    "surrender."
I wanna be thrilled by only you, dear,
I wanna be thrilled by your caress.
I wanna find each dream of mine come
    true, dear,
I wanna be loved!
I wanna be loved!

REFRAIN 2
I wanna be loved with inspiration,
I wanna be loved starting tonight.
Instead of merely holding conversation
Hold me tight!
I wanna be kissed until I tingle,
I wanna be kissed,
Starting tonight.
Embrace me till our heartbeats
    intermingle,
Wrong or right.
I feel like acting my age,
I'm past the stage of merely doving.
I'm in no mood to resist,

And I insist the world owes me a loving.
I wanna be thrilled to desperation,
I wanna be thrilled, starting tonight.
With ev'ry kind of crazy new sensation, I
    wanna be
I wanna be loved!

—Johnny Green

WHEN I FALL IN LOVE

VERSE
Maybe I'm old-fashioned
Feeling like I do,
Maybe I am living in the past.
But when I meet the right one
I know that I'll be true.
My first love will be my last.

REFRAIN
When I fall in love
It will be forever,
Or I'll never fall in love.
In a restless world like this is,
Love is ended before it's begun,
And too many moonlight kisses
Seem to cool in the warmth of the sun.
When I give my heart
It will be completely,
Or I'll never give my heart.
And the moment I can feel that
You feel that way too,
Is when I'll fall in love with you.

—Victor Young

YOU'RE MINE, YOU!

VERSE
The sky possesses the moon,
The earth possesses a tree,

And here am I, and here are you
Taking possession of me.
I'm yours, I give you my heart,
You're mine till death do us part.
Together we will always be
Just as we were from the start.

REFRAIN
You're mine, you!
You belong to me, you!
I will never free you,
You're here with me to stay.
You're mine, you!
You are mine completely,

Love me strong or sweetly,
I need you night and day.
Arm in arm, hand in hand,
We will be found together.
Heart to heart, lips to lips,
We're chained and bound
    together.
I own you,
I don't need to buy love,
You're a slave to my love.
In every way,
You're mine.

—Johnny Green

Ralph Freed (1907–1973)

R ALPH FREED WAS BORN in Vancouver and, like his older brother Arthur, was writing songs by 1934, the year Bing Crosby's recording of his "Little Dutch Mill" was a number-one hit for five weeks. It was probably Freed's biggest hit, but "How About You" has been his most famous lyric, and his best, even when "creative" singers change "Franklin Roosevelt's" looks to, say, "Frank Sinatra's." Among the many movies he wrote for were the Judy Garland/Mickey Rooney *Babes on Broadway* (produced by brother Arthur) and the Sinatra/Gene Kelly *Anchors Aweigh.* And when M-G-M decided that Cole Porter's songs weren't good enough for the film version of his Broadway hit *DuBarry Was A Lady,* Freed contributed such numbers as the goofy "Madame, I Love Your Crepes Suzette."

BABES ON BROADWAY

We're babes on Broadway,
We're going places
When our new faces appear.
It's a wonderful street for babes like us to
    be on,
We're here because we want our names
    in neon.
We left Topeka,
We left Eureka,
And came to seek a career.
Oh, we're milkin' applause instead of
    milkin' a cow,
'Cause we're babes on Broadway now.

—Burton Lane

HOW ABOUT YOU

VERSE
When a girl meets a boy,
Life can be a joy,
But the note they end on

Will depend on
Little pleasures they will share;
So let us compare.

REFRAIN
I like New York in June,
How about you?
I like a Gershwin tune,
How about you?
I love a fireside
When a storm is due.
I like potato chips,
Moonlight and motor trips,
How about you?
I'm mad about good books,
Can't get my fill.
And Franklin Roosevelt's looks
Give me a thrill.
Holding hands in a movie show
When all the lights are low
May not be new,
But I like it,
How about you?

—Burton Lane

You Leave Me Breathless

VERSE

I've seen the famous Rembrandts,
The lovely Mona Lisa,
And I've been told the fortunes they are
    worth.
I've seen the great Niag'ra,
The Pyramids of Egypt,
The seven wonders of the earth.

REFRAIN

But you leave me breathless,
You heavenly thing.
You look so wonderful
You're like a breath of Spring.

You leave me speechless,
I'm just like the birds,
I'm filled with melody,
But at a loss for words.
That little grin of yours,
That funny chin of yours,
Does so much to my heart.
Oh! give your lips to me,
For, darling, that would be
The final touch to my heart.
You leave me breathless,
That's all I can say.
I can't say more, because
You take my breath away.

—*Frederick Hollander*

Paul Francis Webster (1907–1984)

H E M A Y B E more famous for his rhapsodic material of the fifties and for his six-teen Academy Award nominations (resulting in three Oscars), but we can be more grateful for what he brought earlier to the wonderful Ellington numbers "I Got It Bad and That Ain't Good" and "Jump for Joy." Born in New York City and educated at Cornell and NYU, he was a seaman and a dance instructor before turning out his first hit, "Masquerade," at the age of twenty-four. A few years later he was in Hollywood, beginning one of the longest and most successful songwriter careers in movie history. Not only did he write the hit songs for films like *Calamity Jane* ("Secret Love") and *Dr. Zhivago* ("Lara's Theme–Somewhere My Love"), but he was responsible for movie theme songs like the hugely successful "Love Is a Many-Splendored Thing"–a lyric that can stand for an entire genre of overblown film anthems. He wrote that one with the omnipresent composer Sammy Fain (also responsible for "Secret Love"), but his most entertaining collaboration, apart from the one with Ellington, was with Hoagy Carmichael: the highly original "Baltimore Oriole" and the song that defines Betty Hutton, "Doctor, Lawyer, Indian Chief." (It may seem politically incorrect today, but it was a number-one hit in 1945.)

BALTIMORE ORIOLE

Baltimore Oriole
Took a look at the mercury, forty below.
No life for a lady
To be draggin' her feathers around in
　　the snow.

[HE] Leaving me blue,
　　Off she flew

[OR SHE] Leaving her mate,
　　She flew straight

To the Tangipaho,
Where a two-timin' blackbird
Met the divine Miss O!
I'd like to ruffle his plumage!

Baltimore Oriole
Messed aroun' with that big mouth 'til he
　　singed her wing.
Forgivin' is easy,
It's a woman-like, now-and-then-could-
　　happen thing.
Send her back home,
Home ain't home without her warbling;
Make a lonely man happy.
Baltimore Oriole,
Come down from that bough,
Fly back to me now.

–Hoagy Carmichael

BLACK COFFEE

(with Sonny Burke)

I'm feelin' mighty lonesome,
Haven't slept a wink,
I walk the floor
And watch the door
And in between I drink
Black coffee.
Love's a hand-me-down broom.
I'll never know a Sunday,
In this weekday room.
I'm talkin' to the shadows,
One o'clock to four.
And Lord, how slow
The moments go
When all I do is pour
Black coffee.
Since the blues caught my eye
I'm hangin' out on Monday
My Sunday dreams to dry.
Now a man is born to go a-lovin',
A woman's born to weep and fret.
To stay at home and tend her oven,
And drown her past regrets
In coffee and cigarettes!
I'm moonin' all the mornin',
And mournin' all the night,
And in between
It's nicotine
And not much heart to fight
Black coffee.
Feelin' low as the ground.
It's drivin' me crazy,
This waitin' for my baby,
To maybe come around.

> —*Paul Francis Webster and*
>   *Sonny Burke*

DOCTOR, LAWYER, INDIAN CHIEF

There's a doctor livin' in your town.
There's a lawyer and an Indian, too.
Neither doctor, lawyer, or Indian chief
Could love you any more than I do.
There's a barr'l of fish in the ocean
And a lot of little birds in the blue.
Neither fish nor fowl,
Says the wise old owl,
Could love you any more than I do.
No, no, no, it couldn't be true
That anyone else could love you like I do.

1. I'm gonna warn all the dead-eye dicks
   That you're the chick with the slickest
       tricks,
   And ev'ry tick of my ticker ticks
   For you, follow through.

2. And confidentially I confess
   I sent a note to the local press
   That I'll be changin' my home address
   For you, follow through.
   Tell the "doc" to stick to his practice,
   Tell the lawyer to settle his case,
   Send the Injun chief and his
       tommy-hawk
   Back to little Rain-in-the-face.
   'Cause you know, know, know
   It couldn't be true
   That anyone else could love you like
       I do.
   There's a do.
   No, no, you know, know
   That nobody else could love you like
       I do.

> —*Hoagy Carmichael*

I Got It Bad and That Ain't Good

VERSE

The poets say that all who love are blind,
But I'm in love and I know what time
    it is!
The Good Book says, "Go seek and ye
    shall find."
Well, I have sought and, my, what a climb
    it is!
My life is just like the weather,
It changes with the hours.
When he's near I'm fair and warmer,
When he's gone I'm cloudy with showers.
In emotion, like the ocean it's either sink
    or swim
When a woman loves a man like I love him.

REFRAIN I

Never treats me sweet and gentle
The way he should.
I got it bad and that ain't good!
My poor heart is sentimental,
Not made of wood.
I got it bad and that ain't good!
But when the weekend's over
And Monday rolls aroun',
I end up like I start out,
Just cryin' my heart out.
He don't love me like I love him,
Nobody could.
I got it bad and that ain't good.

REFRAIN 2

Like a lonely weeping willow
Lost in the wood,
I got it bad and that ain't good!
And the things I tell my pillow
No woman should.
I got it bad and that ain't good!
Though folks with good intentions

Tell me to save my tears,
I'm glad I'm mad about him,
I can't live without him.
Lord above me, make him love me
The way he should.
I got it bad and that ain't good.

—Duke Ellington

Jump for Joy

VERSE

We're so fed up with the Southland,
That way down South in the Mouthland.
For all these years
We've been bored to tears
With the blues.
Those southern songs are getting tired.
They're sweet, beat, and uninspired.
It's time they were retired.
And we got news.

REFRAIN

Fare thee well, land of cotton,
Cotton, lisle is out of style,
Honey chile,
Jump for joy.
Don't'cha grieve, little Eve,
All the hounds, I do believe,
Have been killed, ain't'cha thrilled,
Jump for joy.
Have you seen pastures groovy?
Green Pastures was just a Technicolor
    movie.
When you stomp up to heaven
And you meet Ol' Saint Pete,
Tell that boy, "Jump for joy."
Step right in, give Pete some skin,
And jump for joy.

—Duke Ellington and Sid Kuller

Love Is a Many-Splendored Thing

VERSE

I walked along the streets of Hong
 Kong town,
Up and down,
Up and down.
I met a little girl in Hong Kong town,
And I said, "Can you tell me, please,
Where's that love I've never found?
Unravel me this riddle, what is love?
What can it be?"
And in her eyes were butterflies
As she replied to me:

REFRAIN

"Love is a many-splendored thing,
It's the April rose that only grows
In the early Spring.
Love is nature's way of giving
A reason to be living,
The golden crown that makes a man a king.
Once on a high and windy hill,
In the morning mist two lovers kissed
And the world stood still.
Then your fingers touched my silent heart
And taught it how to sing,
Yes, true love's a many-splendored thing."

—Sammy Fain

Secret Love

VERSE

Nobody knew, not even you,
When I first started walking on wings.
But how long can a man or woman ever
 hope to hide
Love that's locked up inside?
Ev'ry story worth the spinning
Must have a beginning.

REFRAIN

Once I had a secret love
That lived within the heart of me.
All too soon my secret love
Became impatient to be free.
So I told a friendly star,
The way that dreamers often do,
Just how wonderful you are
And why I'm so in love with you.
Now I shout it from the highest hills,
Even told the golden daffodils;
At last my heart's an open door,
And my secret love's no secret any more.

—Sammy Fain

Two Cigarettes in the Dark

Two,
Two cigarettes in the dark.
He strikes a match till the spark
Clearly thrilled me
And filled me
With romance.
Two,
Two cigarettes in the dark.
Love was the flame and the spark
That inspired
And fired
My heart.
The smoke rings seemed to signify
A story old yet new.
I heard a voice within me cry,
"I love you, I love you, you know that I do."
Two,
Two tender arms hold me tight,
Two loving lips say "goodnight,"
As two silhouettes
Light two cigarettes
In the dark.

—Lew Pollack

Harold Rome (1908–1993)

S ON OF THE PRESIDENT OF the Connecticut Coal and Charcoal Company, Harold Rome was an undergraduate first at Trinity College and then at Yale, before going on to Yale's law school and its architecture school. There was no work for young architects in the Depression mid-thirties, however, so he fell back on his avocation, music, and discovered that he could write songs. With his left-leaning political views, he was drawn to songs of social significance, and in 1937 he provided the words and music for *Pins and Needles,* the most successful revue in Broadway history until *Oh, Calcutta!* (The big hit song was, appropriately, "Give Me a Song of Social Significance.") *Pins and Needles* was a highly satirical political statement, mounted by the International Ladies Garment Workers Union, with performers taken from the union ranks and serendipitously first presented at the old Kern/Wodehouse/Bolton Princess Theater, now renamed the Labor Stage. It soon moved uptown and ran for 1,108 performances. It was during this period that a critic referred to Rome as "a Noel Coward with a social conscience." Rome's second great hit was the snappy postwar revue *Call Me Mister,* and then he had a series of flops until a run of four successful musicals. *Wish You Were Here* retained some elements of Rome's earlier sardonic approach (though its immediate fame came from its onstage swimming pool), and *Fanny* not only starred *South Pacific*'s Ezio Pinza but sounds like a Rodgers and Hammerstein clone: This was 1954, when R & H dominated the American musical. Then came *Destry Rides Again* and *I Can Get It for You Wholesale,* best remembered for having introduced Barbra Streisand to Broadway. Rome's final big project was a musical version of *Gone With the Wind,* which had some success in Tokyo and London but never made it to New York. The output of this composer/lyricist is highly impressive as well as various; he's one of the most underrated figures of his time.

CALL ME MISTER

VERSE

Da-di-da, da-di-da, da-da-dee,
Da-di-da, da-di-da, da-da-dee,
Da-di-dip, da-di-da,
Da-da-dee, da-dee-da, da-di-dum, di-dum.

REFRAIN

It's a beautiful day, ain't it?
So exciting and gay, ain't it?
There's a beautiful hue in the
    beautiful blue.
Call me Mister!
Lovely weather we've got, ain't it?
Not too cold or too hot, ain't it?

There's a beautiful breeze in the beautiful
    trees.
Call me Mister!
There's a lift in the air;
There's a song ev'rywhere;
There's a tang in,
A bang in, just living!
Da-di-ah-da-da,
It's a beautiful time, ain't it?
All the world is in rhyme, ain't it?
It's a beautiful shore from New Jersey to
    Oregon!
Just call me Mister from now on!

Chain Store Daisy

VERSE

When I was young I studied hard and
    thirsted after knowledge,
And often burned the midnight oil so I
    could get to college.
They told me my fine education would
    help improve my situation;
So then I crammed and crammed till I was
    almost in a coma,
And thesised and examed until I got me a
    diploma.
"Ah-hah," they said,
Now comes admission
Into a very high position.
Out I went and looked around,
And Macy's is the place I found,
I filled my blanks and application
And went for my examination.
They took my weight and took my
    height,
And tapped my chest and tested my sight.
Examined my head, took prints of
    my toes,
Looked at my teeth and up my nose.
Examined my throat and measured
    my hips,

And even took prints of my fingertips.
They made me say "ah" and told me to
    grunt.
Examined my back, examined my front.
Then they tested my "I.Q."
And asked me what I'd like to do
And when that exam was through
What there was to know, Macy's knew!
[Spoken]
So I got the job.

REFRAIN

Life is a bitter cup of tea,
Now I'm just salesgirl seventy-three.
I used to be on the daisy chain,
Now I'm a chain store daisy.
Once they gave me the honor seat,
Now I stand up with pains in my feet,
I used to be on the daisy chain
Now shoppers drive me crazy.
I sell smart but thrifty
Corsets at three-fifty,
Better grade four sixty-nine.
I sell bras and girdles
For Mauds and Myrtles
To hold in their plump
Behind this counter.
Once I wrote poems, put folks in tears,
Now I write checks for ladies' brassieres,
I used to be on the daisy chain
Now I'm a chain store daisy.
[Spoken]
Oh! yes, Madam—Oh! no, Madam—
I guess, Madam—That's so, Madam—
Of course, Madam—that's the very best,
Exactly the kind that's worn by Mae West.
For you, Madam—we do, Madam—
That's true, Madam—in blue, Madam—
That one is nineteen seventy-four.
It ought to be expensive
It's the largest in the store.
[Sung]
Once I had a yearning

For all higher learning,
Studied till I made the grade.
I pursued my knowledge
And finished college,
Well look at the
Kind of grade I made.
I'm now selling things to fit in the figure,
[Spoken]
Make the big things small and
The small things bigger!
[Sung]
I used to be on the daisy chain
Now I'm a chain store daisy.

DOING THE REACTIONARY

VERSE

It's darker than the dark bottom,
It rumbles more than the rumba.
If you think that the two-step got 'em
Just take a look at this number.
It's got that certain swing
That makes you want to sing.

REFRAIN

Don't go left, but be polite,
Move to the right,
Doing the reactionary.
Close your eyes to where you're bound,
And you'll be found
Doing the reactionary.
All the best dictators do it,
Millionaires keep stepping to it,
The four hundred love to sing it,
Ford and Morgan swing it.
Hand up high and shake your head,
You'll soon see red,
Doing the reactionary.
So get in it, begin it,
It's smart, oh so very,
To do the reactionary.

DON'T WANNA WRITE ABOUT THE SOUTH

Don't wanna write about the South,
I don't wanna!
There's books to be sold outside.
Ain't gonna write about the South,
I ain't gonna!
But, Baby, there's gold outside.
Though you may think I'm acting formal,
I don't like decline and decay.
I'd rather be growing up normal.
South Ca'lina, please take it away.
(Ay-ay-ay)
I'm not gonna knock, I'm a booster—
Kindly tell that to Simon and Schuster.
I'm gonna shut my mouth,
Not write a word about the Southland
Down by the Gullahs.
How we gonna break the news to Carson
    McCullers?

CODA

Hey, Baby, Southland,
Say, Baby! won't you change your mind?
No! No! No! No!

F.D.R. JONES

VERSE

I hear tell there's a stranger in the Jones
    household,
Yes siree, yes siree, that's what I'm told.
I hear tell there's a new arrival six days old,
Yes siree, yes siree, worth his weight
    in gold.
Come right in and meet the son,
Christ'ning's done,
Time to have some fun,
Yes siree, yes siree, yes siree.
Yes siree, yes siree.

It's a big holiday ev'rywhere,
For the Jones family has a
　　brand-new heir;
He's the joy heaven sent
And they proudly present
Mister Franklin D. Roosevelt Jones.
When he grows up he never will stray
With a name like the one that he's got
　　today.
As he walks down the street,
Folks will say "Pleased to meet"
Mister Franklin D. Roosevelt Jones.
What a smile!
And how he shows it!
He'll keep happy
All day long.
What a name!
I'll bet he knows it.
With that handle
How can he go wrong!
And the folks in the town all agree
He'll be famous, as famous as he can be.
How can he be a dud
Or a stick in the mud
When he's Franklin D. Roosevelt
　　Jones?
Yes siree, yes siree, yes siree,
Yes siree, yes siree.

THE MILITARY LIFE

VERSE

There are ads in all the papers,
There are signs on every truck
With a picture of the soldier's friend,
The good old Ruptured Duck,
And it says beneath the picture,
"Kindly treat with great respect
The guy upon whose coat lapel
This button you detect."
A sentiment very dear to each one here.

But remember what the first columnist—A
　　Greek named Aesop who lived two
　　thousand years ago—wrote:
You can't make a nylon pocketbook out of
　　a pig's ear,
Exclamation point, unquote—
That's a fact you ought to note.
Take the case of Charley Jones
Drafted when the war began,
Now returning to civilian life
A veteran.

REFRAIN I

He was a jerk before he got into the
　　service,
He was a jerk and never on the square.
He would shoot with loaded dice,
Loved to peddle stolen ice,
Stole milk from babies in his
　　spare time.
But oh, the charm of Army life,
The touch of discipline and strife.
Through the muck and the mire,
Through the flack and the fire
The military magic did its work:
From a foreign shore
He is back once more—
Still a jerk.

PATTER I

Oh, the magic of the barracks and the
　　battle and the din,
The magic of the travel and the drill and
　　discipline,
Oh, the military builds a man with lots of
　　root-de-toot,
But even they can make a slight mistake,
And when they do—boy, it's a beaut!
It's a beaut!

REFRAIN 2

He was a slob before he got into the
　　service,

He was a slob, acquaintances would say.
His deportment wasn't nice,
He indulged in every vice
That plagues the Board of Sanitation.
But oh, the charm of Army life,
The touch of discipline and strife.
Through the mash and the mush,
Through the crash and the crush,
The military magic did its job.
With the other men
He's come back again—
Changed in many respects—
Still a slob.

REFRAIN 3

He was a bum before he got into the
    service,
He was a bum when all is said
    and done.
He would beat his ma and dad
For suggesting it was bad
To be a burglar on Sunday.
But oh, the charm of Army life,
The touch of discipline and strife.
Through the blitz and the fluff,
Through the spritz and the stuff,
The military magic made him hum.
With the things he's learned
He has now returned—
Still a bum.

PATTER 2

Oh, the service made a hero out of
    some guys
That were bum guys who we knew.
They can take a heel and make him over
    really
Who's schlemielly through and through.
But a miracle's a miracle and though we
    sound empirical
Believe us there are limits to even
    things that
Nimitz, Halsey and MacArthur can do.

REFRAIN 4

He was a drip before he got into the
    service,
He was a drip, and tighter than a clam.
He would hold on to a dollar
Till he made the Eagle holler,
Foreclosed the mortgage on his mammy.
But oh, the charm of Army life,
The touch of discipline and strife.
Through the slush and the slosh,
Through the mish and the mosh,
The military magic got its grip.
Now he's on his toes in civilian clothes—
Still a drip.

REFRAIN 5

She was a bore before she got into the
    service,
She was a bore—had ants within her
    glance.
She would tear her friends to shreds,
Broke up many double beds,
And drooled at anything with pants on.
But oh, the charm of Army life,
The touch of discipline and strife.
Through the straff and the strafe,
Through the chaff and the chafe,
This gallant little lady did her hitch.
Now she marches by
With her chest held high,
Still—a bore.

THE MONEY SONG

VERSE

Down in Washington, D.C.
Men are working busily
In a place they call the mint.
They make coins and also print
Very excellent engraving,
Which the rest of us keep saving,
Printed up in black and green.

It's the darndest stuff
You've ever seen.

If you've got it,
You don't need it.
If you need it,
You don't got it.
You don't get it,
Shame on you!
Funny, funny, funny
What money can do!
Them that have it
Get more of it.
Less they need it,
More they love it,
And it sticks to
Them like glue.
Funny, funny, funny
What money can do!
Ask the rich man,
He'll confess
Money can't buy
Happiness.
Ask the poor man,
He don't doubt,
But he'd rather be miserable
With than without.
If you spend it,
Please be wiser.
If you save it,
You're a miser.
You don't want it,
You're cuckoo!
Funny, funny, funny
What money can do!

PATTER
A nickel or dime or penny,
La la lu lu,
Is better than not having any,
La la lu lu.
A half a dollar or a quarter,

La la lu lu,
Makes people do a lot of things they
   hadn't ever oughter do!

If you do not
Need it badly,
Banks will give it
To you gladly.
If you need it,
Nuts to you!
Funny, funny, funny
What money can do!
If you're lucky
And you make it,
You're so frightened
Who might take it
Stomach ulcers
Come to you.
Funny, funny, funny
What money can do!
Birds don't got it,
Still they sing,
Eating worms
Upon the wing;
Ideal life,
Some folks affirm.
So O.K., you're a bird,
But suppose you're a worm.
It's a bad thing,
Oh yes, very,
Full of germs un-
Sanitary.
Will I have some?
Oh, thank you!
Funny, funny, funny
What money can do!

(ALL OF A SUDDEN)
MY HEART SINGS

(with Jean-Marie Blanvillain)

VERSE

It comes from out the blue,
The sudden thought of you,
Filling my heart up
And thrilling me through.

REFRAIN 1

All of a sudden my heart sings
When I remember little things.
The way you dance and hold me tight,
The way you kiss and say good night,
The crazy things we say and do,
The fun it is to be with you,
The magic thrill that's in your touch,
Oh darling, I love you so much.
The secret way you press my hand
To let me know you understand,
The wind and rain upon your face,
The breathless world of your embrace,
Your little laugh and half surprise,
The starlight gleaming in your eyes.
Rememb'ring all those little things,
All of a sudden my heart sings.

REFRAIN 2

All of a sudden my heart sings
When I remember little things.
Your voice upon the telephone,
The little laugh that's all your own,
The way a smile lights up your eyes,
The way you look up in surprise,
The magic thrill that's in your touch,
Oh darling, I love you so much.
The funny way you hold your head,
The crazy things you've often said,
The way your hair won't stay in place,
The wind and rain upon your face,
The way you hold my hand at shows,

The way you wrinkle up your nose.
Rememb'ring all those little things,
All of a sudden my heart sings.

—Henri Herpin

NOBODY MAKES A PASS AT ME

VERSE

I want men that I can squeeze,
That I can please, that I can tease.
Two or three or four or more!
What are those fools waiting for?
I want love and I want kissing.
I want more of what I'm missing—
Nobody comes knocking at my front door.
What do they think my knocker's for?
If they don't come soon there won't be
    any more!
What can the matter be?

REFRAIN

I wash my clothes with Lux,
My etiquette's the best.
I spend my hard-earned bucks
On just what the ads suggest.
Oh dear what can the matter be?
Nobody makes a pass at me!
I'm full of Kellogg's bran,
Eat GrapeNuts on the sly,
A date is on the can
Of the coffee that I buy.
Oh dear what can the matter be?
Nobody makes a pass at me!
Oh Beatrice Fairfax, give me the bare facts,
How do you make them fall?
If you don't save me, the things the Lord
    gave me
Never will be of any use to me at all.
I sprinkle on a dash
Of Fragrance d'Amour
The ads say "makes men rash"—

But I guess their smell is poor!
Oh dear what can the matter be?
Nobody makes a pass at me!

PATTER

I use Ovaltine and Listerine,
Barbasol and Musterole,
Lifebuoy soap and Flit,
So why ain't I got it?
I use Coca-Cola and Mazola,
Crisco, Lesco, and Marmola,
Ex-Lax, and Vapex,
So why ain't I got sex?
I use Alboline and Maybelline,
Alka-Seltzer, Bromo-Seltzer,
Odorono and Sensation,
So why ain't I got fascination?
My girdles come from Best.
The *Times* ads say they're chic,
And up above I'm dressed
In the brassiere of the week.
Oh dear what can the matter be?
Nobody makes a pass at me!
I use Pond's on my skin.
With Ry-Krisp I have thinned.
I get my culture in–
I began *Gone with the Wind.*
Oh dear what can the matter be?
Nobody makes a pass at me!
Oh Dorothy Dix, please show me some
    tricks, please.
I want some men to hold.
I want attention and things I won't
    mention–
And I want them all before I get too old.
I use Mum every day
And Angelus Lip-Lure,
But still men stay away.
Just like Ivory Soap I'm 99 and 44/100ths
    percent pure!

I don't know!

RING ON THE FINGER

VERSE

The strongest thing in the world
Is not made of steel,
Iron, stone, cement, or sand.
It's a simple golden band.

REFRAIN I

That ring on the finger,
That little golden band
That's next to the pinky
On a well-dressed left hand.
From the day she is born,
Ev'ry girl is aiming for
That life rearranger,
That last-name changer,
That ring on the finger
From the jew'lry store.
That bliss advertiser,
That kiss legalizer,
That ring on the finger
From the jew'lry store.

REFRAIN 2

That ring on the finger,
That little golden band
That's next to the pinky
On a well-dressed left hand.
From the day she is born,
Ev'ry girl is aiming for
That world populator,
That in-law creator,
That ring on the finger
From the jew'lry store.
That bachelor killer,
That double-bed filler,
That ring on the finger
From the jew'lry store.

It makes more magic than Aladdin's lamp
of yore.
Packs more wallop than a trusty forty-four.
Hides more treasure than King
Solomon's mine,
Hell on wheels and paradise divine.
It holds more tears than all the rivers
flowing by,
More promise than a rainbow in the sky.
Turns the bold ones shy and makes the shy
ones bold.
Sings out the oldest and the newest story
ever told!

REFRAIN 3

That ring on the finger,
That little golden band
That's next to the pinky
On a well-dressed left hand.
From the day she is born,
Ev'ry girl is aiming for
That home entertainer,
That old ball and chainer,
That ring on the finger
From the jew'lry store.
That don't count the kisses,
That hey! Meet the missus,
That ring on the finger
From the jew'lry store.

South America, Take It Away!

VERSE

Up here in the land of the hot dog stand,
The atom bomb and the Good Humor man,
We think our South American neighbors
are grand.
We love them to beat the band!
South America! Ba-ba-lou, ba-ba-lou, ay
yay, ba-ba-lou!

One favor you can do, ay yay, you can do!
You beautiful lands below
Don't know what you began.
To put it plainly, I'm tired of shaking
To that Pan-American Plan!

REFRAIN 1

Take back your samba, ay!
Your rumba, ay!
Your conga, ay, yay, yay!
I can't keep shaking, ay!
My rumble, ay!
Any longer, ay, yay, yay!
Now maybe Latins, ay!
In their middles, ay!
Are built stronger, ay, yay, yay!
But all this makin' with the quakin'
And this shakin' of the bacon
Leaves me achin'!
Holay!
First you shake it and you put it there!
Then you shake it and you put it here!
Then you shake it and you put it there!
That's enough, that's enough, take
it back,
My spine's out of whack!
There's a great big crack
In the back of my sacroiliac!
1. Take back your conga, ay!
Your samba, ay!
Your rumba, ay, yay, yay!
Why can't you send us, ay!
A less strenu-ay!-ous number!
Ay, yay, yay!
It's getting so now, ay!
That even, ay!
In slumber, ay, yay, yay!
I hear the rocking of maracas
And the knocking of the knockers
In my carcass!
Holay!
South America, take it away!

2. Take back your conga, ay!
   Your samba, ay!
   Your rumba, ay, yay, yay!
   Bring back the old days, ay!
   Of dancing I re-mamba,
   Ay, yay, yay!
   My hips are creaking, ay!
   And shrieking, ay!
   Caramba, ay, yay, yay!
   I've got a wriggle and a diddle
   And a jiggle like a fiddle
   In my middle.
   Holay!
   This fancy swishin' in position
   Wears out all of my transmission
   Ammunition!
   Holay!
   I know there's danger really lurking
   If my rear end keeps on working
   At this jerking!
   Holay!
   South America, take it away!

Who Knows?

New York is a wonderful town,
A very stimulating place to be.
It's full of galleries and exhibitions,
Most are absolutely free.
And concerts like at Lewisohn Stadium,
Plus at Carnegie Hall.
We sit way up top,
But it's wonderful acoustics,
That's where it sounds best of all.
Art lectures at the Metropolitan–
I attended Ancient Greece the
     other day.
The modern dance and ballet
At the Y.M. and W.H.A.
And legitimate plays on Broadway.
Don't you think Odets is great?

Not downstairs, of course.
We get last-minute balcony down at Gray's
     cut-rate.
What better way can a single girl
With leisure spare time find
Than to go around, broaden out her
     background,
Also improve her mind?
Plus it give more chances
For meeting up with people, wouldn't
     you say?
Such as certain members of the
     opposite sex
She hopes to get involved with some day.
And who can tell, who knows
When they might come one's way!

REFRAIN

Who knows when I'll see him,
     who knows?
Or why it will be him, who knows?
Perfect he doesn't have to be,
Good-looking, or rich, or smart,
Long as he's crazy after me,
And we see heart to heart.
Who knows when he'll be there, who
     knows?
One day he'll see me there and hold out
     his arms.
Then he'll kiss me, say he loves me, and
     propose.
But why, when, where, who knows?

Wish You Were Here

VERSE
Where is the wonder
As each day would start
That sang with the dawn,
Ran away with my heart?
Where is it gone?

REFRAIN

They're not making skies as blue
This year.
Wish you were here!
As blue as they used to when you
Were near.
Wish you were here!
And the mornings don't seem as new,
Brand-new as they did with you.
Wish you were here!
Wish you were here!
Wish you were here!
Someone's painting the leaves all wrong

This year.
Wish you were here!
And why did the birds change their song
This year?
Wish you were here!
They're not shining the stars as
   bright.
They've stolen the joy from the night.
Wish you were here!
Wish you were here!
Wish you were here!

REPEAT REFRAIN

Johnny Burke (1908–1964)

O NE OF THE MOST talented, successful, and underappreciated of all American lyricists, Johnny Burke is in that small group of top writers who rank just below the Berlins and the Porters. Indeed, after he graduated from the University of Wisconsin (he had been born in California and raised in New York), his first job was with the Chicago office of the Irving Berlin Publishing Company, playing the piano and plugging songs. His first success (with composer Harold Spina) was "Annie Doesn't Live Here Anymore," and they went on turning out hits until Burke left for Hollywood. He had a remarkable career there, first collaborating with Arthur Johnston, then with James Monaco, and finally–and most memorably–with Jimmy Van Heusen. There were two unique constants in Burke's film career: He worked for only one studio, Paramount; and out of the forty-one movies he wrote, twenty-five (including the first six of the seven *Road* pictures) starred Bing Crosby–together they enjoyed more than half a dozen number-one hits, beginning with the perennial "Pennies from Heaven" and ending with the Oscar-winning "Swinging on a Star." Burke worked with Van Heusen on a couple of unsuccessful Broadway musicals, but more than thirty years after his death, a show made up of his songs–*Swinging on a Star*–converted a lot of people to Johnny Burke. It was time he received his due.

AIN'T IT A SHAME ABOUT MAME

VERSE
Can you tell that I'm unhappy,
Can you see that things are bad?
Of course, you know what happened
To the best friend I ever had.

REFRAIN 1
Ain't it a shame about Mame?
She has only herself to blame.
She can't go to the picnics in Hooligans
   Grove,
No corned beef and cabbage is cooked on
   her stove.
She married Sir Reginald
What's his name.
Ain't it a shame–poor Mame.

PATTER
And she has to be social,
Has to go to the nightclubs.
Has to dance like a Cuban
And still act like a lady.
Oh, to
Think that a child of Mike O'Grady
Would marry Sir Reginald
What's his name.
Ain't it a shame about Mame.

REFRAIN 2
Ain't it a crime what she did?
Sure she's only a crazy kid.
Now she has to talk fancy and eat caviar,
And look like those pictures in *Harper's
   Bazaar*
And try to find happiness

Just the same.
Ain't it a shame–poor Mame.

REFRAIN 3
Ain't it a shame about Mame?
Now she lost all her spark and flame.
She wears sables instead of a skirt and a
    blouse,
And has to keep shoes on when she's in the
    house.
She married Sir Reginald
What's his name.
Ain't it a shame–poor Mame.

–James V. Monaco

But Beautiful

VERSE
Who can say what love is?
Does it start
In the mind
Or the heart?
When I hear discussions on what love is,
Ev'rybody speaks a diff'rent part.

REFRAIN
Love is funny
Or it's sad
Or it's quiet
Or it's mad;
It's a good thing
Or it's bad,
But beautiful!
Beautiful
To take a chance
And if you fall, you fall.
And I'm thinking
I wouldn't mind at all.
Love is tearful
Or it's gay;
It's a problem

Or it's play;
It's a heartache
Either way,
But beautiful!
And I'm thinking
If you were mine
I'd never let you go,
And that would be
But beautiful,
I know.

–Jimmy Van Heusen

Good Time Charlie

VERSE
Before you start an argument
On wealth or reconstruction,
Let me introduce a man
Who needs no introduction:

REFRAIN 1
Ev'rybody here knows Good Time
    Charlie:
Charlie is a perfect clown.
Always kills the folks with funny jokes
And turns the parlor upside down.
Ev'rybody sure likes Good Time
    Charlie.
No one ever saw him frown,
But here's the funniest part,
Down deep in his heart,
He's the lonesomest man in town.

REFRAIN 2
Ev'rybody waits for Good Time Charlie:
Charlie's just a grown-up brat.
They roll on the floor and laugh and roar
When he puts on a lady's hat.
Charlie is the life of ev'ry party,
Never has a care to drown.
The girls all kiss him good night,

But out of their sight,
He's the lonesomest man in town.

—*Jimmy Van Heusen*

Here's That Rainy Day

Maybe
I should have saved those leftover dreams;
Funny,
But here's that rainy day.
Here's that rainy day
They told me about,
And I laughed at the thought that it might
    turn out this way.
Where is that worn-out wish that I threw
    aside
After it brought my lover near?
Funny, how love becomes a cold rainy day.
Funny, that rainy day is here.

—*Jimmy Van Heusen*

Imagination

VERSE
Do you remember Don Quixote
Or the Bulpington of Blup?
The things they thought of can't
    compare with
The things my mind makes up.

REFRAIN
Imagination is funny,
It makes a cloudy day sunny,
Makes a bee think of honey,
Just as I think of you.
Imagination is crazy,
Your whole perspective gets hazy,
Starts you asking a daisy,
What to do

What to do?
Have you ever felt a gentle touch,
And then a kiss,
And then and then
Find it's only your imagination again?
Oh, well
Imagination
Is silly,
You go around willy-nilly.
For example, I go around wanting you.
And yet I can't imagine that
You want me too.

—*Jimmy Van Heusen*

It Could Happen to You

VERSE
Do you believe
In charms and spells,
In mystic words and magic wands
And wishing wells?
Don't look so wise,
Don't show your scorn;
Watch yourself,
I warn you.

REFRAIN
Hide your heart from sight,
Lock your dreams at night,
It could happen to you.
Don't count stars or you might stumble,
Someone drops a sigh, and down you
    tumble.
Keep an eye on Spring,
Run when church bells ring,
It could happen to you.
All I did was wonder how your arms
    would be,
And it happened to me!

—*Jimmy Van Heusen*

I've Got a Pocketful of Dreams

VERSE

Happiness comes with success,
And that I guess is true.
But success is more or less
A point of view:

REFRAIN

I'm no millionaire,
But I'm not the type to care,
'Cause I've got a pocketful of dreams.
It's my universe
Even with an empty purse,
'Cause I've got a pocketful of dreams.
Wouldn't take the wealth on Wall
    Street
For a road where nature trods.
And I calculate
I'm worth my weight
In goldenrods.
Lucky, lucky me,
I can live in luxury,
'Cause I've got a pocketful of dreams.

—James V. Monaco

Like Someone in Love

VERSE

This change I feel puzzles me.
It's strange, a real mystery.
Maybe you see it.
If you do see it,
What on earth can it be?

REFRAIN

Lately I find myself out gazing at
    stars,
Hearing guitars
Like someone in love.

Sometimes the things I do astound me,
Mostly whenever you're around me.
Lately I seem to walk as though I had
    wings,
Bump into things
Like someone in love.
Each time I look at you
I'm limp as a glove
And feeling like someone in love.

—Jimmy Van Heusen

Misty

Look at me,
I'm as helpless as a kitten up a tree,
And I feel like I'm clinging to a cloud.
I can't understand,
I get misty
Just holding your hand.
Walk my way,
And a thousand violins begin to play,
Or it might be the sound of your hello,
That music I hear.
I get misty,
The moment you're near.
You can say that you're leading me on,
But it's just what I want you to do.
Don't you notice how hopelessly
    I'm lost?
That's why I'm following you.
On my own
Would I wander through this wonderland
    alone,
Never knowing my right foot from
    my left,
My hat from my glove?
I'm too misty
And too much in love.

—Erroll Garner

Moonlight Becomes You

VERSE

VERSE

Stand there just a moment,
Darling, let me catch my breath.
I've never seen a picture quite so lovely.
How did you ever learn to look so lovely?

REFRAIN

Moonlight becomes you,
It goes with your hair,
You certainly know the right thing
    to wear.
Moonlight becomes you,
I'm thrilled at the sight,
And I could get so romantic tonight.
You're all dressed up to go dreaming,
Now don't tell me I'm wrong.
And what a night to go dreaming!
Mind if I tag along?
If I say I love you,
I want you to know
It's not just because there's moonlight,
    although
Moonlight becomes you so.

—Jimmy Van Heusen

My Heart Is a Hobo

VERSE

When I try to get the habit of doing what I
    should,
I remember George F. Babbitt and wonder
    if I could.
'Tho I try to do my best, dag nab it,
It doesn't do much good.

REFRAIN

My heart is a hobo,
Loves to roam through fields of clover,

Hates to have to think things over,
And 'tho it's wrong,
I string along.
My heart is a hobo,
Loves to go out berry picking,
Hates to hear alarm clocks ticking,
It isn't smart
But that's my heart.
When hopes are out at the elbows
And dreams are run down at the heels,
My heart refuses to worry
Except about rods and reels.
My heart is a hobo,
Loves to quote from Omar Khayyam,
Hates the stodgy guy that I am,
And 'tho it's strange,
I just can't change my heart.

—Jimmy Van Heusen

Pennies from Heaven

VERSE

A long time ago –
A million years B.C. –
The best things in life were
    absolutely free.
But no one appreciated
A sky that was always blue;
And no one congratulated
A moon that was always new.
So it was planned that they would vanish
    now and then
And you must pay before you get them
    back again;
That's what storms were made for
And you shouldn't be afraid . . .

REFRAIN

For ev'ry time it rains, it rains
Pennies from heaven.
Don't you know each cloud contains

Pennies from heaven?
You'll find your fortune falling
All over town.
Be sure that your umbrella
Is upside down.
Trade them for a package of
Sunshine and flowers.
If you want the things you love,
You must have showers.
So when you hear it thunder,
Don't run under a tree,
There'll be pennies from heaven
For you and me.

—Arthur Johnston

PERSONALITY

VERSE

Mary Smith had a college education,
Sally Jones had a scientific streak,
Susie Brown used to lecture
On ancient architecture,
Josie Green spoke Latin and Greek.
Just forgotten girls with forgotten brains
While history explains:

REFRAIN I

When Madame Pompadour
Was on a ballroom floor
Said all the gentlemen, "Obviously
The Madame has the cutest personality."
And think of all the books
About DuBarry's looks,
What was it made her the toast of
     Paree?
She had a well-developed
Personality.
And what did Romeo
See in Juliet,
Or Pierrot in Pierrette,
Or Jupiter

In Juno?
You know!
And when Salome danced
And had the boys entranced,
No doubt it must have been easy to see—
That she knew how to use her
Personality.

REFRAIN 2

A girl can learn to spell
And take dictation well
And never sit on the boss's settee
Unless she's got a perfect
Personality.
A girl can get somewhere
In spite of stringy hair
Or even just a bit bowed at the knee
If she can show a faultless
Personality.
And why are certain girls
Offered certain things
Like sable coats
And wedding rings
By men who wear
Their spats right?
That's right!
So, don't you say I'm smart
And have the kindest heart,
Or what a wonderful sister I'd be.
Just tell me how you like my
Personality.

—Jimmy Van Heusen

POLKA DOTS AND MOONBEAMS

VERSE

Would you care to hear the strangest
     story—
At least it may be strange to you?
If you saw it in a moving picture,
You would say it couldn't be true.

REFRAIN

A country dance was being held in a
    garden,
I felt a bump and heard an "Oh, beg your
    pardon."
Suddenly I saw
Polka dots and moonbeams
All around a pug-nosed dream.
The music started and was I the
    perplexed one,
I held my breath and said, "May I have the
    next one?"
In my frightened arms
Polka dots and moonbeams
Sparkled on a pug-nosed dream.
There were questions
In the eyes of other dancers
As we floated over the floor.
There were questions,
But my heart knew all the answers,
And perhaps a few things more.
Now in a cottage built of lilacs and
    laughter
I know the meaning of the words "ever
    after,"
And I'll always see polka dots and
    moonbeams
When I kiss the pug-nosed dream.

—Jimmy Van Heusen

THE ROAD TO MOROCCO

REFRAIN 1

Let's meet on the road to Morocco,
Instead of the tunnel of love.
The desert night, the Arab tents, the
    harem atmosphere,
It's the best attraction Coney Island has
    this year.
Let's meet on the road to Morocco,
Though our Brooklyn moon shines above.

I'll whisper how I love you to the strains of
    native flutes,
And your arms will thrill me more than all
    the chute-the-chutes.
Tell the gang
So they won't
Hang around.
Like Webster's Dictionary,
We're Morocco bound.

REFRAIN 2

Let's meet on the road to Morocco,
Let's dream for the price of a dime.
We'll ride the magic carpet that looks
    absolutely real,
Don't you think that's more romantic than
    the Ferris wheel?
Let's meet on the road to Morocco,
It beats Central Park any time.
The funny streets are nice and dark, the
    music is unique.
You can be the kidnapped girl and I can be
    the sheik.
Tell the gang
So they won't
Hang around.
Like Webster's Dictionary,
We're Morocco bound.

—Jimmy Van Heusen

SLEIGH RIDE IN JULY

VERSE

If I were the type to play around
It wouldn't be so bad,
But I didn't know my way around,
And what a time I had!

REFRAIN

I was taken for a sleigh ride in July.
Oh, I must have been a set up for a sigh.

A mockingbird was whistling
A sentimental tune
And I didn't know enough to come in
Out of the moonlight.
So, the big romance was only make-
    believe,
Just a sleigh ride on a balmy summer eve.
My dreams were safe all winter,
And then to think that I
Was taken for a sleigh ride in July.

—*Jimmy Van Heusen*

SWINGING ON A STAR

REFRAIN 1

Would you like to swing on a star,
Carry moonbeams home in a jar,
And be better off than you are,
Or would you rather be a mule?

VERSE 1

A mule is an animal with long funny ears,
He kicks up at anything he hears.
His back is brawny and his brain is weak,
He's just plain stupid with a stubborn
    streak.
And by the way, if you hate to go to school,
You may grow up to be a mule.

REFRAIN 2

Or would you like to swing on a star,
Carry moonbeams home in a jar,
And be better off than you are,
Or would you rather be a pig?

VERSE 2

A pig is an animal with dirt on his face,
His shoes are a terrible disgrace.
He's got no manners when he eats
    his food,
He's fat and lazy and extremely rude.

But if you don't care a feather or a fig,
You may grow up to be a pig.

REFRAIN 3

Or would you like to swing on a star,
Carry moonbeams home in a jar,
And be better off than you are,
Or would you rather be a fish?

VERSE 3

A fish won't do anything but swim in a
    brook,
He can't write his name or read a book.
To fool the people is his only thought,
And though he's slippery, he still gets
    caught.
But then if that sort of life is what
    you wish,
You may grow up to be a fish.

REFRAIN 4

And all the monkeys aren't in the zoo,
Ev'ry day you meet quite a few,
So you see it's all up to you.
You can be better than you are.
You could be swinging on a star.

—*Jimmy Van Heusen*

WELCOME TO MY DREAM

VERSE

'Twas such a big surprise to see you
That I really got weak,
Couldn't even speak.
Let me apologize,
I stared and didn't offer my hand.
Hope you understand.

REFRAIN

Welcome to my dream
And how are you?

Will you be here long
Or just passing through?
Brush off that stardust.
Where have you been?
Don't tell me your rainbow
Was late getting in.
Welcome to my dream,
It now seems real.
You're what it needed
To make it ideal.
So glad you got here,
I hope you can stay,
But welcome to my dream
Anyway.

—Jimmy Van Heusen

You May Not Love Me

VERSE 1

HE: Here I am,
　　The same old fervent plea;
　　The would-be Romeo again
　　Waiting for that blow again.
　　Here I am,
　　The same old bended knee;

And yet the same old "No" again
Wouldn't worry me.

REFRAIN

You may not love me, but you may,
So, I don't dare to keep away.
Supposing you get lonely overnight,
You might not need me, but you might.
Perhaps I have no chance with you,
But then again, perhaps I do.
I only hope tomorrow won't be just
　　another day.
You may not love me, but you may.

VERSE 2

SHE: Here I am,
　　The same old hopeful me,
　　The would-be Juliet again
　　Throwing out my net again.
　　Here I am,
　　The same old balcony;
　　And if it's no duet again
　　That won't worry me.

REPEAT REFRAIN

—Jimmy Van Heusen

Don Raye (1909–1985)

H E WAS BORN Donald Macrae Wilhoite, Jr. (in Washington, D.C.), but it was as Don Raye that he became one of the quintessential voices of World War II, author of a string of bouncy, upbeat lyrics that perfectly typify one aspect of wartime America. There were the "boogie" songs–"Cow Cow Boogie" (which gave Ella Mae Morse and the Freddie Slack Orchestra Capitol Records' first hit) and the Andrew Sisters' "Boogie Woogie Bugle Boy" (brought back with a bang by Bette Midler in the seventies) and "Scrub Me Mama with a Boogie Beat." There was the number-one Harry James record of "Mr. Five by Five," and other swingers like "Milkman, Keep Those Bottles Quiet!" and "Beat Me Daddy, Eight to the Bar." And there were ballads, too– "You Don't Know What Love Is" and "I'll Remember April," later turned into a jazz standard by Miles Davis. Don Raye, who was Virginia's dancing champion at the age of fifteen, and who worked in vaudeville and nightclubs before serving in the armed forces, is an unfairly forgotten figure. He helped America make joyous music during an unjoyous time.

BOOGIE WOOGIE BUGLE BOY

(with Hughie Prince)

VERSE

He was a famous trumpet man from out
    Chicago way.
He had a "boogie" style that no one else
    could play.
He was the top man of his craft,
But then his number came up,
And he was gone with the draft.
He's in the army now,
A-blowin' reveille,
He's the Boogie Woogie Bugle Boy of
    Company B.

REFRAIN I

They made him blow a bugle for his
    Uncle Sam,

It really brought him down because he
    couldn't jam.
The captain seemed to understand,
Because the next day the "cap" went out
    and drafted a band,
And now the comp'ny jumps when he plays
    reveille,
He's the Boogie Woogie Bugle Boy of
    Company B.
A toot! A toot!

1. A toot diddle ah da toot. He blows it
    eight to the bar
  In "boogie" rhythm.
  He can't blow a note unless a bass and
    guitar
  Is playin' with 'im.
  He makes the comp'ny jump
  When he plays reveille,

He's the Boogie Woogie Bugle Boy of
Company B.

REFRAIN 2

He puts the boys to sleep with "boogie"
ev'ry night,
And wakes them up the same way in the
early bright.
They clap their hands and stamp
their feet
Because they know how he plays when
someone gives him a beat.
He really breaks it up when he plays
reveille,
He's the Boogie Woogie Bugle Boy of
Company B.

REPEAT 1

—Don Raye and Hughie Prince

I'll Remember April

(with Patricia Johnston)

This lovely day will lengthen into ev'ning.
We'll sigh good-bye to all we've ever had.
Alone,
Where we have walked together,
I'll remember April
And be glad.
I'll be content
You loved me once
In April.
Your lips were warm,
And love and Spring were new.
But I'm not afraid
Of Autumn and her sorrow,
For I'll remember
April and you.
The fire will dwindle into glowing ashes,
For flames and love live such a little while.
I won't forget,

But I won't be lonely,
I'll remember April,
And I'll smile.

—Gene De Paul

Milkman, Keep Those Bottles Quiet!

REFRAIN 1

Milkman, keep those bottles quiet!
Can't use that jive on my milk diet!
So, milkman, keep those bottles quiet!
Been jumpin' on the swing shift all night,
Turnin' out my quota all right.
Now I'm beat right down to the sod
And I've got to dig myself some nod.
So, milkman, keep those bottles quiet!
Quiet! quiet!

PATTER

Now the noise of the riveter I don't
mind it
'Cause the man with the whiskers has a lot
behind it,
But I can't keep punchin' with that
vict'ry crew
When you're makin' me punchy with that
bottled "moo."
I wanta give my all if I'm a-gonna give it,
But I gotta get my shut-eye if I'm gonna
rivet,
So bail out, Bud, with that-a milk
barrage,
'Cause it's unpatriotic, it's a sabotage.

REFRAIN 2

Milkman, stop that Grade A riot!
Cut out if you can't lullaby it!
Oh, milkman, keep those bottles quiet!
Been knockin' out a fat tank all day,
Workin' on a bomber okay.

Boy, you blast my wig with those clinks
And I've got to get my forty winks.
So, milkman, keep those bottles quiet!
Quiet! quiet!

—Gene De Paul

MISTER FIVE BY FIVE

VERSE

Well, twirl my turban! Man alive!
Here comes Mister Five by Five.
He's one of those big fat bouncin' boys,
Solid avoir du pois!

REFRAIN

Mister Five by Five,
He's five feet tall and he's five feet wide,
He don't measure no mo'
From head to toe
Than he do from side to side.
Mister Five by Five,
Got fifteen chins and a line of jive.
He's a mellow ol' cat,
A real "hep fat,"
He be Mister Five by Five.
That man
Can really jump it for a fat man,
The only trouble is there's no way of
    knowin'
Whether he's comin' on or goin'.
Mister Five by Five,

He's slightly plump on the solid side.
He don't shake it no mo'
From head to toe
Than he do from side to side.

—Gene De Paul

YOU DON'T KNOW WHAT LOVE IS

You don't know what love is
Until you've learned the meaning of the
    blues,
Until you've loved a love you've had
    to lose,
You don't know what love is.
You don't know how lips hurt
Until you've kissed and had to pay the cost;
Until you've flipped your heart and you
    have lost,
You don't know what love is.
Do you know
How a lost heart fears the thought of
    reminiscing?
And how lips that taste of tears
Lose their taste for kissing?
You don't know how hearts burn
For love that cannot live, yet never dies.
Until you've faced each dawn with
    sleepless eyes,
You don't know what love is.

—Gene De Paul

Don George (1909–1985)

Unquestionably, Don George's biggest hit was "The Yellow Rose of Texas," to an old minstrel tune, which in 1955 spent six weeks at number one, as recorded by Mitch Miller. But George came from New York, not Texas, and he is more likely to be remembered for his brilliant collaborations with Duke Ellington on "I'm Beginning to See the Light," and others; his work with Nat King Cole; and his notorious memoir of Ellington, *Sweet Man*.

I Ain't Got Nothin' but the Blues

Ain't got the change of a nickel,
Ain't got no bounce in my shoes,
Ain't got no fancy to tickle,
I ain't got nothin' but the blues.
Ain't got no coffee that's perkin',
Ain't got no winnings to lose,
Ain't got a dream that is workin',
I ain't got nothin' but the blues.
When trumpets flare up
I keep my hair up,
I just can't make it come down.
Believe me, Pappy,
I can't get happy,
Since my everlovin' baby left town.
Ain't got no rest on my slumbers,
Ain't got no feelings to bruise,
Ain't got no telephone numbers,
I ain't got nothin' but the blues.

—Duke Ellington

I'm Beginning to See the Light

I never cared much for moonlit skies,
I never wink back at fireflies,
But now that the stars are in your eyes,
I'm beginning to see the light.
I never went in for afterglow,
Or candlelight on the mistletoe,
But now when you turn the lamp down low
I'm beginning to see the light.
Used to ramble through the park,
Shadowboxing in the dark,
Then you came and caused a spark
That's a four-alarm fire now.
I never made love by lantern shine,
I never saw rainbows in my wine,
But now that your lips are burning mine,
I'm beginning to see the light.

—Johnny Hodges, Duke Ellington, and
  Harry James

It Shouldn't Happen to a Dream

Millions of stars playing tag in the skies,
All of my hope living right in your eyes,
So much at stake, and then I wake up—
It shouldn't happen to a dream.
Light-fingered clouds tuck the moon
    into bed,
I feel your lips stand my heart on its head,

Then comes the ache, again I'll wake up—
It shouldn't happen to a dream.
The flowers get happy and dance in
    the lane,
The darkness no longer is deep.
We're meant for each other, it's perfectly
    plain
Each time you walk in my sleep.
Here comes the night cutting capers
    again,
Just for a while you'll be with me,
    and then
The bubble will break, again I'll wake up—
It shouldn't happen to a dream.

       —Johnny Hodges and Duke Ellington

It's Kind of Lonesome Out Tonight

Wish I had a place to walk to,
Wish there was a star in sight,
Wish I had a friend to talk to,
It's kind of lonesome out tonight.
Wish it wasn't getting colder,
Wish the moon would give some light,
Wish my head could find a shoulder,
It's kind of lonesome out tonight.
I look at the passing lovers
That slowly wander by.

My heart shakes its head and whispers,
How many times can I die?
Wish I knew some lips to borrow,
Wish someone would hold me tight,
How I wish it was tomorrow,
It's kind of lonesome out tonight.

       —Duke Ellington

Tulip or Turnip

Tulip or turnip, rosebud or rhubarb,
Filet or plain beef stew,
Tell me, tell me, tell me, dreamface,
What am I to you?
Diamond or doorknob, sapphire or
    sawdust,
Champagne or just home brew,
Tell me, tell me, tell me, dreamface,
What am I to you?
Do I get the booby prize
Or will you be the hero?
Am I heading for blue skies,
Or is my ceiling zero?
Tulip or turnip, moonbeam or mudpie,
Bankroll or I.O.U.,
Tell me, tell me, tell me, dreamface,
What am I to you?

       —Duke Ellington

George Marion, Jr. (1909–1968)

G EORGE MARION, JR., had a varied career—as librettist, scenarist, and short-story writer, as well as lyricist. Born in Boston, he had been educated in Switzerland and at Harvard, perhaps overkill for his early work as a title-writer for such silent films as *It, Ella Cinders,* and *Son of the Sheik*. He wrote lyrics for a number of Hollywood movies, often in collaboration with Richard Whiting, and worked on the screenplays for *The Gay Divorcée* and *Love Me Tonight,* among others. He also wrote the book for a number of Broadway shows, including the Rodgers and Hart *Too Many Girls* and Fats Waller's *Early to Bed* (lyrics as well as book).

THE LADIES WHO SING WITH A BAND

VERSE

There's an inn in Indiana with a very
    goodly clientele
Of junior jerks from the boilerworks who
    thought my singin' swell.
I'd a voice so sweet an' low, I guess my
    dress was even lower still.
Sellin' vocals to those yokels was my first
    important thrill.

REFRAIN

Should your career need a
    springboard,
Here is the best in the land.
Rise and rejoice
For you don't need a voice,
Join the ladies who sing with a band.
Who's in the Hollywood spotlight?
Who do producers demand?
They're making Duses
Of all the chantoosers,
The ladies who sing with a band.
Flat tone,

That tone (wah!)
Can never hurt a singer with curves.
You'll see fans stand
Around your bandstand
If you've a tropical torso
And your digestion is grand.
You may do finer
Than Ginny or Dinah,
The ladies who sing with a band.
Dottie or Janet or Helen or Ina,
They don't need to know from a major or
    minor
The ladies who sing with a band.

—Thomas "Fats" Waller

LOVE IS A RANDOM THING

VERSE I
SHE: Straight from the heart
    department, dear,
    I bring you a sweeping statement:
    You seem to be the mate meant
    for me.
    Why in the name of common sense

Were all of my young dreams wasted?
Never in one your face did I see.
If this is all a big surprise to you,
Me too!

REFRAIN

Why must love be such a random thing?
Unpredictable as early spring.
Why no choir praising the joy I was to find?
And why am I the one to be overwhelmed,
    undermined?
Where's that heart I thought could feel
    no pain?
Where's that detour sign in Lover's Lane?
Why no warning until the bells began to
    ring and sing?
Why must love be such a random thing?

VERSE 2

HE: Dear, in the lovely dream parade
    That marched by my pillow nightly
    You were not even slightly in view.
    There's been a great mistake, I fear.
    I felt it when first you came in,
    Someone would put a claim in
        for you.
    A fugitive from someone else's
        dream,
    You seem!

REPEAT REFRAIN

—*Sammy Fain*

MY FUTURE JUST PASSED

VERSE

You will find my past not spotless
If you care to delve.
Twenty broken hearts and not less
Before I was twelve.
But from then on I stopped;

From the parade I dropped.
Hopes of future loves I'd started to shelve.

REFRAIN

1) HE: There goes the girl I dreamed all
        through school about,
    There goes the girl I'll now be a
        fool about.

2) SHE: He is my fate with capital "F" in it,
    Now in my dreams there'll be
        someone definite.

Ring down the curtain, I'm certain at
    present
My future just passed.
Don't even know if she/he has been
    spoken for,
If she/he is tied, the ties must be
    broken, for
Life can't be that way, to wake me, then
    break me.
My future just passed.

1) HE: Stars in the blue, though you're at
        a distance,
    You can at least do this:
    Sometimes a boy encounters
        resistance.
    Help me to win this miss.
    Here are my arms, may she find
        illusion there,
    Look in my heart, there is no
        confusion there,
    Now that I'm loving, I'm living
        at last,
    My future just passed.

2) SHE: Stars in the blue, though you're at
        a distance,
    You can assure me, but
    Sometimes a girl encounters
        resistance.

Help me to win this boy.
Here are my arms, may he find
    illusion there,
Kiss my two lips, remove all the
    rouge on them,
Now that I'm loving, I'm living
    at last.
My future just passed.

—Richard Whiting

THERE'S A MAN IN MY LIFE

VERSE

Long ago and far away
I met the right love.
He had fortune and he had fame,
Things that put to flight love.
Spring was near and me he viewed
As a winter interlude.

REFRAIN

There's a man in my life
Responsible for
The kind of life I lead.
He's the talk of my heart,
When thoughts of him start
I find myself all a-tremble
Like a windblown reed.
To one who never met him,
This might seem extreme,
Yet his charm still makes me lay down and
    dream.
Every song in my soul,
Each plan in my life,
Has one unattainable goal:
That man in my life,
That man in my life.

—Thomas "Fats" Waller

Johnny Mercer (1909–1976)

J OHNNY MERCER CAME from a well-to-do Savannah family that, during his youth, fell on hard times. Instead of going to college, he went to New York and a struggling existence as a bit player on and off Broadway. A lyric he wrote was incorporated into *The Garrick Gaieties of 1930*, and soon afterward he won a singing competition and joined Paul Whiteman's Orchestra, replacing Bing Crosby and his Rhythm Boys; Mercer was later to write many hits for Crosby. "Lazybones," with music by Hoagy Carmichael, was his first smash hit—it was 1933—and dozens followed, songs in just about every genre and mood, and written with most of the major composers of his day, most importantly Carmichael ("Skylark"); Harold Arlen ("Blues in the Night"); Richard Whiting ("Too Marvelous for Words"); Harry Warren ("You Must Have Been a Beautiful Baby"); Jerome Kern ("You Were Never Lovelier"); and Henry Mancini ("Moon River"). His songs, whether ballads or specialty numbers, all seem easy, relaxed, inevitable—and American. Which may explain why he won four Oscars and holds the record for most number-one songs on the Hit Parade—fourteen. He had remained a terrific singer, and in the forties he became a big recording star: four of his records reached number one, and well over a dozen were in the top ten. Along the way he wrote several memorable Broadway shows—*St. Louis Woman, Top Banana, L'il Abner*. Oh, yes—he was also one of the three founders of Capitol Records.

ACCENTUATE THE POSITIVE

VERSE

Gather 'round me,
Ev'rybody,
Gather 'round me
While I preach some.
Feel a sermon
Comin' on me.
The topic will be sin,
And that's what I'm agin'.
If you wanna
Hear my story,
Then settle back
And just sit tight

While I start reviewin'
The attitude of doin' right.

REFRAIN

You've got to
Accent-tchu-ate the positive,
E-lim-my-nate the negative,
Latch on to the affirmative,
Don't mess with Mister In-between.
You've got to spread joy
Up to the maximum,
Bring gloom down to the minimum,
Have faith, or pandemonium
Li'ble to walk upon the scene.
To illustrate my last remark,

Jonah in the whale, Noah in the Ark,
What did they do
Just when everything looked so dark?
"Man," they said,
"We better
Accent-tchu-ate the positive,
E-lim-my-nate the negative,
Latch on
To the affirmative,
Don't mess with Mister In-between."
No, don't mess with Mister In-between.

—*Harold Arlen*

Arthur Murray Taught Me Dancing in a Hurry

VERSE
Life was so peaceful at the drive-in,
Life was so calm and serene,
Life was très gay
Till that unlucky day
I happened to read that magazine.
Why did I read that advertisement
Where it said . . .
"Since I rumba, Jim thinks I'm sublime."
Why, oh why,
Did I ever try
When I didn't have the talent,
Didn't have the money,
And teacher did not have the time.

REFRAIN
Arthur Murray taught me dancing in a
    hurry.
I had a week to spare.
He showed me the groundwork,
The walkin' around work,
And told me to take it from there.
Arthur Murray then advised me not to
    worry.
It'd come out all right.

To my way of thinkin',
It came out stinkin,'
I don't know my left from my right.
The people around me can all sing
A-one and a-two and a-three,
But any resemblance to waltzing
Is just coincidental with me,
'Cause Arthur Murray taught me dancing
    in a hurry.
And so I take a chance.
To me it resembles the nine-day trembles,
But he guarantees
It's a dance.

—*Victor Schertzinger*

Blues in the Night

My mama done tol' me
When I was in knee pants [pigtails]
My mama done tol' me–son [hon],
A woman'll sweet talk [man's gonna
    sweet talk],
And give ya the big eye,
But when the sweet talkin's done
A woman's a two-face [a man is a two-face],
A worrisome thing
Who'll leave ya t'sing
The blues in the night.
Now the rain's a-fallin',
Hear the train a-callin'
Whooee
(My mama done tol' me).
Hear that lonesome whistle
Blowin' 'cross the trestle,
Whooee
(My mama done tol' me),
A whooee-duh-whooee,
Ol' clickety clack's
A-cchoin' back
The blues in the night.
The evenin' breeze'll start

The trees to cryin'
And the moon'll hide its light,
When you get the blues in the night.
Take my word, the mockingbird'll
Sing the saddest kind of song,
He knows things are wrong
And he's right.
From Natchez to Mobile,
From Memphis to St. Jo,
Wherever the four winds blow;
I been in some big towns
An' heard me some big talk,
But there is one thing I know,
A woman's a two-face [a man is a two-face],
A worrisome thing
Who'll leave ya t'sing
The blues in the night.
My mama was right,
There's blues in the night.

—Harold Arlen

Come Rain or Come Shine

I'm gonna love you
Like nobody's loved you,
Come rain or come shine.
High as a mountain
And deep as a river,
Come rain or come shine.
I guess when you met me
It was just one of those things,
But don't ever bet me,
'Cause I'm gonna be true if you let me.
You're gonna love me
Like nobody's loved me,
Come rain or come shine.
Happy together,
Unhappy together,
And won't it be fine?
Days may be cloudy or sunny,
We're in or we're out of the money,

But I'm with you always,
I'm with you rain or shine!

—Harold Arlen

Day In—Day Out

Day in—day out,
The same old hoodoo follows me about.
The same old pounding in my heart
Whenever I think of you,
And, darling, I think of you
Day in—day out.
Day out—day in,
I needn't tell you how my days begin.
When I awake I awaken with a tingle,
One possibility in view,
That possibility of maybe seeing you.
Come rain, come shine,
I meet you and to me the day is fine.
Then I kiss your lips
And the pounding becomes
The ocean's roar,
A thousand drums.
Can't you see it's love?
Can there be any doubt?
When there it is,
Day in—day out.

—Rube Bloom

Early Autumn

When an early Autumn walks the land
And chills the breeze
And touches with her hand
The Summer trees,
Perhaps you'll understand
What memories I own.
There's a dance pavilion in the rain
All shuttered down,

A winding country lane all russet brown,
A frosty windowpane shows me a town
    grown lonely.
That Spring of ours that started
So April hearted
Seemed made for just a boy and girl.
I never dreamed, did you,
Any Fall could come in view so early, early?
Darling, if you care,
Please let me know,
I'll meet you anywhere,
I miss you so.
Let's never have to share
Another early Autumn.

    —Ralph Burns and Woody Herman

GLOW-WORM

Glow, little glow-worm, fly of fire,
Glow like an incandescent wire,
Glow for the female of the specie,
Turn on the A-C and the D-C.
This night could use a little brightnin',
Light up, you li'l ol' bug of lightnin',
When you gotta glow, you gotta glow,
Glow, little glow-worm, glow.
Glow, little glow-worm, glow and glimmer,
Swim through the sea of night, little
    swimmer,
Thou aer-o-nau-tic-al boll weevil,
Il-lu-mi-nate yon woods primeval.
See how the shadows deep and darken,
You and your chick should get to sparkin',
I got a gal that I love so,
Glow, little glow-worm, glow.
Glow, little glow-worm, turn the key on,
You are equipped with taillight neon.
You got a cute vest-pocket Mazda
Which you can make both slow or
    "Fazda":
I don't know who you took a shine to

Or who you're out to make a sign to,
I got a gal that I love so,
Glow, little glow-worm, glow.

    —Paul Lincke

HOORAY FOR HOLLYWOOD

Hooray for Hollywood!
That screwy bally-hooey Hollywood,
Where any office boy or young mechanic
Can be a panic
With just a good-looking pan,
And any bar maid
Can be star maid,
If she dances with or without a fan.
Hooray for Hollywood!
Where you're terrific if you're even good,
Where anyone at all from Shirley Temple
To Aimee Semple
Is equally understood.
Go out and try your luck,
You might be Donald Duck!
Hooray for Hollywood!
Hooray for Hollywood!
That phony super Coney Hollywood,
They come from Chilicothes and Paducahs
With their bazookas
To get their names up in lights,
All armed with photos from local rotos,
With their hair in ribbons and legs in
    tights.
Hooray for Hollywood!
You may be homely in your neighborhood,
But if you think that you can be an actor,
See Mister Factor,
He'd make a monkey look good.
Within a half an hour,
You'll look like Tyrone Power!
Hooray for Hollywood!

    —Richard A. Whiting

How Little We Know

Maybe it happens this way,
Maybe we really belong together,
But after all, how little we know.
Maybe it's just for a day,
Love is as changeable as the weather,
And after all, how little we know.
Who knows why an April breeze never
    remains?
Why stars in the trees hide when it rains?
Love comes along casting a spell,
Will it sing you a song,
Will it say a farewell?
Who can tell!
Maybe you're meant to be mine,
Maybe I'm only supposed to stay in your
    arms a while,
As others have done.
Is that what I've waited for?
Am I the one?
Oh, I hope in my heart that it's so,
In spite of how little we know.

—Hoagy Carmichael

I Remember You

VERSE
Was it in Tahiti?
Were we on the Nile?
Long, long ago,
Say an hour or so,
I recall that I saw your smile.

REFRAIN
I remember you.
You're the one who made my dreams
    come true
A few kisses ago.
I remember you.

You're the one who said, "I love
    you, too."
I do. Didn't you know?
I remember, too, a distant bell
And stars that fell
Like rain, out of the blue.
When my life is through
And the angels ask me to recall
The thrill of them all,
Then I shall tell them
I remember you.

—Victor Schertzinger

I Thought About You

VERSE
Seems that I read, or somebody said,
That out of sight is out of mind.
Maybe that's so, but I tried to go
And leave you behind,
What did I find?

REFRAIN
I took a trip on the train,
And I thought about you.
I passed a shadowy lane,
And I thought about you.
Two or three cars parked under the
    stars,
A winding stream,
Moon shining down on some
    little town,
And with each beam,
Same old dream.
At ev'ry stop that we made,
Oh, I thought about you.
But when I pulled down the shade,
Then I really felt blue.
I peeked through the crack
And looked at the track,
The one going back to you,

And what did I do?
I thought about you!

—Jimmy Van Heusen

I Wonder What Became of Me

Lights are bright,
Pianos making music all the night,
And they pour champagne just like it
    was rain.
It's a sight to see,
But I wonder what became of me.
Crowds go by,
That merrymaking laughter in their eye,
And the laughter's fine,
But I wonder what became of mine.
Life's sweet as honey
And yet it's funny,
I get a feeling that I can't analyze.
It's like, well, maybe,
Like when a baby
Sees a bubble burst before its eyes.
Oh, I've had my fling,
I've been around and seen most
    ev'rything,
Oh, I've had my thrills,
They've lit my cigarettes with dollar bills,
But I can't be gay,
For along the way
Something went astray.
And I can't explain,
It's the same champagne,
It's a sight to see,
But I wonder what became of me.

—Harold Arlen

I'm Old-Fashioned

VERSE
I am not such a clever one
About the latest fads.
I admit I was never one
Adored by local lads.
Not that I ever try to be a saint,
I'm the type that they classify as quaint.

REFRAIN
I'm old-fashioned,
I love the moonlight,
I love the old-fashioned things—
The sound of rain
Upon a windowpane,
The starry song that April sings.
This year's fancies
Are passing fancies,
But sighing sighs, holding hands,
These my heart understands.
I'm old-fashioned,
But I don't mind it,
That's how I want to be,
As long as you agree
To stay old-fashioned with me.

—Jerome Kern

Jeepers Creepers

VERSE
I don't care what the weatherman says.
When the weatherman says it's raining,
You'll never hear me complaining,
I'm certain the sun will shine.
I don't care how the weathervane points.
When the weathervane points to
    gloomy,
It's gotta be sunny to me,
When your eyes look into mine.

REFRAIN

Jeepers creepers!
Where'd ya get those peepers?
Jeepers creepers!
Where'd ya get those eyes?
Gosh all git up!
How'd they get so lit up?
Gosh all git up!
How'd they get that size?
Golly gee!
When you turn those heaters on,
Woe is me!
Got to put my cheaters on.
Jeepers creepers!
Where'd ya get those peepers?
Oh! Those weepers!
How they hypnotize!
Where'd ya get those eyes?

—Harry Warren

LAURA

VERSE

You know the feeling
Of something half remembered,
Of something that never happened,
Yet you recall it well.
You know the feeling
Of recognizing someone
That you've never met
As far as you could tell; well:

REFRAIN

Laura is the face in the misty light,
Footsteps that you hear down the hall,
The laugh that floats on a summer night
That you can never quite recall.
And you see Laura
On the train that is passing through,
Those eyes, how familiar they seem.
She gave your very first kiss to you.

That was Laura,
But she's only a dream.

—David Raksin

MIDNIGHT SUN

Your lips were like a red and ruby chalice,
Warmer than the summer night.
The clouds were like an alabaster palace
Rising to a snowy height.
Each star its own aurora borealis,
Suddenly you held me tight.
I could see the midnight sun.
I can't explain the silver rain that found me,
Or was that a moonlight veil?
The music of the universe around me,
Or was that a nightingale?
And then your arms miraculously
    found me,
Suddenly the sky turned pale.
I could see the midnight sun.
Was there such a night?
It's a thrill I still don't quite believe.
But after you were gone,
There was still some stardust on my sleeve.
The flame of it may dwindle to an ember,
And the stars forget to shine,
And we may see the meadow in December,
Icy white and crystalline.
But, oh, my darling, always I'll remember
When your lips were close to mine,
And I saw the midnight sun.

—Sonny Burke and Lionel Hampton

MOON RIVER

Moon River,
Wider than a mile:
I'm crossin' you in style

Some day.
Old dreammaker,
You heartbreaker,
Wherever you're goin',
I'm goin' your way.
Two drifters
Off to see the world,
There's such a lot of world
To see.
We're after the same
Rainbow's end
Waitin' 'round the bend,
My huckleberry friend,
Moon River
And me.

—Henry Mancini

MY SHINING HOUR

VERSE

This moment, this minute
And each second in it,
Will leave a glow upon the sky,
And as time goes by,
It will never die.

REFRAIN

This will be my shining hour,
Calm and happy and bright.
In my dreams, your face will flower,
Through the darkness of the night.
Like the lights of home before me,
Or an angel watching o'er me,
This will be my shining hour,
Till I'm with you again.

—Harold Arlen

ON THE ATCHISON, TOPEKA AND THE SANTA FE

Do yuh hear that whistle down the line?
I figure that it's engine number forty-nine,
She's the only one that'll sound that way
On the Atchison, Topeka and the Santa Fe.
See the ol' smoke risin' 'round the bend,
I reckon that she knows she's gonna meet
    a friend.
Folks around these parts get the time o' day
From the Atchison, Topeka and the
    Santa Fe.
Here she comes!
Ooh, Ooh, Ooh,
Hey, Jim! yuh better git the rig!
Ooh, Ooh, Ooh,
She's got a list o' passengers that's
    pretty big,
And they'll all want lifts to Brown's Hotel,
'Cause lots 'o them been travelin' for quite
    a spell,
All the way from Philadelphiay,
On the Atchison, Topeka and the Santa Fe.

—Harry Warren

ONE FOR MY BABY
(AND ONE MORE FOR THE ROAD)

It's quarter to three,
There's no one in the place except you
    and me,
So, set 'em up, Joe,
I've got a little story you oughta know.
We're drinking, my friend,
To the end of a brief episode,
Make it one for my baby
And one more for the road.
I got the routine,
So drop another nickel in the machine.

I'm feelin' so bad,
I wish you'd make the music dreamy
    and sad.
Could tell you a lot,
But you've got to be true to your code,
Make it one for my baby
And one more for the road.
You'd never know it,
But, buddy, I'm kind of a poet
And I've gotta lotta things to say.
And when I'm gloomy,
You simply gotta listen to me,
Until it's talked away.
Well, that's how it goes,
And Joe, I know you're anxious to close,
So thanks for the cheer,
I hope you didn't mind my bending your ear.
This torch, I've found,
Must be drowned or it soon might explode.
Make it one for my baby
And one more for the road,
That long, long road.

—Harold Arlen

Out of This World

You're clear out of this world.
When I'm looking at you
I hear out of this world
The music that no mortal ever knew.
You're right out of a book,
The fairy tale I read when I was so high.
No armored knight out of a book
Was more enchanted by a Lorelei
Than I.
After waiting so long for the right time,
After reaching so long for a star,
All at once, from the long and lonely
    nighttime,
And despite time,
Here you are.

I'd cry out of this world
If you said we were through,
So let me fly out of this world
And spend the next eternity or two
With you.

—Harold Arlen

P.S. I Love You

VERSE
What is there to write,
What is there to say?
Same things happen ev'ry day.
Not a thing to write,
Not a thing to say,
So I take my pen in hand and start
The same old way.

REFRAIN
Dear, I thought I'd drop a line,
The weather's cool,
The folks are fine;
I'm in bed each night at nine.
P.S. I love you.
Yesterday we had some rain,
But all in all
I can't complain.
Was it dusty on the train?
P.S. I love you.
Write to the Browns just as soon as
    you're able,
They came around to call.
I burned a hole in the dining room table,
And let me see, I guess that's all.
Nothing else for me to say,
And so I'll close,
But by the way,
Ev'rybody's thinking of you.
P.S. I love you.

—Gordon Jenkins

Satin Doll

Cigarette holder
Which wigs me.
Over her shoulder
She digs me.
Out cattin',
That satin doll.
Baby, shall we go
Out skippin'?
Careful, amigo,
You're flippin'.
Speaks Latin,
That satin doll.
She's nobody's fool,
So I'm playin' it cool as can be.
I'll give it a whirl,
But I ain't for no girl catchin' me.
Telephone numbers,
Well, you know.
Doin' my rumbas,
With uno,
And that's my satin doll.

—Duke Ellington and Billy Strayhorn

Skylark

Skylark,
Have you anything to say to me?
Won't you tell me where my love can be?
Is there a meadow in the mist
Where someone's waiting to be kissed?
Skylark,
Have you seen a valley green with Spring
Where my heart can go a-journeying,
Over the shadows and the rain
To a blossom-covered lane?
And in your lonely flight,
Haven't you heard the music in the
   night,

Wonderful music,
Faint as a "will-o-the-wisp,"
Crazy as a loon,
Sad as a gypsy serenading the moon.
Oh, skylark,
I don't know if you can find these
   things,
But my heart is riding on your wings,
So if you see them anywhere,
Won't you lead me there?

—Hoagy Carmichael

Something's Gotta Give

When an irresistible force such as you
Meets an old immovable object like me,
You can bet as sure as you live,
Something's gotta give,
Something's gotta give,
Something's gotta give.
When an irrepressible smile such as
   yours
Warms an old implacable heart such
   as mine,
Don't say no, because I insist
Somewhere, somehow,
Someone's gonna be kissed.
So, en garde, who knows what the fates
   have in store
From their vast mysterious sky?
I'll try hard ignoring those lips I adore,
But how long can anyone try?
Fight, fight, fight, fight,
Fight it with all of our might.
Chances are, some heavenly star-spangled
   night
We'll find out as sure as we live,
Something's gotta give,
Something's gotta give,
Something's gotta give.

TANGERINE

VERSE

South American stories
Tell of a girl who's quite a dream,
The beauty of her race.
Though you doubt all the stories
And think the tales
Are just a bit extreme,
Wait till you see her face.

REFRAIN

Tangerine,
She is all they claim,
With her eyes of night
And lips as bright as flame.
Tangerine,
When she dances by,
Señoritas stare
And caballeros sigh.
And I've seen
Toasts to Tangerine
Raised in ev'ry bar
Across the Argentine.
Yes, she has them all on the run,
But her heart belongs to just one.
Her heart belongs to Tangerine.

—Victor Schertzinger

THAT OLD BLACK MAGIC

That old black magic has me in its spell,
That old black magic that you weave
    so well.
Those icy fingers up and down my spine,
The same old witchcraft when your eyes
    meet mine.
The same old tingle that I feel inside,
And then that elevator starts its ride,
And down and down I go,

'Round and 'round I go
Like a leaf that's caught in the tide.
I should stay away,
But what can I do?
I hear your name
And I'm aflame,
Aflame with such a burning desire
That only your kiss
Can put out the fire.
For you're the lover I have waited for,
The mate that fate had me created for,
And ev'ry time your lips meet mine,
Darling, down and down I go,
'Round and 'round I go
In a spin,
Loving the spin I'm in,
Under that old black magic called love!

—Harold Arlen

TOO MARVELOUS FOR WORDS

VERSE

I search for phrases
To sing your praises,
But there aren't any magic adjectives
To tell you all you are.

REFRAIN

You're just too marvelous,
Too marvelous for words,
Like glorious, glamorous,
And that old standby, amorous.
It's all too wonderful,
I'll never find the words
That say enough,
Tell enough,
I mean, they just aren't swell enough.
You're much too much,
And just too very very!
To ever be in Webster's Dictionary.
And so I'm borrowing

A love song from the birds,
To tell you that you're marvelous,
Too marvelous for words.

—*Richard A. Whiting*

You Must Have Been a Beautiful Baby

VERSE

Does your mother realize
The stork delivered quite a prize
The day he left you on the family tree?
Does your dad appreciate
That you are merely super-great,
The miracle of any century?
If they don't, just send them both
    to me.

REFRAIN

You must have been a beautiful baby,
You must have been a beautiful child.
When you were only startin'
To go to kindergarten,
I bet you drove the little boys wild.
And when it came to winning blue
    ribbons,
You must have shown the other
    kids how.
I can see the judges' eyes
As they handed you the prize,
I bet you made the cutest bow.
Oh! You must have been a
    beautiful baby,
'Cause, baby, look at you now.

—*Harry Warren*

You Were Never Lovelier

VERSE

I was never able
To recite a fable
That would make the party bright.
Sitting at the table
I was never able
To become the host's delight.
But now you've given me
My after-dinner story,
I'll just describe you
As you are in all your glory.

REFRAIN

You were never lovelier,
You were never so fair.
Dreams were never lovelier,
Pardon me if I stare.
Down the sky
The moonbeams fly
To light your face;
I can only say
They chose the proper place.
You were never lovelier,
And to coin a new phrase,
I was never luckier
In my palmiest days.
Make a note,
And you can quote me,
Honor bright.
You were never lovelier
Than you are tonight.

—*Jerome Kern*

Frank Loesser (1910–1969)

O F ALL the major songwriters, Frank Loesser is the one with a career most sharply divided in two: his early period in Hollywood, writing lyrics to other composers' music, and his later Broadway career as composer/lyricist of an extraordinary group of ambitious hit shows. The latter period, of course, is the better known—for the classic *Guys and Dolls* first and foremost, but also for *Where's Charley?, How to Succeed in Business Without Really Trying* (which won the Pulitzer Prize for drama), and the music drama *Most Happy Fella.* These shows made him one of only a handful of writers who supplied both music and words for a series of major Broadway successes. Loesser, whose family occupation was classical music, was born in New York City and worked as a reporter, a pianist, a singer, a caricaturist in vaudeville, even a process-server, but he quickly established himself in Hollywood in the mid-thirties, writing hit songs for such diverse stars as Dorothy Lamour ("Moon of Manakoora"); Bette Davis ("They're Either Too Young or Too Old"); Bob Hope and Shirley Ross ("Two Sleepy People"); Marlene Dietrich ("The Boys in the Backroom"); Betty Hutton ("Murder, He Says"); and Esther Williams, Ricardo Montalban, and friends. ("Baby, It's Cold Outside"), which won an Oscar. During World War II, while serving in the armed forces, he wrote several successful war songs, including the number-one hit "Praise the Lord and Pass the Ammunition." By then he was composing his own tunes, and when peace came, he was off to Broadway and his lasting place in theater history.

ADELAIDE'S LAMENT

VERSE 1

[Reads] It says here:
[Sung] The av'rage unmarried female,
Basically insecure,
Due to some long frustration, may react
With psychosomatic symptoms,
Difficult to endure,
Affecting the upper respiratory tract.
In other words, just from waiting around
For that plain little band of gold,
A person can develop a cold.
You can spray her wherever you figure

The streptococci lurk,
You can give her a shot
For whatever she's got
But it just won't work.
If she's tired of getting the fish-eye
From the hotel clerk,
A person can develop a cold.

VERSE 2

[Reads] It says here:
[Sung] The female remaining single,
Just in the legal sense,
Shows a neurotic tendency. See note,
[Spoken] Note:

[Sung] Chronic, organic syndromes,
Toxic or hypertense,
Involving the eye,
The ear and the nose and the throat.
In other words, just from worrying
　　whether
The wedding is on or off,
A person can develop a cough.
You can feed her all day with the vitamin A
And the Bromo Fizz,
But the medicine never gets
　　anywhere near
Where the trouble is.
If she's getting a kind of name for herself
And the name ain't "his,"
A person can develop a cough.
And furthermore,
Just from stalling and stalling
And stalling the wedding trip,
A person can develop la grippe.
When they get on the train for Niag'ra,
And she can hear church bells chime,
The compartment is air-conditioned,
And the mood sublime.
Then they get off at Saratoga
For the fourteenth time,
A person can develop la grippe.
La grippe,
La post-nasal drip,
With the wheezes and the sneezes,
And a sinus that's really a pip!
From a lack of community property
And a feeling she's getting too old,
A person can develop a bad, bad cold.

BABY, IT'S COLD OUTSIDE

REFRAIN 1
SHE: I really can't stay!
HE: But baby it's cold outside!
SHE: I've got to go 'way!

HE: But baby it's cold outside!
SHE: This evening has been . . .
HE: Been hoping that you'd drop in!
SHE: So very nice.
HE: I'll hold your hands, they're just
　　like ice.
SHE: My mother will start to worry . . .
HE: Beautiful, what's your hurry?
SHE: And Father will be pacing the
　　floor . . .
HE: Listen to the fireplace roar!
SHE: So really I'd better scurry.
HE: Beautiful, please, don't hurry.
SHE: Well, maybe just a half a
　　drink more.
HE: Put some records on while I pour.
SHE: The neighbors might think . . .
HE: But baby it's bad out there.
SHE: Say, what's in this drink?
HE: No cabs to be had out there.
SHE: I wish I knew how . . .
HE: Your eyes are like starlight now.
SHE: To break the spell.
HE: I'll take your hat. Your hair looks
　　swell.
SHE: I ought to say, "No, no, no, sir!"
HE: Mind if I move in closer?
SHE: At least I'm gonna say that I tried.
HE: What's the sense of hurting my
　　pride?
SHE: I really can't stay . . .
HE: Oh baby don't hold out.
SHE: Ah, but it's . . .
HE: Baby it's . . .
BOTH: Cold outside.

REFRAIN 2
SHE: I simply must go!
HE: But baby it's cold outside!
SHE: The answer is No!
HE: But baby it's cold outside!
SHE: The welcome has been . . .

HE: How lucky that you dropped in!

SHE: So nice and warm.

HE: Look out the window at that storm.

SHE: My sister will be suspicious . . .

HE: Gosh, your lips look delicious.

SHE: My brother will be there at the door . . .

HE: Waves upon a tropical shore!

SHE: My maiden aunt's mind is vicious . . .

HE: Gosh, your lips are delicious.

SHE: Well, maybe just a cigarette more.

HE: Never such a blizzard before.

SHE: I've got to get home . . .

HE: But baby you'd freeze out there.

SHE: Say, lend me a comb . . .

HE: It's up to your knees out there.

SHE: You've really been grand . . .

HE: I thrill when you touch my hand.

SHE: But don't you see . . .

HE: How can you do this thing to me?

SHE: There's bound to be talk tomorrow . . .

HE: Think of my lifelong sorrow.

SHE: At least there will be plenty implied . . .

HE: If you caught pneumonia and died . . .

SHE: I really can't stay . . .

HE: Get over that old doubt . . .

SHE: Ah, but it's

HE: Baby it's

BOTH: Cold outside.

THE BOYS IN THE BACKROOM

VERSE

See what the boys in the backroom
    will have
And tell them I'm having the same.

Go see what the boys in the backroom
    will have
And give them the poison they name.

REFRAIN

And when I die,
Don't spend my money on flowers
Or my pictures in a frame,
Just see what the boys in the backroom
    will have
And tell them I sighed,
And tell them I cried,
And tell them I died of the same!
And when I die,
Don't buy a casket of silver
With the candles all aflame.
Just see what the boys in the backroom
    will have
And tell them I sighed,
And tell them I cried,
And tell them I died of the same!
And when I die,
Don't pay the preacher for speaking
Of my glory and my fame.
Just see what the boys in the backroom
    will have
And tell them I sighed,
And tell them I cried,
And tell them I died of the same!

—Frederick Hollander

FUGUE FOR TINHORNS

VERSE I

I got the horse right here,
The name is Paul Revere,
And here's a guy that says if the weather's
    clear,
Can do, can do.
This guy says the horse can do.

If he says the horse can do,
Can do, can do.
For Paul Revere I'll bite,
I hear his foot's all right,
Of course it all depends if it rained last
    night.
Likes mud, likes mud,
This "X" means the horse likes mud.
If that means the horse likes mud,
Likes mud, likes mud.
I tell you Paul Revere,
Now this is no bum steer,
It's from a handicapper that's real
    sincere.
Can do, can do,
This guy says the horse can do.
If he says the horse can do,
Can do, can do,
Paul Revere,
I got the horse right here.

VERSE 2

I'm pickin' Valentine,
'Cause on the morning line
The guy has got him figured at five
    to nine.
Has chance, has chance,
This guy says the horse has chance,
If he says the horse has chance,
Has chance, has chance.
I know it's Valentine,
The morning works look fine.
Besides, the jockey's brother's a friend
    of mine.
Needs race, needs race,
This guy says the horse needs race.
If he says the horse needs race,
Needs race, needs race.
I go for Valentine,
'Cause on the morning line
The guy has got him figured at five
    to nine.
Has chance, has chance,

This guy says the horse has chance.
Valentine
I got the horse right here.

VERSE 3

But look at Epitaph.
He wins it by a half,
According to this here in the *Telegraph*.
Big threat, big threat,
This guy calls the horse big threat.
If he calls the horse big threat,
Big threat, big threat.
And just a minute, boys,
I got the feed box noise.
It says the great-grandfather was
    Equipoise.
Shows class, shows class,
This guy says the horse shows class.
If he says the horse shows class,
Shows class, shows class.
So make it Epitaph,
He wins it by half
According to this here in the *Telegraph*.
Epitaph!
I got the horse right here!

GUYS AND DOLLS

VERSE

What's playing at the Roxy?
I'll tell you what's playing at the Roxy,
A picture about a Minnesota man
So in love with a Mississippi girl
That he sacrifices everything
And moves all the way to Biloxi,
That's what's playing at the Roxy.
What's in the *Daily News*?
I'll tell you what's in the *Daily News*,
Story about a guy who bought his wife a
    small ruby
With what otherwise would have been his
    union dues.

That's what's in the *Daily News.*
What's happening all over?
I'll tell you what's happening all over.
Guy's sitting home by a television set,
    who once
Used to be something of a rover,
That's what's happening all over.
Love is the thing that has licked 'em,
And it looks like Nathan's just another
    victim.

REFRAIN 1
[Spoken] Yes sir!
[Sung] When you see a guy
Reach for stars in the sky,
You can bet
That he's doing it for some doll.
When you spot a John waiting out in
    the rain,
Chances are he's insane as only a John
Can be for a Jane.
When you meet a gent
Paying all kinds of rent
For a flat
That could flatten the Taj Mahal.
Call it sad, call it funny,
But it's better than even money
That the guy's only doing it for some doll.

REFRAIN 2
When you see a Joe
Saving half of his dough
You can bet
There'll be mink in it for some doll.
When a bum buys wine like a bum can't
    afford,
It's a cinch that the bum is under the thumb
Of some little broad.
When you meet a mug
Lately out of the jug,
And he's still lifting platinum fol-de-rol,
Call it hell, call it heaven,
It's probable twelve to seven

That the guy's only doing it for
    some doll.

REFRAIN 3
When you see a sport
And his cash has run short,
Make a bet
That he's banking it with some doll.
When a guy wears tails with the front
    gleaming white,
Who the hell do you think he's
    tickling pink
On Saturday night?
When a lazy slob
Takes a good steady job
And he smells from Vitalis and Barbasol,
Call it dumb, call it clever,
Ah, but you can give odds forever
That the guy's only doing it
For some doll, some doll,
The guy's only doing it for some doll!

I Believe in You

You have the cool clear eyes
Of a seeker of wisdom and truth,
Yet there's that upturned chin
And the grin of impetuous youth.
Oh I believe in you,
I believe in you.
I hear the sound of good
Solid judgment whenever you talk,
Yet, there's the bold brave spring
Of the tiger that quickens your walk.
Oh I believe in you,
I believe in you.
And when my faith in my fellow man
All but falls apart,
I've but to feel your hand grasping mine
And I take heart,
I take heart.
To see the cool clear eyes

Of a seeker of wisdom and truth,
Yet there's that slam-bang tang
Reminiscent of gin and vermouth.
Oh I believe in you,
I believe in you.

I Don't Want to Walk
Without You

VERSE

All our friends keep knocking at the door,
They've asked me out a hundred times
    or more,
But all I say is, "Leave me in the gloom,"
And here I stay within my lonely room,
'Cause

REFRAIN

I don't want to walk without you, baby,
Walk without my arm about you, baby.
I thought the day you left me behind,
I'd take a stroll and get you right off
    my mind,
But now I find that
I don't want to walk without the sunshine.
Why'd you have to turn off all that
    sunshine?
Oh, baby, please come back
Or you'll break my heart for me,
'Cause I don't want to walk without you,
No siree.

—Jule Styne

I Hear Music

VERSE

Not that I'm a Punchinello,
Just an optimistic fellow
With a lot of very mellow
Music in my soul.

Not that I'm a Pollyanna
Shoutin' out a loud Hozanna,
It's my singing heart I can't control.

REFRAIN

I hear music,
Mighty fine music,
The murmur of a morning breeze up
    there,
The rattle of the milkman on the stair.
Sure that's music,
Mighty fine music,
The singing of a sparrow in the sky,
The perking of the coffee right nearby.
There's my favorite melody,
You, my angel, phoning me.
I hear music,
Mighty fine music,
And any time I think my world is wrong,
I get me out of bed and sing this song.

—Burton Lane

I Wish I Didn't Love You So

VERSE

After all this time without you,
After all this time I find
That it's still no use to say to myself:
"Out of sight, out of mind."

REFRAIN

I wish I didn't love you so,
My love for you
Should have faded long ago.
I wish I didn't need your kiss,
Why must your kiss
Torture me as long as this?
I might be smiling by now with some new
    tender friend,
Smiling by now with my heart on
    the mend,

But when I try,
Something in that heart says "No,"
You're still there,
I wish I didn't love you so.

IF I WERE A BELL

Ask me how do I feel,
Ask me now that we're cozy and clinging.
Well, sir, all I can say is,
If I were a bell I'd be ringing.
From the moment we kissed tonight,
That's the way I've just got to behave.
Boy, if I were a lamp I'd light,
And if I were a banner I'd wave.
Ask me how do I feel,
Little me with my quiet upbringing.
Well, sir, all I can say is,
If I were a gate I'd be swinging.
And if I were a watch I'd start popping my
      spring
Or if I were a bell I'd go
Ding, dong, ding, dong, ding.
Ask me how do I feel
From this chemistry lesson I'm
      learning.
Well, sir, all I can say is,
If I were a bridge I'd be burning.
Yes, I knew my morale would crack
From the wonderful way that you
      looked.
Boy, if I were a duck I'd quack
Or if I were a goose I'd be cooked.
Ask me how do I feel,
Ask me now that we're fondly caressing.
Pal, if I were a salad
I know I'd be splashing my dressing.
Ask me how to describe
This whole beautiful thing,
Well, if I were a bell I'd go
Ding, dong, ding, dong, ding.

THE LADY'S IN LOVE WITH YOU

VERSE
Have you ever seen the dawn of love?
Little things that mean the dawn of love?
Why wait for her to say that she
      adores you?
Long before the first kiss
Have you ever seen this?

REFRAIN 1
If there's a gleam in her eye
Each time she straightens your tie,
You'll know the lady's in love with you.
If she can dress for a date
Without that waiting you hate,
It means the lady's in love with you.
And when your friends ask you over to join
      their table
But she picks that faraway booth for two,
Well, sir, here's just how it stands,
You've got romance on your hands,
Because the lady's in love with you.

REFRAIN 2
If you've been traveling by plane
And she says, "Please take the train,"
Betcha three to one the lady's in love
      with you.
And if she writes you every day
Though she hasn't got a darn thing to say,
You're a cinch, the lady's in love. How true!
And if she phones, but she doesn't reverse
      the charges
Like all kinds of lady friends often do,
Well, sir, here's just how it stands,
You've got romance on your hands,
Because the lady's in love with you.

REFRAIN 3
If she goes deaf, dumb, and blind
While you've got things on your mind,

You'll know the lady's in love with you.
If she has met your old flames
And she remembers their names,
It means the lady's in love with you.
And Sunday night when you take her to
   that movie
And she says, "The balcony seats
   will do,"
Well, sir, here's just how it stands
You've got romance on your hands,
Because the lady's in love with you.

—Burton Lane

LUCK BE A LADY TONIGHT

VERSE

They call you Lady Luck,
But there is room for doubt.
At times you have a very unladylike way of
   running out.
You're on this date with me,
The pickings have been lush,
And yet before this evening is over
You might give me the brush.
You might forget your manners,
You might refuse to stay,
And so the best that I can do is pray.

REFRAIN I

Luck, be a lady tonight.
Luck, be a lady tonight.
Luck, if you've ever been a lady to
   begin with,
Luck, be a lady tonight.
Luck, let a gentleman see
How nice a dame you can be.
I know the way you've treated other guys
   you've been with,
Luck, be a lady with me.
A lady doesn't leave her escort,
It isn't fair, it isn't nice.

A lady doesn't wander all over
   the room
And blow on some other guy's dice.
So let's keep the party polite,
Never get out of my sight,
Stick with me, baby, I'm the fellow you
   came in with,
Luck, be a lady,
Luck, be a lady,
Luck, be a lady tonight.

MAKE A MIRACLE

VERSE

SHE: Our future will be marvelously
      exciting.
HE: [Spoken] Exciting!
SHE: [Sung] For progress is a thing there's
      no use fighting,
HE: [Spoken] Progress!
SHE: [Sung] They say it will seem like
      emerging into the light
      From a dismal penitenti'ry.
HE: [Spoken] What are you talking
      about?
SHE: [Spoken] The twentieth century!
HE: [Spoken] Don't change the
      subject!
SHE: I've just read a book on what's to be
      expected,
      They'll have wireless telegraphy
      perfected,
      Electric lights
      And fountain pens,
      And machines by which a lie can be
      detected!
HE: But this is eighteen ninety-three!
      What about you and me?
SHE: Horseless carriages on the road,
      Breakfast cereals that explode.
HE: Yes, I know, I know,
      I know, I know, I know.

REFRAIN I

HE: Someday they'll have horseless
carriages that fly,

SHE: Horseless carriages that fly.

HE: Horseless carriages, and someday,
They'll be roaring all about the sky.

SHE: Spelling out slogans–
"Buy a beer at Hogan's."

HE: But who knows
When that age of miracles will come
to be,
So meanwhile,
Darling, make a miracle and
marry me.

SHE: Horseless carriages! I
Can't believe it, no, I can't.

HE: Someday they'll have stereopticons
that move.

SHE: Stereopticons that move.

HE: Stereopticons appearing
In cathedrals larger than the
Louvre.

SHE: How romantic!

HE: Colossal!

SHE: Gigantic!

HE: But who knows
When that great, great cultural event
will shine,
So, meanwhile,
Darling, make a miracle and say
you're mine.

SHE: Stereopticons, I
Can't believe it, no, I can't.

HE: And I
Will see the wonders of the future in
your eyes,
Brightly gleaming wonders
That I challenge modern science to
devise.
Oh, yes, I know that someday
After we've grown very, very old.

SHE: Oh! so very, very old.

HE: Old enough to bury . . .

SHE: Someone rather bright will cure the
common cold.

HE: Not the British! (Sniff)

SHE: Never the British!

HE: And someday
Just a small white pill will feed a
family.
But, meanwhile,
Let's have steak and kidney pie,
And, meanwhile,

SHE: What a future!

HE: Let's be sure our feet are dry,
And, meanwhile,

SHE: What a future full of . . .

HE: Darling, make a miracle and marry
me.

SHE: Horseless carriages, I can't believe
it, no, I . . .
Stereopticons, I can't believe it,
no, I . . .

REFRAIN 2

HE: Someday
They'll be wearing skirts way up
to here.

SHE: Daring skirts way up to here.

HE: Wearing skirts way up to . . .
Someday, with a neckline equally
sincere.

SHE: Ah, the future, to peer into the
future.

HE: A vision that, alas, I may not be alive
to see,
So meanwhile, darling, make a
miracle and marry me.

SHE: Wearing skirts way up to–can't
believe it, no, I can't . . .

HE: Someday, life will be one sweet
domestic dream.

SHE: Be one sweet domestic dream.

HE: On that sweet domestic someday
They'll be heating cottages with
steam.

SHE: Not the British.

HE: Never the British!

SHE: Never the British!

HE: But somehow, can't you warm this
    heart
    Until that dream comes true?
    Yes, yes, meanwhile darling, make a
    miracle and say "I do."

SHE: Heating cottages, I can't believe it–
    no, I can't.

HE: And I will see the wonders of the
    future in your eyes,
    Brightly gleaming wonders
    That I challenge modern science to
    devise.
    Oh yes, I know that
    Someday, when your mind keeps
    harboring a grouch . . .

SHE: Ouch!

HE: Someday, Doctor Bones will place
    you on a couch,
    And listen to your sad, sad story for a
    handsome fee,
    But, meanwhile, let's get one big
    Morris chair,
    And, meanwhile . . .

SHE: What a future!

HE: Tell me all your troubles there,
    And, meanwhile . . .

SHE: What a future!

HE: Darling, make a miracle and
    marry me.

SHE: Stereopticons, I can't believe it,
    No, I can't believe it.

HE: Marry me.

SHE: No, I–
    Heating cottages, I can't believe it,
    No, I–
    Wearing skirts way up to . . .

HE: Marry me.

MURDER, HE SAYS

VERSE

Finally found a fellow
Almost completely divine,
But his vocabulary
Is killing this romance of mine!
We get into an intimate situation
And then begins this Romeo's
    conversation:

REFRAIN 1

He says, "Murder," he says,
Ev'ry time we kiss,
He says, "Murder," he says,
At a time like this,
He says "Murder," he says.
Is that the language of love?
He says, "Solid," he says,
Takes me in his arms,
And says, "Solid," he says,
Meaning all my charms,
He says, "Solid," he says.
Is that the language of love?
He says, "Chick, Chick, you torture me,
Zoot! Are we livin'!"
I'm thinking of leaving him flat.
He says, "Dig, dig, the jumps the old
    ticker is givin',"
Now he can talk plainer than that.
He says, "Murder," he says,
Ev'ry time we kiss,
He says, "Murder," he says,
Keep it up like this,
And that "Murder" he says,
In that impossible tone,
Will bring on nobody's murder but
    his own.

REFRAIN 2

He says, "Jackson," he says,
And my name's Marie,

He says, "Jackson," he says,
"Shoot the snoot to me,"
He says, "Jackson," he says.
Is that the language of love?
He says, "Woof, woof," he says,
When he likes my hat,
He says, "Tsk, tsk," he says,
What the heck is that?
He says, "Woo, woo," he says,
Is that the language of love?
He says, "Hep hep, with Helium,
Now, babe, we're cookin' "
And other expressions, to wit:
He says, "We're in the groove
And the groove is good-lookin'."
He sounds like his uppers don't fit.
He says, "Murder," he says,
Ev'ry time we kiss,
He says, "Murder," he says,
Keep it up like this,
And that "Murder" he says,
In that impossible tone,
Will bring on nobody's murder but
    his own.
He says, "Murder,"
He says, "Murder,"
And the way he says "Murder" in that
    impossible tone,
I've told him over and over and over again
It'll be nobody else's murder but his own.

—Jimmy McHugh

My Darling, My Darling

VERSE 1
HE: Till a moment ago we were "Mister"
        and "Miss,"
    Discussing the weather, avoiding
        each other's eye,
    Till a moment ago when we happened
        to kiss,

And we kissed the "Mister" and
    "Miss" good-bye.
Now at last I can sigh,

REFRAIN 1
My darling, my darling,
I've wanted to call you my darling
For many and many a day.
My darling, my darling,
I flutter'd and fled like a starling,
My courage just melted away.
Now all at once you've kissed me,
And there's not a thing I'm sane enough
    to say,
Except, my darling, my darling,
Get used to that name of my darling,
It's here to stay.

VERSE 2
SHE: Till a moment ago we were "Kitty"
        and "Jack,"
     So distant, so proper, the
        meaningless repartee,
     But a moment ago I was taken aback,
     When you swept the "Kitty" and
        "Jack" away.
     In reply, let me say:

REPEAT REFRAIN

Once in Love with Amy

VERSE
I caught you, sir,
Having a look at her,
As she went strolling by.
Now, didn't your heart go
Boom, boom, boom, boom, boom,
And didn't you sigh a sigh?
I warn you, sir,
Don't start to dream of her,
Just bid such thoughts be gone,

Or it will be boom, boom
Boom, boom, boom, boom, boom,
Boom, boom, boom, boom
From then on,

REFRAIN

For once in love with Amy,
Always in love with Amy,
Ever and ever fascinated by her,
Sets your heart a-fire to stay.
Once you're kissed by Amy,
Tear up your list, it's Amy,
Ply her with bon-bons, poetry and flowers,
Moon a million hours away.
You might be quite the fickle-hearted rover,
So carefree and bold;
Who loves a girl, and later thinks it over,
And just quits cold.
But once in love with Amy,
Always in love with Amy.
Ever and ever
Sweetly you'll romance her.
Trouble is, the answer will be
That Amy'd rather stay in love with me!

SAND IN MY SHOES

VERSE

"Out of sight, out of mind,"
That's what I told myself,
So I left you behind,
And I controlled myself;
Yet some mysterious thing
Makes every memory cling,
It makes me want to take wing
Again tonight,
And know the delight
Of holding you tight–

REFRAIN

Sand in my shoes,
Sand from Havana,

Calling me to that ever so heavenly shore,
Calling me back to you once more.
Dreams in the night,
Dreams of Havana,
Dreams of a love I haven't the strength to
     refuse;
Darling, the sand is in my shoes.
Deep in my veins
The sensuous strains of the soft guitars;
Deep in my soul
The thundering roll of a tropic sea
Under the stars.
That was Havana,
You are the moonlit mem'ry I can't seem
     to lose,
That's why my life's an aimless cruise:
All that is real is the feel
Of that sand in my shoes!

—Victor Schertzinger

SIT DOWN, YOU'RE ROCKIN' THE BOAT

VERSE I

I dreamed last night
I got on a boat to Heaven
And by some chance
I had brought my dice along,
And there I stood
And I hollered, "Someone fade me,"
But the passengers, they knew right from
     wrong.

REFRAIN

For the people all said, "Sit down,
Sit down, you're rockin' the boat."
People all said, "Sit down,
Sit down, you're rockin' the boat.
And the devil will drag you under
By the sharp lapel of your
     checkered coat;

Sit down, sit down, sit down,
   sit down,
Sit down, you're rockin' the boat."

VERSE 2
I sailed away
On that little boat to Heaven
And by some chance
Found a bottle in my fist,
And there I stood
Nicely passin' out the whiskey,
But the passengers were bound to
   resist.
For the people all said, "Beware,
You're on a heavenly trip."
People all said, "Beware,
Beware you'll scuttle the ship.
And the devil will drag you under
By the fancy tie 'round your wicked
   throat;
Sit down, sit down, sit down, sit down.
Sit down, you're rockin' the boat."

VERSE 3
And as I laughed
At those passengers to Heaven,
A great big wave
Came and washed me overboard.
And as I sank
And I hollered, "Someone save me,"
That's the moment I woke up,
Thank the Lord.
And I said to myself, "Sit down,
Sit down, you're rockin' the boat."
Said to myself, "Sit down,
Sit down, you're rockin' the boat.
And the devil will drag you under
With a soul so heavy you'd never
   float.
Sit down.
Sit down, sit down, sit down,
Sit down, you're rockin' the boat."

SOMEBODY, SOMEWHERE

Somebody, somewhere
Wants me and needs me,
That's very wonderful
To know.
Somebody lonely
Wants me to care,
Wants me of all people
To notice him there.
Well, I want to be wanted,
Need to be needed,
And I'll admit I'm all
Aglow.
'Cause somebody, somewhere
Wants me and needs me,
Wants lonely me to smile
And say hello.
Somebody, somewhere
Wants me and needs me,
And that's very wonderful
To know.

SPRING WILL BE A LITTLE LATE THIS YEAR

VERSE
January and February were never so empty
   and gray.
Tragic'lly I feel like crying,
"Without you, my darling, I'm dying,"
But let's rather put it this way:

REFRAIN
Spring will be a little late this year,
A little late arriving
In my lonely world over here.
For you have left me,
And where is our April of old?
You have left me
And Winter continues cold,

As if to say
Spring will be a little slow to start,
A little slow reviving
That music it made in my heart.
Yes, time heals all things,
So I needn't cling to this fear,
It's merely that
Spring will be a little late this year.

Take Back Your Mink

VERSE

He bought me the fur thing five
    Winters ago
And the gown the following fall.
Then the necklace, the bag, the gloves,
    and the hat,
That was late forty-eight, I recall.
Then last night in his apartment
He tried to remove them all!
And I said as I ran down the hall:

REFRAIN

"Take back your mink,
Take back your pearls,
What made you think
That I was one of those girls?
Take back the gown, the shoes, and
    the hat,
I may be down, but I'm not flat as
    all that.
I thought that each expensive gift you'd
    arrange
Was a token of your esteem.
Now when I think of what you want in
    exchange,
It all seems a horrible dream.
So, take back your mink
To from whence it came,
And tell them to Hollanderize it
For some other dame."

REPEAT VERSE

I thought that each expensive gift you'd
    arrange
Was a token of your esteem.
But when I think of what you want in
    exchange,
It all seems a horrible dream (eek!).
Take back your mink,
Those old worn-out pelts,
And go shorten the sleeves
For somebody else.

They're Either Too Young or Too Old

VERSE

You marched away and left this town
As empty as can be.
I can't sit under the apple tree
With anyone else but me.
For there is no secret lover
That the draft board didn't discover.

REFRAIN 1

They're either too young or too old,
They're either too gray or too grassy
    green,
The pickins are poor and the crop is lean,
What's good is in the army,
What's left will never harm me.
They're either too old or too young,
So darling, you'll never get stung.
Tomorrow I'll go hiking with that Eagle
    Scout unless
I get a call from Grandpa for a snappy
    game of chess.
I'm finding it easy to stay good as gold.
They're either too young or too old.

REFRAIN 2

They're either too warm or too cold,
They're either too fast or too fast asleep,

So, darling, believe me, I'm yours to keep,
There isn't any gravy,
The gravy's in the navy.
They're either too fresh or too stale,
There is no available male.
I will confess to one romance I'm sure you
　　will allow,
He tries to serenade me but his voice is
　　changing now.
I'm finding it easy to keep things
　　controlled.
They're either too young or too old.

REFRAIN 3
They're either too bald or too bold,
I'm down to the wheelchair and bassinet,
My heart just refuses to get upset,
I simply can't compel it to
With no marines to tell it to.
I'm either their first breath of spring,
Or else I'm their last little fling.
I either get a fossil or an adolescent pup,
I either have to hold him off or have to
　　hold him up.
The battle is on, but the fortress will hold.
They're either too young or too old.

INTERLUDE
I'll never, never fail ya
While you are in Australia,
Or out in the Aleutians
Or off among the Rooshians,
Or flying over Egypt,
Your heart will never feel gypped,
And when you get to India,
I'll still be what I been to ya.
I've looked the field over
And lo and behold–
They're either too young or too old.

　　　–Arthur Schwartz

TWO SLEEPY PEOPLE

VERSE
I guess we haven't got a sense
Of responsibility,
Our young romance is so intense
We're close to imbecility.
Tick, tock! Cuckoo!

REFRAIN
Here we are,
Out of cigarettes,
Holding hands and yawning,
Look how late it gets.
Two sleepy people, by dawn's early
　　light,
And too much in love to say "Good
　　night."
Here we are,
In the cozy chair,
Picking on a wishbone
From the Frigidaire,
Two sleepy people, with nothing to say
And too much in love to break away.
Do you remember
The nights we used to linger in the hall?
Father didn't like you at all.
Do you remember
The reason why we married in the fall?
To rent this little nest,
And get a bit of rest.
Well, here we are,
Just about the same,
Foggy little fella,
Drowsy little dame.
Two sleepy people, by dawn's early
　　light,
And too much in love to say "Good
　　night."

　　　–Hoagy Carmichael

Bobby Troup (1910–1999)

B OBBY (Robert William, Jr.) Troup, born in Harrison, Pennsylvania, may be the only good songwriter to have graduated from the Wharton School of Business. What he graduated *to* was the Tommy Dorsey Orchestra, for which he was a staff writer, and the Marine Corps, in which he served during World War II. He became a successful pianist and singer, then leader of a trio, recording for a number of major labels. For three years he was the narrator of the TV show *Stars of Jazz,* perched on a script-boy stool. He acted in several movies–*The Five Pennies,* the bandleader in *The Gene Krupa Story,* and a minor role in *M*A*S*H.* He may also be remembered as the neurosurgeon Dr. Joe Early on the television drama *Emergency* from 1972 to 1977; it featured as well his wife of forty years, the sultry singing star Julie London. But his chief claim to fame is as a songwriter–the Nat King Cole signature song "Route 66," Eartha Kitt's "Daddy," and a small but select group of witty and appealing numbers particularly suited to his own casual, laid-back singing style.

BABY, BABY ALL THE TIME

VERSE

Once I loved a man
And he loved me, too,
But that just couldn't last,
Good things never do;
'Cause my man has gone away,
Yes, my man has gone away.

REFRAIN

Once I had a man
As sweet as he could be,
Once I had a man
And he was, oh, so right for me,
Kinda sandy hair,
Eyes so soft and blue
That you couldn't help but care
When he looked at you.
He called me Baby,
Baby all the time.

He said, "Baby, try to see,
Baby understand,
Baby, you're for me,
Won't you take my hand?"
But I pushed him away,
Wouldn't let him near,
Pushed him far away,
Now I'm wishing I could hear him call
    me Baby,
Baby all the time.
It's so lonely through the day,
Lonely, oh the night,
Lonely, lonely hours without that guy I
    held so tight.
Lord, I pray that you will listen to
    my plea,
Help him to forgive
So he'll come back to me and call
    me Baby,
Baby all the time.

Daddy

Hey! listen
To my story 'bout
A gal named Daisy Mae,
Lazy Daisy Mae.
Her disposition
Is rather sweet and charming;
At times alarming,
So they say.
She had a man, rich, tall, dark, handsome,
    large and strong,
To whom she used to sing this song:

Hey! Daddy!
I want a diamond ring,
Bracelets, ev'rything.
Daddy!
You oughta get the best for me.
Hey! Daddy! Gee!
Won't I look swell in sables,
Clothes with Paris labels,
Daddy!
You oughta get the best for me.
Here's 'n amazing revelation:
With a bit of stimulation
I'd be a great sensation,
I'd be your inspiration. Daddy!
I want a brand-new car,
Champagne, caviar,
Daddy!
You oughta get the best for me.

(Get Your Kicks On) Route 66!

If you ever plan to motor west,
Travel my way, take the highway that's
    the best,
Get your kicks on Route Sixty-six!
It winds from Chicago to L.A.,
More than two thousand miles all
    the way.
Get your kicks on Route Sixty-six!
Now you go thru Saint Looey and Joplin,
    Missouri,
And Oklahoma City is mighty pretty.
You'll see Amarillo,
Gallup, New Mexico,
Flagstaff, Arizona,
Don't forget Winona,
Kingman, Barstow, San Bernardino.
Won't you get hip to this timely tip?
When you make that California trip,
Get your kicks on Route Sixty-six!

You're in Love

Have you ever awakened to find that
    you're glad to be awake?
Hamburger tastes like steak,
You're in love!
Have you ever experienced the thrill of a
    fall that feels like spring?
Then you have felt the sting,
You're in love

1. Have you found when she's around that
    you are so enthused?
  You don't make sense, but what's the
    difference, you're glad to be
    confused.
  It's quite easily explained biologically,
    you have found a mate,
  Might I reiterate,
  You're in love.

2. When he's near do you appear to be so
    ill at ease?
  You try to hide your pounding side and
    calm your shaking knees.

Have you ever sincerely imagined that
    you could walk on air?
You're broke but you don't care,
You're in love.

Unmistakably
Your symptoms prove to me
That you're in love.

You're Lookin' at Me

Who had the girl turning handsprings,
Crazy to love him, claimed he?
Who could so misunderstand things?
You're lookin' at me.

Who was so sure of his conquest,
Sure as a human could be?
Who would up losing the contest?
You're lookin' at me, you're lookin' at me.
Where is the boy
Who was certain his charms couldn't fail?
Where is the boy
Who believed every word of this
    ridiculous tale?
Who was so childishly flattered,
Thought he'd swept her right off her feet?
Who woke to find his dream shattered?
Might I repeat? might I repeat?
For you needn't strain your eyes
To see what I want you to see,
That's right! You're lookin' at me.

Mack David (1912–1993)

Mack David, older brother of lyricist Hal David, was born in New York and educated at Cornell and St. John's University law school. He was writing hits by the thirties, and before he was through, he had provided the lyrics for a string of number-one hits–"Moon Love," for Glenn Miller; "It's Love, Love, Love," for Guy Lombardo; "Candy," for Johnny Mercer and Jo Stafford; "Chi-Baba, Chi-Baba," for Perry Como; "Cherry Pink and Apple Blossom White," for Perez Prado. David wrote the score for several Disney films and is responsible for the themes of TV's "Sunset Strip" and "Hawaiian Eye." He had the thankless task of putting words to "Tara's Theme" from *Gone With the Wind* ("My Own True Love") and provided the words for the very successful English version of Edith Piaf's "La Vie en Rose." But probably the best-known song with which he is associated is "Hello, Dolly!": He sued Jerry Herman, claiming that it was partially taken from "Sunflower"; they settled out of court.

CANDY

(With Joan Whitney and Alex Kramer)

VERSE

Some say that love is sweet as a rose,
Some say it's honey and the bee.
Well, sit right down and let me tell you
What my love is to me.

REFRAIN

"Candy,"
I call my sugar "Candy,"
Because I'm sweet on "Candy"
And "Candy's" sweet on me.
She understands me,
My understanding "Candy,"
And "Candy's" always handy
When I need sympathy.
I wish that there were four of her
So I could love much more of her.
She has taken my complete heart,
Got a sweet tooth for my sweetheart,

"Candy,"
It's gonna be just dandy,
The day I take my "Candy"
And make her mine all mine.

I'M JUST A LUCKY SO-AND-SO

VERSE

Some people need a lot of money
And nothin' else but money
To make their life complete.
Not me, not me.
I haven't got a lot of money,
But life is milk and honey.
Yes, life is mighty sweet.
You see
This is my philosophy.

REFRAIN

As I walk down the street
Seems ev'ryone I meet

Gives me a friendly, "Hello."
I guess I'm just a lucky so-and-so.
The birds in ev'ry tree
Are all so neighborly,
They sing wherever I go.
I guess I'm just a lucky so-and-so.
If you should ask me the amount
In my bank account,
I'd have to confess that I'm slippin',
But that don't worry me.
Confidentially,
I've got a dream that's a pippin'.
And when the day is through
Each night I hurry to
A home where love waits, I know.
I guess I'm just a lucky so-and-so.

—*Duke Ellington*

A SINNER KISSED AN ANGEL

VERSE
This is an age-old story,
It's happened many times before,
And I was there, that night of nights,
When heaven opened up its door.
Stars
In the sky were dancing
One night
Perfect for romancing,
The night a sinner kissed an angel.
He wanted thrills,
She wanted love.
Oh,
But his sighs were tender
As he
Begged her to surrender,
The night a sinner kissed an angel
And she believed
That it was love.
How was she to know that ev'ry lovely vow
Was part of the game he was playing?

But to his surprise he realized somehow,
He meant ev'ry word he was saying.
Yes,
Miracles can happen,
I know,
'Cause I saw one happen
That night a sinner kissed an angel,
That was the night
I fell in love.

—*Ray Joseph*

SUNFLOWER

VERSE I
I was born in Kansas,
I was bred in Kansas,
And when I get married, I'll be wed in
    Kansas.
There's a true blue gal who promised she
    would wait;
She's a sunflower from the Sunflower
    State.

REFRAIN
She's a sunflower,
She's my sunflower,
And I know we'll never part.
She's a sunflower,
She's my one flower,
She's the sunflower of my heart.

VERSE 2
Skies are fair in Kansas,
Clouds are rare in Kansas,
Never saw a place that could compare with
    Kansas,
So I'm goin' home to keep a weddin' date
With a sunflower from the Sunflower
    State.

REPEAT REFRAIN

VERSE 3

Troubles end in Kansas,
Folks unbend in Kansas,
Ev'ryone you meet will be your friend in
    Kansas,
And they'll all be there to help me
    celebrate
With my sunflower from the Sunflower
    State

REPEAT REFRAIN

VERSE 4

Oh, the moon is brighter,
And the stars are bluer,
And the gals are sweeter and their hearts
    are truer,
And I'm here to state there's one who's
    really great,
She's a sunflower from the Sunflower
    State.

REPEAT REFRAIN

Jack Lawrence (1912–   )

BORN IN Brooklyn and educated at Long Island University, Jack Lawrence has had a long and varied career. "Ciribiribin" became Harry James's theme song; "Linda" was written to celebrate the birth of Linda Eastman McCartney; and he gave first hits to Sarah Vaughan ("Tenderly," which went on to become a jazz standard); Dinah Shore ("Yes, My Darling Daughter"); Frank Sinatra ("All or Nothing at All"); and the Ink Spots ("If I Didn't Care"). His first published song, "Play, Fiddle, Play," was a hit in 1932; "Sleepy Lagoon" was a number one for Harry James ten years later; and in 1946, five different recordings of "Symphony" reached the top ten. At least one of his assaults on Broadway had a superior score—*I Had a Ball*—and he wrote songs for many movies, from *Dinner at Eight* and *Torch Song* to *Fedora* and *The Pawnbroker.* What's more, he got out of Hollywood, returning East not once but twice.

ALL OR NOTHING AT ALL

All or nothing at all!
Half a love never appealed to me.
If your heart never could yield to me,
Then I'd rather have nothing at all!
All or nothing at all!
If it's love, there is no in between.
Why begin, then cry for something that
    might have been?
No, I'd rather have nothing at all!
But, please, don't bring your lips so close
    to my cheek.
Don't smile or I'll be lost beyond recall.
The kiss in your eyes, the touch of your
    hand makes me weak,
And my heart may grow dizzy and fall.
And if I fell under the spell of your call,
I would be caught in the undertow.
So, you see, I've got to say No! No!
All or nothing at all!

    —*Arthur Altman*

FOOLIN' MYSELF

I tell myself, "I'm through with you
And I'll have nothing more to do
    with you."
I stay away, but ev'ry day
I'm just foolin' myself!
I tell my friends that I don't care,
I shrug my shoulders at the whole affair;
But they all know it isn't so,
I'm just foolin' myself.
And ev'ry time I pass
And see my face in a looking glass,
I tip my hat and say,
"How do you do, you fool;
You're throwing your life away."
I'm acting gay, I'm acting proud,
And ev'ry time I see you in a crowd
I may pretend, but in the end
I'm just foolin' myself.

    —*Peter Tinturin*

LINDA

VERSE

The story is simple;
The girl has a dimple,
The guy is as shy as can be.
Now she doesn't know it,
For he doesn't show it,
But he loves her secretly.
Night and day
Here's all he can say:

REFRAIN

"When I go to sleep
I never count sheep,
I count all the charms about Linda.
And lately it seems
In all of my dreams
I walk with my arms about Linda.
But what good does it do me,
For Linda doesn't know I exist.
Can't help feeling gloomy,
Think of all the lovin' I've missed.
We pass on the street,
My heart skips a beat,
I say to myself,
'Hello, Linda.'
If only she'd smile
I'd stop her a while
And then I would get to know Linda.
But miracles still happen,
And when my lucky star begins to shine,
With one lucky break
I'll make Linda mine."

THE OTHER HALF OF ME

Somewhere there has to be
The other half of me,
The other half of me
I've yet to meet.

One special someone whose heart has a
    similar leaning.
If she were right for me,
Day and night for me
Would have meaning.
The other half of me,
That unknown quantity,
That unseen destiny
Would make me complete.
Is there a chart for the heart, or a graph?
Will we meet on the street with a welcome
    laugh?
Will we know one another
If I ever meet my other half?
The other half of me.

—Stan Freeman

SLEEPY LAGOON

A sleepy lagoon,
A tropical moon,
And two on an island.
A sleepy lagoon
And two hearts in tune
In some lullaby land.
The fireflies' gleam
Reflects in the stream,
They sparkle and shimmer.
A star from on high
Falls out of the sky
And slowly grows dimmer.
The leaves from the trees
All dance in the breeze
And float on the ripples.
We're deep in a spell,
As nightingales tell
Of roses and dew.
The memory of
This moment of love
Will haunt me forever.
A tropical moon,

A sleepy lagoon,
And you!

—*Eric Coates*

TENDERLY

VERSE

The evening breeze
Caressed the trees
Tenderly.
The trembling trees
Embraced the breeze
Tenderly.
Then you and I
Came wandering by
And lost in a sigh
Were we.
The shore was kissed
By sea and mist
Tenderly.
I can't forget
How two hearts met
Breathlessly.
Your arms opened wide
And closed me inside–
You took my lips,
You took my love
So tenderly.

—*Walter Gross*

WHAT'S YOUR STORY, MORNING GLORY

(with Paul Webster)

What's your story, morning glory,
What makes you look so blue?
The way that you've been acting, I don't
     know what to do,
For I love you, sure as one and one
     makes two.
What's your story, morning glory,
Got a feeling there's a lot you're
     concealing.
So won't you tell me that you love
     me, too?
What's your story, morning glory,
You've got me worried, too.
A postman came this morning and left a
     note for you.
Did you read it? Then you know that I
     love you.
What's your story, morning glory,
If I guess it, darling, will you
     confess it?
Oh, won't you tell me that you love
     me, too?

—*Mary Lou Williams*

Tom Adair (1913–1988)

BORN IN Kansas but having grown up and been educated in Los Angeles, Tom Adair found his main career in writing scripts for films and television–he was a sitcom expert *(My Three Sons, My Favorite Martian, The Munsters)*–and for night-club acts. He also worked on various projects for Disney, including Disneyland and Disney World. But in the forties, he was also an important and very special lyricist, particularly in his collaboration with singer/composer Matt Denis. Their sophisti-cated and feeling songs were pounced upon by most of the major song interpreters of the day, particularly Frank Sinatra, who first sang them with the Tommy Dorsey Orchestra. Disney's gain was music's loss.

EVERYTHING HAPPENS TO ME

VERSE

Black cats creep across my path
Until I'm almost mad,
I must have 'roused the devil's wrath,
'Cause all my luck is bad.

REFRAIN

I make a date for golf
And you can bet your life it rains,
I try to give a party
And the guy upstairs complains,
I guess I'll go through life
Just catchin' colds and missin'
    trains.
Ev'rything happens to me.
I never miss a thing,
I've had the measles and the mumps,
And ev'ry time I play an ace
My partner always trumps,
I guess I'm just a fool
Who never looks before he jumps.
Ev'rything happens to me.

At first my heart thought you could break
    this jinx for me,
That love would turn the trick to end
    despair,
But now I just can't fool this head that
    thinks for me,
I've mortgaged all my castles in
    the air.
I've telegraphed and phoned,
I sent an "Air-mail Special," too.
Your answer was "good-bye,"
And there was even postage due.
I fell in love just once
And then it had to be with you.
Ev'rything happens to me.

—Matt Dennis

LET'S GET AWAY FROM IT ALL

VERSE

I'm so tired of this dull routine,
Up to town on the eight-fifteen,

Back at night, off to bed and then
Get up and start it all over again.

REFRAIN

Let's take a boat to Bermuda–
Let's take a plane to Saint Paul–
Let's take a kayak
To Quincy or Nyack,
Let's get away from it all.
Let's take a trip in a trailer–
No need to come back at all–
Let's take a powder
To Boston for chowder,
Let's get away from it all.
We'll travel 'round from town
     to town,
We'll visit ev'ry state.
I'll repeat "I love you, Sweet!"
In all the forty-eight.
Let's go again to Niag'ra,
This time we'll look at the Fall.
Let's leave our hut, Dear,
Get out of our rut, Dear,
Let's get away from it all.

—*Matt Dennis*

The Night We Called It a Day

VERSE

Authors and poets in prose and in
     rhyme
Seem to agree that night is the time
Of lovers' meetings,
Romantic greetings.
To my misfortune, I found this a lie,
For it was night when you whispered
     "Good-bye,"
A night of madness
That turned to sadness,
Much too soon.

REFRAIN

There was a moon out in space,
But a cloud drifted over its face,
You kissed me and went on your way,
The night we called it a day.
I heard the song of the spheres
Like a minor lament in my ears,
I hadn't the heart left to pray,
The night we called it a day.
Soft through the dark
The hoot of an owl in the sky,
Sad though his song,
No bluer was he than I.
The moon went down,
Stars were gone,
But the sun didn't rise with the dawn.
There wasn't a thing left to say,
The night we called it a day.

—*Matt Dennis*

Violets for Your Furs

VERSE

It was Winter in Manhattan,
Falling snowflakes filled the air,
The streets were covered with a film of ice.
But a little simple magic
That I'd heard about somewhere
Changed the weather all around,
Just within a trice.

REFRAIN

I bought you violets for your furs,
And it was Spring for a while,
Remember?
I bought you violets for your furs,
And there was April in that December.
The snow drifted down on the flowers
And melted where it lay.
The snow looked like dew on the blossoms–

As on a summer day.
I bought you violets for your furs
And there was blue in the wintry sky.
You pinned the violets to your furs
And gave a lift to the crowds passing by.
You smiled at me so sweetly,
Since then one thought occurs,
That we fell in love completely
The day that I bought you violets for
    your furs.

—*Matt Dennis*

WILL YOU STILL BE MINE?

VERSE

Ever since my heart took such a tumble
I've wondered if your love for me would last.
When landmarks fall and institutions
    crumble,
Will it be just a mem'ry of the past?

REFRAIN

When lovers make no rendezvous
To stroll along Fifth Avenue,
When this familiar world is
    through,
Will you still be mine?
When cabs don't drive around
    the park,
No windows light the summer dark,
When love has lost its secret spark,
Will you still be mine?
When moonlight on the Hudson's not
    romancy
And Spring no longer turns a young man's
    fancy,
When glamour girls have lost their
    charms,
When sirens just mean false alarms,
When lovers heed no call to arms,
Will you still be mine?

—*Matt Dennis*

Sammy Cahn (1913–1993)

SAMMY CAHN (previously Cohen, Cohn, and Kahn) got his start collaborating with Saul Chaplin (previously Kaplan). Their first hit was the 1935 "Rhythm Is Our Business," but their greatest success came from their role in adapting a Yiddish folk song into the huge 1938 hit "Bei Mir Bist Du Schoen," which also launched the Andrews Sisters. Post-Chaplin, Cahn's most successful partnerships were with Jule Styne and Jimmy Van Heusen. With the former he wrote such hit songs as "Saturday Night Is the Loneliest Night of the Week," "It's Magic," "Let It Snow, Let It Snow, Let It Snow," and the Oscar-winning "Three Coins in the Fountain," as well as his one Broadway success, *High Button Shoes;* with the latter, a long string of hits, many of them for Frank Sinatra–"The Second Time Around," "The Tender Trap," "Come Fly with Me," "Only the Lonely," "Love and Marriage"–and his three other Oscar winners, "Call Me Irresponsible," "All the Way," and "High Hopes." In other words, he was the prime commercial lyricist of what can loosely be called the Sinatra era, the forties into the sixties. Born in New York to a poor Jewish family, forced by his mother to play the violin, apprenticed in vaudeville, he got to Hollywood by the time he was twenty-seven and never looked back, except when reminiscing, which he did joyously until his death, at eighty. His autobiography, *I Should Care,* reflects his generous opinion of himself, but he was clear-sighted as well. In an interview for Max Wilk's book *They're Playing Our Song,* he lays it on the line: "Now, you ask which comes first, the words or the music? I'll tell you which–the *money*!"

ALL THE WAY

When somebody loves you,
It's no good unless he loves you
All the way.
Happy to be near you
When you need someone to cheer you
All the way.
Taller than the tallest tree is,
That's how it's got to feel;
Deeper than the deep blue sea is,
That's how deep it goes,
If it's real.
When somebody needs you,

It's no good unless he needs you
All the way.
Through the good or lean years
And for all the in-between years,
Come what may.
Who knows where the road will lead us?
Only a fool would say.
But if you let me love you,
It's for sure I'm gonna love you
All the way.
All the way.

—Jimmy Van Heusen

CALL ME IRRESPONSIBLE

VERSE

Seems I'm always making resolutions,
Like ev'ry night for me is New Year's Eve.
Things they chisel on those institutions,
The lofty thoughts I never quite achieve.
Each time I'm taking bows 'cause
    ev'rything went well,
Things go awry,
And there am I
Saying I meant well

REFRAIN

Call me irresponsible,
Call me unreliable,
Throw in undependable, too.
Do my foolish alibis bore you?
Well, I'm not too clever;
I just adore you.
Call me unpredictable,
Tell me I'm impractical,
Rainbows I'm inclined to pursue.
Call me irresponsible
Yes, I'm unreliable
But it's undeniably true—
I'm irresponsibly mad for you!

—Jimmy Van Heusen

COME FLY WITH ME

VERSE

When Dad and Mother
Discovered one another
They dreamed of the day when they
Would love and honor and obey.
And during all their modest spooning,
They'd blush and speak of honeymooning.
And if your memory recalls,
They spoke of Niagra Falls.

But today, my darling, today,
When you meet the one you love, you say—

REFRAIN

Come fly with me! Let's fly! Let's
    fly away!
If you can use some exotic booze
There's a bar in far Bombay.
Come fly with me!
Let's fly! Let's fly away!
Come fly with me!
Let's float down to Peru!
In llama land, there's a one-man band
And he'll toot his flute for you.
Come fly with me!
Let's take off in the blue!
Once I get you up there
Where the air is rarefied,
We'll just glide, starry-eyed.
Once I get you up there
I'll be holding you so near,
You may hear angels cheer
'Cause we're together.
Weather-wise it's such a lovely day!
Just say the words and we'll beat the birds
Down to Acapulco Bay.
It's perfect for a flying honeymoon,
    they say.
Come fly with me!
Let's fly! Let's fly away!

—Jimmy Van Heusen

DAY BY DAY

Day by day
I'm falling more in love with you,
And day by day
My love seems to grow.
There isn't any end to my devotion;
It's deeper, dear, by far than any ocean.
I find that day by day

You're making all my dreams come true,
So come what may
I want you to know–
I'm yours alone
And I'm in love to stay,
As we go through the years
Day by day.

—Axel Stordahl and Paul Weston

GUESS I'LL HANG MY TEARS OUT TO DRY

VERSE

The torch I carry is handsome,
It's worth its heartache in ransom.
And when the twilight steals,
I know how the lady in the harbor feels.

REFRAIN

When I want rain
I get sunny weather;
I'm just as blue as the sky.
Since love is gone,
Can't pull myself together.
Guess I'll hang my tears out to dry.
Friends ask me out,
I tell them I'm busy;
Must get a new alibi.
I stay at home and ask myself where is she.
Guess I'll hang my tears out to dry.
Dry little teardrops,
My little teardrops,
Hanging on a string of dreams.
Fly, little mem'ries.
My little mem'ries
Remind her of our crazy schemes.
Somebody said
Just forget about her.
I gave that treatment a try.
Strangely enough,
I got along without her,

Then one day she passed me right by.
Oh well, I guess I'll hang my tears out
to dry.

—Jule Styne

I FALL IN LOVE TOO EASILY

VERSE

There are those who can leave love or
take it,
Love to them is just what they make it.
I wish that I were the same,
But love is my fav'rite game.

REFRAIN

I fall in love too easily,
I fall in love too fast.
I fall in love too terribly hard
For love to ever last.
My heart should be well schooled
'Cause I've been fooled in the past.
And still I fall in love too easily,
I fall in love too fast.

—Jule Styne

I SHOULD CARE

VERSE

I know I should pity me,
But I don't, because, you see,
I have loved and I have learned,
And as far as I'm concerned:

REFRAIN

I should care,
I should go around weeping.
I should care,
I should go without sleeping.
Strangely enough, I sleep well

'Cept for a dream or two.
But then I count my sheep well.
Funny how sheep can lull you to sleep.
So I should care,
I should let it upset me.
I should care,
But it just doesn't get me.
Maybe I won't find someone as lovely as you,
But I should care, and I do.

—Axel Stordahl and Paul Weston

I'LL WALK ALONE

VERSE
They call, no date,
I promised you I'd wait.
I want them all to know
I'm strictly single-o.

CHORUS
I'll walk alone,
Because to tell you the truth,
I'll be lonely.
I don't mind being lonely
When my heart tells me you
Are lonely too.
I'll walk alone,
They'll ask me why and I'll tell them I'd
    rather.
There are dreams I must gather,
Dreams we fashioned the night
You held me tight.
I'll always be near you,
Wherever you are,
Each night in ev'ry prayer.
If you call I'll hear you
No matter how far.
Just close your eyes and I'll be there.
Please walk alone,
And send your love and your kisses to
    guide me.

Till you're walking beside me,
I'll walk alone.

—Jule Styne

IT'S MAGIC

VERSE
I've heard about Houdini and the rest
    of them
And I'd put you up against the best
    of them.
As far as I'm concerned, you're the tops,
And you don't resort to props.
Things I used to think were inconceivable,
You've a way of making them believable.
And upon a night like this,
I'm afraid you just can't miss.

REFRAIN
You sigh, the song begins,
You speak and I hear violins,
It's magic.
The stars desert the skies
And rush to nestle in your eyes,
It's magic.
Without a golden wand or mystic charms
Fantastic things begin when I am in
    your arms.
When we walk hand in hand
The world becomes a wonderland,
It's magic.
How else can I explain
Those rainbows when there is no rain,
It's magic.
Why do I tell myself
These things that happen are all
    really true?
When in my heart I know
The magic is my love for you.

—Jule Styne

LET IT SNOW! LET IT SNOW! LET IT SNOW!

VERSE

The snowman in the yard is frozen hard,
He's a sorry sight to see.
If he had a brain, he'd complain,
Bet he wishes he were me.

CHORUS

Oh, the weather outside is frightful,
But the fire is so delightful,
And since we've no place to go,
Let it snow! Let it snow! Let it snow!
It doesn't show signs of stopping,
And I brought some corn for popping.
The lights are turned way down low,
Let it snow! Let it snow! Let it snow!
When we finally kiss good night,
How I'll hate going out in the storm!
But if you'll really hold me tight,
All the way home I'll be warm.
The fire is slowly dying
And, my dear, we're still goodbye-ing.
But as long as you love me so,
Let it snow! Let it snow! Let it snow!

—Jule Styne

LOVE AND MARRIAGE

Love and marriage, love and marriage,
Go together like a horse and carriage.
This I tell ya, brother,
Ya can't have one without the other.
Love and marriage, love and marriage,
It's an institute you can't disparage.
Ask the local gentry
And they will say it's element'ry.
Try, try, try to separate them,
It's an illusion.
Try, try, try and you will only come
To this conclusion:
Love and marriage, love and marriage,
Go together like a horse and carriage.
Dad was told by Mother
You can't have one,
You can't have none.
You can't have one without the other.

—Jimmy Van Heusen

PUT 'EM IN A BOX, TIE 'EM WITH A RIBBON
(AND THROW 'EM IN THE DEEP BLUE SEA)

VERSE

I not only was burned by love
But I was scorched,
And instead of forgetting
I torched and torched and torched.
Whether you represent the Gallup poll
    or not,
You're welcome to these opinions of love
    I've got:

REFRAIN I

You can take the moon,
Gather up the stars
And the robins that sing merrily.
Put 'em in a box, tie 'em with a ribbon,
And throw 'em in the deep blue sea.
You can take the flow'rs
Down in lover's lane
And that sentimental poetry.
Put 'em in a box, tie 'em with a
    ribbon,
And throw 'em in the deep blue sea.
Not for me
All that stuff,
The dreams that ruin your sleep.
Not for me,

Had enough,
Love is one thing you can keep.
You can take the plans
And the wedding bells
And whoever sings "Oh, Promise Me."
Put 'em in a box, tie 'em with a ribbon,
And throw 'em in the deep blue sea.
'Cause love and I, we don't agree.

REFRAIN 2
Hansoms thru the park,
Kisses in the dark,
All the promises made faithfully.
Put 'em in a box, tie 'em with a ribbon,
And throw 'em in the deep blue sea.
And you won't go wrong
If you take a song
Sung by Frankie Boy or Mister C.
Put 'em in a box, tie 'em with a ribbon,
And throw 'em in the deep blue sea.
Not for me,
Had enough,
Love is one thing you can keep.
You know what to do
With old "Tea for Two"
And "The Boy for You, the Girl for Me."
Put 'em in a box, tie 'em with a ribbon,
And throw 'em in the deep blue sea.
'Cause love and I, we don't agree.

—*Jule Styne*

THE SECOND TIME AROUND

Love is lovelier
The second time around.
Just as wonderful with both feet on the
    ground.
It's that second time you hear your love
    song sung
Makes you think perhaps that love, like
    youth, is wasted on the young.

Love's more comf'table the second time
    you fall,
Like a friendly home the second time
    you call.
Who can say what led us to this miracle we
    found?
There are those who'll bet
Love comes but once, and yet—
I'm, oh so glad we met,
The second time around.

—*Jimmy Van Heusen*

TEACH ME TONIGHT

Did you say I've got a lot to learn?
Well, don't think I'm trying not to learn.
Since this is the perfect spot to learn,
Teach me tonight.
Starting with the A-B-C of it,
Right down to the X-Y-Z of it,
Help me solve the mystery of it,
Teach me tonight.
The sky's a blackboard high above you.
If a shooting star goes by,
I'll use that star to write I love you
A thousand times across the sky.
One thing isn't very clear, my love,
Should the teacher stand so near, my love?
Graduation's almost here, my love.
Teach me tonight.

—*Gene DePaul*

(LOVE IS) THE TENDER TRAP

You see a pair of laughing eyes
And suddenly you're sighing sighs,
You're thinking nothing's wrong,
You string along, boy,
Then, snap!

Those eyes, those sighs,
They're part of the tender trap.
You're hand in hand beneath the trees
And soon there's music in the breeze,
You're acting kind of smart
Until your heart
Just goes whap!
Those trees, that breeze,
They're part of the tender trap.
Some starry night
When her kisses make you tingle,
She'll hold you tight
And you'll hate yourself for being
    single.
And all at once it seems so nice,
The folks are throwing shoes and rice,
You hurry to a spot
That's just a dot
On the map.
You wonder how it all came about.
It's too late now, there's no getting out,
You fell in love,
And love is the tender trap!

       —Jimmy Van Heusen

THE THINGS WE DID LAST SUMMER

VERSE
The weeks go quickly by
When hearts are gay;
They seem to fly away,
Too soon they're gone.
Throughout the lonely nights
How hard you try
To lose the memories
That linger on.

REFRAIN
The boat rides we would take,
The moonlight on the lake,

The way we danced and hummed our
    fav'rite song.
The things we did last summer
I'll remember
All winter long.
The midway and the fun,
The kewpie dolls we won,
The bell I rang to prove that I was strong.
The things we did last summer,
I'll remember
All winter long.
The early morning hike,
The rented tandem bike,
The lunches that we used to pack;
We never could explain
That sudden summer rain,
The looks we got when we got back.
The leaves began to fade
Like promises we made.
How could a love that seemed so right go
    wrong?
The things we did last summer
I'll remember
All winter long.

       —Jule Styne

TIME AFTER TIME

VERSE
What good are words I say to you?
They can't convey to you
What's in my heart.
If you could hear instead
The things I've left unsaid—

REFRAIN
Time after time
I tell myself that I'm
So lucky to be loving you.
So lucky to be
The one you run to see

In the evening
When the day is through.
I only know what I know,
The passing years will show
You've kept my love so young, so new.

And time after time
You'll hear me say that I'm
So lucky to be loving you.

—Jule Styne

William Engvick (1914–)

WILLIAM ENGVICK was born in Oakland, California, and majored in art at the University of California at Berkeley, but soon he was in New York trying to break into the theater world. It was 1939, and he had written the lyrics for what he hoped would become a revue. An agent introduced him to Alec Wilder, and a collaboration began that lasted forty years, almost until Wilder's death. In the fifties, the two men went to Hollywood, having been invited to write a film score; when they got there, the producer was fired, and the film was scrapped, too. Apart from their songs, Wilder and Engvick wrote a book, *Lullabies and Night Songs,* illustrated by Maurice Sendak. But although the Wilder/Engvick songs–"While You're Young," "Crazy in the Heart"–remain admired standards, Engvick's most popular song by far was written with someone else. It was "The Song from Moulin Rouge" ("Where Is Your Heart?"), to the music of the classical composer Georges Auric; the lyrics heard in the film, translated into English from the French, were discarded and Engvick came to the rescue. The result: a number-one hit for Percy Faith in 1953.

CRAZY IN THE HEART

I see roses in December,
Think it's April in November,
And it's all because I'm crazy in the heart.
I hear trumpets when I'm talking,
Think I'm flying when I'm walking,
And it's all because I'm crazy in the heart.
I used to be the kind
That acted sober, acted wise,
Until I saw the magic
That happens in your eyes.
But though I'm batty as a hatter,
Baby, don't let it matter,
Don't you worry if I'm not so very smart.
It only means you've got me
Crazy in the heart.

—Alec Wilder

WHILE WE'RE YOUNG

VERSE
We must fulfill this golden time
When hearts awake so shyly, softly.

REFRAIN
Songs were made to sing
While we're young.
Ev'ry day is spring
While we're young.
None can refuse,
Time flies so fast,
Too dear to lose
And too sweet to last.
Though it may be just
For today,
Share our love we must,
While we may.
So blue the skies,

All sweet surprise
Shines before our eyes
While we're young.

—Alec Wilder and Morty Palitz

WHO CAN I TURN TO?

Who can I turn to,
Where can I go,
How can I face it alone . . . now,
After the moments we've known,
Who can I turn to now?
Who can I sing to,

How can I smile,
How can I wish on a star . . . how?
Knowing the way that you are,
Who can I turn to now?
We walked in the spell of the summer;
We kissed in the wind and the rain.
But now the enchantment is over,
The echo and I remain.
People are strangers who talk through
     the town,
Ghosts in a lonely parade.
Oh, where are the dreams that we made?
Who can I turn to now?

—Alec Wilder

Hugh Martin (1914–)
and Ralph Blane (1914–1995)

ALTHOUGH Martin was primarily the composer of this partnership, and Blane the lyricist, both men worked on both aspects of their craft, and their work always carried the byline "Words and music by Hugh Martin and Ralph Blane." Martin grew up in Birmingham, Alabama, and began his career as a singer and vocal arranger; Blane (Ralph Blane Hunsecker) was born (and died) in Broken Arrow, Oklahoma, and also started out as a singer/arranger. The two men were singers together in *Hooray for What* and *Louisiana Purchase,* and from 1940 to 1942 they were part of a vocal quartet known as the Martins. They were brilliant arrangers–for *The Boys from Syracuse, Cabin in the Sky, Pal Joey, Gentlemen Prefer Blondes,* and *DuBarry Was a Lady,* among others. Their most successful Broadway score was for *Best Foot Forward* ("Buckle Down, Winsocki"), and their most famous movie was Judy Garland's *Meet Me in St. Louis.* (Years later, Martin was Garland's accompanist for her first Palace Theater gig.) Martin went on alone to write the scores of *Look Ma, I'm Dancin'* and *High Spirits;* Blane occasionally wrote solo, too–"Spring Isn't Everything"–and at one point he was named Oklahoma Ambassador of Goodwill.

AN OCCASIONAL MAN

I got an island
In the Pacific
And ev'rything about it is terrific.
I got the sun to tan me,
Palms to fan me and . . .
An occasional man.
I love my island,
It's very lazy.
If I should ever leave it, I'd be crazy.
I got papayas, peaches,
Sandy beaches and . . .
An occasional man.
When I go swimmin',
I am always dressed in style;

'Cause I go swimmin',
Wearin' just a great big smile.
My little island
Was made for pleasure,
And in the cool of evening it's a
    treasure.
And when the hour grows later,
What is greater than . . .
An occasional man?
My little island is such a beauty,
You may forget to heed the call of duty.
But if you give the slip
To your ship,
Miss your trip,
Take a tip and blame . . .
An occasional dame!

Ev'ry Time

VERSE

False or true?
I wish I had a clue or two.
Where I stood I thought I knew,
Or should.
True or false?
Life was a never-ending waltz.
Then it caught the somersaults
For good.
Might have known
It would.

REFRAIN I

SHE: Ev'ry time my heart begins to dance,
The world steps on my little toes.
Ev'ry time I take a little chance,
I pay right through my little nose.
Ev'ry time I fly my little kite,
It catches on a tree.
Ev'ry time I throw an anchor out,
It pulls me in the sea.
Ev'ry time I feel a little glow,
I always get a little shock.
Ev'ry time I stick my little chin out,
I always get a little knock.
And when I aim my arrows at the sun,
They always miss their mark,
Leaving just a lonely lady in the dark.
Leaving just a lonely lady in the dark.

REFRAIN 2

HE: Ev'ry time I feel a little brave,
I always get a little scare.
Ev'ry time I want a little bone,
I always find the cupboard bare.
Ev'ry time I play a little golf,
I'm always over par.
Ev'ry time I sail my little boat,
She's never very far.
Ev'ry time I feel a little warm,
I always catch a little cold.
Ev'ry time I feel a little young,
I always grow a little old
And when I build my cabin in
the sky,
It tumbles from its mark,
Leaving just a lonely fellow in
the dark.

Have Yourself a Merry Little Christmas

VERSE

Christmas future is far away,
Christmas past is past.
Christmas present is here today,
Bringing joy that will last.

REFRAIN

Have yourself a merry little Christmas,
Let your heart be light,
From now on, our troubles will be out of
sight.
Have yourself a merry little Christmas,
Make the Yuletide gay,
From now on, our troubles will be
miles away.
Here we are as in olden days,
Happy golden days of yore.
Faithful friends who are dear to us
Gather near to us once more.
Through the years we all will be
together,
If the Fates allow.
Hang a shining star upon the highest
bough,
And have yourself a merry little
Christmas now.

I Never Felt Better

REFRAIN 1

When I try makin' money,
I never have much luck–
I never earn a dime, much less a buck.
Are my finances in a mess?
Yes!!
But I never felt better,
So I couldn't care less!
I don't buy polo ponies,
Or fly a private plane,
I never order beer, much less champagne.
But do I need a lot of dough?
No!!
'Cause I never felt better,
So I couldn't feel low.
Not low,
No, no!
I'm high,
Here's why.
I never have a worry,
I never have a care,
About what I should buy or what to wear.
And do I find my future bright?
Right!
'Cause I never felt better,
And I'm doin' all right.

REFRAIN 2

When summer's at its hottest,
The rain must keep me cool,
'Cause I don't own a creek, much less
    a pool.
What do I do when warm as toast?
Boast!!
That I never felt better,
So I simply won't roast!
When winter's at its coldest,
I shiver and I shrink,
I haven't got a coat, much less a mink.
But does that mean I'm losin' hope?

Nope!!
Since I never felt better,
Tell me why should I mope?
Why mope?
No soap!
Won't cry,
Not I.
The days I go out shoppin',
I buy each thing I see,
I charge 'em, then I feel I got 'em free.
So where will I receive my mail!
Jail!
But I never felt better,
So I'm cruisin' full sail.

PATTER

The thing I dearly love to do is worry,
I dearly love to worry and complain.
So help me check my list,
And see if I have missed
A possible source of misery and pain–
A possible source of misery and pain.
How's your appetite? / Tremendous!
How's your energy? / Stupendous!
Are you strong? / So strong I have to watch
    my step.
How're your eyes? / Bright as a penny.
And your sleep? / I don't need any, but I'm
    always on the ball and full of pep.
How's your heart? / It must be tickin',
    'cause I feel alive and kickin'.
How's your brain? / Well, it's insane but
    kinda quick.
How's your love life? / I got plenty.
How's your vision? / Twenty-twenty, must
    confess that I'm depressingly unsick!

REFRAIN 3

If I'm to cross the ocean,
I better learn to float,
I can't afford a raft, much less a boat!
But would I love to see Paree?
Oui!!

Still I never felt better,
So Pomona suits me!
And Heidelburg would thrill me,
I'd buy a dress of chintz
And go right out and land a student
    prince.
But will I ever cross the Rhine?
Nein!!
Still I never felt better,
So the beach will do fine.
No Rhine,
That's fine!
Won't see
Paree.
I haven't got a worry,
I haven't got a care
About what I should buy or what to wear.
Got no diamond solitaire:
So what?
Y'know what?
I consider diamonds kinda square.
Besides, I never felt better, and I'm
    walkin'
On
Air!!

LOVE

REFRAIN 1

Love
Can be a moment's madness,
Love
Can be insane,
Love
Can be a life of sadness and pain.
Love
Can be a summer shower,
Love
Can be the sun,
Love
Can be two hearts that flower as one.
It can be

Fine and free,
But it's true,
It doesn't always happen to you.
Love
Can be a dying ember,
Love
Can be a flame,
Love pledged in September
May be dead in December.
You may not even remember
It came.
Oh, love
Can be a joy forever,
Or
An empty name,
Love
Is almost never
Ever
The same.

REFRAIN 2

Love
Can be a cup of sorrow,
Love
Can be a lie,
Love
Can make you wake tomorrow and sigh.
Love
Can be a snow-capped mountain,
Love
Can be the truth,
Love
Can be an endless fountain of youth.
It can be
Ecstasy,
But that kind
Is not so very easy to find.
Love
Can be the force for failure,
Love
Can bring you fame,
Love fresh as the morning
May be wild when it's borning.

And then without any warning
It's tame.
Oh, love's
A tie that's hard to sever,
Or
A losing game,
Love
Is almost never
Ever
The same.

Spring Isn't Everything

(Ralph Blane alone)

Spring
Isn't ev'rything, it's true.
There's a lot to be said for Summer,
Summer has beauty too.
With the world full out of its shell,
You'll be caught in its sunny spell;
Oh, Spring
Isn't ev'rything.
Spring
Isn't ev'rything, it's true.
There's a lot to be said for Autumn,
Autumn has beauty too.
Though the breeze may chill with its blow,
You'll be caught in its golden glow;
Oh, Spring
Isn't ev'rything.
There's a lot to be said when Winter brings
The snow to hide the heather;
Don't worry your head with what Winter
    brings,
It's only the weather.
Spring
Isn't ev'rything, it's true.
Though a lot can be said when Summer
And Autumn and Winter sing,
If you're together
Life is a golden ring.

Oh, Spring
Isn't ev'rything.

—Harry Warren

That Face

HE: Never touched a drop last night,
    Stuck to soda pop last night,
    But I went on a sympathetic binge.
    While others wassail-cupped it up,
    I always Seven-Upped it up
    But savored every alcoholic twinge.
SHE: Congratulations on all your
        abnegations,
    But why shy from rye
    Or steer clear of beer?
HE: I keep my eyes from getting bleary,
    The better to see you with, my dearie.

    That face,
    That funny, sunny face,
    No smile as wileful, beguileful as
        yours.
    I case
    That happy, happy face,
    And want to smother my other
        amours.
    That face
    Is such a silly face,
    But it's a treasure of pleasure and
        grace.
    There's obviously no face
    That ever can replace
    That chiller-thriller, killer-diller
        face.

SHE: That face,
    That darling, snarling face,
    Though it's an eyeful, I stifle
        each yen.

I face
Your helter-skelter face,
You most attractive, reactive of men.
That face
Makes every blonde give chase,
But with brunettes, too, it gets to
     first base.
There's absolutely no face
That ever can replace
That jazzy, snazzy, razzmatazzy face.

The Trolley Song

VERSE

With my high starched collar
And my high-topped shoes
And my hair piled high upon my head,
I went to lose a jolly
Hour on the trolley
And lost my heart instead.
With his light brown derby
And his bright green tie,
He was quite the handsomest of men.
I started to yen,
So I counted to ten,
Then I counted to ten again.

REFRAIN

"Clang, clang, clang," went the trolley,
"Ding, ding, ding," went the bell,
"Zing, zing, zing," went my heartstrings,

For the moment I saw him I fell.
"Chug, chug, chug," went the motor,
"Bump, bump, bump," went the brake.
"Thump, thump, thump," went my
     heartstrings,
When he smiled, I could feel the car
     shake.
He tipped his hat
And took a seat.
He said he hoped he hadn't stepped upon
     my feet.
He asked my name,
I held my breath,
I couldn't speak
Because he scared me half to death.
"Buzz, buzz, buzz," went the buzzer.
"Plop, plop, plop," went the wheels,
"Stop, stop, stop," went my heartstrings,
1. As he started to go
    Then I started to know
    How it feels
    When the universe reels.
2. As he started to leave,
    I took hold of his sleeve with my hand,
    And as if it were planned,
    He stayed on with me
    And it was grand,
    Just to stand with his hand
    Holding mine,
    To the end of the line.

—Hugh Martin

Robert Wright (1914–)
and George Forrest (1915–1999)

T HE WRITING partnership of Robert Wright and George Forrest is probably the
longest in musical history: over seventy years. They met in school, in Miami–
Forrest (born George Forrest Chichester, Jr.) was, at thirteen, already playing the
piano in night spots, while Wright–aged fourteen–was conducting his own radio show
as well as Sunday concerts. Before they were twenty, they were off on an extended tour
of cabarets, and eventually fetched up in Hollywood, at M-G-M. Their breakthrough
came when they stitched together out of classical oddments a score for the Jeanette
MacDonald/Nelson Eddy *Maytime*–including a completely invented opera, *La Tsa-
rita,* based on Tchaikovsky's Fifth Symphony. In the same year, they wrote the semi-
immortal "Donkey Serenade," based on a Rudolf Friml melody–Allan Jones sings it to
MacDonald and some mules in *The Firefly.* They were putting on revues for New York's
glamorous Copacabana nightclub when they began work on the first of their major triumphs in the theater–the 1944 *Song of Norway,* about Edvard Grieg, and using his
music. In 1948 came *The Great Waltz* and in 1953, came *Kismet,* based on the music
of Alexander Borodin and featuring "Stranger in Paradise." In 1989, *Grand Hotel,*
revamped by them and others from a version written thirty years earlier, opened on
Broadway and ran for more than a thousand performances.

AND THIS IS MY BELOVED

Dawn's promising skies,
Petals on a pool drifting;
Imagine these in one pair of eyes,
And this is my beloved.
Strange spice from the south,
Honey through the comb sifting;
Imagine these on one eager mouth,
And this is my beloved.
And when she speaks,
And when she talks to me,
Music!
Mystery!

And when she moves,
And when she walks with me,
Paradise comes suddenly near!
All that can stir,
All that can stun,
All that's for the heart's
Lifting;
Imagine these in one perfect one,
And this is my beloved!
And this is my beloved!

–Alexander Borodin

Baubles, Bangles, and Beads

Baubles, bangles,
Hear how they jing-jing-a-ling-a,
Baubles, bangles,
Bright shiny beads.
Sparkles, spangles,
My heart will sing, sing-a-ling-a,
Wearing baubles, bangles, and beads.
I'll glitter and gleam so,
Make somebody dream so
That someday he may buy me
A ring, ring-a-ling-a,
I've heard that's where it leads,
Wearing baubles, bangles, and beads.

—Alexander Borodin

It's a Blue World

VERSE
You were the light that brightened my life,
My stars, and moon, and sun.
Then with your flight came the night in
my life,
No laughs, no love, no fun.

REFRAIN
It's a blue world
Without you,
It's a blue world
Alone.
My days and nights
That once were filled with heaven,
With you away,
How empty they have grown.
It's a blue world
From now on,
It's a through world
For me.
The sea, the sky, my heart, and I,

We're all an indigo hue,
Without you
It's a blue, blue world.

Strange Music

VERSE
Soft breeze!
Whispering trees!
The summer winds are sighing,
The leaves are lullabying.
Violins are all around you,
I can hear the chords resound
Of bounding brass that seems to say,
I've found you!
I've found you!
I've found you!

REFRAIN
Strange music in my ears,
Only now as you spoke, did it start.
Strange music of the spheres,
Could its lovely hum be coming from my
heart?
You appear, and I hear song sublime,
Song that I'm
Incapable of.
So dear, let me hold you near,
While we treasure ev'ry measure,
So that time can never change
The strange
New music of love.

—Edvard Grieg

Stranger in Paradise

Take my hand,
I'm a stranger in paradise,
All lost in a wonderland,
A stranger in paradise.

If I stand starry-eyed,
That's a danger in paradise,
For mortals who stand beside
An angel like you.
I saw your face
And I ascended
Out of the commonplace
Into the rare!
Somewhere in space
I hang suspended
Until I know

There's a chance that you care.
Won't you answer the fervent prayer
Of a stranger in paradise?
Don't send me in dark despair
From all that I hunger for,
But open your angel's arms
To the stranger in paradise
And tell him that he need be
A stranger no more.

—Alexander Borodin

Irving Gordon (1915–1996)

BORN IN Brooklyn, Irving Gordon studied the violin as a child, and was soon working in Catskill resorts, writing parody songs. Like so many other beginning lyricists, he went to work for Mills Music, but soon he was established as a reliable songwriter, responsible for both music and words. Because of the success of the Natalie Cole version of "Unforgettable"–her voice superimposed on that of her late father, Nat–that song is now Gordon's best-known work, but he had other real successes: Duke Ellington's "Prelude to a Kiss," "What Will I Tell My Heart?," "Be Anything (But Be Mine)." And how many songwriters produced hits for both Billie Holiday ("Me, Myself and I") and Patti Page ("(Throw) Mama From the Train (a Kiss, a Kiss))?

BE ANYTHING (BUT BE MINE)

Be a beggar, be a thief,
Be my sunshine or my grief,
Be anything, but darling, be mine.
Be a wise one, be a fool,
Treat me tender or be cruel,
Be anything, but darling, be mine.
Climb to the top of the ladder,
Be master of all you survey,
Fail and it still doesn't matter,
If you love me ev'rything is O.K.
Be the angel of my pray'rs,
Be the Devil who cares,
Be anything, but darling, be mine.

PRELUDE TO A KISS

(with Irving Mills)

If you hear a song in blue
Like a flower crying for the dew,
That was my heart serenading you,
My prelude to a kiss.
If you hear a song that grows
From my tender sentimental woes,
That was my heart trying to compose
A prelude to a kiss.
Though it's just a simple melody
With nothing fancy, nothing much,
You could turn it to a symphony,
A Schubert tune with a Gershwin touch.
Oh! How my love song gently cries
For the tenderness within your eyes.
My love is a prelude that never dies,
A prelude to a kiss.

—Duke Ellington

UNFORGETTABLE

Unforgettable,
That's what you are.
Unforgettable,
Though near or far.
Like a song of love that clings to me,
How the thought of you does things
   to me.
Never before

Has someone been more
Unforgettable,
In ev'ry way,
And forever more,
That's how you'll stay.

That's why, darling,
It's incredible,
That someone so unforgettable
Thinks that I am unforgettable,
    too.

Jay Livingston (1915–   )
and Ray Evans (1915–   )

O NE OF the most successful songwriting teams of our time, Jay Livingston (from McDonald, Pennsylvania) and Ray Evans (from Salamanca, New York) met at the University of Pennsylvania, and began working together in dance bands and nightclub orchestras. Their first successful song, "G'bye Now," was written for the musical *Hellzapoppin'* in 1941; after the war, their careers began in earnest. They became the chief writers for Paramount, producing half a dozen number-one songs (three different recordings of "To Each His Own" got to number one: Eddy Howard's, Freddy Martin's, and the Ink Spots'–now that's a *hit*). And three of their songs won Oscars: "Buttons and Bows," "Mona Lisa," and "Whatever Will Be, Will Be" ("Que Sera, Sera"). (While at Paramount, they even appeared in the party scene in *Sunset Boulevard.*) In 1958 their show *Oh Captain!* was modestly successful on Broadway. Throughout their decades-long partnership, Livingston has been the composer while collaborating with Evans on the lyrics. In their post-Paramount days they've worked together on lyrics for other composers, including Jimmy McHugh and Henry Mancini.

BUTTONS AND BOWS

VERSE

A western ranch is just a branch of
   Nowhere Junction to me.
Gimme the city where livin's pretty and
   the gals wear finery.

REFRAIN

East is east and west is west
And the wrong one I have chose;
Let's go where I'll keep on wearin'
Those frills and flowers and buttons
   and bows,
Rings and things and buttons and bows.
Don't bury me in this prairie,
Take me where the cement grows;
Let's move down to some big town

Where they love a gal by the cut o' her
   clothes,
And I'll stand out in buttons and bows.
I'll love you in buckskin
Or skirts that I've homespun,
But I'll love ya' longer, stronger,
Where yer friends don't tote a gun.
My bones denounce the buckboard bounce
And the cactus hurts my toes;
Let's vamoose where gals keep usin'
Those silks and satins and linen that
   shows,
I'm all yours in buttons and bows.
And gimme eastern trimmin' where
   women are women
In high silk hose and peekaboo clothes
And French perfume that rocks the room
And I'm all yours in buttons and bows.

FEMININITY

VERSE

Why can't I be the girl that I want to be?
Why can't I be the girl that I'm not?
Why do men always look as they look when
    they look at me?
I must have something, but what have
    I got?
I say I'd like to join the married class;
The man says, "Yes my dear," then makes
    a pass.

REFRAIN

Femininity, femininity,
I guess I'm over-blessed with femininity.
I want a family life, woman's career,
But all that I get is a pinch on the rear.
Femininity, my femininity
Just seems to bring out basic masculinity.
There's only thing they want, that's
    understood,
I tell them I shouldn't, they tell me I should.
There must be other ways to make a man
    feel good.
All I do is simply stand there,
All at once I feel a hand there,
Begging for my femininity.
Femininity, my femininity,
Just seems to bring a crowd to my vicinity.
Other girls have the same these, them,
    and those,
But they always manage to stay in their
    clothes.
Personality, my personality,
It makes them all expect my hospitality.
When a man brings me home, I ask him in,
I only intend to have one little gin,
Why do I always end up on the tiger skin?
There are times I can't help feeling,
As I'm staring at the ceiling,
What's the point of femininity?

HAVEN'T GOT A WORRY

VERSE

Feelin' fine, feelin' great,
I got a reason to celebrate,
Feelin' great, feelin' fine,
Caught me some happiness on my line!

REFRAIN I

Birds can fly, so can I,
I'm so happy I'm flyin' high;
Haven't got a worry to my name!
She's my friend, he's my pal,
Ev'rybody's my guy and gal;
Haven't got a worry to my name!
I do ev'rything I do with brand-new
    rhythm;
Tell those lucky stars I'm movin' right in
    with 'em.
Fly the flags, ring the bells,
What a future my fortune tells!
Feel so free I'll never be the same;
I haven't got a worry to my name.
Haven't got a worry!
Who's got time to worry?
Haven't got a worry to my name!

REFRAIN 2

There are some who study nights to be a
    mourner;
Me, I have a new adventure 'round each
    corner.
Fly the flags, ring the bells,
What a future my fortune tells!
Feel so free I'll never be the same;
I haven't got a worry to my name.
Haven't got a worry!
Who's got time to worry?
Haven't got a worry to my name!

KEEP IT SIMPLE

Keep it simple,
Don't make too much of love.
Keep it simple,
Let's enjoy each touch of love.
Don't end up with self-reproach,
Don't bring your dramatic coach,
Take that direct approach,
Why be tricky, grab a quicky.
Come with me, but
Don't pack a big valise.
Take my key, but
Don't expect a long-term lease.
For tonight, c'est la guerre,
And tomorrow who knows where?
Keep it simple,
And we'll have a simply splendid affair.
I'm not standoff,
And I'm frustration-free,
"Take your hands off,"
This you'll never hear from me.
Here is my moral code,
Have your fun and hit the road,
Keep it simple,
Sweet and simple,
And we'll have a simply splendid affair.

MONA LISA

VERSE

In a villa in a little old Italian town
Lives a girl whose beauty shames
    the rose.
Many yearn to love her, but their hopes all
    tumble down.
What does she want? No one knows!

REFRAIN

Mona Lisa, Mona Lisa,
Men have named you:

You're so like the lady with the mystic
    smile.
Is it only 'cause you're lonely
They have blamed you
For that Mona Lisa strangeness in your
    smile?
Do you smile to tempt a lover, Mona Lisa,
Or is this your way to hide a broken heart?
Many dreams have been brought to your
    doorstep.
They just lie there,
And they die there.
Are you warm, are you real, Mona Lisa,
Or just a cold and lonely, lovely work of art?

NEVER LET ME GO

Never let me go,
Love me much too much.
If you let me go,
Life would lose its touch.
What would I be without you?
There's no place for me without you.
Never let me go.
I'd be so lost if you went away,
There'd be a thousand hours in the day
Without you, I know.
Because of one caress my world was
    overturned,
At the very start, all my bridges burned
By my flaming heart.
You'd never leave me, would you?
You couldn't hurt me, could you?
Never let me go,
Never let me go.

TO EACH HIS OWN

VERSE

Wise men have shown
Life is no good alone,

Day needs night,
Flowers need light,
I need you,
I need you.

REFRAIN

A rose must remain with the sun and
     the rain
Or its lovely promise won't come true.
To each his own, to each his own,
And my own is you.
What good is a song
If the words just don't belong,
And a dream must be a dream for two.
No good alone, to each his own,
For me there's you.
If a flame is to grow there must be a glow,
To open each door there's a key.
I need you, I know,
I can't let you go,
Your touch means too much to me.
Two lips must insist on two more to be
     kissed
Or they'll never know what love can do.
To each his own, I've found my own
One and only you.

WHATEVER WILL BE, WILL BE
(QUE SERA, SERA)

REFRAIN I

When I was just a little girl
I asked my mother,
"What will I be?
Will I be pretty?
Will I be rich?"
Here's what she said to me:
"Que sera, sera,

Whatever will be will be;
The future's not ours to see.
Que sera sera!
What will be will be!"
When I grew up and fell in love,
I asked my lover,
"What lies ahead?
Will we have rainbows day after
     day?"
Here's what my lover said:
"Que sera, sera,
Whatever will be will be;
The future's not ours to see.
Que sera sera!
What will be will be!"

REFRAIN 2

When I was just a child in school,
I asked my teacher,
"What should I try?
Should I paint pictures?
Should I sing songs?"
This was her wise reply:
"Que sera, sera,
Whatever will be will be;
The future's not ours to see.
Que sera sera!
What will be will be!"
Now I have children of my own,
They ask their mother,
"What will I be?
Will I be pretty?
Will I be rich?"
I tell them tenderly:
"Que sera, sera,
Whatever will be will be;
The future's not ours to see.
Que sera, sera!
What will be will be!"

Bob Russell (1915–1970)

SIDNEY KEITH, "Bob Russell," seems to have moved steadily westward: He was born in New Jersey, went to college in St. Louis, and ended up in Beverly Hills. His output ranges widely, too–from his Ellington collaborations to his big-band hits ("Frenesi," number one for Artie Shaw; "Maria Elena," number one for Jimmy Dorsey) to the schmaltzy but effective "Ballerina," ten weeks at the top of the charts for Vaughn Monroe in 1947, and on into the world of Neil Diamond in 1970, with "He Ain't Heavy, He's My Brother." And let's not forget "Brazil," which kept turning up in movie musicals through the forties: in *The Gang's All Here,* sung by Carmen Miranda; in *The Road to Rio;* in *The Eddie Duchin Story;* and in something actually *called Brazil,* featuring popular Mexican singer Tito Guizar and Carmen Miranda's sister.

BALLERINA

Dance, ballerina, dance,
And do your pirouette in rhythm with your
    aching heart.
Dance, ballerina, dance,
You mustn't once forget a dancer has to
    dance the part.
Whirl, ballerina, whirl,
And just ignore the chair that's empty in
    the second row.
This is your moment, girl,
Although he's not out there applauding as
    you steal the show.
Once you said
His love must wait its turn.
You wanted fame instead–
I guess that's your concern,
We live and learn.
And love is gone, ballerina, gone,
So on with your career,
You can't afford a backward glance.
Dance on and on and on;

A thousand people here have come to see
    the show
As 'round and 'round you go,
So ballerina dance, dance, dance.

–Carl Sigman

CRAZY SHE CALLS ME

I say I'll move the mountains,
And I'll move the mountains
If she wants them out of the way.
Crazy she calls me,
Sure I'm crazy, crazy in love, I'd say.
I say I'll go through fire, and I'll go
    through fire,
As she wants it so it will be.
Crazy she calls me,
Sure I'm crazy,
Crazy in love, you see.
Like the wind that shakes the bough
She moves me with a smile.

The difficult I'll do right now,
The impossible will take a little while.
I say I'll care forever,
And I mean forever
If I have to hold up the sky.
Crazy she calls me,
Sure I'm crazy,
Crazy in love am I.

—*Carl Sigman*

DON'T GET AROUND MUCH ANYMORE

VERSE
When I'm not playing solitaire,
I take a book down from the shelf,
And what with programs on the air
I keep pretty much to myself.

REFRAIN
Missed the Saturday dance,
Heard they crowded the floor,
Couldn't bear it without you,
Don't get around much anymore.
Thought I'd visit the club,
Got as far as the door,
They'd have asked me about you,
Don't get around much anymore.
Darling, I guess
My mind's more at ease,
But nevertheless,
Why stir up memories?
Been invited on dates,
Might have gone, but what for?
Awf'lly diff'rent without you,
Don't get around much anymore.

—*Duke Ellington*

I DIDN'T KNOW ABOUT YOU

VERSE
If they would ask me I would say,
I have had a thrill or so.
But that goes back to yesterday,
A long time ago.

REFRAIN
I ran around with my own little crowd,
The usual laughs, not often but loud,
And in the world that I knew,
I didn't know about you.
Chasing after the ring on the merry-go-
    round,
Just taking my fun where it could be
    found,
And yet what else could I do?
I didn't know about you.
Darling, now I know I had the loneliest
    yesterday,
Ev'ry day.
In your arms I know for once in my life
I'm living.
Had a good time ev'ry time I went out,
Romance was a thing I kidded about,
How could I know about love?
I didn't know about you.

—*Duke Ellington*

YOU CAME A LONG WAY FROM ST. LOUIS

You came a long way from St. Louis,
You climbed the ladder of success.
I've seen the Town and Country cars that
    were parked out in front
Of your fancy address.
You came a long way from St. Louis,
You broke a lotta hearts between.

I've met a gang of gloomy guys who were
     doin' all right
Till you came on the scene.
You blew in from the Middle West,
And certainly impressed
The population hereabouts.
Well, baby, I got news for you,
I'm from Missouri, too,

So natcherly I got my doubts.
You got 'em droppin' by the wayside,
A feelin' I ain't gonna know.
You came a long way from St. Louis,
But, baby, you still got a long way
     to go.

—John Benson Brooks

Bart Howard (1915–)

B ORN HOWARD GUSTAFSSON IN Burlington, Iowa, Bart Howard–his father was the town bootlegger–got his start at age sixteen, playing for a dance marathon. He graduated to hotel bands, and then to vaudeville, accompanying an act featuring Siamese twins, then on to the army, and finally to New York. His first important sponsor was Mabel Mercer; not only did she sing his early songs, but she hired him as her accompanist, a gig that lasted four years. In 1952 he became the emcee and musical director of the Blue Angel, one of New York's most fashionable nightclubs. He was there until 1960, by which time New York, nightclubs, and popular music itself had changed. By then, he had turned out many sophisticated yet expressive songs, of which the most famous, by far, is "Fly Me to the Moon"; it's been recorded more than one thousand times.

FLY ME TO THE MOON
(IN OTHER WORDS)

VERSE

Poets often use many words to say a simple
    thing.
It takes thought and time and rhyme to
    make a poem sing.
With music and words I've been playing,
For you I have written a song,
To be sure that you'll know what I'm
    saying
I'll translate as I go along.

REFRAIN

Fly me to the moon, and let me play
    among the stars;
Let me see what Spring is like on Jupiter
    and Mars.
In other words, hold my hand!
In other words, darling, kiss me!
Fill my heart with song, and let me sing
    forever more;

You are all I long for, all I worship and
    adore.
In other words, please be true!
In other words, I love you!

WHO BESIDES YOU

When you hear me say "darling" or "dear"
To another man, or see me blow another
    man a kiss,
I don't know what you can do, do you?
Other than, darling, ask yourself this:

Who besides you
Could I see beside me
All alone on a tropical isle?
And who could I see
Besides you beside me
When I dream with my lips in a smile?
And where besides here in these arms of
    yours
Am I nearer to heaven above?

But why take the time
To ask questions in rhyme
When there's you beside me to love?
But why take the time
To ask questions in rhyme
When there's you beside me beside you
    beside me beside you beside me
    to love?

Would You Believe It?

VERSE

I bought a great big hat
With a bright red feather and a bow.
I sold my stocks, bought some
    mink-dyed fox,
And I'm riding high instead of hiding low.
But remember the way I used to be,
Kind of huffy, plain stuffy, all the day?
Never used any kind of cologne
When I hadn't a man of my own.
Today you can smell my Chanel a
    mile away.

REFRAIN

Would you believe it,
After all that I said
About romance not bothering me?
Would you believe it,
Used to have a level head,
Now I'm now in love as love can be?
I was immune
To June,
I never ventured out in the park,

No butterfly
Was I,
Now get me, I'm gay as a lark.
I'm really giddy,
Why to tell you the truth,
I'm like a bird let out of a cage,
A chickabiddy
Who mixes gin and vermouth,
Might even try my luck on the stage.
I used to sing
About birdies in the Spring,
Then love gave me a twirl.
Would you believe it,
Now I'm a real gone girl.

Year After Year

Here we stand on the brink of tomorrow
Too helplessly happy to think of
    tomorrow,
But as long as you're looking at me,
Oh, what a joy my tomorrows would be!
Let my love be the love you remember,
Let my heart be the heart you'll keep,
Let my face be the face you'll dream of
Every time you smile in your sleep.
Let my lips be the lips you long for
And my song be the song you sing,
Let my love be the love you'll remember
Spring after Spring after Spring.
Let my arms be the arms you are seeking
When the dawn is creeping near,
Let my love be the love you'll remember
Year after year after year.

Billy Strayhorn (1915–1967)

ALTHOUGH BILLY STRAYHORN was born in Dayton, Ohio, he grew up in Pittsburgh, like so many other important figures in jazz (including his friend Lena Horne). He was raised in classical music, but an early exposure to the music of Duke Ellington converted him, and by 1938 they were working together. Their collaboration was of an extraordinary kind: The somewhat retiring Strayhorn (he was known as "Swee' Pea" by his friends) became less an employee or co-worker than an alter ego. He and Ellington were together for more than twenty-five years. Strayhorn played piano, did arrangements, co-wrote; he and Ellington worked together on many compositions and songs. Sometimes Strayhorn wrote music, sometimes words, sometimes both—as in the case of the Ellington theme song "Take the A Train." His most famous song is the extremely complicated "Lush Life," sung by countless recording artists and cabaret singers, but by no one more affectingly than Nat "King" Cole.

A LONELY COED

I just can't seem to get that campus
   bloom.
When I come in, the boys all leave
   the room.
I just don't seem to attract.
I'm just a lonely coed.
I wear my clothes like all the other girls,
I wear my hair in all the latest curls,
They just don't seem to react.
I'm just a lonely coed.
Maybe I don't know enough of the
   tricks,
Maybe I lack technique,
Maybe there's something I could fix,
Maybe my line is weak.
While everybody else is making love
I sit with folded hands, the picture of
A total failure, a flop.
I'm just a lonely, lonely coed.

LUSH LIFE

I used to visit all the very gay places,
Those come-what-may places,
Where one relaxes on the axis of the wheel
   of life
To get the feel of life
From jazz and cocktails.
The girls I knew had sad and sullen gray
   faces,
With distingué traces
That used to be there.
You could see where
They'd been washed away
By too many through the day
Twelve o'clock tails.
Then you came along
With your siren song
To tempt me to madness.
I thought for a while
That your poignant smile
Was tinged with the sadness

Of a great love for me.
Ah, yes, I was wrong,
Again, I was wrong!
Life is lonely again,
And only last year
Ev'rything seemed so sure.
Now life is awful again,
A troughful of hearts could only be a bore.
A week in Paris will ease the bite of it.
All I care is to smile in spite of it.
I'll forget you, I will,
While yet you are still
Burning inside my brain.
Romance is mush, stifling those who
    strive.
I'll live a lush life in some small dive,
And there I'll be, while I rot with the rest
Of those whose lives are lonely too.

SOMETHING TO LIVE FOR

VERSE
I have almost ev'rything
A human could desire,

Cars and houses, bearskin rugs
To lie before my fire.
But there's something missing,
Something isn't there.
It seems I'm never kissing
The one whom I could care for.

REFRAIN
I want something to live for,
Someone to make my life
An adventurous dream.
Oh, what wouldn't I give for
Someone who'd take my life
And make it seem
Gay as they say it ought to be.
Why can't I have love like that brought
    to me?
My eye is watching the noon
    crowds,
Searching the promenades,
Seeking a clue
To the one who will someday be
My something to live for.

—with Duke Ellington

Betty Comden (1917–)
and Adolph Green (1915–)

THE SPECTACULAR CAREER of this partnership–they've worked only with each other–began in 1939, when they wrote for and performed in a fresh and sophisticated cabaret act (with Judy Holliday) called the Revuers. Soon they linked up with another couple of talented youngsters–Leonard Bernstein and Jerome Robbins–to write their first musical, the 1944 smash hit *On the Town,* based on Robbins's first ballet, *Fancy Free.* There followed a long list of shows, among them *Wonderful Town* (with Bernstein again, and starring Rosalind Russell); the Mary Martin *Peter Pan; Bells are Ringing,* for their old friend Judy Holliday; *Do Re Mi* for Phil Silvers and Nancy Walker; and with Cy Coleman, *On the Twentieth Century* and *The Will Rogers Follies.* And although they are pure New Yorkers, born and bred, they were highly successful in Hollywood, too, as part of the famous "Freed unit" at M-G-M: They wrote the screenplays for *Singin' in the Rain* and *The Band Wagon,* among other top movie musicals. In addition, they have been indefatigable performers of their own work, starring in the one-woman/one-man show aptly titled *A Party with Comden and Green.* It's been a long and wonderful party!

ADVENTURE

HE: You should have married Seymour
    Brilkin.
A better life you would be leading.
Respectable, secure,
So comfortable and sure,
A regular Mrs. Counselor-at-law.
You should have married Seymour
    Brilkin!
Down on his knees you heard him
    pleading.
He tore his hair and cried,
Yet you threw him aside,
Why didn't you listen to your maw!?

SHE: Ah yes, ah yes,

I'd have two fur coats
And a black beaded dress,
Two cars, two houses,
Two safe deposit boxes,
Two poodles, and oodles
Of dripping silver foxes . . .

HE: You should have married Seymour
    Brilkin!
Oh what a lush life it would be.
You'd be living high.

SHE: So kindly tell me why
The wealthy Mrs. Brilkin is jealous
    of me?
'Cause I've got
Adventure . . . adventure,
With you every day is an adventure.

I wake with the dawn
And before I can yawn
There's a knock at the door.
Who knows what lies in store?
Are you under arrest?
Have we been dispossessed?
Will we find ourselves out on the
   street?
Yes I've got . . .
Adventure . . . adventure.
So dear Mrs. Brilkin,
Go keep all your silken,
And satin and mink lingerie.
My life is a ball.
It's the "Perils of Paul-
Ine," with my name up on the
   marquee!
It's adventure for me!

HE: You should have married Sheldon
   Miller
And have the million things you're
   missing.
A dope,
A brain of wood,
In plastics he made good,
So you could be Mrs. "Plastic-
   garment-bag."
You should have married Sheldon
   Miller,
The ground you walked on he was
   kissing.
But you told him "Drop dead"
And you picked me instead—
If you were his wife your mom
   could brag!

SHE: Ah, so . . . ah, so . . .
I'd have full-time maids
And an old French chateau,
Two yachts,
Two airplanes,
A home with two golf courses,
French labels,
And stables

Of fiery racing horses.

HE: You should have married Sheldon
   Miller.
Oh, what a lush life that would be,
Built of solid gold.

SHE: So why is it I'm told
The horsey Mrs. Miller is jealous
   of me?
'Cause I've got
Adventure . . . adventure,
With you may I say it's an
   adventure.
You've passed a bum check
And the guy's on your neck,
So we dash out of town for a spree.
The place that we stay
Is in Far Rockaway,
With a heavenly view of the sea.
But the bill soon arrives,
So we run for our lives.
Out the window, by dark,
We continue our lark.
We drop to the streets
On a ladder of sheets,
It's an unobserved drop,
All except for one cop.
We flee, hand in hand,
Down in the damp midnight sand,
By a great piece of luck
There's the back of a truck.
It bumps us to town,
I'm still in my nightgown—
Well, the weekend's been chic,
And it's tune in next week.
So dear Mrs. Mill-
Er, go beep your chinchill-
A, 'Cause even if Sheldon were free,
I'd give up each ruby
And stick to my Hubie.
It's adventure . . . adventure . . .
For me!
Ah well, Seymour Brilkin,
Ah well, Sheldon Miller,

Oh well, what's a girl gonna do?
Hubert Cram, I love you.

—Jule Styne

ALL OF MY LIFE

All of my life
I've been dreaming the wrong dream,
Hoping the wrong hope,
Singing the wrong song . . . all of
    my life.
All of my life
I've been picking the wrong horse,
Saying the wrong things,
Making the wrong bets . . . all of my life.
I thought there was nothing to life
But wait for that lucky hunch.
Just land that lucky punch
Wham!
You too can be the champ.
Yesterday you batted zero.
Hit a homer, you're a hero.
I thought there was nothing to life
But wait for that lucky hunch.
There must be something more to it,
Somewhere along the line I blew it!
All of my life
I've been seeing the wrong crowd,
Wearing the wrong ties,
Dancing the wrong steps,
All of my life.
All of my life
I've been off on the wrong beam,
Backing the wrong team,
Dreaming the wrong dream,
All of my life,
All of my life,
All of my no-good life.
I thought the American dream was:
Wait for your one big break.
Just give the dice a shake.

You too can be on top. Be an overnight
    sensation,
Meet the press and face the nation.
I thought the American dream was:
Wait for your one big break
There must be something more to it,
Somewhere along the line I blew it!
All of my life
I've been learning the wrong tricks,
Pulling the wrong strings,
Making the wrong moves,
All of my life.
All of my life
I've been off on the wrong beam,
Backing the wrong team,
Dreaming the wrong dream,
All of my life,
All of my life,
All of my whole damn life!

—Jule Styne

CONGA

What do you think of the USA–NRA–TVA?
What do you think of our Mother's Day?
What do you think of the–
Conga!
What do you think of our native squaws,
Charles G. Dawes,
Warden Lawes–
What's your opinion of Santa Claus?
What do you think of the–
Conga!
Good neighbors, good neighbors,
Remember our policy–
Good neighbors–I'll help you,
If you'll just help me–
Conga!
What's your opinion of Harold Teen,
Mitzi Green,
Dizzy Dean?

Who do you love on the silver screen?
What do you think of the—
Conga!
What do you think of our rhythm bands,
Monkey glands,
Hot dog stands?
What do you think of Stokowski's hands?
What do you think of the—
Conga!
Good neighbors—good neighbors,
Remember our policy—
Good neighbors—I'll help you,
If you'll just help me—
Conga!
What's your opinion of women's clothes,
Major Bowes,
Steinbeck's prose?
How do you feel about Broadway Rose?
What do you think of the—
Conga!
What do you think of our rocks and rills,
Mother Sills'
Sea-sick pills?
How do you feel about Helen Wills?
What do you think of the—
Conga!
Good neighbors, good neighbors,
Remember our policy—
Good neighbors—I'll help you,
If you'll just help me—
What do you think of our double malts,
Family vaults,
Epsom salts?
Wouldn't you guys like to learn to waltz?
I know—you just want to—Conga!

—Leonard Bernstein

I CAN COOK, TOO

Oh, I can cook, too, on top of the rest,
My seafood's the best in the town.

And I can cook, too,
My fish can't be beat,
My sugar's the sweetest aroun'.
I'm a man's ideal of a perfect meal
Right down to the demitasse.
I'm a pot of joy for a hungry boy,
Baby, I'm cooking with gas!
Oh, I'm a gumdrop,
A sweet lollipop,
A brook trout right out of the brook,
And what's more, baby, I can cook!
Some girls make magazine covers,
Some girls keep house on a dime,
Some girls make wonderful lovers,
But what a lucky find I'm.
I'd make a magazine cover,
I do keep house on a dime,
I'd make a wonderful lover,
I should be paid overtime!
'Cause I can bake, too, on top of the lot,
My oven's the hottest you'll find.
Yes, I can roast, too,
My chickens just ooze,
My gravy will lose you your mind.
I'm a brand-new note
On a table d'hôte,
But just try mine à la carte.
With a single course
You can choke a horse.
Baby, you won't know where to start!
Oh, I'm an hors d'oeuvre,
A jelly preserve
Not in the recipe book,
And what's more, baby, I can cook!
Baby, I'm cooking with gas!
Oh, I'm a gumdrop,
A sweet lollipop,
A brook trout right out of the brook.
And what's more, baby, I can cook!
Some girls make wonderful jivers,
Some girls can hit a high "C,"
Some girls make good taxi drivers,
But what a genius is me.

I'd make a wonderful jiver,
I even hit a high "C,"
I'd make the best taxi driver,
I rate a big navy "E"!
'Cause I can fry, too, on top of
    the heap,
My Crisco's as deep as a pool.
Yes, I can broil, too,
My ribs win applause,
My lamb chops will cause you to drool.
For a candied sweet
Or a pickled beet,
Step up to my smorgasbord.
Walk around until
You get your fill.
Baby, you won't ever be bored!
Oh, I'm a paté,
A marron glacé,
A dish you will wish you had took.
And what's more, baby, I can cook!!

—Leonard Bernstein

IF YOU HADN'T—BUT YOU DID

VERSE

VERSE

There he goes as usual,
My man,
Breaking my foolish heart.
I really don't know what to do
About him,
I've told myself I've got to do
Without him.
There he goes as usual,
My man,
Tearing my heart apart.
He's made my life a mess.
I've got to do this, I guess.
Good-bye, Joe,
From here I kiss you.
Good-bye, Joe,
I hope I don't miss you.

REFRAIN 1

If
You had been on the square and had
    treated me fair we'd have not had
    a tiff.
If
You had not said I should go and jump
    right off the nearest cliff.
If
You had stayed off the make and you
    never had taken to coming home
    stiff.
If
I had not smelled perfume with a nasty
    unfamiliar whiff.
I'm gonna miss you, baby.
Things could have been terriff.
Ah! What's the diff!
If
You had not had the cheek to stay out for a
    week saying "Back in a jiff."

1. If
    You were not such a two-timing guy.
    If you
    Weren't,
    If you hadn't,
    If you didn't,
    If you weren't,
    If you
    Hadn't,
    If you didn't,
    But you were and you have
    And you went and you did,
    And so good-bye.

REFRAIN 2

If
I had not seen you take Geraldine on the
    lake in your flat-bottomed skiff.
If
You were not found with Sue with your
    arms around her bare midriff.

If
I had not seen you pen sexy letters to Gwen
    in your own hieroglyph.
If
You had not left me home when you had
    two seats for *South Pacif*!!
I'm gonna miss you, baby.
You were too darn proliff!
Ah! What's the diff!
If
You were not such a hound who when
    game was around always picked up the
    sniff.

REPEAT I

REFRAIN 3
If
When I asked where you'd been you
    had not clipped my chin with a
    beautiful biff.
If
I had not always found purple lipstick on
    your handkerchief.
If
You had not told me lies and then looked
    in my eyes with a smile beautiff.
If
When I caught you with Kate you had not
    said: "It's of no signiff."
I'm
Going to miss you baby, and I could get
    specif.
Ah. What's the diff!
If,
The best years of my life weren't spent as
    your wife with no marriage certiff.

REPEAT I

—Jule Styne

JUST IN TIME

VERSE
I was resting comfortably
Facedown in the gutter,
Life was serene,
I knew where I was at.
"There's no hope for him,"
My dearest friends would mutter.
I was something dragged in by
    the cat.
Then

REFRAIN
Just in time,
I found you just in time,
Before you came, my time
Was running low.
I was lost,
The losing dice were tossed,
My bridges all were crossed,
Nowhere to go.
Now you're here,
And now I know just where I'm going,
No more doubt or fear,
I've found my way.
For love came just in time.
You found me just in time,
And changed my lonely life,
That lovely day.

—Jule Styne

A LITTLE BIT IN LOVE

Mm,
I'm a little bit in love,
Never felt this way before.
Mm,
Just a little bit in love,
Or perhaps a little bit more.

When he looks at me
Ev'rything's hazy and all out of focus.
When he touches me
I'm in the spell of a strange
    hocus-pocus.
It's so,
I don't know,
I'm so,
I don't know,
I don't know, but I know
If it's love, then it's lovely!
Mm,
It's so nice to be alive
When you meet someone
Who bewitches you.
Will he be my all,
Or did I just fall
A little bit,
A little bit in love.

—Leonard Bernstein

LONELY TOWN

VERSE

Gabey's comin'–
Gabey's comin' to town–
So what–
Who cares?
Back on the ship–
It seemed such a snap–
You'd tap a girl on the shoulder–
She'd turn around–
And then she'd say, "I love you"–
But once on shore–
It's not such a snap–
You get the cold shoulder–
The old runaround–
You're left with no one but you–
Gabey's coming–
Gabey's coming to town.

REFRAIN

A town's a lonely town
When you pass through
And there is no one waiting there for you,
Then it's a lonely town.
You wander up and down–
The crowds rush by,
A million faces pass before your eye,
Still it's a lonely town.
Unless there's love,
A love that's shining like a harbor light–
You're lost in the night
Unless there's love–
The world's an empty place
And every town's
A lonely town.

(ALTERNATE VERSE)

New York, New York–or a village in Ioway;
The only diff'rence is the name.
If you're alone
Whether on Main Street or on Broadway,
If you're alone they are both the same.

—Leonard Bernstein

LUCKY TO BE ME

VERSE

I used to think it might be fun to be
Anyone else but me.
I thought that it would be a pleasant
    surprise
To wake up as a couple of other guys.
But now that I've found you
I've changed my point of view,
And now I wouldn't give a dime to be
Anyone else but me.

REFRAIN

What a day–
Fortune smiled and came my way–

Bringing love I never thought I'd see.
I'm so lucky to be me.
What a night–
Suddenly you came in sight–
Looking just the way I hoped you'd be.
I'm so lucky to be me.
I am simply thunderstruck
At this change in my luck.
Knew at once I wanted you.
Never dreamed you'd want me too.
I'm so proud
You chose me from all the crowd.
There's no other guy I'd rather be–
I could laugh out loud,
I'm so lucky to be me.

—Leonard Bernstein

MAKE SOMEONE HAPPY

Make someone happy,
Make just one someone happy,
Make just one heart the heart you
    sing to.
One smile that cheers you,
One face that lights when it nears you,
One girl you're ev'rything to.
Fame,
If you win it,
Comes and goes
In a minute.
Where's the real
Stuff in life to cling to?
Love
Is the answer,
Someone to love is the answer.
Once you've found her,
Build your world around her.
Make
Someone happy,
Make just one
Someone happy,

And you
Will be happy too.

—Jule Styne

NEW YORK, NEW YORK

VERSE 1

We've got one day here, and not another
    minute
To see the famous sights;
We'll find the romance and danger waiting
    in it
Beneath the Broadway lights.
But we've hair on our chest,
So what we like the best
Are the nights,
Sights! Lights! Nights!

REFRAIN 1

New York, New York,
A helluva town.
The Bronx is up and the Battery's down,
And people ride in a hole in the
    ground.
New York, New York,
It's a helluva town!

VERSE 2

The famous places to visit are so many,
Or so the guidebooks say;
I promised Daddy I wouldn't miss
    on any,
And we have just one day.
Gotta see the whole town
Right from Yonkers on down
To the bay
In just one day.

REFRAIN 2

New York, New York,
A visitor's place.

Where no one lives on account of
    the pace,
But seven million are screaming for space.
New York, New York,
Is a visitor's place!

VERSE 3

Manhattan women are dressed in silk and
    satin,
Or so the fellows say;
There's just one thing that's important in
    Manhattan
When you have just one day.
Gotta pick up a date,
Maybe seven or eight
On your way,
In just one day.

REPEAT REFRAIN I

—*Leonard Bernstein*

NOT MINE

See her eager face,
Her charm,
Her grace,
Her glance,
Her stance,
Her style,
Walks nice,
Talks nice,
Suits me fine.
Trouble is
The girl is his, not mine.
Not mine, and note the light perfume
She lends
A room,
Her flair,
Her air,
Her smile.
Looks good,

Cooks good,
Warm as wine,
[or]
Thrills me,
Kills me,
She's divine.

Touch not,
Clutch not,
Stay in line.
The only trouble is
The girl is his, not mine!

—*Jule Styne*

THE PARTY'S OVER

VERSE

I'm in love with a man,
But the girl that he loves isn't me.
I'll never see him again,
And that's how it has to be.

REFRAIN

The party's over,
It's time to call it a day.
They've burst your pretty balloon
And taken the moon away.
It's time to wind up
The masquerade.
Just make your mind up,
The piper must be paid.
The party's over,
The candles flicker and dim.
You danced and dreamed through the
    night,
It seemed to be right,
Just being with him.
Now you must wake up,
All dreams must end.
Take off your makeup,
The party's over,

It's all over,
My friend.

—Jule Styne

SOME OTHER TIME

VERSE

SHE: Twenty-four hours can go
    so fast,
You look around—the day has
    passed—
When you're in love—
Time is precious stuff—
Even a lifetime isn't enough.

REFRAIN

Where has the time all gone to?
Haven't done half the things we want to—
Oh, well—
We'll catch up
Some other time.
This day was just a token,
Too many words are still unspoken,
Oh, well—
We'll catch up
Some other time.
Just when the fun is starting
Comes the time for parting,
But let's be glad for what we've had
And what's to come.
There's so much more embracing
Still to be done, but time is racing—
Oh, well—
We'll catch up
Some other time.

SHE: Didn't get half my wishes—
Never have seen you dry the
    dishes—
Oh, well—
We'll catch up
Some other time.

Can't satisfy my craving—
Never have watched you while
    you're shaving.
Oh, well—
We'll catch up
Some other time . . .

HE: Haven't had time to wake up—
Seeing you there without your
    makeup,
Oh, well—we'll catch up some
    other time.

TOGETHER: Just when the fun is starting
Comes the time for parting,
But let's be glad for what
    we've had—
And what's to come.
There's so much more
    embracing
Still to be done, but time is
    racing.
Oh, well—
We'll catch up some
    other time.

—Leonard Bernstein

THANKS A LOT, BUT NO THANKS

VERSE

I'm watching and waiting,
I'm waiting and watching,
I hope and I yearn
Just for his return.

REFRAIN

Thanks for the present of the silver
    blue mink,
Thanks for the plane and the ice
    skating rink,
Thanks for the yacht and for the solid
    gold sink,
Thanks a lot, but no thanks.

Thanks for the Scrabble set with platinum
    board,
Thanks for the factory once known as
    Ford,
Thank you for finding me the famous
    "Lost Chord,"
Thanks a lot, but no thanks.
For I am just a faithful lassie
Waiting for her faithful lad.
And there's no gift however classy
By which this lassie can be had.
Thanks for the banks and for the Santa
    Fe line,
Thanks for the darling uranium mine,
But I'm a gal with only one valentine,
Thanks a lot, but no thanks.

    —André Previn

You Mustn't Feel Discouraged

When you think you've hit the bottom,
And you're feeling really low,
You mustn't feel discouraged!—
There's always one step further down
    you can go.
When you're lying in the gutter,
Feeling just a bit unsure,
Just wait until tomorrow—
You may be lying flat face down in a
    sewer.
Don't be afraid of a little raindrop.
That don't mean nothing, Bud!
Just remember one little raindrop
Started the Johnstown Flood
(In Pennsylvania)!
When you're living on a park bench,
Eating grass 'cause you've no dough,
Your luck will change mañana—
You may be six feet under helping
    it grow!
So just remember when you're lower
    than low,
There's always one step further down
You can go.

    —Jule Styne

John Latouche (1917–1956)

WHO KNOWS what John Latouche would have done if he had lived even into middle age! At his death, at the age of thirty-eight, he had just finished revising his libretto and lyrics for the Americana opera *The Ballad of Baby Doe,* and he might have continued on in opera, or returned to musical comedy, or gone on exploring alternatives to these genres or producing variants of them. His most successful musical was the great *Cabin in the Sky,* his first collaboration with Vernon Duke (*Banjo Eyes,* with Eddie Cantor, came later), starring Ethel Waters, staged by George Balanchine, and featuring "Takin' a Chance on Love." He wrote the liberal/patriotic "Ballad for Americans," which he described as a "pamphlet for democracy." He was involved with Harold Rome's *Pins and Needles* and Leonard Bernstein's *Candide.* Today he is perhaps best known for *The Golden Apple,* an Off-Broadway musical that moved briefly to Broadway and remains a cult show. It was based on *The Odyssey* (yes, Homer's) and won the New York Drama Critics Circle award as best musical of the 1954–55 season. Is it a daring and revolutionary new step or a pretentious cul-de-sac? Luckily, it was recorded, so we can make up our own minds.

CABIN IN THE SKY

VERSE

In this cloudy sky overhead now,
There's no guiding star I can see.
I would be lost,
By each wild tempest tossed,
If I didn't know
Of a place we two can go.

REFRAIN 1

There's a little cabin in the sky,
Baby,
For me and for you,
I feel that it's true somehow.
Can't you see that cabin in the sky,
Mister,
An acre or two
Of heavenly blue to plow?

We will be oh so gay,
Eat fried chicken ev'ry day
As the angels go sailing by.
That is why my heart is flying high,
Mister,
'Cause I know we'll have a
Cabin in the sky.

REFRAIN 2

There may be a little cabin in the sky,
Baby,
Yet I am a boy
Who's headed for joy below.
There may be an acre way up high,
Lady,
But I ain't got wings
And I want the things I know.
I done heard preachers pray
'Bout that chicken ev'ry day,

But I'd settle for gravy now.
Since I guess I'll never learn to fly,
Lady,
I'm jes passing by that
Cabin in the sky.

—Vernon Duke

Honey in the Honeycomb

VERSE

What have I got that the others ain't
That always seems to please?
Ain't my perfume nor my fancy paint,
But
When I charm
The men all swarm
Just like they was bees.

REFRAIN 1

There's honey in the honeycomb,
There's sugar in the cane.
There's oysters in a real oyster stew
And bubbles in sweet champagne.
There's jelly in the jelly roll
And sap in ev'ry tree.
Oh, there's honey in the honeycomb
And, honey, there is love in me.

REFRAIN 2

There's honey in the honeycomb,
There's stuffing in a squab.
There's hot meat in a barbecue roast
And corn liquor on the cob.
There's cherries in the cherry tart
And fish in ev'ry sea.
Oh, there's honey in the honeycomb,
And, baby, there is love in me.

REFRAIN 3

There's honey in the honeycomb,
There's nectar in the peach.

There's candy in the coconut shell
And muscles on every beach.
There's money in the savings bank
And I pers'nally guarantee
There's honey in the honeycomb,
Then, baby, there is love in me.

—Vernon Duke

Lazy Afternoon

It's a lazy afternoon
And the beetle bugs are zoomin',
And the tulip trees are bloomin',
And there's not another human
In view
But us two.
It's a lazy afternoon
And the farmer leaves his reapin',
In the meadows cows are sleepin',
And the speckled trout stop leapin'
Upstream
As we dream.
A fat pink cloud hangs over the hill
Unfolding like a rose.
If you hold my hand and sit real still
You can hear the grass as it grows.
It's a lazy afternoon
And my rockin' chair will fit yer,
And my cake was never richer,
And I've made a tasty pitcher
Of tea.
So spend this lazy afternoon with me.
A fat pink cloud hangs over the hill
Unfolding like a rose.
If you hold my hand and sit real still
You can hear the grass as it grows.
It's a lazy afternoon
And I know a place that's quiet
'Cept for daisies running riot,
And there's no one passing by it
To see.

Come spend this lazy afternoon
With me.

—Jerome Moross

Love Turned the Light Out

VERSE

Leave me, love, and never come back,
I'm gonna face the end alone
Here in the twilight of the lovely love
    we've known.
Mourning dove, your feathers are
    black,
Your voice is like a night wind's moan.
Somewhere there's dawn in view,
But not for you.

REFRAIN

Love turned the light out,
Now there's no end to the darkness
    I see;
Empty shadows blinding me.
Love turned the light out,
Now it won't matter wherever I go,
In this gloomy afterglow.
Last night
The moon was shining for joy
Like an electric light.
Last night
I reached for stars overhead,
But instead
Mister Love turned the light out.
He took the stars from the sky up
    above,
Now I'm left with loveless love.

—Vernon Duke

Maybe I Should Change My Ways

VERSE

I never could qualify as a saint
Or pose for a Sunday school mural.
I've romped with the fillies and dallied
    with dillies,
My pleasures have always been plural.
Then, all of a sudden, a girl I meet
Who seems to believe I'm a special treat,
On the primrose path I'm stumbling.
Are my bad intentions crumbling?
Have I been wrong all along?

REFRAIN

Maybe I should change my ways,
Maybe sweet romancing pays.
Maybe I am overdue
For a love that's true.
What if I should try
To let temptation pass me by,
And really concentrate upon
A girl who'd lead me to my place in
    the sun?
Maybe if I could resist
All the lips I've never kissed,
If I anchored down my heart
Would the magic start?
I should change my ways,
But something deep inside me says
That love undying is a sham,
I guess I'll stay the way I am!

—Duke Ellington

Not a Care in the World

VERSE

Rent overdue,
My sister has measles.

Hole in my shoe,
My belt's drawn tight.
My income is nil,
My in-laws are weasels.
My present is dark,
My future's a fright.
But as long as you are there,
What in the world do I care?

REFRAIN I
Though hope is low,
I'm aglow when you smile at me.
Life is simple as A-B-C.
Not a thought in my head,
Not a care in the world.
Though skies are gray,
I'm as gay as a Disney cow,
Not a wrinkle upon my brow.
Not a cent in the red,
Not a care in the world.
I view the scene
Like that old queen of Russia;
As Kate the Great
Used to state long ago,
"Nichevo!"
So if I move
In a groove with a giddy trot,
I'm a-trottin' because I've got
Not a bean in my pot,
Not a care in the world!

REFRAIN 2
Though I can't jive,
I revive when I see your face.
Not a limp in my merry pace,
Not a crimp in my style,
Not a care in the world.
Though I'm a wreck,
I can peck if you take a chance.
Not a shine on my blue serge pants,
Not a crack in my smile,
Not a care in the world.
Why should I fret

When I bet on a sure thing?
Like Nick the Greek
Used to say ev'ry day,
"Yip-i-ay!"
So if I'm struttin'
With nuttin' ahead in store,
There's a reason I said before.
I'll repeat it once more,
Not a care in the world!

—*Vernon Duke*

SUMMER IS A-COMIN' IN

VERSE
Heigh-ho,
Summer comes along.
It comes once a year,
But it's always gay.
Heigh-ho,
Try to sing a song
Of how people feel
When summer's on the way.
The season that Rachel and Rube
      adore,
When Nature cuts up tricks,
Was best described by a troubadour
Way back in twelve twenty-six,
In the year of twelve twenty-six.

REFRAIN I
Summer is a-comin' in,
Loud sing cuckoo.
Girlie strolleth in the park,
Cupid striketh up a spark,
Sing cuckoo.
Summer is a-comin' in,
Loud sing cuckoo.
Ev'ry poet dreameth dream,
Salmon scrammeth up the stream,
Life is new.
Club woman planteth in a pot

Forsythia and hydrangea,
And my poor heart's in danger.
Twit, twit, twit,
Jug, jug, jug.
Summer is a-comin' in,
Tomcat doth mew.
Balmy breezes smell like gin,
Why the hell don't thou give in,
Sing cuckoo.
Twit, twit, twit,
Jug, jug, jug.
A down, a down, a derry
Cuckoo.

REFRAIN 2

Summer is a-comin' in,
Loud sing cuckoo.
Lovers flirteth on ye bus,
Birdie kicketh up a fuss,
Life is new.
Summer is a-comin' in,
Sky turneth blue.
Pollen floateth on ye breeze
Bringing countless allergies,
Sing cuckoo.
In ev'ry dark and stagnant pool,
The primitive amoeba
Divides and signs, "Ich liebe."
Twit, twit, twit,
Jug, jug, jug.
Summer is a-comin' in,
Loud sing cuckoo.
Each libido goeth pop,
Marg'ret Sanger closeth shop,
Sing cuckoo.
Twit, twit, twit,
Jug, jug, jug.
A down, a down, a derry
Cuckoo.

—*Vernon Duke*

TAKING A CHANCE ON LOVE

(with Ted Fetter)

VERSE

I thought love's game was over,
Lady luck had gone away.
I laid my cards on the table,
Unable to play.
Then I heard good fortune say,
"They're dealing you a new hand
today!"

REFRAIN I

Oh
Here I go again,
I hear those trumpets blow again,
All aglow again,
Taking a chance on love.
Here I slide again,
About to take that ride again,
Starry-eyed again,
Taking a chance on love.
I thought that cards were a frame-up,
I never would try.
But now I'm taking the game up,
And the ace of hearts is high.
Things are mending now,
I see a rainbow blending now,
We'll have our happy ending now,
Taking a chance on love.

REFRAIN 2

Here I come again,
I'm gonna make things hum again,
Acting dumb again,
Taking a chance on love.
Here I stand again,
About to beat the band again,
Feeling grand again,
Taking a chance on love.
I never dreamed in my slumbers,
And bets were taboo.

But now I'm playing the numbers
On a little dream for two.
Wading in again,
I'm leadin' with my chin again,
I'm startin' out to win again,
Taking a chance on love.

REFRAIN 3
Here I slip again,
About to take that trip again,
Got my grip again,
Taking a chance on love.
Now I prove again

That I can make life move again,
In the groove again,
Taking a chance on love.
I walk around with a horseshoe,
In clover I lie.
And brother rabbit, of course you
Better kiss your foot good-bye.
On the ball again,
I'm ridin' for a fall again,
I'm gonna give my all again,
Taking a chance on love.

—Vernon Duke

Bob Hilliard (1918–1971)

B OB HILLIARD WROTE two fairly successful Broadway shows—*Hazel Flagg* and the revue *Angel in the Wings,* which featured the very politically incorrect "Civilization" ("Bongo, Bongo, Bongo, I Don't Want to Leave the Congo")—but he's probably best known for the score of the animated Disney *Alice in Wonderland* ("I'm Late") and a series of specialty numbers, among them "Mention My Name in Sheboygan" and "The Coffee Song," written for New York's Copacabana nightclub. There were ballads, too—Sinatra's "In the Wee Small Hours of the Morning," "How Do You Speak to an Angel?," and the once-ubiquitous "Dear Hearts and Gentle People." In other words, he did lots of things rather well and a few things very well.

CIVILIZATION
(BONGO, BONGO, BONGO)

VERSE I

Each morning a missionary advertise with
neon sign,
He tell the native population that
civilization is fine.
And three educated savages holler from a
bamboo tree
That civilization is the thing for me to see.
But,

REFRAIN I

Bongo, bongo, bongo, I don't want to
leave the Congo,
Oh, no, no, no, no, no!
Bingle, bangle, bungle,
I'm so happy in the jungle I refuse to go.
Don't want no bright lights, false teeth,
doorbells, landlords,
I make it clear
That, no matter how they coax me,
I'll stay right here!

VERSE 2

Each look through a magazine the
missionary's wife conceal,
I see how people who are civilized bang
you with automobile.
At the movies they have got to pay many
coconuts to see
Uncivilized pictures that the newsreel
takes of me.
So,

REFRAIN 2

Bongo, bongo, bongo, I don't want to
leave the Congo,
Oh, no, no, no, no, no!
Bingle, bangle, bungle,
I'm so happy in the jungle I refuse to go.
Don't want no penthouse, bathtub,
streetcars, taxis, noise in my ear.
So, no matter how they coax me,
I'll stay right here!
They have things like the atom bomb,
So I think I'll stay where I "om."
Civilization, I'll stay right here!

VERSE 3

Each hurry like savages to get aboard an
    iron train.
And, though it's smoky and it's crowded,
    they're too civilized to complain.
When they've got two weeks' vacation
    they hurry to vacation ground.
They swim and they fish but that's what I
    do all year 'round.
So,

REFRAIN 3

Bongo, bongo, bongo, I don't want to
    leave the Congo,
Oh, no, no, no, no, no!
Bingle, bangle, bungle,
I'm so happy in the jungle I refuse to go.
Don't want no jailhouse, shotgun, fish
    hooks, golf clubs, I've got my spear.
So, no matter how they coax me, I'll stay
    right here!
They have things like the atom bomb,
So I think I'll stay where I "om."
Civilization, I'll stay right here!

—*Carl Sigman*

THE COFFEE SONG
(THEY'VE GOT AN AWFUL LOT OF
COFFEE IN BRAZIL)

REFRAIN I

Way down among Brazilians
Coffee beans grow by the billions,
So they've got to find those extra cups
    to fill.
They've got an awful lot of coffee in
    Brazil.
You can't get cherry soda
'Cause they've got to sell their quota
And the way things are I guess they
    never will.

They've got a zillion tons of coffee in
    Brazil.
No tea!
Or tomato juice.
You'll see
No potato juice.
'Cause the planters down in Santos all say,
    "No! No! No!"
A politician's daughter
Was accused of drinking water
And was fined a great big
    fifty-dollar bill.
They've got an awful lot of coffee in
    Brazil.

REFRAIN 2

You date a girl and find out later
She smells like a percolator,
Her perfume was made right on the
    grill.
Why, they could percolate the ocean in
    Brazil.
And when their ham and eggs need
    savor,
Coffee ketchup gives them flavor,
Coffee pickles way outsell the dill.
Why, they put coffee in the coffee in
    Brazil.
No tea!
Or tomato juice.
You'll see
No potato juice.
'Cause the planters down in Santos all say,
    "No! No! No!"
So you'll add to the local color
Serving coffee with a cruller,
Dunking doesn't take a lot of skill.
They've got an awful lot of coffee in
    Brazil.

—*Dick Miles*

In the Wee Small Hours of the Morning

VERSE

When the sun is high in the
    afternoon sky,
You can always find something
    to do.
But from dusk till dawn, as the clock
    ticks on,
Something happens to you.

REFRAIN

In the wee small hours of the morning,
While the whole wide world is fast asleep,
You lie awake and think about the girl
And never ever think of counting sheep.
When your lonely heart has learned its
    lesson,
You'd be hers if only she would call.
In the wee small hours of the morning,
That's the time you miss her most of all.

—David Mann

Alan Jay Lerner (1918–1986)

T HE TEAM OF Alan Jay Lerner and Frederick ("Fritz") Loewe is one of Broadway's most renowned partnerships, yet it produced only three major shows and one major movie. Lerner came from a wealthy New York family–his father owned a successful chain of apparel stores–and was educated in England and America before going on to Harvard, where he wrote two Hasty Pudding shows. While trying his hand at writing for an ad agency and for such radio shows as the *Philco Hall of Fame,* he met the much older Fritz Loewe, who casually suggested that they try to work together. Three shows later came *Brigadoon,* then, after the mildly successful *Paint Your Wagon,* one of the greatest hits in musical comedy history: *My Fair Lady,* which ran for more than six years and whose cast album was the number-one LP for fifteen weeks. *My Fair Lady* was more than a hit, it was a worldwide phenomenon, and the movie–with Audrey Hepburn in place of Julie Andrews–won the Oscar for best picture, despite being a little stately. *Camelot,* which followed, ran a mere two years, but the movie *Gigi* also won the Oscar. Lerner was *Gigi*'s scriptwriter as well as lyricist, just as he had been for the Loewe stage musicals and for the work he was to do with other composers after Loewe's retirement. But the post-Loewe years never approached the earlier successes. There was *On a Clear Day You Can See Forever,* written with Burton Lane, better known in its movie version starring Barbra Streisand, and *Coco,* the musical about Chanel, written with André Previn and starring Katharine Hepburn, which ran for almost a year on star power, but there was a series of flops, too. Nor could he build on his early screenwriting career–back in 1951 he had written the Astaire *Royal Wedding* as well as *An American in Paris.* The success of Lerner's lyrics lies to a great extent in their almost miraculous relationship to Loewe's music; they don't make themselves felt as brilliant light verse as, say, Hart's or Porter's or Coward's can, and he generally didn't move easily from composer to composer the way Hammerstein did. Perhaps this explains his somewhat unhappy final years–tax problems, health problems, and the financial (and emotional) problems resulting from eight marriages.

ALMOST LIKE BEING IN LOVE

VERSE
Maybe the sun gave me the pow'r,
For I could swim Loch Lomond
And be home in
Half an hour.

Maybe the air gave me the drive,
For I'm aglow and alive!

REFRAIN
What a day this has been!
What a rare mood I'm in!
Why, it's . . . almost like being in love!

There's a smile on my face
For the whole human race!
Why, it's . . . almost like being in love!
All the music of life seems to be
Like a bell that is ringin' for me!
And from the way that I feel
When that bell starts to peal,
I would swear I was falling,
I could swear I was falling,
It's almost like being in love.

—Frederick Loewe

CAMELOT

It's true! It's true! The crown has made it
      clear:
The climate must be perfect all the year.
A law was made a distant moon ago here,
July and August cannot be too hot;
And there's a legal limit to the snow here
In Camelot.
The winter is forbidden till December,
And exits March the second on the dot.
By order Summer lingers through
      September
In Camelot.
Camelot! Camelot!
I know it sounds a bit bizarre;
But in Camelot, Camelot
That's how conditions are.
The rain may never fall till after sundown,
By eight the morning fog must
      disappear.
In short, there's simply not
A more congenial spot
For happ'ly-ever-aftering than here
In Camelot.
Camelot! Camelot!
I know it gives a person pause,
But in Camelot, Camelot
Those are the legal laws.

The snow may never slush upon the
      hillside.
By nine P.M. the moonlight must appear.
In short, there's simply not
A more congenial spot
For happ'ly-ever-aftering than here
In Camelot.
Each evening from December to
      December
Before you drift to sleep upon your cot,
Think back on all the tales that you
      remember
Of Camelot.
Ask ev'ry person if he's heard the story,
And tell it strong and clear if he has not:
That once there was a fleeting wisp of
      glory
Called Camelot.
Camelot! Camelot!
Now say it out with love and joy!
Camelot! Camelot!
Yes, Camelot, my boy . . .
Where once it never rained till after
      sundown;
By eight A.M. the morning fog had flown . . .
Don't let it be forgot
That once there was a spot
For one brief shining moment that was
      known
As Camelot. . . .

—Frederick Loewe

COME BACK TO ME

Hear my voice where you are;
Take a train, steal a car;
Hop a freight, grab a star—
Come back to me.
Catch a plane, catch a breeze;
On your hands, on your knees;
Swim or fly, only please

Come back to me!
On a mule; in a jet;
With your hair in a net,
In a towel wringing wet–
I don't care, this is where
You should be.
From the hills, from the shore,
Ride the wind to my door.
Turn the highway to dust.
Break the law if you must.
Move the world, only just
Come back to me.
Blast your hide, hear me call;
Must I fight City Hall?
Here and now, damn it all!
Come back to me.
What on earth must I do,
Scream and yell, 'til I'm blue?
Curse your soul, when will you
Come back to me?
Have you gone to the moon
Or the corner saloon
And to rack an' to "roon"?
Madem'selle, where in hell can you be?
Leave a sign on your door,
"Out to lunch evermore."
In a Rolls or a van;
Wrapped in mink or Saran;
Any way that you can–
Come back to me.
Hear my voice through the din;
Feel the waves on your skin
Like a call from within–
Come back to me.
Leave behind all you own;
Tell your flowers
You will phone;
Let your dog walk alone–
Come back to me.
Let your tub overflow.
If a date waits below,
Let him wait for Godot.
Ride a rail, come by mail C.O.D.,

Come in pain or in joy,
As a girl, as a boy,
In a bag or a trunk,
On a horse or a drunk,
In a Ford or a funk,
Come back to me.
Come back to me.
Come back to me.

—*Burton Lane*

THE HEATHER ON THE HILL

VERSE

Can't we two go walkin' together
Out beyond the valley of trees,
Out where there's a hillside of heather
Curtseyin' gently in the breeze?
That's what I'd like to do:
See the heather–but with you.

REFRAIN

The mist of May is in the gloamin',
And all the clouds are holdin' still.
So take my hand and let's go roamin'
Through the heather on the hill.
The mornin' dew is blinkin' yonder;
There's lazy music in the rill;
And all I want to do is wander
Through the heather on the hill.
There may be other days as rich and rare;
There may be other Springs as full and fair;
But they won't be the same–they'll come
    and go;
For this I know:
That when the mist is in the gloamin',
And all the clouds are holdin' still,
If you're not there I won't go roamin'
Through the heather on the hill,
The heather on the hill.

—*Frederick Loewe*

A HYMN TO HIM

What in all of heaven could have
    prompted her to go
After such a triumph at the ball?
What could have depressed her?
What could have possessed her?
I cannot understand the wretch at all!
Women are irrational, that's all there is
    to that!
Their heads are full of cotton, hay,
    and rags!
They're nothing but exasperating,
    irritating,
Vacillating, calculating, agitating,
Maddening and infuriating hags!
Pickering, why can't a woman be more like
    a man?
Yes, why can't a woman be more like
    a man?
Men are so honest, so thoroughly square;
Eternally noble, historically fair;
Who when you win will always give your
    back a pat.
Why can't a woman be like that?
Why does ev'ry one do what the others do?
Can't a woman learn to use her head?
Why do they do everything their
    mothers do?
Why can't they grow up like their fathers
    instead?
Why can't a woman take after a man?
Men are so pleasant, so easy to please;
Whenever you're with them, you're always
    at ease.
Would you be slighted if I didn't speak for
    hours?
Of course not.
Would you be livid if I had a drink or two?
Nonsense.
Would you be wounded if I never sent you
    flowers?

Never.
Why can't a woman be like you?
One man in a million may shout a bit.
Now and then there's one with slight
    defects,
One perhaps whose truthfulness you
    doubt a bit.
But by and large we are a marvelous sex!
Why can't a woman behave like a man?
Men are so friendly, good-natured,
    and kind;
A better companion you never will find.
If I were hours late for dinner, would you
    bellow?
Of course not.
If I forgot your silly birthday, would
    you fuss?
Nonsense.
Would you complain if I took out another
    fellow?
Never.
Why can't a woman be like us?
Why can't a woman be more like a man?
Men are so decent, such regular chaps.
Ready to help you through any mishaps.
Ready to buck you up whenever you are
    glum.
Why can't a woman be a chum?
Why is thinking something women
    never do?
Why is logic never even tried?
Straightening up their hair is all they
    ever do.
Why don't they straighten up the mess
    that's inside?
Why can't a woman be more like a man?
If I were a woman who'd been to a ball,
Been hailed as a princess by one and
    by all,
Would I start weeping like a bathtub
    overflowing?
And carry on as if my home were in
    a tree?

Would I run off and never tell me where
    I'm going?
Why can't a woman be like me?

—Frederick Loewe

I Could Have Danced All Night

VERSE

Bed! Bed! I couldn't go to bed!
My head's too light to try to set it down!
Sleep! Sleep! I couldn't sleep tonight!
Not for all the jewels in the crown!

REFRAIN

I could have danced all night!
I could have danced all night!
And still have begged for more.
I could have spread my wings
And done a thousand things
I've never done before.
I'll never know
What made it so exciting;
Why all at once
My heart took flight.
I only know when he
Began to dance with me,
I could have danced, danced, danced all
    night!

—Frederick Loewe

I Left My Hat in Haiti

I left my hat in Haiti,
In some forgotten flat in Haiti;
I couldn't tell you how I got there,
I only know it was so hot there.
She took my hat politely
And wound her arms around me tightly,

But I remember nothing clearly
Except the flame when she came near me.
Her eyes had the fire of surrender
And her touch, it was tender;
And with someone as fi'ry as that
You forget about your hat!
So if you go to Haiti,
There is a girl I know in Haiti.
If you can find her
You'll adore-a;
Just look around
Till you've found
Someone who has a blue gray fedora.
I think of that gorgeous creature when I'm
    all alone,
Whenever I do, from down inside there
    comes a groan.
That son of a gun in Haiti
Has got the prettiest hat I own.
And when it is bleak and chilly
And life is flat,
I think of that Haitian dilly.
And think I'd better go get my hat.

—Burton Lane

I Remember It Well

HE: We met at nine.
SHE: We met at eight.
HE: I was on time.
SHE: No, you were late.
HE: Ah yes! I remember it well.
    We dined with friends.
SHE: We dined alone.
HE: A tenor sang.
SHE: A baritone.
HE: Ah yes! I remember it well.
    That dazzling April moon!
SHE: There was none that night.
    And the month was June.
HE: That's right! That's right!

SHE: It warms my heart
      To know that you
      Remember still
      The way you do.
 HE: Ah yes! I remember it well.
      How often I've thought of that
          Friday—
SHE: —Monday
 HE: . . . night,
      When we had our last rendezvous.
      And somehow I've foolishly
          wondered if you might
      By some chance be thinking of it too.
      That carriage ride . . .
SHE: You walked me home.
 HE: You lost a glove.
SHE: I lost a comb.
 HE: Ah yes! I remember it well.
      That brilliant sky.
SHE: We had some rain.
 HE: Those Russian songs.
SHE: From sunny Spain.
 HE: Ah yes! I remember it well.
      You wore a gown of gold.
SHE: I was all in blue.
 HE: Am I getting old?
SHE: Oh no! Not you!
      How strong you were,
      How young and gay;
      A prince of love
      In ev'ry way.
 HE: Ah yes! I remember it well.

—Frederick Loewe

IF EVER I WOULD LEAVE YOU

If ever I would leave you,
It wouldn't be in Summer.
Seeing you in Summer, I never would go.
Your hair streaked with sunlight . . .
Your lips red as flame . . .

Your face with a luster
That puts gold to shame.
But if I'd ever leave you,
It couldn't be in Autumn.
How I'd leave in Autumn, I never
    would know.
I've seen how you sparkle
When Fall nips the air.
I know you in Autumn
And I must be there.
And could I leave you running merrily
    through the snow?
Or on a wintry evening when you catch the
    fire's glow?
If ever I would leave you,
How could it be in Springtime,
Knowing how in Spring I'm bewitched by
    you so?
Oh, no, not in Springtime!
Summer, Winter or Fall!
No, never could I leave you at all.

REPEAT FINAL SIX LINES

—Frederick Loewe

I'M GLAD I'M NOT YOUNG ANY MORE

VERSE

Poor boy. Poor boy.
Down-hearted and depressed and in
    a spin.
Poor boy. Poor boy.
Oh, youth can really do a fellow in.

REFRAIN I

How lovely to sit here in the shade
With none of the woes of man and maid.
I'm glad that I'm not young any more.
The rivals that don't exist at all;
The feeling you're only two feet tall;

I'm glad that I'm not young any more.
No more confusion.
No morning-after surprise.
No self-delusion
That when you're telling those lies,
She isn't wise.
And even if love comes through the door;
The kind that goes on for evermore,
For evermore is shorter than before.
Oh, I'm so glad that I'm not young
    any more.

REFRAIN 2

The tiny remark that tortures you;
The fear that your friends won't like
    her too;
I'm glad I'm not young any more.
The longing to end a stale affair
Until you find out she doesn't care.
I'm glad that I'm not young any more.
No more frustration.
No star-crossed lover am I.
No aggravation.
Just one reluctant reply:
Lady, good-bye.
The fountain of youth is dull as paint.
Methuselah is my patron saint.
I've never been so comfortable before.
Oh, I'm so glad that I'm not young
    any more.

—Frederick Loewe

I'VE GROWN ACCUSTOMED TO HER FACE

REFRAIN I

I've grown accustomed to her face!
She almost makes the day begin.
I've grown accustomed to the tune
She whistles night and noon.
Her smiles, her frowns,

Her ups, her downs,
Are second nature to me now;
Like breathing out and breathing in.
I was serenely independent and content
    before we met;
Surely I could always
Be that way again—and yet
I've grown accustomed to her looks;
Accustomed to her voice;
Accustomed to her face.

PATTER

Marry Freddie! What an infantile
    idea! What
A heartless, wicked, brainless thing
    to do!
But she'll regret it! She'll regret it. It's
Doomed before they even take the vow!
I can see her now:
Mrs. Freddie Eynsford-Hill,
In a wretched little flat above a store.
I can see her now:
Not a penny in the till,
And a bill collector beating at the door.
She'll try to teach the things I taught her,
And end up selling flow'rs instead;
Begging for her bread and water,
While her husband has his breakfast
    in bed!
In a year or so
When she's prematurely gray
And the blossoms in her cheek have
    turned to chalk,
She'll come home and lo!
He'll have upped and run away
With a social-climbing heiress from
    New York!
Poor Eliza!
How simply frightful!
How humiliating!
How delightful!

REPEAT REFRAIN I

But I'm so used to hear her say,
"Good morning" every day.
Her joys, her woes,
Her highs, her lows
Are second nature to me now;
Like breathing out and breathing in.
I'm very grateful she's a woman
And so easy to forget;
Rather like a habit
One can always break–and yet
I've grown accustomed to the trace
Of something in the air;
Accustomed to her face.

—*Frederick Loewe*

ON A CLEAR DAY YOU CAN SEE FOREVER

Could anyone among us
Have an inkling or a clue
What magic feats of wizardry
And voodoo you can do?
And who would ever guess
What powers you possess?
And who would have the sense
To change his views
And start to mind
His ESP's and Q's?
For who would ever dream
Of hearing phones before they ring,
Or ordering the earth
To send you up a little Spring?
Or finding you've been crowned
The Queen of Lost and Found?
And who would not be stunned
To see you prove
There's more to us
Than surgeons can remove?
So much more than we ever knew,

So much more we were born to do;
Should you draw back the curtain,
This, I am certain,

You'll be impressed with you.
On a clear day
Rise and look around you
And you'll see who you are.
On a clear day
How it will astound you
That the glow of your being
Outshines ev'ry star.
You feel part of
Ev'ry mountain, sea, and shore;
You can hear from far and near
A world you've never heard before,
And on a clear day,
On that clear day,
You can see forever
And ever, and ever, and evermore!

—*Burton Lane*

ON THE STREET WHERE YOU LIVE

Darling, there's the tree you run to
When it starts to rain.
See the way it's filled with bloom.
And isn't there a garland 'round the
    windowpane?
That could only be your room.
This street is like a garden and your door a
    garden gate,
What a lovely place to wait.

I have often walked down this street
    before,
But the pavement always stayed beneath
    my feet before.

All at once am I
Several storeys high,
Knowing I'm on the street where you live.
Are there lilac trees in the heart of town?
Can you hear a lark in any other part
    of town?
Does enchantment pour
Out of ev'ry door?
No, it's just on the street where you live.
And oh, the towering feeling,
Just to know somehow you are near;
The overpowering feeling
That any second you may suddenly
    appear.
People stop and stare. They don't
    bother me.
For there's nowhere else on earth that I
    would rather be.
Let the time go by,
I won't care if I
Can be here on the street where you live.

—Frederick Loewe

Paris Is Paris Again

Night in the sky . . .
From the street comes the cry
Of the rooster in search of the hen.
And Paris is Paris again.
Stars on their beat
Looking down on the sweet
Intertwining of women and men.
And Paris is Paris again.
Lovers in closets and shoes in the drawer;
Screams on the Rue Madeleine.
Swords in the park,
A shot in the dark,
And Paris is spicely,
Vicely Paris again.
Moon burning bright,
And like bats in the night

Come the well-feathered demimondaine.
And Paris is Paris again.
Ladies you know
Arm in arm with their low
Classanovas meander the Seine.
And Paris is Paris again.
Meetings at nine that tomorrow will be
Meetings with lawyers at ten.
Handfuls of hair,
A tooth on the chair,
And Paris is gallicly, phallicly
Paris again.
The song of the cuckold is heard in
    the land
Hailing La Vie Parisienne.
Joy and remorse,
Delight and divorce,
And Paris is gaudily, bawdily,
Physically,
Aph-er-o-disically
Paris again.

—Frederick Loewe

The Rain in Spain

Poor Professor Higgins!
Poor Professor Higgins!
Night and day
He slaves away!
Oh, poor Professor Higgins!
All day long
On his feet;
Up and down until he's numb;
Doesn't rest;
Doesn't eat;
Doesn't touch a crumb!
Poor Professor Higgins!
Poor Professor Higgins!
On he plods
Against all odds;
Oh, poor Professor Higgins!

Nine P.M.

Ten P.M.

On through midnight ev'ry night.

One A.M.

Two A.M.

Three . . . !

Quit, Professor Higgins!

Quit, Professor Higgins!

Hear our plea

Or payday we

Will quit, Professor Higgins!

"Ay" not "I,"

"O" not "Ow,"

Pounding, pounding in our brain.

"Ay" not "I,"

"O," not "Ow,"

Don't say "Rine," say "Rain" . . .

SHE: The rain in Spain stays mainly in the plain.

HE: What was that?

SHE: The rain in Spain stays mainly in the plain.

HE: Again.

SHE: The rain in Spain stays mainly in the plain.

HE: I think she's got it! I think she's got it!

SHE: The rain in Spain stays mainly in the plain!

HE: By George, she's got it!
By George, she's got it!
Now once again, where does it rain?

SHE: On the plain! On the plain!

HE: And where's that soggy plain?

SHE: In Spain! In Spain!

ALL: The rain in Spain stays mainly in the plain!
The rain in Spain stays mainly in the plain!

HE: In Hertford, Hereford and Hampshire . . . ?

SHE: Hurricanes hardly happen.
How kind of you to let me come!

HE: Now once again, where does it rain?

SHE: On the plain! On the plain!

HE: And where's that blasted plain?

SHE: In Spain! In Spain!

ALL: The rain in Spain stays mainly in the plain!
The rain in Spain stays mainly in the plain!

—*Frederick Loewe*

WOULDN'T IT BE LUVERLY?

All I want is a room somewhere,

Far away from the cold night air;

With one enormous chair . . .

Oh, wouldn't it be luverly?

Lots of choc'late for me to eat;

Lots of coal makin' lots of heat;

Warm face, warm hands, warm feet . . . !

Oh, wouldn't it be luverly?

Oh, so luverly sittin' absobloominlutely still,

I would never budge till Spring

Crept over me windersill.

Someone's head restin' on my knee,

Warm and tender as he can be,

Who takes good care of me . . .

Oh, wouldn't it be luverly?

Luverly! Luverly!

Luverly! Luverly!

—*Frederick Loewe*

Jack Segal (1918–)

S OMEHOW, Minneapolis-born Jack Segal found his way from political science studies at the University of Wisconsin and the New School of Social Research to Paramount Pictures' music department. In Hollywood, he contributed to such late-forties losers as *Manhattan Angel,* starring Gloria Jean, and *Make Believe Ballroom,* in which non-stars Jerome Courtland and Virginia Welles, collegiate carhops, win top prize in a musical quiz show. At that point, poli-sci must have looked good! Nonetheless, Segal went on to write a scattering of distinguished lyrics, including the jazz standard "When Sunny Gets Blue."

I Keep Going Back to Joe's

I keep going back to Joe's,
To that table in the corner,
Sippin' wine and starin' at the door.
Our old waiter knows we're through,
Still he sets the place for you,
Everything the way it was before.
I keep going back to Joe's,
But the man who plays piano
Never plays your fav'rite melody.
Joe keeps busy at the bar,
Never asks me where you are,
He was there when you walked out on me.
Now I pray you'll walk back in
And you'll say what fools we've been,
And we'll celebrate our happy new
    beginning.
Chances are you'll never show,
But you'll know just where to find me
Ev'ry night until it's time to close.
Just in case you miss me too,
I'll be there to welcome you,
That's why I keep going back to Joe's.

—*Marvin Fisher*

Nothing Ever Changes My Love for You

The earth may change from summer green
    to winter white,
The brightest day can change into the
    darkest night,
A gray cloud may change a sky of blue,
But nothing ever changes my love for you.
A gentle breeze can blow into a hurricane,
A happy song can change into a sad
    refrain,
The oak leaf will fall when autumn's
    through,
But nothing'll ever change my love
    for you.
Time will alter
Gibraltar,
The seas may run dry,
But you'll see
That we'll be
The same you and I.
A million things are bound to change as
    time rolls on,
A million springs will come and go and
    when they're gone,

My darling, the thrill will still be new,
For nothing ever changes my love for you.

—Marvin Fisher

WHEN SUNNY GETS BLUE

When Sunny gets blue,
Her eyes get gray and cloudy.
Then the rain begins to fall.
Pitter patter, pitter patter,
Love is gone, so what can matter?
No sweet lover man comes to call.
When Sunny gets blue,
She breathes a sigh of sadness,
Like the wind that stirs the trees.
Wind that sets the leaves to swayin',
Like some violins are playin'
Weird and haunting melodies.
People used to love
To hear her laugh, see her smile.
That's how she got her name.
Since that sad affair,
She's lost her smile, changed her style.
Somehow she's not the same.
But mem'ries will fade,
And pretty dreams will rise up
Where her other dream fell through.
Hurry, new love, hurry here

To kiss away each lonely tear,
And hold her near when Sunny gets blue.
Hold her near when Sunny gets blue.

—Marvin Fisher

WIND IN THE WILLOW

Wind in the willow, why do you weep?
Wind in the willow, how can I sleep?
My love is gone now, just let me be.
All of your sighing won't bring her to me.
Moon on my pillow, why shine so bright,
Making me restless all through the
    night?
When you appear now, I miss her so.
She isn't here now, sharing your glow.
Blow wind, through the midnight air.
Sing your saddest song until she cries.
Go moon, find my love somewhere,
Shine the lovelight back into her eyes.
Wind, whisper sweetly things I would say.
Moon, make her meet me, show her
    the way.
Wind in the willow, moon high above,
Don't stay and haunt me, go and find
    my love.

—Marvin Fisher

Ervin Drake (1919–)

NEW YORKER Ervin Drake (Ervin Maurice Druckman) began writing lyrics in the early forties–"Tico Tico" appeared in the Disney *Saludos Amigos*–and, twenty years later, he entered the Juilliard School to continue his musical studies. (He had studied graphic arts and the social sciences at City College.) He added the words to Juan Tizol's "Perdido," an Ellington specialty, and wrote "Good Morning, Heartache" and Sinatra's "It Was a Very Good Year." But he was a more important figure in the world of television, writing and producing some seven hundred network shows, including several important series and forty or so spectaculars for such stars as Ethel Merman, Julie Andrews, Tony Bennett, Nichols and May, and Eddie Cantor. He also served from 1973 to 1982 as president of the American Guild of Authors and Composers, deeply involved in the successful campaign for passage of the 1976 U.S. Copyright Law.

THE FRIENDLIEST THING
(TWO PEOPLE CAN DO)

Drinks are okay,
They break the ice.
Dancing this way
Is also nice.
But why delay
The friendliest thing
Two people can do?
If you are free,
No strings attached,
And you're like me,
No wings attached,
Then it can be
The friendliest thing
Two people can do.
Some fellers take
And boast of it;
Some ladies make
The most of it.
Why do they fake

The friendliest thing
Two people can do?
When it can be
The sweetest and,
Let's face it,
The completest and friendliest thing
Two people can do!

IT WAS A VERY GOOD YEAR

When I was seventeen,
It was a very good year,
It was a very good year
For small-town girls and soft summer
    nights.
We'd hide from the lights
On the village green
When I was seventeen!
When I was twenty-one,
It was a very good year,
It was a very good year

For city girls who lived up the stair,
With perfumed hair
That came undone,
When I was twenty-one!
When I was thirty-five,
It was a very good year,
It was a very good year
For blue-blooded girls of independent
    means.
We'd ride in limousines
Their chauffeurs would drive
When I was thirty-five!
But now the days are short,
I'm in the Autumn of the year,
And now I think of my life
As vintage wine from the old kegs.
From the brim to the dregs
It poured sweet and clear;
It was a very good year!

JUST FOR TODAY

VERSE I
Candle, climb upward;
Tallow, return;
Lengthen, burnt wick,
Do me this trick,
Unburn! Unburn! Unburn!

REFRAIN I
Make me a child again,
Just for today;
Foolish and wild again,
Just for today.
Make me unwise again,
Teach me surprise again,

Seen through young eyes again,
Just for today!

VERSE 2
Wisdom, desert me,
Folly, return;
Brain of my youth,
Wrinkled by truth:
Unlearn! Unlearn! Unlearn!

REFRAIN 2
Children who cared for me,
Come out and play.
Don't hide in memory,
Just for today.
Kitten, be found again,
I'll chase you 'round again,
Free and unfrowned again,
Just for today!

REFRAIN 3
All that is beautiful,
Bring back once more;
Leave all that's dutiful
Outside my door.
Tell me the prayer to pray,
Tell me the price to pay,
For one sweet yesterday,
Just for today!

CODA
Candle, climb upward;
Tallow, return;
Lengthen, burnt wick,
Do me this trick,
Unburn! Unburn! Unburn!

Bob Merrill (1920–1998)

A STRANGE CAREER. On the one hand, wildly successful and not very respected novelty songs–"If I Knew You Were Comin' I'd've Baked a Cake," "How Much for That Doggie in the Window?," "Mambo Italiano"; on the other, a series of successful musicals on Broadway: *New Girl in Town* (George Abbott, Bob Fosse, Gwen Verdon, based on *Anna Christie*); *Take Me Along* (Jackie Gleason, based on *Ah, Wilderness*); *Carnival!* (David Merrick, Gower Champion); all with music and words by Merrill. And then, in 1964, his greatest hit, *Funny Girl.* This one had music by Jule Styne, and of course it had Streisand. After that, nothing of any consequence, and several disasters, none greater than the 1993 *The Red Shoes,* for which Styne enlisted him to rewrite the lyrics. It was the last fling for both of them, but Merrill at least had the sense to keep his name off the show. In his youth he had struggled to find work in the New York theater, then hitchhiked to Hollywood, where he eventually became a radio writer and songwriter. He is quoted as saying about his songs, "They are all about America, they are all wholesome, and they are all happy." And then, "Clichés make the best songs. I put down every one I can find." He may well have meant it.

Don't Rain on My Parade

Don't tell me not to fly,
I've simply got to.
If someone takes a spill, it's me and
    not you.
Don't bring around a cloud
To rain on my parade.
Don't tell me not to live,
Just sit and putter.
Life's candy and the sun's a ball of butter.
Who told you you're allowed to rain on my
    parade?
I'll march my band out,
I'll beat my drum,
And if I'm fanned out,
Your turn at bat, sir,
At least I didn't fake it.
Hat, sir,

I guess I didn't make it!
But whether I'm the rose of sheer
    perfection
Or freckle on the nose of life's
    complexion,
The cinder on the shiny apple of its eye,
I gotta fly once,
I gotta try once,
Only can die once,
Right, sir?
Oooh, love is juicy,
Juicy, and you see
I gotta have my bite, sir.
Get ready for me, love, 'cause I'm a comer.
I simply gotta march, my heart's a
    drummer.
Don't bring around a cloud to rain on my
    parade.
I'm gonna live and live now!

Get what I want,
I know how!
All that the law will allow!
One roll for the whole shebang!
One throw, that bell will go clang!
Though I'm alone, I'm a gang!
Eye on the target and wham!
One shot, one gunshot, and bam!
Hey, world, here I am!
Get ready for me, love, 'cause I'm a comer.
I simply gotta march, my heart's a
    drummer.
Nobody, no nobody
Is gonna rain on my parade.

—*Jule Styne*

MUSIC THAT MAKES ME DANCE

VERSE
To me, to me love is no go
Till fiddle and oboe start weeping,
Wailing.
That's my failing.
He may be wrong for me,
But his is the only song for me.

REFRAIN
I know he's around when the sky and the
    ground start in ringing.
I know that he's near by the thunder I hear
    in advance.
His words, and his words alone, are the
    words that can start my heart singing.
And his is the only music that makes me
    dance.
He'll sleep and he'll rise in the light of two
    eyes that adore him.
Bore him it might, but he won't leave my
    sight for a glance.
In ev'ry way, ev'ry day, I need less of
    myself, and need more him,

More him,
'Cause his is the only music that makes me
    dance.

—*Jule Styne*

PEOPLE

People,
People who need people
Are the luckiest people
In the world.
We're children
Needing other children,
And yet letting our grown-up pride
Hide all the need inside,
Acting more
Like children,
Than children.
Lovers
Are very special people,
They're the luckiest people
In the world.
With one person,
One very special person,
A feeling deep in your soul
Says you were half, now you're whole.
No more hunger and thirst,
But first, be a person who needs
    people.
People who need people
Are the luckiest people
In the world.

—*Jule Styne*

STAYING YOUNG

VERSE
I'm glad I'm not getting old like that
And wind up losing my hold like that.

Should the truth be known, he's resentful
    of the young
'Cause he's over the hill looking back,
And his hindsight's all out of whack.
I'm glad I'm not getting old like that
And wind up losing my hold like that.

REFRAIN
The moon has a few new wrinkles,
He shines a bit more silver now
    than gold.
I'm staying, I'm staying young,
But everyone around me's growing old.
When life only rains in sprinkles,

You've got to gather all your hands
    can hold.
I'm staying young, I'm staying young,
But everyone around me's growing old.
While love is still my jewel of recollection,
No valentine too frayed and frail to fold,
So I'll go my heart's direction,
My story's in the telling, not the told.
I'm staying young,
I'm staying young,
It's wonderful the way I hold my own
When everything surrounding me has
    grown
So old.

Peggy Lee (1920-   )

P EGGY LEE (born Norma Delores Engstrom) was one of America's most successful and admired vocalists for more than forty years. After surviving a difficult childhood in North Dakota, she broke into professional singing with the Will Osborne Band in Minneapolis. Then, in 1941, she became Benny Goodman's singer and in a few years was singing for the newly created Capitol Records. Her sultry voice and emotionally direct and simple delivery have kept her a favorite ever since–a respected *interpreter* of popular music, not just a voice. Lee appeared in several films, notably *Pete Kelly's Blues,* for which she won an Oscar nomination, and she is the main voice you hear in Disney's animated *The Lady and the Tramp.* And of all the traditional singers who have tried their hand at writing songs, she is by far the most successful; with her then husband, Dave Barbour, and later with Cy Coleman, she turned out a number of very effective lyrics, the most famous of which–her recording of it was the number-one hit for nine weeks in 1948–is the charming, if politically ambiguous "Mañana."

I DON'T KNOW ENOUGH ABOUT YOU

I know a little bit about a lot of things,
But I don't enough about you.
Just when I think you're mine
You try a different line,
And, baby, what can I do?
I read the latest news, no buttons on my
        shoes,
But, baby, I'm confused about you.
You get me in a spin,
Oh what a stew I'm in,
'Cause I don't know enough about you.
Jack of all trades, master of none,
And isn't it a shame?
I'm so sure that you'd be good for me,
If you'd only play my game.
You know I went to school
And I'm nobody's fool,
That is to say until I met you.

I know a little bit about a lot of things,
But I don't know enough about you.
I know a little bit about biology,
And a little more about psychology,
I'm a little gem in geology,
But I don't know enough about you.

—Dave Barbour

I LOVE BEING HERE WITH YOU

I love the east, I love the west,
And north or south, they're both the best,
But I'd only go there as a guest,
For I love being here with you.
I love the sea, I love the shore,
I love the rocks, and what is more
With you they'll never be a bore,
'Cause I love being here with you.
Singing in the shower,

Laughing by the hour,
Life is such a breezy game.
Love all kinds of weather
'Long as we're together,
I love to hear you say my name.
I like good wine and fine cuisine,
And candlelight, I like the scene,
But baby, if you know what I mean,
I love being here with you.
I like a dance by Fred Astaire,
And Brando's eyes, Yul Brynner's hair,
But I think to tell you's only fair
That I love being here with you?
And Cary Grant, oh doo-da-day,
His utter charm takes me away,
But don't get me wrong, how do you say
That I love being here with you.
Oh, the Basie band is swinging, I like Ella
    singing,
Because they're something else, you know.
They know how to say it, they know how to
    play it,
They wind it up and let it go.
I love the thrill of New York shows,
I love to kiss Durante's nose,
But I'd like to say before I close
That I love being here with you.

—*Bill Schluger*

I'm Gonna Go Fishin'

Woke up this mornin',
Wanted to cry.
Then I remembered—
Yes, I knew why.
He's a real good one
For havin' his cake,
I'm gonna go fishin'
Or jump in the lake!
I'm goin' fishin',

That's what I'll do,
Think about nothin',
Not even you.
Catch a real big one,
A big speckled trout
Snappin' in the water,
I'll pull him on out!
Sweet-talkin' liar,
Spin me a yarn,
Tell me a story
Big as a barn.
Gonna stop list'nin',
I won't hear you out,
I'm gonna go fishin'
And catch me a trout!
If a man is a liar,
A man is a fool,
Playin' for keepers
And breakin' the rule.
He'll be the loser,
Yes, he'll find out,
I'm gonna go fishin'
And catch me a trout!
Here in the water,
Look at him shine,
There goes a big one,
That one is mine!
Cast off the reel now,
I've got the feel now,
Snap! Goes the fine fly rod,
I'll catch me a trout!
Sweet-talkin' liar,
You're in for a fall,
You tell me a story,
You talk to the wall!
Gonna go my way
On down the highway,
I'm gonna go fishin'
And catch me a trout!

—*Duke Ellington*

It's a Good Day

(words and music with Dave Barbour)

VERSE

I looked at my horoscope
And it said to me,
Don't be a dope,
'Cause ev'rything you do
Will turn out right,
'Cause it's a good day
From mornin' till night:

REFRAIN

Yes, it's a good day
For singin' a song,
And it's a good day
For movin' along.
Yes, it's a good day,
How could anything go wrong?
A good day from mornin' till night.
Yes, it's a good day
For shinin' your shoes,
And it's a good day
For losin' the blues,
Ev'rything to gain
And nothin' to lose,
'Cause it's a good day from mornin' till
    night.
I said to the sun,
"Good mornin' sun,
Rise and shine today."
You know, you've gotta get goin'
If you're gonna make a showin',
And you know you've got the right
    of way.
'Cause it's a good day
For payin' your bills,
And it's a good day
For curin' your ills,
So take a deep breath
And throw away your pills,

'Cause it's a good day from mornin' till
    night.

Mañana

(Is Soon Enough for Me)

(words and music with Dave Barbour)

The faucet she is dripping
And the fence she's falling down.
My pocket needs some money
So I can't go into town.
My brother isn't working
And my sister doesn't care.
The car she needs a motor,
So I can't go anywhere.
Mañana, mañana, mañana is soon enough
    for me.
My mother's always working;
She's working very hard.
But ev'ry time she looks for me
I'm sleeping in the yard.
My mother thinks I'm lazy
And maybe she is right.
I'll go to work mañana, but I gotta sleep
    tonight.
Mañana, mañana, mañana is soon enough
    for me.
Oh, once I had some money
But I gave it to my friend.
He said he'd pay me double,
It was only for a lend.
But he said a little later that
The horse she was so slow.
Why he gave the horse my money
Is something I don't know.
Mañana, mañana, mañana is soon enough
    for me.
My brother took his suitcase
And he went away to school.
My father said he only learned
To be a silly fool.

My father said that I should learn
To make a chili pot.
But then I burned the house down,
The chili was too hot.
Mañana, mañana, mañana is soon enough
    for me.
The window she is broken
And the rain is coming in.
If someone doesn't fix it
I'll be soaking to my skin.
But if we wait a day or two
The rain may go away.
And we don't need a window
On such a sunny day.
Mañana, mañana, mañana is soon enough
    for me.

THAT'S MY STYLE

That's my style
And I know it when I see it,
And I see it,
And I know it,
And I just can't quite forgo it.
He's got that chemistry

That melts me down and ruins me.
Yes, that's my style.
And there's that smile
A little lopsided,
And it's wicked,
And it's crooked,
And I know it's got me hook-ed.
Don't even mention eyes
Or walk or talk or shape or size,
Yes, that's my style.
I give up,
I give in,
'Cause I already know that he's
    gonna win.
I'm all through,
So what's new,
And there's no use worrying what he's
    gonna do.
'Cause that's my style,
A stormy, smoldering fire,
I can't fight it,
I can't fake it,
And I know I just can't make it.
Call out those engines now,
Clang those bells, I'm burning wild,
Eee-yeah, that's my style.

George David Weiss (1921–   )

A NEW YORKER educated at Brooklyn College and Juilliard, George David Weiss is the relatively unknown writer of numerous hits, including million-record sellers like "Rumors Are Flying" (for Frankie Carle); "Wheel of Fortune" (for Kay Starr); "Can't Help Falling in Love" (for Elvis Presley); and "The Lion Sleeps Tonight" (for the Tokens). He was involved with several Broadway musicals, including Sammy Davis, Jr.'s, *Mr. Wonderful*. And he wrote "What a Wonderful World," Louis Armstrong's posthumous and final hit.

LULLABY OF BIRDLAND

Lullaby of birdland,
That's what I
Always hear
When you sigh.
Never in my wordland
Could there be ways to reveal,
In a phrase,
How I feel!
Have you ever heard two
Turtledoves
Bill and coo
When they love?
That's the kind of magic
Music we make with our lips
When we kiss!
And there's a weepy old willow,
He really knows how to cry!
That's how I'd cry in my pillow
If you should tell me farewell and
    good-bye!
Lullaby of birdland,
Whisper low,
Kiss me sweet
And we'll go
Flyin' high in birdland,

High in the sky up above
All because we're in love!

—George Shearing

OH! WHAT IT SEEMED TO BE

*(words and music with Bennie Benjamin
and Frankie Carle)*

VERSE
When I'm walking through the park,
I'm not in the park at all.
Ordinary things that happen to me
Are never what they seem to be.

REFRAIN
It was just a neighborhood dance,
That's all that it was,
But oh, what it seemed to be!
It was like a masquerade ball
With costumes and all,
'Cause you were at the dance with me.
It was just a ride on a train,
That's all that it was,
But oh, what it seemed to be!
It was like a trip to the stars,

To Venus and Mars,
'Cause you were on the train with me.
And when I kissed you,
Darling,
It was more than just a thrill for me.
It was the promise,
Darling,
Of the things that fate had willed
    for me.
It was just a wedding in June,
That's all that it was,
But oh, what it seemed to be!
It was like a royal affair
With ev'ryone there,
'Cause you said "Yes, I do," to me.

Too Close for Comfort

*(words and music with Jerry Bock and
Larry Holofcener)*

VERSE

The men of science are a brilliant clan.
Just think, just think,
They can tell how far it is from here to a
    star above.
And yet they cannot measure the safest
    distance between

A woman and man in love.
Since I cannot consult a book of
    knowledge
That may be lying on a shelf,
I guess I'll have a confidential discussion
    with myself.

REFRAIN

Be wise, be smart,
Behave, my heart,
Don't upset your cart
When she's so close.
Be soft, be sweet,
But be discreet,
Don't go off your beat.
She's too close for comfort,
Too close, too close for comfort.
Please not again,
Too close, too close to know just when
    to say
"When."
Be firm, be fair,
Be sure, beware,
On your guard, take care–
While there's such temptation,
One thing leads to another,
Too late to run for cover,
She's much too close for comfort now!

Richard Adler (1921–   )
and Jerry Ross (1926–1955)

A s a team, Adler and Ross had one of the most meteoric (and briefest) careers in Broadway musical history–two giant hits, *The Pajama Game* and *Damn Yankees,* before Ross died of leukemia at the unthinkable age of twenty-nine. Adler, son of a concert pianist, went into advertising after college and the navy; Ross (born Jerold Rosenberg) was a child star and juvenile lead in the Yiddish theater. In 1953, early in their joint career, they wrote "Rags to Riches," which sold over a million records in the Tony Bennett version and was the number-one song in America for eight weeks. They also contributed songs to *John Murray Anderson's Almanac.* But it wasn't until they became protégés of Frank Loesser that they were given their big chance by a new production team that included the young Hal Prince. In 1954 came *Pajama Game* ("Hey There," "Hernando's Hideaway"), in 1955 *Damn Yankees* ("Heart," "Whatever Lola Wants"), and six months later Ross was gone. Both shows ran for more than a thousand performances, outliving their co-author before going on to become highly successful movies. Afterward, Richard Adler wrote several shows on his own, including the ambitious *Kwamina;* had success writing commercial jingles; wrote several extended symphonic compositions; and staged White House shows for Presidents Kennedy and Johnson; but he never achieved alone what he and Jerry Ross had accomplished together.

Heart

You've gotta have heart,
All you really need is heart.
When the odds are sayin'
You'll never win,
That's when the grin
Should start.
You've gotta have hope,
Mustn't sit around and mope,
Nothin's half as bad as it may appear,
Wait'll next year
And hope.

When your luck is battin' zero,
Get your chin up off the floor;
Mister, you can be a hero,
You can open any door,
There's nothin' to it,
But to do it.
You've gotta have heart,
Miles 'n' miles 'n' miles of heart.
Oh, it's fine to be a genius of course,
But keep that old horse
Before the cart.
First you've gotta have heart!

HERNANDO'S HIDEAWAY

I know a dark secluded place,
A place where no one knows your face,
A glass of wine, a fast embrace,
It's called Hernando's Hideaway!
Olay!
All you see are silhouettes,
And all you hear are castanets,
And no one cares how late it gets,
Not at Hernando's Hideaway!
Olay!
At the Golden Fingerbowl or any place
    you go,
You will meet your Uncle Max and
    ev'ryone you know.
But if you go to the spot that I am
    thinkin' of,
You will be free
To gaze at me
And talk of love!
Just knock three times and whisper low,
That you and I were sent by Joe,
Then strike a match and you will know,
You're in Hernando's Hideaway!
Olay!

HEY THERE

Hey there,
You with the stars in your eyes.
Love never made a fool of you,
You used to be too wise!
Hey there,
You on that high-flying cloud.
Though she won't throw a crumb to you,
You think someday
She'll come to you.
Better forget her,
Her with her nose in the air,
She has you dancing on a string,

Break it and she won't care!
Won't you take this advice
I hand you like a brother?
Or are you not seeing things too clear,
Are you too much in love to hear,
Is it all going in one ear
And out the other?

THERE ONCE WAS A MAN

HE: There once was a man
SHE: There once was a woman
HE: Who loved a woman.
SHE: Who loved a man.
HE: She was the one he slew a dragon for!
SHE: He was the one that she took
    poison for!
HE: They say that nobody ever loved as
    much as he-ee,
SHE: They say that nobody ever loved as
    much as she-ee,
HE: But me-ee.
SHE: But me-ee.
HE: I love you more!
SHE: I love you more!
HE: And there once was a man
SHE: And there once was a woman
HE: Who loved a woman.
SHE: Who loved a man.
HE: She was the one he gave his
    kingdom for.
SHE: He was the one she swam the
    channel for.
HE: They say that nobody ever loved as
    much as he-ee,
SHE: They say that nobody ever loved as
    much as she-ee,
HE: But me-ee.
SHE: But me-ee.
HE: I love you more!
SHE: I love you more!
HE: My love is a giant,

SHE: My love's meteoric,
HE: Fierce and defiant.
SHE: It's merely historic,
HE: But how can I prove it to you?
SHE: A whirlwind, a cyclone on wheels!
HE: Ain't got no kingdom,
SHE: It rocks "muh" whole solar
plexus.
HE: No dragon,
SHE: It's bigger 'n Texas.
HE: To back up my braggin'.
SHE: I just can't tell you how it feels!
HE: How can I show what I would do?
HE: I only know there once was a man
SHE: I only know there once was a woman
HE: Who loved a woman.
SHE: Who loved a man.
HE: She was the one he ate that apple for.
SHE: Loved him enough to cause the
Trojan War.
HE: They say that nobody ever loved as
much as he-ee,
SHE: They say that nobody ever loved as
much as she-ee,

HE: But me-ee.
SHE: But me-ee.
HE: I love you more!
SHE: I love you more!

WHATEVER LOLA WANTS (LOLA GETS)

Whatever Lola wants, Lola gets,
And little man, little Lola wants you.
Make up your mind to have no regrets,
Recline yourself, resign yourself, you're
through.

I always get what I aim for,
And your heart and soul is what I came for.

Whatever Lola wants, Lola gets,
No use to fight, don't you know–you can't
win!
You're no exception to the rule
I'm irresistible, you fool,
Give in!–give in!–give in!

Joseph McCarthy, Jr. (1922–1975)

WHEREAS HIS FATHER, the notable Tin Pan Alley lyricist Joseph McCarthy, started out singing in cafés, Joseph McCarthy, Jr., studied at Juilliard. Although he contributed to the mildly successful *John Murray Anderson's Almanac* of 1953 and the *Ziegfeld Follies of 1956* (it closed out of town, Tallulah Bankhead and all), McCarthy's hits came in the pop world. "Why Try to Change Me Now?," introduced by Frank Sinatra, was his first conspicuous success—it was Cy Coleman's first, too; they were to score together again with "The Riviera," popularized by Mabel Mercer, and "I'm Gonna Laugh You Right Outa My Life," introduced by Nat King Cole.

CLOUDY MORNING

Cloudy morning
Dark as night,
Tops of buildings
Lost from sight.
A sign of spring was nowhere to be seen,
The trees in Central Park were anything
    but green.
And then that cloudy morning
Slowly cleared,
Tops of buildings
Reappeared.
Then suddenly I saw you come my way,
And I knew that this would be a
    lovely day.

—Marvin Fisher

I'M GONNA LAUGH YOU RIGHT OUT OF MY LIFE

I'm gonna laugh you right out of my life,
Laugh and forget this affair.
Guess I was foolish to care.

So I'm gonna dance you right out of my
    dreams,
Try to be carefree and gay.
I guess I'll learn to play
The part.
'Cause when our friends begin that
    heartless rumor,
I know I'll need my sense of humor.
I'm gonna laugh you right out of my life,
Making a beautiful joke,
No one will know you broke
My heart.
But if I find you and I
Really meant that last good-bye,
Then I'm gonna laugh so hard I'll cry.

—Cy Coleman

THE RIVIERA

The Riviera,
On every street a gay casino
Where continentals sip their vino
And leave their fortune to chance.
The Riviera,

Where matrons draped in Paris fashions
Prolong the twilight of their passions
In mad pursuit of romance.
Every gay mademoiselle
Is disarming some maharajah
With the daring of her décolletage.
Life is so completely zany and free
By the Mediterranean Sea.
Ah, the Riviera,
Where every golden coat of suntan
Has cost the gold of more than one man
Who wasn't warned in advance.
He may take to his heart
All the wonders of France,
Then as a token for the dough that
    he's sunk
He gets a little label slapped on his
    trunk,
The Riviera.

    —Cy Coleman

WHY TRY TO CHANGE ME NOW?

I'm sentimental, so I walk in the rain.
I've got some habits even I can't explain.
Could start for the corner, turn up in
    Spain,
But why try to change me now?
I sit and daydream, I've got daydreams
    galore.
Cigarette ashes, there they go on the
    floor.
I'll go away weekends, leave my keys in
    the door,
But why try to change me now?
Why can't I be more conventional?
People talk, people stare, so I try.
But that's not for me,
'Cause I can't see
My kind of crazy world go passing
    me by.
So let people wonder, let them laugh, let
    them frown,
You know I'll love you till the moon's
    upside down.
Don't you remember, I was always your
    clown,
Why try to change me now?

    —Cy Coleman

Marshall Barer (1923–1998)

BORN IN Queens, New York, Marshall Barer began as an illustrator, then went on to work for Golden Records and on various industrial/commercial projects and television shows. In his sixties he became a successful cabaret performer. But his chief distinction was as a writer: of the successful shows *New Faces of 1956, Once Upon a Mattress* (libretto and lyrics), and *The Mad Show,* the latter two with Mary Rodgers, as well as of individual songs for a variety of today's leading cabaret artists. Nor should we forget his "Mighty Mouse Theme (Here I Come to Save the Day)"!

BEYOND COMPARE

VERSE
How do I love thee?
Let me count the ways:
One, two, three, four, five, six million–
This could take me days and days
    and days!

REFRAIN
Shall I, my love, compare thee to
Baba au rhum or summer's day?
Handel chorale, or Malibu?
Rubens, Ravel, or Mel Tormé?
Is there a better metaphor
For how I melt beholding you,
Or shall the glow I so adore
Only be felt enfolding you?
Racking my brain for fitting praise!
Seeking, in vain, the perfect phrase!
Poring through piles of poems and plays!
Haunting the aisles at Doubleday's!
I might convey the state I'm in
If I could play the mandolin;
Since I cannot, I'll just declare
You are beyond compare

And leave it right there!
Who could compose your Valentine?
Not Billy Rose, nor Gertrude Stein!
Only a "heart" like Larry might
Tell you what burns in mine tonight!
That which of which there's only one
Simply defies comparison.
So I repeat, in sweet despair,
You are beyond compare
And leave it right there!

—David Ross

HERE COME THE DREAMERS

Please hang a moon up and tune up the
    cellos,
For here come the dreamers.
Tell all the fellows to varnish their
    trumpets,
Butter the crumpets and garnish the
    Jell-Os.
Let us get to it and do it up right,
Welcome the dreamers with all of our
    might.

Here come a few of the true punchinellos,
The beautiful dreamers.
Here comes a clown in motley of yellows
Made from a gown of Dolores Costello's,
Giddy and gaudy and bawdy and bright,
Here come the dreamers to light up the
    night.
They
May arrive in a sleigh
Or the ghost of a gay
Painted
Steamboat,
Dreamboat.
What does it matter who scatter confetti
And string up the streamers,
Cover the table with strawberry satin,
Put out the platinum sugar and
    creamers,
Tell every sorrow to slip out of sight?
Here come the dreamers to put them to
    flight.

—Hugh Martin

On Such a Night As This

VERSE

There's something in the air that you can
    sense,
Elusive, yet unbearably intense!
The stars are all hanging there in bright
    suspense,
As they prepare to light immense events!

REFRAIN I

On such a night as this,
Did young Lorenzo swear
He'd gladly swim a thousand seas, to
    please his lady fair?
On such a night, did Wagner write the
    "Evening Star"?

'Neath such a moon stood Lorna Doone
    and Lochinvar.
If someone waits for you in yonder leafy
    glade
On such a night, who knows,
He might compose
A serenade.
Hurry, my sweet, wings on your feet,
You mustn't miss
The sheer delight of such a night as this.

REFRAIN 2

'Twas such a night as this,
When Judy Garland swore,
"I just adore him, how can I ignore the boy
    next door?"
On such a night, did Gershwin write his
    Rhapsody.
On such a did young Jeanette sing,
"Lover, come back to me."
On such a night as this, did Robert
    Taylor sigh,
As Garbo gave a little cough
And wandered off
To die.
Lately I find I'm disinclined
To reminisce,
Except, perhaps, on such a night as this.

—Hugh Martin

Shall We Join the Ladies?

VERSE

At a quarter to seven we sat down to dine.
The porter was heaven, the filet was fine.
The mere fact that you thought it a quarter
    to nine
When it's going on ten is an excellent sign
And a clear corroboration that whenever
    you combine

A little sparkling conversation with an
    educated wine
You bring about a combination one may
    rightfully define
As: "Simply frightfully, delightfully
    divine!"
But banana flambé and Havana cigar
And Jamaica with lime as sublime as
    they are
Seem to have the effect on this kind
    of song
Of extending the verse just a wee bit
    too long.
And so now without further ado, let us do
What a gent of good breeding's expected
    to do.
If postprandially speaking, if all are
    agreed,
You may follow my lead as I hasten
    to heed
The clear need to proceed.
Shall we now? Now indeed!
Now indeed, shall we now,

REFRAIN

Shall we join the ladies?
Yes, do, let's join the ladies
And make one great big lady.
Taken sep'rately, the girls can be
    confusing,
But as a whole they might, I think, be
    quite amusing.
I'd rather have one enormous lady with
    two tremendous eyes
Than twenty with forty of ord'n'ry size.
So shall we join those darling
    daughters?
I mean, join them to each other
And make one great huge mother?
You maintain that if she's
Big she'll be ungainly,
But I maintain that you're a prig
Who spouts inanely.

My cousin Denise weighed seven hundred
    pounds and wasn't fat at all:
She was, indeed, quite slender (though
    terribly tall)!
Oh, what a fine finale to such a
    summer's day,
For in the damp and sultry weather,
The ladies seem to tend to stick together
Anyway.
Shall we join the ladies?
I mean *really* join the ladies
And make one great big lady?
Whadda you say?!

—*David Ross*

VERY SOFT SHOES

VERSE

I am far from sentimental or romantic,
And I like to think I'm strictly up to date.
But at times the dancing gets a bit too
    frantic
In these hectic days of fourteen twenty-
    eight.
So, indulge me if I pause to raise my
    chalice
To a quaint and charming dance they used
    to do
In the days when my dear father played the
    palace,
Back in thirteen ninety-two.

REFRAIN

My Dad was debonair
And quite as light as air
In his very soft shoes.
How he could dip and glide,
And skip and slip and slide
In his very soft shoes.
I used to stand and watch him ev'ry day;
He was always smooth and cool.

I used to love to hear the people say,
He's a regular dancing fool.
He barely touched the ground
And never made a sound,
But I've noticed in all his reviews
That when he took his bow

To the crowd and the crown,
The crowd went crazy and the house
   came down
When Daddy wore his very soft shoes.

   —Mary Rodgers

Sandy Wilson (1924–   )

S ANDY WILSON WAS educated at Harrow and Oxford, where he wrote for and appeared in various undergraduate productions. By 1948 he was providing songs for revues in London–*Slings and Arrows, Oranges and Lemons*–and in 1953 he was asked to provide the book, music, and lyrics for a one-hour show to be called *The Boy Friend.* A loving look back at the musicals of the twenties, it opened at the tiny Player's Theatre, then was expanded and moved into a larger theater, and finally opened in the West End, where it played for over five years. It was also a hit in New York–it's the show that introduced Julie Andrews to America (she went straight from it into *My Fair Lady.*) Alas, the 1971 film version, made by Ken Russell, didn't have the charm of the show; in fact, it had no charm at all. Wilson went on to write other shows in London, most noticeably *Valmouth*, but it's *The Boy Friend* that secures his reputation.

THE BOY FRIEND

VERSE

Any girl who's reached the age
Of seventeen or thereabouts
Has but one desire in view.
She knows she has reached the stage
Of needing one to care about;
Nothing else will really do.
Childhood games are left behind,
And her heart takes wing,
Hoping that it soon will find
Just one thing.

REFRAIN 1

We've got to have,
We plot to have,
For it's so dreary not to have,
That certain thing called the boy friend.
We scheme about,
And dream about,
And we've been known to scream about,
That certain thing called the boy friend.

He is really a necessity
If you want to get on.
And we might as well confess it, he
Is our *sine qua non.*
We sigh for him,
And cry for him,
And we would gladly die for him,
That certain thing called the boy friend.

REFRAIN 2

We plead to have,
We need to have,
In fact our poor hearts bleed to have,
That certain thing called the boy friend.
We'd save for him,
And slave for him,
We'd even misbehave for him,
That certain thing called the boy friend.
Life without us is impossible
And devoid of all charms.
No amount of idle gossip'll
Keep them out of our arms.
We're blue without,

Can't do without,
Our dreams just won't come true
    without,
That certain thing called the boy friend.

It's Never Too Late to Fall in Love

VERSE

I may be too old to run a mile . . .
Run a mile?
Yes, run a mile.
But there's one thing I still do very well.
I may be too old to jump a stile . . .
Jump a stile?
Yes, jump a stile.
But there's one thing at which I still
    excel.
Although my hair is turning gray . . .
Yes, it's rather gray.
I still believe it when I say . . .
Well, what do you say?

REFRAIN 1

It's never too late to have a fling,
For autumn is just as nice as spring,
And it's never too late to fall in love.
Boop-a-doop, boop-a-doop, boop-a-doop.
It's never too late to wink an eye,
I'll do it until the day I die,
And it's never too late to fall in love.
Boop-a-doop, boop-a-doop, boop-a-doop.
If they say I'm too old for you,
Then I shall answer, "Why, sir,
One never drinks the wine that's new,
The old wine tastes much nicer."
A gentleman never feels too weak
To pat a pink arm, or pinch a cheek,
And it's never too late to fall in love.
Says who?
Says me.
Says you,

Says we.
Says both of us together.
It's never too late to fall in,
Never too late to fall in love.

REFRAIN 2

It's never too late to whisper words
Concerning the ways of bees and birds,
And it's never too late to fall in love.
Wack-a-doo, wack-a-doo, wack-a-doo.
It's never too late to flirt and spoon,
A fiddle that's old is more in tune,
And it's never too late to fall in love.
Wack-a-doo, wack-a-doo, wack-a-doo.
The modern artists of today
May paint their pictures faster.
But when it comes to skill, I say:
"You can't beat an Old Master."
It's never too late to bill and coo.
At any age one and one make two,
And it's never too late to fall in love.
Says who?
Says me.
Says you,
Says we.
Says both of us together.
It's never too late to fall in,
Never too late to fall in love.

A Room in Bloomsbury

VERSE

HE: A life of wealth does not appeal to
        me at all.
    Do you agree at all?
SHE: I do!
HE: The mere idea of living in a
        palace is
    So full of fallacies.
SHE: That's true.
HE: I've got a very diff'rent sort of
        scheme in mind,

It's just a dream designed for two.
Would you care to hear about
    it, dear?
SHE: Would I care to? Can you doubt
    it, dear?

REFRAIN I
HE: All I want is a room
In Bloom-
Sbury,
Just a room that will do
For you and me.
One room's enough for us,
Though it's on the top floor.
Life may be rough for us,
But its troubles we'll ignore.
On a wintery night
I'll light
A fire.
Ev'rything I shall do
As you
Desire.
I'll be sitting
And you'll be knitting,
And so contented we'll be,
In our dear little room

In Bloom-
Sbury.

REFRAIN 2
SHE: All I want is a room
In Bloom-
Sbury,
Just a room that will do
For you
And me.
I'll sew the covers for
Two old cozy armchairs.
Neighbors will love us, for
We shall laugh at all our cares.
While you're reading a book,
I'll cook
A stew.
Then I'll bake a plum duff,
Enough
For two.
BOTH: In our attic
We'll be ecstatic
As lovebirds up in a tree.
All we want is a room
In Bloom-
Sbury.

Lee Adams (1924–)

L EE ADAMS WAS BORN in Ohio and was educated at the University of Ohio and the Columbia School of Journalism. He was working at *Newsweek* in New York when he started up his partnership with Charles Strouse, a partnership that led to three solid Broadway hits: *Bye Bye Birdie, Golden Boy,* and *Applause,* the Lauren Bacall musical based on *All About Eve.* Undoubtedly, though, their most widely heard work was "Those Were the Days," the theme song of *All in the Family,* performed at the start of each episode by Jean Stapleton and Carroll O'Connor.

But Alive

I feel groggy and weary and tragic,
Punchy and bleary and fresh out of magic,
But alive, but alive, but alive!
I feel twitchy and bitchy and manic,
Calm and collected and choking with
	panic,
But alive, but alive, but alive!
I'm a thousand diff'rent people,
Ev'ry single one is real.
I've a million diff'rent feelings.
O.K., but at least I feel!
And I feel rotten yet covered with roses,
Younger than Springtime and older than
	Moses,
But alive, but alive, but alive!
I feel wicked and wacky and mellow,
Firm as Gibraltar and shaky as Jell-O,
But alive, but alive, but alive!
I feel half Tiajuana, half Boston,
Partly Jane Fonda and partly Jane
	Austen,
But alive! That's the thing! But alive!
This kaleidoscope of feelings
Whirls around inside my brain,
I admit I'm slightly coo-coo,

But it's dull to be too sane!
And I feel brilliant and brash and
	bombastic,
Limp as a puppet and simply fantastic,
Frisky as a lamb, lazy as a clam, crazy, but I
	am alive!

—*Charles Strouse*

Kids!

Kids!
I don't know what's wrong with these kids
	today!
Kids!
Who can understand anything they say?
Kids!
They are disobedient,
Disrespectful oafs!
Noisy crazy sloppy lazy loafers!
While we're on the subject:
Kids!
You can talk and talk till your face is blue!
Kids!
But they still do just what they want to do!
Why can't they be like we were,

Perfect in ev'ry way?
What's the matter with kids today?
Kids!
I don't know what's wrong with these kids
    today!
Kids!
Who can understand anything they say?
Kids!
They are disobedient,
Disrespectful oafs!
Noisy crazy sloppy lazy loafers!
Why are they so dreadful?
Kids!
They are just impossible to control!
Kids!
With their awful clothes and their rock
    and roll!
Why can't they be like we were,
Perfect in ev'ry way?
What's the matter with
Kids today?
Kids!
I don't know what's wrong with these kids
    today!
Kids!
Even I don't understand what they say!
Kids!
They are so ridiculous
And so immature!
I don't see why anybody wants 'em!
Why are they so dreadful?
Kids!
What the devil's wrong with these kids
    today?
Kids!
Who could guess that they would turn out
    that way!
Why can't they be like you were,
Perfect in ev'ry way?
What's the matter with
Kids today?

—Charles Strouse

ONCE UPON A TIME

Once upon a time
A girl with moonlight in her eyes
Put her hand in mine
And said she loved me so.
But that was once upon a time,
Very long ago.
Once upon a hill
We sat beneath a willow tree,
Counting all the stars
And waiting for the dawn.
But that was once upon a time.
Now the tree is gone.
How the breeze
Ruffled through her hair,
How we always laughed as though
    tomorrow wasn't there.
We were young
And didn't have a care.
Where did it go?
Once upon a time
The world was sweeter than we knew.
Ev'rything was ours;
How happy we were then.
But somehow once upon a time
Never comes again.

—Charles Strouse

PUT ON A HAPPY FACE

Gray skies are gonna clear up,
Put on a happy face.
Brush off the clouds and cheer up,
Put on a happy face.
Take off the gloomy mask of tragedy,
It's not your style;
You'll look so good that you'll be
    glad ya' de-
Cided to smile!

Pick out a pleasant outlook,
Stick out that noble chin,
Wipe off that "full of doubt" look,
Slap on a happy grin!
And spread
Sunshine
All over the place,
Just put on a happy face!

—*Charles Strouse*

THOSE WERE THE DAYS

Boy, the way Glenn Miller played
Songs that made the hit parade.
Guys like me, we had it made.
Those were the days.
Didn't need no welfare state,
Ev'rybody pulled his weight,

Gee, our old LaSalle ran great.
Those were the days.
And you knew who you were then,
Girls were girls and men were men.
Mister, we could use a man like Herbert
    Hoover again.
People seemed to be content,
Fifty dollars paid the rent,
Freaks were in a circus tent.
Those were the days.
Take a little Sunday spin,
Go to watch the Dodgers win.
Have yourself a dandy day, that cost you
    under a fin.
Hair was short and skirts were long.
Kate Smith really sold a song.
I don't know just what went wrong,
Those were the days.

—*Charles Strouse*

Sheldon Harnick (1924–)

BORN IN CHICAGO, Sheldon Harnick tried his hand at various kinds of writing while also playing the violin when he could find jobs; then, in 1943, he went into the army for three years. After Northwestern University, he came to New York and met composer Jay Gorney and lyricist Yip Harburg, who encouraged him to concentrate on lyrics. He had several clever songs in *New Faces of 1952* and, a few years later, he met Jerry Bock, the composer with whom he was to have one of the most fruitful collaborations of the day. Their first hit was *Fiorello!* (the third musical to win the Pulitzer Prize), and later they scored with *She Loves Me, The Apple Tree,* and *The Rothschilds,* but of course their great triumph—one of the greatest in musical comedy history—was *Fiddler on the Roof,* which opened in 1964 and ran for eight years. There was to be no improving on *that* show.

THE BOSTON BEGUINE

VERSE

Tropical nights . . .
Orchids in bloom . . .
Sultry perfume . . .
Intrigues and dangers
With passionate strangers,
I've seen it all . . .
As I recall . . .

REFRAIN

I met him in Boston
In the native quarter.
He was from Harvard
Just across the border.
It was a magical night
With romance everywhere.
There was something in the air,
There always is . . . in Boston.
We went to the Casbah,
That's an Irish bar there,

The underground hideout
Of the D.A.R. there.
Something inside of me said,
"Watch your heart, mad'moiselle,
And it might be just as well
To watch your purse . . . in Boston."
We danced in a trance
And I dreamed of romance
Till the strings of my heart
Seemed to be knotted,
And even the palms seemed to be
    potted.
The Boston Beguine
Was casting its spell
And I was drunk with love . . .
And cheap Muscatel.
We walked to the Common,
That's a pretty park there.
As I remember,
It was pretty dark there.
In this exotic locale
By a silver lagoon

Underneath a voodoo moon . . .
We fell asleep . . . in Boston.
That was the story of my one romance
    there,
Our dream of adventure didn't stand a
    chance there,
How could we hope to enjoy all the
    pleasures ahead
When the books we should have read
Were all suppressed . . . in Boston?
Exotic Boston . . . land of the free . . . home
    of the brave . . .
Home of the Red Sox . . . home of the
    bean . . .
And home . . . of the Boston Beguine!

IF I WERE A RICH MAN

If I were a rich man,
Dai-dle, dee-dle, dai-dle, dig-guh, dig-
    guh, dee-dle, dai-dle, dum,
All day long I'd bid-dy, bid-dy, bum,
If I were a wealthy man.
Wouldn't have to work hard,
Dai-dle, dee-dle, dai-dle, dig-guh, dig-
    guh, dee-dle, dai-dle, dum,
If I were a bid-dy, bid-dy rich,
Dig-guh, dig-guh, dee-dle, dai-dle man.

I'd build a big tall house with rooms by the
    dozen
Right in the middle of the town;
A fine tin roof with real wooden floors
    below.
There would be one long staircase just
    going up
And one even longer coming down,
And one more leading nowhere just
    for show.
I'd fill my yard with chicks and turkeys and
    geese

And ducks for the town to see and hear,
Squawking just as noisily as they can.
And each loud quack and cluck and gobble
    and honk
Will land like a trumpet on the ear,
As if to say here lives a wealthy man.

I see my wife, my Golde, looking like a rich
    man's wife with a proper double chin,
Supervising meals to her heart's delight.
I see her putting on airs and strutting like
    a peacock.
Oy! What a happy mood she's in,
Screaming at the servants day and night.
The most important men in town will
    come to fawn on me.
They will ask me to advise them
Like a Solomon the wise,
"If you please, Reb Tevye, pardon me, Reb
    Tevye,"
Posing problems that would cross a
    rabbi's eyes.
Boi, boi, boi, boi, boi, boi, boi, boi, boi,
    boi, boi.
And it won't make one bit of diff'rence
If I answer right or wrong.
When you're rich, they think you
    really know.
If I were rich, I'd have the time that I lack
To sit in the synagogue and pray,
And maybe have a seat by the eastern wall.
And I'd discuss the holy books with the
    learned men
Seven hours ev'ry day.
This would be the sweetest thing of all.

If I were a rich man,
Dai-dle, dee-dle, dai-dle, dig-guh, dig-
    guh, dee-dle, dai-dle, dum,
All day long I'd bid-dy, bid-dy bum,
If I were a wealthy man.
Wouldn't have to work hard,

Dai-dle, dee-dle, dai-dle, dig-guh, dig-
    guh, dee-dle, dai-dle, dum.
Lord, who made the lion and the lamb,
You decreed I should be what I am.
Would it spoil some vast eternal plan
If I were a wealthy man?

—*Jerry Bock*

LITTLE TIN BOX

Mr. "X," may we ask you a question?
It's amazing, is it not,
That the city pays you slightly less
Than fifty bucks a week
Yet you've purchased a private yacht!

I am positive Your Honor must be joking.
Any working man can do what I have done.
For a month or two I simply gave up
    smoking
And I put my extra pennies one by one
Into
A little tin box,
A little tin box,
That a little tin key unlocks.
There is nothing unorthodox
About a little tin box.
There is honor and purity
Lots of security
In a little tin box.

Mr. "Y," we've been told you don't
    feel well
And we know you've lost your voice.
But we wondered how you managed on the
    salary you make
To acquire a new Rolls-Royce.

You're implying I'm a crook and I say,
    No sir!
There is nothing in my past I care to hide.

I've been taking empty bottles to the grocer
And each nickel that I got was put aside
Into
A little tin box,
A little tin box,
That a little tin key unlocks.
There is nothing unorthodox
About a little tin box.
In a little tin box,
A little tin box,
There's a cushion for life's rude shocks.
There is faith, hope, and charity,
Hard-won prosperity,
In a little tin box.

Mr. "Z," you're a junior official
And your income's rather low,
Yet you've kept a dozen women
In the very best hotels.
Would you kindly explain how so?

I can see Your Honor doesn't pull his
    punches,
And it looks a trifle fishy, I'll admit,
But for one whole week I went without my
    lunches,
And it mounted up, Your Honor, bit by bit.
It's just
A little tin box,
A little tin box,
That a little tin key unlocks.
There is nothing unorthodox
About a little tin box.
In
A little tin box,
A little tin box,
All a-glitter with blue chip stocks.
There is something delectable,
Almost respectable,
In a little tin box,
In a little tin box!

—*Jerry Bock*

MATCHMAKER

VERSE 1

Matchmaker, matchmaker, make me a
   match,
Find me a find,
Catch me a catch;
Matchmaker, matchmaker, look through
   your book
And make me a perfect match.

REFRAIN 1

Matchmaker, matchmaker,
I'll bring the veil,
You bring the groom,
Slender and pale;
Bring me a ring, for I'm longing to be
The envy of all I see.
For Poppa,
Make him a scholar,
For Momma, make him rich as a king.
For me, well, I wouldn't holler
If he were as handsome as anything.

VERSE 2

Matchmaker, matchmaker,
Make me a match,
Find me a find,
Catch me a catch;
Night after night in the dark I'm alone,
So find me a match of my own.

REFRAIN 2

Matchmaker, matchmaker,
You know that I'm
Still very young,
Please take your time;
Up to this minute, I misunderstood
That I could get stuck for good.
Dear Momma,
See that he's gentle,
Remember you were also a bride.

It's not that I'm sentimental.
It's just that I'm terrified.
Matchmaker, matchmaker,
Plan me no plans,
I'm in no rush,
Maybe I've learned
Playing with matches, a girl can get
   burned.
So bring me no ring,
Groom me no groom,
Find me no find,
Catch me no catch;
Unless he's a matchless match!

—Jerry Bock

(THE BALLAD OF) THE SHAPE OF THINGS

Completely round is the perfect pearl
The oyster manufactures.
Completely round is the steering wheel
That leads to compound fractures.
Completely round is the golden fruit
That hangs in the orange tree.
Yes, the circle shape is quite renowned,
And sad to say, it can be found
In the dirty low-down runaround
My true love gave to me,
Yes, my true love gave to me.

Completely square is the velvet box
He said my ring would be in.
Completely square is the envelope
He wrote farewell to me in.
Completely square is the handkerchief
I flourish constantly,
As it dries my eyes of the tears I've shed,
And blows my nose 'til it turns bright red,
For a perfect square is my true love's head.
He will not marry me,
No, he will not marry me.

Rectangular is the hotel door
My true love tried to sneak through.
Rectangular is the transom
Over which I had to peek through.
Rectangular is the hotel room
I entered angrily.
Now, rectangular is the wooden box
Where lies my love 'neath the grazing
    flocks.
They said he died of the chicken pox,
In part I must agree;
One chick too many had he.

Triangular is the piece of pie
I eat to ease my sorrow.
Triangular is the hatchet blade
I plan to hide tomorrow.
Triangular the relationship
That now has ceased to be.
And the self-same shape is a garment thin,
That fastens on with a safety pin
To a prize I had no wish to win;
It's a lasting memory
That my true love gave to me.

SHE LOVES ME

VERSE

Well, well, well, well, well,
Well, well, well, well, well,
Will wonders never cease?
I didn't like her.
Didn't like her?
I couldn't stand her.
Couldn't stand her?
I wouldn't have her.
I never knew her.
But now I do
And I could
And I would
And I know:

REFRAIN

She loves me,
And to my amazement,
I love it
Knowing that she loves me!
She loves me!
True, she doesn't show it.
How could she
When she doesn't know it?
Yesterday she loathed me. *Bah!*
Now today she likes me. *Hah!*
And tomorrow,
Tomorrow,
Ah!
My teeth ache
From the urge to touch her.
I'm speechless,
For I mustn't tell her.
It's wrong now.
But it won't be long now
Before my love discovers
That she and I are lovers.
Imagine how surprised she's bound to be!
She loves me!
She loves me!

I love her!
Isn't that a wonder?
I wonder
Why I didn't want her.
I want her.
That's the thing that matters,
And matters
Are improving daily.
Yesterday I loathed her. *Bah!*
Now today I love her. *Hah!*
And tomorrow,
Tomorrow,
Ah!
I'm tingling
Such delicious tingles.
I'm trembling.

What the heck does that mean?
I'm freezing.
That's because it's cold out.
But still I'm incandescent
And like some adolescent,
I'd like to scrawl on ev'ry wall I see:
She loves me!
She loves me!

—Jerry Bock

Someone's Been Sending Me Flowers

REFRAIN 1
Someone's been sending me flowers.
Oh, what a sweet thing to do.
Ev'ry new day brings another bouquet
And I don't know who to say "Thank
    you" to.
Sometimes they're thrown through my
    window
Or down through my chimney they fall.
Sometimes at night when I've turned out
    my light
They come through a crack in the wall.
Now that my house is a garden,
Bursting with blossom and bloom,
I stand there for hours admiring my
    flowers;
I'd like to lie down but there just isn't room.
Someone's been sending me flowers,
More than I ever have had.
Remarkable stuff
But enough is enough.
If I see another bouquet,
I'll go mad.

INTERLUDE
Flowers are the language of love, I'm told,
A language divine.

Ev'ry dainty little blossom has a message
    to unfold,
All except mine.
If flowers are the language of affection,
How can I interpret my collection?

REFRAIN 2
He started by sending me bluebells.
Oddly enough, they were gray.
Each faded bloom had a nasty perfume.
Besides being gray they were papier-
    mâché.
There followed a garland of fungus
And then as a tropical treat,
He sent me a plant that proceeded
    to pant
And later began to eat meat.
The cactus corsage touched me deeply,
A beautiful plant in its prime.
I felt much the same when the rock
    garden came,
One rock at a time.
Somebody madly adores me.
I know not whom to suspect.
Since I cannot afford to be madly adored,
I do wish you'd stop sending flowers
Collect!

—David Baker

Sunrise, Sunset

VERSE 1
Is this the little girl I carried?
Is this the little boy at play?
I don't remember growing older.
When did they?
When did she get to be a beauty?
When did he grow to be so tall?
Wasn't it yesterday when they were
    small?

REFRAIN

Sunrise, sunset,
Sunrise, sunset,
Swiftly flow the days;
Seedlings turn overnight to sunflow'rs,
Blossoming even as we gaze.
Sunrise, sunset,
Sunrise, sunset,
Swiftly fly the years;
One season following another,
Laden with happiness and tears.

VERSE 2

Now is the little boy a bridegroom,
Now is the little girl a bride.
Under the canopy I see them,
Side by side.
Place the gold ring around her finger,
Share the sweet wine and break the glass;
Soon the full circle will have come to pass.

REPEAT REFRAIN

—*Jerry Bock*

TONIGHT AT EIGHT

I'm nervous and upset
Because this girl I've never met
I get to meet
Tonight at eight.
I'm taking her to dinner
At a charming old café,
But who can eat
Tonight at eight?
It's early in the morning
And our date is not till eight o'clock
    tonight,
And yet already I can see
What a nightmare this whole day will be.
I haven't slept a wink,
I only think

Of our approaching tête-à-tête
Tonight at eight.
I feel a combination
Of depression and elation;
What a state to wait
Till eight.
Three more minutes, two more seconds,
Ten more hours to go.
In spite of all I've written,
She may not be very smitten
And my hopes, perhaps,
May all collapse,
Ka-put,
Tonight at eight!

I wish I knew exactly
How I'll act and what will happen
When we dine
Tonight at eight.
I know I'll drop the silverware,
But will I spill the water
Or the wine
Tonight at eight?
Tonight I'll walk right up and sit
    right down
Beside the smartest girl in town
And then it's anybody's guess.
More and more I'm breathing less
    and less.
In my imagination
I can hear our conversation
Taking shape
Tonight at eight.
I'll sit there saying absolutely nothing
Or I'll jabber like an ape
Tonight
At eight.
Two more minutes, three more seconds,
Ten more hours to go.
I'll know when this is done
If something's ended or begun
And if it goes all right,
Who knows, I might

Propose
Tonight at eight!

—Jerry Bock

(I'll Marry) The Very Next Man

VERSE

I shall marry the very next man who
   asks me,
You'll see.
Next time I feel
That a man's about to kneel,
He won't have to plead or implore.
I'll say "Yes" before his knee hits the floor.

REFRAIN

No more waiting around,
No more browsing through *True Romance*.

I've seen the light, so while there's a
   chance
I'm gonna marry the very next man who
   asks me.
Start rehearsing a choir—
Tie some shoes on my Chevrolet—
Pelt me with rice and catch my bouquet—
I'm gonna marry the very next man if he
   adores me.
What does it matter if he bores me?
If I allow a man to carry me off,
No more will people try to marry me off.
New York papers, take note,
Here's a statement that you can quote:
"Waiting for ships that never come in,
A girl is likely to miss the boat."
I'm through being wary,
I'll marry
The very next man.

—Jerry Bock

Alan Bergman (1925–) and Marilyn Bergman (1929–)

T HE BERGMANS ARE the most successful husband/wife team in the business. Both of them were born in Brooklyn–he went to the Ethical Culture School, she to the High School of Music & Arts–and both, after college, began writing for radio and television (among other things, they wrote the themes for *Maude, Good Times,* and *Alice*). The heartfelt anthems for which they are best known have won them two Grammy awards, two Golden Globes, four Emmys, and three Oscars–one for "The Windmills of Your Mind," one for "The Way We Were," one for the score of Barbra Streisand's *Yentl.* In 1994, Marilyn became president and chairman of the board of ASCAP; she has been a leading advocate for the protection of the rights of all American songwriters. Alan, encouraged early on by Johnny Mercer to pursue his songwriting career, has (in imitation of his mentor?) recently taken up singing professionally, performing at the Russian Tea Room in New York and the Jazz Bakery in L.A.

SUMMER ME, WINTER ME

Summer me, Winter me,
And with your kisses morning me,
    evening me,
And as the world slips far away, star away,
Forever me with love!
Wonder me, wander me, then by a fire
Pleasure me, peaceful me,
And in the silence quietly whisper me,
Forever me with love!
Forever me with love!
And ev'ry day I'll gentle you, tender you,
And oh, the way I'll velvet you, clover you.
I'll wrap you up and ribbon you,
    rainbow you,
And shower you with shine!
Suddenly, magic'ly,
We found each other,
There we were, here we are.

I plan to let you happy me,
Summer me, Winter me,
Always be mine!

   –Michel Legrand

THE WAY WE WERE

Mem'ries–
Light the corners of my mind.
Misty watercolor mem'ries
Of the way we were.
Scattered pictures
Of the smiles we left behind,
Smiles we gave to one another
For the way we were.
Can it be that it was all so simple then,
Or has time rewritten ev'ry line?
If we had the chance to do it all again,

Tell me, would we?
Could we?
Mem'ries
May be beautiful, and yet,
What's too painful to remember
We simply choose to forget.
So it's the laughter
We will remember,
Whenever we remember
The way we were;
The way we were.

—Marvin Hamlisch

THE WINDMILLS OF YOUR MIND

Round like a circle in a spiral,
Like a wheel within a wheel,
Never ending or beginning
Or an ever-spinning reel.
Like a snowball down a mountain
Or a carnival balloon,
Like a carousel that's turning,
Running rings around the moon.
Like a clock whose hands are sweeping
Past the minutes of its face,
And the world is like an apple
Whirling silently in space.
Like the circles that you find
In the windmills of your mind
Like a tunnel that you follow
To a tunnel of its own,
Down a hollow to a cavern
Where the sun has never shown.
Like a door that keeps revolving
In a half-forgotten dream,
Or the ripples of a pebble
Someone tosses in a stream.
Like a clock whose hands are sweeping
Past the minutes of its face,
And the world is like an apple
Whirling silently in space.

Like the circles that you find
In the windmills of your mind.
Keys that jingle in your pocket,
Words that jangle in your head.
Why did Summer go so quickly?
Was it something that you said?
Lovers walk along a shore
And leave their footprints in the sand.
Is the sound of distant drumming
Just the fingers of your hand?
Pictures hanging in a hallway
And the fragments of a song.
Half remembered names and faces,
But to whom do they belong?

1. BOY: When you knew that it was over
          You were suddenly aware
          That the Autumn leaves were
              turning
          To the color of her hair.
2. GIRL: When you knew that it was over
          In the Autumn of good-byes,
          For a moment you could not
              recall
          The color of his eyes.
Like a circle in a spiral,
Like a wheel within a wheel,
Never ending or beginning
On an ever spinning reel,
As the images unwind,
Like the circles that you find
In the windmills of your mind.

—Michel Legrand

YOU MUST BELIEVE IN SPRING

When lonely feelings chill the meadows of
    your mind,
Just think if Winter comes, can Spring be
    far behind?
Beneath the deepest snows,

The secret of a rose
Is merely that it knows you must believe in
    Spring!
Just as a tree is sure its leaves will
    reappear;
It knows its emptiness is just a time
    of year.
The frozen mountain dreams
Of April's melting streams,
How crystal clear it seems.
You must believe in Spring!

You must believe in love and trust it's on
    its way,
Just as the sleeping rose awaits the kiss
    of May.
So in a world of snow,
Of things that come and go,
Where what you think you know,
You can't be certain of,
You must believe in Spring and love.

—*Michel Legrand*

Carolyn Leigh (1926–1983)

CAROLYN LEIGH WAS BORN in the Bronx and was educated at Hunter, Queens College, and NYU. She began as an office worker, once describing herself as a secretary "who couldn't take dictation." Possibly her work as a copywriter was some help in teaching her to write lyrics, because she started professionally at the age of twenty-five and within two years had written her first hit, "Young at Heart." Her partnership with composer Cy Coleman was particularly productive–the shows *Wildcat,* for Lucille Ball, and *Little Me,* for Sid Caesar; the pop hit "Witchcraft"–but she also collaborated successfully with Moose Charlap on the 1954 Mary Martin *Peter Pan.* Her work was sung appreciatively by the leading song stylists of the fifties and sixties– Frank Sinatra, Mabel Mercer, and Tony Bennett recorded her frequently–and today she is generally regarded as the finest woman songwriter since Dorothy Fields.

THE BEST IS YET TO COME

REFRAIN
Out of the tree of life
I just picked me a plum.
You came along and ev-
'Rything's startin' to hum.
Still, it's a real good bet
The best is yet to come.
The best is yet to come
And, babe, won't it be fine?
You think you've seen the sun,
But you ain't seen it shine.
Wait till the warm-up's under way,
Wait till our lips have met,
Wait till you see that sunshine day,
You ain't seen nothin' yet!
The best is yet to come
And, babe, won't it be fine?
The best is yet to come,
Come the day you're mine.

INTERLUDE
I'm gonna teach you to fly,
We've only tasted the wine.
We're gonna drain the cup dry.
Wait till your charms are ripe
For these arms to surround.
You think you've flown before,
But you ain't left the ground.

Wait till you're locked in my
    embrace,
Wait till I draw you near;
Wait till you see that sunshine place,
Ain't nothin' like it here!
The best is yet to come
And, babe, won't it be fine;
The best is yet to come,
Come the day you're mine.

–Cy Coleman

Hey, Look Me Over

REFRAIN
Hey, look me over,
Lend me an ear,
Fresh out of clover,
Mortgaged up to here.
But don't pass the plate, folks,
Don't pass the cup;
I figure whenever you're down and out,
The only way is up.
And I'll be up like a rosebud,
High on the vine;
Don't thumb your nose, bud,
Take a tip from mine.
I'm a little bit short of the elbow room,
But let me get me some,
And look out, world, here I come.

INTERLUDE
Nobody in the world was ever without a
    pray'r;
How can you win the world if nobody
    knows you're there?
Kid, when you need the crowd, the tickets
    are hard to sell;
Still, you can lead the crowd, if you can get
    up and yell:

REPEAT REFRAIN

—*Cy Coleman*

How Little We Know
(How Little It Matters)

How little we know,
How much to discover,
What chemical forces flow
From lover to lover?
How little we understand

What touches off that tingle,
That sudden explosion
When two tingles intermingle.
Who cares to define
What chemistry this is?
Who cares with your lips on mine
How ignorant bliss is,
So long as you kiss me
And the world around us shatters?
How little it matters,
How little we know.
How little we know.

—*Philip Springer*

I Walk a Little Faster

VERSE
Up Madison, down Park,
Ev'ry day and often after dark.

REFRAIN
Pretending that we'll meet
Each time I turn a corner,
I walk a little faster.
Pretending life is sweet
'Cause love's around the corner,
I walk a little faster.
Can't begin to see my future shine
    as yet,
No sign as yet,
You're mine as yet.
Rushing t'ward a face I can't divine
    as yet,
Keep bumping into walls,
Taking lots of falls.
But even though I meet
At each and ev'ry corner
With nothing but disaster,
I set my chin a little higher,
Hope a little longer,
Build a little stronger

Castle in the air;
And thinking you'll be there,
I walk a little faster.

—*Cy Coleman*

It Amazes Me!

VERSE

My height: just av'rage.
My weight: just av'rage.
And my I.Q. is like you'd estimate,
Just av'rage.
But evidently she does not agree.
Consequently, if I seem at sea:

REFRAIN

It amazes me,
It simply amazes me,
What she sees in me
Dazzles me, dazes me!
That I've learned to clip my wings
And soften my ways,
These are ordinary things
Unworthy of praise.
Yet she praises me
Just knowing I'd try for her
When so many would,
If they could,
Die for her!
I'm the one who's worldly wise,
And nothing much fazes me,
But to see me in her eyes,
It just amazes me!
Yes, to see me in her eyes,
It just amazes me!

—*Cy Coleman*

I've Got Your Number

VERSE

You've got
No time for me,
You've got
Big things to do!
Well, my
Sweet chickadee,
I've got
Hot news for you!

REFRAIN

I've got your number,
I know you inside out,
You ain't no Eagle Scout,
You're all at sea!
Oh, yes, you'll brag a lot,
Wave your own flag a lot,
But you're unsure a lot,
You're a lot like me.
Oh, I've got your number
And what you're looking for,
And what you're looking for
Just suits me fine!
We'll break the rules a lot,
We'll be damn' fools a lot,
But then why should we not,
How could we not
Combine,
When I've got your number
And I've got the glow you've got,
I've got your number
And, baby,
You know you've got mine!

—*Cy Coleman*

Real Live Girl

REFRAIN I
Pardon me, Miss,
But I've never done this
With a real
Live
Girl.
Strayed off the farm
With an actual arm-
Ful of real
Live
Girl.
Pardon me if your affectionate squeeze
Fogs up my goggles and buckles
    my knees.
I'm simply drowned in the sight and the
    sound and the scent
And the feel
Of a real
Live
Girl.

REFRAIN 2
Nothing can beat
Getting swept off your feet
By a real
Live
Girl.
Dreams in your bunk
Don't compare with a
Hunk
Of a real
Live
Girl.

Speaking of miracles, this must be it,
Just when I started to learn how
    to knit.
I'm all in stitches from finding what
    riches a waltz

Can reveal
With a real
Live
Girl.

    —Cy Coleman

The Rules of the Road

So these are the ropes,
The tricks of the trade,
The rules of the road.
You're one of the dopes
For whom they were made,
The rules of the road.
You follow that kiss
And recklessly miss
A bend of the road.
Then suddenly this:
The end of the road.
So love is a hoax,
A glittering string
Of little white lies,
But these are the jokes,
And what if they bring
The tears to your eyes?
Well, love often shows
A funny return,
The brighter it glows,
The longer you burn,
And Lord only knows
Love has little concern
For the fools of the road!
But that's how it goes,
You live and you learn
The rules of the road!

    —Cy Coleman

WHEN IN ROME
(I DO AS THE ROMANS DO)

VERSE

Though now and then your problems fall
Within the errant mate department,
Forget the transatlantic call,
Don't notify the State Department.
For when on foreign shores I am,
Very truly yours I am,
But if inclined to play I am,
Dear heart, that's the way I am.

REFRAIN 1

When in Spain,
For reasons I don't explain,
I remain
Enjoying a brew;
Don't deplore
My fondness for fundador,
You know how a fundador
Can lead to a few.
And baby, when in Rome,
I do as the Romans do!
And though from Italy
I lie to you prettily,
Why think of me bitterly?
You know that I'm true.
'Cept now and then in Rome,
I get that old yen in Rome
And nat'rally, when in Rome,
I do as the Romans do!

REFRAIN 2

If perchance
I'm saying farewell to France,
And romance
Drops in from the blue;
Chère amour,
I beg of you, please endure
My taking a brief detour

With somebody new.
It's just that when in Rome,
I do as the Romans do!
If I write happily
Best wishes from Napoli,
Don't cable me snappily
To tell me we're through.
'Cause once again in Rome,
In somebody's den in Rome,
Well, Pussycat, den in Rome,
I do as de Romans do!
If I write
Disregard the signs and the omens,
When in Rome I do
As the Romans do!

—Cy Coleman

WITCHCRAFT

VERSE

Shades of old Lucretia Borgia!
There's a devil in you tonight,
'N' although my heart adores ya,
My head says it ain't right.
Right to let you make advances, oh no!
Under normal circumstances, I'd go,
But oh!

REFRAIN

Those fingers in my hair,
That sly, come-hither stare
That strips my conscience bare,
It's witchcraft.
And I've got no defense for it,
The heat is too intense for it,
What good would common sense for
    it do?
'Cause it's witchcraft,
Wicked witchcraft.
And although I know it's strictly taboo,

When you arouse the need in me,
My heart says, "Yes, indeed" in me,
"Proceed with what you're leadin'
    me to!"
It's such an ancient pitch,
But one I wouldn't switch,
'Cause there's no nicer witch than you!

    —Cy Coleman

YOU FASCINATE ME SO

I have a feeling that beneath the little halo
    on your noble head
There lies a thought or two the devil might
    be int'rested to know.
You're like the finish of a novel that I'll
    fin'lly have to take to bed,
You fascinate me so!
I feel like Christopher Columbus when
    I'm near enough to contemplate
The sweet geography descending from
    your eyebrow to your toe.
The possibilities are more than I can
    possibly enumerate,
That's why you fascinate me so.
So sermonize and preach to me,
Make your sanctimonious little speech
    to me,
But oh, my darling, you'll forgive my
    inability to concentrate.
I think I'm dealing with a powder keg
    that's just about to blow.
Will the end result deflate me,
Or will you annihilate me?
You fascinate me so!
You aggravate me,

You irritate me,
You fascinate me so!

    —Cy Coleman

YOUNG AT HEART

Fairy tales can come true,
It can happen to you
If you're young at heart.
For it's hard, you will find,
To be narrow of mind
If you're young at heart.
You can go to extremes
With impossible schemes,
You can laugh when your dreams
Fall apart at the seams,
And life gets more exciting with each
    passing day,
And love is either in your heart or on
    the way.
Don't you know that it's worth
Ev'ry treasure on earth
To be young at heart?
For, as rich as you are,
It's much better by far
To be young at heart.
And if you should survive
To a hundred and five
Look at all you'll derive
Out of being alive,
And here is the best part,
You have a head start
If you are among
The very young at heart.

    —Johnny Richards

Fran Landesman (1927–)

F RAN LANDESMAN WAS BORN in New York and educated at Columbia and Temple, but her entry into the music world took place in St. Louis, when she, her husband, and her in-laws opened a hip hangout called the Crystal Palace. There, in 1951, she began her brilliant collaboration with composer Tommy Wolf, producing a series of songs Wolf was later to refer to as "American lieder." During the decade or so that this partnership lasted, Landesman wrote the words for such anthemic songs as "Spring Can Really Hang You Up the Most" and "The Ballad of the Sad Young Men," which took on even more resonance in the age of AIDS. In 1959, a number of Wolf/ Landesman songs were brought together in a show called *The Nervous Set,* which didn't fare well in New York but produced a much-admired cast album. Landesman moved to London in the early sixties, and has worked there ever since, both as a poet/songwriter and as a performer.

THE BALLAD OF THE SAD YOUNG MEN

REFRAIN 1

Sing a song of sad young men,
Glasses full of rye;
All the news is bad again,
Kiss your dreams good-bye.
All the sad young men
Sitting in the bars,
Knowing neon nights,
Missing all the stars.
All the sad young men,
Drifting through the town,
Drinking up the night,
Trying not to drown.
All the sad young men
Singing in the cold,
Trying to forget
That they're growing old;
All the sad young men
Choking on their youth;

Trying to be brave,
Running from the truth.
Let your gentle light
Guide them home again,
All the sad young men.

REFRAIN 2

Autumn turns the leaves to gold,
Slowly dies the heart;
Sad young men are growing old,
That's the cruelest part.
All the sad young men
Seek a certain smile,
Someone they can hold
For a little while.
Tired little girl
Does the best she can,
Trying to be gay
For a sad young man
While a grimy moon
Watches from above.
All the sad young men

Play at making love;
Misbegotten moon,
Shine for sad young men
Trying to be brave,
Running from the truth.
Let your gentle light
Guide them home again,
All the sad young men.

—*Tommy Wolf*

PHOTOGRAPHS

Here's a picture of me
When I was three, and here's my pony, too.
Here's a picnic we had, and Jane, with Dad,
Here's me in love with you.
Here's our house, up in Maine,
And me, again,
I always loved that view.
There are lots in this book,
How young we look!
That's me in love with you.
Life isn't quite what we expected.
At times it seems so strange.
Of all the pictures we've collected
There's only one that doesn't change.
If you want a few laughs,
Old photographs
Are fun to rummage through.
Here's our house in the snow
So long ago,
And me in love with you.

—*Alec Wilder*

SAY "CHEESE!"

When you're sad and down in the dumps,
Say "cheese."
Feeling bad and getting your lumps,

Say "cheese."
See the corners of your mouth turn up,
You stop acting like an underpup,
You'll look sweet as a little buttercup
When you say "cheese."
Lift your chin and turn on a smile,
Wear a grin and you'll be in style,
Say "cheese."
When the movie stars and glamour
    queens
Sell deodorants and nicotines,
Smiling gladly in the magazines,
They all say "cheese."
If they're selling cars or beer,
This is what you'll always hear,
Take the pose, Madonna, please,
All right, smile, come on, say "cheese."
Feeling tragic, just want to cry,
Say "cheese."
Works like magic, give it a try,
Say "cheese."
Show more ivory than a crocodile,
That's the way, my little honey chile,
You'll feel better in a little while,
When you say "cheese."
When your back is to the wall
That's the time to stand up tall,
Just forget those miseries,
Come on, smile, just try,
Say "cheese."
Though you've got a pain in the neck,
Say "cheese."
Even if they're stacking the deck,
Say "cheese."
Though you're tired of the human race,
Don't start acting like a hardship case,
Fool the people with a sunny face,
When you say "cheese."
So get off your knees and give gloom a
    teasin'
And you'll be breezin' along,
Singing song after song,
When you say

Camembert,
Roquefort,
Brie.

—Tommy Wolf

SPRING CAN REALLY HANG YOU UP THE MOST

VERSE

Once I was a sentimental thing,
Threw my heart away each Spring.
Now a Spring romance
Hasn't got a chance.
Promised my first dance
To Winter,
All I've got to show's
A splinter
For my little fling!

REFRAIN I

Spring this year has got me feeling
Like a horse that never left the post.
I lie in my room,
Staring up at the ceiling,
Spring can really hang you up the most!
Morning's kiss wakes trees and flowers,
And to them I'd like to drink a toast.
I walk in the park
Just to kill lonely hours,
Spring can really hang you up the most!
All afternoon
Those birds twitter twit,
I know the tune:
"This is love, this is it!"

Heard it before
And I know the score,
And I've decided that Spring is a bore!
Love seemed sure around the New Year,
Now it's April, love is just a ghost.
Spring arrived on time,
Only Spring can really hang you up
    the most!

REFRAIN 2

Spring is here, there's no mistaking,
Robins building nests from coast to coast.
My heart tries to sing
So they won't hear it breaking.
Spring can really hang you up the most!
College boys are writing sonnets,
In the "tender passion" they're
    engrossed,
But I'm on the shelf
With last year's Easter bonnets,
Spring can really hang you up the most!
Love came my way,
I hoped it would last,
We had our day,
Now it's all in the past.
Spring came along,
A season of song
Full of sweet promise, but something went
    wrong!
Doctors once prescribed a tonic:
"Sulphur and molasses" was the dose.
Didn't help a bit,
My condition must be chronic,
Spring can really hang you up the most!

—Tommy Wolf

Gene Lees (1928–   )

G ENE LEES TRAINED as a commercial artist in Ontario, Canada, where he was born, but he became instead a reporter and foreign correspondent, and eventually the editor of *Downbeat,* America's leading jazz magazine. (Later, he was to begin *Jazzletter,* his own highly influential monthly.) In the early sixties, he started writing lyrics, adapting several of Antonio Carlos Jobim's wonderful songs into English, with considerable success. He has written with the great jazz pianist Bill Evans and for Sarah Vaughan, and has recorded widely. Finally, he is the author of many valuable books: biographies of Woody Herman and Oscar Peterson; several collections of pieces—*Waiting for Dizzy, Meet Me at Jim and Andy's, Cats of Any Color;* a book on arrangers; and a rhyming dictionary for lyricists.

QUIET NIGHTS OF QUIET STARS

(CORCOVADO)

(based on a lyric by Antonio Carlos Jobim)

Quiet nights of quiet stars,
Quiet chords from my guitar
Floating on the silence
That surrounds us.
Quiet thoughts and quiet dreams,
Quiet walks by quiet streams,
And a window looking on the mountains
    and the sea—
How lovely!
This is where I want to be,
Here with you so close to me
Until the final flicker
Of life's ember.
I who was lost and lonely,
Believing life was only
A bitter, tragic joke,
Have found with you

The meaning of existence,
O my love.

—*Antonio Carlos Jobim*

THE RIGHT TO LOVE

My love and I asked little of the world—
The right to sigh together in the rain
And walk with heads up in the sun
And share our joys and our pain.
And yet they said that we were wrong,
That we hadn't a right to our love,
That this love was shameful to see.
And yet we treasured our love.
And so we go our solitary way,
Indifferent to the cold unfriendly
    stares,
Indifferent to the whispered talk—
We don't care at all.
We have all we need,
As long as we can be together.

We find our consolation in each
    other's eyes—
The sweet look of wonder.
We know that we have earned the precious
    right
To love.

    —Lalo Schifrin

Waltz for Debby

Populated by dolls and clowns
And a prince and a big purple bear,
Lives my favorite girl,
Unaware of the worried frowns

That we weary grownups all wear.
In her own sweet world,
Songs that are spun of gold
In the sun
She dances to silent music
Somewhere in her own little head.
One day all too soon
She'll grow up and she'll leave
    her dolls
And her prince and her silly old bear.
When she goes they will cry
As they whisper good-bye.
They will miss her I fear,
But then so will I.

    —Bill Evans

Stephen Sondheim (1930–   )

B Y F A R the most inventive, individual, and influential voice in the musical theater of the past four decades has been Stephen Sondheim. Having been transplanted from New York to Doylestown, Pennsylvania, at the age of eleven, he met and was befriended by neighbor Oscar Hammerstein II. As Sondheim matured, Hammerstein encouraged and advised him, and helped in practical ways, too; at seventeen, as an undergraduate at Williams College, Sondheim served as a production assistant for Rodgers and Hammerstein's problematic *Allegro.* Having done apprentice work in college shows, summer theater, TV, and incidental music for straight plays, he made his first public splash as the lyricist of *West Side Story*–you can't get splashier than that! A couple of years later came the glories of *Gypsy,* and then–having collaborated with Leonard Bernstein and Jule Styne–Sondheim was ready with his first Broadway solo effort, the madcap *A Funny Thing Happened on the Way to the Forum,* starring Zero Mostel; it ran for almost a thousand performances. The next triumph, a landmark both for its structure and its mordant bite, was *Company,* in 1970; then *Follies* and *A Little Night Music.* After the controversial *Pacific Overtures,* Sondheim had three major hits: *Sweeney Todd, Sunday in the Park with George* (which won the Pulitzer Prize), and *Into the Woods.* Since then, he has had a spotty commercial record, but he has never lost the fascinated attention of serious theatergoers and critics, nor has his reputation diminished–and not just with lounge singers who've worked up "Send in the Clowns." He remains the benchmark composer/lyricist of his (and our) time.

ALL I NEED IS THE GIRL

Once my clothes were shabby.
Tailors called me "cabbie."
So I took a vow,
Said, "This bum'll
Be Beau Brummell."
Now I'm smooth and snappy,
Now my tailor's happy.
I'm the cat's meow!
My wardrobe is a wow!
Paris silk,
Harris tweed.

There's only one thing I need:
Got my tweed pressed,
Got my best vest,
All I need now is the girl!
Got my striped tie,
Got my hopes high,
Got the time and the place and I got
    rhythm,
Now all I need's the girl to go with 'em.
If she'll
Just appear, we'll
Take this big town for a whirl.
And if she'll say, "My darling, I'm yours,"

I'll throw away my striped tie
And my best pressed tweed,
All I really need
Is the girl!

—Jule Styne

America

Puerto Rico,
You lovely island,
Island of tropical breezes.
Always the pineapples growing,
Always the coffee blossoms
    blowing.
Puerto Rico,
You ugly island,
Island of tropic diseases.
Always the hurricanes blowing,
Always the population growing,
And the money owing,
And the babies crying,
And the bullets flying.
I like the island Manhattan.
Smoke on your pipe and put that in!
I like to be in America!
O.K. by me in America!
Everything free in America
For a small fee in America!

I like the city of San Juan. / I know a boat
    you can get on.
Hundreds of flowers in full bloom. /
    Hundreds of people in each room!

Automobile in America,
Chromium steel in America,
Wire-spoke wheel in America,
Very big deal in America!

I'll drive a Buick through San Juan. / If
    there's a road you can drive on.

I'll give my cousins a free ride.
How you get all of them inside?

Immigrant goes to America,
Many hellos in America,
Nobody knows in America,
Puerto Rico's in America!

I'll bring T.V. to San Juan. / If there's a
    current to turn on!
I'll give them new washing machine. /
    What have they got there to keep
    clean?

I like the shores of America!
Comfort is yours in America!
Knobs on the doors in America,
Wall-to-wall floors in America!

When I will go back to San Juan, / When
    you will shut up and get gone?
Everyone there will give big cheer! /
    Everyone there will have moved here!

I like to be in America!
O.K. by me in America!
Everything free in America
For a small fee in America!

—Leonard Bernstein

Another Hundred People

Another hundred people just got off of the
    train
And came up through the ground,
While another hundred people just got off
    of the bus
And are looking around
At another hundred people who got off of
    the plane
And are looking at us

Who got off of the train
And the plane and the bus
Maybe yesterday.

It's a city of strangers–
Some come to work, some to play–
A city of strangers–
Some come to stare, some to stay,
And every day
The ones who stay
Can find each other in the crowded streets
   and the guarded parks,
By the rusty fountains and the dusty trees
   with the battered barks,
And they walk together past the postered
   walls with the crude remarks,
And they meet at parties through the
   friends of friends who they never know.
Will you pick me up or do I meet you there
   or shall we let it go?
Did you get my message? 'Cause I looked
   in vain.
Can we see each other Tuesday if it
   doesn't rain?
Look, I'll call you in the morning or my
   service will explain . . .
And another hundred people just got off
   the train.
And another hundred people just got off
   the train.
And another hundred people just got off
   the train.
And another hundred people just got off
   the train.
And another hundred people just got off
   the train. . . .

Comedy Tonight

Something familiar,
Something peculiar,
Something for everyone:

A comedy tonight!
Something appealing,
Something appalling,
Something for everyone:
A comedy tonight!
Nothing with kings,
Nothing with crowns.
Bring on the lovers, liars, and clowns!
Old situations,
New complications,
Nothing portentous
Or polite;
Tragedy tomorrow,
Comedy tonight!

Something convulsive,
Something repulsive,
Something for everyone:
A comedy tonight!
Something esthetic,
Something frenetic,
Something for everyone:
A comedy tonight!
Nothing of gods,
Nothing of Fate.
Weighty affairs will just have to wait.
Nothing that's formal,
Nothing that's normal,
No recitations to recite!
Open up the curtain!
Comedy tonight!

Something erratic,
Something dramatic,
Something for everyone:
A comedy tonight!
Frenzy and frolic,
Strictly symbolic,
Something for everyone:
A comedy tonight! . . .

Something that's gaudy,
Something that's bawdy,

Something for everybawdy:
Comedy tonight!
Nothing that's grim,
Nothing that's Greek!
She plays Medea later this week.
Stunning surprises,
Cunning disguises,
Hundreds of actors out of sight!

Pantaloons and tunics!
Courtesans and eunuchs!
Funerals and chases!
Baritones and basses!
Panderers!
Philanderers!
Cupidity!
Timidity!
Mistakes!
Fakes!
Rhymes!
Mimes!
Tumblers!
Grumblers!
Fumblers!
Bumblers!
No royal curse,
No Trojan horse,
And a happy ending, of course!
Goodness and badness,
Man in his madness:
This time it all turns out all right!
Tragedy tomorrow!
Comedy tonight!

EVERYBODY SAYS DON'T

Everybody says don't,
Everybody says don't,
Everybody says don't—it isn't right,
Don't—it isn't nice!
Everybody says don't,
Everybody says don't,

Everybody says don't walk on the
    grass,
Don't disturb the peace,
Don't skate on the ice.

Well, I
Say,
Do.
I say
Walk on the grass, it was meant to feel!
I
Say,
Sail!
Tilt at the windmill,
And if you fail, you fail.

Everybody says don't,
Everybody says don't,
Everybody says don't get out of line.
When they say that, then,
Lady, that's a sign:
Nine times out of ten,
Lady, you are doing just fine!

Make just a ripple.
Come on, be brave.
This time a ripple,
Next time a wave!
Sometimes you have to start small,
Climbing the tiniest wall,
Maybe you're going to fall—
But it's better than not starting
    at all!

Everybody says no,
Everybody says stop,
Everybody says mustn't rock the boat!
Mustn't touch a thing!
Everybody says don't,
Everybody says wait,
Everybody says can't fight City Hall,
Can't upset the cart,
Can't laugh at the King!

Well, I
Say,
Try!
I
Say,
Laugh at the kings, or they'll make you cry.
Lose
Your
Poise!
Fall if you have to,
But, lady, make a noise!

Everybody says don't.
Everybody says can't.
Everybody says wait around for
    miracles,
That's the way the world is made!
I insist on
Miracles, if *you* do them!
Miracles—nothing to them!
I say don't:
Don't be afraid!

Everything's Coming Up Roses

I had a dream,
A dream about you, Baby!
It's gonna come true, Baby!
They think that we're through,
But Baby,

You'll be swell, you'll be great,
Gonna have the whole world on a plate!
Starting here, starting now,
Honey, everything's coming up roses!
Clear the decks, clear the tracks,
You got nothing to do but relax!
Blow a kiss, take a bow—
Honey, everything's coming up roses!
Now's your inning—
Stand the world on its ear!

Set it spinning,
That'll be just the beginning!
Curtain up, light the lights,
You got nothing to hit but the heights!
You'll be swell,
You'll be great,
I can tell—
Just you wait!
That lucky star I talk about is due!
Honey, everything's coming up roses for
    me and for you!

You can do it,
All you need is a hand.
We can do it,
Momma is gonna see to it!
Curtain up, light the lights,
We got nothing to hit but the heights!
I can tell,
Wait and see!
There's the bell,
Follow me,
And nothing's gonna stop us till we're
    through!
Honey, everything's coming up roses and
    daffodils,
Everything's coming up sunshine and
    Santa Claus,
Everything's gonna be bright lights and
    lollipops,
Everything's coming up roses for me and
    for you!

    —*Jule Styne*

Gee, Officer Krupke

Dear kindly Sergeant Krupke,
You gotta understand,
It's just our bringin' upke
That gets us out of hand.

Our mothers all are junkies,
Our fathers all are drunks.
Golly Moses,
Natcherly we're punks!

Gee, Officer Krupke, we've very upset;
We never had the love that every child
oughta get.
We ain't no delinquents, we're
misunderstood.
Deep down inside us there is good!
There is good!
There is good, there is good, there is
untapped good.
Like inside, the worst of us is good!

Dear kindly Judge, Your Honor,
My parents treat me rough.
With all their marijuana,
They won't give me a puff.
They didn't wanna have me,
But somehow I was had.
Leapin' lizards, that's why I'm so bad!

Right!
Officer Krupke, you're really a square;
This boy don't need a judge, he needs an
analyst's care!
It's just his neurosis that oughta be curbed.
He's psychologically disturbed!
I'm disturbed!
We're disturbed, we're disturbed, we're
the most disturbed,
Like we're psychologically disturbed.

My father is a bastard,
My ma's an S.O.B.
My grandpa's always plastered,
My grandma pushes tea.
My sister wears a mustache,
My brother wears a dress.
Goodness gracious, that's why I'm a mess!

Yes!
Officer Krupke, you're really a slob.
This boy don't need a doctor, just a good
honest job.
Society's played him a terrible trick,
And sociologically he's sick!
I am sick!
We are sick, we are sick, we are sick,
sick, sick,
Like we're sociologically sick!

Dear kindly social worker,
They say go earn a buck,
Like be a soda jerker,
Which means like be a schmuck.
It's not I'm antisocial,
I'm only anti-work.
Gloryosky,

That's why I'm a jerk!
Eek!
Officer Krupke, you've done it again,
This boy don't need a job, he needs a year
in the pen.
It ain't just a question of misunderstood;
Deep down inside him, he's no good!
I'm no good!
We're no good, we're no good, we're no
earthly good,
Like the best of us is no damn good!

The trouble is he's crazy.
The trouble is he drinks.
The trouble is he's lazy.
The trouble is he stinks.
The trouble is he's growing.
The trouble is he's grown!
Krupke, we got troubles of our
own!

Gee, Officer Krupke, we're down on our
knees,

'Cause no one wants a fellow with a social
    disease.
Gee, Officer Krupke, what are we to do?
Gee, Officer Krupke, krup you!

—Leonard Bernstein

I NEVER DO ANYTHING TWICE
(MADAM'S SONG)

When I was young and simple
(I don't recall the date),
I met a handsome Captain of the Guard.
He visited my chambers one evening
    very late,
In tandem with a husky St. Bernard.
At first I was astonished,
And tears came to my eyes.
But later when I asked him to resume
He said, to my surprise,
"My dear, it isn't wise.
Where love is concerned, one must
    freshen the bloom."

Once, yes, once for a lark.
Twice, though, loses the spark.
One must never deny it,
But after you try it, you vary the diet.
Said my handsome young guard,
Yes, I know that it's hard,
But no matter how nice,
I never do anything twice. . . ."

I think about the baron
Who came at my command
And proffered me a riding crop and chains.
The evening that we shared was
    meticulously planned:
He took the most extraordinary pains.
He trembled with excitement,
His cheeks were quite aglow.

And afterwards he cried to me, "Encore!"
He pleaded with me so
To have another go.
I murmured caressingly, "Whatever for?

Once, yes, once is a lark.
Twice, though, loses the spark.
Once, yes, once is delicious,
But twice would be vicious or just
    repetitious.
Someone's bound to be scarred.
Yes, I know that it's hard,
But no matter the price,
I never do anything twice. . . ."

And then there was the abbot
Who worshiped at my feet,
Who dressed me in a wimple and in veils.
He made a proposition which I found
    rather sweet,
And handed me a hammer and some nails.
In time we lay contented
And he began again
By fingering the beads around our waists.
I whispered to him then,
"We'll have to say amen,"
For I had developed more Catholic
    tastes.

Once, yes, once for a lark.
Twice, though, loses the spark.
As I said to the abbot,
"I'll get in the habit, but not in the
    habit.
You've my highest regard.
And I know that it's hard.
Still, no matter the vice,
I never do anything twice."

Once, yes, once can be nice.
Love requires some spice.
If you've something in view,

Something to do, totally new,
I'll be there in a trice,
But I never do anything twice, except . . .
No, I never do anything twice!

I'm Still Here

Good times and bum times,
I've seen them all and, my dear,
I'm still here.
Plush velvet sometimes,
Sometimes just pretzels and beer,
But I'm here.
I've stuffed the dailies
In my shoes,
Strummed ukuleles,
Sung the blues,
Seen all my dreams disappear,
But I'm here.

I've slept in shanties,
Guest of the W.P.A.
But I'm here.
Danced in my scanties,
Three bucks a night was the pay.
But I'm here.
I've stood on breadlines
With the best,
Watched while the headlines
Did the rest.
In the Depression was I depressed?
Nowhere near.
I met a big financier,
And I'm here.

I've been through Gandhi,
Windsor and Wally's affair,
And I'm here.
Amos 'n' Andy,
Mah-jongg and platinum hair,
And I'm here.

I got through "Abie's Irish Rose,"
Five Dionne babies,
Major Bowes,
Had heebie jeebies for Beebe's
    Bathysphere.
I lived through Brenda Frazier
And I'm here.

I've gotten through Herbert and J. Edgar
    Hoover,
Gee, was that fun and a half.
When you've been through Herbert and J.
    Edgar Hoover,
Anything else is a laugh.

I've been through Reno,
I've been through Beverly Hills,
And I'm here.
Reefers and vino,
Rest cures, religion, and pills,
And I'm here.
Been called a pinko
Commie tool,
Got through it stinko
By my pool.
I should have gone to an acting school,
That seems clear.
Still someone said, "She's sincere,"
So I'm here.

Black sable one day,
Next day it goes into hock,
But I'm here.
Top billing Monday,
Tuesday you're touring in stock,
But I'm here.
First you're another sloe-eyed vamp,
Then someone's mother,
Then you're camp.
Then you career from career to career.
I'm almost through my memoirs,
And I'm here.

I've gotten through "Hey, lady, aren't you
  Whoozis?
Wow! What a looker you were."
Or better yet, "Sorry, I thought you were
  'Whoozis.'
Whatever happened to her?"

Good times and bum times,
I've seen them all and, my dear,
I'm still here.
Plush velvet sometimes,
Sometimes just pretzels and beer,
But I'm here.
I've run the gamut,
A to Z.
Three cheers and dammit,
C'est la vie!
I got through all of last year
And I'm here.
Lord knows at least I was there,
And I'm here!
Look who's here!
I'm still here!

In Buddy's Eyes

Life is slow, but it seems exciting
'Cause Buddy's there.
Gourmet cooking and letter writing
And knowing Buddy's there.
Every morning, don't faint, I tend the
  flowers.
Can you believe it?
Every weekend I paint for umpteen hours.
And yes, I miss a lot, living like a shut-in.
No, I haven't got cooks and cars and
  diamonds.
Yes, my clothes are not Paris fashions, but
  in Buddy's eyes
I'm young, I'm beautiful.
In Buddy's eyes,
I don't get older.

So life is ducky and time goes flying
And I'm so lucky I feel like crying. . . .

In Buddy's eyes,
I'm young, I'm beautiful.
In Buddy's eyes,
I can't get older.
I'm still the princess,
Still the prize.
In Buddy's eyes,
I'm young, I'm beautiful.
In Buddy's arms, on Buddy's shoulder,
I won't get older.
Nothing dies.
And all I ever dreamed I'd be,
The best I ever thought of me,
Is every minute there to see
In Buddy's eyes.

The Ladies Who Lunch

Here's to the ladies who lunch–
Everybody laugh–
Lounging in their caftans and planning a
  brunch
On their own behalf.
Off to the gym,
Then to a fitting,
Claiming they're fat,
And looking grim
'Cause they've been sitting,
Choosing a hat–
Does anyone still wear a hat?
I'll drink to that.

Here's to the girls who stay smart–
Aren't they a gas?
Rushing to their classes in optical art,
Wishing it would pass.
Another long exhausting day,
Another thousand dollars,
A matinée, a Pinter play,

Perhaps a piece of Mahler's—
I'll drink to that.
And one for Mahler.

Here's to the girls who play wife—
Aren't they too much?
Keeping house but clutching a copy
    of *Life*
Just to keep in touch.
The ones who follow the rules
And meet themselves at the schools,
Too busy to know that they're fools—
Aren't they a gem?
I'll drink to them.
Let's *all* drink to them.

And here's to the girls who just watch—
Aren't they the best?
When they get depressed, it's a bottle of
    Scotch
Plus a little jest.
Another chance to disapprove,
Another brilliant zinger,
Another reason not to move,
Another vodka stinger—
Aaaahh—I'll drink to that.

So here's to the girls on the go—
Everybody tries.
Look into their eyes and you'll see what
    they know:
Everybody dies.
A toast to that invincible bunch,
The dinosaurs surviving the crunch—
Let's hear it for the ladies who lunch—
Everybody rise! Rise!
Rise! Rise! Rise! Rise! Rise! Rise!

LOSING MY MIND

The sun comes up,
I think about you.

The coffee cup,
I think about you.
I want you so,
It's like I'm losing my mind.
The morning ends,
I think about you.
I talk to friends,
I think about you.
And do they know?
It's like I'm losing my mind.
All afternoon, doing every little chore,
The thought of you stays bright.
Sometimes I stand in the middle of the
    floor,
Not going left,
Not going right.
I dim the lights
And think about you,
Spend sleepless nights
To think about you.
You said you loved me,
Or were you just being kind?
Or am I losing my mind?

REMEMBER?

Remember? Remember?
The old deserted beach that we
    walked,
Remember?
The café in the park where we talked,
Remember?
The tenor on the boat that we
    chartered,
Belching "The Bartered
Bride."
Ah, how we laughed! Ah, how we cried.
Ah, how you promised
And ah, how I lied.

That dilapidated inn,
Remember, darling?

The proprietress's grin,
Also her glare . . .
Yellow gingham on the bed,
Remember, darling?
And the canopy in red,
Needing repair . . .
I think you were there.

Remember? Remember?
The funny little games that we played,
Remember?
The unexpected knock of the maid,
Remember?
The wine that made us both rather
    merry
And oh so very
Frank.
Ah, how we laughed!
Ah, how we drank!
You acquiesced
And the rest is a blank.

What we did with your perfume,
Remember, darling?
The condition of the room
When we were through . . .
Our inventions were unique,
Remember, darling?
I was limping for a week,
You caught the flu . . .
I think it was you.

SEND IN THE CLOWNS

Isn't it rich?
Are we a pair?
Me here at last on the ground,
You in mid-air.
Send in the clowns.

Isn't it bliss?
Don't you approve?

One who keeps tearing around,
One who can't move.
Where are the clowns?
Send in the clowns.

Just when I'd stopped
Opening doors,
Finally knowing
The one that I wanted was yours,
Making my entrance again
With my usual flair,
Sure of my lines,
No one is there.

Don't you love farce?
My fault, I fear.
I thought that you'd want what I want–
Sorry, my dear.
But where are the clowns?
Quick, send in the clowns.
Don't bother, they're here.

Isn't it rich?
Isn't it queer?
Losing my timing this late
In my career?
And where are the clowns?
There ought to be clowns.
Well, maybe next year . . .

SOME PEOPLE

Some people can get a thrill
Knitting sweaters and sitting still–
That's okay for some people who don't
    know they're alive;
Some people can thrive and bloom,
Living life in a living room–
That's perfect for some people of one
    hundred and five!
But I
At least gotta try,

When I think of all the sights that I gotta
    see yet,
All the places I gotta play,
All the things that I gotta be yet—
Come on, Poppa, whaddaya say?
Some people can be content
Playing bingo and paying rent—
That's peachy for some people,
For some humdrum people
To be,
But some people ain't me!

I had a dream,
A wonderful dream, Poppa,
All about June and the Orpheum
    Circuit—
Give me a chance and I know I can
    work it!
I had a dream
Just as real as can be, Poppa—
There I was in Mr. Orpheum's office
And he was saying to me,
"Rose!
Get yourself some new orchestrations,
New routines and red velvet curtains,
Get a feathered hat for the Baby,
Photographs in front of the theater,
Get an agent—and in jig time
You'll be being booked in the big time!"
Oh, what a dream,
A wonderful dream, Poppa,
And all that I need.
Is eighty-eight bucks, Poppa!
That's what he said, Poppa,
Only eighty-eight bucks . . .

Goodbye
To blueberry pie!
Good riddance to all the socials
I had to go to,
All the lodges I had to play,
All the Shriners I said hello to—
Hey, L.A., I'm coming your way!

Some people sit on their butts,
Got the dream—yeah, but not the guts!
That's living for some people,
For some humdrum people,
I suppose.
Well, they can sit and rot,
But not
Rose!

    —*Jule Styne*

SOMEWHERE

There's a place for us,
Somewhere a place for us.
Peace and quiet and open air
Wait for us somewhere.
There's a time for us,
Some day a time for us,
Time together with time to spare,
Time to learn, time to care,
Some day!
Somewhere
We'll find a new way of living,
We'll find a way of forgiving,
Somewhere . . .

There's a place for us,
A time and place for us.
Hold my hand and we're halfway there.
Hold my hand and I'll take you there
Somehow,
Some day,
Somewhere!

    —*Leonard Bernstein*

TOGETHER WHEREVER WE GO

Wherever we go,
Whatever we do,

We're gonna go through it
Together.
We may not go far,
But sure as a star,
Wherever we are,
It's together!
Wherever I go,
I know he goes.
Wherever I go,
I know she goes.
No fits, no fights, no feuds
And no egos,
Amigos
Together!
Through thick and through thin,
All out or all in,
And whether it's win, place or show,
With you for me
And me for you,
We'll muddle through
Whatever we do,
Together, wherever we go!

Wherever we go,
Whatever we do,

We're gonna go through it
Together.
Wherever we sleep,
If prices are steep,
We'll always sleep cheaper
Together.
Whatever the boat I row,
You row.
Whatever the row I hoe,
You hoe.
And any I.O.U. I owe,
You owe.
No, we owe
Together!
We all take the bow,
Including the cow,
Though business is lousy and slow.
With Herbie's vim, Louise's verve,
Now all we need is someone with
    nerve,
Together,
Wherever we go!

—Jule Styne

Lionel Bart (1930–1998)

BORN IN the East End of London, the son of a tailor, Lionel Bart (Lionel Begleiter) first studied art on a scholarship and worked as a graphic artist. But by the late fifties he was writing successful pop songs, and quickly he became a notable figure in the British theater, writing the songs for Joan Littlewood's *Fings Ain't Wot They Seem* and the Mermaid Theatre's *Lock Up Your Daughters*. In 1960, with those hits still running, he wrote the music, lyrics, and book for *Oliver!*, which played for more than six years in London, breaking the record for long-running musicals. *Oliver!* enjoyed a comparable success on Broadway—Bart was to win a Tony for the show's music and lyrics—and eventually became an Oscar-winning movie. His later work, however, was far less successful, and he signed away his rights to *Oliver!* when trying to rescue a flop called *Twang!* Noël Coward had advised him to "never invest in your own show, Lionel," but unfortunately he didn't listen.

AS LONG AS HE NEEDS ME

VERSE

He doesn't act as though he cares,
But deep inside I know he cares,
And this is why
I'm tied right by his side.

REFRAIN

As long as he needs me,
I know where I must be.
I'll cling on steadfastly,
As long as he needs me.
As long as life is long,
I'll love him, right or wrong;
And somehow I'll be strong
As long as he needs me.
If you are lonely
Then you will know
When someone needs you,
You love them so.
I won't betray his trust

Though people say I must.
I've got to stay true, just
As long as he needs me.

FINGS AIN'T WOT THEY USED T'BE

VERSE

I used to lead a lovely life of sin,
Dough! I charged a ton!
Now it's become an undercover game.
Who wants to read a postcard in a window,
"Massaging done?"
Somehow the bus'ness doesn't seem
    the same.
It's a very diff'rent scene,
Well you know what I mean.

REFRAIN I

There's toffs wiv toffee noses
And poofs in coffeehouses,
And fings ain't wot they used ter be.

Short-time low-priced mysteries
Wivaht proper histories,
Fings ain't wot they used ter be.
There used ter be class,
Doin' the town, buyin' a bit o' vice,
And that's when a brass
Couldn't go down
Under the Union price,
Not likely!
Once in golden days of yore
Ponces killed a lazy whore,
Fings ain't wot they used ter be.
Did their lot, they used ter,
Fings ain't wot they used ter be!

REFRAIN 2
Cops from universities,
Dropsy, wot a curse it is!
Fings ain't wot they used ter be.
Big hoods now are little hoods,
Gamblers now do Littlewoods,
Fings ain't wot they used ter be.
There used ter be schools,
Fahsands o' pounds
Passing across the beize.
There used ter be tools,
Flashin' around,
Oh, for the bad old days!
Remember,
'Ow we used ter pull for them,
I've got news for Wolfenden,
Fings ain't wot they used ter,
Did their lot, they used ter,
Fings ain't wot they used ter be!

REVIEWING THE SITUATION

A man's got a heart,
Hasn't he? Joking apart–
Hasn't he?
And though I'd be the first one to say that I
    wasn't a saint,

I'm finding it hard to be really as black as
    they paint.
I'm reviewing the situation.
Can a fellow be a villain all his life?
All the trials
And tribulation,
Better settle down and get myself a wife.
And a wife would cook and sew for me,
And come for me and go for me
(And go for me), and nag at me,
The fingers she would wag at me,
The money she would take from me,
A misery she'd make from me
I think I'd better think it out again.

A wife you can keep,
Anyway. I'd rather sleep
Anyway.
Left without anyone in the world and I'm
    starting from now,
So how to win friends and to influence
    people, so how?
I'm reviewing the situation.
I must quickly look up ev'ryone I know.
Titled people
With a station
Who can help me make a real
    impressive show.
I will own a suite at Claridges,
And run a fleet of carriages,
And wave at all the duchesses
With friendliness, as much as is
Befitting of my new estate,
"Good morrow to you, Magistrate!"
I think I'd better think it out again.

So where shall I go?
Somebody? Who do I know?
Nobody!
All my dearest companions have always
    been villains and thieves,
So at my time of life I should start turning
    over new leaves?

I'm reviewing the situation.
If you want to eat you've got to earn a bob!
Is it such a
Humiliation
For a robber to perform an honest job?
So a job I'm getting possibly,
I wonder who my boss'll be?
I wonder if he'll take to me?
What bonuses he'll make to me?
I'll start at eight, and finish late,
At normal rate and all, but wait!
I think I'd better think it out again.

What happens when I'm
Seventy? Must come a time,
Seventy,
When you're old and it's cold and who
    cares if you live or you die.

Your one consolation's the money you
    may have put by.
I'm reviewing the situation.
I'm a bad 'un and a bad 'un I shall stay!
You'll be seeing
No transformation.
But it's wrong to be a rogue in ev'ry
    way.
I don't want nobody hurt for me,
Or made to do the dirt for me.
This rotten life is not for me.
It's getting far too hot for me.
There is no in between for me,
But who will change the scene for me?
Don't want no one to rob for me,
But who will find a job for me?
I think I'd better think it out again!
Hey!

Leslie Bricusse (1931–)

L ESLIE BRICUSSE BEGAN his career writing for the Footlights Club shows at Cambridge University. Soon he was in London, performing his own material in *An Evening with Beatrice Lillie,* and by the end of the fifties he had begun his partnership with Anthony Newley: Their shows *Stop the World, I Want to Get Off!* and *The Roar of the Greasepaint, The Smell of the Crowd* were to triumph both in the West End and on Broadway. In the sixties he was writing for the movies–the theme for *Goldfinger,* the Rex Harrison *Doctor Dolittle,* the Petula Clark/Peter O'Toole *Goodbye Mr. Chips.* The 1965 show *Pickwick* was not a success, but then in 1970 came the film *Willie Wonka and the Chocolate Factory,* and the Sammy Davis, Jr., number-one version of Bricusse's *Candy Man.* In recent years, Bricusse has written for two long-running Broadway shows: the Julie Andrews *Victor/Victoria* and *Jekyll & Hyde.*

THE CANDY MAN

(words and music with Anthony Newley)

VERSE

I can't stop
Eating sweets!
All those wonderful Willy Wonka treats.
You can keep the others,
'Cause I'm a Wonkerer.
When it comes to candy,
Willy's the conqueror.

REFRAIN

Who can take a sunrise,
Sprinkle it with dew,
Cover it in choc'late and a miracle or two?
The candy man,
The candy man can.
Who can take a rainbow,
Wrap it in a sigh,
Soak it in the sun and make a strawb'ry
    lemon pie?

The candy man,
The candy man can.
The candy man can,
'Cause he mixes it with love
And makes the world taste good,
World taste good.
The candy man makes
Ev'rything he bakes
Satisfying and delicious.
Talk about your childhood wishes!
You can even eat the dishes!
Who can take tomorrow,
Dip it in a dream,
Separate the sorrow and collect up all the
    cream?
The candy man,
The candy man can.
The candy man can,
'Cause he mixes it with love
And makes the world taste good.
And the world tastes good
'Cause the candy man thinks it should.

GOLDFINGER

(with Anthony Newley)

Goldfinger!
He's the man,
The man with the Midas touch,
A spider's touch.
Such a cold finger
Beckons you
To enter his web of sin.
But don't go in.
Golden words he will pour in
    your ear,
But his lies can't disguise what
    you fear,
For a golden girl
Knows when he's kissed her.
It's the kiss of death from
    Mister
Goldfinger.

Pretty girl,
Beware of this heart of gold.
This heart is cold. Golden cold.
He loves only gold,
Only gold.
He loves gold.
He loves only gold,
Only gold.
He loves gold.
He loves gold.

—*John Barry*

WHAT KIND OF FOOL AM I?

*(words and music with
Anthony Newley)*

What kind of fool am I
Who never fell in love?
It seems that I'm the only one

That I have been thinking of.
What kind of man is this?
An empty shell,
A lonely cell in which
An empty heart must dwell.
What kind of lips are these
That lied with ev'ry kiss?
That whispered empty words
Of love that left me
Alone like this.
Why can't I fall in love
Like any other man?
And maybe then I'll know
What kind of fool I am.
What kind of fool I am.
What kind of clown am I?
What do I know of life?
Why can't I cast away
The mask of play
And live my life?
Why can't I fall in love
Till I don't give a damn,
And maybe then I'll know
What kind of fool I am.
What kind of fool I am.

WHO CAN I TURN TO

(WHEN NOBODY NEEDS ME?)

*(words and music with
Anthony Newley)*

Who can I turn to
When nobody needs me?
My heart wants to know,
And so I must go
Where destiny leads me.
With no star to guide me,
And no one beside me,
I'll go on my way, and after the
    day
The darkness will hide me.
And maybe tomorrow

I'll find what I'm after.
I'll throw off my sorrow,
Beg, steal, or borrow
My share of laughter.

With you I could learn to,
With you on a new day,
But who can I turn to
If you turn away?

Jerry Herman (1931-)

BORN IN New York and raised in Jersey City, Jerry Herman first trained to be an interior decorator, then went to the University of Miami to study drama. After contributing songs to a few Off-Broadway shows, he had a hit with his first venture for Broadway, *Milk and Honey,* but all it really had was Mollie Picon and theater parties. Then, in 1964, came one of the greatest successes in Broadway history, *Hello, Dolly!,* with Carol Channing–2,844 performances; she was still tottering through it more than thirty years later. *Mame,* for Angela Lansbury, ran a mere 1,508 performances, then there were no more hits until the 1983 *La Cage aux Folles,* which ran for four years. Herman's most admired flop, *Mack and Mabel,* came in between. His strongest point is writing showstoppers for his leading ladies (or, in the case of *Cage,* leading men), but his work–both words and music–has been on a consistently high professional level.

BEFORE THE PARADE PASSES BY

Before the parade passes by,
I'm gonna go and taste Saturday's high life;
Before the parade passes by,
I'm gonna get some life back into my life.
I'm ready to move out in front,
I've had enough of just passing by life;
With the rest of them,
With the best of them,
I can hold my head up high,
For I've got a goal again,
I've got a drive again,
I'm gonna feel my heart comin' alive again,
Before the parade passes by.
Look at the crowd up ahead,
Listen and hear that brass harmony
      growing;
Look at that crowd up ahead,
Pardon me if my old spirit is showing.
All of those lights over there
Seem to be telling me where I'm going;
When the whistles blow
And the cymbals crash
And the sparklers light the sky,
I'm gonna raise the roof,
I'm gonna carry on.
Gimme an old trombone, gimme an old
      baton,
Before the parade passes by.

HELLO, DOLLY!

VERSE
I went away from the lights of Fourteenth
      Street
And into my personal haze;
But now that I'm back in the lights of
      Fourteenth Street,
Tomorrow will be brighter than the good
      old days!

REFRAIN

Hello, Dolly,
Well, hello, Dolly,
It's so nice to have you back where you
    belong.
You're looking swell, Dolly,
We can tell, Dolly,
You're still glowin',
You're still crowin',
You're still goin' strong.
We feel the room swayin',
For the band's playin'
One of your old fav'rite songs from 'way
    back when.
1. So
    Take her wrap, fellas,
    Find her an empty lap, fellas,
    Dolly'll never go away again!

REPEAT REFRAIN

2. So
    Golly gee, fellas,
    Find her a vacant knee, fellas,
    Dolly'll never go away,
    Dolly'll never go away,
    Dolly'll never go away again!

I Won't Send Roses

I won't send roses
Or hold the door;
I won't remember
Which dress you wore,
My heart is too much in control.
The lack of romance in my soul
Will turn you gray, kid,
So stay away, kid.
Forget my shoulder
When you're in need.
Forgetting birthdays
Is guaranteed.
And should I love you, you would be

The last to know.
I won't send roses,
And roses suit you.

My pace is frantic,
My temper's cross;
With words romantic
I'm at a loss.
I'd be the first one to agree
That I'm preoccupied with me.
And it's inbred, kid,
So keep your head, kid.
In me you'll find things
Like guts and nerve,
But not the kind of things
That you deserve.
And so while there's a fighting chance,
Just turn and go.
I won't send roses,
And roses suit you so.

If He Walked into My Life

VERSE

Where's that boy with the bugle?
My little love who was always my big
    romance.
Where's that boy with the bugle?
And why did I ever buy him those damn
    long pants?

REFRAIN

Did he need a stronger hand?
Did he need a lighter touch?
Was I soft or was I tough?
Did I give enough?
Did I give too much?
At the moment that he needed me,
Did I ever turn away?
Would I be there when he called,
If he walked into my life today?
Were his days a little dull?

Were his nights a little wild?
Did I overstate my plan?
Did I stress the man
And forget the child?
And there must have been a million
    things
That my heart forgot to say.
Would I think of one or two,
If he walked into my life today?
Should I blame the times I pampered him,
Or blame the times I bossed him;
What a shame I never really found the boy
Before I lost him.
Were the years a little fast?
Was his world a little free?
Was there too much of a crowd,
All too lush and loud
And not enough of me?
Though I'll ask myself my whole life long,
What went wrong along the way;
Would I make the same mistakes
If he walked into my life today?
If that boy with the bugle
Walked into my life today.

MAME

You coax the blues right out of the horn,
Mame.
You charm the husk right off of the corn,
Mame.
You've got the banjoes strummin'
And plunkin' out a tune to beat the band.
The whole plantation's hummin'
Since you brought Dixie back to
    Dixieland.
You make the cotton easy to pick,
Mame.
You give my old mint julep a kick,
Mame.
You make the old magnolia tree
Blossom at the mention of your name,

You've made us feel alive again,
You've given us the drive again
To make the South revive again,
Mame.

You've brought the cakewalk back into
    style,
Mame.
You make the weepin' willow tree smile,
Mame.
Your skin is Dixie satin,
There's rebel in your manner and your
    speech.
You may be from Manhattan,
But Georgia never had a sweeter peach.
You make our black-eyed peas and our
    grits,
Mame,
Seem like the bill of fare at the Ritz,
Mame.
You came, you saw, you conquered and
Absolutely nothing is the same.
Your special fascination'll
Prove to be inspirational,
We think you're just sensational,
Mame.

TAP YOUR TROUBLES AWAY

Tap your troubles away.
You've bounced a big check,
Your mom has the vapors.
Tap your troubles away.
Your car had a wreck,
They're serving you papers.
When you're the one that it always rains on,
Simply
Try putting your Mary Janes on.
Your boss just gave you the ax,
There's years of back tax
You simply can't pay.
If a sky full of crap

Always lands in your lap,
Make a curtsy and
Tap your troubles away.
Tap your troubles away.
You're sued for divorce,
Your brother gets locked up.
Tap your troubles away.
You're fat as a horse,
And find that you're knocked up.
When you need something to turn your
    mind off,
Why not
Try tapping your poor behind off.
Your boat goes over the falls,
The plane you're on stalls,
The pilot yells, "Pray!"
When your parachute strap
Is beginning to snap,
Smile a big smile and
Tap your troubles away.

Tap your troubles away.
A raging typhoon,
An earthquake in Java,
Tap your troubles away.
The rats in Rangoon,
The oncoming lava.
Some people constantly take a licking,
But you'll never know
When your cleats are clicking.

So through the mire and mud,
Through fire and flood,
Sincerely I say:
When the wolf's at your door,
There's a bluebird in store
If you glide 'cross the floor
Till your ankles get sore,
Just tap your troubles away.

Time Heals Everything

Time heals ev'rything,
Tuesday, Thursday,
Time heals ev'rything
April, August.
If I'm patient, the break will mend
And one fine morning the hurt will end.
So make the moments fly,
Autumn, Winter,
I'll forget you by
Next year, some year.
Though it's hell that I'm going through,
Some Tuesday, Thursday,
April, August,
Autumn, Winter,
Next year, some year.
Time heals ev'rything,
Time heals ev'rything but loving you.
Time heals ev'rything but loving you.

Fred Ebb (1932–   )

F RED EBB WAS BORN in New York and educated there, at NYU and Columbia. He wrote several successful songs in the early sixties and did a couple of more or less invisible shows in New York. Then he met John Kander, and they began a collaboration that has lasted for decades. They had a pop success with Barbra Streisand's recording of their "My Coloring Book," and then, in 1965, came their first Broadway show together, *Flora, the Red Menace.* It starred Liza Minnelli, and although it ran only a few months, it began their collaboration with Minnelli, who was to win an Oscar for her performance in the film version of their *Cabaret.* (Years later, she would appear in *The Act* and *The Rink.*) *Cabaret* and *Chicago* are two great Kander and Ebb hits, running for years in their original stagings, and then for more years when revived in the nineties. *Woman of the Year,* for Lauren Bacall, ran for almost two years, but their later work has been less interesting than their earlier—on the whole, it lacks the bite that makes *Cabaret* and *Chicago* so special. Kander and Ebb keep going; with luck, they'll find a subject closer to their strengths. The closest they've come in recent years was *Kiss of the Spider Woman,* although *Steel Pier* has its advocates.

AND ALL THAT JAZZ

Come on, babe,
Why don't we paint the town,
And all that jazz!
I'm gonna rouge my knees
And roll my stockings down,
And all that jazz!
Start the car,
I know a whoopee spot
Where the gin is cold
But the piano's hot.
It's just a noisy hall
Where there's a nightly brawl,
And all that jazz!
Slick your hair
And wear your buckle shoes,
And all that jazz!

I hear that Father Dip is gonna blow the
	blues,
And all that jazz!
Hold on, hon, we're gonna bunny hug,
I bought some aspirin down at
	United Drug
In case we shake apart and want a brand-
	new start
To do that jazz!
Oh,
You're gonna see your Sheba shimmy
	shake.
(And all that jazz!)
Oh,
I'm gonna shimmy till my garters break.
(And all that jazz!)
Show
Me where to park my girdle,

Oh,
My mother's blood'd curdle
If she'd hear her baby's queer
For all that jazz!
Find a flask, we're playing fast and loose,
And all that jazz!
Right up here is where I store the juice,
And all that jazz!
Come on, babe,
We're gonna brush the sky,
I betcha Lucky Lindy never flew so high,
'Cause in the stratosphere
How could he lend an ear
To all that jazz!
No, I'm no one's wife,
But oh, I love my life
And all that jazz!

—John Kander

CABARET

What good is sitting alone in your room?
Come hear the music play;
Life is a cabaret, old chum,
Come to the cabaret.
Put down the knitting, the book and the
    broom,
Time for a holiday;
Life is a cabaret, old chum,
Come to the cabaret.
Come taste the wine,
Come hear the band,
Come blow the horn, start celebrating,
Right this way, your table's waiting.
No use permitting some prophet of doom
To wipe ev'ry smile away.
Life is a cabaret, old chum,
Come to the cabaret.
Start by admitting from cradle to tomb
Isn't that long a stay.
Life is a cabaret, old chum,

Come to the cabaret.
Only a cabaret, old chum,
So come to the cabaret.

—John Kander

CLASS

What ever happened to fair dealing
And pure ethics and nice manners?
Why is it ev'ryone now is a pain in the ass?
What ever happened to class?
Class?
What ever happened to "Please, may I?"
And "Yes, thank you," and "How
    charming!"
Now ev'ry son of a bitch is a snake in the
    grass.
What ever happened to class?
Class!
Ah,
There ain't no gentlemen to open up the
    doors,
There ain't no ladies now, there's only pigs
    and whores,
And even kids'll knock ya down so's they
    can pass.
Nobody's got no class.
What ever happened to old values
And fine morals and good breeding?
Now no one even says "Oops"
When they're passing their gas.
Whatever happened to class?
Class!
Ah,
There ain't no gentlemen who's fit for
    any use,
And any girl'd touch your privates for a
    deuce.
And even kids'll kick your shins and give
    ya sass.
Nobody's got no class.

All you read about today is rape and theft.
Jesus Christ!
Ain't there no decency left?
Nobody's got no class.
Ev'rybody you watch
S'got his brains in his crotch.
Holy crap, holy crap,
What a shame, what a shame.
What's become of class?

—John Kander

The Happy Time

Remember the Christmas morning long
    ago,
The frosted glass, the dancing snow,
The happy time?
Remember the painted horse, the
    carousel,
The choc'late kiss, the caramel,
The happy time?
Remember the pale pink sky,
Your first Easter hat?
And if you should ask me why,
The reason I ask you this is that
I want to remember you
Remembering the happy time.
Remember the day you found the
    dollar bill,
Or roller-skating down the hill,
The happy time?
Remember the compliment you once
    received,
The lie you told they all believed,
The happy time?
Remember your first school play,
The sound of applause?
Why do I go on this way?
I'm only reminding you because
I want to remember you
Remembering the happy time.

Remember the dearest love you
    ever knew,
The day she said, "Hello" to you.
The happy time?
Remember the tulip trees you walked
    among,
The game was old, the player young,
The happy time?
Remember a long deep sigh,
A tentative kiss?
And if you should ask me why,
The reason I ask you that is this:
I'm longing to see you smile
And hear you laugh
So I can have the photograph
And remember you.
Remembering the happy time.

—John Kander

My Coloring Book

In case you fancy coloring books,
And lots of people do,
I've a new one for you.
A most unusual coloring book,
The kind you never see.
Crayons ready, very well, begin to
    color me.

These are the eyes that watched him as he
    walked away,
Color them gray.
This is the heart that thought he would
    always be true,
Color it blue.
These are the arms that held him and
    touched him, then lost him somehow,
Color them empty now.
These are the beads I wore until she came
    between.
Color them green.

This is the room I sleep in and walk in and
    weep in and hide in that nobody sees,
Color it lonely, please.
This is the man, the one I depended upon.
Color him gone.

—John Kander

Nowadays

It's good, isn't it?
Grand, isn't it?
Great, isn't it?
Swell, isn't it?
Fun, isn't it?
Nowadays.
There's men ev'rywhere,
Jazz ev'rywhere,
Booze ev'rywhere,
Life ev'rywhere,
Joy ev'rywhere,
Nowadays.
You can like the life you're living,
You can live the life you like.
You can even marry Harry
But mess around with Ike.
And that's good, isn't it?
Grand, isn't it?
Great, isn't it?
Swell, isn't it?
Fun, isn't it?

But nothing stays.
In fifty years or so
It's gonna change, you know.
But oh, it's heaven
Nowadays.

—John Kander

A Quiet Thing

When it all comes true,
Just the way you planned,
It's funny, but the bells don't ring.
It's a quiet thing.
When you hold the world
In your trembling hand,
You'd think you'd hear a choir sing.
It's a quiet thing.
There are no exploding fireworks
Where's the roaring of the crowds?
Maybe it's the strange new atmosphere,
'Way up here among the clouds.
But I don't hear the drums,
I don't hear the band,
The sounds I'm told such moments bring,
Happiness comes in on tiptoe.
Well, whatd'ya know!
It's a quiet thing,
A very quiet thing.

—John Kander

Dave Frishberg (1933–)

B ORN IN ST. PAUL and educated at the University of Minnesota, Dave Frishberg
is a notably successful jazz pianist, a superb performer of his own wryly obser-
vant, if not satirical, songs, and a highly original composer and lyricist. During the sixties, he was in New York, playing with other jazz figures ranging from Eddie Condon
and Ben Webster to Zoot Sims and Carmen McRae. In the early seventies, he moved to
Los Angeles to work as a studio musician while staying active in jazz circles. Since the
mid-eighties, he has lived in Portland, Oregon, working with other Portland musicians
and recording. Lately, it almost seems you can't have a cabaret act without singing
"Peel Me a Grape."

ANOTHER SONG ABOUT PARIS

Lovers in the rain and flowers in the stall
On the rue Madeleine near the Place
    Pigalle,
How amusing
When the gypsies stole our wine.
Remember
Notre Dame where we chatted with the
    hunchback,
The dim café where we had to send the
    lunch back.
Ah! Paris in the spring!
It was all too, too divine.
Another song about Paris.
Is there room for one more?
Is there really a note or a word we all
    haven't heard before?
Is there one thing about Paris
Left to sing, left to say?
Though they still may be gay
On the rue de la Paix
Near the Champs-Elysées
In that sidewalk café
Where Maurice Chevalier

Ordered café au lait,
I'm afraid that today
It's become–how you say?–
More or less a cliché.
To sing a song about Paris,
Charming though it may be,
Another song about Paris
Is like another cup of water in the sea.
So spare us
Another song about Paris,
'Cause all the songs about Paris,
Sound exactly the same
To me.

Pigeons on the grass on the rue Soufflot,
Pigeons under glass at the Deux Magots.
How confusing
When we couldn't find Montmartre.
Remember
The small hotel where we didn't tip the
    waiter,
The way we felt when we met the waiter
    later.
Ah! Breakfast at Maxim's!
It was toujours à la carte.

I could sing songs about Paris
'Til I ran out of breath.
I defy you to find me just one
That hasn't been done to death.
It's all been said about Paris.
Let it lie, let it be!
Though they still say "oui oui"
And they sigh "c'est la vie"
As they gulp their Chablis
On the rue Rivoli
I'm afraid, mon ami,
One more gay melody
Sung for Lady Paree
Is a fait accompli,
A cold cup of tea.
There's nothing wrong about Paris.
It's a nice place to be.
You may feel strong about Paris
And maybe fifty million Frenchmen will
    agree.
But spare us
Another song about Paris,
'Cause all the songs about Paris
Sound exactly the same
To me.
Merci.

I'M HIP

I'm hip.
I'm no square.
I'm alert, I'm awake, I'm aware.
I am always on the scene, makin' the
    rounds, diggin' the sounds.
I read *Playboy* magazine 'cause I'm hip.
I'm dig.
I'm in step.
When it was hip to be hep I was hep.
I don't blow, but I'm a fan. Look at me
    swing, ring-a-ding-ding!
I even call my girlfriend "man," 'cause
    I'm hip.

Every Saturday night
With my suit buttoned tight and my
    suedes on,
I'm gettin' my kicks
Diggin' arty French flicks with my
    shades on.
I'm too much.
I'm a gas.
I am anything but middle-class.
When I hang around the band, poppin' my
    thumbs, diggin' the drums,
Squares don't seem to understand why
    I flip.
They're not hip
Like I'm hip.
I'm hip.
I'm alive.
I enjoy any joint where there's jive.
I'm on top of every trend. Look at me go!
    vo-de-o-do!
Sammy Davis knows my friend, I'm so hip.
I'm hip,
But not weird.
Like you notice I don't wear a beard.
Beards were in, but now they're out. They
    had their day, now they're passé.
Just ask me if you're in doubt, 'cause
    I'm hip.
Now I'm deep into Zen
Meditation, and macrobiotics,
And as soon as I can,
I intend to get into narcotics.
'Cause I'm cool
As a cuke.
I'm a cat, I'm a card, I'm a kook.
I get so much out of life, really I do,
    skooba dee boo.
One more time play "Mack the Knife"!
    Let 'er rip!
I may flip.
But I'm hip.

—Bob Dorough

Peel Me a Grape

Peel me a grape, crush me some ice,
Skin me a peach, save the fuzz for my
    pillow.
Start me a smoke, talk to me nice.
You gotta wine me
And dine me.
Don't try and train me,
Chow mein me.
Best way to serve me:
Hors d'œuvre me.
I'm gettin' hungry.
Peel me a grape.

Pop me a cork, french me a fry,
Crack me a nut, bring a bowl fulla
    bon-bons.
Chill me some wine, keep standin' by.
Just entertain me,
Champagne me.
Best way to smell me:
Chanel me.
Best way to cheer me:
Cashmere me.
I'm gettin' hungry.
Peel me a grape.

Here's how to be an agreeable chap:
Love me and leave me in luxury's lap.
Hop when I holler,
Skip when I snap.
When I say, "Do it,"
Jump to it.
Send out for Scotch, call me a cab.
Cut me a rose, make my tea with the
    petals.

Just hang around, pick up the tab.
Never out-think me,
Just mink me.
Polar bear rug me,
Don't bug me.
New Thunderbird me,
You heard me.
I'm gettin' hungry.
Peel me a grape.

Van Lingle Mungo

Heenie Majeski, Johnny Gee,
Eddie Joost, Johnny Pesky, Thornton Lee,
Danny Gardella,
Van Lingle Mungo.
Whitey Kurowski, Max Lanier,
Eddie Waitkus and Johnny Vandermeer,
Bob Estalella,
Van Lingle Mungo.
Augie Bergamo, Sigmund Jakucki,
Big Johnny Mize and Barney McCosky,
Hal Trosky.
Augie Galan and Pinky May,
Stan Hack and Frenchy Bordagaray,
Phil Cavaretta, George McQuinn,
Howie Pollett and Early Wynn,
Art Passarella,
Van Lingle Mungo.
John Antonelli, Ferris Fain,
Frankie Crosetti, Johnny Sain,
Harry Brecheen and Lou Boudreau,
Frankie Gustine and Claude Passeau,
Eddie Basinski,
Ernie Lombardi,
Hughie Mulcahy,
Van Lingle . . . Van Lingle Mungo.

Richard Maltby, Jr. (1937–)

R ICHARD MALTBY, JR., the son of a bandleader, was educated at Yale, where he began his collaboration with composer David Shire; songs that they wrote in the early seventies went into the 1977 Off-Broadway musical *Starting Here, Starting Now*. In 1978, Maltby conceived and directed the brilliant Fats Waller musical *Ain't Misbehavin'*, which won him a Tony award, and then worked with Shire again on the musicals *Baby, Closer Than Ever,* and *Big*. With Charles Strouse he wrote the songs for *Nick & Nora,* and he co-wrote the lyrics for *Miss Saigon*. In 1985 he directed and cowrote the lyrics for *Song and Dance*. In 1999, he conceived and directed the Tony Award–winning *Fosse*.

I DON'T REMEMBER CHRISTMAS

I was standing in the bedroom
When it suddenly came clear
That at last I don't remember
That at one time you were here.
All that stuff that used to haunt me
Like your robe behind the door,
For the first time I don't notice
That they're not here any more.
And I don't remember Summer,
And I don't remember Fall,
So it's possible December
Never happened after all.
Did we trim the tree together?
I can't get the image through.
'Cause I don't remember Christmas
And I don't remember you.

Later on to my astonishment
I did not feel a tug
When I walked into the living room
And saw that sheepskin rug.
All those pesky little echoes,
They're all gone without a trace.

It was good to know I could grow
Unaccustomed to your face,
'Cause I don't remember Easter
Or the rainy day we met.
Did we really have some good times?
Come on, tell me, I forget.
Did I think that you were Springtime?
It's all vanished in the blue,
'Cause I don't remember Christmas
And I don't remember you.

If she wants to leave you, well let her,
Says a practical voice in my head.
Any sensible man would forget her,
Forget her,
Forget her . . .

So Thanksgiving never happened
And Bermuda is a blur,
And I'm not the type to waste time
Over things that never were.
Were you really my obsession
'Til our ship of pleasure sank?
No, I guess I must have dreamt you,
'Cause the whole year is a blank.

And I don't remember crying,
And I can't recall your touch,
'Cause I'd never be so stupid
As to open up so much.
Did I really say I need you?
No, the words just don't ring true,
'Cause I don't remember talking,
And I don't remember laughing,
And I don't remember wanting,
And I don't remember needing,
I do not remember April,
I do not remember Tuesday,
And I don't remember Christmas,
And I don't remember you.

—David Shire

A LITTLE BIT OFF

I'm a little bit off.
I'm a little bit shot.
I am falling in love
And I wish I were not.
I feel a little bit warm,
Suddenly weak.
I would like to say "Stop,"
But I find I can't speak.
A beautiful dam I had built
Is about to break through.
Knowing it's going
To happen with you
Puts me a little on edge,
A little on fire,
A little bit off.

You're a little too fast,
I'm a little too tense.
I feel aimless and shameless
And nothing makes sense.
For you're a little too close
And I'm too upset
I want to get wet,

But not yet, oh, not yet.
I know an explosion is coming
I've not felt before.
Just give me a few minutes more.
And then in one blast
I'll go tearfully, cheerfully off!

I feel suddenly cold,
I feel suddenly thin,
I am suddenly very
Aware of my skin.
I'm feeling totally mad,
Have doubts about my soul.
I am boozy and woozy
And losing control.
I've waited so long to be feeling
Like crossing the line.
Now you are here
And you're totally mine!
And I'm a bit rocked,
A little displaced.
Prepared to be shocked
And a little disgraced.
I know I'm half-cocked,
But it's time to go thrillingly off.

—David Shire

TODAY IS THE FIRST DAY OF THE REST OF MY LIFE

Here I stand
With life ahead of me,
No place to hide.
Today is the first day of the rest of my life.
Though it's true
What some have said of me,
That I'm untried,
Today is the first day of the rest of my life.
Hushed and scared
And flushed and wary,
I watch for dawn.

All my waiting years
Suddenly are gone.
Wait, don't move,
I'm still not ready yet,
I need more time
To steady my heart.
But it's too late.
For now I
Start.

Beat by beat
My pulse is quickening
And growing strong.
Today is the first day of the rest of my life.
One might say
My plot's been thickening

For far too long.
Today is the first day of the rest of
    my life.
There, right there,
The future's gleaming.
It blinds my eyes.
Soon my world will grow
Wider than the skies.
Wait, don't move,
I'm still not grown enough,
And yet it's time
To own my heart.
I'm not prepared,
But let it start.

—David Shire

CODA

BY THE LIGHT OF THE SILVERY MOON
Edward Madden, 1909

VERSE 1

Place park,
Scene dark,
Silv'ry moon is shining through the
    trees.
Cast two,
Me, you,
Sound of kisses floating on the breeze.
Act one
Begun,
Dialogue, "Where would you like to
    spoon?"
My cue
With you,
Underneath the silv'ry moon.

REFRAIN

By the light
Of the silvery moon,
I want to spoon,
To my honey I'll croon
Love's tune.
Honeymoon,
Keep a-shining in June.
Your silv'ry beams
Will bring love's dreams,
We'll be cuddling soon,
By the silvery moon.

VERSE 2

Act two,
Scene new,

Roses blooming all around the place.
Cast three,
You, me,
Preacher with a solemn-looking face.
Choir sings,
Bell rings,
Preacher: "You are wed forevermore!"
Act two, all through,
Ev'ry night the same encore.

REPEAT REFRAIN

—*Gus Edwards*

I'VE GOT RINGS ON MY FINGERS
R. P. Weston and F. J. Barnes, 1909

VERSE 1

Jim O'Shea was cast away upon an
    Indian isle.
The natives there, they liked his hair, they
    liked his Irish smile,
So made him chief Panjundrum, the nabob
    of them all,
They called him Ji-ji-boo Jhai
And rigged him out so gay,
So he wrote to Dublin Bay
To his sweetheart just to say:

REFRAIN

"Sure, I've got rings on my fingers,
Bells on my toes,
Elephants to ride upon,
My little Irish rose.
So come to your nabob

And next Patrick's day,
Be Mistress Mumbo Jumbo Jijiboo J.
O'Shea."

VERSE 2
O'er the sea went Rose McGee to see her
    nabob grand,
He sat within his palanquin and when
    she'd kissed his hand
He led her to his harem, where he had
    wives galore.
She started shedding a tear;
Said he, "Now have no fear!
I'm keeping these wives here
Just for ornament, my dear."

REPEAT REFRAIN

VERSE 3
Em'rald green he robed his queen to share
    with him his throne,
'Mid eastern charms and waving palms
    they'd shamrocks, Irish grown,
Sent all the way from Dublin to Nabob J.
    O'Shea.
But in his palace so fine,
Should Rose for Ireland pine,
With smiles her face will shine
When he murmurs, "Sweetheart mine."

REPEAT REFRAIN

—*Maurice Scott*

HEAVEN WILL PROTECT THE WORKING GIRL

Edgar Smith, 1910

VERSE 1
A village maid was leaving home with
    tears, her eyes was wet,

Her mother dear was standing near
    the spot.
She says, "Neuralgia, dear, I hope you
    won't forget
That I'm the only mother you have got.
The city is a wicked place as anyone
    can see,
And cruel dangers 'round your path
    may hurl.
So ev'ry week you'd better send your
    wages back to me,
For Heaven will protect a working girl.

REFRAIN 1
You are going far away,
But remember what I say
When you are in the city's giddy
    whirl,
From temptations, crimes, and follies,
Villains, taxicabs, and trolleys,
Oh! Heaven will protect a working girl."

VERSE 2
Her dear old mother's words proved true,
    for soon the poor girl met
A man who on her ruin was intent.
He treated her respectful as those villains
    always do,
And she supposed he was a perfect gent.
But she found diff'rent when one night she
    went with him to dine
Into a table d'hote so blithe and gay,
And he says to her, "After this we'll have a
    demitasse."
Then to him these brave words the girl
    did say:

REFRAIN 2
"Stand back, villain! Go away. Here I will
    no longer stay,
Although you were a Marquis or an Earl.
You may tempt the upper classes

With your villainous demitasses,
But Heaven will protect a working girl."

—*A. Baldwin Sloane*

PUT YOUR ARMS AROUND ME, HONEY

Junie McCree, 1910

VERSE I

Nighttime am a fallin',
Ev'rything is still,
And the moon am a-shinin' from above.
Cupid am a-callin'
Ev'ry Jack and Jill,
It's just about the time for making love.
Someone is awaiting all alone for me,
No more hesitating, I must go and see.
How de do, dear.
It's with you, dear,
That I love to be.

REFRAIN

Put your arms around me, honey,
Hold me tight.
Huddle up and cuddle up
With all your might.
Oh, Babe, won't you roll dem eyes,
Eyes that I just idolize.
When they look at me my heart begins to
    float,
Then it starts a-rockin' like a motorboat.
Oh, oh,
I never knew
Any girl
Like you.

VERSE 2

Music am a-playin'
Such a lovin' glide
That my feet keep a-moving to and fro.

And with you a-swayin'
I'll be satisfied
To dance until we hear the roosters crow.
I love seven 'leven, I love chicken, too,
Nearest thing to heaven is to be
    with you.
For I'm spoony, moony, loony,
But my love is true.

REPEAT REFRAIN

—*Albert Von Tilzer*

MY MELANCHOLY BABY

George Norton, 1912

VERSE I

Come, sweetheart mine,
Don't sit and pine,
Tell me of the cares that make you feel
    so blue.
What have I done?
Answer me, Hon,
Have I ever said an unkind word to you?
My love is true,
And just for you.
I'd do almost anything at any time.
Dear, when you sigh
Or when you cry,
Something seems to grip the very heart
    of mine.

REFRAIN

Come to me, my melancholy baby,
Cuddle up and don't be blue.
All your fears are foolish fancies,
    maybe;
You know, dear, that I'm in love
    with you.
Ev'ry cloud must have a silver lining,
Wait until the sun shines through.

Smile, my honey dear,
While I kiss away each tear,
Or else I shall be melancholy too.

VERSE 2
Birds in the trees,
Whispering breeze,
Should not fail to lull you into peaceful
    dreams.
So tell me why
Sadly you sigh,
Sitting at the window where the pale moon
    beams.
You shouldn't grieve,
Try and believe
Life is always sunshine when the heart
    beats true.
Be of good cheer,
Smile though your tears,
When you're sad it makes me feel the same
    as you.

REPEAT REFRAIN

—*Ernie Burnett*

Row, Row, Row

William Jerome, 1912

VERSE 1
Young Johnnie Jones, he had a cute
    little boat,
And all the girlies he would take for a
    float.
He had girlies on the shore,
Sweet little peaches by the score,
But Johnnie was a Weisenheimer,
    you know,
His steady girl was Flo,
And ev'ry Sunday afternoon
She'd jump in his boat and they would
    spoon.

REFRAIN
And then he'd row, row, row,
Way up the river
He would row, row, row,
A hug he'd give her,
Then he'd kiss her now and then,
She would tell him when,
He'd fool around and fool around and then
    they'd kiss again.
And then he'd row, row, row
A little further he would row
Oh, oh, oh, oh!
1) Then he'd drop both his oars,
    Take a few more encores,
And then he'd
Row,
Row,
Row.

2) With her head on his breast,
    Then there's twenty bars rest,
And then he'd
Row,
Row,
Row.

VERSE 2
Right in his boat he had a cute
    little seat,
And ev'ry kiss he stole from Flo was so
    sweet,
And he knew just how to row,
He was a rowing Romeo.
He knew an island where the trees were so
    grand,
He knew just where to land.
Then tales of love he'd tell to Flo,
Until it was time for them to go,

REPEAT REFRAIN

—*James V. Monaco*

Ballin' the Jack
Jim Burris, 1913

VERSE 1

Folks in Georgia's 'bout to go insane
Since that new dance down in
 Georgia came.
I'm the only person who's to blame,
I'm the party introduced it there.
So! Give me credit to know a thing
 or two,
Give me credit for springing
 something new.
I will show this little dance to you;
When I do, you'll say that it's a bear.

REFRAIN

First you put your two knees close up
 tight,
Then you sway 'em to the left, then you
 sway 'em to the right,
Step around the floor kind of nice and
 light,
Then you twist around and twist around
 with all your might.
Stretch your lovin' arms way out in
 space,
Then you do the Eagle Rock with style and
 grace.
Swing your foot way 'round, then bring
 it back,
Now that's what I call "Ballin' the Jack."

VERSE 2

It's being done at all the cabarets,
All society now has got the craze,
It's the best dance done in modern days,
That is why I rave about it so.
Play some good rag that will make you
 prance,
Old folks, young folks, all try to do the
 dance.

Join right in now while you got the chance;
Once again the steps to you I'll show.

REPEAT REFRAIN

—Chris Smith

The St. Louis Blues
W. C. Handy, 1914

VERSE 1

I hate to see de evening sun go down,
Hate to see de evenin' sun go down.
Cause my baby, he done lef dis town.
Feelin' tomorrow lak ah feel today,
Feel tomorrow lak ah feel today,
I'll pack my trunk, make ma gitaway.
St. Louis woman, wid her diamon' rings
Pulls dat man 'roun' by her apron strings.
'Twant for powder an' fer store-bought hair,
De man ah love would not gone
 nowhere.

REFRAIN 1

Got de St. Louis blues, jes blue as ah
 can be.
Dat man got a heart lak a rock cast in
 the sea,
Or else he wouldn't gone so far from me.

VERSE 2

Doggone it!
Been to de Gypsy to get ma fortune tole,
To de Gypsy done got ma fortune tole,
Cause I'm is wile 'bout ma Jelly Roll.
Gypsy done tole me, "Don't you wear no
 black,"
Yes, she done tole me, "Don't you wear no
 black.
Go to St. Louis, you can win him back."
Help me to Cairo, make St. Louis by
 maself,

Git to Cairo, find ma ole friend Jeff.
Gwine to pin maself close to his side.
If ah flag his train, I sho can rise.

REFRAIN 2

I loves dat man lak a schoolboy loves
    his pie,
Lak a Kentucky Col'nel loves his mint
    and rye.
I'll love ma baby till de day ah die.

VERSE 3

You ought to see that stovepipe brown
    of mine,
Lak he owns de Dimon Joseph line.
He'd make a crosseye woman go stone blin'.
Blacker than midnight, teeth lak flags of
    truce,
Blackest man in de whole St. Louis.
Blacker de berry, sweeter are the juice.
About a crap game he knows a
    pow'ful lot,
But when worktime comes, he's on
    the dot.
Gwine to ask him fer a cold ten-spot.
What it takes to git it, he's cert'nly got.

K-K-K-KATY

Geoffrey O'Hara, 1918

VERSE I

Jimmy was soldier brave and bold,
Katy was a maid with hair of gold.
Like an act of fate,
Kate was standing at the gate,
Watching all the boys on dress
    parade.
Jimmy with the girls was just a gawk,
Stuttered ev'ry time he tried to talk.
Still, that night at eight
He was there at Katy's gate,
Stuttering to her this lovesick cry:

REFRAIN

"K-K-K-Katy, beautiful Katy,
You're the only g-g-g-girl that I
    adore.
When the m-m-m-moon shines
Over the cowshed,
I'll be waiting at the k-k-k-kitchen
    door."

VERSE 2

No one ever looked so nice and neat,
No one could be just as cute and sweet.
That's what Jimmy thought
When the wedding ring he bought,
Now he's off to France the foe to meet.
Jimmy thought he'd like to take a
    chance,
See if he could make the Kaiser dance.
Stepping to a tune
All about the silv'ry moon,
This is what they hear in far-off
    France:

REPEAT REFRAIN

AND HER MOTHER CAME TOO!

Dion Titheradge, 1921

VERSE I

I seem to be the victim of a cruel jest,
It dogs my footsteps with the girl I love
    the best.
She's just the sweetest thing that I have
    ever known,
But still we never get the chance to
    be alone.

REFRAIN I

My car will meet her–
And her mother comes too!
It's a two-seater–
Still her mother comes too!

At Ciro's when I am free,
At dinner, supper, or tea,
She loves to shimmy with me–
And her mother does too!
We buy her trousseau–
And her mother comes too!
Asked *not* to do so–
Still her mother comes too!
She simply can't take a snub,
I go and sulk at the club,
Then have a bath and a rub–
And her brother comes too!

VERSE 2

There may be times when couples need a
    chaperone,
But mothers ought to learn to leave a chap
    alone.
I wish they'd have a heart and use their
    common sense,
For three's a crowd, and more, it's treble
    the expense.

REFRAIN 2

We lunch at Maxim's–
And her mother comes too!
How large a snack seems–
When her mother comes too!
And when they're visiting me,
We finish afternoon tea,
She loves to sit on my knee–
And her mother does too!
To golf we started–
And her mother came too!
Three bags I carted–
When her mother came too!
She fainted just off the tee,
My darling whispered to me–
"Jack, dear, at last we are free!"–
But her mother came to!

—Ivor Novello

I'M NOBODY'S BABY
Benny Davis and Lester Santly, 1921

VERSE

I used to be my mother's baby,
When I was near my dad went wild.
Whenever we had company
They'd bounce me on their knee.
The neighbors thought I was a darling
    child.
Once I was ev'rybody's baby,
But right now I'm lonesome as can be.
You see . . .

REFRAIN

I'm nobody's baby,
I wonder why.
Each night and day I pray the Lord up
    above,
Please send me down somebody
    to love.
But nobody wants me,
I'm blue somehow.
Won't someone hear my plea
And take a chance with me,
Because I'm nobody's baby now.

—Milton Ager

MY BLUE HEAVEN
George Whiting, 1925

VERSE 1

Day is ending,
Birds are wending
Back to the shelter of
Each little nest they love.
Night shades falling,
Lovebirds calling.
What makes the world go 'round?
Nothing but love.

REFRAIN

When whippoorwills call
And evening is nigh,
I hurry to
My
Blue
Heaven.
A turn to the right,
A little white light
Will lead you to
My
Blue
Heaven.
You'll see a smiling face, a fireplace, a
    cozy room,
A little nest that's nestled where the roses
    bloom.
Just Mollie and me,
And Baby makes three.
We're happy in
My
Blue
Heaven.

VERSE 2

Moonbeams creeping,
Flow'rs are sleeping
Under a starlit way,
Waiting another day.
Time for resting,
Birds are nesting,
Resting their weary wings,
Tired from play.

REPEAT REFRAIN

—Walter Donaldson

SLEEPY TIME GAL

*Raymond Egan and Joseph Reed
Alden,* 1925

VERSE 1

Wouldn't it be a change for you and me
To stay at home once in a while?
We cabaret until the break of day;
I'll bet we've danced many a mile.
I'd like to see a movie once more,
They don't keep people stayin' up
    until four.
Wouldn't it be a pleasant novelty
To tumble in early once more?

REFRAIN

Sleepy time gal,
You're turning night into day.
Sleepy time gal,
You've danced the ev'ning away.
Before each silvery star fades out of sight,
Please give me one little kiss,
Then let us whisper "Good night."
It's gettin' late and,
Dear, your pillow's waitin'.
Sleepy time gal,
When all your dancin' is through,
Sleepy time gal,
I'll find a cottage for you.
You'll learn to cook and to sew,
What's more you'll love it, I know,
When you're a stay-at-home,
Play-at-home,
Eight o'clock,
Sleepy time gal.

VERSE 2

Wouldn't it be a pleasant sight
To see a kitchenette only for you?
Wouldn't it be a pleasant sight
To see a table set only for two?

I'll get a big Victrola, and then
We'll start in dancing ev'ry new dance
    again.
Then it will be a pleasant novelty
To tumble in just about ten.

REPEAT REFRAIN

    —*Richard Whiting and Ange Lorenzo*

SWEET GEORGIA BROWN

*Ben Bernie, Maceo Pinkard, and
Kenneth Casey,* 1925

VERSE I
She just got here yesterday,
Things are hot here now they say,
There's a big change in town.
Gals are jealous, there's no doubt,
Still the fellows rave about
Sweet, Sweet Georgia Brown;
And ever since she came
The colored folks all claim:
Say,

REFRAIN I
1. No gal made
    Has got a shade
    On Sweet Georgia Brown.
    Two left feet,
    But oh so neat,
    Has Sweet Georgia Brown.
    They all sigh
    And wanna die
    For Sweet Georgia Brown.
    I'll tell you just why,
    You know I don't lie,
    Not much!
It's been said
She knocks 'em dead
When she lands in town.

Since she came
Why it's a shame
How she cools 'em down.
Fellers
She can't get
Are fellers
She ain't met.
Georgia claimed her,
Georgia named her,
Sweet Georgia Brown.

VERSE 2
Brown-skin gals, you'll get the blues,
Brown-skin pals, you'll surely lose,
And
There's but one excuse.
Now I've told you who she was
And I've told you what she does,
Hand this gal her dues,
This colored maiden's pray'r
Is answer'd anywhere.
Say,

REFRAIN 2
REPEAT I
All those tips
The porter slips
To Sweet Georgia Brown,
They buy clothes
At fashion shows
With one dollar down.
Oh boy,
Tip your hats
Oh joy,
She's the "cat's,"
Who's that, mister?
'Tain't her sister,
Sweet Georgia Brown.

She's Funny That Way
(I Got A Woman, Crazy for Me)
Richard A. Whiting, 1928

VERSE 1

Once she dressed in silks and lace,
Owned a Rolls-Royce car;
Now she seems quite out of place,
Like a fallen star.
Draped around my kitchen sink,
Happy as can be,
I just have to stop and think
Why she fell for me.

REFRAIN 1

I'm not much to look at,
Nothin' to see,
Just glad I'm livin'
And lucky to be,
I got a woman, crazy for me,
She's funny that way.
I can't save a dollar,
Ain't worth a cent,
She doesn't holler,
She'd live in a tent.
I got a woman, crazy for me,
She's funny that way.
Though she loves to work and slave
For me ev'ry day,
She'd be so much better off
If I went away.
But why should I leave her,
Why should I go?
She'd be unhappy
Without me I know,
I got a woman, crazy for me,
She's funny that way.

VERSE 2

She should have the very best,
Anyone can see;
Still she's diff'rent from the rest,
Satisfied with me.
While I worry, plan and scheme,
Over what to do,
Can't help feeling it's a dream,
Too good to be true.

REFRAIN 2

I never had nothin',
No one to care,
That's why I seem to
Have more than my share,
I got a woman, crazy for me,
She's funny that way.
When I hurt her feelings
Once in a while,
Her only answer
Is one little smile,
I got a woman, crazy for me,
She's funny that way.
I can see no other way
And no better plan,
End it all and let her go
To some better man.
But I'm only human,
Coward at best,
I'm more than certain
She'd follow me west,
I got a woman, crazy for me,
She's funny that way.

—Neil Moret

That's My Weakness Now
Sam H. Stept (with Bud Green),
1928

VERSE 1

Love, love, love, love,
What did you do to me?
The things I never missed
Are things I can't resist.
Love, love, love, love,

Isn't it plain to see?
I just had a change of heart,
What can it be?

She's got eyes of blue,
I never cared for eyes of blue,
But she's got eyes of blue,
And that's my weakness now.
She's got dimpled cheeks,
I never cared for dimpled cheeks,
But she's got dimpled cheeks,
And that's my weakness now.
Oh! my, oh! me,
Oh! I should be good, I would be good,
    but gee–
She likes to bill and coo,
I never liked to bill and coo,
But she likes to bill and coo,
And that's my weakness now.

VERSE 2

Love, love, love, love,
Gee! but I'm glad I fell.
Just think of what I missed
By never being kissed.
Love, love, love, love,
Couldn't resist your spell.
Guess you know the reason now.
Well, can't you tell?

REFRAIN 2

She talks baby talk,
I never cared for baby talk,
But she talks baby talk,
And that's my weakness now.
She likes 'gagement rings,
I never liked engagement rings,
But she likes 'gagement rings,
And that's my weakness now.
Oh! yes, oh! yes,
And we're headin' for the parson's door, I
    guess.

She likes a family,
I never liked a family,
But she likes a family,
And that's my weakness now.

I May Be Wrong
(But I Think You're Wonderful!)
Harry Ruskin, 1929

VERSE I

HE: When I play roulette,
    When I place a bet,
    I have been a loser all my life.
    Like a two-year-old
    I pick 'em bad, I'm told,
    Still I think I'd find in you the
        perfect wife.

REFRAIN I

I may be wrong, but–
I think you're wonderful!
I may be wrong, but–
I think you're swell!
I like your style, say–
I think it's marvelous.
I'm always wrong, so
How can I tell?
All of my shirts are unsightly,
All of my ties are a crime.
If, dear, in you I've picked rightly,
It's the very first time.
You came along, say–
I think you're wonderful!
I think you're grand, but–
I may be wrong.

VERSE 2

SHE: Though your lot is sad,
    I am just as bad.
    Mine is really quite a hopeless case.
    Oculists advise
    Glasses for my eyes,

Without them I can't even see
your face.

REFRAIN 2

I may be wrong, but–
I think you're wonderful!
I may be wrong, but–
I think you're swell!
I like your style, say–
I think it's marvelous.
But I can't see, so
How can I tell?
Deuces to me are all aces,
Life is to me just a bore,
Faces are all open spaces,
You might be John Barrymore.
You came along, say–
I think you're wonderful!
I think you're grand, but–
I may be wrong.

—*Henry Sullivan*

IF I HAD YOU

Jimmy Campbell and Reginald Connelly, 1929

VERSE I

I dreamed all my dreams
And schemed all my schemes,
But somehow it just seemed wrong.
Until I met you
And then, dear, I knew
To me you must belong.

REFRAIN

I could show the world how to smile,
I could be glad all of the while,
I could change the gray skies to blue
If I had you.
I could leave the old days behind,
Leave all my pals,

I'd never mind,
I could start my life all anew
If I had you.
I could climb the snowcapped mountains,
Sail the mighty ocean wide,
I could cross the burning desert,
If I had you by my side.
I could be a king, dear, uncrowned,
Humble or poor, rich or renowned,
There is nothing I couldn't do
If I had you,

VERSE 2

My whole life would be
Just heaven to me,
Dear, if you'd learn to care.
To know all the bliss
Of your loving kiss
Was waiting for me somewhere.

REPEAT REFRAIN

—*Ted Shapiro*

A COTTAGE FOR SALE

Larry Conley, 1930

VERSE I

Love in a bungalow high on a hill,
That was the way we had planned it,
Now it's a bungalow empty and still,
Needing your love to command it.

REFRAIN I

Our little dream castle
With ev'ry dream gone
Is lonely and silent,
The shades are all drawn,
And my heart is heavy
As I gaze upon
A cottage for sale.
The lawn we were proud of

Is waving in hay,
Our beautiful garden
Has withered away,
Where you planted roses
The weeds seem to say
"A Cottage for Sale."
From ev'ry single window,
I see your face,
But when I reach a window,
There's empty space.
The key's in the mailbox
The same as before,
But no one is waiting
For me anymore,
The end of our story
Is told on the door:
A cottage for sale.

VERSE 2
Do I imagine it or is it real,
Someone is standing beside me,
Sharing the sorrow and sadness I feel,
What is this new hope inside me?

REPEAT REFRAIN

—*Willard Robison*

GEORGIA ON MY MIND
Stuart Gorrell, 1930

VERSE
Melodies bring memories,
Mem'ries of a song.
A song that sings of Georgia,
Back where I belong.

REFRAIN
Georgia, Georgia,
The whole day through;
Just an old sweet song
Keeps Georgia on my mind.

Each day, Georgia,
A song of you
Comes as sweet and clear
As moonlight through the pines.
Other arms reach out to me,
Other eyes smile tenderly,
Still in peaceful dreams I see
The road leads back to you.
Georgia, Georgia,
No peace I find,
Just an old sweeet song
Keeps Georgia on my mind.

—*Hoagy Carmichael*

PAPER DOLL
Johnny S. Black, 1930 (1915)

I'm goin' to buy a paper doll that I can call
    my own,
A doll that other fellows cannot steal.
And then the flirty, flirty guys
With their flirty, flirty eyes
Will have to flirt with dollies that are real.
When I go home at night she will be
    waiting,
She'll be the truest doll in all this world.
I'd rather have a paper doll to call my own
Than have a fickle-minded, real live girl.

ALL OF ME
Seymour Simons and Gerald Marks,
1931

VERSE
You took my kisses and you took my love,
You taught me how to care.
Am I to be just the remnant of
A one-sided love affair?
All you took, I gladly gave;
There's nothing left for me to save.

REFRAIN

All of me,
Why not take all of me?
Can't you see
I'm no good without you?
Take my lips,
I want to lose them.
Take my arms,
I'll never use them.
Your good-bye
Left me with eyes that cry,
How can I
Go on living without you?
You took the part
That once was my heart,
So why not take
All of me?

WHEN YOUR LOVER HAS GONE
E. A. Swan, 1931

VERSE I

For ages and ages
The poets and sages
Of love, wondrous love, always sing.
But ask any lover
And you'll soon discover
The heartaches that romance can bring.

REFRAIN

When you're alone,
Who cares for starlit skies?
When you're alone,
The magic moonlight dies.
At break of dawn
There is no sunrise,
When your lover has gone.
What lonely hours
The evening shadows bring,
What lonely hours,
With mem'ries lingering,

Like faded flowers
Life can't mean anything,
When your lover has gone.

VERSE 2

What good is the scheming,
The planning and dreaming,
That comes with each new love affair?
The love that you cherish
So often may perish
And leave you with castles in air.

REPEAT REFRAIN

IT'S THE TALK OF THE TOWN
Marty Symes and A. J. Neiburg,
1933

I can't show my face,
Can't go anyplace,
People stop and stare,
It's so hard to bear.
Ev'rybody knows you left me,
It's the talk of the town.
Ev'rytime we meet,
My heart skips a beat,
We don't stop to speak,
Though it's just a week.
Ev'rybody knows you left me,
It's the talk of the town.
We sent out invitations
To friends and relations
Announcing our wedding day.
Friends and our relations
Gave congratulations.
How can you face them?
What can you say?
Let's make up, sweetheart,
We can't stay apart,
Don't let foolish pride
Keep you from my side.

How can love like ours be ended?
It's the talk of the town.

—Jerry Livingston

ON THE GOOD SHIP LOLLIPOP
Sidney Clare, 1934

VERSE
I've thrown away my toys,
Even my drum and trains.
I wanna make some noise
With real live aeroplanes.
Someday I'm going to fly.
I'll be a pilot, too,
And when I do
How would you
Like to be my crew?

REFRAIN
On the good ship
Lollipop
It's a sweet trip
To a candy shop
Where bon-bons play
On the sunny beach of
    Peppermint Bay.
Lemonade stands
Ev'rywhere,
Crackerjack bands
Fill the air,
And there you are
Happy landing on a chocolate bar.
See the sugar bowl do a Tootsie Roll
With the big bad Devil's food cake.
If you eat too much, ooh, ooh,
You'll awake with a tummy ache.
On the good ship
Lollipop
It's a night trip,
Into bed you hop

1. With this command:
    "All aboard for Candy Land."

2. And dream away
    On the good ship Lollipop.

—Richard Whiting

AUTUMN IN NEW YORK
Vernon Duke, 1935

VERSE
It's time to end my lonely holiday
And bid the country a hasty farewell.
So on this gray and melancholy day
I'll move to a Manhattan hotel.
I'll dispose of my rose-colored chattels
And prepare for my share of adventures
    and battles.
Here on the twenty-seventh floor,
Looking down on the city I hate
And adore!

REFRAIN I
Autumn in New York,
Why does it seem so inviting?
Autumn in New York,
It spells the thrill of first-nighting.
Glittering crowds and shimmering
    clouds
In canyons of steel,
They're making me feel
I'm home.
It's Autumn in New York,
That brings the promise of new love;
Autumn in New York
Is often mingled with pain.
Dreamers with empty hands
May sigh for exotic lands;
It's Autumn in New York,
It's good to live it again.

REFRAIN 2

Autumn in New York,
The gleaming rooftops at sundown.
Autumn in New York,
It lifts you up when you're rundown.
Jaded roués and gay divorcées
Who lunch at the Ritz,
Will tell you that "it's
Divine!"
This Autumn in New York
Transforms the slums into Mayfair;
Autumn in New York,
You'll need no castles in Spain.
Lovers that bless the dark
On benches in Central Park
Greet Autumn in New York;
It's good to live it again.

SUMMERTIME

Dubose Heyward, 1935

Summertime
And the livin' is easy,
Fish are jumpin',
And the cotton is high.
Oh, your daddy's rich,
And your ma is good lookin',
So hush, little baby,
Don' yo' cry.
One of these mornin's
You goin' to rise up singin',
Then you'll spread yo' wings
An' you'll take to the sky.
But till that mornin',
There's a-nothin' can harm you
With Daddy and Mammy
Standin' by.

—George Gershwin

ZING! WENT THE STRINGS OF MY HEART

James F. Hanley, 1935

VERSE

Never could carry a tune,
Never knew where to start.
You came along
When ev'rything was wrong,
And put a song in my heart.

REFRAIN

Dear, when you smiled at me,
I heard a melody,
It haunted me from the start.
Something inside of me
Started a symphony,
Zing! went the strings of my heart.
'Twas like a breath of spring,
I heard a robin sing
About a nest set apart.
All nature seemed to be
In perfect harmony,
Zing! went the strings of my heart.
Your eyes made skies seem blue again,
What else could I do again
But keep repeating through again,
"I love you, love you."
I still recall the thrill,
I guess I always will,
I hope 'twill never depart.
Dear, with your lips to mine,
A rhapsody divine,
Zing! went the strings of my heart.

THE GLORY OF LOVE

Billy Hill, 1936

You've got to give
A little,
Take

A little,
And let your poor heart break
A little.
That's the story of,
That's the glory of love.
You've got to laugh
A little,
Cry
A little,
Before the clouds roll by
A little.
That's the story of,
That's the glory of love.
As long as there's the two of us,
We've got the world and all its charms.
And when the world is through with us,
We've got each other's arms.
You've got to win
A little,
Lose
A little,
And always have the blues
A little.
That's the story of,
That's the glory of love.

STRANGE FRUIT

Lewis Allan, 1939

Southern trees bear a strange fruit,
Blood on the leaves and blood at the root,
Black body swinging in the Southern
    breeze,
Strange fruit hanging from the poplar
    trees.
Pastoral scene of the gallant South,
The bulging eyes and the twisted mouth,
Scent of magnolia sweet and fresh,
And the sudden smell of burning flesh!
Here is a fruit for the crows to pluck,
For the rain to gather, for the wind
    to suck

For the sun to rot, for a tree to drop,
Here is a strange and bitter crop.

HOW HIGH THE MOON

Nancy Hamilton, 1940

Somewhere there's music,
How faint the tune!
Somewhere there's heaven,
How high the moon!
There is no moon above
When love is far away, too;
Till it comes true,
That you love me
As I love you.
Somewhere there's music,
It's where you are;
Somewhere there's heaven,
How near, how far!
The darkest night would shine
If you would come to me soon;
Until you will,
How still my heart,
My aching heart,
How high the moon!

—Morgan Lewis

GOD BLESS THE CHILD

*Arthur Herzog, Jr., and Billie
Holiday,* 1941

Them that's got shall get,
Them that's not shall lose,
So the Bible said, and it still is news.
Mama may have,
Papa may have,
But God bless the child that got his own!
That's got his own.
Yes, the strong gets more
While the weak ones fade.

Empty pockets don't ever make the grade.
Mama may have,
Papa may have,
But God bless the child that's got his own!
That's got his own.
Money, you got lots o' friends
Crowdin' round the door.
When you're gone and spendin' ends,
They don't come no more.
Rich relations give, crust of bread
    and such,
You can help yourself, but don't take
    too much!
Mama may have,
Papa may have,
But God bless the child that's got his own!
That's got his own.

I'M GLAD THERE IS YOU
(IN THIS WORLD OF
ORDINARY PEOPLE)
Paul Madeira, 1942

VERSE

Said I many times,
"Love is illusion,
A feeling,
Result of confusion!"
With knowing smile and blasé sigh,
A cynical so and so was I.
I felt so sure,
So positive,
So utterly unchangingly certain,
That I never was aware of love and you,
'Til suddenly I realized there was love
    and you,
And I.

REFRAIN

In this world
Of ordinary people,
Ext'rodinary people,

I'm glad there is you.
In this world
Of overrated pleasures,
Of underrated treasures,
I'm glad there is you.
I'll live to love,
I'll love to live with you beside me.
This role is new,
I'll muddle through
With you to guide me.
In this world
Where many, many play at love,
And hardly any stay in love,
I'm glad there is you,
More than ever,
I'm glad there is you.

—Jimmy Dorsey

JUKEBOX SATURDAY NIGHT
Al Stillman, 1942

VERSE

Soft drinks and hot music
And nothing over a dime;
Me and lover
Pay no cover,
We just spend the time.

REFRAIN

Moppin' up soda pop rickeys
To our heart's delight,
Dancin' to swingeroo quickies,
Jukebox Saturday night.
Goodman and Kyser and Miller
Help to make things bright,
Mixin' hot licks with vanilla,
Jukebox Saturday night.
They put nothin' past us,
Me and honey lamb,
Making one Coke last us
Till it's time to scram.

Money, we really don't need that,
We make out all right,
Lettin' the other guy feed that
Jukebox Saturday night.

—Paul McGrane

Moonlight in Vermont
*John Blackburn and Karl
Suessdorf,* 1944

Pennies in a stream,
Falling leaves, a sycamore,
Moonlight in Vermont.
Icy finger waves,
Ski trails on a mountainside,
Snowlight in Vermont.
Telegraph cables
They sing down the highway
And travel each bend in the road.
People who meet
In this romantic setting
Are so hypnotized
By the lovely
Ev'ning summer breeze,
Warbling of a meadowlark,
Moonlight in Vermont,
You and I and moonlight in Vermont.

'Round Midnight
Bernie Hanighen, 1944

It begins to tell
'Round midnight, 'round midnight.
I do pretty well
Till after sundown.
Suppertime, I'm feeling sad.
But it really gets bad
'Round midnight,
Mem'ries always start
'Round midnight, 'round midnight.

Haven't got the heart
To stand those mem'ries
When my heart is still with you,
And old midnight knows it too.
When some quarrel we had
Needs mending,
Does it mean that our love
Is ending?
Darling, I need you;
Lately I find
You're out of my arms
And I'm out of my mind.
Let our love take wing
Some midnight, 'round midnight.
Let the angels sing
For your returning,
Let our love be safe and sound
When old midnight comes around.

—Cootie Williams and Thelonious Monk

Sentimental Journey
Bud Green, 1944

VERSE

Ev'ry rolling stone gets to feel alone
When home, sweet home is far away.
I'm a rolling stone who's been so alone
Until today.

REFRAIN

Gonna take a sentimental journey,
Gonna set my heart at ease,
Gonna make a sentimental journey
To renew old memories.
Got my bag, I got my reservation,
Spent each dime I could afford.
Like a child in wild anticipation,
Long to hear that "All aboard."
Seven,
That's the time we leave, at seven,
I'll be waitin' up for Heaven,

Countin' ev'ry mile of railroad track
That takes me back.
Never thought my heart could be so
    yearn-y.
Why did I decide to roam?
Gotta take this sentimental journey,
Sentimental journey home.

—Les Brown and Ben Homer

WE'LL BE TOGETHER AGAIN
Frankie Laine, 1945

VERSE

Here in our moment of darkness
Remember the sun has shone.
Laugh and the world will laugh
    with you,
Cry, and you cry alone.

REFRAIN

No tears, no fears,
Remember there's always tomorrow.
So what if we have to part?
We'll be together again.
Your kiss, your smile
Are mem'ries I'll treasure forever.
So try thinking with your heart,
And we'll be together again.
Times when I know you'll be
    lonesome,
Times when I know you'll be sad.
Don't let temptation surround you,
Don't let the blues make you bad.
Some day, some way
We both have a lifetime before us.
For parting is not good-bye,
We'll be together again.

—Carl Fischer

WE'LL GATHER LILACS
Ivor Novello, 1945

VERSE 1

Although you're far away
And life is sad and gray,
I have a scheme, a dream to try,
I'm thinking, dear, of you
And all I meant to do
When we're together, you and I.
We'll soon forget our care and pain
And find such lovely things to share
    again.

REFRAIN

We'll gather lilacs in the spring
Again
And walk together down an Eng-
Lish lane
Until our hearts have learned to sing
Again
When you come home once more.
And in the evening by the firelight's glow
You'll hold me close and never let
    me go.
Your eyes will tell me all I want to know,
When you come home once more.

VERSE 2

We'll learn to love anew
The simple joys we knew
And shared together night and day.
We'll watch without a sigh
The moments speeding by
When life is free and hearts are gay.
My dream is here for you to share
And in my heart my dream becomes a
    prayer.

REPEAT REFRAIN

The Christmas Song
Robert Wells, 1946

Chestnuts roasting on an open fire,
Jack Frost nipping at your nose.
Yuletide carols being sung by a choir
And folks dressed up like Eskimos.
Ev'rybody knows a turkey and some
    mistletoe
Help to make the season bright.
Tiny tots with their eyes all aglow
Will find it hard to sleep tonight.
They know that Santa's on his way;
He's loaded lots of toys and goodies on his
    sleigh.
And ev'ry mother's child is gonna spy
To see if reindeer really know how to fly.
And so I'm offering this simple phrase
To kids from one to ninety-two.
Although it's been said many times,
    many ways,
"Merry Christmas to you."

—Mel Tormé

The End of a Love Affair
Edward C. Redding, 1950

REFRAIN
So I walk a little too fast,
And I drive a little too fast,
And I'm reckless, it's true,
But what else can you do,
At the end of a love affair?
So I talk a little too much,
And I laugh a little too much,
And my voice is too loud
When I'm out in a crowd,
So that people are apt to stare.
Do they know, do they care, that it's only

That I'm lonely and low as can be?
And the smile on my face
Isn't really a smile at all!
So I smoke a little too much,
And I drink a little too much,
And the tunes I request
Are not always the best,
But the ones where the trumpets blare!
So I go at a maddening pace,
And I pretend that it's taking her place,
But what else can you do,
At the end of a love affair?

INTERLUDE
Dear Dorothy Dix:
I'm in an awful fix,
I thought she was in love with me,
But found that she was only up to her old
    tricks!
Dear Emily Post:
No wiser, I, than most.
Please exercise your nimble brain,
And tell me how a girl can entertain
A ghost!
So I'm writing to you for advice,
Ladies, the situation isn't very nice,
Ladies, I find myself completely at a loss,
Ladies, my heart, and not my mind,
    is boss!

REPEAT REFRAIN

Guess Who I Saw Today
Elisse Boyd, 1952

VERSE
You're so late getting home from the
    office,
Did you miss your train?
Were you caught in the rain?
No, don't bother to explain.

Can I fix you a quick martini?
As a matter of fact, I'll have one with you,
For to tell you the truth
I've had quite a day too!

REFRAIN
Guess who I saw today, my dear!
I went in town to shop around for
    something new
And thought I'd stop and have a bite when
    I was through.
I looked around for someplace near,
And it occurred to me where I had parked
    the car
I'd seen a most attractive French café
    and bar.
It really wasn't very far.
The waiter showed me to a dark, secluded
    corner,
And when my eyes became accustomed to
    the gloom,
I saw two people at the bar who were so
    much in love
That even I could spot it clear across
    the room.
Guess who I saw today, my dear!
I've never been so shocked before;
I headed blindly for the door,
They didn't see me passing through.
Guess who I saw today!
I saw you!

—*Murray Grand*

ANGEL EYES
Earl Brent, 1946

Try to think that love's not around,
Still it's uncomfort'bly near.
My old heart ain't gainin' no ground
Because my angel eyes ain't here.

Angel eyes that old Devil sent,
They glow unbearably bright.
Need I say that my love's misspent,
Misspent with angel eyes tonight.
So drink up, all you people,
Order anything you see.
Have fun, you happy people,
The drink and the laugh's on me.
Pardon me, but I "gotta run,"
The fact's uncommonly clear.
Gotta find who's now "number one,"
And why my angel eyes ain't here.
'Scuse me while I disappear.

—*Matt Dennis*

NO MOON AT ALL
Redd Evans and Dave Mann, 1947

No moon at all,
What a night,
Even lightnin' bugs have dimmed their
    light,
Stars have disappeared from sight,
And there's no moon at all.
Don't make a sound.
It's so dark,
Even Fido is afraid to bark.
What a perfect chance to park,
And there's no moon at all.
Should we want atmosphere
For inspiration, dear,
One kiss will make it clear
That tonight is right, and bright
    moonlight might interfere.
No moon at all
Up above,
This is nothing like they told us of.
Just to think we fell in love,
And there's no moon at all.

I Wish You Love

(Que reste-t-il de nos amours?)

Albert A. Beach, 1955
(French lyric by Charles Trenet)

VERSE

Good-bye,
No use leading with our chins.
This is where our story ends,
Never lovers, ever friends.
Good-bye,
Let our hearts call it a day,
But before you walk away
I sincerely want to say:

REFRAIN

I wish you bluebirds in the Spring
To give your heart a song to sing;
And then a kiss, but more than this
I wish you love.
And in July, a lemonade,
To cool you in some leafy glade;
I wish you health and more than wealth,
I wish you love,
My breaking heart and I agree
That you and I could never be,
So with my best, my very best,
I set you free.
I wish you shelter from the storm,
A cozy fire to keep you warm;
But most of all, when snowflakes fall,
I wish you love.

—*Charles Trenet*

Something Cool

Billy Barnes, 1957

Something cool,
I'd like to order something cool,

It's so warm here in town,
And the heat gets me down,
Yes, I'd like something cool.
My, it's nice
To simply sit and rest a while.
Now I know it's a shame,
I can't think of your name,
I remember your smile.
I don't ordinarily drink with strangers,
I most usually drink alone,
But you were so awfully nice to ask me
And I'm so terribly far from home.
Like my dress?
I must confess it's very old,
But it's simple and neat,
It's just right for the heat,
Save my furs for the cold.
A cigarette?
Well, I don't smoke them as a rule,
But I'll have one,
It would be fun with something . . .

Bet you couldn't imagine
That I one time had a house
With so many rooms
I couldn't count them all!
I'll bet you couldn't imagine
I had fifteen diff'rent beaus
Who would beg and beg
To take me to a ball.
I'll bet you couldn't picture me
The time I went to Paris in the Fall.
And who would think the man I loved
Was quite so handsome, quite so tall?
Well, it's through,
It's just a memory I had,
One I almost forgot,
'Cause this weather's so hot
And I'm feeling so bad
About a date,
Oh! Wait!
I'm such a fool,

He's just a guy
Who stopped to buy me something cool.

THE MORNING AFTER
Dory Langdon Previn, 1962

Love is a twelve o'clock notion,
Love is a bedtime potion,
Just a laugh in the night,
A sundown delight,
Just a laugh in the night,
And then the fun's up,
Then the fun's up,
When the sun's up.

If I didn't have to face the morning after,
If I only could erase the day in store,
That lonely feeling I know I'll never shake,
That lonely ceiling that waits for me
    to wake,
Achin' once more.
If I only could survive the morning after
When the room is still alive with love you
    swore.
How could you love me, then leave me to
    get through
The morning after the night with you?

With you
Away
How blue
The day.

—*Harold Arlen*

ONE
Edward Kleban, 1975

One singular sensation,
Ev'ry little step she takes.

One thrilling combination,
Ev'ry move that she makes.
One smile and suddenly nobody else
    will do.
You know you'll never be lonely with you
    know who.
One moment in her presence and you can
    forget the rest,
For the girl is second best to none, son.
Oooh! Sigh!
Give her your attention.
Do I
Really have to mention,
She's the one?
She walks into a room
And you know she's uncommonly rare,
Very unique,
Peripatetic, poetic, and chic.
She walks into a room
And you know from her maddening poise,
    effortless whirl,
She's the special girl
Strolling.
Can't help all of her qualities extolling.
Loaded with charisma
Is my jauntily, sauntering, ambling
    shambler.

She walks into a room
And you know
You must shuffle along, join the
    parade.
She's the quintessence of making the
    grade.
This is whatcha call trav'ling!
Oh, strut your stuff.
Can't get enough of her.
Love her.
I'm a son of a gun,
She is one of a kind.

—*Marvin Hamlisch*

ACKNOWLEDGMENTS

THE EDITORS WISH to thank the many people who helped guide and support them through the three years it took to create this book, beginning with our friends at Pantheon: Dan Frank, editorial director, whose idea the book was; Janice Goldklang, publishing director; Kristen Bearse, designer; Archie Ferguson, art director; Susan Norton, production editor; Kathy Grasso, production manager; Jennifer Weh, editorial assistant, who triumphantly and cheerfully struggled with the permissions; Erik Simon, who—with his manly manner and Southernish drawl—took up the torch from Jennifer and, to mix metaphors, wrestled the permissions problem to the ground; and, first and foremost, Altie Karper, managing editor, without whom. . . .

We were fortunate enough to be able to speak with some of our lyricists, all of whom were unfailingly generous with assistance: Richard Adler, Betty Comden, Ervin Drake, Fred Ebb, William Engvick, Doris Fisher, David Frishberg, Adolph Green, Jack Lawrence, Gene Lees, Richard Maltby, Jr., Hugh Martin, Stephen Sondheim, Robert Wright.

A number of performing artists offered advice and practical help: Richard Rodney Bennett, William Bolcom, Eric Comstock, Lorna Dallas, Michael Feinstein, Mary Cleere Haran, Barbara Lea, Jo Sullivan Loesser, Susannah McCorkle, John McGlinn, Peter Mintun, Joan Morris, Bobby Short, K.T. Sullivan, Paul Trueblood, Margaret Whiting, Ronny Whyte.

We received major assistance from such experts and collectors as David A. Jasen, Miles Kreuger, Robert Lissauer, Sandy Marrone, David Sanjek (of BMI), Jim Steinblatt (of ASCAP), and Donald J. Stubblebine.

Among the many others who stood by with general advice, reminiscences, help in acquiring permissions, etc., are Fred Ahlert, Jr., June Ahlert, Lisa Alter, Samuel Arlen, Amy Asch, Mary Ellin Barrett, Jeanine Basinger, Helene Blue, Ken Bloom, Beebe Bourne, Martha Buck, Tita Cahn, Hoagy Bix Carmichael, Susan Caruso, Ted Chapin, Joe Chiplock, Steven Clar, Suzanne Colin, Robert Cornfield, Monica Corton, Lynnae Crawford, Kendall Crilly, Lee Davis, Barry Day, Alvin Deutsch, Ellen Donaldson, Robert Dorough, Linda Emmet, Frank Fain, David Farneth, Tommie Frazier, Terry Fricon, Rosemarie Gawelko, Gary Giddins, Mark Trent Goldberg, Linda Golding, Nicholas Gottlieb, Lawrence J. Greene, Flora Griggs, Ernie Harburg, Chris Harding, Sidney Herman, Elliott Hoffman, Molly Hyman, Lee Hubner, Kay Duke Ingalls, Edward Jablonski,

David R. Jones, Donald Kahn, Abigail, Philip, and Miranda Kimball, Camille Kuznetz, David Lahm, Maxyne Lang, Bella Linden, Paul McKibbins, Frank Military, Robert H. Montgomery, Jr., Dan Morgenstern, Dr. Gregory A. Morris, Tara Mullaney, Dave Olsen, Steve Nelson, Julia Riva, Irwin Robinson, Deena Rosenberg, David Rosner, Meyer Sack, Harold Samuel, Paul Schwartz, Vince Scuderi, Barry Singer, Larry Spier, Roberta Staats, Michael Strunsky, Richard M. Sudhalter, Caroline Underwood, Leslie Wallake, Joseph Weiss, Deborah Grace Winer, Mary Jane Wolf, and Vincent Youmans III. Special thanks to Jay Morgenstern, without whom this book could not have existed, and to Will Friedwald for his encyclopedic knowledge, endless readiness to assist, and unfailing good nature.

Finally, in addition to *Variety* and the *New York Times,* a shelf-full of books contributed to our knowledge:

American Musical Theatre, by Gerald Boardman

American Popular Song, by Alec Wilder

American Song, by Ken Bloom

ASCAP Biographical Dictionary

Black and Blue, by Barry Singer

Blue Book of Tin Pan Alley, by Jack Burton

Broadway Sheet Music, by Donald J. Stubblebine

Cinema Sheet Music, by Donald J. Stubblebine

The Complete Lyrics of Irving Berlin, edited by Robert Kimball and Linda Emmet

The Complete Lyrics of Ira Gershwin, edited by Robert Kimball

The Complete Lyrics of Lorenz Hart, edited by Robert Kimball

The Complete Lyrics of Cole Porter, edited by Robert Kimball

Encyclopedia of American Popular Song, by Stanley Green

The Hollywood Musical, by Clive Hirschhorn

Hollywood Song, by Ken Bloom

I Should Care, by Sammy Cahn

Lissauer's Encyclopedia of Popular Music in America, by Robert Lissauer

Lullaby of Broadway, by Patricia Dubin McGuire

The Melody Lingers On, by Roy Hemming

Poets of Tin Pan Alley, by Philip Furia

Show Tunes, by Steven Suskin

Sweet and Lowdown, by Warren Craig

Swing!, edited by Steve Knapper

Tin Pan Alley, by David A. Jasen

They're Playing Our Song, by Max Wilk

The Unsung Song Writers, by Warren W. Vaché

"You Must Remember This . . .", by Mark White

INDEX OF SONG TITLES

This index provides the publication date of each song and the name or names of the performers who introduced it if it began life in a show or a movie. Sometimes the names of other performers indelibly associated with the song are included as well (e.g., Fred Astaire with "Puttin' on the Ritz"); a slash mark separates the original performer from later ones.

There can be confusion about dates, particularly when the sheet music of a show was copyrighted and published just before or just after the year the show itself opened; we provide the actual copyright year. In an effort to provide as accurate information as possible about performance, we have tried to confirm data given by previous sources, and in some cases–after watching old movies, or tracking down old *Playbills*–have come up with new identifications. Of course, we may have slipped into errors of our own.

The key: (s) indicates that a song came from a show; (f) from a film; (nc) from a nightclub act; (TV) from television; (GB) from Great Britain. Songs with no such attribution were written as pop songs and introduced through live performance, recordings, and sheet music.

Permissions Acknowledgments

WARNER BROS. PUBLICATIONS U.S. INC., Miami, FL 33014. **Make Someone Happy** © 1960 Betty Comden, Adolph Green and Jule Styne. © Renewed Stratford Music Corporation, Owner of Publication and Allied Rights throughout the World, Chappell & Co., Administrator. All Rights Reserved. WARNER BROS. PUBLICATIONS U.S. INC., Miami, FL 33014. **New York, New York** © 1945 (Renewed) Warner Bros. Inc. All Rights Reserved. WARNER BROS. PUBLICATIONS U.S. INC., Miami, FL 33014. **Not Mine** © 1967 CHAPPELL & CO. Copyright Renewed. All Rights Reserved. WARNER BROS. PUBLICATIONS U.S. INC., Miami, FL 33014. **The Party's Over** © 1956 Betty Comden, Adolph Green and Jule Styne. © Renewed Stratford Music Corporation, Owner of Publication and Allied Rights throughout the World, Chappell & Co., Administrator. All Rights Reserved. Used by Permission. WARNER BROS. PUBLICATIONS US, INC., Miami, FL 33014. **Some Other Time** © 1945 WARNER BROS. INC. (Renewed). All Rights Reserved. WARNER BROS. PUBLICATIONS US, INC., Miami, FL 33014. **Thanks a Lot, But No Thanks** © 1954 (Renewed) EMI FEIST CATALOG INC. All Rights Reserved. Used by Permission. WARNER BROS. PUBLICATIONS U.S. INC., Miami, FL 33014 **You Mustn't Feel Discouraged** © 1964 CHAPPELL & CO. Copyright Renewed. All Rights Reserved. WARNER BROS. PUBLICATIONS U.S. INC., Miami, FL 33014.

JOHN LATOUCHE. **Cabin in the Sky** © 1940 (Renewed) EMI MILLER CATALOG INC. All Rights Reserved. Used by Permission. WARNER BROS. PUBLICATIONS U.S. INC., Miami, FL 33014. **Honey in the Honeycomb** © 1940 (Renewed) EMI MILLER CATALOG INC. All Rights Reserved. Used by Permission. WARNER BROS. PUBLICATIONS U.S. INC., Miami, FL 33014. **Lazy Afternoon** © 1954 (Renewed) CHAPPELL & CO. and SONY TUNES, INC. All Rights Reserved. WARNER BROS. PUBLICATIONS U.S. INC., Miami, FL 33014. **Love Turned the Light Out** © 1940 (Renewed) EMI MILLER MUSIC CATALOG INC. All Rights Reserved. Used by Permission. WARNER BROS. PUBLICATIONS U.S. INC., Miami, FL 33014. **Maybe I Should Change My Ways** © 1946 (Renewed) CHAPPELL & CO. and FISHER MUSIC CORP. © 1950 Sony/ATV Tunes LLC and Warner Chappell (Renewed). All rights on behalf of Sony/ATV Tunes LLC administered by Sony/ATV Music Publishing, 8 Music Square West, Nashville, TN 37203. All Rights Reserved. WARNER BROS. PUBLICATIONS U.S. INC., Miami, FL 33014. **Not a Care in the World** © 1941 (Renewed) EMI ROBBINS MUSIC CATALOG INC. All Rights Reserved. Used by Permission. WARNER BROS. PUBLICATIONS U.S. INC., Miami, FL 33014 **Summer Is a-Comin' In** © 1941 (Renewed) FRANK MUSIC CORP. All Rights Reserved. **Taking a Chance on Love** © 1940 (Renewed) EMI MILLER CATALOG INC. All Rights Reserved. Used by Permission. WARNER BROS. PUBLICATIONS U.S. INC., Miami, FL 33014.

BOB HILLIARD. **Civilization (Bongo, Bongo, Bongo)** © Copyright 1947 (Renewed) by EDWIN H. MORRIS & COMPANY, A Division of MPL COMMUNICATIONS, INC. and BETTER HALF MUSIC. All Rights Reserved. International Copyright Secured. **The Coffee Song (They've Got an Awful Lot of Coffee in Brazil)** TRO–© Copyright 1946 (Renewed) Cromwell Music, Inc., New York, NY. Used by Permission. **In the Wee Small Hours of the Morning** © Copyright 1955 by Better Half Music and Rytvoc Music. Copyright Renewed. All Rights Reserved. International Copyright Secured.

ALAN JAY LERNER. **Almost Like Being in Love** © 1947 (Renewed) Alan Jay Lerner (ASCAP) and Frederick Loewe (ASCAP). World Rights Assigned to CHAPPELL & CO., INC. All Rights Reserved. WARNER BROS. PUBLICATIONS U.S. INC., Miami, FL 33014. **Camelot** © 1960 (Renewed) Alan Jay Lerner (ASCAP) and Frederick Loewe (ASCAP). Chappell & Co. owner of Publication and Allied Rights throughout the World. All Rights Reserved. Used by Permission. WARNER BROS. PUBLICATIONS US, INC., Miami, FL 33014. **Come Back to Me** © 1965 Alan Jay Lerner and Burton Lane. Copyright Renewed. WB Music Corp. and Chappell & Co., Publishers in the United States, its territories and possessions by agreement with the Heirs of Alan Jay Lerner and Burton Lane. Chappell & Co. owner of Publications and Allied Rights throughout the World. All Rights Reserved. Used by Permission. WARNER BROS. PUBLICATIONS US, INC., Miami, FL 33014 **The Heather on the Hill** © 1947 (Renewed) Alan Jay Lerner (ASCAP) and Frederick Loewe (ASCAP). World Rights Assigned to CHAPPELL & CO., INC. All Rights Reserved. WARNER BROS. PUBLICATIONS U.S. INC., Miami, FL 33014. **A Hymn to Him** © 1956 (Renewed) Alan Jay Lerner (ASCAP) and Frederick Loewe (ASCAP). World Rights Assigned to CHAPPELL & CO., INC. All Rights Reserved. WARNER BROS. PUBLICATIONS U.S. INC., Miami, FL 33014. **I Could Have Danced All**

(Renewed) CHAPPELL & CO. LTD. (PRS) All Rights for the U.S. and Canada Controlled by CHAP-PELL & CO. (ASCAP). All Rights Reserved. Used by Permission.

LEE ADAMS. **But Alive** Copyright © 1970 Renewed Strada Music (ASCAP). All Rights Reserved. Used by Permission of Helene Blue Musique Ltd. **Kids!** Copyright © 1960 Renewed Strada Music (ASCAP). All Rights Reserved. Used by Permission of Helene Blue Musique Ltd. **Once Upon a Time** Copyright © 1960 Renewed Strada Music (ASCAP). All Rights Reserved. Used by Permission of Helene Blue Musique Ltd. **Put on a Happy Face** Copyright © 1962 Renewed. Strada Music (ASCAP). All Rights Reserved. Used by Permission of Helene Blue Musique Ltd. **Those Were the Days** © 1971 (Renewed) EMI ROBBINS CATALOG INC. All Rights Reserved. Used by Permission. WARNER BROS. PUBLICATIONS U.S. INC., Miami, FL 33014.

SHELDON HARNICK. **The Boston Beguine** © 1952 (Renewed) CHAPPELL & CO. All Rights Reserved. Used by Permission. WARNER BROS. PUBLICATIONS U.S. INC., Miami, FL 33014. **If I Were a Rich Man** Copyright © 1964 (Renewed 1992) by Mayerling Productions, Ltd. (Administered by R&H Music) and Jerry Bock Enterprises (USA). Reprinted by Permission. All Rights Reserved. **Little Tin Box** Copyright © 1959 (Renewed 1987) by Mayerling Productions, Ltd. (Administered by R&H Music) and Jerry Bock Enterprises (USA). Reprinted by Permission. All Rights Reserved. **Matchmaker** Copyright © 1964 (Renewed 1992) by Mayerling Productions, Ltd. (Administered by R&H Music) and Jerry Bock Enterprises (USA). Reprinted by Permission. All Rights Reserved. **(The Ballad of) The Shape of Things** Copyright © 1950, 1966 by Mayerling Productions, Ltd. (Administered by R&H Music) Reprinted by Permission. All Rights Reserved. International Copyright Secured. **She Loves Me** Copyright © 1962 (Renewed 1990) by Mayerling Productions, Ltd. (Administered by R&H Music) and Jerry Bock Enterprises (USA). Reprinted by Permission. All Rights Reserved. **Someone's Been Sending Me Flowers** Copyright © 1955 (Renewed 1983) by Mayerling Productions, Ltd. (Administered by R&H Music). Reprinted by Permission. All Rights Reserved. **Sunrise, Sunset** Copyright © 1964 (Renewed 1992) by Mayerling Productions, Ltd. (Administered by R&H Music) and Jerry Bock Enterprises (USA). Reprinted by Permission. All Rights Reserved. **Tonight at Eight** Copyright © 1962 (Renewed 1990) by Mayerling Productions, Ltd. (Administered by R&H Music) and Jerry Bock Enterprises (USA). Reprinted by Permission. All Rights Reserved. **(I'll Marry) The Very Next Man** Copyright © 1959 (Renewed 1987) by Mayerling Productions, Ltd. (Administered by R&H Music) and Jerry Bock Enterprises (USA). Reprinted by Permission. All Rights Reserved.

ALAN BERGMAN AND MARILYN BERGMAN. **Summer Me, Winter Me** © 1969 (Renewed) WB Music Corp. All Rights Reserved. WARNER BROS. PUBLICATIONS U.S. INC., Miami, FL 33014. **The Way We Were** © 1973 Colgems-EMI Music Inc. (ASCAP). All Rights Reserved. International Copyright Secured. Used by Permission. **The Windmills of Your Mind** © 1968 UNITED ARTISTS MUSIC CO., INC. © Assigned to EMI U CATALOG INC. © Renewed. All Rights Reserved. Used by Permission. WARNER BROS. PUBLICATIONS U.S. INC., Miami, FL 33014. **You Must Believe in Spring** © 1967, 1968 (Copyrights Renewed) PRODUCTIONS MICHEL LEGRAND and PRODUCTIONS FRANCIS LEMARQUE. All Rights in USA and Canada administered by EMI U CATALOG INC. All Rights Reserved. Used by Permission.

CAROLYN LEIGH. **The Best Is Yet to Come** © 1959, 1961 (Renewed 1987, 1989) NOTABLE MUSIC CO., INC. AND JUNES TUNES LTD. PARTNERSHIP and EMI CARWIN MUSIC INC. All Rights on behalf of NOTABLE MUSIC CO., INC. Administered by WB MUSIC CORP. All Rights Reserved. WARNER BROS. PUBLICATIONS U.S. INC., Miami, FL 33014. **Hey, Look Me Over** © 1960, 1961 (Renewed 1988, 1989) NOTABLE MUSIC CO., INC. AND JUNES TUNES LTD. PARTNERSHIP and EMI CARWIN MUSIC INC. All Rights on behalf of NOTABLE MUSIC CO., INC. Administered by WB MUSIC CORP. Print Rights on behalf of EMI CARWIN CATALOG INC. Administered by WARNER BROS. PUBLICATIONS INC. All Rights Reserved. WARNER BROS. PUBLICATIONS U.S. INC., Miami, FL 33014. **How Little We Know (How Little It Matters)** © 1956 June's Tunes Ltd. Partnership and Philip Springer and EDWIN H. MORRIS & COMPANY, a Division of MPL Communications, Inc. All Rights Reserved. Used by Permission. **I Walk a Little Faster** © 1958, 1963 (Copyrights Renewed) NOTABLE MUSIC CO., INC. AND JUNES TUNES LTD. PARTNERSHIP and EMI CARWIN MUSIC INC. and EDWIN H. MORRIS & COMPANY, A Division of MPL Communications, Inc. All Rights on behalf of NOTABLE MUSIC CO., INC. Administered by WB MUSIC CORP. All Rights Reserved. WARNER BROS. PUBLICATIONS U.S. INC., Miami, FL 33014. **It Amazes Me!**

© 1958 (Renewed) NOTABLE MUSIC CO., INC. AND JUNES TUNES LTD. PARTNERSHIP and EMI CARWIN MUSIC INC. All Rights on behalf of NOTABLE MUSIC CO., INC. Administered by WB MUSIC CORP. All Rights Reserved. WARNER BROS. PUBLICATIONS U.S. INC., Miami, FL 33014. **I've Got Your Number** © 1962 (Renewed 1990) NOTABLE MUSIC CO., INC. AND JUNES TUNES LTD. PARTNERSHIP and EMI CARWIN MUSIC INC. All Rights on behalf of NOTABLE MUSIC CO., INC. Administered by WB MUSIC CORP. Print Rights on behalf of EMI CARWIN CATALOG INC. Administered by WARNER BROS. PUBLICATIONS INC. All Rights Reserved. WARNER BROS. PUB-LICATIONS U.S. INC., Miami, FL 33014. **Real Live Girl** © 1962 (Renewed 1990) NOTABLE MUSIC CO., INC. AND JUNES TUNES LTD. PARTNERSHIP and EMI CARWIN MUSIC INC. All Rights on behalf of NOTABLE MUSIC CO., INC. Administered by WB MUSIC CORP. Print Rights on behalf of EMI CARWIN CATALOG INC. Administered by WARNER BROS. PUBLICATIONS INC. All Rights Reserved. WARNER BROS. PUBLICATIONS U.S. INC., Miami, FL 33014. **The Rules of the Road** © 1961, 1963 (Renewed) NOTABLE MUSIC CO., INC. AND JUNES TUNES LTD. PARTNERSHIP and EMI CARWIN MUSIC INC. All Rights on behalf of NOTABLE MUSIC CO., INC. Administered by WB MUSIC CORP. All Rights Reserved. WARNER BROS. PUBLICATIONS U.S. INC., Miami, FL 33014. **When in Rome (I Do As the Romans Do)** © 1965 (Renewed) NOTABLE MUSIC CO., INC. AND JUNES TUNES LTD. PARTNERSHIP. All Rights on behalf of NOTABLE MUSIC CO., INC. Administered by WB MUSIC CORP. All Rights Reserved. WARNER BROS. PUBLICATIONS U.S. INC., Miami, FL 33014. **Witchcraft** © 1957 (Renewed) NOTABLE MUSIC CO., INC. AND JUNES TUNES LTD. PARTNERSHIP and MORLEY MUSIC CO. All Rights on behalf of NOTABLE MUSIC CO., INC. Administered by WB MUSIC CORP. All Rights Reserved. WARNER BROS. PUBLICATIONS U.S. INC., Miami, FL 33014. **You Fascinate Me So** © 1958 (Renewed 1987) NOTABLE MUSIC CO., INC. AND JUNES TUNES LTD. PARTNERSHIP and EMI CARWIN MUSIC INC. All Rights on behalf of NOTABLE MUSIC CO., INC. Administered by WB MUSIC CORP. All Rights Reserved. WARNER BROS. PUBLICATIONS U.S. INC., Miami, FL 33014. **Young at Heart** © 1954 CHERIO CORP. © Renewed CHERIO CORP. and JUNE'S TUNES. All Rights Reserved.

Fran Landesman. **The Ballad of the Sad Young Men** © 1959 Assigned to Wolfland 1987. Administered by Fricout Music Co., (ASCAP), a division of Fricon Entertainment, 11 Music Square East, Suite 301, Nashville, TN 37203, (615) 826-2288. Used by Permission–All Rights Reserved. **Photographs** TRO–© Copyright 1968 (Renewed) Musical Comedy Productions, Inc., New York, NY. Used by Permission. **Say "Cheese!"** © 1956 Assigned to Wolfland 1987. Administered by Fricout Music Co., (ASCAP) a division of Fricon Entertainment, 11 Music Square East, Suite 301, Nashville TN 37203, (615) 826-2288. Used by Permission. All Rights Reserved. **Spring Can Really Hang You Up the Most** © 1956 Assigned to Wolfland 1987. Administered by Fricout Music Co., (ASCAP) a division of Fricon Entertainment, 11 Music Square East, Suite 301, Nashville, TN 37203, (615) 826-2288. Used by Permission–All Rights Reserved.

Gene Lees. **Quiet Nights of Quiet Stars** © Copyright 1962 Universal–MCA Music Publishing, Inc., a division of Universal Studios, Inc. (BMI) and WARNER BROS. MUSIC, INC. International Copyright Secured. All Rights Reserved. WARNER BROS. PUBLICATIONS U.S. INC., Miami, FL 33014. **The Right to Love** © 1965 Published by Scherzo Music, Inc. **Waltz for Debby** TRO–© Copyright 1964 (Renewed) 1965 Renewed 1966 (Renewed) Folkways Music Publishers, Inc., New York, NY. Used by Permission.

Stephen Sondheim. **All I Need Is the Girl** © 1959 (Renewed) WILLIAMSON MUSIC, INC. and STRATFORD MUSIC CORPORATION. All Rights on behalf of WILLIAMSON MUSIC, INC. and STRATFORD MUSIC CORPORATION Administered by CHAPPELL & CO. All Rights Reserved. WARNER BROS. PUBLICATIONS U.S., INC., Miami, FL 33014. **America** © Copyright 1956, 1957, 1959 by Amberson Holdings LLC and Stephen Sondheim. Copyright Renewed. Leonard Bernstein Music Publishing Company LLC, Publisher, Boosey & Hawkes, Inc., Sole Agent. Reprinted by permission. **Another Hundred People** © 1970–RANGE ROAD MUSIC, INC., QUARTET MUSIC INC. and RILTING MUSIC, INC. Copyright renewed. All rights administered by HERALD SQUARE MUSIC INC. Used by permission. All Rights Reserved. **Comedy Tonight** © 1962 (Renewed 1990) BURTHEN-MUSIC CO INC. All Rights on behalf of BURTHEN-MUSIC CO INC. Owner and publication and allied rights for the world CHAPPELL & CO. All Rights Reserved. WARNER BROS. PUBLI-